Hungary

THE ROUGH GUIDE

Written and researched by
Dan Richardson
and Charles Hebbert

With additional contributions by
Jill Denton, Simon Broughton
and Dan Landin

THE ROUGH GUIDES

Hungary

THE ROUGH GUIDE

Other available Rough Guides
Amsterdam • Andalucia • Australia • Barcelona • Berlin
Brazil • Brittany & Normandy • Bulgaria • California • Canada
Corsica • Crete • Czech & Slovak Republics • Cyprus • Egypt • England
Europe • Florida • France • Germany • Greece • Guatemala & Belize
Holland, Belgium & Luxembourg • Hong Kong • Ireland • Italy • Kenya
Mediterranean Wildlife • Mexico • Morocco • Nepal • New York
Nothing Ventured • Pacific Northwest • Paris • Peru • Poland • Portugal
Prague • Provence • Pyrenees • St Petersburg • San Francisco
Scandinavia • Scotland • Sicily • Spain • Thailand • Tunisia • Turkey
Tuscany & Umbria • USA • Venice • Wales • West Africa
Women Travel • Zimbabwe & Botswana

Forthcoming
India • Malaysia & Singapore • Classical Music • World Music

Rough Guide Credits

Text Editors:	Kate Berens and John Fisher
Series Editor:	Mark Ellingham
Editorial:	Martin Dunford, Jack Holland, Jonathan Buckley, Richard Trillo
Production:	Susanne Hillen, Gail Jammy, Andy Hilliard, Vivien Antwi
Finance:	Celia Crowley

Acknowledgements

Many **thanks** to friends in *Magyarország* for their kind hospitality and advice: Anni, Csaba, Csilla, István, Judit, Laci, Margo, Sola, Szabolcs, Tibor, Zoltán, Zsolt and, last but not least, Zsuzsi. On the production front, thanks in particular to Kate Berens and John Fisher (for incisive editing), Andy Hilliard (for battling with accents and revisions) and Gareth Nash (for proofing).

We'd also like to thank the many **readers of the previous edition** of the guide who took time to annotate our errors, omissions and lapses of taste. The roll of honour (in alphabetical order) reads: Martin Armstrong; Gary M Bilkus; Mike Billington; Martina Chamberlain; Kathryn J. Chinn; Nate Clement; Judy Colin; Keith Crane; Rosemary Creeser; Attila Domby; T C Dunn; Julian Duplain; Kester J Eddy; Peter Foersom; R E Fricke; Danny Gallagher; Simon Gill; Susan Greenberg; Rebecca Grinter; Martyn Harris; Pat Kelly; Martin Kender; Sophia Lambert; Andrew Lawler; Margaret Levene; Richard Levy; Bill Lomax; Alastair Macaulay; Maureen (who missed the fair at Kecskemét); John McClelland; Dave Major; Michael O'Hare & Sally Manders; Henry Race; Ed Raw; Dr L J Ray; Rodney Read & Jill Turner; Adam Roch; Keneth Ross; Byron Russell; Rosemary E Silva; Martin Stafford; Karin Steininger; Anne Tillyer; Hazel Walmsley; Dick Wash; Lorraine Weber. Apologies to anyone whose name we missed or whose signature we couldn't quite decipher.

The publishers and authors have done their best to ensure the accuracy and currency of all information in *The Rough Guide to Hungary*, however, they can accept no responsibility for any loss, injury, or inconvenience sustained by any traveller as a result of information or advice contained in the guide.

This second edition published 1992 by Rough Guides Ltd, 1 Mercer St, London WC2H 9QJ.
Reprinted 1993 and twice 1994.
Distributed by the Penguin Group:

Penguin Books Ltd, 27 Wrights Lane, London W8 5TZ
Penguin Books USA Inc., 375 Hudson Street, New York 10014, USA
Penguin Books Australia Ltd, 487 Maroondah Highway, PO Box 257, Ringwood, Victoria 3134, Australia
Penguin Books Canada Ltd, 10 Alcorn Avenue, Toronto, Ontario, Canada M4V 1E4
Penguin Books (NZ) Ltd, 182–190 Wairau Road, Auckland 10, New Zealand

Previous edition published in the UK by Harrap Columbus.
Previously published in the US and Canada as *The Real Guide Hungary*.

Typeset in Linotron Univers and Century Old Style to an original design by Andrew Oliver.
Printed in the United Kingdom by Cox and Wyman Ltd (Reading).
Illustrations in Part One and Part Three by Edward Briant.
Basics illustration by Hilary McManus; Contexts illustration by Tommy Yamaha.

368p. Includes index.

A catalogue record for this book is available from the British Library.

ISBN 1-85828-021-4

CONTENTS

Introduction viii

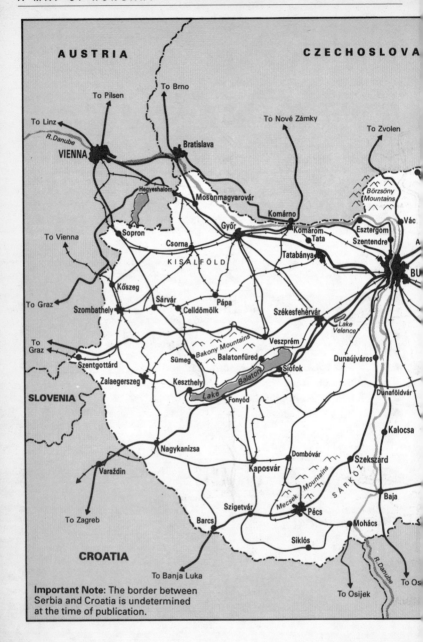

INTRODUCTION

Visitors who refer to **Hungary** as a Balkan country risk getting a lecture on how this small, landlocked nation of eleven million people differs from "all those Slavs". Natives are strongly conscious of Hungary (likened by the poet Ady to a "river ferry, continually travelling between East and West, with always the sensation of not going anywhere but of being on the way back from the other bank") as a nation, one that identifies with "Western values", and of themselves as Magyars – a race that transplanted itself from Central Asia into the heart of Europe. Any contradiction between nationalism and cosmopolitanism is resolved by what the Scottish expatriate Charlie Coutts called the Hungarian "genius for not taking things to their logical conclusion". Having embarked on reforming state socialism long before Gorbachev, Hungary made the transition to multi-party democracy without a shot being fired, while the removal of the iron curtain along its border set in motion the events leading to the fall of the Berlin Wall. Since the election of a conservative government in 1990, traditional values and institutions have made a comeback, but at the same time contemporary Western influences pervade every aspect of life.

Hungary's capital, **Budapest**, inspires a feeling of déjà vu. It's not just the vast Gothic parliament and other monuments of a bygone imperial era that seem familiar, but the latest fashions on the streets, or a poster advertising something that was all the rage back home a year before. In coffee houses, Turkish baths, and the fad for Habsburg bric-à-brac, there's a strong whiff of *Mitteleuropa* – that ambient culture that welcomed Beethoven in Budapest and Hungarian-born Liszt in Vienna. Meanwhile a wave of new clubs and restaurants and a burgeoning sex industry reflects the advent of nouveau riche entreprenuers, and a massive influx of tourists and foreign investment.

After Budapest, **Lake Balaton** and the **Danube Bend** vie for popularity. The Balaton, with its string of brash resorts, styles itself as the "Nation's Playground," and enjoys a fortuitous proximity to the Badacsony wine-producing region. The Danube Bend has more to offer in terms of scenery and historic architecture, as do the **Northern Uplands** and **Transdanubia**. The beautiful old parts of Sopron, Győr and Pécs are, rightfully, the main attractions in Transdanubia, though for castle buffs the Zempléni range and the lowlands of southern Transdanubia also have several treats in store; while in the Uplands the famous wine centres of Tokaj and Eger are the chief draw. On the **Great Plain** Szeged hosts a major festival, and its rival city, Debrecen, serves as the jumping-off point for the archaic Erdőhát region and the mirage-haunted Hortobágy *puszta*. See the **chapter introductions** for more details about each region.

When to go

Most visitors come in the summer, when nine or ten hours of sunshine can be relied on most days, sometimes interspersed with short, violent storms. The humidity that causes these is really only uncomfortable in Budapest, where the crowds don't help; elsewhere the **climate** is agreeable. Budapest, with its spring and autumn festivals, sights and culinary delights, is a standing invitation to come out of season. But other parts of Hungary have little to offer during the winter, and the weather doesn't become appealing until late spring. May, warm but showery, is the time to see the Danube Bend, Tihany or Sopron before everyone else arrives; June is hotter and drier, a pattern reinforced throughout July, August and September. There's little variation in **temperatures** across the country: the Great Plain is drier, and the highlands are wetter, during summer, but that's about as far as climatic changes go. The number of **tourists** varies more – the popular areas can be mobbed in summer, but rural areas receive few visitors, even during the high season.

	Jan	Feb	March	April	May	June	July	August	Sept	Oct	Nov	Dec
AVERAGE DAYTIME TEMPERATURES												
Budapest												
°F	29	32	42	53	61	68	72	70	63	52	42	34
°C	-2	0	6	12	16	20	22	21	17	11	6	1
Debrecen												
°F	27	31	41	51	60	66	70	68	61	51	41	32
°C	-3	-1	5	10	16	19	21	20	16	11	5	0

PART ONE

THE
BASICS

GETTING THERE FROM NORTH AMERICA

The quickest way to reach Hungary from the US or Canada is to fly to Budapest, on a one- or two-stop direct flight via another European city; there are no non-stop flights. Direct flights are comparatively expensive, however, so you might be better off flying to Paris, London, Frankfurt or Vienna, and making your way overland from there (see "Getting There from Europe"). Names and addresses of agents specialising in travel to Hungary and details of the various options are given below. Unless specified otherwise, prices quoted are for round-trip tickets and include taxes.

FLIGHTS FROM THE US

If saving time and minimising hassle are more important than finding the cheapest fare, you can get to Budapest from most US cities in around fifteen hours. Airlines offering **direct flights from the US to Budapest** include *Malév*, the Hungarian national airline, who fly via Frankfurt; *Delta* (via Frankfurt and Vienna); *Lufthansa* (via Frankfurt); *SAS* (via Copenhagen); and *American* (via London or Zurich). Schedules and routings are subject to change, but at the time of writing the last leg of the journey is likely to be on *Malév* no matter which airline you buy your ticket from. To confuse things further, *Malév* also buys seats on other carriers and sells them as its own.

APEX fares (which allow a maximum stay of 21 days) are virtually identical on all these carriers. Low season rates start at around $750 from New York and $1100 from West Coast cities, rising to $1000 and $1350 respectively during high season. If you want to stay longer, the next level of ticket is good for visits of up to six months but costs around $150 more. **One-way tickets** are hard to get, and the return flight from Hungary will cost at least as much as a round-trip APEX from the US. However, *Malév* does offer an "Early Bird Special" (which must be booked and paid for two months in advance) that brings the cost of high-season travel down to as low as $759 from New York, $1050 from the West Coast. These fares are available only through **travel agencies specialising in Eastern Europe**, such as *Hungaria Travel* and *Sir Bentley* (see box). Both agencies are excellent sources of advice on travelling in Hungary, and your best bet for finding out about any bargains that might be available.

Full-time students and anyone under 26 can take advantage of the excellent deals offered by **student/youth travel agencies** such as *Council Travel*, *STA* and *Nouvelles Frontières* (see box). Their flights on major carriers like *British Airways* or *Air France* can cost as little as $750 from the East Coast, $950 from the West Coast, even in high season. A further advantage to these

TOLL-FREE AIRLINE NUMBERS	
Air France ☎1-800/237-2747	**Malév** (East Coast) ☎1-800/223-6884
American ☎1-800/433-7300	**Malév** (West Coast) ☎1-800/262-5380
British Airways ☎1-800/247-9297	**SAS** ☎1-800/221-2350
ČSA ☎1-800/223-2365	**SwissAir** ☎1-800/221-4750
Delta ☎1-800/241-4141	**TWA** ☎1-800/892-4141
KLM ☎1-800/777-5553	**United** ☎1-800/538-2929
Lufthansa ☎1-800/645-3880	

COUNCIL TRAVEL IN THE US

Head Office: 205 E 42nd St, New York, NY 10017; ☎212/661-1450.

CALIFORNIA
2486 Channing Way, Berkeley, CA 94704; ☎415/848-8604.
UCSD Price Center, Q-076, La Jolla, CA 92093; ☎619/452-0630.
1818 Palo Verde Ave, Suite E, Long Beach, CA 90815; ☎213/598-3338.
1093 Broxton Ave, Suite 220, Los Angeles, CA 90024; ☎213/208-3551.
4429 Cass St, San Diego, CA 92109; ☎619/270-6401.
312 Sutter St, Suite 407, San Francisco, CA 94108; ☎415/421-3473.
919 Irving St, Suite 102, San Francisco, CA 94122; ☎415/566-6222.
14515 Ventura Blvd, Suite 250, Sherman Oaks, CA 91403; ☎818/905-5777.

COLORADO
1138 13th St., Boulder, CO 80302; ☎818/905-5777.

CONNECTICUT
Yale Co-op East, 77 Broadway, New Haven, CT 06520; ☎203/562-5335.

DISTRICT OF COLUMBIA
1210 Potomac St, NW Washington, DC 20007; ☎202/337-6464.

GEORGIA
12 Park Place South, Atlanta, GA 30303; ☎404/577-1678.

ILLINOIS
1153 N Dearborn St, Chicago, IL 60610; ☎312/951-0585.
831 Foster St, Evanston, IL 60201; ☎708/475-5070.

LOUISIANA
8141 Maple St, New Orleans, LA 70118; ☎504/866-1767.

MASSACHUSETTS
79 South Pleasant St, 2nd Floor, Amherst, MA 01002; ☎413/256-1261.
729 Boylston St, Suite 201, Boston, MA 02116; ☎617/266-1926.
1384 Massachusetts Ave, Suite 206, Cambridge, MA 02138; ☎617/497-1497.
Stratton Student Center MIT, W20-024, 84. Massachusetts Ave, Cambridge, MA 02139; ☎617/497-1497.

MINNESOTA
1501 University Ave, SE, Room 300, Minneapolis, MN 55414; ☎612/379-2323.

NEW YORK
35 W 8th St, New York, NY 10011; ☎212/254-2525.
Student Center, 356 West 34th St, New York, NY 10001; ☎212/643-1365.

NORTH CAROLINA
703 Ninth St, Suite B-2, Durham, NC 27705; ☎919/286-4664.

OREGON
715SW Morrison, Suite 600, Portland, OR 97205; ☎503/228-1900.

RHODE ISLAND
171 Angell St, Suite 212, Providence, RI 02906; ☎401/331-5810.

TEXAS
2000 Guadalupe St, Suite 6, Austin, TX 78705; ☎512/472-4931.
Exec. Tower Office Center, 3300 W Mockingbird, Suite 101, Dallas,TX 75235; ☎214/350-6166.

WASHINGTON
1314 Northeast 43rd St, Suite 210, Seattle, WA 98105; ☎206/632-2448.

WISCONSIN
2615 North Hackett Ave, Milwaukee, WI; ☎414/332-4740.

STA IN THE US

BOSTON
273 Newbury St, Boston, MA 02116; ☎617/266-6014.

HONOLULU
1831 S. King St, Suite 202, Honolulu, HI 96826; ☎808/942-7755.

LOS ANGELES
920 Westwood Blvd, Los Angeles, CA 90024; ☎213/824-1574.
7204 Melrose Ave, Los Angeles, CA 90046; ☎213/934-8722.

2500 Wilshire Blvd, Los Angeles, CA 90057; ☎213/380-2184.

NEW YORK
17 E. 45th St, Suite 805, New York, NY 10017; ☎212/986-9470;☎ 800/777-0112.

SAN DIEGO
6447 El Cajon Blvd, San Diego, CA 92115; ☎619/286-1322.

SAN FRANCISCO
166 Geary St, Suite 702, San Francisco, CA 94108; ☎415/391-8407.

TRAVEL CUTS IN CANADA

Head Office: 187 College St., Toronto, Ontario M5T 1P7; ☎416/979-2406

ALBERTA
MacEwan Hall Student Centre, Univ. of Calgary, Calgary T2N 1N4, (☎403/282-7687); 10424A 118th Ave, Edmonton T6G 0P7; (☎403/471-8054).

BRITISH COLUMBIA
Room 326, TC, Student Rotunda, Simon Fraser University, Burnaby, British Columbia V5A 1S6, (☎604/291-1204); 1516 Duranleau St, Granville Island, Vancouver V6H 3S4, (☎604/687-6033); Student Union Building, University of British Columbia, Vancouver V6T 1W5, (☎604/228-6890); Student Union Building, University of Victoria, Victoria V8W 2Y2, (☎604/721-8352).

MANITOBA
University Centre, University of Manitoba, Winnipeg R3T 2N2; ☎204/269-9530

NOVA SCOTIA
Student Union Building, Dalhousie University, Halifax B3H 4J2, (☎902/424-2054), 6139 South St, Halifax B3H 4J2, (☎902/494-7027).

ONTARIO
University Centre, University of Guelph, Guelph N1G 2W1, (☎519/763-1660);. Fourth Level Unicentre, Carleton University, Ottawa, K1S5B6, (☎613/238-5493. 60); Laurier Ave E, Ottawa K1N 6N4, (☎613/238-8222); Student Street, Room G27, Laurentian University, Sudbury P3E 2C6, (☎705/673-1401); 96 Gerrard St E, Toronto M5B 1G7;, (☎416/977-0441); University Shops Plaza, 170 University Ave W, Waterloo N2L 3E9, (☎519/886-0400).

QUÉBEC (Known as *Voyages CUTS*)
Université McGill, 3480 rue McTavish, Montréal H3A 1X9, (☎514/398-0647); 1613 rue St Denis, Montréal H2X 3K3, (☎514/843-8511); Université Concordia, Edifice Hall, Suite 643, SGW Campus, 1455 bd de Maisonneuve Ouest, Montréal H3G 1M8, (☎514/288-1130); 19 rue Ste Ursule, Québec G1R 4E1, (☎418/692-3971).

SASKATCHEWAN
Place Riel Campus Centre, University of Saskatchewan, Saskatoon S7N 0W0; ☎306/975-

NOUVELLES FRONTIÈRES

In the United States
NEW YORK 12 E 33rd St, New York, NY 10016 ☎212/779-0600.
LOS ANGELES 6363 Wilshire Blvd, Suite 200, Los Angeles, CA 90048; ☎213/658-8955.
SAN FRANCISCO 209 Post St, Suite 1121, San Francisco, CA 94108; ☎415/781-4480.

In Canada
MONTRÉAL 800 East Bd de Maison Neuve, Montréal, Québec ;☎514/288-9942.
QUÉBEC 176 Grande Allée Ouest, Québec, P.Q. G1R 2G9; ☎418/525-5255.

OTHER DISCOUNT AGENCIES

Access International (☎1-800/825-3633). Good East Coast and central US deals.
250 West 57th St, Suite 511, New York, NY 10107, ☎212/465-0707.

Airkit. West Coast consolidator, with seats from Los Angeles and San Francisco.
1125 West 6th St, Los Angeles, CA 90017, ☎213/957-9304.

Forum Travel International, 91 Gregory Lane, Pleasant Hill, CA 94523 ;☎415/671-2900.

Moments Notice, 425 Madison Ave, New York, NY 10017; ☎212/486-0503.

Travel Avenue, 180 N Jefferson St, Chicago IL; ☎1-800/333-3335.

Worldwide Discount Travel Club, 1674 Meridian Ave, Miami Beach, FL 33139; ☎305/534-2082.

AGENCIES SPECIALISING IN EASTERN EUROPE

Hungaria Travel, 1603 Second Ave, New York NY (☎212/249-9342).

Sir Bentley, 17280 Newhope St, Fountain Valley, CA; ☎714/559-6946 or ☎1-800/675-0559.

student fares is that you can **stop over en route** for little or no extra charge, which can't be done on an APEX ticket. Those who don't meet the student/youth requirements can still save some money by buying tickets through **discount agencies** like those listed in the box on p.5.

If your travel plans are flexible or you've left buying a ticket until the last minute, the best deals are available through **seat consolidators** such as *TFI Tours* (34 W 32nd St, New York, NY; ☎212/736-1140 or ☎1-800/825-3834). Scan the ads in the back pages of the Sunday travel sections of *The New York Times* or your local paper, and phone around. These tickets are impossible to change once you've paid for them, so be certain about your dates and the routing of the flight, since many involve long stopovers and several changes of plane. That said, they can be great value, with peak-season fares running as low as $750 from New York, $950 from Los Angeles or Seattle.

PACKAGE TOURS

Package tours can save you time and effort, and sometimes even money. *Travel Travel* runs week-long all-inclusive trips to Budapest (and Prague) for as little as $799. Fully fledged guided tours are offered by *Fugazy International, Magyar Tours* and the Hungarian national tourist organisation *IBUSZ* (see p.15), which has a range of packages focusing on various aspects of Hungarian culture, plus horse-riding, walking and cycling tours. The latter are also available from *Forum Travel* (see box for addresses).

PACKAGE TOUR OPERATORS

Forum Travel, 91 Gregory Lane, Pleasant Hill, CA; ☎510/671-2900.

Fugazy International, 770 US-1, North Brunswick, NJ; ☎1-800/828-4488.

Magyar Tours; ☎718/816-6828.

Travel Travel, 10 E 39th St, New York, NY; ☎212/547-0737.

If you're simply interested in **booking accommodation** and transport within Hungary, contact *Sir Bentley* or *Hungaria Travel* (see above). Information on accommodation can also be obtained through *Hungarian Hotels Sales* (6033 W Century Blvd, Los Angeles, CA; ☎310/277-6915 or ☎1-800/231-8704), but bookings must be made through one of the agencies above.

FLIGHTS FROM CANADA

The only airline to fly **from Canada to Budapest** (via Frankfurt) is *Lufthansa*. Fares start at CDN$1000 from Toronto and CDN$1250 from Vancouver during the low season, rising to CDN$1200 and CDN$1550 over summer. The alternatives are to travel to the US and then fly from there (see above), or fly to a European city and then carry on to Hungary by air or overland. Though London is the cheapest "gateway" city, a bargain flight to Frankfurt or Vienna might prove less expensive in the long run.

GETTING THERE FROM AUSTRALASIA

There are no direct flights from Australasia to Budapest and it's usually cheaper to fly to Athens, London, Frankfurt, Rome or Vienna and then travel on to Hungary.

Olympic Airways to Athens is usually a good bet. You could also try *British Airways* and *Alitalia*, which have onward connections to Budapest from London and Rome respectively, or *Lauda Air* via Bangkok or Phuket to Vienna, only a short journey from the border.

Whether or not you qualify for **student or youth discounts**, it's worth enquiring first through an agent like *STA Travel*. They have more than twenty offices in Australia, including 1a Lee St, Railway Sq, Sydney 2000 (☎02/519 9866) and 224 Faraday St, Carlton, Victoria 3053 (☎03/347 4711). Their ten offices in New Zealand include high street branches at 147 Cuba St, Palmerston North, Wellington, and 10 High St, Auckland (☎09/309 9723 for telephone sales).

GETTING THERE FROM EUROPE

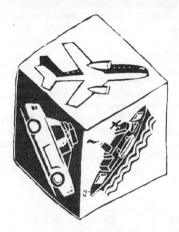

Situated in the heart of Europe, Hungary is easily accessible by air, rail or road from a dozen countries. While travellers flying in from North America generally favour Britain as a springboard, it is equally feasible to reach Hungary from Germany, Austria or Czechoslovakia.

FLIGHTS FROM BRITAIN

At the time of writing, three specialist companies handle the majority of reasonably priced *British Airways* or *Malév* scheduled return flights **from London to Budapest**. Departures are from Heathrow, and travellers are required to stay at least one Saturday night. All APEX flights must be booked and paid for in full at least fourteen days in advance; confirmed bookings can't be changed.

Hungarian Air Tours offers a variety of deals. In the so-called "Money Miser" category, there are weekend flights limited to set periods (for example Thurs–Sun, Thurs–Tues, Fri–Mon) costing £192 during April, May and October, and £230 between June and September; plus six- to thirty-day return flights costing £214 and £230 for the same periods. Their Midweek APEX flights (Tues & Wed) go for £268, while regular APEX returns, subject to the same restrictions but valid for up to three months, cost £304 irrespective of the season. *Danube Travel* offers similar weekend savers – ranging from £184 (Nov–March) to £199 (April, May & Oct) – and week-long trips (£198 and £219 for the same periods): all cost £235 during high season (June–Sept). Should anyone be interested, they also do one-way flights for £268. Lastly, *Canterbury Travel* does return flights to Budapest (valid for up to one month) for £220 (low season) or £240 (June–Sept).

By approaching *Malév, Air France, Austrian Airlines, KLM, Lufthansa* or *British Airways* directly, you might shave £10–30 off the above prices, but it's easier to let specialised **agents** do the work. *STA Travel* and *Campus Travel*, both with branches around the country, are highly reliable; they also offer special **student discount** deals – a Heathrow–Budapest return with *British Airways* currently costs £190. Another possibility is to go for a bargain **flight to Frankfurt or Vienna**, available from *Jetsave, Pegasus* and various "bucket shops" (see ads in the London

---

FLIGHT OPERATORS AND AGENTS

Airlines

Air France, 158 New Bond St, London W1Y 0BD (☎071/499 9511).

Austrian Airlines, 50–51 Conduit St, London W1R 0NP (☎071/439 0741).

British Airways, 156 Regent St, London W1 (☎081/897 4000).

KLM, 8 Hanover St, London W1 (☎081/750 9000).

Lufthansa, 23 Piccadilly, London W1V 9PF (☎ 071/408/0322).

Malév, 10 Vigo St, London W1X 1AJ (☎071/439 0577).

Independent travel specialists

Campus Travel, 52 Grosvenor Gardens, London SW1 (☎071/730 3402). Branches in Bristol, Cambridge, Oxford and Edinburgh.

STA Travel, 86 Old Brompton Rd, London SW7; 117 Euston Road, London NW1 (☎071/937 9921). Branches in Bristol, Cambridge, Oxford and Manchester.

Evening Standard and listing magazine *Time Out*, or the classified sections of the quality Sunday newspapers). Round-trips can cost as little as £90 ($153) for Frankfurt and £148 ($252) for Vienna, but of course exclude the expense of travelling to and from Hungary, plus accommodation en route.

The cost of direct flights **from other European cities** to Budapest isn't always proportionate to their proximity to Hungary. However, it's certainly worthwhile checking out *Malév, Air France, KLM, Alitalia* or *Lufthansa* in any country.

PACKAGE DEALS FROM BRITAIN

The following is merely intended to give an idea of what's available. Send off for brochures if you're interested, and compare the various deals carefully, since there are variations in seasonal price-bands and accommodation amongst the various companies. Unless stated otherwise, prices below are per person sharing the cheapest available double room during the high season, and include return flights.

Hungarian Air Tours, 3 Heddon Street, London W1R 7LE (☎071/437 9405). 3- to 7-night Budapest City Breaks (£299–365); week-long spa holidays in Budapest (£1179), Hévíz (£1014) or Bükfürdő (£1135); Budapest Spring Festival (£480) and Christmas (£459) packages; 3–7 nights in Vienna and Budapest (£276–350); riding holidays and car rental.

Danube Travel, 6 Conduit St, London W1R 9TG (☎071/493 0263). Similar packages at comparable prices, plus various tours around Hungary by coach (from £590); fly/drive deals (£277); and City Breaks combining Budapest with Vienna (£381), Bratislava and Prague (£979), or Prague and Warsaw (£999).

Canterbury Travel, 248 Streatfield Rd, Kenton, Harrow, Middlesex HA3 9BY (☎081/206 0411). 2- to 7-night Budapest City Breaks (£323–437), and combinations featuring Prague and/or Warsaw, or Vienna and Prague. For the Budapest-only tour, you can travel to Hungary on the luxury *Venice–Simplon Orient Express* for £980 extra.

Thompson Holidays (bookings through any travel agent). 3- to 7-night City Breaks in Budapest (£385–527) and twin-centre package with 4 nights in Vienna (£519).

Crystal Holidays (bookings through travel agents, or ☎081/390 9900). Similar 2- to 7-night City Breaks (£339–579), and twin-centre deals (£569).

Red Square, 41 Datchet House, London NW1 3TH (☎071/387 2104). Custom-made coach tours of Eastern Europe, avoiding "the naff and tacky" in favour of horse-riding, bison-spotting or other activities with a generic theme, for groups of 12–30.

Attila Tours, 36a Kilburn High Rd, London NW6 5UA (☎071/372 0470). A week's accommodation on a Budapest campsite and coach travel to and from Hungary for £115 from May to September. Coaches also run out of season (£80–100).

New Millennium Holidays (☎021/711232). Similar operator offering week-long holidays near Hévíz in the Balaton region for as little as £120. Return transport is also by coach.

Bike Tours, PO Box 75, Bath BA1 1BX (☎0225/480130). Well-run two-week cycling tours of Budapest, the Danube Bend and Lake Balaton (£540); Eger, Hortobágy and Tokaj (£540); or Kecskemét, Kiskunság National Park, Tiszafüred and Eger (£595). Prices exclude return flight (£225) and insurance premium (£19) for each person.

BY TRAIN

As an alternative to a direct flight **from Britain**, travelling by rail has the obvious advantage of allowing you to see more of Europe on your trip, and is attractive economically if you're a **student**, **under 26** or **over 60**.

Those in the first two categories qualify for the discount BIJ tickets offered by **Eurotrain**, which are valid for two months and allow unlimited stopovers along a pre-determined route. A return ticket to Budapest costs £174–186,

depending on whether you travel directly (via Ostend, Aachen, Frankfurt and Vienna) or make a detour via Amsterdam. Another option for under-26s is the *Eurotrain* **"Eastern Explorer"** (£190), valid for a two-month circuit of cities such as Berlin, Prague and Budapest. Should you decide to venture off the circuit, both sorts of ticket entitle you to 25–30 percent off other railway journeys within Hungary.

Alternatively, if you're under 26 and have been resident in Europe for at least six months, you can buy an **InterRail pass**, currently sold for £180 at major *British Rail* stations and travel agents. This entitles the holder to one month's travel on most European railways including Hungary's, plus around a third off rail travel in Britain and discounts on cross-Channel ferries. The **InterRail "26-plus" pass**, for those aged 26 and over, costs £260 for a month, or £180 for fifteen days, but doesn't cover ferry crossings or travel in Britain. If you're sixty or over and hold a *BR* Senior Citizen Railcard, you can get a **Rail Europe Senior Card** (£7.50) which gives up to fifty percent reductions on rail fares throughout Europe, including Hungary. Ask at any *British Rail* station or agent for details.

Although **US and Canadian citizens** aren't eligible for *InterRail*, they can buy **Eurail passes** (before arrival in Europe), which come in various forms. Over-26s usually go for a **regular** pass, which covers first-class travel for 15 days ($430), 21 days ($550), or one ($680), two ($920) or three months ($1150). There is also the **Eurail Youth Pass**, valid for those under 26, good for one ($470) or two ($640) months' travel; and the **Eurail Saverpass**, allowing 15 days of unlimited first-class travel for two people for $340 each between March and October (you need 3 people to qualify between April and Sept). With the **Eurail Flexipass**, you only pay for the number of days that you actually travel: 5 days within 15 consecutive days costs $280; 9 days within 21 days costs $450; and 14 days within one month costs $610. The **Eurail Youth Flexipass**, for under-26s, is valid for 15 days within two months ($420). Finally, the **Eurail Drive Pass** gives three days' rail travel and three days' car rental for $269 per person; extra days cost $40.

Australians and New Zealanders can also buy *Eurail* passes, which must again be purchased before arrival in Europe. As a guide to prices, a one-month *Eurail Youth Pass* costs Aus$590, a *Eurail Youth Flexipass* (15 days over 3 months) Aus$470.

If you don't qualify for any discounts, the **regular fare** from London to Budapest is dearer than most flights, with a second-class return costing £251–261 or £258–273 (depending on whether you go via Paris or Ostend), on top of which you'll probably want a couchette (£8). **The journey from London's** Victoria Station takes about 27 hours, including the ferry crossing. For those with money to burn, there's the option of travelling instead on the **Venice-Simplon**

Orient Express – an opulent, 1920s-style pullman train whose dining car serves haute cuisine to passengers dressed in furs and jewels. A one-way ticket to Budapest costs about £1000. This touristic fantasy is not to be confused with the "real" *Orient Express*, which is thoroughly prosaic as far as Hungary, and grimly awful for the final leg down to Bucharest in Romania.

FROM CONTINENTAL EUROPE

For travellers starting on the continent, there are two trains **from Paris** (Gare de l'Est) – the above-mentioned *Orient Express*, and the midday connection for the *Wiener Waltzer*. Both take roughly 21 hours to reach Keleti Station in Budapest. Munich, Frankfurt and Berlin are the main points of departure **from Germany**; Frankfurt to Budapest takes around 12 hours. Travellers coming **from Czechoslovakia** have a choice of half a dozen trains from Prague and Bratislava, while Warsaw, Kraków and Czestochowa are the points of departure **from Poland**. Most of the half-dozen services **from Vienna** leave from the Westbahnhof, arriving at Keleti Station three to four hours later. If you're coming back the same way, it's worth buying a return ticket (roughly £16/$27) in Vienna, as singles cost more in Hungary. (See under "Hitching", below, for advice on staying in Vienna.) On some trains from Austria you can exchange money or travellers' cheques after crossing the Hungarian border, saving you from queuing at an exchange desk in one of the main Budapest stations.

BY BUS

Buses are an economical alternative to trains from **London to Budapest**, particularly if you're over 26. The best deals are offered by *Attila Travel* which charges £80–100 for a ten-day return ticket (see the "Agents" box for details of travel-plus-accommodation deals). To stay longer than this, however, you will probably have to use *Eurolines*, which runs one to four buses weekly from Victoria Coach Station to Győr, Budapest and Siófok. A return ticket costs £149 ($254) at the standard rate, or £139 ($236) for under-26s. *Eurolines* coaches drop you at Erzsébet tér bus station in downtown Pest, while *Attila Tours* should deposit you at the *Hotel Wien* in the suburbs of Buda (take bus #139 to Moskva tér, then switch to the metro). With either company the journey takes about 28 hours.

TRAIN AND BUS ENQUIRIES

Trains

British Rail European Travel Centre, Victoria Station, London SW1 (☎071/834 2345).

Eurotrain, 52 Grosvenor Gardens, London SW1 (☎071/730 3402).

Buses

Attila Travel, 36a Kilburn High Rd, London NW6 5UA (☎071/372 0470).

Eurolines, Victoria Coach Station, 164 Buckingham Palace Rd, London SW1 (☎071/730 0202; bookings through any *National Express* agent).

Senior citizens and under-26s could make savings by bussing it **via Vienna**, since both pay only £99 ($168) for a return ticket on the weekly *Eurolines* service to the Austrian capital. From the Wien Mitte bus station (Landstrasser Hauptstrasse 1/b), where coaches from London arrive at 10.30am, you can catch a *Blagluss* bus on to Budapest at 5pm (or 7am the following day). The single (£13/$22) and thirty-day return (£22/$37) fares are payable in Austrian schillings.

For details of **buses from other cities in Western Europe**, contact *Deutsche Touring Gmbh*, Hauptbahnhof Europabus (2, Arnulfstrasse 3) or *Ungarn und Osteuropapareisen* (Altheimer Eck 1) in **Munich**; *Romeatour* (Lista di Spagna 134) in **Venice**; or *Heribert Matzer Reisebüro* (Draisgasse 18 and Lendplatz 38) in **Graz**. Travellers coming **from Romania** can take advantage of services from Cluj, Timişoara, Oradea, Tîrgu Mureş and other cities in Transylvania.

BY CAR – DRIVING AND HITCHING

The most direct **route** from London to Budapest runs via Ostend, Brussels, Aachen, Cologne, Frankfurt, Nürnberg, Linz and Vienna. It's a distance of 1732km, and you shouldn't bank on driving it in under 36 hours. To avoid the long queues at Hegyeshalom and other main border crossings over summer, consider entering Hungary instead from Deutsch-Kreutz, just south of Eisenstadt. See "Driving", below, regarding licences, insurance and driving inside Hungary.

Hitching along the same route can take up to three days, so you'd be wise to pack rainwear, a tent, a good road map, and some Deutschmarks and/or food. On all European motorways it's illegal to hitch anywhere but at petrol stations and motels, and police are generally tough with violators although their attitude to "law-abiding" hitchers varies. The ideal ride would be with a *Hungarocamion* lorry going home, but it's realistic to settle for anything heading towards Austria. Hitching from London to Dover isn't worth the hassle, but prospects should improve from Ostend onwards, particularly between Germany and Vienna.

To economise on **the Vienna stopover**, stay at the *Hostel Ruthensteiner* (XV, Robert-Hamerling-Gasse 24; ☎83-46-93 or 83-08-265), five minutes' walk from the Westbahnhof, which costs around £5 ($8) a night. There is a campsite on the Linz side of town (Metro U4 to Hütteldorf, then bus #52B). To carry on towards Budapest, ride the Schnellbahn to Gross Schwechat and then walk 500m to the crossroads, where hitching is easy. A *Wien 72 hour* ticket covers both trains, and other transport within the city limits.

Hitching back from Hungary, you might consider contacting the *Kenguru* agency in Budapest (VIII, Kőfaragó utca 15; ☎138-2019; Mon–Sat 8am–6pm), which pairs up drivers (*autos*) and hitchers (*utas*) heading the same way. The hitcher pays a set amount according to the distance (eg 6600Ft – roughly £47/$80 – to London), of which the driver gets the lion's share. It helps to have a Hungarian friend to explain matters over the phone. For independent hitchhikers, German is the lingua franca of the road: *Wo fahren sie?* means "Where are you going?", and hitching signs should carry the word *Richtung* ("direction"). Sticking to routes through German-speaking countries and Belgium, it's possible to make the English Channel in 24 hours; but avoid France, where the hitching's awful.

BY HYDROFOIL FROM VIENNA

Although the frequency of **hydrofoils from Vienna** varies seasonally, the journey to Budapest always takes four and a half hours. Departures are at 8am daily during the low season (March 1–30 & Sept 4–Oct 1), and 2.30pm daily from May 1 to Sept 3, with an extra daily service at 8am during the high season (July 3–Sept 3) – but check this in Vienna, as schedules may change. Make bookings at least 24 hours in advance at *IBUSZ*, Kärtnerstrasse 26 (☎53-26-86), or the *DDSG boat station*, Praterkai, II. Mexiko Platz 8 (☎26-56-36), where the hydrofoils depart; the one-way fare costs around £35/ $60, payable in Austrian schillings.

VISAS AND RED TAPE

Citizens of the United States, Canada and EC countries (except Portugal) no longer require visas, and simply receive a tiny green stamp in their passport at the border, which allows a stay of up to ninety days. Australians, New Zealanders and other nationalities, however, must still obtain a visa – either from a Hungarian consulate abroad, or on arrival at Budapest airport or any road crossing along the border. Visas are not issued at rail crossings or the passenger dock for hydrofoils from Vienna.

Assuming that you require a visa, applications can be made to any Hungarian consulate abroad in person or by post. **Tourist visas** are valid for thirty days' stay, with the option of single, double or multiple entries, while **transit visas** entitle you to 48 hours' stay. Besides two passport photos, you will need to submit your passport and the requisite fee (currently £12 for a single-entry visa obtained in Britain; consulates in Eastern Europe require payment in US$).

Applications in person are generally processed within 24 hours, though some consulates will issue visas the same day for a surcharge. To apply by post, obtain an application form by sending a SAE to the consulate; then send the completed form and your passport by registered post, including a postal order (in Britain) or certified cheque (in the US), plus an SAE for return. Applications can also be made through *IBUSZ* (1 Parker Plaza, Suite 1004, Fort Lee NJ 07024; ☎1-800/367-7878) in the US, or *Danube Travel* (6 Conduit St, London W1R 9TG; ☎071/493 0263) in Britain, which levy a surcharge.

VISA EXTENSIONS AND REGISTRATION

In practice, visitors can stay up to ninety days by getting two thirty-day visa **extensions** from the police. Applications must be made 48 hours

HUNGARIAN CONSULATES ABROAD

AUSTRALIA: 79 Hopetown Circuit, Yarralumia ACT 2600 Canberra (☎82-32-26); 351/a Edgecliff Rd, Edgecliff NSW 2027 Sydney (☎328-7859).

AUSTRIA: 1, Bank Gasse 4–6, A–1010 Wien (☎62-36-21).

BRITAIN: 35b Eaton Place, London SW1 (☎071/ 235 2664; open Mon–Fri 10am–noon).

CANADA: 7 Delaware Ave, Ottawa K2P 0Z2 Ontario (☎613-232-1711).

DENMARK: Strandvej 170, 2920 Charlottenlund, Copenhagen (☎451/63-16-88).

GERMANY: 5300 Bonn 2 (Plittersdorf) Trumstr. 30 (☎37-67-97).

NETHERLANDS: La Haye Hoheweg 14, Den Haag (☎500-405).

NORWAY: Sophus Lies gt. 3 Oslo 2 (☎47-2/56-46-88).

SWEDEN: Laboratoriegaten 2, 11527 Stockholm (☎47-8/61-67-62).

USA: 3910 Shoemaker St NW, Washington DC 20008 (☎202/362-6730; visa enquiries ☎202/362-6795); 223 E 52nd St, New York NY (☎212/752-0661).

before the visa expires, and you may be asked to show evidence of funds. In Budapest, go to the district police station (*kerületi rendőrség*) nearest to your place of residence; in provincial towns, apply to police headquarters (*főkapitányság*). The process usually takes about fifteen minutes.

After thirty days' stay, all visitors are required to register their address (and any subsequent changes of address) with the local police. In practice, however, **registration** need only concern those staying in "unofficial" accommodation (eg with friends), since residents in hotels, hostels, pensions, guesthouses and campsites are automatically registered. Should you need to register, get an Alien's Registration form (*Lakcímbejelentő lap küföldiek részére*) from any post office and have it countersigned by your host before taking it to the police station.

Lost passports must be reported to the police (who'll issue a visa, if necessary) and your own consulate. If found, they will be forwarded to *KEOKH* (the aliens' registration office) in Budapest (VI, Andrássy út 93; Mon 8am–4pm, Tues–Fri 8.30am–noon).

CUSTOMS

Customs formalities are normally painless, though visitors arriving from Austria or Romania by road may get stuck in long queues at the border crossings. Visitors can bring in 250 cigarettes (or 250g of tobacco), 2 litres or wine and 1 litre of spirits. There is no **import duty** on personal effects such as bicycles, cameras, portable cassette recorders and TV sets, but items with a high resale value (eg laptop computers and video cameras) are liable to customs duty and 25 percent VAT unless you can prove that they are for personal use.

These customs regulations change fairly frequently, so it's worth checking the latest rules at a Hungarian consulate or tourist office before leaving home. You might also ask about the **export ban** on certain goods (including citrus fruits, coffee, meat products and chocolate at the time of writing). In practice, however, officials turn a blind eye to modest quantities, and shouldn't object to you taking home a salami or two.

HEALTH AND INSURANCE

No inoculations are required for Hungary, and standards of public health are good. Tap water is safe everywhere, while potable springs (*forrás*) and streams are designated on maps, and with signs, as *ivóvíz*. The national health service (*Sz.T.K.*) will provide free emergency treatment in any hospital or doctor's office – and EC citizens are covered for longer stays in hospital – but there is a charge for drugs and non-emergency care.

Even so, it's a very good idea to have some kind of **travel insurance**, since with this you're covered for loss of possessions and money, as well as the cost of all medical and dental treatment. Among **British insurers**, Endsleigh are about the cheapest, offering a month's cover for around £20. Their policies are available from most youth/student travel specialists or direct from their offices at 97–107 Southampton Row, London WC1 (☎071/580 4311). You can also buy a policy from just about any travel agent, insurance broker or major bank.

In the **US and Canada** you should check the insurance policies you already have carefully before taking out a new one. You may discover that you're already covered for medical and other losses while abroad. Canadians especially are usually covered by their provincial health plans, and holders of ISIC cards are entitled to be reimbursed for $3000-worth of emergency care, plus hospital costs of up to $100 a day for up to sixty days within the period the card is valid. Students may also find their health coverage extends during vacations, and many bank and charge accounts include some form of travel cover; insurance is also sometimes included if you pay for your trip with a credit card. If you do want a specific travel insurance policy, there are numerous kinds to choose from: short-term combination policies covering everything from baggage loss to broken legs are the best bet and cost around $25 for ten days, plus $1 a day for trips of 75 days or more. You might also consider a policy which covers trip cancellation (especially for APEX tickets which are non-refundable). One thing to bear in mind is that none of the currently available policies covers theft; they only cover loss while in the custody of an identifiable person – though even then you must make a report to the police and get their written statement. Two companies you might try are *Travel Guard*, 110 Centrepoint Drive, Steven Point, WI 54480 (☎715/345-0505 or 800/826-1300), or *Access America International*, 600 Third Ave, New York, NY 10163 (☎212/949-5960 or 800/284-8300). Specialist policies covering evacuation expenses are available through *Travel Assistance International* (☎1-800/368-7878) or *International SOS Assistance Abroad* (Box 11568, Philadelphia PA 19116; ☎800/523-8930).

With all these policies you have to pay up front and **reclaim the money** when you get home, producing hospital receipts or a police report to verify your claim.

HEALTH CARE AND HOSPITALS

Sunburn (*napszúrás*) and insect bites (*rovarcsípés*) are the most common **minor complaints**: suntan lotion is sold in supermarkets and chemists stock *Vietnámi balzsam* (Vietnamese-made "Tiger Balm" – the best bug repellent going) and bite ointment. Mosquitoes are pesky, but the bug to beware of in forests is the *kullancs*, which bites and then burrows into human skin, causing inflammation. The risk seems fairly small – we've never encountered any – but if you get a bite which seems particularly painful, it's worth having it inspected at a **pharmacy**. All towns and some villages have a *gyógyszertár* or *patika*, with staff (most likely to understand German) authorised to issue a wide range of drugs, including painkillers. However, pharmaceutical products are mainly of East European origin, so anyone requiring specific medication should bring a supply with them. Opening hours are normally Monday–Friday 9am–6pm, Saturday 9am–noon or 1pm; signs in the window give the location or telephone number of the nearest all-night (*éjjeli* or *ügyeleti szolgálat*) pharmacy.

In **more serious cases**, provincial tourist offices can direct you to local medical centres or doctors' offices (*orvosi rendelő*), while your embassy in Budapest will have the addresses of foreign-language speaking **doctors** and **dentists**, who'll probably be in private (*magán*) practice. Private medicine is much cheaper than in the West, as attested to by the thousands of Austrians who come here for treatment. For muscular, skin or gynaecological complaints, doctors often prescribe a soak at one of Hungary's numerous **medicinal baths** (*gyógyfürdő*), whose curative properties are described in an *IBUSZ* booklet.

In **emergencies**, dial ☎04 for the *Mentők* ambulance service, or catch a taxi to the nearest *Kórház*. The standard of **hospitals** varies enormously, but low morale and shortages of beds testify to poor wages and the general underfunding of the health service. Depending on local conditions, Westerners might get the best available treatment, or be cold-shouldered; in the event of the latter, it's worth trying to bribe the staff as a last resort.

COSTS, MONEY AND BANKS

Hungary began moving towards a market economy long before Poland and Czechoslovakia, enabling the post-Communist government to avoid imposing the shock therapy currently being applied in Russia. Even so, most Hungarians complain of "paying Swedish taxes on an Ethiopian wage" and the rising cost of living, which is now approaching Western levels.

Although foreigners no longer find Hungary a really cheap place to visit, it's still good value on the whole. Depending on the exchange rate (currently £1 = 130Ft, $1 = 75Ft) and where you go, most **costs** are two-thirds to three-quarters of what you'd pay at home, except in Budapest and the Lake Balaton resorts, which are dearer than other parts of Hungary. Wherever you are, the biggest item on your budget will be **accommodation**. Outside of Budapest and the Balaton, the average three-star hotel charges £35–40 ($60–68) for a double room with bath, while the same in a private guesthouse costs about £8 ($13). Although you can get stung for more in some **restaurants**, a three-course meal with wine can generally be had for £5–10 ($8–17). With flat fares (roughly 10p or 20¢) in urban areas, and cheap inter-city trains and buses (averaging under £2–3/$3–5), **transport** will be the least of your expenses.

INFLATION

With **inflation** running at over 30 percent, forint prices quoted in this guide will inevitably become outdated, but unless your own currency slips badly, real costs should remain fairly stable.

If you're keeping to a tight budget, remember that *Eurotrain/BIJ* ticket-holders get reductions on domestic railway tickets, and that some campsites and hostels give discounts to holders of IUS cards (see "Directory", below). Further **savings** can be made by hitching, making or buying your own food, or eating in public canteens.

MONEY

The Hungarian unit of currency is the **forint** (Ft or HUF), which comes in notes of 10, 20, 50, 100, 500, 1000 and 5000Ft, with 1, 2, 5, 10, and 20Ft coins; the little *fillér* (100 fillér = 1Ft) coins are practically useless though still in circulation. Forints can't be exchanged outside the country; and while they can be bought at a favourable rate around Vienna's Mexiko Platz, importing or exporting banknotes exceeding 500Ft is illegal. There's no restriction on bringing in or taking out convertible currency – although if all your cash is in small denominations, declare this on entry (or a zealous customs person might suspect you of smuggling them on the way out).

TRAVELLERS' CHEQUES AND CREDIT CARDS

Although a modest amount of low-denomination dollar bills or Deutschmarks can be useful, it's safest to carry the bulk of your money in **travellers' cheques**. Travellers' cheques issued by American, Australian, British, Dutch, Norwegian and German banks are all accepted; but for speedy refunds in case of loss, *American Express* (represented in Budapest at Deák Ferenc utca 10) is much the most reliable brand. You can cash **Eurocheques** up to the value of 15,000Ft at places displaying the Eurocheque logo. *Amex, Visa, Mastercard, Diners' Club, Carte Blanche* and *Eurocard* **credit and charge cards** can be used to hire cars, buy airline tickets, or pay your bills directly in the fancier hotels and restaurants and in shops catering mainly to tourists. But in everyday Hungarian life, and out in the sticks, they're pretty useless.

BANKS AND CHANGING MONEY

Providing you produce your passport, **changing money** or travellers' cheques is a painless operation at any *IBUSZ* or regional tourist office, or the majority of large hotels and campsites; *valuta* desks in **banks** take longer over transactions, and work shorter hours (Mon–Fri 8.30am–3.30pm) than tourist offices. While commissions range from one to two percent (there is no charge at *OTP* banks), exchange rates are the same everywhere. Keep the **receipts**, as these are required to pay for international tickets in forints and to re-exchange forints back into hard currency when you leave Hungary. At road checkpoints, fifty percent of any remaining forints can be re-exchanged up to the value of $50. The advantages of changing money on the illegal **black market** are minimal (ten percent above the official rate), and scalpers are skilled at cheating.

If you're planning a lengthy stay you can open a **hard currency account** at one of the new commercial banks. Visitors can **transfer money from abroad** through the Hungarian National Bank in Budapest (V, Szabadság tér 6; ☎132-7114; Mon–Fri 8.30am–1.30pm) by having it telexed. *Barclays* and *Midland* bank can do this in a couple of days; other banks can take a week or longer.

INFORMATION AND MAPS

A large number of photo-packed brochures, maps and special-interest leaflets are available free from *IBUSZ*, the Hungarian tourist organisation, and distributed by their agents abroad.

The most useful are the large road map (which is perfectly adequate for travelling around Hungary); a pamphlet detailing the year's festivals and events; and the *Hotels* and *Camping* booklets, which list accommodation on a town-by-town basis, together with the tourist offices that handle bookings. Unfortunately, neither is fully comprehensive, omitting many of the pensions featured in the privately published *Tourism Almanac* (available in Budapest), which only lists places that have paid to be included. There is also a rather dated map designed for campers, and a useful booklet on cycling tours.

TOURIST AGENCIES IN HUNGARY

In Hungary itself you'll find *IBUSZ* offices in almost every town, together with **other tourist agencies** that operate on a regional basis (eg *Savaria Tourist*) or strictly locally. Addresses and opening hours are given in the guide section of this book. There are also three agencies operating nationwide, on a limited basis. *Volántourist* – linked to the *Volán* bus company – specialises in handling travel bookings and tour groups, while *Cooptourist* deals with car and apartment hire, for relatively upmarket travellers. Lastly, there is

IBUSZ AGENTS ABROAD

Australia: Suite 401, 115 Pitt St, Sydney NSW (☎61 2/223-41-97).

Britain: *Danube Travel Ltd*, 6 Conduit St, London W1R 9TG (☎071/493 0263).

Germany: 6000 Frankfurt am Main, Schaftergasse 17 (☎49 69/299-88-70); 2000 Hamburg, Holzdamm 53 (☎49 40/24-59-62); 8000 München, Dachauer Str. 5 (☎49 89/557-217); 5000 Köln, Mauritiussteinweg 114–116 (☎49 221/20-64-50); 7000 Stuttgart, Kronprinz Str. 6 (☎49 711/296-233).

Holland: Strawinskylaan 1425, 1077 Amsterdam (☎31 20/644-98-51).

Sweden: 10326 Stockholm, Beridarebanan 1 (☎46 8/23-20-30).

USA: 1 Parker Plaza, Suite 1104, Fort Lee, NJ 07024 (☎201/592-8585 or ☎1-800/367-7878); M/ C79/50 5000 Airport Plaza Drive, Long Beach, Los Angeles CA (☎213/593-2952).

the "youth travel" agency *Express*, which no longer confines itself to the under-35s and will now book anyone into its stable of hotels and campsites, or college hostels that are vacant at weekends and over holidays. Generally, the regional offices and *IBUSZ* are the most helpful with information, and stock a free monthly magazine, *Programme*, which details tourist **events** throughout Hungary.

MAPS

For reasons of scale, our **town maps** lack some of the details, accents and tram and bus routes that appear on Hungarian *városi-térkép*. These cost between 40Ft and 130Ft and are available from local tourist offices or, failing that, from bookshops (*könyvesbolt*). Better value is the **Magyar Auto Atlasz**, which contains plans of most towns (some of the street names may be out of date) plus road maps, and can be bought from bookshops for 120Ft. Bookshops also stock **hiking maps** or *turistatérkép* covering the Mátra, Bükk and other highland regions (50–100Ft), which should be purchased in advance wherever possible, as they may not be available on the spot. They are not totally reliable, however, so hikers should always carry a compass. *IBUSZ* issues a variety of useful, free **road maps**, including one showing Budapest's one-way streets and bypasses.

GETTING AROUND

Although it doesn't break any speed records, public transport reaches most parts of Hungary and, despite recent price increases, remains remarkably cheap.

The only problem is *információ*, for the staff rarely speaks anything but Hungarian, the only language used for notices and announcements (except around Lake Balaton, where German is widely spoken). You'll find some pertinent phrases in the *Contexts* section of this guide, while the following should be useful for **deciphering timetables**. *Érkező járatok* (or *érkezés*) means "arrivals", and *induló járatok* (or *indulás*) "departures". Trains or buses to (*hova*) a particular destination leave from a designated platform

(for example *vágány 1*) or bus-stand (*kocsiállás*); and the point of arrival for services from (*honnan*) a place may also be indicated. Some services run (*közlekedik; köz.* for short) *munkaszüneti napok kivételével naponta köz.* – daily, except on rest days, meaning Sunday and public holidays; *munkanapkon (hetfőtől-péntekig) köz.* – weekdays, Monday to Friday; *munkaszüneti napokon köz.* – on rest days; or *09.30–tól 12-ig vasárnap köz.* – on Sunday 9.30am–midnight. *Átszállás* means "change"; *át* "via"; and *kivételével* "except".

TRAINS

The centralisation of the **MÁV** railway network means that many cross-country journeys are easier if you travel via Budapest rather than on branch lines where services are slower and less frequent. Timetables are in yellow (for departures) or white (for arrivals), with the different types of fast **trains** in red. The fastest are *Express* trains (marked "*Ex*" on timetables), stopping at major centres only, and costing ten percent more than *gyorsvonat* and *sebesvonat* services, which stop more regularly. The slowest trains (*személyvonat*) halt at every hamlet along the way, and since the fare is the same as on a *gyorsvonat*, you might as well opt for the latter. Do not use international trains for journeys within Hungary, as this can prove expensive and entail a lot of hassle.

> **TRAVEL DETAILS**
>
> Regional transport schedules are summarised under **"Travel Details"** at the end of each chapter.

All trains have first- and second-class (*osztály*) sections, and many also feature a buffet car (indicated on timetables). International services routed through Budapest have **sleeping cars** and **couchettes** (*hálókocsi* and *kusett*), for which tickets can be bought at *MÁV* offices in advance, or sometimes on the train itself. More details are available from the *UTASELLÁTÓ* company in Budapest (☎114-0803), which runs the catering side of *MÁV*. Hungary also runs a **car train** on the Budapest–Dresden line, which travellers to Germany might find useful, although it doesn't carry camper vans or minibuses.

If you're planning to travel a lot by rail, or take trains to neighbouring countries, it's worth investing in the **timetables** available from the *MÁV* office in Budapest (VI, Andrássy út 35) or large railway stations. Domestic services are covered by the chunky *Hivatalos Menetrend* (120Ft), which details boat and ferry services on the Danube and the Balaton as well as all internal trains. International services are listed in the *Nemzetközi Menetrend* (60Ft), a slimmer paperback. In both cases you'll need to spend a while decoding them; an English-language section at the front explains the symbols used.

TICKETS AND FARES

Tickets (*jegy*) for domestic services can safely be bought at the station (*pályaudvar* or *vasútállomás*) on the day of departure, although it's possible to reserve them up to sixty days in advance. You can break your journey once between the point of departure and the final destination, but must get your ticket punched within an hour of arrival at the interim station. It is also possible to claim a refund if you only use part of the ticket, but only at the station where it was issued. Most Hungarians purchase one-way tickets (*egy útra*), so specify a *retur* or *oda-vissza* if you want a return ticket. If you're found travelling without a ticket you have to buy one at many times the normal price.

Seat bookings (*fielyjegy*), in the form of a separate numbered bit of card, are obligatory for services marked ☐R on timetables (mostly international or express trains), and optional on those designated by an ⓡ. They cost 30Ft on most domestic routes, 100Ft on express trains, and 170Ft on international services, and can be made up to two months in advance at any *MÁV* or *Volántourist* office.

It's best to buy tickets for **international trains** (*nemzetközi gyorsvonat*) at least 36 hours in advance, since demand is heavy. Holders of IUS cards (see "Directory", below) are entitled to fifty percent reductions on services to Czechoslovakia and Poland, forty percent for Ukraine and Russia, and thirty percent to Bulgaria. The "Hungarian stage" of the journey can be paid for in forints, but the "international" phase must be paid for in hard currency unless you can produce an exchange receipt for the sum concerned. The central *MÁV* ticket office in Budapest, which handles bookings, gets crowded during summer; and staff and customers won't thank anybody who tries to pay by cheque or credit card.

Concessions in the form of reduced fares on domestic services are available for groups of ten or more people (25 percent), *BIJ/Eurotrain* ticket holders (50 percent) and pensioners with rail permits (33 percent), while *InterRail* passes allow free travel. Children under four travel free if they don't occupy a separate seat. *MÁV* itself issues various **season tickets**, valid on domestic lines nationwide (but not on the international trains within Hungary) for a week or ten days, but you'd need to travel fairly intensively to make savings with a seven-day national *Runaround* (3900Ft first-class/2600Ft second-class). Budapest season tickets are detailed under "Getting Around" in *Budapest*.

BICYCLES AND LUGGAGE

Bicycles can only be carried in the guard's van on *személyvonat*, which severely restricts your choice of trains, meaning that complicated cross-country journeys can take days. Most stations have a **left-luggage** office (*ruhatár*), which charges 30Ft per day for each item deposited – sometimes including "each item" strapped to your backpack. Beware of huge queues for baggage at Budapest's main stations (and some Balaton termini) during the summer, and keep *all* of the scrappy little receipts, or you'll never get your gear back. A few main stations have automatic luggage lockers, which take two 20Ft coins and store your baggage for up to 24 hours. **Lost property** is kept for two months at the station where it was handed in, and then forwarded to the regional *MÁV* headquarters (except for passports, which are sent to the aliens registration office – *KEOKH*, VI, Andrassy út 93, Budapest – immediately).

BUSES

Regional **Volán** ("Wheel") companies run the bulk of Hungary's **buses**, which are called *busz* (pronounced "boose" as in "loose", *not* "bus", which means "fuck" in Hungarian). Buses are often the quickest way to travel **between towns**, and while fares are higher than on the railways they're still cheap (roughly 2Ft per km). To save you from buying the eleven-volume national timetable (volume one covers inter-city services from Budapest and cross-country routes, the others local services), we have detailed useful routes in the guide. In any case, schedules are clearly displayed in bus stations (*autóbuszállomás* or *autóbusz pályaudvar*) in every Hungarian town. Arrive early to confirm the departure bay (*kocsiállás*) and be sure of getting a seat. For long-distance services originating in Budapest or major towns, you can buy tickets with a seat booking up to half an hour before departure; after that you get them from the driver, and risk standing throughout the journey. Services **in rural areas** may be limited to one or two a day, and tickets are only available on board the bus. As on trains, children under four travel free unless they occupy a separate seat, and at half-fare up to the age of ten; otherwise there are no concessions.

Volán also runs **international services** to neighbouring countries and a few points further west. The main depot for these is Erzsébet tér in Budapest (see p.45), but services also run from provincial towns like Siófok, Szombathely, Győr, Miskolc, Szeged, Baja, Mohács and Debrecen (detailed under those towns in the guide). It's fractionally cheaper to travel from Budapest to Vienna by bus, but other destinations may cost less by train. Unless you present a receipt showing that your forints were obtained legally, tickets on all international coaches must be purchased in hard currency.

URBAN PUBLIC TRANSPORT

Public transport **within towns** is generally excellent, with buses and trolleybuses (*trolibusz*), and sometimes trams (*villamos*), running from dawn until around 10.30 or 11pm. Express buses (numbered in red and prefixed by an "E") halt only at main stops, or not at all between termini, so be careful about boarding these. **Tickets** for all services are sold in strips at tobacconists and

street stands, and should be punched on board the vehicle. Municipalities set their own flat rates, causing some variation in prices nationwide. Generally, the local fare for trams and trolleybuses is identical, so the same kind of ticket can be used on both services; buses require different, slightly more costly tickets. Tickets from one town aren't supposed to be used in another. In Budapest, various types of **passes** are available (see "Getting Around" in Chapter One).

DRIVING AND HITCHING

Hungary's geographical location means that the country plays an important part in overland communications across Europe. To drive in Hungary you'll need an **international driving permit** (issued by national motoring organisations for a small fee; contact the AA in Britain, AAA in the US) and **third-party insurance**. If you're taking your own car, check with your insurance company to see if you're covered; you'll probably need a **Green Card**. You can also purchase insurance at the border, but this only covers damage to third parties in Hungary and pays out in forints, so it's wiser to fix it up before leaving home.

ROADS AND SERVICES

Hungary's roads fall into four categories. **Motorways** (*autopálya*) – prefixed by an "M" – link Budapest to Győr (M1) and Lake Balaton (M7), with other routes – currently half-finished and extremely hazardous – running towards Miskolc (M3) and Kecskemét (M5). Lesser **highways** (numbered with a single digit from 1 to 8) radiate from Budapest like spokes in a wheel; linked by **secondary roads** identified by two or three digits (the first one indicates the highway which the road joins, for example roads 82 and 811 both meet route 8 at some point). Lastly, there are unnumbered, bumpy **back-country roads**, which tourists seldom use. **Pedestrian zones** (found in many towns and shaded light blue on maps) are indicated by "Restricted Access" signs – *kivéve célforgalom*. Information on nationwide **driving conditions** can be obtained from *ÚTINFORM* (☎122-7643); conditions in Budapest are monitored by *FŐVINFORM* (☎117-1173).

The arrival of Western competitors has caused *AFOR*, the state **petrol** company, to enter into joint ventures with *BP* and *Agip*, and improve its act. Most stations (*benzinkút*) stock 98 octane *extra*; 92 octane *szuper*, 86 octane *normál*, and diesel. **Lead-free** petrol (*olomentes benzin*) is available at stations in big cities and along major routes; the *AFOR* ones are shown on a free map published by the Hungarian Automibile Club, while *Shell* sells a map of its own outlets. Petrol stations usually function from 6am to 10pm, except on highways and in the capital, where many operate around the clock.

RULES AND REGULATIONS

Drinking and driving is totally prohibited, and offenders with in excess of eight milligrams of alcohol are liable to felony charges. The state requires cars to be roadworthy (steering, brakes and all lights must work); and carry certain **mandatory equipment** – a triangular break-down sign; spare bulbs for the indicators, head-, rear- and brake-lights; a first-aid box; and a supplementary mud-guard made of a non-rigid material, attached to rear bumpers. Passengers must wear three-point safety belts in the front seats, where children are forbidden to travel.

Speed limits for vehicles are 120kph on motorways, 100kph on highways, 80kph on other roads, and 60kph in built-up areas. Offenders can expect to be heavily fined on the spot. In rural areas, wagons, cyclists, livestock and pedestrians are potential **traffic hazards**, so you should drive slowly – especially at night. Besides driving on the right, the most important **rules** are the prohibitions against repeatedly switching from lane to lane on highways; overtaking near pedestrian crossings; and sounding the horn in built-up areas unless to avert accidents. At crossroads, vehicles coming from the right have right of way, unless otherwise indicated by signs, and pedestrians have priority over cars turning onto the road. Remember that trams *always* have right of way, and that some traffic islands serve as bus or tram stops. On highways and secondary roads it's illegal to reverse, make U-turns, or stop at islands.

ACCIDENTS AND EMERGENCIES

Accidents should be reported to the *Hungaria Biztositó* insurance department in Budapest (XIV, Gvadányi út 69; ☎252-6333 Mon & Thurs 7.30am–7pm, Tues & Wed 7.30am–4pm or ☎183-6527 Mon & Thurs 8am–6pm, Tues & Wed 8am–4pm, Fri 8am–3pm) within 24 hours; if someone is injured the police must also be notified (☎07).

In Budapest you can summon the "Yellow Angels" **24-hour breakdown service** (☎252-8000), which is free if the repairs take no longer than one hour to complete and your own motoring organisation belongs to the *FIA* or *AIT* federations, to which the **Hungarian Automobile Club** – *MAK* – is also affiliated. The *MAK's* national headquarters is at Rómer Flóris utca 4A in Budapest's II district (☎166-6404; Mon–Thurs 8am–4pm, Fri 8am–3pm); but their depot for **technical assistance** in the capital is at Boldizsár utca 2 in the XI district (☎185-0722). **Spare parts** for foreign cars are easiest to find in Budapest (see "Listings" in Chapter One).

CAR RENTAL

Renting a car is easy provided you're 21 or older, with a valid national driving licence that's at least one year old. You can order a car through any *Avis*, *Hertz* or *Europcar* bureau in the world, and from hotel reception desks or certain travel agencies within Hungary, using cash or credit cards. In Budapest these agencies are *Cooptourist* (IX, Ferenc körút 43; ☎113-1466); *IBUSZ* (V, Martinelli tér 8; ☎118-4158); and *FŐTAXI* (☎122-1471); *IBUSZ*, *Volántourist* and *Cooptourist* offices offer the same service in the provinces. Rental **costs** vary from £12 ($20) per day/£72 ($122) per week for a *Lada Nova*, to £28 ($48)/£176 ($300) for a *Toyota* or *VW Golf*, or £37 ($63)/£235 ($400) for a *VW* minibus. There's a minimum deposit of around £90 ($153), plus a charge of 10–40p (20–80¢) per km and £3.50–7 ($6–12) per day insurance to add to this – not to mention the cost of petrol. The latter is not included in the price of **fly/drive holidays**.

HITCHING

Autostop or **hitchhiking** is widely practiced by young Magyars, and only forbidden on motorways. A fair number of drivers seem willing to give lifts, although your prospects at weekends are poor since cars are usually packed with families. Solo **women travellers** risk hassles, and perhaps worse, so a few precautions are recommended. Establish the driver's destination before revealing your own; note how the door opens when you get in; never accept rides from men in pairs; and keep an eye on the road signs.

PLANES AND BOATS

Malév doesn't operate any **domestic flights**, since Hungary is such a small country, but many of their **flights abroad** (departing from Ferihegy airport) are a good deal. If you're heading on to Greece or Turkey, they may prove an attractive alternative to trains — especially for holders of IUS cards, who sometimes qualify for substantial discounts. *Malév* central office (Roosevelt tér 2; ☎118-6614) is the place to make enquiries, while you can also make bookings at desks in the main Budapest hotels, or by telephone (☎118-4333).

The *MAHART* company organises **passenger boats** in Hungary, which operate on Lake Balaton, between Budapest and Esztergom, and on the section of the Danube running through the capital. Between March and November, *MAHART* also operates a daily **hydrofoil service between Vienna and Budapest**. It's a four-and-a-half-hour journey downriver to Budapest; an hour longer if you travel upriver to Vienna. Tickets to Vienna are sold at the International Boat Station on the Belgrád rakpart (the Pest embankment), where the hydrofoil departs, or at *IBUSZ* (V, Károly körút 3C); in Vienna, tickets are available from *IBUSZ* (I. Kärntnerstrasse 26; ☎43 1/515-55) or the Austrian company *DDSG* (II. Mexiko Platz 8). A one-way ticket costs about 690 Austrian schillings (£35/$60).

BIKES

The only potential drawback to **motorcycling** is that spare parts could be problematic should you have a breakdown. Motorcyclists must be over eighteen, wear a helmet, and have a log book or other registration document, plus a Green Card (see "Driving"). Aside from being required to use dimmed headlights by day, the rules of the road (and speed limits) are the same as for cars.

Given the generally flat terrain, and the light winds and small amount of rain from July until the end of September, **cycling** should also be a good way to see Hungary. In practice, however, there are several caveats. Cyclists are not allowed on main roads (with single digit numbers), and on some secondary roads between "peak hours" (7–9.30am and 4–6pm); bikes can only be carried on slow trains (*személyvonat*), severely limiting your choice of services; and in towns, there are sunken tramlines and slippery cobbled streets to contend with. All things considered, it is best to pre-plan an itinerary which avoids or at least minimises these problems. The *Cycling Tours in Hungary* booklet produced by *IBUSZ* describes over three dozen routes, graded according to effort. The most scenic areas are the Northern Uplands, the Danube Bend and parts of Transdanubia and the Bakony, where you'll find a few stiff climbs and lots of rolling hills. Conversely, the easiest cycling terrain — the Great Plain — tends to be visually monotonous. It is possible **to rent bikes** (by the day or week) in most large towns and the Balaton resorts, from *MÁV*, private operators or certain campsites (details are given in the guide). Unfortunately, most machines are low-slung and heavy, with limited gears, although superior models may gradually become available now that the *Csepel Bicycle Co* has gone into partnership with a German firm. Your best chance of getting **spares and repairs** is in Budapest (see p.50).

ACCOMMODATION

The move towards a fully capitalist economy has meant a steep rise in hotel prices and the closure of many provincial tourist hostels. On the plus side, competitively priced pensions and guesthouses are springing up everywhere, and tourists can now stay in holiday complexes formerly reserved for trade unionists, or hostels attached to colleges. All in all, it shouldn't prove difficult to find somewhere that suits your tastes and budget.

Most towns have several hotels and pensions, private lodgings for rent, and quite often a campsite or hostel within easy reach of the centre. That said, the cheapest places tend to fill up during high season (June–Sept), so it's wise to make **reservations** if you're on a tight budget or bound for somewhere with limited possibilities. This can be done **from abroad** either through travel agents (*Danube Travel* in Britain charges £10 for any number of bookings) or by telexing places yourself. The telex numbers for hotels, campsites and pensions appear in the *Hotel* and *Camping* booklets and the *Tourism Almanac* (see below). **Inside Hungary**, bookings for the three nationwide upmarket hotel chains are handled through their respective head offices in Budapest: *HungarHotels* (V, Petőfi utca 16; ☎118-3393), *Pannonia* (VIII, Rákóczi út 9; ☎114-1886) and *Danubius* (V, Martinelli tér 8; ☎117-3652). Less expensive hotels and private lodgings in the provinces are reservable through regional tourist offices or local branches of *IBUSZ*, while beds in college dormitories can usually be booked through the local *Express* agency or regional tourist office.

In the absence of any single, comprehensive **guide to accommodation** in Hungary, you'll have to make do with the free *Camping* and *Hotels* booklets stocked by most tourist offices, or invest in the *Tourism Almanac* – a trilingual volume (150Ft) known to Hungarians as the *Idegenforgalmi Almanach Magyarország*. This lists numerous pensions and campsites not mentioned in the booklets, but omits others that are. All three make useful supplements to this book.

HOTELS

Although natives call **hotels** *szálló* or *szállóda*, everyone understands the English term. Aside from smaller places in the provinces and a number of "international" hotels in Budapest, most belong to the *HungarHotels*, *Pannonia* or *Danubius* chains. Although all have an official three- or four-star rating (five-star establishments are restricted to Budapest and the Balaton), this gives only a vague idea of **prices**, which vary according to the locality and the time of year. At the time of writing there are five seasonal price-bands, with different rates for Hungarians and foreigners – but this complicated system is liable to be changed soon. As an indication of the way things are going, many places simply post current rates in Deutschmarks (although you pay in forints). More predictably, prices in Budapest and the Balaton region are 15–35 percent higher than in other areas.

Bearing this in mind, you can expect to pay between £85 and £180 ($144–306) for a double room in a five-star hotel **in Budapest or the Balaton**; £40–95 ($68–162) for a four-star place; and £35–75 ($60–128) in a three-star hotel – all of which have private bathrooms, TV and central heating. Assuming you can find one in Budapest, a double room in a two-star hotel costs about £35 ($60). The price of a double room **in the provinces** ranges from £30 to £62 ($51–140) in a four-star establishment; £21–57 ($35–97) in three-star places, whose prices overlap those of some two-star hotels (£21–37/$35–63); down to £8–28 ($13–47) in a one-star place. All of these rates are for the **high season** (June–Sept) and can drop by as much as thirty percent over **winter**. Breakfast is always included in the price.

As with prices, **standards** vary. While four- and five-star establishments are reliably comfortable, three-star places can be soulless in gone-to-seed Seventies fashion, or redolent of "old" Central Europe (a few are ensconced in former stately homes or castles). One- and two-star hotels probably won't have private bathrooms, but might have a sink in the room.

Single rooms are rare and **solo travellers** will generally have to fork out for a double.

ACCOMMODATION PRICES

With the exception of campsites, all accommodation listed in the guide is given a symbol that corresponds to one of **seven price categories**, and generally refers to the cost of a double room during high season. In cases where the ① symbol stands for a bed rather than a room, this will be indicated in the text.

① Under 650Ft (under £5/$8/DM14).
② 650–1300Ft (£5–10/$8–17/DM14–28).
③ 1300–2000Ft (£10–15/$17–25/DM28–40).
④ 2000–3000Ft (£15–23/$25–40/DM40–65).

⑤ 3000–4500Ft (£23–35/$40–60/DM65–100).
⑥ 4500–8000Ft (£35–60/$60–100/DM100–170).
⑦ Over 8000Ft (over £60/$100/DM170).

PENSIONS, INNS AND MOTELS

Other types of accommodation are likewise categorised with one to three stars. Private (often family owned) **pensions** are appearing in all the towns and villages frequented by tourists, where they often undercut hotels with the same star rating. While some are purpose-built, with a restaurant on the premises, others are simply someone's house with a TV in the lounge and a few rooms upstairs. There's no correlation between their appearance and title – some style themselves *panzió* (or *penzió*), others as *fogadó*. The latter designation is also used for **inns**, which can be a pension under another name, or more of a motel. Places that actually describe themselves as **motels** are usually on the edge of town, or farther out along the highway. Some coexist with bungalows and a campsite to form a tourist complex; quite a few are near a thermal bath or swimming pool, with restaurants and sports facilities.

Although the rating system bears some relation to **prices**, local circumstances – and the trade-off between cost and convenience – are more relevant. In some towns, a centrally located pension might cost more than an older one- or two-star hotel, whereas elsewhere they could be the best alternative to a pricey three-star establishment. Similarly, some motels are really cheap, and others on par with equivalently rated hotels in a better location. Even the rule of thumb that places get cheaper the further you are from Austria or Budapest doesn't always hold, since a pension in a remote village might exploit its monopoly to the hilt.

PRIVATE ROOMS AND FARMSTEAD ACCOMMODATION

In Budapest and many towns, **private rooms** in Magyar households are often the cheapest options in the centre. This type of accommodation (termed *Fiz*, short for *fizetővendégszolgálat*) can be arranged by local tourist offices for a fee, or by knocking on the door of places advertising *szoba kiadó* or *Zimmer frei* – which abound along the west bank of the Danube Bend, both shores of Lake Balaton, and thermal spas throughout Hungary. In Budapest and the Balaton region, the **price** of a double room is generally around £8–10 ($13–17); elsewhere £5–7 ($8–12) is the norm, although places accustomed to an influx of Germans and Austrians sometimes charge

premium rates. Unfortunately, many rentiers charge thirty percent extra if you stay fewer than three nights, and a general lack of single rooms means that solo travellers have to pay for a double.

Although tourist offices rent sight unseen, you can still exercise judgement when **choosing a room** by rejecting dubious-sounding locations; some private rooms are not at all appealing, others are excellent. As a rule of thumb, a town's *Belváros* (inner sector) is likely to consist of spacious apartments with parquet floors, high ceilings, and a balcony overlooking a courtyard, whereas the outlying zones are probably charmless, high-rise modern developments. Either way, your hostess (widows and divorcees are the biggest renters) will probably be helpful and then self-effacing, but a few words of Hungarian will make you seem less of a stranger. Use of the washing machine comes free, and some landladies will provide breakfast for a fee, although most leave early for work. For this reason, it's usually impossible to take possession of the room before 5pm; after that you can come and go with a key.

It's possible to rent whole **apartments** in some towns and resorts, while in western and southern Hungary many tourist offices can arrange rural **farmstead accommodation** in old buildings converted into holiday homes with kitchen facilities. Both come more expensive than private rooms, but if there's a group of you, or you're travelling with children, they could prove to be just the thing.

HOSTELS

Although many are due to close or become private pensions in the future, hostels are currently the cheapest lodgings going. There are two kinds of official **tourist hostels**: *Túristaszálló* – generally found in provincial towns – and *Túristaház*, located in highland areas favoured by hikers. Both are graded "A" or "B" depending on the availability of hot water and the number of beds per room. *Túristaszálló* rates range from £1.50 to £8 ($2.50–13): the former for a bed, the latter for a double or triple room. In *Túristaház*, which rarely have separate rooms, a dormitory bed goes for £1.50–3 ($2.50–5). It's generally advisable to make bookings through the regional tourist office.

In many towns, you can also stay in vacant **college dormitories** for about £2 ($3) a night.

Generally, these accept tourists at weekends throughout the year, and over the whole of the summer vacation (roughly July 1–Aug 11). It is usually possible to make bookings through the local *Express* agency or the regional tourist office, but otherwise you can just turn up at the designated college (*kollégium*) and ask if there are any beds going.

BUNGALOWS AND CAMPSITES

Throughout Hungary, bungalows and campsites come together in complexes where tourists of the world unite. **Bungalows** (*üdölőház*) proliferate around resorts, where many were previously reserved for trade union members but now take anyone to balance their books. Rates for hiring bungalows (aka *faház*, literally "wooden houses") range from £3.50 to £14 ($4–23), depending on their amenities and size (usually 2–4 persons). The first-class bungalows – with well-equipped kitchens, hot water and a sitting room or terrace – are excellent, while the most primitive at least have clean bedding and don't leak.

Campsites – usually signposted *Kemping* – similarly range across the spectrum from "deluxe" to third class. The more elaborate places boast a restaurant and shops (sometimes even a disco) and tend to be overcrowded; second- or third-class sites often have a nicer ambience, with lots of old trees rather than a manicured lawn ineffectually shaded by saplings, and acres of campers and trailers. Expect to pay at least £1.50–2 ($2.50–3), or twice that around Lake Balaton, which has the dearest sites in Hungary. Fees are calculated on a basic ground rent, plus a charge per head and for any vehicle (eg 100Ft + 150Ft + 100Ft), plus, for non-students, an obligatory local tax (*kurtaxe*). There are **reductions** of 25–30 percent during "low" season (Oct–May) when fewer sites are open, and during the high season for members of the *FICC* (International Camping & Caravaning Club). While a few resorts and towns have semi-official **free campsites** (s*zabad kemping*), **camping rough** is illegal, although young Hungarians sometimes do it in highland areas where there are "rain shelters" (*esőház*).

EATING AND DRINKING

Even under Communism, Hungary was renowned for its abundance of food: material proof of the "goulash socialism" that amazed visitors from Romania and the Soviet Union. Nowadays, there is more choice than ever, particularly in Budapest, where almost every cuisine in the world is available.

For foreigners the archetypal Magyar dish is "goulash" – historically the basis of much **Hungarian cooking.** The ancient Magyars relished cauldrons of *gulyás* (pronounced "gouyash") – a soup made of potatoes and whatever meat or fish was available, which was later flavoured with paprika and beefed up into a variety of stews, modified over the centuries by various foreign influences. Hungary's Slav neighbours probably introduced native cooks to yogurt and sour cream (vital ingredients in many dishes); while the influence of the Turks, Austrians and Germans is apparent in a variety of sticky pastries and strudels, plus recipes featuring sauerkraut or dumplings. Another influence was that of France, which revolutionised Hungarian cooking in the Middle Ages and again in the nineteenth century. Today, the influences are "international", with fast food such as pizzas, hamburgers and kebabs spreading from the capital to provincial towns, and even signs of vegetarian and nouvelle cuisine. Perhaps in reaction to these trends, some foodies now advocate *Reform konyha* (literally "Calvinist cooking") – allegedly healthier, simple meat-and-veg dishes, recommended for good Christians!

DISHES AND TERMS

What follows is by no means a comprehensive list of Hungarian dishes, but by combining names and terms it should be possible to decipher anything that you're likely to see on a menu. Alcoholic and soft drinks are covered in the text, as are desserts and pastries, which are best sampled in the ubiquitous *cukrászda*.

Basics, and how to order

bors	pepper	*kenyér*	bread	*só*	salt
cukor	sugar	*kifli*	croissant	*vaj*	butter
ecet	vinegar	*méz*	honey	*zsemle* or	bread rolls
egészségedre!	Cheers!	*mustár*	mustard	*péksütemeny*	
jó étvágyat!	Bon appetit!	*rizs*	rice		

Legyen szives ("Would you be so kind . . ".) is the polite way of attracting a waiter's attention; while you can say *Kérnék* . . . or *Szeretnék* . . . ("I'd like . . ".), or *Kaphatok* . . . ("Can I have . . . ?") **to order**. Using these grammatical forms, Hungarians add a suffix (*-t, -et, -ot* or *-at*) to the item being requested, so that *vaj* becomes *vajat, kávé, kávét*, and so on.

Appetizers (*előételek*), soups (*levesek*), and salads (*saláták*)

bécsi hering-saláta	Viennese-style herring with vinegar	*gulyásleves*	meat, vegetable and paprika soup
halmajonéz	fish with mayonnaise	*kunsági pandúrleves*	chicken or pigeon soup seasoned with nutmeg, paprika, ginger and garlic
majonézes kukorica	sweetcorn with mayonnaise		
bakonyi betyárleves	"Outlaw soup" of chicken, beef, noodles and vegetables, richly spiced	*lencseleves*	lentil soup
		meggyleves	delicious chilled sour cherry soup
csirke-aprólék	mixed vegetable and giblet soup	*palócleves*	mutton, bean and sour cream soup
csontleves	bland bone and noodle consommé	*paradicsomleves*	tomato soup
bajai halászlé	fish and tomato soup	*szegedi halászlé*	Szeged-style mixed-fish soup
bableves	beans and meat soup – a meal in itself	*zöldségleves*	vegetable soup
burgonyaleves	potato, onion and paprika soup	*alföldi saláta*	"Puszta salad" – sliced sausages in a vinaigrette dressing
gombaleves	mushroom soup		
(*kalocsai*) *halászleves*	spicy fish soup (with red wine)	*almás cékla*	dressed apple and beetroot slices

The names of other **salads** are easy to work out if you refer to the section on vegetables. **Cream** and **sour cream** feature in dishes whose name includes the words *tejszín, kem*, and *tejföl*.

Fish dishes (*halételek*)

csuka tejfölben sütve	fried pike with sour cream	*paprikás ponty*	carp in paprika sauce
fogas	a local fish of the pike-perch family	*ponty filé gombával*	carp fillet in mushroom sauce
fogasszeletek Gundel modra	breaded fillet of fogas	*pisztráng tejszín mártásban*	trout baked in cream
kecsege	sterlet (small sturgeon)	*rostélyos töltött ponty*	carp stuffed with bread, egg, herbs and fish liver or roe
. . *tejszínes paprikás mártásban*	. . . in a cream and paprika sauce	*sült hal*	fried fish
nyelvhal	sole	*tökehal*	cod
		tonhal	tuna

Meat (*húsételek*) and poultry (*baromfi*) dishes

alföldi marha-rostélyos	steak with a rich sauce and stewed vegetables	*nyúl*	rabbit
bográcsgulyás	what foreigners mean by "Goulash"	*paprikás-csirke*	chicken in paprika sauce
		rablóhús nyárson	kebab of pork, veal and bacon
borjúpörkölt	veal stew seasoned with garlic	*sertésborda*	pork chop
csabai szarvascomb	venison stuffed with spicy sausage	*sonka*	ham
		töltött-káposzta	cabbage stuffed with meat and rice, in a tomato sauce
cigányrostelyos	"Gypsy-style" steak with brown sauce	*töltött-paprika*	peppers stuffed with meat and rice, in a tomato sauce
csikós tokány	strips of beef braised in bacon, onion rings, sour cream and tomato sauce	*vaddisznó borókamártással*	wild boar in juniper sauce
		virsli	frankfurter
csirke	chicken		
erdélyi rakott-káposzta	layers of cabbage, rice and ground pork baked in sour cream – a Transylvanian speciality	**Terms**	
		comb	leg
		félig nyersen	underdone/rare
fasírozott	meatballs	*főve*	boiled
hortobágyi rostélyos	steak "Hortobágy style"; braised in stock, with a large dumpling	*jól megsütve*	well done (fried)
		jól megfőzve	well done (boiled)
kacsa	duck	*pörkölt*	stewed slowly
kolbász	spicy sausage	*rántott*	in breadcrumbs
liba	goose	*roston sütve*	grilled
máj	liver	*sülve*	roasted
marhahús	beef	*sült/sütve*	fried

Sauces (*mártásban*)

Many restaurants serve meat or fish dishes in rich **sauces** – a legacy of French culinary influence.

almamártásban	in an apple sauce	*kapormártásban*	in a dill sauce
bormártásban	in a wine sauce	*meggymártásban*	in a morello cherry sauce
gombamártásban	in a mushroom sauce	*paprikás mártásban*	in a paprika sauce
ecetes torma	with horse radish	*tárkonyos mártásban*	in a tarragon sauce
fehérhagyma mártásban	in an onion sauce	*vadasmártásban*	in a brown sauce (made of mushrooms, almonds, herbs and brandy)
fokhagymás mártásban	in a garlic sauce		

Vegetables (*zöldség*)

bab	beans	*fokhagyma*	garlic	*paprika – édes* or *erős*	peppers – sweet or hot
borsó	peas	*gomba*	mushrooms	*paradicsom*	tomatoes
burgonya (krumpli)	potatoes ("spuds")	*hagyma*	onions	*sárgarepa*	carrots
		káposzta	cabbage	*spárgá*	asparagus
ecetes uborka	gherkin	*karfiol*	cauliflower	*uborka*	cucumber
fejes	lettuce	*kukorica*	sweet corn	*zöldbab*	green beans

Fruit (*gyümölcs*) and cheese (*sajt*)

alma	apples	*málna*	raspberries	*füstölt*	a term covering several smoked cheeses, one of which unwinds like licorice laces
barack	apricots	*mandula*	almonds		
citrancs	grapefruit	*meggy*	morello cherries		
citrom	lemon				
dió	walnuts	*mogyoró*	hazelnuts	*karaván*	tasty smoked cheese
eper	strawberries	*narancs*	oranges	*márvány*	Stilton-like blue cheese
füge	figs	*őszibarack*	peaches		
(görög) dinnye	(water) melon	*szilva*	plums	*trappista*	rubbery, Edam-type cheese
körte	pears	*szőlő*	grapes		

BREAKFAST AND SNACKS

As a nation of early risers, Hungarians like to have a calorific **breakfast** (*reggeli*). Commonly, this includes cheese, eggs or salami together with bread and jam, and in rural areas is often accompanied by a shot of *pálinka* (brandy) to "clear the palate" or "aid digestion". By 8am, cafés and snack bars are already functioning, and the rush hour is prime time for *Tej-bár* or *Tejivó*. These stand-up milk bars serve mugs of hot milk (*meleg tej*) and sugary cocoa (*kakaó*), cheese-filled pastry cones (*sajtos pogácsa*) and rolls (*sajtos-rollo*), envelopes of dough filled with curds (*túrós táska*), spongy milk-bread with raisins (*mazsolás kalács*), and other dunkable pastries.

Everyone is addicted to **coffee**. At intervals throughout the day, people consume tiny glasses of *kávé* – super-strong, served black and sweetened to taste – a brew that can double your heart beat. **Coffee houses** were once the centres of Budapest's cultural and political life, hotbeds of gossip where penurious writers got credit and the clientele dawdled for hours over the free newspapers. Sadly this is no longer the case, but you'll find plenty of unpretentious *kávéház* serving the beverage with milk (*tejeskávé*) or whipped cream (*tejszínhabbal*) should you request it. Most coffee houses have some pastries on offer, although you'll find much more choice in the patisseries (see "Cakes and ice cream", below) which, of course, also serve coffee. **Tea**-drinkers are a minority here, perhaps because Hungarian tea with milk (*tejes tea*) is so insipid – although *tea citrommal* (with lemon) is fine.

A whole range of places purvey **snacks**, notably *Csemege* or **delicatessens**, which display a tempting spread of salads, open sandwiches, pickles and cold meats, and are really superior takeouts (in a few, you can eat on the premises). Unfortunately, many delis (like *Tej-bár*) use the system whereby customers order and pay at the cash desk (*kassa*) in return for a receipt to be exchanged at the food counter. If your Hungarian is minimal, this can throw up a few misunderstandings. For sit-down nibbles, people patronise **bisztró**, which tend to offer a couple of hot dishes besides the inevitable salami rolls; *snackbár*, which are superior versions of the same, with leanings in the direction of being a patisserie; and *büfé*. These last are found in department stores and stations, and are some-times open around the clock. The food on offer, though, is often limited to tired sandwiches and greasy sausages filled with rice (called *hurka* and *kolbász*).

On the streets, according to season, vendors preside over vats of *kukorica* (corn on the cob) or trays of *gesztenye* (roasted chestnuts); while fried fish (*sült hal*) shops are common in towns near rivers or lakes. *Szendvics*, *hamburger* and *gofri* (waffle) stands are mushrooming in the larger towns, while *McDonald's* and *Burger King* are set to spread from Budapest to other cities. **Around resorts**, another popular munch is *lángos*: the native, mega-size equivalent of doughnuts, often sold with a sprinkling of cheese or a dash of syrup. Fruit, too, is sold by street vendors (see the food list) and **in markets**, where you'll also find various greasy spoons forking out *hurka* and the like. Outdoor markets (*piac*) are colourful affairs, sometimes with the bizarre sight of rows of poultry sheltered beneath sunshades; in market halls (*vásárcsarnok*), people select their fish fresh from glass tanks, and their mushrooms from a staggering array of *gomba*, which are displayed alongside toxic fungi in a "mushroom parade" to enable shoppers to recognise the difference.

No list of snacks is complete without mentioning **bread** (*kenyér*), which is so popular, as the old saying has it, that "Hungarians will even eat bread with bread". The white loaves produced by the state bakeries are unsatisfyingly bland – hence the popularity of privately run *házi-kenyér* ("Home Bread") vans – but their brown (*barna*) and rye (*rozs*) breads, stocked by *Malomipari* shops and large supermarkets, are fine.

MAIN MEALS

Traditionally, Hungarians take their main meal at midday; so the range of dishes offered by restaurants is greater for lunch (*ebéd*) than for dinner (*vacsora*) in the **evenings**. Sunday evenings in particular are the worst time to eat out, with stale bread and limited menus. Another point worth noting is that the kitchens in many places begin to close down at 10pm. There's some compensation, though, in the bands of musicians that play in many restaurants at lunchtime and in the evening, their violin airs and melodic plonkings of the cimbalom an essential element of the "Hungarian scene".

All eating places display signs signifying their class, or *osztály* (*oszt.*). This categorisation from I to IV is a fair guide to **comparative prices**, but doesn't necessarily reflect the quality of the food served. Some excellent meals can be had in humble III *oszt.* joints, while a restaurant's I *oszt.* rating may derive solely from its flashy decor. Places used to tourists often have **menus** in German (and sometimes English), a language that most waiters and waitresses have a smattering of. Particularly in Budapest, tourist-oriented establishments may give you a menu without prices – a sure sign that they're expensive, or plan to rip you off. **Overcharging** is unfortunately on the increase, and even fluent Hungarian speakers can get burned if they don't check the bill carefully. While some restaurants offer a set menu (*napi menü*) of basic dishes for about £1.50 ($2.50), the majority of places are strictly *à la carte*. For a three-course meal with a beer, expect to pay £3.50–5 ($6–8) in an average class II restaurant, twice that in downtown Budapest. A service charge isn't usually included in the bill and the staff depend on customers **tipping** (ten percent of the total is customary).

Hungarians have a variety of words implying fine distinctions among **restaurants** – in theory an **étterem** is a proper restaurant, while a **vendéglő** approximates the Western notion of a bistro – but in practice the terms are often used interchangeably. The Sixties saw the advent of **kisvendéglő** – basically smaller versions of bistros that became youth hangouts; nowadays this title may also denote seedy, raucous dives in the vicinity of factories and stations, where women on their own are likely to attract unwelcome attention. The old word for an inn, **csárda**, applies to posh places specialising in certain dishes (eg a "Fishermen's inn" or **halászcsárda**), restaurants alongside roads, or with rustic pretensions, as well as the humbler rural establishments that it originally signified. At the bottom of the heap are **Önkiszolgáló, self-service** restaurants mostly open 8am to 8pm on weekdays. They're rock-bottom cheap and you can see the food while ordering it (removing the uncertainty inherent in menus or the cash desk system), but the grubby decor and the prospect of lukewarm food outside peak hours (midday and around 6–7pm) are both disadvantages.

When they can afford to be, Hungarians are enthusiastic eaters, so as a (presumably rich) Westerner you'll be asked if you want **starters** (*előételek*) – generally a soup or salad. Nobody will mind, however, if you just have one of the dishes offered as the **main course** (*fő ételek*) or, alternatively, order just a soup and a starter. Bread is supplied almost automatically, on the grounds that "a meal without bread is no meal". **Drinks** are normally listed on the menu under the heading *italok*.

OPTIONS FOR VEGETARIANS

Despite the emergence of *vegetarianus* restaurants in Budapest, and a growing understanding of the concept, the outlook for **vegetarians** remains poor: most Hungarians are amazed that anyone might forgo meat willingly. Aside from cooked vegetables (notably *rántott gomba*, mushrooms in breadcrumbs), the only meatless dish that's widely available is **eggs** – fried (literally "mirror" – *tükörtojás*), soft-boiled (*lágy tojás*), scrambled (*tojásrántotta*), or in mayonnaise (*kaszínótojás*). Even innocuous vegetable soups may contain meat stock, and the pervasive use of sour cream and animal fat in cooking means that avoiding animal products or by-products is difficult. However, greengrocers (*zöldségbolt*) and markets sell excellent produce which, combined with judicious shopping in *ABC* supermarkets (for pulses, grains, etc) should see you through.

CAKES AND ICE CREAM

Numerous **patisseries** (*cukrászda*) pander to the Magyar fondness for sweet things. **Pancakes** (*palacsinta*) **with fillings** – *almás* (apple), *diós* (walnuts), *fahej* (cinnamon), *mákos* (poppy seeds), *mandula* (almonds) or *Gundel*-style, with nuts, chocolate sauce, cream and raisins – are very popular, as are **strudels** (*rétes*) made with curds and dill (*kapros túrós rétes*), poppy seeds (*mákosrétes*) or plums (*szilvás rétes*). Even the humble dumpling is transformed into a *somlói galuska*, flavoured with vanilla, nuts and chocolate and served in an orange and rum sauce. But the frontrunners in the rich 'n' sticky stakes have to be chestnut pureé with whipped cream (*gesztenyepüré*); chocolate soufflé (*kapucineres felfújt*); baked apple with vanilla, raisins and cream (*töltött alma*); and the staggering array of **cakes**. *Dobostorta* (chocolate cream cake topped with caramel) and the pineapple-laden *ananásztorta* are just two; the average *cukrászda* displays a dozen or more types, all temptingly priced around 50Ft. If you're still not satiated, there's **ice cream** (*fagylalt*), the opium of the masses, sold by the scoop (*gomboc*) and priced low enough so that anyone can afford a cone. The most common flavours are *vanília*, *csokoládé*, *puncs* (fruit punch), *citrom* and *kávé*; but mango, pistachio, and various nutty flavours can be found – see the fruit section of the food box for the Magyar names. And finally there's *metelt* – a rather unlikely-sounding but quite tasty dessert of chopped sweet noodles, served cold with poppy seeds or some other topping.

DRINKING: WINE, BEER AND SPIRITS

Hungary's mild climate and diversity of soils is perfect for **wine** (*bor*), which is perennially cheap, whether you buy it by the bottle (*üveg*) or the glass (*pohár*). The main wine-growing regions surround Pécs, Eger, Kecskemét, Sopron and Tokaj, and cover large areas of the Balaton and Mátra highlands. Standards are constantly rising as more vineyards try to win the right to label their bottles *minőségi bor* (quality wine), the equivalent of *appelation contrôlée*. By day, people often drink wine with water or soda water, specifying a *fröccs* or a yet more diluted *hosszú lépés* (literally, a "long step"). **Wine bars** (*borozó*) are ubiquitous and generally far less pretentious than in the West; true devotees of the grape make pilgrimages to the extensive **wine cellars** (*borpince*) that honeycomb towns like Tokaj and Eger.

Hungarian **red wines** (*Vörös bor*) can be divided into light-bodied and full-bodied types. Examples of the former are *Villányi burgundi*, *Vaskúti kadarka* and *Egri pinot noir*; in the full-bodied category are *Villányi medoc noir*, *Tihanyi merlot*, *Soproni kékfrankos* and the famous *Egri bikavér*, or "Bulls' Blood of Eger". **White wines** (*fehér bor*) are classified as sweet (*édes*) or dry (*száraz* or *furmint*). *Olasz riszling* wines tend to be sweet, with the exception of the "Sand Wines" produced on the sandy soil between the Tisza and the Danube. Other sweet whites include *Balatonfüredi szemelt*, *Akali zöldszilváni*, and the richest of the Tokaj wines, *Tokaji aszú*. In the dry category are three wines from the Badacsony vineyards, *kéknyelű*, *szürkebarát* and *zöldszilváni*; *Egri Leányka* from the Gyöngyös region; and two varieties of Tokaj, *furmint* and *szamorodni* (which means "as it's grown"). *Tököly* and *Pannonia* are sparkling wines.

Hungarians enjoy the ritual of **toasting**, so the first word to get your tongue around is *egészségedre* ("EGG-aish-shaig-edreh") – cheers! When toasting more than one other person, it's grammatically correct to change this to *egészségünkre* (Cheers to us!). Hungarians only consider it appropriate to toast with wine or spirits.

As long as you stick to native brands, **spirits** are also cheap. The best-known type of *pálinka* – brandy – is distilled from apricots (*barack*), and is a speciality of the Kecskemét region, but spirits are also produced from peaches (*őszibarack*), pears (*körte*), and any other fruits available. This is particularly true of *szilva* – a lethal spirit produced on cottage stills in rural areas, allegedly based on plums. Hungarians with money to burn order whisky (*viszki*) to impress, but most people find its cost prohibitive. Vodka isn't popular, despite the availability of excellent Russian *Stolichnaya* in *ABC*s.

Bottled **beer** (*sör*) of the lager type (*világos*) predominates, although you might come across brown ale (*barna sör*) and draught beer (*csapolt sör*). Western brands like *Tuborg*, *Wernesgrünner* and *Gold Fassel* are imported or brewed under licence at Nagykanizsa, and the famous old Austro-Hungarian beer *Dreher* has made a comeback, displacing cheaper Magyar brands such as *Kőbányai*, or imported Czech *Urquell* Pilsen. Other brands to try are *Arany Aszok*, a very cheap light beer, and *Pannonia Sör*, a pleasant hoppy beer from Pécs. **Beer halls** (*söröző*) range from plush establishments sponsored by foreign breweries to humble stand-up joints where you order either a small glass (*pohár*) or a half-litre mug (*korsó*).

SOFT DRINKS

Pepsi and Coke and various sugary, fruit-flavoured **soft drinks** are sold from street stalls and in coffee houses and patisseries. A few (mostly German) brands of unsweetened fruit juices can be found in supermarkets and *Vitamin Porta* shops. Most *ABC*s also stock bottled *limonád*, mineral water (*ásvány víz*), soda water (*szóda víz*) and Hungarian *Kóla*.

COMMUNINCATIONS: POST, PHONES AND MEDIA

minutes after 6pm), though some of the older machines only take 2Ft coins. **Long-distance calls** are more problematic, for while lines between Budapest and provincial centres are okay, communications between smaller towns are poor and all incoming or outgoing calls must be placed by the post office or the operator (☎01). This goes for all numbers prefixed by the locality's name rather than an area code. Elsewhere, it should be possible to make direct calls by dialling ☎06 (which gives a strange tone), followed by the area code and the subscriber's number. Even so, you might still achieve better results by getting the post office or operator to place the call.

In downtown Budapest and the Balaton resorts there are now booths taking **phone-cards**, which can be bought from main post offices for 270Ft or 540Ft – an innovation that is sure to spread to provincial cities such as Pécs or Szeged. This has already happened with the special red or grey booths (taking 10Ft and 20Ft coins) that allow you to make **international calls**. Dial ☎00, then the country code (see box below), the area code and finally the number – and keep your fingers crossed. Alternatively, you can place calls through the international operator (☎09), the Central Telephone Bureau in Budapest, or fancy hotels in the provinces (which levy a hefty surcharge).

POST OFFICES

Post offices (*posta*) are usually open 8am–6pm Monday to Friday and until noon on Saturday, although in Budapest you'll find several offices functioning around the clock. Mail from abroad should be addressed "*poste restante, posta*" followed by the name of the town; tell your friends to write your surname first, Hungarian-style, and underline it; even this may not prevent your mail being misfiled, so ask them to check under all your names. To collect, show your passport and ask "*Van posta a részemre?*". A more secure "drop" is the American Express office in Budapest (V, Deák Ference utca 10), or their former office, the 24-hour *IBUSZ* bureau (V, Petőfi tér 3) – where letters marked "c/o American Express" are lovingly guarded until collection, and the staff speak English. Letters (*levél*) can be sent to anywhere in the West for 40Ft, postcards for 30Ft – plus a surcharge for air mail. It's quicker to buy stamps (*bélyeg*) at tobacconists; post offices are often full of people making complicated transactions or sending telegrams (*távirat*), which can also be dictated by dialling ☎02.

PHONES

Hungary's **telephone network** is being improved and expanded, but remains patchy and inefficient at the time of writing. In towns and cities, **local calls** can be made from public phones where 5Ft gets you three minutes (six

---

TELEPHONE CODES
International codes (dialling from Hungary):
Australia ☎61
Austria ☎43
Czechoslovakia ☎42
Irish Republic ☎353
Netherlands ☎31
New Zealand ☎64
Poland ☎48
UK ☎44
USA and Canada ☎1

Country code for Hungary (calling from abroad): ☎36.

Area codes for Hungarian towns and cities appear in the guide section.

MEDIA

Without a knowledge of Hungarian you can only appreciate certain aspects of the **media**. Foreign cable and satellite television have made huge inroads, and there is a rash of tabloids and magazines devoted to soft porn and celebrity trivia. Many papers are now owned by foreign press barons such as Rupert Murdoch.

Western programmes are much in evidence on the two national **television** stations, TV1 and TV2, which many Hungarians augment by subscribing to *Sky*, *MTV* or *Super Channel*, with whole apartment blocks sharing the cost of installation. Hungary not only broadcasts *Neighbours*, but produces its own equivalent, *Szomszédok*, which is set – and filmed – on a Buda housing estate. Editorially speaking, TV1 and TV2 are respectively pro- and anti-government – a policy intended to satisfy both the ruling and opposition parties.

The serious **press** is similarly partisan, with *Új Magyarország* supporting the conservative government, while *Népszabadság* (formerly Communist, but now avowedly socialist) adopts a critical stance, and the daily *Magyar Hírlap* (purchased by the late Robert Maxwell) swings both ways. Having made a big splash as Hungary's first "independent" paper in 1988, the tabloid weekly *Reform* no longer attracts much attention with its mix of scandal and page-three girls.

In Budapest you can buy papers and magazines **in English** and other languages, notably *The Times*, *Guardian*, *Herald Tribune*, *Newsweek* and *Time*; German publications are also sold around Lake Balaton. *Budapest Weekly*, produced by expatriate Americans, combines listings and entertainment features with limited coverage of Hungarian affairs. Similar listings and press agency reports from around the world appear in the *Daily News*, a publication which almost followed Communism into oblivion, but now hopes to come out regularly again.

If these don't appeal, drop into the British or American cultural centres in Budapest, or try the **radio**. A new German-language station, *Radio Danubius*, lets rip with pop, rap and ads, broadcasting on a daily basis from 6.30am to 10pm throughout the summer until October 31 (100.5, 103.3, or 102 MHz VHF); while *Radio Petőfi* broadcasts news in English at 11am (weekdays) and 11.57am (Sat) from June to August. Alternatively, tune into the *BBC World Service* on 24.80, 30.77, 48.54, or 49.59 MHz, or 12.095, 9.75, 6.18 or 6.05 Metres. The lower frequencies (MHz) tend to give better results early in the morning and late at night, the higher ones during the middle of the day.

OPENING HOURS AND HOLIDAYS

During the week, most public buildings are open from 8.30am to 5pm, but it's worth remembering that the staff at lesser institutions usually take an hour off around noon for lunch. Aside from shops and tourist offices, the most obvious exceptions are museums, which almost always close on Monday. Otherwise, opening times are affected by the shift to and from summer time (see "Directory", p.38), and by public holidays, when most things shut down. These are December 25 and 26, January 1, March 15, Easter Monday, May 1, August 20 and October 23. Should any of these holidays fall on a Tuesday or Thursday, the day between it and the weekend also becomes a holiday.

MUSEUMS

Museums are generally open Tuesday to Sunday 10am–6pm (winter 9am–5pm, or earlier), but there are many exceptions so it is best to check details under each town in the guide. As public subsidies are withdrawn, many of the smaller museums could close down altogether over winter. Admission charges vary from 10Ft to 100Ft and IUS/ISIC cards (see "Directory") secure reductions, or free entry in many cases. Some places have free admission on Saturdays or Wednesdays. Hungary has about 600 museums, whose contents range from the crown jewels down to the dullest junk. Almost none of them have captions in any language but Hungarian, although important museums in provincial centres and the capital might sell catalogues in German, French or English. For surmounting the language barrier, **Skanzens** or **Village Museums** are probably the most effective – fascinating ensembles of buildings and domestic objects culled from old settlements around the country, assembled on the outskirts of Szentendre, Nyíregyháza, Zalaegerszeg and Szombathely, or preserved in situ at Szalafő and Hollókő.

CHURCHES AND SYNAGOGUES

Hungary's few remaining mosques (*djami*) now qualify as museums rather than places of worship, but getting into **churches** (*templom*) may pose problems. The really important ones charge a small fee to see their crypts and treasures, and may prohibit sightseeing during services (*szertartás*, or *Gottdienst* in German). In small towns and villages, however, churches are usually kept locked except for worship in the early morning and/or the evening (between around 6 and 9pm). A small tip is in order if you rouse the verger to unlock the building during the day; he normally lives nearby in a house with a doorbell marked *plébánia csengője*. Visitors are expected to wear "decorous" dress – that is, no shorts or sleeveless tops.

Most of Hungary's **synagogues** were ransacked during World War II and subsequently left derelict or given over to other functions. Although a fair number have been reopened and restored since the late 1980s, only Budapest retains a sizeable Jewish community.

The Hungarian terms for the main **religious denominations** are: *Katolikus* (Catholic), *Református* (Reformed or Calvinist), *Evangélicus* (Lutheran), *Görög* (Greek Orthodox), *Görög-Katolikus* (Uniate) and *Zsidó* (Jewish).

ENTERTAINMENTS AND FESTIVALS

Music and dance are probably the easiest paths through the thicket of language that surrounds Hungarian culture, but they're not the only accessible forms of entertainment. During the summer in particular, you'll find plays or films in foreign languages – or festivals where language is a minor obstacle – in many of the main towns and resorts.

GYPSY AND FOLK MUSIC

No visitor to Hungary should fail to experience **Gypsy music** or *cigányzene*, which is widely performed in restaurants during the evening, usually by one or two violinists, a bass player and a guy on the cimbalom – a stringed instrument played with little hammers. *Mulatni* means "to be possessed by music", and the Gypsies have always venerated the range of sounds and emotions produced by the violin, the playing of which – *bashavav* – has traditionally had magical associations. The sense of awe that great violinists used to inspire, and their bohemian lifestyles, are well captured in Walter Starkie's book *Raggle Taggle* (see "Books" in *Contexts*).

Hungarians are keen to make requests or sing along when the *Prímás* (band leader) comes to the table, soliciting tips. If approached yourself, it is acceptable (though rather awkward) to decline with a *nem, köszönöm*. Nowadays, most musicians are townspeople and graduates of the *Rajkó* music school, rather than wandering, self-taught artists like János Bihari, Czinka Panna and Czermak (a nobleman turned vagabond) – who were legendary figures during the nineteenth century. However, it's still common for sons to follow their fathers into the profession.

Confusingly, this archetypal "Hungarian" music is neither Hungarian nor Gypsy in its origins. The music performed by Gypsies among their own communities (in Szabolcs-Szatmár county, for example) is actually far closer to the music of India and Central Asia, and inaccessible to outsiders unless they catch a concert by the Gypsy group *Kalyi Jag* (Black Flame).

Hungarian folk music (*Magyar népzene*) is different again, having originated around the Urals and the Turkic steppes over a millennium ago. The haunting rhythms and pentatonic scale of this "Old Style" music (to use Bartók's terminology) were subsequently overlaid by "New Style" European influences – which have been discarded by twentieth-century enthusiasts in the folk revival centred around **Táncház**. These "Dance Houses" encourage people to build and learn to play archaic instruments, besides providing the site for **dances** which are usually fast and furious – particularly the wild, foot-stamping *csárdás*, or "tavern dance". Aside from Dance Houses, you can hear folk music at various festivals (see below), and at concerts by **groups** like *Muzsikás* and the *Kalamajka* and *Sebö* ensembles. For a selection of folk records, see "Music and Records" in *Contexts*.

POPULAR MUSIC AND JAZZ

At Budapest clubs and Balaton discos, the most **popular music** is whatever was the rage in the West six months earlier. Depending on the venue, this is likely to be Eurorock, House or rap music – either imported straight from New York or Berlin, or cooked up by a sound-alike group in Budapest. Live music – at least outside the capital – is pretty much limited to the obligatory summer concerts by native pop stars (advertised in *Programme* magazine), or appearances by bands in smoky local clubs (look for flyposters carrying the word *zene*, music).

Budapest itself, since it became established on the international concert circuit in the mid-Eighties, has been visited by such diverse **foreign acts** as the Talking Heads and Dylan, Springsteen and Tina Turner. Concerts usually take place in one of the city's football stadiums over summer.

At the time of writing **the contemporary music scene** is derivative and uninspiring. The charts are dominated by Kylie Minogue clones such as *Dora* and *Szandi*, or heavy metal/thrash groups like *Ossian*, *V. Moto-rock* and *Bikini*. The punky female duo *Pa-dö-dö* is also popular at the moment. Aside from these, there are several groups dating back to the Seventies – notably *Locomotiv GT* (playing a mix of styles from folk to

heavy metal) and the country music parodists *Folk Celsius 100* – plus new wave bands from the late Eighties, of which the best is probably *Vágtazo Halott Kémek* (The Galloping Coroners). The local club circuit also throws up skinhead bands like *Akció, Egység* (Action, Unity) and *Egészéges Fejbőr* (Healthy Headskin), whose neo-Nazi fans are best avoided.

Though nowhere near as popular, **jazz** is currently undergoing a revival. The Budapest club scene offers the widest choice, but aficionados should check *Programme* magazine for advance notice of jazz **festivals** at Debrecen, Tatabánya, Székesfehérvár, Nagykanizsa or Zalaegerszeg – usually over summer. *Aladár Pege* and the *Benkó Dixieland Band* have both achieved success outside Hungary, but foreign jazz fans have yet to cotton on to pianist György Szabados, who works on the interface between jazz and classical music.

CLASSICAL MUSIC, OPERA AND DANCE

Bartók, Kodály and Liszt still enjoy pride of place in the field of **classical music**, but modern composers can be heard at the *Interforum* festival, staged at Keszthely every three years (scheduled next for 1993). The "**Spring Days**" in late March see a host of concerts in Budapest, Szeged, Debrecen, Kecskemét and other towns, with similar "seasons" over **summer** (in Szeged) and **autumn** (in Budapest and Nyíregyháza). Aside from these landmarks, the concert year features Haydn's and Beethoven's works (performed in the palatial surroundings of the Esterházy and Brunswick mansions); orchestral concerts at Veszprém and Diósgyőr castles; organ recitals in the main churches of Pécs, Buda, Debrecen, Eger, Miskolc, Szeged and Tihany; and chorales in the Gothic churches at Köröshegy and Nyírbátor (mainly over summer). Performers to watch out for are Dezső Ránki and Zoltán Kocsis, whose names will be inverted on posters, Hungarian style (see "Directory").

The reputation of the state **opera** continues to grow, with singers like Adrienne Csengery winning rapturous acclaim abroad. The Budapest Opera's **ballet** company is classically oriented, and most of the impetus for **modern dance** comes from the Pécs and Győr companies, whose superb reputations make it difficult to get tickets when they visit the capital. Details of performances and the addresses for making bookings appear in *Programme* magazine.

CINEMA

Hungarian cinema is going through an identity crisis, its former role as licensed social critic no longer relevant in a post-Communist Hungary, where people would rather watch Hollywood blockbusters and soft porn movies. Directors seem at a loss now that censorship has been abolished: ideological subtleties count for nothing, and they are expected to cater for lowbrow tastes. Their uncertainty is compounded by the reduction of subsidies and the need to find commercial support. For this reason, the annual **Hungarian Film Festival** did not occur in 1991, while in 1992 it only did so with the backing of private enterprise. Should the festival survive, February is the time to catch new Hungarian films, dubbed or subtitled for the benefit of foreign critics.

Unlike István Szabó – whose big-budget international productions *Colonel Redl* and *Mephisto* have made him well known (and wealthy) abroad – other talented **directors** still dwell on the darker side of Hungarian life, tackling subjects such as abortion (Pál Zolnay), rape (Judit Elek), incest (Zsolt Kézdi-Kovács) and Stalinism (Péter Bacsó, Márta Mészáros). Understandably, their compatriots prefer to watch foreign films, the majority of them dubbed into Magyar (indicated by *m.b.* or *Magyarul beszelő* on posters); the Hungarian for cinema is *filmszínház* or *mozi*.

FESTIVALS

The **festival year** kicks off with the **Mohács Carnival** of masked revellers re-enacting ancient spring rites and ritual abomination of the Turks on March 1, followed later in the month by the **Spring Days** (*Tavasi Napok*) of music and drama in Budapest, Szeged, Kecskemét, Debrecen and other towns. On **March 15**, wreaths are laid at monuments to commemorate the anniversary of the 1848 Revolution against the Habsburgs. Nowadays, **May 1** is just a public holiday, shorn of the Soviet-style parades that characterised it during the Communist period.

With the onset of tourists and fine weather, the summer months soon get crowded with events. With the exception of the week-long *Téka Tábor* **festival of folk arts** at Nagykálló (in late July), most of them are listed in *Programme* magazine.

You can see **historical pageants** at Veszprém, Tihany, Visegrád, Gyula or Esztergom; and **equestrian shows** with a "rodeó atmosphere and amazing displays of horsemanship at Nagyvázsony, Apajpuszta, Tamási, Kisbér, Szántódpuszta and Hortobágy. The two-day Hortobágy Bridge Fair and the **Szeged Weeks** of music and drama reach their climax on **St Stephen's Day** (Aug 20), which honours the death of Hungary's patron saint and "founding father" with parades and fireworks in Budapest, a Flower Carnival in Debrecen, and lesser displays in provincial towns.

Budapest's **Autumn Music Weeks** (late Sept–late Nov) more or less round off the year. **October 23**, the anniversary of the 1956 Uprising, has lost the emotional potency it had as a "forbidden anniversary" under Communism, since its belated commemoration with patriotic pageantry and cathartic reburials in 1990.

Although Saint Stephen's relics attract multitudes of worshippers to the great Basilica in Pest, **religious festivals** aren't widely observed in contemporary Hungary. The most obvious exception is Easter, when the churches and cathedrals are packed – particularly in Esztergom, the seat of Hungarian Catholicism. Another, more remote focus for religious fervour is the village of Máriapócs in eastern Hungary, which draws thousands of pilgrims on August 15 and September 8 (see p.306).

It is also worth knowing about the tradition of **name-day celebrations**, which are as important to Hungarians as birthdays are in other countries. Customarily, the celebrant invites relatives and friends to a party, and receives gifts and salutations. Lest you forget someone's name-day, tradition allows congratulations to be rendered up to a week afterwards.

SPORTS

Since hosting the 1988 World Ice Skating Championships, Hungary has been angling for other major sporting events to supplement its annual Budapest Marathon and Hungarian Grand Prix. Full details of these, and national championships in everything from parachuting to canoeing are available from *IBUSZ*, regional tourist offices, and in *Programme* magazine.

Several pages of the weekly paper *Népsport* are devoted to **football** (*labdarúgás*), Hungary's most popular sport. Current First Division contenders include the Budapest teams *Kispest Honvéd*, *Ferencváros* (aka "Fradi") and *Újpesti TE*; and *Győri Rába ETO*, *DVTK* and *Váci Izzó MTE* from the provinces. Players to look out for are Lajos Détári, Kálmán Kovács, Zsolt Petry and József Gregor. Tickets for matches are cheap, as are facilities at local **sports halls** (*Sportcsarnok*).

Windsurfing (*szörf*) and **sailing** equipment can be hired (*kölcsönző*) at the main Balaton boat stations and Lake Velence, and **tennis** (*tenisz*) courts are often attached to more upmarket hotels in Budapest and main resorts. Hungary's topography rules out any dramatic or lengthy slopes, but that doesn't stop enthusiasts from **skiing** in the Mátra Mountains and the Buda Hills. Visitors into **hiking** can avail themselves of detailed maps of the highland regions (see box below).

HIKING SYMBOLS

Mountain trails are generally marked with multi-coloured symbols (painted on tree trunks or boulders) which correspond with routes marked by the following initial letters, on maps:

K – kek (blue) S – saga (yellow)
R – piros (red) F – zöld (green)

HORSE-RIDING

Hungarians profess a lingering attachment to the horse – their equestrian ally since the time of the great migration and the Magyar conquest – and the horseherds or *csikós* of the Plain are romantic figures of national folklore. Most native **horses** are mixed breeds descended from Arab and English thoroughbreds, crossed in recent years with Hanoverian and Holstein stock. The adjective most commonly used to describe their character is "spirited" or "mettlesome".

Horse-riding tours, organised by *Pegazus Tours* (V, Ferenciek tere 5; ☎117-1644; Mon–Fri 9am–5pm) in Budapest, come in various forms. There are several itineraries around the Balaton, the northern uplands and the Great Plain, lasting from a week to ten days, with meals, lodgings and guide included; and somewhat bizarre expeditions by **covered wagons**, which tourists drive and navigate across the puszta. To give you an idea of prices, an eight-day tour starts at around £535/$910.

Regional tourist offices and local enterprises offer equestrian programmes and instruction at **riding schools** (*Lovarda*), namely: Alag, Üllő-Tornyoslöb and Ady-liget **near Budapest**; Taliándorog, Nagyvázsony, Nagyberek, Szentbékkálla, Szántódpuszta, Siófok and Keszthely **around the Balaton**; Tata, Szombathely, Sárvár, Radiháza, Nagycenk and Dunakiliti **in Transdanubia**; Visegrád on the **Danube Bend**; Szilvásvárad in the **Northern Uplands**; and Hortobágy, Bugac, Tiszafüred, Makó and Szatymaz on the **Great Plain**. Ask *IBUSZ* for their *On Horseback* booklet, and check with local tourist offices if you're interested. The schools provide saddlery, but you'll need your own riding clothes.

WORK AND STUDY

Teaching English is the main opportunity for work in Hungary, where a command of the language is now required for university entrance examinations (replacing Russian, which was compulsory until 1989). Native speakers are in great demand and language teaching is a big business, particularly in Budapest. As most teaching is at an intermediate or advanced level, you are seldom required to speak much (if any) Hungarian.

Assuming you can get enough clients, the most profitable option is **giving private lessons**. Qualified teachers can charge up to 1000Ft an hour, but as few Hungarians can afford this, it's more realistic to settle for 400–600Ft per hour. This is roughly twice what you'd get **working in a language school**, where monthly salaries average 20,000–30,000Ft (minus 20 percent tax and health insurance) for around twenty hours per week. The most reputable schools in Budapest are *IHB* (V, Cukor utca 4; ☎118-4467) and *IHLS* (II, Bimbó utca 11), both of which require experience, if not a TEFL certificate. *ILS* (V, Bajscy-Zsilinszky út 62) is less fussy, but doesn't give contracts and may not provide enough work to pay for renting a flat in Budapest (15,000–30,000Ft per month). Some employers will arrange **work permits**, but others leave it up to you. The process involves a lot of paperwork and medical reports.

Although **teaching in primary or secondary schools** pays much less (around 2000Ft per month), the deal usually includes subsidised or free accommodation. Expect to work fifteen hours

a week, mostly in the morning. Primary school work is not exam oriented and largely involves playing games with pupils aged 6–14. Secondary school classes are smaller, but teachers will need at least basic Hungarian, since the exam is based on translation. The former may take anyone who seems capable and enthusiastic; the latter are likely to require at least a TEFL and/or a PGCE certificate.

Recruitment for state schools is handled by several agencies abroad (see below) and three clearing houses inside Hungary. The *Budapest Pedagogical Institute* (VIII, Horváth Mihály tér 8) recruits for schools in the capital; the *English Teacher's Association of the National Pedagogical Institute* (II, Bolyai utca 14), also in Budapest, recruits for the provinces; while *IATEFL* in the southern town of Kecskemét (Academia körút 20), does likewise.

Better still you can make arrangements abroad. Qualified teachers (with a degree or TEFL certificate) are currently being recruited **in Britain** by the *Eastern European Partnership*, 15 Princeton Court, 53–55 Felsham Road, London SW15 1AZ (☎081/780 2841). The two-year contract includes travel, accommodation and medical expenses. Other agencies such as the British Council may also advertise for teachers (usually in the *TES* or *Guardian* between April and June).

Native-speaking sixth-formers, students or teachers (up to the age of 45) can apply for jobs at English-language **summer camps** (generally 3 weeks during July/Aug). Besides giving Hungarian 15- to 17-year-olds the chance to practice their English, you're expected to organise sports and/or drama and musical activities – so previous experience in these areas is desirable. Board and accommodation is provided but applicants must pay for their own travel to Hungary; applications should be made to the *Youth Exchange Centre*, Seymour Mews House, Seymour Mews, London W1H 9PE (☎071/486 5101 ext 24) by the end of March.

In the **United States** volunteer teachers can apply to the Peace Corps (1990 K Street NW, Washington DC 20526) for two-year assignments; the Fulbright Program (which offers a round-trip fare, salary and housing); or George Washinton University (PO Box 2798, Washington DC 20057).

SUMMER COURSES

Eager to publicise their cultural achievements and earn foreign exchange, the Hungarians also organise **summer courses** in everything from folk art to environmental studies. Full details are contained in a booklet published in the spring, which can be obtained by writing to *TIT* (the Society for the Dissemination of Scientific Knowledge), H-1088 Budapest, VIII, Bródy Sándor utca 16. The deadline for most applications is May 1, so it's advisable to write months in advance. Students are of all ages and come from countries as diverse as Switzerland and Venezuela, so the chance to meet people can be as much an attraction as the subject to be studied. These include photography (at Vác), Hungarian language and culture (Debrecen), fine arts (Zebegény), Esperanto (Gyula), Baroque recorder music (Sopron), jazz (Tatabánya), orchestral music (Pécs and Kecskemét), music-teaching by the Kodály method (Esztergom and Kecskemét), folk art (Zalaegerszeg) and nature studies (Keszthely). Fees include room and board and various excursions and entertainments.

TROUBLE AND SEXUAL HARASSMENT

The Hungarian police (*Rendőrség*) always had a milder reputation than their counterparts in other Eastern bloc states, and are keen to present a favourable image. Foreign tourists are generally handled with kid gloves unless suspected of black-marketeering, drug-smuggling, driving under the influence of alcohol, or of being illegal immigrants (who, like Hungary's Gypsy minority, are roughly treated).

However, since police in towns occasionally ask to inspect passports and visas, you should make sure that everything's in order. In border regions, solo travellers may be (politely and briefly) questioned by plain-clothes secret policemen; but here too, if your stamps are in order, there shouldn't be any problem. Most police officers have at least a smattering of German, but rarely any other foreign language. If you need the police, dial ☎07 in **emergencies**; should you be arrested or need legal advice, ask to contact your embassy or consulate (see "Listings" in *Budapest* for the addresses).

Although **theft** and violent crime are rare, their incidence is growing, not least because of the widening gap between rich and poor. Budapest in particular is no longer utterly safe at night, though still far less risky than any Western capital. There has also been a worrying upsurge in **racist attacks** on Africans, Asians and Arabs, in some cases encouraged by foreign neo-Nazis. That said, **trouble** can be avoided. Don't sunbathe nude or topless unless everyone else is, or deal on the black market, and you've eliminated the likeliest causes.

SEXUAL HARASSMENT

The exception is **sexual harassment**, which is mainly a problem for women travelling alone, and more likely in certain situations than in others. "Provocative" clothing may encourage unwelcome male attention if you visit rural or working-class *italbolt* (bars), or hitchhike alone. It is advisable to avoid travelling on the "black train" (see p.267), and walking around Budapest's VIII district or in Miskolc after dark.

Mostly, harassment is of the annoying rather than the frightening variety, and it's probably not worth responding with "*ne fogdoss!*" (keep your hands to yourself!) or "*menj a fenébe!*" (go to hell!). The important word to remember is *segítség!* – help! – although it's unlikely that you'll need to use it.

DIRECTORY

ACCENTS For technical reasons, street names on the maps in this book have not always been given the proper accents.

ADDRESSES usually begin with the postcode, which indicates the town or city and locality. The most common terms are *utca* (street, abbreviated to *u.*), *út* (or *útja*, avenue), *tér* (or *tere*, square) and *körút* (ring boulevard). You may also encounter *rakpart* (embankment), *sétány* (promenade), *hid* (bridge), *köz* (lane), *hegy* (hill) or *liget* (wood). Town centres are signposted *Belváros*, *Városközpont* or *Centrum*. A *lakótelep* is a high-rise housing estate.

BRING . . . any specific medication or contact lens sundries that you might need. Western fashion and pop magazines are much appreciated in trendy (*divatos*) circles. Passport-sized photos come in handy for season tickets, student cards, etc.

CAMPERS should bring a primus stove, which takes local *spiritusz*, since camping gas canisters are hard to find. Candles – *gyertya* – are sold in supermarkets; buy lots if you're going on to Romania or Bulgaria, since they're hard to find there, and may be so poor that they won't burn.

CHILDREN (*gyerek*) qualify for reductions on most forms of public transport (see "Getting Around"), and fifty percent off the cost of camping up to the age of 14. Separate visas aren't required for children under 14 who are included on their parent's passport (assuming they need

one at all). The best facilities and entertainments for kids are in Budapest and the Balaton resorts. Children are forbidden to ride in the front seat of a car. Most supermarkets stock baby food and *Libero* disposable nappies.

CIGARETTES are sold in tobacconists (*dohánybolt*), supermarkets, bars and restaurants. *Marlboro* and *Camel* made under licence are cheaper than imports, but still more expensive than "native" brands like charcoal-filtered *Helikon* and *Sopianae*, or throat-rasping *Symphonia* and *Munkás*. Matches are *gyufa*. *Tilos a dohányzás* means "no smoking", and applies to cinemas, the Metro, all buses, trams and trolleybuses.

CONTRACEPTIVES Hungarian or German-made condoms (*óvszer*, *gumi* or *kondom*) are available at the cash tills in chemists, and in some food stores. Reliable, locally manufactured contraceptive pills and morning-after pills are available on prescription, although it's always more sensible to bring your own.

ELECTRIC POWER 220 volts. Round, two-pin plugs are used. A standard continental adaptor allows the use of 13 amp, square-pin plugs. Televisions and VCRs brought from Britain will only function if they are dual-system, or adjusted to Secam.

FILM Kodak, Fuji, Agfa and Konica film is readily available, and most towns offer colour processing services. Mini-labs in Budapest and major towns can process and print films in a couple of hours.

GAY MEN AND LESBIANS are emerging from the closet, but caution is still the watchword. Although the age of consent for lesbians and gay men is 18, they remain liable to police harassment and public disapproval. The organisation *HOMEROS-Lambda*, founded in 1988, maintains a low profile, fearful of antagonising the newly powerful Catholic Church, which allegedly pressured the government into halting advertisments for condoms and safer sex. A law passed under the Communists permits the compulsory blood-testing of "suspected" HIV-carriers. Given this, and public homophobia, it's hardly surprising that visible manifestations of gay life are limited to Budapest (see p.101).

LAUNDRY Self-service launderettes (*mosoda*) are rare, and *Patyolat* (local cleaning services) are unlikely to have your washing or dry-cleaning back in less than 48 hours. Staying in private lodgings, you may be allowed to use your host's washing machine. All supermarkets sell detergent.

NUDISM (often known by the German initials *FKK*) is gaining ground – with nudist camps outside Budapest, Szeged, Mohács and Balatonberény, and nude sunbathing on segregated terraces at some pools – but you can't assume that it's permitted. However, a fair number of women do get away with going topless around the Balaton and on certain campsites – there's safety in numbers, it seems. For more information, contact the *Naturisták Egyesülete* (Naturist Union) in Budapest (XIII, Kárpát utca 8).

SHOPS AND SUPERMARKETS in larger towns are usually open 9am–7pm (8pm on Thurs) during the week, on Saturday until midday or 5pm. Budapest and a few other places also have 24-hour food shops; the signs to look for are *Non-Stop*, *0–24* or *Éjjel-Nappali*. Generally, supermarkets are called *ABC* and department stores *Áruház*, while shops are usually named after their wares, for example *húsbolt* (butchers), *italbolt* (drink), *papírirószerbolt* (stationery shop) and *ciposbolt* (shoe shop).

STUDENT CARDS entitle you to small reductions at some hostels and campsites, free or reduced admission to museums, and significant discounts on certain international railway tickets and *Malév* flights. The East European student organisation, IUS, produces its own card, which in the past has been the only one to give discounts; it may, however, be superseded by the ISIC card in the future. For the time being, it's best to bring an ISIC card with you and then to get an IUS card in Hungary from an *Express* office or railway station. *Express* offices in Budapest might issue cards without asking for proof that you're a full-time student (photo required).

SURNAMES precede forenames in Hungary, to the confusion of foreigners. In this book, the names of historical personages are rendered in the Western fashion – for instance, Lajos Kossuth rather than Kossuth Lajos (Hungarian-style) – except when referring to buildings, streets, etc.

TIME Hungary is one hour ahead of GMT in Britain, and six hours ahead of EST and nine ahead of PST in North America. During summertime (from the end of March to the end of Sept) these differences increase by one hour.

THE
GUIDE

CHAPTER ONE

BUDAPEST

The importance of **BUDAPEST** to Hungary is difficult to overestimate. Over two million people – one fifth of the population – live here, and everything converges on Budapest: the roads and railways; flights to Ferihegy (the only civilian airport); opportunities, wealth and power; industry, commerce and culture. Like Paris, it has a tradition of revolutions – in 1849, 1918 and 1956 – buildings, parks and avenues on a monumental scale, and a reputation for hedonism, style and parochial pride; in short, it's a city worthy of comparison with other great European capitals.

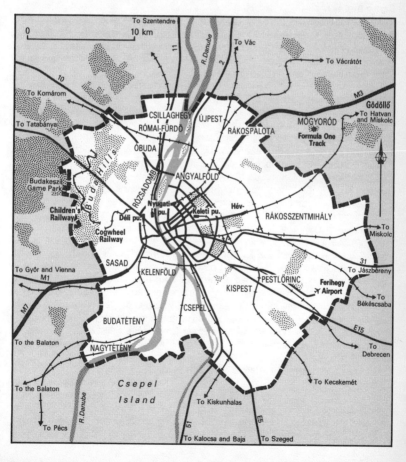

Surveying Budapest from the embankments or the bastions of Castle Hill, it's obvious why the city was dubbed the "Pearl of the Danube". Its grand buildings and sweeping bridges look magnificent, especially when floodlit or illuminated by the barrage of fireworks launched from Gellért Hill on St Stephen's Day. The eclectic inner-city and radial boulevards combine brash commercialism with a *fin-de-siècle* sophistication, while a distinctively Hungarian character is highlighted by the sounds and appearance of the Magyar language at every turn.

Long known as the liveliest city in the Eastern bloc, Budapest has experienced a new surge of energy since the end of Communism. The choice of restaurants, bars and entertainments has never been greater – and there's also a sleazy side to the city that accounts for its reputation as the "Bangkok of Europe". While some Hungarians fear the corruption and ultimate erosion of their culture by foreign influences, others herald the start of a new golden age, with Budapest as the foremost city in *Mitteleuropa*.

Some history

Though Budapest has formally existed only since 1873 – when the twin cities of Buda and Pest were united in a single municipality – the history of settlement here goes back to the second millennium BC, or even earlier. During the first Age of Migrations, the area was settled by waves of peoples, notably Scythians from the Caucasus and Celts from what is now France.

During the first century BC, the Celtic Eravisci tribe were absorbed into the Roman Empire as part of the vast province of Pannonia. Pannonia was subsequently divided into two regions; one of them, *Pannonia Inferior*, governed from **Aquincum**, a garrison town on the west bank of the Danube, where the ruins of a camp, villas, baths and an amphitheatre can be seen today. When the Romans pulled out early in the fifth century AD, the Huns moved in to claim Aquincum; Attila's brother, Buda, probably gave his name to the west bank.

Germanic tribes, Lombards, Avars and Slavs succeeded one another during the second Age of Migrations, until finally the **Magyars** arrived in about 896. According to the medieval chronicler Anonymous, the clan of Árpád settled on Csepel Island, the other tribes spreading out across the Carpathian basin. It was under the Árpád dynasty that Hungary became a Christian state, ruled first from Esztergom and then from Székesfehérvár.

The **development of Buda and Pest** did not really begin until the twelfth century, and was largely thanks to French, Walloon and German settlers, working and trading here under royal protection. Both towns were devastated by the Mongols in 1241, but rebuilt by colonists from Germany, who named Buda *Ofen*, after its numerous lime-kilns (the name Pest, which is of Slav origin, also means "oven"). Under the Angevin kings of the fourteenth century, Buda became a **royal seat**, with a succession of palaces on Castle Hill, that reached its apogee under the Renaissance monarchy of "Good King" Mátyás and his Italian-born queen, Beatrice.

Hungary's catastrophic defeat at Mohács in 1526 paved the way for the **Turkish occupation** of Buda and Pest, which lasted 160 years before a pan-European army finally recaptured Buda Castle – after a six-week siege – at the twelfth attempt. Under **Habsburg rule**, with control exerted from Vienna or Pozsony (Bratislava), recovery was followed by a period of intensive growth during the second half of the eighteenth century. During the first decades of the next century, Pest became the centre of the **Reform movement** led by Count Széchenyi – whose vision of progress was embodied in the **Chain Bridge**, the first permanent link between Buda and Pest (which had hitherto relied on pontoon bridges or barges).

When the Habsburg empire was shaken by revolutions across Europe in **March 1848**, local reformists and radicals seized the moment. While Kossuth dominated Parliament, Petőfi and his fellow revolutionaries from the *Café Pilvax* mobilised crowds on the streets of Pest. After the War of Independence ended in defeat for the Hungarians, Habsburg repression was epitomised by the hilltop Citadella, built to cow the citizenry with its guns.

Following the Compromise of 1867, which established the Dual Monarchy familiarly known to its subjects as the *K & K* (from the German for "Emperor and King"), the twin cities underwent rapid **expansion** and formally merged. Pest was extensively remodelled, acquiring the Great Boulevard and the grand thoroughfare that runs from the Belváros to the Városliget, where Hősök tere (Heroes' Square) and Vajdhunyad Castle were constructed for Hungary's **millennial anniversary celebrations** in 1896. New suburbs were created to house the burgeoning population, which was by now predominantly Magyar, although there were still large German and Jewish communities. Early this century Budapest's **cultural efflorescence** rivalled that of Vienna, its café society that of Paris – a Belle Époque doomed by World War I.

In the aftermath of defeat, Budapest experienced the tumultuous **Republic of Councils** under Béla Kun, and occupation by the Romanian army. The *status quo ante* was restored by **Admiral Horthy**, self-appointed Regent for the exiled Karl IV (the "Admiral without a fleet, for the king without a kingdom"). His regency was characterised by gala balls and hunger marches, bombastic nationalism and anti-Semitism. Yet Horthy was a moderate compared to the Arrow Cross fascists, whose power grew as **World War II** raged.

Anticipating Horthy's defection from the Axis in 1944, Nazi Germany staged a coup, installing an Arrow Cross government, which helped them begin to massacre the **Jews** of Budapest; and blew up the Danube bridges to hamper the advancing Red Army. The six-month-long **siege of Budapest** reduced Castle Hill to rubble and severely damaged much of the rest of the city, making **reconstruction** the first priority for the post-war coalition government.

As the **Communists** gained ascendancy, the former Arrow Cross torture chambers filled up again. A huge statue of the Soviet dictator (whose name was bestowed upon Budapest's premier boulevard) symbolised the reign of terror carried out by **Mátyás Rákosi**, Hungary's "Little Stalin". However, his liberally inclined successor, Imre Nagy, gave hope to the people, who refused to tolerate a comeback by the hardliners in **1956**. In Budapest, peaceful protests turned into a city-wide **uprising** literally overnight: men, women and children defying Soviet tanks on the streets.

After Soviet power had been bloodily restored, **János Kádár** – initially reviled as a quisling – gradually normalised conditions, embarking on cautious reforms to create a **"goulash socialism"** that made Hungary the envy of its Warsaw Pact neighbours and the West's favourite Communist state during the late Seventies. A decade later, the regime saw the writing on the wall and anticipated Gorbachev by promising **free elections**, hoping to reap public gratitude. Instead – as Communism was toppled in Berlin and Prague – the Party was simply voted out of power in Hungary.

The removal of the red star from Budapest's Parliament building and the restoration of old street names throughout the city are symbolic of a desire to go back to **the future** – but many of the changes unfolding bring with them new uncertainties. What will happen to venerated institutions taken over by foreign capital, or the refugees interned to discourage others from hustling on Váci utca? Will Budapest **EXPO 1996** prove to be a costly fiasco or crown the city's renaissance? And so people pass time, arguing over a flow of *káva* and cigarettes, or wallowing in Turkish baths that remind them that troubles pass, but Budapest is enduring.

Orientation, arrival and information

The River Danube – which is never blue – determines basic **orientation**, with Buda on the hilly west bank and Pest covering the plain across the river. More precisely, you can refer to Budapest's 22 districts (*kerület*), designated on maps and street signs by Roman numerals; or use the historic names of quarters (some only recently restored after decades of official disfavour). In **Buda**, the focus of attention is the I district, comprising Castle Hill and the Watertown; the XI, XII, II and III districts are worth visiting for the Gellért and Buda hills, Óbuda and Római-Fürdő. **Pest** revolves around the downtown Belváros (V district) within the Small Boulevard, beyond which lie the VI, VII, VIII and IX districts, respectively known as the Lipótváros Terézváros, Erzsébetváros, Józsefváros and Ferencváros.

It's easier to make sense of this in practice than the welter of names might suggest. Districts and streets are well signposted, and those in Pest conform to an overall plan based on radial avenues and semicircular boulevards. The finer points of addresses are covered in the box below.

BUDAPEST ADDRESSES

For everyday purposes, **Budapest addresses** begin with the number of the district – for example, V, Petőfi tér 3 – a system used throughout this chapter. When addressing letters, however, a four-digit postal code is used instead, the middle digits indicating the district (so that 1054 refers to a place in the V district). Far more relevant to visitors is the wholesale **renaming of streets** on a district-by-district basis (which has so far spared Marx tér). To help people adjust, the new signs show the old names, too, but crossed out in red.

As a rule of thumb, **street numbers** ascend away from the Danube, or the Kossuth utca/Rákóczi út axis in Pest. Even numbers are generally on the left-hand side, odd numbers on the right. One number may refer to several premises or an entire apartment block, while an additional combination of numerals denotes the floor and number of individual **apartments** (eg III/24). Confusingly, some old blocks in Pest are designated as having a half-floor (*félemelet*) or upper ground floor (*magas földszint*) between the ground (*földszint*) and first floor (*első emelet*) proper – so that what a Briton would call the second floor, an American the third, Hungarians describe as the first. This stems from a nineteenth-century taxation fiddle, whereby landlords avoided the higher tax on buildings with more than three floors.

Arrival

Other than the airport, all points of **arrival** are fairly central, most within walking distance or just a few stops by metro from downtown Pest. Depending on when and where you arrive, consider either arranging somewhere to stay before leaving the terminal (there are reservation services at all of them), or stashing your luggage before setting out to look on your own.

By air

Ferihegy Airport has two terminals: Ferihegy 1, which is used by most airlines, and Ferihegy 2, serving *Malév, Air France* and *Lufthansa*. Unfortunately, the bus-shuttle that used to run to Erzsebet tér in downtown Pest has recently stopped operating, leaving you with only two ways to get into town. The cheap method is to catch a #93 bus to Kőbánya-Kispest, and then switch to metro line 3, alighting ten stops later at Deák tér; a journey of about forty minutes. Alternatively, there are taxis, which invariably charge way over the official fare (it should be roughly £6/$10) and demand payment in hard currency – there appears to be a tightly-run "Mafia" that ensures honest drivers can't work at the airport. Any of the tourist offices at Ferihegy can reserve accommodation.

By train

The Hungarian word *pályaudvar* (abbreviated to *pu.* in writing only) is used to designate seven of Budapest's **railway stations**, only three of which are useful to tourists and on the metro. Translated into English, their names refer to the direction of services handled rather than location, so that the Western Station (*Nyugati pu.*) is actually north of downtown Pest, and the Southern Station (*Déli pu.*) further north than the Eastern Station (*Keleti pu.*).

Trains from Vienna's Westbahnhof terminate at **Nyugati Station**, by Marx tér on the northern edge of Pest's Great Boulevard; there's a left-luggage office inside the waiting room beside platform 13 and an *IBUSZ* office on platform 10. With pickpockets working the queue, it's safer to change money at *Cooptourist* or *Budapest Tourist* in the metro arcade outside the station, where you can also book rooms. To reach Deák tér, ride the metro two stops in the direction of Kőbánya-Kispest.

Pest's **Keleti Station**, on Baross tér in the VIII district, is even worse for thieves and hustlers, especially at night, when it's taken over by prostitutes and the homeless. In summer there are long queues at the left-luggage, *IBUSZ* and *Express* offices, making it better to do business with *Budapest Tourist* at Baross tér 3 (beyond the overpass on the other side of the square) or Erzsébet körút 41 (a 10-min walk). Keleti is three stops from Deák tér by Déli pu.-bound metro.

Déli Station itself is 500m behind Castle Hill in Buda. Rooms and exchange are handled by *IBUSZ* and *Budapest Tourist* in the mall by the metro entrance (left-luggage is around the corner), or you can cross the park towards Castle Hill to deal with *Cooptourist* at Attila út 107. Déli Station is four stops from Deák tér by any metro train.

By bus

International bus services invariably wind up at the **Erzsébet tér bus station**, just by Deák tér on the edge of downtown Pest. Its left-luggage office is smaller than those at the railway stations but rarely busy, and there are several tourist offices in the vicinity. You'll find *Omnibusz* in the bus station, *Dunatours* and *Budapest Tourist* at Bajcsy-Zsilinszky út 17, 150m north, and *IBUSZ* at Károly körút 21, slightly further in the other direction. *TOURINFORM* (see below) is just around the corner and the 24-hour *IBUSZ* bureau on the Pest embankment is less than ten minutes' walk away.

Coming from another part of Hungary, you might arrive instead at **Népstadion bus station** in the XIV district, or the **Árpád híd bus station** in the XIII. Neither has any tourist facilities, but they're both just four or five metro stops from the centre of Pest.

By hydrofoil
Hydrofoils from Vienna dock at the **international landing stage** on the Belgrád rakpart (embankment), near downtown Pest. *Volántourist* is just outside the terminal and there are two *IBUSZ* offices five minutes' walk north, on Ferenciek tere inland of the Erzsébet Bridge, and Március 15. tér by the big hotels along the embankment.

Information and maps

Leaving aside the business of finding accommodation, the best source of **information** is **TOURINFORM** at V, Sütő utca 2 (daily 8am–8pm; ☎117-9800), just around the corner from Deák tér metro. Their friendly polyglot staff can answer just about any question on Budapest, or travel elsewhere in Hungary.

Get hold of a proper **map** of the city at the earliest opportunity. The small freebies supplied by tourist offices give an idea of Budapest's layout and principal monuments, but lack the detail of the larger, folding maps sold all over the place. The *Inner City of Budapest* map covers just that, in excellent detail, but for total coverage you can't beat the light-blue **Budapest Atlasz** (215Ft), showing every street, bus and tram route; the location of restaurants, museums and suchlike; and even marking the numbers on many streets. It also contains enlarged maps of Castle Hill, central Pest, Margit Island and the Városliget, plus a comprehensive index.

Details of **what's on** can be found in the free, bilingual magazine *Programme*, the trendier paper *Budapest Week* (50Ft), and the Hungarian-language listings weekly *Pesti Műsor*. For more on this, see "Entertainments" later in the chapter.

Tours
Although Budapest can easily be explored without a guide, visitors hard-pressed for time might appreciate a **city tour**. The cheapest one going (currently 900Ft) is the three-hour, air-conditioned coach tour offered by *Jade Imperial*, VI, Teréz körút 55 (☎112-8671), which starts at 10am from the car park outside *McDonald's* in Nyugati Station. Of the plethora of other tours available, the only one worth considering is the **tour of Parliament** – which can't be visited otherwise – combined with the Mátyás Church or the National Gallery, organised by *Budapest Tourist*, V, Roosevelt tér 5 (☎117-3555).

The phone code for Budapest is ☎1

Getting around

Budapest's excellent **public transport** system ensures that few parts of the city are more than thirty minutes' journey from the centre, and much of it can be reached in half that time. The language and local geography may be unfamiliar, but it doesn't take long to pick up the basics and start using the system to full effect. It's also extremely cheap – unlike **taxis** (which may take advantage of tourists) – and preferable to **driving** or **cycling** amidst the traffic jams and fumes that afflict Budapest's thoroughfares. Most of the backstreets and historic quarters, however, are eminently suited to **walking** – and this is much the best way to appreciate their character. Budapest's outer suburbs are well served by overground **HÉV trains**, while Danube **ferries** and the **Children's Railway** in the Buda Hills offer fun excursions.

Metro

Running at two- to five-minute intervals between 4.30am and 11.10pm, Budapest's **metro** reaches most areas of interest to tourists, its three lines intersecting at Deák tér in downtown Pest (see map). From nearby Vörösmarty tér, **line 1** (coded yellow) runs out beneath Andrássy út to Mexikoi út, beyond the Városliget. The red **line 2** connects Déli Station in Buda with Keleti Station and Örs vezér tere in Pest; and the blue **line 3** describes an arc from Kőbánya-Kispest to Újpest-Központ, via Ferenciek tere and Nyugati Station. There's little risk of going astray once you've learned to recognise the signs *bejárat* (entrance), *kijárat* (exit), *vonal* (line) and *felé* (towards). Drivers announce the next stop between stations.

   Tickets must be punched aboard the trains on line 1, and at the entrance barriers on lines 2 and 3. Sticking to one line, you can travel for up to an hour and break your journey as often as you like using a single ticket; but each change of line requires a new ticket.

Buses, trams and trolley buses

Buses (*autóbusz*) are useful for journeys that can't be made by metro – especially around Buda, where Moszkva tér (on metro line 2) and Móricz Zsigmond körtér (southwest of Gellért Hill) are the main bus depots. Most buses run every five to fifteen minutes from 6am to 11pm. Regular services are numbered in black; buses with red numbers make fewer stops en route; and those with an "E" suffix run non-stop between terminals (be careful about boarding these). Busy routes are also served by **night buses** (one to four an hour) with black numbers and an "É" suffix. You can board and exit through any door, but buses will only stop if there is someone waiting to get on or off (push the button above the door if you want the driver to stop). You should cancel your own ticket on board using the orange punch-machines; if you can't reach one, ask fellow passengers to oblige.

   Yellow **trams** (*villamos*) are chiefly good for travelling around the Great Boulevard or along the embankments. Services run from early in the morning to 10 or 11pm (*Utolsó kocsi indul . . .* means "the last one leaves . . ."), with **night trams** (from one to four an hour) along a limited number of routes. From May to September, special 1920s **"nostalgia trams"** run along the Pest embankment on Saturdays and the Buda embankment on Sundays. Intended for sightseeing, these cost 60Ft – way above the ordinary tram fare.

Tourists have little need to use **trolley buses** (*trolibusz*), since none of the thirteen routes are especially notable. The reason the route numbers start at 70 is allegedly because the first trolley bus line was inaugurated on Stalin's seventieth birthday in 1949.

Tickets and passes

Yellow **tickets** valid for the metro, buses, trams, trolley buses and suburban HÉV lines (see below) are sold at metro stations, newspaper kiosks and tobacconists, and currently cost 18Ft. You can also buy **day passes** (*Napijegy*), costing 150Ft, which are valid for unlimited travel until midnight, and worth buying if only to avoid queuing and punching tickets all the time. Two types of **season ticket** are also sold at metro stations. The cheaper version covers trams, trolley buses, the metro, HÉV and cogwheel railway; the other can be used on buses too. They cost, respectively, 310Ft or 430Ft for a week; 420Ft or 580Ft for two weeks; and 620Ft or 860Ft for a month. Bring a photo along as you'll also need to buy a photocard.

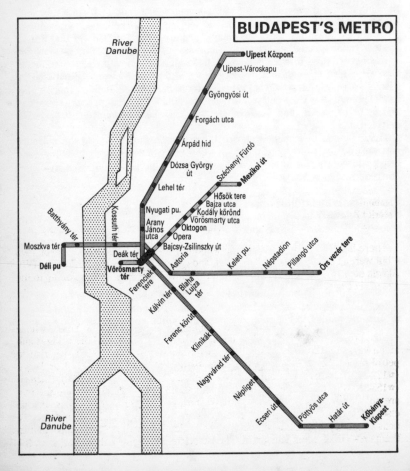

BUDAPEST'S METRO

SOME USEFUL BUS AND TRAM ROUTES

BUSES

#1 Kelenföld Station–Deák tér–Hősök tere–Mexikoi út (for the Gellért Baths, National Museum and Széchenyi Baths).

#7 Bosnyák tér–Keleti Station–Móricz Zsigmond körtér–Kelenföld Station (via Rákóczi út, Ferenciek tere, the Gellért, Rudas and Rác Baths).

#16 Erzsébet tér–Dísz tér (Castle Hill).

#22 Moszkva tér–Budakeszi Game Park.

#26 Marx tér–Szent István körút–Margit Island.

#27 Móricz Zsigmond körtér–Gellért Hill.

#56 Moszkva tér–Szilyági E. fasor–Hűvösvölgy.

#65 Kolosy tér–Pál-völgyi Cave–Hármasmatár-hegy.

#86 Gellért tér–the Watertown–Flórián tér (Óbuda).

#105 Lékai J. tér–Chain Bridge–Deák tér–Hősök tere.

#116 Március 15. tér–Dísz tér (Castle Hill).

NIGHT BUSES

#6É Moszkva tér–Margit Island–Nyugati Station–Great Boulevard–Móricz Zsigmond körtér.

#78É Örs vezér tere–Keleti Station–Buda side of the Erzsébet Bridge,

following the route of metro line 2 most of the way.

#182É Kőbánya-Kispest–Újpest along the route of metro line 3.

TRAMS

#2 Along the Pest embankment.

#4 Moszkva tér–Margit Island–Nyugati Station–Great Boulevard–Boráros tér–Schönherz Zoltán utca.

#6 Moszkva tér–Margit Island–Nyugati Station–Great Boulevard–Boráros tér–Móricz Zsigmond körtér.

#19 Batthyány tér–the Watertown–Kelenföld Station.

#56 Moszkva tér–Szilyági E. fasor–Hűvösvölgy.

There is a 600Ft **fine** for travelling without a ticket, reduced to 50Ft if you own – but weren't carrying – a season ticket, and can produce it at the *BKV* office (VII, Akácfa utca 15, near Blaha Lujza tér metro) within three days. **Children** up to the age of six travel free.

Taxis

Budapest has 18,000 registered **taxis** (more per head than New York), whose drivers proved themselves a force in 1990, when they blockaded the bridges and motorways for three days, until the government rescinded a massive rise in petrol prices. Some belong to the **state firms** *Volántaxi* (☎166-6666) or *Fõtaxi* (☎122-2222); others to **cooperatives** such as *Budataxi* (☎120-4000), *Citytaxi* (☎153-3633), *Gábriel Taxi* (☎155-5000) and *Rádió Taxi* (☎127-1271); and the rest are **solo operators** – the ones with Western cars charging more than anyone else. While those in the first two categories are generally reliable, many freelance taxis are dodgy, operating without meters (which is illegal) or "forgetting" to turn them on – check when you get in. The best **drivers** display a merit badge on the dashboard, for so many hundred thousand accident-free kilometres, and post their **prices** – currently 20–30Ft to start, then 30Ft per kilometre, with a surcharge after midnight. The worst ones hang around the airport and stations, charging six times the official fare from the airport into town, and demanding payment in hard currency.

Taxis can be flagged down or engaged at ranks throughout the city. Ordering by phone, you must give your address, full name and telephone number; most companies can take orders in English.

Driving and car rental

All things considered, **driving** in Budapest can't be recommended. Road manners are non-existent (the bigger the car, the meaner the driver), parking space is scarce and traffic jams are frequent. The Pest side of the Chain Bridge and the roundabout before the tunnel under Castle Hill are notorious for collisions. Careering trams, smoke-belching Trabants and unexpected one-way systems make things worse. If you do have a car, you might be better off parking it somewhere outside the centre and using public transport to get in and out.

If you're going **to rent a car**, eschew cheaper, unreliable Ladas (from £9/$15 a day) in favour of Western models (upwards of £12/$20 a day). Most agencies also rent minivans. Payment must be in hard currency and incurs 25 percent tax, and you can also expect to pay a substantial deposit (of £60–120/$100–200). See "Listings", p.107, for agency addresses.

Cycling

Cyclists must contend with the same hazards as drivers, plus sunken tram-lines and slippery cobbles – and are banned from major thoroughfares. Although biking under these conditions is hardly feasible, Budapest is the best place in Hungary **to get repairs or buy a bike** for use elsewhere. Given that state retailers sell bikes unassembled and it takes ten days for them to be put together at a depot (XIV, Egressy út 17–21), it's not surprising that private bike shops are mushrooming. Try the *Kerékpár Műhely* at V, Kálmán Imre utca 23 (Mon–Fri 10am–6pm, Sat 9am–1pm; ☎131-3184), off Bajcsy-Zsilinszky út. On the other hand, the cumbersome old Soviet bikes cost under £40/$68, as opposed to at least £150/$255 for a non-Soviet model.

Walking

Many areas of Budapest are best explored **on foot**, starting from the nearest metro station. Traffic is restricted in downtown Pest and around Castle Hill in Buda, and fairly light in the residential backstreets off the main boulevards, which are the nicest areas to wander around. Be careful on main roads, though, as drivers are careless of pedestrians – even at crossings. Personal security can also be an issue **at night**, particularly in the VIII (red-light) district and around mainline railway stations. Though rarer than in most Western cities, muggings do occur. Last year, there was even a robbery at gunpoint in broad daylight on Gellért Hill (another place to avoid after dark).

HÉV trains

Overground **HÉV trains** provide easy access to Budapest's suburbs, running at least four times an hour between 6.30am and 11pm. As far as tourists are concerned, the most useful line is the one **from Batthyány tér** (on metro line 2) out **to Szentendre**, north of Budapest, which passes through Óbuda, Aquincum and Római-Fürdő. The other lines originate in Pest, with one running northeast **from Örs vezér tere** (also on metro line 2) **to Gödöllő** via the Formula 1 racing track at Mogyoród; the other southwards **from Soroksári út** (bus #23 or #54 from Boráross tér) **to Ráckeve**, on Csepel Island. Szentendre, Gödöllő and Ráckeve are attractions in their own right, covered in chapters Two, Five and Six respectively. On all these routes, a yellow ticket will take you to the city limits, beyond which you must punch additional tickets according to the distance travelled.

Ferries and other rides

Although **ferries** play little useful part in the transport system, they do offer an enjoyable ride. From May to September there are regular excursion boats from the Vigadó tér dock on the Pest embankment, south to Boráross tér and north to Jászi Mari tér – both brief, scenic routes (7am–7pm; every 15–30 min). From May to August, there is also a boat from the Jászi Mari tér dock to Pünkösfürdő in northern Buda (1 hr), though you might prefer to disembark at Margit Island, before the boat reaches dismal Békásmegyer. Ferry tickets can be obtained from kiosks (where timetables are posted) or machines at the docks.

Other pleasure rides can be found in the Buda Hills, on the **Cogwheel Railway**, the **Children's Railway** (largely staffed by kids) and the **chairlift** between Zugliget and János-hegy. Details are given in the "Buda Hills" section (see p.75).

Accommodation

With only 60,000 beds to cope with five-million-plus visitors a year, the **accommodation** situation in Budapest is hardly ideal – but it's better than in any other capital in the former Soviet bloc. Predictably, the heaviest demand and highest prices occur over summer, when the city feels like it's bursting at the seams. Christmas and New Year, the Grand Prix and the Autumn Music Weeks are also busy periods, with higher rates in most hotels. Even so it should always be possible to find somewhere affordable, if not well sited, providing you know the score.

ACCOMMODATION PRICES

With the exception of campsites, all accommodation listed in the guide is given a symbol that corresponds to one of **seven price categories**, and generally refers to the cost of a double room during high season. In cases where the symbol stands for a bed rather than a room, this will be indicated in the text.

① Under 650Ft (under £5/$8/DM14).

② 650–1300Ft (£5–10/$8–17/DM14–28).

③ 1300–2000Ft (£10–15/$17–25/DM28–40).

④ 2000–3000Ft (£15–23/$25–40/DM40–65).

⑤ 3000–4500Ft (£23–35/$40–60/DM65–100).

⑥ 4500–8000Ft (£35–60/$60–100/DM100–170).

⑦ Over 8000Ft (over £60/$100/DM170).

Budget travellers will find most **hotels** affordable only during low season (Nov–March, excluding the New Year period), though a few remain viable options year round. **Pensions** are cheaper, but tend to fill up quickly as most are quite small. Your safest bet is a **private room**, arranged through a tourist agency. Though its location might not be perfect, the price should be reasonable, and you can be sure of finding one at any time of year, day or night. The cheapest options are **hostels** – which fill rapidly but can be unbeatable bargains – and **campsites**, where tent space can usually be found, even if all the **bungalows** are taken. The listings below are divided according to the type of accommodation, then arranged by area.

ACCOMMODATION BOOKING AGENCIES

Budapest Tourist
Private rooms, apartments and bungalows
Ferihegy airport
Nyugati Station, in the metro arcade outside (Mon–Sat 8am–8pm, Sun 2–8pm; ☎132-4911).
VIII, Baross tér 3, across from Keleti Station (Mon–Sat 8am–8pm, Sun 2–8pm; ☎133-6587).
Déli Station, in the mall by the metro entrance (Mon–Sat 8am–8pm, Sun 2–8pm; ☎115-4296).
VII, Erzsébet körút 41 (Mon–Sat 8am–8pm; ☎142-6521).
V, Roosevelt tér 5 (Mon–Fri 8am–7.30pm, Sat & Sun 9am–noon; ☎118-6600).

Cooptourist
Private rooms and apartments
Ferihegy (☎147-7328).
Skála Metro department store opposite Nyugati Station (Mon–Sat 8am–5pm; ☎112-1007).
V, Bajcsy-Zsilinszky út 17 (Mon–Sat 8am–5pm; ☎111-7034).
V, Kossuth tér 13 (Mon–Sat 8am–5pm; ☎112-1007).
I, Attila út 107 (Mon–Sat 8am–5pm; ☎116-0651).

Danubius
V, Martinelli tér 8 (☎117-3652).

Express
Hostels and student accommodation
VIII, Baross tér, Keleti Station (24-hour).

V, Semmelweiss utca 4 (Mon–Thurs 8am–5pm, Fri 8am–4.30pm; ☎117-6634 or 117-8600).
V, Szabadság tér 16 (daily 8am–4pm; ☎131-7777). Group bookings only.

HungarHotels
V, Petőfi utca 16 (☎118-3933).
VII, Erzsébet körút 47 (☎122-8668).

IBUSZ
Private rooms, apartments, Pannonia and HungarHotels hotel chains
Ferihegy airport
Nyugati Station, platform 10 (daily 8am–8pm; ☎149-1770).
Keleti Station (daily 8am–8pm; ☎142-9572).
Déli Station, in the mall by the metro entrance (daily 8am–6pm; ☎155-2133).
Ferenciek tere 5, by the metro stop (Mon–Fri 8am–5pm, Sat & Sun 8am–noon; ☎118-1120).
V, Petőfi tér 3, on the embankment (24 hr; ☎118-5707).
VII, Károly körút 17–19 (Mon–Fri 8am–5pm, Sat & Sun 8am–noon; ☎122-5429).

Pannonia Service
V, Kigyó utca 4–6 (☎118-3910).
VIII, Rákóczi út 9 (☎114-1886).

Volántourist
Private rooms and apartments
International landing stage on the Belgrád rakpart (embankment) (Mon–Sat 8am–5pm; ☎118-2133).
Bajcsy-Zsilinszky út 16 (Mon–Sat 8am–5pm; ☎117-2150).

Hotels

To get the pick of hotels you must **book** before leaving home (see "Accommodation" in *Basics*), or, failing that, through an agency (*HungarHotels*, *Pannonia* or *Danubius*) or any airport tourist office on arrival. Most hotels belong to the *HungarHotels* or *Pannonia* chains (indicated below by an *H* or *P*), but accept bookings through *IBUSZ*. See the box below for addresses.

Hotel star ratings give a fair idea of **standards**, though facilities at some of the older three-star places don't compare with their Western equivalents. Air conditioning is comparatively rare, for example. Most hotels vary their **prices** according to season – hence the ranges in price codes given below.

Buda

Buda has fewer hotels than Pest, with less choice in the mid-range in particular, though there are some cheaper places in the northern suburbs, (if the best locations seem beyond your means, check out the section on hostels, a few of which enjoy superb settings). Broadly speaking, Buda hotels are in four main areas:

CASTLE HILL AND THE WATERTOWN

The charm and cachet of this historic locality is reflected in the hotel prices.

Budapest Hilton, I, Hess András tér 1–3 (☎175-1000). By the Mátyás Church on Castle Hill, with superb views across the river. Luxurious to a fault, with doubles costing £140/$240 upwards. ⑦.

Dunapart Hotel, I, Szilágyi Dezső tér 33 (☎155-9244). A floating hotel moored upriver from the Chain Bridge, open all year unless ice endangers the boat. ⑤–⑦.

Victoria Hotel, I, Bem rakpart 11 (☎201-8644). On the embankment overlooking the Chain Bridge. The manager is in dispute with the council after adding an extra floor without permission. ⑥–⑦.

Alba Hotel, I, Apor Péter utca 3 (☎175-9244). Brand new four-star hotel in the Watertown below Castle Hill. Rooms with baths or showers, TV and direct-dial phone. ⑦.

AROUND TABÁN AND GELLÉRT HILL

Another pricey area – also far less scenic if you're behind Castle Hill and away from the river.

Orion Hotel, I, Döbrentei utca 13 (☎175–5418 *P*). Small, modern place in the Tabán district, just south of Castle Hill. All rooms have private baths, A/C, TV and video. ⑤–⑦.

Buda Penta Hotel, I, Krisztina körút 41–43 (☎156-6333). Equally comfortable block on the far side of Castle Hill, near Déli Station. ⑥–⑦.

Hotel Gellért, XI, Gellért tér 1 (☎185-2200). The facade and thermal pool are magnificent, but the rooms are nothing special. Rates rise by twenty percent to around £120/$210 during events like the Formula 1 race. ⑦.

Flamenco Occidental, XI, Tas vezér utca 7 (☎161-2250 *H*). Behind Gellért Hill, with quiet grounds and indoor tennis facilities. ⑥–⑦.

Novotel, XII, Alkotás utca 63–67 (☎186-9588), off Hegyalja út, 1km from the Erzsébet Bridge. Eighties complex with air-conditioning, indoor pool and bowling alley. Children under 16 share their parents' room for free. ⑦.

BUDA HILLS

Not much cheaper, but most of these places enjoy a nice location, and are within easy reach of Moszkva tér.

Hotel Budapest, II, Szilágyi E. fasor 47 (☎202-0044 *H*). Cylindrical tower facing the Buda Hills, opposite the lower terminal of the Cogwheel Railway, 500m from Moszkva tér. ⑤.

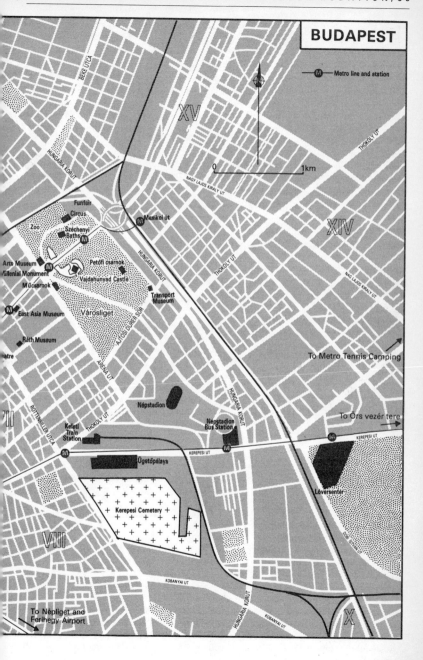

Hotel Rege, II, Pálos utca 2 (☎176-7311), near the foot of Janos-hegy (bus #22 from Moszkva tér). Another three-star place; pool, gym and disco. ⑥.

Hotel Olympia, XII, Eötvös út 40 (☎156-8011 *P*), at Normafa (bus #21E from Moszkva tér). Seventies low-rise with pool and tennis courts. ⑤–⑦.

Hotel Panoráma, XII, Rege utca 21 (☎175-0522 *H*), on Széchenyi-hegy, reached by Cogwheel Railway. Alpine-style place with a sauna and pool. Also bungalows (see below). ⑤–⑥.

NORTHERN SUBURBS

The cheapest places in Buda are out in Aquincum and Római-Fürdő, mostly near stops on the HÉV line from Batthyány tér.

Polo Hotel, III, Mozaik utca 1–3 (☎180-3022). New one-star place between Óbuda and Aquincum (Filatorigát HÉV stop), behind the long white building to the east of the tracks. Shared bathrooms. ④.

Hotel Tusculanum, III, Záhony utca 10 (☎188-7673). Another new establishment, near the Roman ruins of Aquincum and the HÉV stop and pension of the same name. ⑤.

Lido Sport Hotel, III, Nánási út 67 (☎188-6865). An older place with tennis courts, sauna and solarium, near the Danube. Bus #134 from Flórián tér stops nearby, or you can walk from Aquincum or Római-Fürdő HÉV stop. Shared bathrooms. ③.

Margit Island

The island's hotels cater to wealthy tourists who come for the seclusion and fresh air – and for the thermal springs that made this a fashionable spa resort around the turn of the century.

Thermal Hotel, XIII, Margitsziget (☎111-1000). Modern luxury hotel with thermal bath and pool, sauna, gym and other facilities. ⑦.

Ramada Grand Hotel, XIII, Margitsziget (☎132-1100). The island's original, *fin-de-siècle* spa hotel, now totally refurbished, with similar facilities and rates. ⑦.

Pest

Staying in **Pest** offers greater choice, and more in the way of restaurants and nightlife, but traffic noise and fumes are worse. Most of the outlying locations are easily accessible by metro.

DOWNTOWN

These hotels are all within (or on) the Small Boulevard.

Atrium Hyatt, V, Roosevelt tér 2 (☎138-3000 *P*). Overlooking the Chain Bridge and the Danube, this five-star block has air-conditioning, a pool, a sauna, and a landscaped atrium. Doubles from £125/$220. Apartments available too. ⑦.

Hotel Forum, V, Apáczai Csere János utca 12–14 (☎117-8088 *H*). Similarly equipped four-star pile beside the Danube, where Richard Burton used to stay incognito. Doubles from £130/$230; also apartments. ⑦.

Duna Intercontinental, V, Apáczai Csere János utca 4 (☎117-5122 *H*). All rooms in this five-star air-conditioned block overlook the Danube. Doubles from £120/$210; also apartments. ⑦.

Taverna Hotel, V, Váci utca 20 (☎138-3522). Shoehorned into place on the trendy thoroughfare where everyone promenades. ⑥–⑦.

Hotel Erzsébet, V, Károlyi M. utca 11–15 (☎138-2111). Further south, on the unfashionable side of Ferenciek tere. Soundproofed rooms. ⑥–⑦.

Astoria Hotel, V, Kossuth utca 19 (☎117-3411 *H*). Completely refurbished, famous old hotel which lends its name to the junction of Kossuth utca and the Small Boulevard (metro line 2). ⑥–⑦.

Korona Hotel, V, Kecskeméti utca 14 (☎117-4111 *P*). Brand new, post-modernist edifice beside Kálvin tér (metro line 3), a short walk from the National Museum. Every facility, including a pool and sauna. ⑥–⑦.

AROUND THE GREAT BOULEVARD

While most of the following places are on (or just off) the Great Boulevard, a couple are further out, near Keleti Station.

Emke Hotel, VII, Akácfa utca 1–3 (☎122-9230 *P*). Sixties block near the junction of Rákóczi út and the Great Boulevard, off Blaha Lujza tér (metro line 2). ⑤–⑥.

Nemzeti Hotel, VIII, József körút 4 (☎133-9160 *P*). Small Art Nouveau-style place overlooking Blaha Lujza tér (metro line 2). ⑤–⑦.

Palace Austrotel, VIII, Rákóczi út 43 (☎113-6000 *P*). Grander Art Nouveau pile around the corner, once the headquarters of the Social Democratic Party. ④–⑥.

Metropol Hotel, VIII, Rákóczi út 58 (☎142-1175 *P*). Similar vintage but far less flash. ④–⑤.

Grand Hotel Hungária, VII, Rákóczi út 90 (☎122-9050 *H*). Sited opposite Keleti Station, this classic railway hotel was totally refurbished in 1985. ⑥–⑦.

Hotel Park, VIII, Baross tér 10 (☎113-1420). Also near Keleti, but rather noisy. ④–⑤.

Hotel Royal, VII, Erzsébet körút 47–49 (☎153-3133 *H*). Following renovation, this nineteenth-century hotel should reopen in 1993. Located midway round the Great Boulevard.

MEDOSZ Hotel, VI, Jókai tér 9 (☎153-1700). Next to the Puppet Theatre on "Broadway", just off Andrássy út near the Oktogon (metro line 1). ⑥.

Hotel Radisson Béke, VI, Teréz körút 43 (☎132-3300 *H*). Refurbished vintage hotel on the Great Boulevard, 200m south of Nyugati Station. Sauna and pool. Doubles from £100. ⑦.

FURTHER OUT

These are all within fifteen minutes of the centre by metro. The first four are near big parks: the Városliget and Népliget.

Benczúr Hotel, VI, Benczúr utca 35 (☎142-7970). Quietly situated two blocks from Andrássy út and Hősök tere, near Bajza utca (metro line 1). ⑤–⑥.

Hotel Liget, VI, Aréna út 106 (☎111-0493). Stylish new hotel opposite the Fine Arts Museum on Hősök tere, bordering the Városliget. Noisy but great location. TV, direct-dial phones; some rooms air-conditioned. ⑥.

Hotel Délibab, VI, Délibab utca 35 (☎122-8763). Also across from Hősök tere, in a former Esterházy mansion. ⑤.

Hotel Palatanus, X, Könyves Kálmán körút 44 (☎133-6057). On a major thoroughfare opposite the Népliget (metro line 3). ③–⑤.

Stadion Hotel, Ifjúság útja 1–3 (☎252-9333 H). In the sports complex near Népstadion bus station (metro line 2). ⑥.

Hotel Volga, XIII, Dózsa György út 65 (☎129-0200 H). Another three-star place, by the line 3 Dózsa György út metro stop, 1km beyond Nyugati Station. ⑤–⑥.

Pensions

Pensions vary considerably, as do their prices, but they are all likely to fill up fast during summer, so reservations are pretty much essential. In most cases, you need to phone them direct. The following places are all **in Buda** and listed according to location, from south to north.

Jäger–Trió Panzió, XI, Ördögorom út 20D (☎185-1880). In the Sasad district behind Gellért Hill; bus #8 from Március 15. tér to the end of the line, then a ten-minute walk. March 15–Nov 15. ④.

Bara Panzió, I, Hegyalja út 34–36 (☎185-3445). On the main road to Vienna, below Gellért Hill. ④–⑥.

Molnár Panzió, XII, Fodor utca 143 (☎161-1167). In the Orbánhegy district of the Buda Hills; bus #102 from Déli Station runs nearby. Some three-bed rooms. ⑤.

Buda Panzió, XII, Kiss Aron utca 6 (☎176-2679). In the Buda Hills; bus #28 runs along Kütvölgyi út nearby. ⑤.

Beatrix Panzió, II, Szehér út 3 (☎176-3730). Near Hárshegy campsite in the Buda Hills; bus #56 from Moszkva tér. ⑤.

San Marcó Panzió, III, San Marcó utca 6 (☎188-9997); bus #60 from Batthyány tér. Small, friendly pension in Óbuda, run by Mrs Steininger. Shared bathrooms. ③.

Pál Vendégház Panzió, III, Pálvölgyi köz 15 (☎188-7099), near the Pál-völgyi Stalactite Cave; bus #65 from Kolosy tér in Óbuda. Eight double rooms. ③.

Aquincum Panzió, III, Szentendrei út 105 (☎168-7868). Near the Köles utca HÉV stop, one stop before Aquincum. Reservations through Omnibusz in the Erzsébet tér bus station (daily 8am–5pm; ☎117-2248). Some three-bed rooms. ④.

Private rooms and apartments

There are **private rooms** throughout the city, many in the sort of locations where a hotel would be unaffordable. Depending on location and amenities, **prices** for a double room range from 800Ft to 1500Ft a night. On the downside, solo travellers will almost certainly have to pay for a double, and rates are thirty percent higher if you stay fewer than four nights (making pensions or hostels more economical for short-staying visitors). **Apartments**, from 3000Ft a night, are not as common as rooms, but you should be able to find an agency with one on its books.

It's easy enough to get a room from one of the **touts** at the railway stations, but it's safer to go through a tourist agency, where you book and pay at the counter signposted *fizetővendég*. The four main **agencies** – *Budapest Tourist, IBUSZ, Cooptourist* and *Volántourist* – have offices all over the city (see box on p.52 for addresses), but the ones in the stations and central Pest are obviously the most convenient for new arrivals.

Since rooms are rented sight unseen, it pays to take some trouble over your choice. Your host and the premises should give no cause for complaint (both are checked out), but the **location** or ambience might. For atmosphere and comfort, you can't beat those nineteenth-century blocks where spacious, high-ceilinged flats surround a courtyard with wrought-iron balconies – most common in Pest's V, VI and VII districts, and the parts of Buda nearest Castle Hill. Elsewhere – particularly in Újpest, Csepel or Óbuda – you're likely to end up in a box on the twelfth floor of a *lakótelep*. The *Budapest Atlasz* is invaluable for checking the location of sites and access by public transport.

Because many proprietors go out to work, you might not be able to take possession of the room until 5pm – if so, the tourist office will say. Some knowledge of Hungarian facilitates **settling in**; guests normally receive an explanation of the boiler system and multiple door keys (*kulcs*), and may have use of the washing machine (which requires another demonstration).

Hostels

If you don't have a tent, a dormitory bed in a **hostel** is the cheapest alternative – most also have rooms at much the same price as private accommodation (and with no surcharge for staying fewer than four nights). In summer, you can't be sure of getting a bed in the hostel of your choice without **booking** in advance through *Express* (see box on p.52 for addresses). Out of season, only two hostels are open, so reservations are still advisable. There don't seem to be any age or membership requirements, but an IYHF card can be obtained from *Express* if needed.

Unlike the permanently open *Citadella* and *Hotel Expressz*, **college hostels** only function during the summer and change location from year to year, so check with *Express* for the latest situation. All except the last of the following are in Buda.

Citadella, I, Citadella sétány (☎166-5794); bus #27 from Móricz Zsigmond körtér. Romantically sited atop Gellért Hill, the citadel offers doubles with showers, Budapest's cheapest dormitory beds, and breathtaking views. Reserve well ahead through *Budapest Tourist* (not *Express*), or check for vacancies every morning. Open all year . ①–②.

Donáti Kollégium, I, Donáti utca 46 (☎201-1929). Conveniently located just below Castle Hill, in a side street near Batthyány tér, this is the cheapest accommodation in the area. Dormitory beds. July & Aug only. ①.

KÉK Somogyi Kollégium, XI, Szüret utca 2–18 (☎185-2369). Around the back of Gellért Hill, two stops from Móricz Zsigmond körtér by #27 bus. Dormitory beds. July 15–Aug 22. ①.

Hotel Expressz, XII, Beethoven utca 7–9 (☎175-2528). In the backstreets south of Déli Station – two stops by tram #59. Curiously, *Express* claims that its "youth hotel" is always full, even when it isn't, so ring direct or just turn up. Doubles with shared bathrooms. Open all year. ②.

Felvinci Kollégium, II, Felvinci út 8 (☎135-0668); below the exclusive Rózsadomb quarter, close to Moszkva tér (metro line 2). A no-frills college hostel with dormitory beds. July 10–Aug 22. ①.

ELTE Kollégium, XI, Budaörsi út 95–101 (☎166-7788); bus #139 from Moszkva tér, get off before the *Hotel Wien*. Similarly priced beds in a dismal suburb along the Vienna highway. July 10–Aug 22. ①.

SOTE–Balassa Kollégium, VIII, Tömő utca 37–41 (☎133-8916). Just north of Üllői út, near the Klinikák stop (metro line 3) in Pest. July 10–Aug 22. ①.

Campsites and bungalows

You can save a lot of money by **camping** in Budapest. The sites, which are mostly located in the Buda Hills or the outer suburbs of Pest, generally offer good facilities, though they can become unpleasantly crowded between June and September and the smaller ones might run out of space. It is illegal to camp anywhere else, and the parks are patrolled to enforce this. The police tolerate people **sleeping rough** in railway stations, but there's a high risk of theft (or worse) – especially at Keleti.

BUDA
Buda's sites are the more pleasant, with trees and grass and maybe even a pool. The first three listed below are in the Buda Hills, twenty minutes' bus ride from Moszkva tér; the last is in the northern suburbs, accessible by HÉV train from Batthyány tér.

Hárshegy Camping, Hárshegyi út 5–7 (☎115-1482); bus #22 stops at nearby Denes utca. Pleasant, shady hillside site run by *Budapest Tourist*. Open May 1–Oct 15, charging 160Ft per person, tent and vehicle; bungalows range from 650Ft for a double without shower to 3000Ft for one with four beds, a bathroom and breakfast.

Zugligeti Niche Camping, XII, Zugligeti út 101 (☎156-8641); at the end of the #158 bus route, opposite the chairlift up to János-hegy. Small, terraced ravine site in the woods, with good facilities; the office and buffet occupy disused trams. March 15–Oct 15: charges 170Ft per person, 200Ft per car and tent.

Tündérhegyi-Feeburg Camping, XII, Szillássy út 8 (no phone); at the end of the #28 bus route, also near the chair-lift. Nice, very small site close to a nature reserve. Open all year. Prices about the same.

Római-Fürdő Camping, III, Szentrendrei út 189 (☎168-6260) in Római-Fürdő; 25min by HÉV. Huge site beside the road to Szentendre; higher than average rates include use of the nearby swimming pool. May 1–Oct 15. Also has bungalows (③) – book through *Budapest Tourist*.

PEST

Located in the dusty outer suburbs, these are all accessible by bus from Örs vezér tere, at the end of metro line 2.

Expo AutoCamp, X, Dobi István út 10 (☎147-0990); bus #100. Shadeless, gravelled expanse near gate IV of the International Fairground, used by caravanners. July & Aug only: 260Ft per person, 240Ft per tent and 275Ft per car.

Rózsakert Camping, X, Pilisi utca 7 (no phone); off Kerepesi út, three stops by #45 or #46 bus. Small, privately owned site. 160Ft per person, 130Ft per tent.

Metro Tennis Camping, XVI, Csömöri út 158 (☎163-8505); three stops by #31 bus. Larger site with tennis courts. April–Oct: 200Ft per person, 160Ft per tent, 100Ft per car.

Bungalows

Budapest Tourist (see p.52 for addresses) can arrange detached **bungalows** of various sizes at Hárshegy and Római-Fürdő campsites (see above), and the following locations:

Panoráma Bungalows, XII, Rege út 21 (☎175-0522). Upmarket complex by the *Panoráma Hotel*. Bungalows with baths, sleeping four or five; obligatory breakfast. Open all year. ⑤–⑥.

Csillaghegyi Strand, III, Pusztakúti út 3 (☎167-1999); one HÉV stop past Római-Fürdő. Set in a wooded area with bathing. Cheaper second- and third-class bungalows. April 15–Oct 15. ②.

Haladás Motel, IV, Üdülősor 8 (☎189-1114); bus #104 from the Árpad híd (metro line 3). Second-class bungalows beside the Danube in Újpest. May–Sept. ②–③.

Buda

Seen from the embankments of the Danube, **BUDA** forms a collage of palatial buildings, archaic spires and outsize statues, crowning craggy massifs. This glamorous image conceals more mundane aspects, but at times, in the right place, the city can really live up to it. To experience **Castle Hill** at its best, come early in the morning before the crowds arrive. Then you can beat them to the **museums**, wander off for lunch or a soak in one of the Turkish baths, and return to catch street life in full swing during the afternoon. The outlying **Buda Hills** – accessible by chairlift and the Children's Railway – are obviously less visited during the week, while **Gellért Hill**, the **Rózsadomb** and **Roman ruins** can be seen any time the weather's fine.

Castle Hill

Castle Hill (*Várhegy*) is Buda's most prominent feature, a long plateau laden with bastions, mansions and a huge palace, commanding the Watertown below. Its grandiosity and strategic utility have long gone hand in hand: Hungarian kings built their palaces here because it was easy to defend, a fact appreciated by the Turks, Habsburgs and other occupiers. Its buildings, a legacy of bygone Magyar glories, have been almost wholly reconstructed from the rubble of 1945, when the

Wehrmacht and the Red Army battled over the Hill while Buda's inhabitants cowered underground.

Though the Hill's appearance has changed much since building began in the thirteenth century, its main **streets** still follow their medieval courses, with Gothic arches and stone carvings half-concealed in the courtyards and passages of eighteenth- and nineteenth-century Baroque **houses**, whose facades are embellished with fancy ironwork grilles. Practically every building displays a *Mtemlék* plaque giving details of its history.

There are several **approaches** to Castle Hill, mostly starting from the Watertown (described on p.68). The simplest is to ascend to the palace by **Sikló** – a renovated nineteenth-century funicular that runs from Clark Ádám tér near the Chain Bridge (daily 7.30am–10pm; 20–60Ft according to season). Alternatively you can start from Moszkva tér (on Metro line 2) and walk up to the Vienna Gate or take the Várbusz – a minibus that terminates on Dísz tér. Finally from Batthány tér (Metro line 2), you can proceed along Fő utca **on foot** until you see the spires. From this point in the Watertown, various flights of steps (*lepcső*) climb up to the Fishermen's Bastion and the Mátyás Church, where most people begin their tour of Castle Hill. **From Pest**, the easiest journey is by bus #16 bus from Erzsébet tér or bus #116 from Marcius 15. tér (south of the Erzsébet bridge) to Dísz tér, but it's probably more enjoyable to head for the Watertown and approach from there.

The Fishermen's Bastion and Mátyás Church

The **Fishermen's Bastion** (*Hálászbástya*) could have been dreamed up by the illusionist artist Escher: an undulating white rampart of cloisters and flights of steps, intersecting at turrets, like one of his Endless Stairways. Although fishermen from the Watertown reputedly defended this stretch of the Hill during the Middle Ages, the existing structure is purely decorative, providing a perfect frame for the Mátyás Church and the view of Parliament across the river. The seven tent-like turrets, designed by Frigyes Schulek at the turn of the century, allude to the seven Magyar tribes that gave rise to the nation a thousand years earlier. By day the bastion is besieged by tourists, buskers and vendors, its cloisters awash with countrywomen selling embroidery from Transylvania.

THE MÁTYÁS CHURCH

Occupying centre stage right in the middle of the hill, the **Mátyás Church** is an example of neo-Gothic run riot, with diamond-patterned roof tiles and a multitude of toothy spires, wildly asymmetrical but nevertheless coherent in form. Officially dedicated to Our Lady but popularly named after "Good King Mátyás", the building is a superb nineteenth-century recreation by Frigyes Schulek, grafted onto those portions of the original thirteenth-century church that survived the siege of 1686. Prior to that date it had served as a mosque, the *Büyük Dzjami*, whose Turkish occupants whitewashed over the medieval murals and removed the furnishings.

Entering the church through its **Mary Portal**, visitors gape at the richness of the interior. Painted leaves and geometric motifs run up columns and under vaulting, while shafts of light fall through rose windows onto gilded altars and statues with stunning effect. Most of the **frescoes** were executed by Károly Lotz or Bertalan Székely, the foremost historical painters of the late nineteenth century.

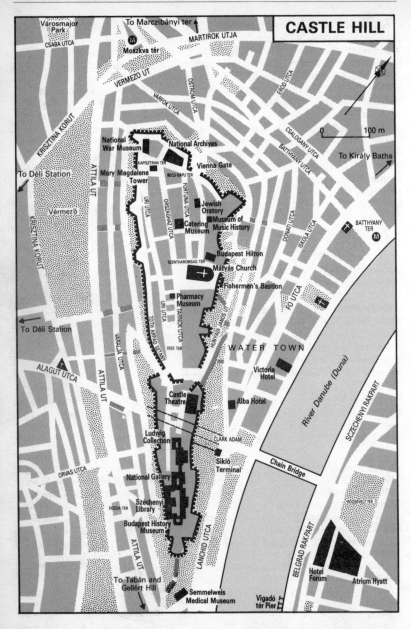

CASTLE HILL

Városmajor Park

To Marczibányi ter

CSABA UTCA

Moszkva tér

MARTIROK UTJA

VERMEZO UT

VARFOK UTCA

OSTROM UTCA

ERŐ UTCA

0   100 m

CSALOGANY UTCA

BATTHYANY UTCA

To Király Baths

National War Museum

National Archives

KRISZTINA KORUT

ATTILA UT

KAPISZTRAN TER

Mary Magdalene Tower

Vienna Gate

To Déli Station

BECSI KAPU TER

FORTUNA UTCA

Jewish Oratory

Vérmező

URI UTCA

ORSZAGHAZ UTCA

Catering Museum

Museum of Music History

DONATI UTCA

ISKOLA UTCA

BATTHYANY TER

KRISZTINA KORUT

Budapest Hilton

SZENTHAROMSAG TER

Mátyás Church

Fishermen's Bastion

FŐ UTCA

URI UTCA

Pharmacy Museum

VARALJA UTCA

ATTILA UT

ALAGUT UTCA

TOTH ARPAD SETANY

TARNOK UTCA

HUNYAD JANOS

DISZ TER

WATER TOWN

To Déli Station

River Danube (Duna)

SZECHENYI RAKPART

Victoria Hotel

Castle Theatre

Alba Hotel

Ludwig Collection

CLARK ADAM

Chain Bridge

ORVAS UTCA

Sikló Terminal

National Gallery

DOZSA TER

Széchenyi Library

Budapest History Museum

LANCHID UTCA

BELGRAD RAKPART

ROOSEVELT TER

ATTILA UT

To Tabán and Gellért Hill

Semmelweis Medical Museum

Vigadó tér Pier

Hotel Forum

Atrium Hyatt

The **coat of arms of King Mátyás** can be seen on the wall to your left, inside the entrance; his family name, Corvinus, comes from the raven (*corvus* in Latin) that appeared on his heraldry and every volume in the famous *Biblioteca Corvinus*.

Around the corner beneath the south tower is the **Loreto Chapel**, containing a Baroque Madonna. Across the way, two medieval capitals, carved with monsters and a bearded figure with a book, lurk below the Béla Tower, so-called after the fourth king of that name. His predecessor lies in the second chapel along, sharing a double sarcophagus with Anne of Chatillon. Originally located in Székesfehérvár, the **tomb of Béla III** and his queen was moved here after its discovery in 1848. Although Hungary's medieval kings were crowned at Székesfehérvár, it was customary to make a prior appearance in Buda – hence yet another sobriquet, the "Coronation Church".

The church's **crypt** and collection of **ecclesiastical treasures** (daily April–Sept 8.30am–8pm; Oct–March 9am–7pm) are reached by a portal to the right of the chancel. From here, stairs ascend to **Saint Stephen's Chapel**, decorated with scenes from the king's life, whence another staircase leads to the **Royal Oratory**, exhibiting the coronation robes and thrones of emperors Franz Josef and Karl IV, and a **replica of the Hungarian Crown Jewels** (the originals are in the National Museum).

Mass is still held here every morning, and more frequently on Sundays, and the church also hosts **concerts** during the Spring Festival and the summer season.

SZENTHÁROMSÁG TÉR

Beyond the Mátyás Church lies **Szentháromság tér** (Holy Trinity Square), which derives its name from a Trinity Column erected in 1713, in thanks for the abatement of a plague – there are many such monuments in Central Europe. The copper and glass facade of the **Budapest Hilton**, which incorporates chunks of a medieval Dominican church and monastery, reflects the image of the church and the Fishermen's Bastion. Around the back is a fine equestrian **statue of King Stephen**. On Szentháromság utca, running off by the Old Town Hall building, **Ruszwurm's patisserie** has thrived at no. 7 since 1827, on a site where a gingerbread shop stood in the Middle Ages. It's invariably too crowded to get a table, but worth a look before you strike out towards Buda Palace or the Vienna Gate, and you can buy cakes to munch on the way.

KING STEPHEN

If you commit only one figure from Hungarian history to memory, make it **King Stephen**, for it was *István* (as Hungarians know him) who welded the tribal Magyar fiefdoms into a state and won recognition from Christendom. Like his father, Prince Géza, Stephen strove to Christianise the pagan Magyars and to develop Hungary with the help of foreign preachers, craftsmen and merchants. By marrying Gizella of Bavaria in 996, he was able to use her father's knights to crush a pagan revolt after Géza's death, and subsequently received an apostolic cross and crown from Pope Sylvester II for his coronation on Christmas Day in 1000 AD.

Though noted for his enlightened admonitions (such as the need for tolerance and the desirability of multi-racial nations), he could act ruthlessly when necessary. After his only son Imre died in an accident and a suspected pagan seemed likely to inherit, Stephen had the man blinded and poured molten lead into his ears, before choosing another successor. Posthumously canonised, **Saint Stephen** became a national talisman; his mummified right hand a sacred relic; and his Coronation regalia the symbol of statehood. Despite downplaying his cult for decades, even the Communists eventually embraced it in a bid for some legitimacy.

To the Vienna Gate and back

The following circuit covers the sector up to the Vienna Gate, at the northern end of Castle Hill. Depending on where you begin, places can be seen more or less in the order described here by cutting back and forth through the side streets. Otherwise, drop in on your way back from the gate. Almost immediately you set off in this direction you'll pass a couple of fine examples of the Hill's ancient buildings on Hess András tér: the *Fortuna* restaurant at no. 4 occupies the site of Hungary's first printing press, while the medieval *Red Hedgehog* inn (no. 3) is now a private residence.

Head up Fortuna utca and you'll find the intriguing **Museum of Commerce and Catering** (Tues–Sun 10am–6pm) at no. 4, where the *Fortuna Inn* was located between 1784 and 1868. Three rooms smelling of vanilla relate the history of confectionery – a serious art in a country that heralded the creator of the *dobostorta* as a hero – while across the corridor is a fine collection of posters, shop windows and illuminated signs, from before and after World War I.

By returning to Hess András tér and following Táncsics Mihály utca to the former Erdödy Palace at no. 7, you can visit the **Museum of the History of Music** (Mon 4–9pm, Wed–Sun 10am–6pm). Beethoven once stayed here and Bartók had his workshop in the building. Its Baroque decor is as much an attraction as the antique instruments within. Next door is the former prison where the writer Mihály Táncsics was held for nationalist agitation, until freed during the 1848 Revolution. During the Middle Ages this street was chiefly inhabited by Jews (Italians, Germans and French congregated in neighbouring quarters), hence the **Jewish Oratory** at no. 26, displaying artefacts and gravestones from that era (May–Oct Tues–Fri 10am–2pm, Sat & Sun 10am–6pm).

AROUND THE VIENNA GATE AND KAPISZTRÁN TÉR

At the end of the road lies **Bécsi Kapu tér**, known as the "Saturday" (market) square before its devastation in 1686. Given a new and sombre cast when it was rebuilt in the eighteenth century, it was subsequently renamed after the chunky **Vienna Gate** (*Bécsi Kapu*) that was erected on the 250th anniversary of the recapture of Buda from the Turks. To the west loom the neo-Romanesque **National Archives** (closed to the public) and the **National War Museum** (Tues–Sun 10am–6pm). The latter is entered from the Tóth Árpád sétány, a promenade overlooking Buda's western districts. Inside are weapons and uniforms galore, and a courtyard full of armoured vehicles.

The museum flanks one corner of **Kapisztrán tér**, named after Friar John Capistranus, who exhorted the Hungarians to victory over the Turks at the siege of Belgrade in 1456. On the south side of the square rises the **Mary Magdalene Tower** (whose accompanying church had to be pulled down after World War II), which now serves as a private picture gallery. From here, you can head back along one of two historic streets, Országház utca or Úri utca.

ORSZÁGHÁZ UTCA AND ÚRI UTCA

During the 145 years of Turkish occupation the Hill's main thoroughfare was known as the "street of the baths" (*Hamam Yolu*), and the Castle district contained 34 mosques, three Dervish monasteries and over 100 tanneries – all of which have long vanished. However, many curious architectural features have survived along what is now **Országház utca** (Parliament Street), so-called after the parliamentary sessions held in a building here during the 1780s.

Heading south you'll pass the *Régi Orságház* restaurant, whose gate's keystone bears a relief of a croissant; the gateway of no. 9 contains a set of niches with lily-ended traceries (thought by some to have served as stalls for merchants). Across the street, no. 22 retains some Renaissance graffiti on the bottom of its bay window, while no. 20 has a trefoil-arched cornice dating back to the fourteenth century.

Historic architecture also dignifies Úri utca (Gentlemen's Street), where the Hungarian Jacobins were imprisoned at no. 52 prior to being excecuted below the Hill in 1795. Allegorical statues of the four seasons decorate the first-floor niches at nos. 54–56, while Gothic sedilia embellish the gateway of nos. 48–50. The facade of no. 31 is almost entirely Gothic, and medieval gateways are incorporated in the houses across the street. The main attraction, however, lies underground, a couple of blocks beyond the equestrian statue at junction with Szentháromság utca.

Here, at Úri utca 9, you'll find the entrance to the **labyrinth of caves** beneath Castle Hill (10am–6pm; closed Tues; 200Ft). During the Middle Ages, ten kilometres of galleries were tunnelled between cavities in the bedrock, and wells were dug to make them habitable in case of siege. The cellars of many houses connected directly to the labyrinth, which served as air-raid shelter and field hospital in the winter of 1944–45. Nowadays part is given over to a dank **waxworks**, with tableaux of the goriest events in Magyar history; a guide ensures that visitors don't stray and get lost in the tunnels.

South towards the Palace

Heading south from Szentháromság tér or continuing down Úri utca, you can easily reach Tárnok utca (named after the royal treasurers who once lived here), whose nineteenth-century inhabitants impressed John Paget with their "sedateness of air" and "pompous vacancy of expression". At the top of the street stands the seventeenth-century *Golden Eagle* apothecary, now a **Pharmacy Museum** of dubious nostrums and wicked-looking instruments (Tues–Sun 10.30am–5.30pm). The *Arany Hordó* restaurant, 20m south, occupies one of the few buildings on the Hill to have kept its original *sgraffiti* – a red and orange checkerboard pattern covering the facade.

Both Tárnok utca and Úri utca end in **Dísz tér** (Parade Square), whose cobbled expanses are guarded by a statue of a hussar. From here on ramparts and gateways buttress the hillside and control access to the palace grounds. Straight ahead lies the scarred hulk of the old Premier's residence, the last

---

HUSSARS

Hussars were a Hungarian innovation later adopted by armies throughout Europe. The first such unit of light cavalry was organised by King Mátyás in 1480; armed with sabres, pikes and daggers, it excelled in surprise attacks and rapid manoeuvres. By the time of the Napoleonic Wars every national army fielded hussars and most infantry wore hussar-style cylindrical felt or leather hats (called *shako*, from the Magyar word for a peaked hat) instead of metal helmets. Although Hussar is one of the few Hungarian words to have entered the English language, it is thought to derive from the Latin *cursor* (runner) rather than the Magyar *húsz* (meaning twenty). In Hungary their romantic image endures, and costumed riders sometimes appear on the Hill in summer, to popular approval.

outbuilding of the palace complex still to be restored, while to your left stands the **Castle Theatre**. A Carmelite church until the order was dissolved by Emperor Josef II, its conversion was supervised by Farkas Kempelen, inventor of a chess-playing automaton. Here, the first ever play in Hungarian was staged in 1790, and Beethoven performed in 1808.

Around the corner of the theatre is the upper terminal of the Sikló funicular, overlooked from the terrace of Buda Palace by a bronze **Turul statue**, honouring the mythical bird that begat Álmos, father of Árpád, who led the Magyar tribes into Europe.

Buda Palace

As befits a former royal residence, the lineage of **Buda Palace**, the *Budavári Palota*, can be traced back to medieval times, and the rise and fall of various palaces on the Hill is symbolic of the changing fortunes of the Hungarian state. The first fortifications and dwellings here, hastily erected by Béla III after the thirteenth-century Mongol invasion, were replaced by ever more luxurious palaces by the Angevin kings, who ruled in more prosperous and stable times. The zenith was attained in the reign of Mátyás Corvinus (1458–90), whose palace was a Renaissance extravaganza to which artists and scholars from all over Europe were drawn by the blandishments of Queen Beatrice and the prospect of lavish hospitality. After the Turkish occupation, and the long siege that ended it, only ruins were left – these the Austrian Habsburgs, Hungary's new rulers, levelled to build a palace of their own.

From Maria Theresa's modest beginnings (a mere 203 rooms, which she never saw completed), the **Royal Palace** expanded inexorably throughout the nineteenth century, though no monarch ever dwelt here, only the Habsburg Palatine (viceroy). After the collapse of the empire, Admiral Horthy inhabited the building with all the pomp of monarchy until he was deposed by a German coup in October 1944. The palace was left unoccupied, and it wasn't long before the siege of Buda once again resulted in total devastation: since then Pest has been the seat of all decision making. Reconstruction work began in the 1950s, and the sombre wings of the Palace now contain a clutch of museums and medieval structures discovered in the course of excavation.

THE LUDWIG COLLECTION

The northern (A) wing of the palace formerly housed the Museum of the Working Class Movement, giving the Communist Party's view of history. In 1990, the museum staff made amends for decades of misinformation by organising a huge exhibition called *RÁ-KO-SI STA-LIN* (the chant, naming the leaders of Hungary and the USSR, that was obligatory at rallies of the time), dealing with the Stalinist era. Sadly, this fascinating display has since been replaced in turn by the **Ludwig Collection** (daily 10am–6pm; may be closed Nov–Feb), a privately assembled hoard of modern art that includes the odd Lichtenstein and Picasso, accompanied by temporary exhibitions. Find out what's showing before forking out the 100Ft admission (students/pensioners half price; free on Mon).

THE NATIONAL GALLERY

The central and southern wings of the palace contain the **National Gallery** (daily April–Nov 10am–6pm; Dec–March 10am–4pm; free Sat), devoted to Hungarian art since the Middle Ages. Few visitors see every section, which have separate entrances (though one ticket suffices for all of them); the main entrance is on the eastern side of Building C, in the courtyard with the stone lions.

To follow it chronologically, start with the ground floor of **Building D**, displaying **Romanesque** and **Gothic stone carvings** from Ják, Esztergom and Veszprém. On the floor above, in what used to be the throne room, are **Renaissance altarpieces** from churches in what is now Slovakia, and **Baroque ecclesiastical art**, much of it confiscated from private owners in the Fifties. The ground floors of **Buildings B and C** are used for temporary exhibits, while those above are devoted to **Hungarian painting since the nineteenth century**, from genre painting to Impressionism, historicism to avant garde. Don't miss the vast painting by Csontváry (see p.214) on the landing between the second and third floors, which cover twentieth-century art. The Nagybánya and Szentendre artists' colonies are well represented, as is József Rippl-Rónai, the chief Hungarian exponent of Art Nouveau. **Contemporary art** is displayed on the third floor of Building D.

THE MÁTYÁS FOUNTAIN AND SZÉCHENYI LIBRARY

In the outer courtyard of the palace, flanked by A, B and C wings, stands the **Mátyás Fountain**, whose bronze figures recall the legend of Szép Ilonka. This beautiful peasant girl supposedly met the king while he was hunting incognito, fell in love with him, and died of a broken heart after discovering his identity and realising the futility of her hopes. The figure on the king's right is his Italian chronicler, who recorded the story for posterity (it is also enshrined in a folk song).

To the west of the inner **Lion Courtyard** stands the **Széchenyi Library**, a repository for publications in Hungarian, and material relating to the country from around the world. By law, the Library receives a copy of every book, newspaper and magazine that is published in Hungary. Like the Hungarian Academy, it was founded by Count Széchenyi during the Reform era. Its central reading room is open to the public, and there are exhibitions on diverse themes (Mon 1–9pm, Tues–Sat 10am–6pm).

THE BUDAPEST HISTORY MUSEUM AND THE SOUTHERN BASTIONS

The palace's E wing, on the far side of the Lion Courtyard, contains the **Budapest History Museum** (Tues–Sat 10am–6pm), which incorporates marbled and flagstoned halls from the Renaissance palace, unearthed during post-war excavations. These are far below the current street level, giving visitors "the sensation of burrowing into the history of the city". In the Renaissance Room are portraits of Mátyás and Beatrice (whose coat of arms decorates the Beatrice Courtyard outside). Upstairs are old prints, ceramics and other artefacts tracing the evolution of Óbuda, Buda and Pest over the centuries.

The southern end of the Hill, once terraced with vineyards, now supports a maze of paths and promenades, guarded by the **Mace Tower** and the Lihegő Gate, leading into the **Round Bastion**. From 1961 to 1984, the **Youth Park** *(Ifjúsági Park)* on the hillside overlooking the embankment played a vital role in Hungarian pop culture, since practically every band played here or aspired to do so. It still hosts occasional rock concerts in the summer; Frank Zappa performed a couple of numbers during the festivities to mark the departure of Soviet troops in June 1991. Down at the bottom, you can either backtrack through the Watertown or head south towards Gellért Hill.

The Watertown

The **Watertown** (*Víziváros*), between Castle Hill and the Danube, was originally a poor quarter housing fishermen, craftsmen and their families, which became depopulated during the seventeenth century save for a few "Turkified Hungarians selling fruit". Today it's a reclusive neighbourhood of old blocks and mansions meeting at odd angles on the hillside, reached by alleys which mostly consist of steps rising from the main street – **Fő utca**. Many are still lit by gas lamps, looking quite Dickensian on misty evenings. The following account progresses southwards from Batthyány tér; see p.72 for details of the northern sector where the Király Baths are located.

BATTHYÁNY TÉR

The Watertown's main square, named **Batthyány tér** after the nineteenth-century prime minister, was originally called Bomba (bomb) tér after an ammunition depot sited here. Now home to a long-established market and the underground interchange between Metro line 2 and the HÉV railway to Szentendre, it's always busy with shoppers and commuters. To the right of the market is a sunken, two-storey building that used to be the *White Horse Inn*, where Casanova reputedly once stayed – this is now a nightclub, predictably named after him. The twin-towered **Watertown Parish Church** on the southern corner of the square sports the Buda coat of arms on its tympanum.

Heading south along Fő utca, you'll see a spiky polychrome-tiled church on **Szilágyi Desző tér**, and a floating hotel moored alongside the embankment. It was here that the Arrow Cross massacred hundreds of Jews and dumped their bodies in the river in the bitterly cold January of 1945, when Eichmann and the SS had already fled the city, which was by then encircled by the Red Army. An inconspicuous plaque commemorates the victims. Further on, you can see the old Capuchin Church featuring Turkish window arches, at no. 30 on the left-hand side. A couple of blocks later you emerge onto Clark Ádám tér, facing the Chain Bridge.

TIIE CHAIN BRIDGE

The majestic **Chain Bridge** (*lánchíd*) has a special place in the hearts of locals as the first permanent link between Buda and Pest, and as a symbol of civic endurance. Austrian troops tried and failed to destroy it in 1849, but in 1945 it fell victim to the Wehrmacht, who dynamited all of Budapest's bridges in a bid to check the Red Army. Their reconstruction was one of the first tasks of the postwar era, the Chain Bridge being reopened on November 21, 1949, the exact centenary of its inauguration.

The bridge was instigated by **Count István Széchenyi**, a horse-fancying Anglophile with a passion for innovation, who founded the National Library and brought steam engines to Hungary, amongst other achievements (see p.195). Designed by **William Tierney Clark**, it was constructed under the supervision of a Scottish engineer, **Adam Clark** (no relation), who personally thwarted the Austrian attempts to destroy it by flooding the chain-lockers. While Széchenyi died in an asylum having witnessed the triumph of Kossuth and revolution – his worst nightmare – Adam Clark married a Hungarian woman and settled happily in Budapest. Clark also built the **tunnel** (*alagút*) under Castle Hill which, Budapesters joked, could be used to store the new bridge when it rained.

THE SIKLÓ AND KILOMETRE ZERO

Near the tunnel entrance is the lower terminal of the **Sikló**, a lovingly restored nineteenth-century funicular running up to the Palace (daily 7.30am–10pm). Constructed on the initiative of Ödön, Széchenyi's son, it was only the second funicular in the world when it was inaugurated in 1870, and functioned without a hitch until wrecked by a shell in 1945. The yellow carriages are exact replicas of the originals, but are now lifted by an electric winch rather than a steam engine, as before. In the small park further south stands "Kilometre Zero", a zero-shaped monument whence all distances from Budapest are measured.

Tabán, Gellért Hill and beyond

South of Castle Hill lies the **Tabán** district, once Buda's artisan quarter, largely inhabited by Serbs (known as *Rác* in Hungarian), but almost totally destroyed by redevelopment in the 1930s. Nowadays it seems to consist mostly of parks and motorways, but there are a few survivors worth seeking out. The **Semmelweiss Medical Museum** (Tues–Sun 10am–6pm), at Apród utca 1–3, honours the "saviour of mothers", Ignác Semmelweiss (1815–65), who discovered the cause of puerperal fever (a form of blood poisoning contracted in childbirth) and a simple method for preventing the disease, which until then was usually fatal. Inside are displayed medical instruments and mementoes of Semmelweiss. The real reason to come to Tabán, though, is the Turkish baths – the place to immerse yourself in history.

THE RÁC AND RUDAS BATHS

The relaxing and curative effects of Buda's **mineral springs** have been appreciated for 2000 years. The Romans built splendid bathhouses at Aquincum, and while these declined with the empire, interest revived after the Knights of Saint John built a hospice on the site of the present Rudas baths, near where Saint Elizabeth cured lepers in the springs below Gellért Hill. However, it was the Turks who consolidated the habit of bathing (as Muslims, they were obliged to wash five times daily in preparation for prayer) and created proper bathhouses which function to this day.

The **Rác Baths** (Mon–Sat 7.30am–6pm), on Hadnagy utca below the Hegyalja út flyover, have an octagonal stone pool from Turkish times, but were otherwise rebuilt in the last century. The sulphurous water (40°C) is good for skin complaints and conditions effecting the joints. There are separate admission days for men (Mon, Wed & Fri) and women (Tues, Thurs & Sat). Heading on towards the Rudas Baths, you pass the Ivocsarnok (Water Hall) below the road to the Erzsébet Bridge – drinking water from three nearby springs is sold here (Mon, Wed & Fri 11am–6pm, Tues & Thurs 7am–2pm).

The **Rudas Baths** (Mon–Fri 6.30am–6pm, Sat 6am–1pm), south of the Erzsébet bridge, are outwardly nondescript, but the interior has hardly changed since it was constructed in 1556 on the orders of Pasha Sokoli Mustapha. Tselebi called this place the "bath with green pillars", and these columns can still be seen supporting the vaulted ceiling beneath which bathers wallow in an octagonal stone pool, watching steam billowing around the shadowy recesses. Illumination is provided by star-shaped apertures in the domed ceiling. Despite being designated **for men only**, the Rudas has a much less obvious gay scene than the Király Baths.

BATHING MATTERS

Most bathhouses are divided into a **swimming** area and a separate section for **thermal baths** (*gyógyfürdő*), sauna, steamrooms and sometimes even mud baths. To enter this section, you must exchange your swimming costume for an apron (for women) or loincloth (for men). A basic ticket covers three hours in the pools, *szauna* and steamrooms (*gőzfürdő*); buy supplementary tickets for a massage (*masszázs*), tub (*kadfürdő*) or mud bath (*iszapfürdő*) if desired. Swimmers are required to wear a bathing cap, which can be rented if necessary (as can costumes and towels).

Gellért Hill

Gellért Hill (*Gellérthegy*) is as much a feature of the waterfront panorama as Castle Hill and the Parliament building: a craggy dolomite cliff rearing 130m above the embankment, surmounted by the Liberation Monument and the Citadella. The hill is named after Bishop Ghirardus (Gellért in Hungarian), who converted pagan Magyars to Christianity at the behest of King Stephen. After his royal protector's demise, vengeful heathens strapped Gellért to a barrow and toppled him off the cliff where a **statue of Saint Gellért** now stands astride a waterfall facing the Erzsébet Bridge.

To reach the summit you can either climb one of the paths from the statue or the *Hotel Gellért* (10–15mins), or travel to Móricz Zsigmond körtér and catch a #27 bus to the top. The **panoramic view** is stunning, drawing one's eye slowly along the curving river, past bridges and the monumental landmarks, and then on to the Buda Hills and Pest's suburbs, merging hazily with the distant plain.

THE GELLÉRT HOTEL AND BATHS

Before ascending the hill, take a look at the **Gellért Hotel**, a famous Art-Nouveau establishment opened in 1918, which Admiral Horthy commandeered after his triumphal entry into "sinful Budapest" in 1920. During the Thirties and Forties, its balls were the highlight of Budapest's social calendar, debutantes dancing on a glass floor laid over its pool. The **Gellért Baths** are magnificently appointed with majolica tiles and columns, lion-headed spouts gushing into its thermal pool (Mon–Sat 6am–7pm, Sun 6.30am–1pm; mixed sex). At the far end of the pool, stairs lead down to the Turkish baths, with ornate plunge pools at different levels and separate areas for men and women; there's also an outdoor summer pool with a wave-machine and terraces for nude sunbathing.

Sadly the staff are unhelpful and prices double over summer (bring a cap and towel to save money), but even if you don't plan on taking a dip, you should at least take a peek into the foyer, entered via the portal carved with writhing figures.

THE CITADELLA AND LIBERATION MONUMENT

The hilltop **Citadella** was built by the Habsburgs in the aftermath of the 1848–49 Revolution to dominate the city with its cannons. When the historic "Compromise" was reached in 1867, citizens breached the walls to affirm that it no longer posed a threat to them. Since World War II, when an SS regiment holed up in the fortress, nothing more sinister than fireworks has been launched from the citadel. Today, it contains a casino and a tourist hostel, plus a "museum" comprising a few display cabinets; to gain free admission enter through the gate marked "hotel", which is always open.

From the ramparts you get a fine view of the towering **Liberation Monument** beside the citadel – a female figure brandishing the palm of victory over 100 feet aloft – which is too large to be properly appreciated when you stand directly below it. The monument's history is ironic, since it was originally commissioned by Admiral Horthy in memory of his son – killed in the "Crusade against Bolshevism" – but was ultimately dedicated to the Soviet soldiers who died liberating Budapest from the Nazis*. Its sculptor, Zsigmond Kisfaludi-Strobl, simply added smaller figures of Soviet armymen around the base to gain approval as a "Proletarian Artist". Having previously specialised in busts of the aristocracy, he was henceforth known by his compatriots as "Kisfaludi-Strébel" (*strébel* means "to climb" or "step from side to side").

Further afield

South of the hill, along the embankment, Budapest's **Technological University** (*Műszaki Egyetem*) sometimes opens its halls of residence to tourists in the summer, while in term time there are concerts and discos in the *E*- and *R-klubs* (see "Entertainments"). Unless you venture further afield into the XI or XXII districts, however, there are no real "sights" here.

Way over to the northwest, the Wolf's Meadow or **Farkasréti Cemetery** (tram #59 from Moszkva tér to the end of the line) contains the **tomb of Béla Bartók**, whose remains were ceremonially reinterred here in July 1988 following their return from America, where the composer died in exile in 1945. His will forbade reburial in Hungary so long as there were any streets named after Hitler or Mussolini – but his return was delayed for decades to prevent the Communists from capitalising on the event. More impressive than his tomb is the amazing crypt in the cemetery chapel, whose wooden vault resembles the oesophagus or belly of a beast – a typically striking design by **Imre Mákovecz** (see p.122).

If you're willing to make a 10km journey south by #3 bus from Móricz Zsigmond körtér, you can get a feel for how the old nobility lived at the **Nagytétény Castle Museum**, XXII, Kastélymúzeum utca 9 (Tues–Sun 10am–6pm). Built for the Rudnyánszky family in the mid-eighteenth century, this Baroque mansion contains a collection of antique furniture from Hungary and other countries (some dating from the fifteenth century), and huge tiled stoves. In the same general direction lies the **Erdliget housing estate** in the Budaörs district, where *Szomszédok* – the Hungarian equivalent of *Neighbours* – is set and filmed. If you're curious to watch the programme, it's broadcast after the news on Thursdays.

Around Moszkva tér and the Rózsadomb

The area immediately north of Castle Hill is largely defined by the transport hub of **Moszkva tér** and the reclusive residential quarter covering the **Rózsadomb** (Rose Hill). The interest here lies in the ambience of the latter, a couple of minor

---

*In reality, joy at being rid of the Nazis was rapidly dispelled as the Red Army raped and looted its way across Hungary. Once Communist rule became entrenched, mention of the very word rape was forbidden in the media; and a protest delegation of writers received a chilling rebuff from the Communist leader, Rákosi. "What is there to write about? In Hungary there are, say, 3000 villages. Supposing the Russians violated, say, three women in every village. Nine thousand in all. Is that so much? You writers have no idea of the law of large numbers".

sights in the backstreets, and easy access to the Buda Hills. For practical purposes, this section also includes the initial stretch of Szilágyi Erzsébet fasor and the Király Baths at the northern end of Fő utca.

Moszkva tér and Szilágyi Erzsébet fasor

It's difficult to predict whether **Moszkva tér** – Moscow Square – will keep its present name but, being of pre-war vintage, it might well survive; especially given the complications involved in changing the name of such a major transport nexus. Among the useful services that run from here are bus #22 to Budakeszi Game Park; bus or tram #56 to Hüvösvölgy; and tram #6 to Margit Island and Pest's Great Boulevard. Aside from **transport**, Moszkva tér is only notable for the flower and vegetable **markets** in the sidestreets to the north, and **Varosmajor Park**, where chess fans play beneath the elms.

Alongside the park, **Szilágyi Erzsébet fasor** runs past the cylindrical **Hotel Budapest** – nicknamed "the dustbin" for its shape – and the terminal of the **Cogwheel Railway** (see p.75), across the road. One kilometre on, you can glimpse on the right a red marble **monument to Raoul Wallenberg**, the "Righteous Gentile", who gave up a playboy life in neutral Sweden to help the Jews of Hungary in 1944. Armed with diplomatic status and money for bribing officials, Wallenberg and his assistants plucked thousands from the cattle trucks and lodged them in "safe houses", manoeuvring to buy time until the Russians arrived. Shortly after they did, Wallenberg was arrested as a spy and vanished into the Gulag, where he probably died in 1953. The monument was unveiled just before Budapest hosted the World Jewish Congress in 1987.

Around the Király Baths and Bem tér

The area **north of Batthyány tér** strictly belongs to the Watertown, but you're likely to visit it en route to the Rószadomb. The easiest way to do this is to start by heading up Fő utca to the Király Baths, or catch a #86 bus along the embankment to Bem tér and walk west from there. On the former route you'll pass the gloomy block of the **Military Court of Justice** (nos. 70–72), where Imre Nagy and other leaders of the 1956 Uprising were tried and executed in 1958. The square outside has recently been renamed after Nagy, whose body lay in an unmarked grave for over thirty years.

You can identify the **Király Baths** at Fő utca 82–86 by the four copper cupolas, shaped like tortoise shells, poking from its eighteenth-century facade. The octagonal pool – lit by star-staped apertures in the dome – was built by the Turks in 1570, for the Buda garrison. The bath's name, meaning "king", comes from that of the König family who owned it in the eighteenth century. Perhaps because there are separate days for men (Mon, Wed & Fri) and women (Tues, Thurs & Sat), the baths have become a major centre of Budapest's **gay life**; this may be why they are often closed despite the official opening hours (Mon–Fri 6.30am–6pm, Sat 6.30am–1pm).

A little further north, **Bem tér** was named after the Polish general Joseph Bem, who fought for the Hungarians in the 1849 War of Independence. Traditionally a site for demonstrations, it was here that crowds assembled on October 23, 1956, prior to marching on Parliament bearing Hungarian flags with the hammer and sickle cut out, hours before the Uprising. The square was also the focus for peace demonstrations and protests against the Nagymaros Dam during the Eighties.

At Bem utca 20, 200m in the direction of the Rózsadomb, the **Foundry Museum** (Tues–Sun 10am–5pm) is housed in the ironworks founded by Abrahám Ganz in 1844, which grew into a massive industrial complex. The huge ladles and jib-cranes are still in their original setting, while the museum's collection includes some fine cast-iron stoves.

By continuing northwards past the Margit Bridge instead, you can find the Neoclassical **Lukács Baths**, where there's both a thermal pool (daily 6.30am–8pm: men Tues, Thurs, Sat & Sun; women Mon, Wed & Fri) and a mixed swimming pool (Mon–Sat 6am–8pm, Sun 6am–7pm). The adjacent **Császár Baths** have a Turkish bath-hall dating from the sixteenth century, still in use. The entrances to both are on Üstökös utca, around the back, rather than on the embankment side of the building.

The Rózsadomb

Budapest's most exclusive neighbourhood lies beyond smog-ridden **Mártirok útja** (Martyrs' Avenue) and the backstreets off Moszkva tér. If you're coming from Bem tér, consider a preliminary detour to the **tomb of Gül Baba** on Mecset utca, just above Mártirok útja. This small octagonal building is a shrine to the "Father of the Roses", a Sufi Dervish who participated in the Turkish capture of Buda but died during the thanksgiving service afterwards: ever since, Muslim pilgrims have come here for *baraka* (blessings). Carpets, examples of calligraphy and Gül Baba's personal effects line the walls of the shrine, which fittingly stands in a rose garden (May–Oct Tues–Sun 10am–6pm).

The **Rózsadomb** itself is as much a social category as a neighbourhood, for a list of residents would read like a Hungarian Who's Who. During the Communist era this included the top Party *funcionárusok*, whose homes featured secret exits that enabled several ÁVO chiefs to escape lynching during the Uprising. Nowadays, wealthy film directors and entrepreneurs predominate, and the sloping streets are lined with spacious villas and parked Mercedes.

Óbuda and Római-Fürdő

The district of **Óbuda**, north of the Rózsadomb, is the oldest part of Budapest, though that's hardly the impression given by the factories and high-rises that dominate the area today, hiding such ancient ruins as remain. Nonetheless it was here that the Romans built a legionary camp and a civilian town, later taken over by the Huns and named Buda, supposedly in honour of Attila's brother. This developed into an important town under the Hungarian Árpád dynasty, but after the fourteenth century it was eclipsed by the Castle district, and the original settlement became known as Óbuda (Old Buda). The best preserved ruins lie further north, in the **Római-Fürdő** district, accessible by HÉV train from Batthyány tér or the Margit Bridge.

THE OLD QUARTER

The section of Óbuda **around Fő tér** blends gaudy Baroque with modern art and overpriced gastronomy, all within a minute's walk of the Árpád híd HÉV stop. At Szentlélek tér 1, the former Zichy mansion has been coverted into the **Vásárhely Museum** (Tues–Sun 10am–6pm), displaying eyeball-throbbing Op-Art paintings by Viktor Vásárhely, one of the founders of the genre. On cobbled

Fő tér, just around the corner, you'll find the *Sipos Halászkert* and *Postakocsi* restaurants (see "Eating and Drinking"). Whatever the weather there are always several figures sheltering beneath umbrellas here: life-sized sculptures by Imre Varga, whose *ceuvre* is the subject of the nearby **Varga Museum** at Laktanya utca 7 (Tues–Sun 10am–6pm). A sense of humour pervades his sheet-metal, iron and bronze effigies of famous personages.

ROMAN RUINS IN ÓBUDA

Although the largest site lies in the Római-Fürdő district, Óbuda does have several excavated ruins to show for its past. The finest of them is the weed-choked, crumbling **amphitheatre** at the junction of Nagyszombat and Pacsirtamező utca: this once covered a greater area than the Colosseum in Rome, seating up to 16,000 spectators. The *amfiteátrum* can be reached by bus #86 (from Batthyány tér or anywhere along the embankment), or by walking 400m north from the Kolósy tér (near the Szépvölgyi út HÉV stop). Having seen it, you can continue to the next batch of ruins by bus #6 or #84.

The **Camp Museum**, a modern block at Pacsirtamező utca 63, displays sarcophagi, the ruins of a bathhouse, fragmented murals and other relics of the legionary camp (May–Oct Tues–Fri 10am–2pm, Sat & Sun 10am–6pm). This was situated near modern-day Flórián tér, where graceful columns now stand incongruously amid a shopping plaza, while the old **military baths** and other finds are huddled beneath the Szentendrei út flyover.

Ten minutes' walk to the northwest, behind apartment block 19–21 on Meggyfa utca, three blue canopies shelter the remains of the **Hercules Villa** (May–Oct Tues–Fri 10am–2pm, Sat & Sun 10am–6pm). The villa gets its name from the third-century AD **mosaic floor** beneath the largest canopy, which depicts Hercules about to vomit at a wine festival, and was originally composed of some 60,000 stones, carefully selected and arranged in Alexandria before shipment to Hungary. Another mosaic depicts the centaur Nessus abducting Deianeira, whom Hercules had to rescue as one of his twelve labours.

Aquincum

The legionary garrison of 6000 spawned a settlement of camp followers – Aquincum – which, over time, became a *Municipum* and later a *Colonia*, the provincial capital of Pannonia Inferior. The **ruins of Aquincum** (May–Oct Tues–Fri 10am–2pm, Sat & Sun 10am–6pm), easily visible from the Aquincum HÉV stop, lie along the Szentendre road a couple of kilometres north of Flórián tér: further up are the remains of an **aqueduct** and another **amphitheatre** near the next HÉV stop, Római-Fürdő (Roman Bath).

Enough foundation walls and underground piping survive to give a fair idea of the **layout** of Aquincum, although you'll need to pay a visit to the museum and use considerable imagination to envisage the town during its heyday in the second to third century AD. A great concourse of people would have filled the main street, doing business in the Forum and law courts (near the site entrance), and steaming in the public baths. Herbs and wine were burned before altars in sanctuaries holy to the goddesses Epona and Fortuna Augusta, while fraternal societies met in the Collegiums and bath-houses further east. The **museum** contains oddments of the imperium – cake moulds, a bronze military diploma, buttons used as admission tickets to the theatre – and statues of gods and goddesses.

The Buda Hills

Thirty minutes' journey from Moszkva tér, the **Buda Hills** provide a welcome respite from Budapest's summertime heat. While particular hills are often busy with people at the weekend, it's possible to ramble through the woods for hours and see hardly a soul during the week. If your time is limited, the most rewarding options are the "railway circuit" or a visit to **Budakeszi Game Park** (daily 9am–5pm), which is reached by taking bus #22 from Moskva tér to the Korányi Sanatorium stop, and then following the *Vadaszpark* signs. Beyond a recreational forest and an exhibition centre, the woods and fields are inhabited by red, roe and shovel-antlered fallow deer, wild pigs, mallards, pheasants and other birds.

The "railway circuit"

The railway circuit begins with a short tram (#18 or #56) or bus (#56) ride from Moskva tér out along Szilágyi Erzsébet fasor, to the lower terminal of the **Cogwheel Railway**. From here, every ten minutes or so, a small train clicks up through the **Svábhegy** suburb, past the world-famous **Pető Institute** for conductive therapy, to the summit of Széchenyi-hegy.

The terminal of the **Children's Railway**, a narrow-gauge line that's almost entirely run by 13- to 17-year-olds, is a short walk across the park. Built by youth brigades in 1948, this enables kids who fancy a career with MÁV to get hands-on experience. Watching them wave flags, collect tickets and salute departures with solemnity, you can see why it appealed to the Communists. Until a few years ago, it was known as the Pioneers' Railway after the organisation that replaced the disbanded Scouts and Guides movements (now reformed). Except on Mondays, when the line is often closed for maintenance, the open trains run every thirty to forty minutes (summer 9am–6.30pm; winter 9am–5pm), stopping at various points en route to Hűvösvölgy. The 11km journey takes about 45 minutes.

The first stop, **Normafa**, is a popular excursion centre with a modest **ski-run**. Its name comes from a performance of the aria from Bellini's *Norma*, given here by the actress Rozália Klein in 1840. János-hegy, three stops on, is the highest point in Budapest. On the 527-metre-high summit, fifteen minutes' climb from the station, the **Erzsébet lookout tower** offers a panoramic view of Budapest and the Buda Hills. By the buffet below the summit is the upper terminal of the **chairlift** (9am–5pm; off-season 9.30am–4pm) down to Zugliget, whence #158 buses return to Moszkva tér.

From the main road by the next stop, **Szépjuhászné**, you can catch a #22 bus to Budakeszi Game Park. **Wild boars** (which prefer to roam during the evening and sleep by day) are occasionally sighted in the forests above **Hárshegy**, one stop before Hűvösvölgy. Also linked directly to Moskva tér by #56 and #56E (non-stop) buses, **Hűvösvölgy** is the site of a small **amusement park** and the popular *Náncsi Néni* restaurant (see "Eating and Drinking").

Stalactite caves and other sights

The hills further to the northwest harbour a second clutch of attractions, best reached in a separate excursion from Kolósy tér in Óbuda (by Szépvölgyi út HÉV stop). From here, ride bus #65 five stops out to Szépvölgyi út 162 to find the **Pál-völgyi Stalactite Caves** (April–Oct Tues–Sat 10am–6pm). Hourly guided tours of this spectacular labyrinth start on the lowest level, boasting rock formations like the "Organ Pipes" and "Beehive". From "John's Lookout" in the largest chamber, you ascend a crevice onto the upper level, there to enter "Fairyland" and finally "Paradise", overlooking the hellish "Radium Hall" 50m below.

From the Pál-völgyi cave another stalactite labyrinth and the Kiscelli Museum are each just twenty minutes' walk away – in opposite directions. Buses also run to both from Kolósy tér. The **Szemlőhegy Cave** at Pusztaszeri út 35 (9am–4pm; closed Tues) abounds in pea-shaped formations and aragonite crystals resembling bunches of grapes. Coming from Kolósy tér by bus #29, alight at the fourth stop near the Pusztaszeri út turn-off. The **Kiscelli Museum** (Tues–Sun April–Oct 10am–6pm; Nov–March 10am–4pm) occupies a former Trinitarian monastery and church at Kiscelli utca 108. Its collection includes antique printing presses and the furnishings of the *Golden Lion* apothecary. Bus #158 from Kolósy tér turns around to begin its return journey near the museum.

Alternatively, ride bus #65 from Pál-völgyi to the end of the line at **Hármashatár-hegy**. This hill provides a fabulous **view** of Budapest from a different perspective, while **hang-gliders** launch themselves off from the western side. It is also the best spot in the hills for **mushroom hunting**, a pastime that's almost as popular amongst Budapesters as it is with city folk in Russia and Poland. People can take their fungi to special *gomba* stalls, where experts distinguish the edible from the toxic ones (there's one in the market near Moszkva tér).

Margit Island

A saying has it that "love begins and ends on **Margit Island**" (*Margit-sziget*), for this verdant expanse has been a favourite spot for lovers since the nineteenth century, although a stiff admission charge deterred the poor before 1945. Today, it is one of the most popular recreation grounds in the city, its thermal springs feeding outdoor pools and ritzy spa-hotels. The easiest way of **getting there** is to catch a #26 bus, which runs all the way along the island, from Marx tér in Pest; or to walk from the middle of Margit Bridge, where trams #4 and #6 (from Moszkva tér or the Great Boulevard) stop. Motorists can only approach from the north, via the Árpád Bridge.

The southern part of the island features a **Casino** and the **Hajós Alfréd Swimming Pool**, named after the winner of the 100m and 1200m swimming races at the 1896 Olympics. Hajós was also an architect, who designed the indoor pool. Further north, before the rose garden on the right, are the **ruins of a Franciscan church** from the late thirteenth century. On the other side of the road, the **Palatinus Baths** (open daily May–Sept) can hold as many as 10,000 people at a time in seven open-air thermal pools, complete with a water chute, wave machine, and segregated terraces for nude sunbathing.

The **outdoor theatre** (*Szabadtéri Színpad*) hosts plays and operas during summer, and together with the nearby Water Tower provides a convenient landmark to help you locate the **ruined Dominican church and convent**. Legend has it that Béla IV vowed to bring his daughter up as a nun if Hungary survived the Mongol invasion, and duly confined nine-year-old Princess **Margit** (Margaret) when it did. She apparently made the best of it, acquiring a reputation for curing lepers and other saintly deeds; being beatified after her death in 1271, and belatedly canonised in 1943. The convent itself fell into ruin during the Turkish occupation, when the island was turned into a harem.

Northeast of the Water Tower is a **Premonstratensian Chapel** whose Romanesque tower dates back to the twelfth century, when the order first established a monastery on the island. The tower's fifteeenth-century bell is one of the oldest in Hungary. Beyond lie the fin-de-siècle **Ramada Grand Hotel** and the modern **Thermal Hotel**, both catering to wealthy invalids. Warm springs in the rock garden beside the latter sustain tropical fish and giant water lilies.

Csepel Island

In the south of the city, the far greater expanse of **Csepel Island** is the polar opposite to its northern counterpart. Heavily industrialised and predominantly working class, Csepel is the XXI district of the city, and the bit that tourists rarely visit. Its northern tip is dominated by the vast **Iron and Metal Works** founded by Manfred Weiss in the 1880s and nationalised after World War II. Traditionally known as "Red Csepel" for its militant workforce, the complex bore the name of Rákosi during the Stalinist era, when the dictator chose this as his own parliamentary constituency. Ironically, its arms factories and workers played a major role in the 1956 Uprising, their factory councils holding out for weeks after the Soviets had crushed resistance elsewhere. In recent years the complex was broken down into smaller units, many of which then went bankrupt or were taken over by foreign companies, leaving swaths of derelict land which will probably become the site of **Budapest Expo 1996**.

Further south, beyond the belt of high-rise *lakótelep*, are tumbledown cottages surrounded by market gardens, and the now abandoned Soviet base at Tököl, whose tanks engaged insurgents during the first days of the Uprising. The remainder of the island is mostly lush semi-wilderness, except near Ráckeve, 50km south of Budapest (see p.268).

Not a great deal of history attaches to Csepel: according to the scribe Anonymous, Prince Árpád was so impressed by the island's fertility that he built a palace here; and the name is said to have been borrowed from a Cumanian master-of-horse called Shepel. If you're interested in **visiting**, the northern end of the island is easily reached by HÉV train from Boráros tér, near the Petőfi Bridge. It is not a good idea to look rich or foreign, or hang around after dark, however.

Pest

PEST is busier, more populous and vital than Buda: the place where things are decided, made and sold. While Buda grew up around Castle Hill's forts and palaces, the east bank was settled by merchants and artisans, and commerce has always been its lifeblood. Much of the architecture and layout dates from the late nineteenth-century, giving Pest a homogenous appearance compared to other European capitals. Boulevards, public buildings and apartment houses were built on a scale appropriate to the Habsburg empire's second city, and the capital of a nation which celebrated its millennial anniversary in 1896. Now bullet-scarred and grimy –or in the throes of restoration– these grand edifices form the backdrop to life in the **Belváros** (inner city) and the residential districts, hulking gloomily above the cafés, wine cellars and courtyards where people socialise. While there's plenty to see and do, it's the less tangible ambience that sticks in one's memory.

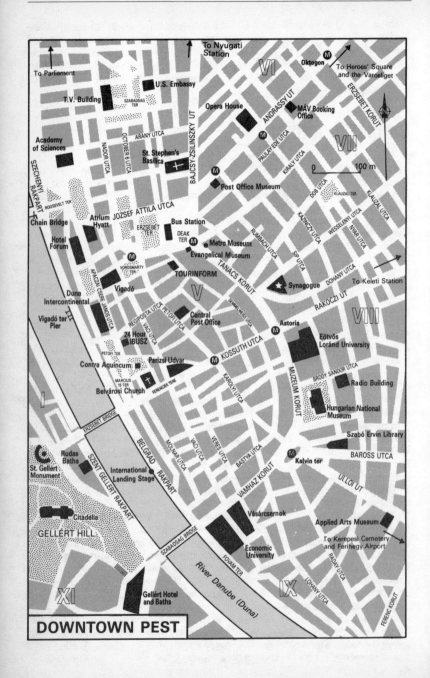

To Parliament

T.V. Building

U.S. Embassy

SZABADSAG TER

Academy of Sciences

ARANY UTCA

OCTOBER 6 UTCA

NADOR UTCA

St. Stephen's Basilica

SZECHENYI RAKPART

ROOSEVELT TER

Chain Bridge

Atrium Hyatt

JOZSEF ATTILA UTCA

ERZSEBET TER

Hotel Forum

Bus Station

DEAK TER

Metro Museum

Evangelical Museum

VOROSMARTY TER

TANACS KORUT

TOURINFORM

Duna Intercontinental

Vigadó

APACZAI CSERE JANOS UTCA

REGI POSTA UTCA

PETOFI UTCA

VACI UTCA

V

Central Post Office

SEMMELWEIS UTCA

Vigadó ter Pier

24 Hour IBUSZ

PETOFI TER

Contra Aquincum

Parizsi Udvar

KOSSUTH UTCA

MARCIUS 15 TER

Belvárosi Church

FERENCIEK TERE

KAROLYI UTCA

VACI UTCA

I

ERZSEBET BRIDGE

BELGRAD RAKPART

MOLNAR UTCA

VERES UTCA

BASTYA UTCA

St. Gellért Monument

Rudas Baths

SZENT GELLERT RAKPART

International Landing Stage

VAMHAZ KORUT

Kalvin ter

Citadella

GELLÉRT HILL

XI

SZABADSAG BRIDGE

Gellért Hotel and Baths

FOVAM TER

Vásárcsarnok

Economic University

River Danube (Duna)

IX

To Nyugati Station

VI

Oktogon

To Heroes' Square and the Varosliget

Opera House

ANDRASSY UT

MÁV Booking Office

ERZSEBET KORUT

PAULAY EDE UTCA

KIRALY UTCA

VII

DOB UTCA

KLAUZAL TER

0   100 m

Post Office Museum

KAZINCZY UTCA

WESSELENYI UTCA

NYAR UTCA

KLAUZAL UTCA

RUMBACH UTCA

SIP UTCA

DOHANY UTCA

Synagogue

To Keleti Station

RAKOCZI UT

Astoria

VIII

Eötvös Lorónd University

BRODY SANDOR UTCA

Radio Building

MUZEUM KORUT

Hungarian National Museum

Szabó Ervin Library

BAROSS UTCA

ULLOI UT

Applied Arts Museum

To Kerepesi Cemetery and Ferihegy Airport

RADAY UTCA

LONAY UTCA

FERENC KORUT

DOWNTOWN PEST

Away from the waterfront, you'll find that two semicircular boulevards are fundamental to **orientation**. The inner city lies within the **Small Boulevard** (*Kiskörút*), made up of József Attila utca, Károly körút, Múzeum körút and Vámház körút. Farther out, the **Great Boulevard** (*Nagykörút*) sweeps through VI, VII, VIII and IX districts, where it is called Szent István körút, Teréz körút, Erzsébet körút, József körút and Ferenc körút. Pest is also defined by **avenues** (*út* or *útja*) radiating out beyond the Great Boulevard – notably Andrássy út, leading to the **Városliget** (City Park); Bajcsy-Zilinszky út; and Rakóczi út, for Nyugati and Keleti **stations**. As the meeting point of three Metro lines and several main avenues, Deák tér makes a good jumping-off point for explorations.

The Belváros

The **Belváros** or inner city (V district) corresponds almost exactly to the original walled, medieval town of Pest. Like the old town it's very cosmopolitan, consciously reacting to foreign influences. For many centuries Pest's population was predominantly German-speaking or Jewish, arousing the mistrust of provincial Hungarians (the more bigoted of whom referred to "Judapest"). Charges of "alien cosmopolitanism" lingered long after an influx of Magyars and a florescence of Hungarian cultural life during the nineteenth century had rendered them irrelevant. Even nowadays, as the Belváros revels in its international connections, the same undercurrent of hostility occasionally surfaces – as in the recent controversy over hustlers on Váci utca.

Along the Embankment

Luxury hotels occupy most of the prime sites along the **Belgrád rakpart** embankment, but the occasional views of Castle Hill amply compensate for the lack of obvious "sights". Such historic architecture as remains can easily be seen during a fifteen-minute stroll between the Erzsébet and Chain bridges. The following account starts near the former: should you tire of the waterfront, almost any sidestreet will lead you to Váci utca within a few minutes.

Immediately to the north of the Erzsébet Bridge ramp, the grimy facade of the **Belvárosi Church** conceals Renaissance niches, Baroque barrel-vaulting and a *mihrab* from the time of the Turkish occupation, indicating the direction of Mecca. The name of the squre on which it stands, **Március 15. tér**, refers to March 15 1848, the date when the Revolution began. Also on the square are for the **ruins of a Roman fort** – Contra-Aquincum – which served as an outpost of their settlement across the river.

Further north, an adjoining square and statue honour Sándor Petőfi (1823–49), poet of the *puszta* and revolutionary firebrand, whose *National Song* – the anthem of 1848 – and romantic death in battle made him a patriotic icon (see p.280). **Petőfi tér** is a traditional site for **demonstrations** against authority – usually on March 15, when the statue is decked out with flags and flowers. Anniversary celebrations have been forbidden (or heavily policed) under autocrats of every political hue. There is a **24-hour IBUSZ bureau** at Petőfi tér 3.

VIGADÓ TÉR

North of Petőfi tér, the **Duna Intercontinental** interposes itself between the embankment and the street parallel, Apáczai Csere János utca, as far north as

Vigadó tér. Here stands the **Vigadó**, a splendidly romantic concert hall, the name of which translates as "having a ball" or "making merry". Since it opened in 1865, the Vigadó has hosted performances by Liszt (a Hungarian), Mahler (who also directed the Budapest Opera) and Wagner. The modern block on the right occupies the site of the *Angol királynő* (English Queen) hotel, where the likes of the Shah of Persia and Emperor Dom Pedro of Brazil used to stay during the city's Belle Époque.

On the square itself, notice the maritime reliefs and ships' hulls decorating the headquarters of **MAHART**, the state shipping company, which is responsible for the pleasure cruisers and ferries to the Danube Bend that leave from the **Vigadó tér pier**. A little further upriver the **Kossuth Museum Ship**, a 1913-vintage steamer, contains an exhibition on the history of the Danube (April–Oct Tues–Sun 10am–6pm) and an expensive restaurant.

ROOSEVELT TÉR

At the Pest end of the Chain Bridge, **Roosevelt tér** is overlooked by the **Atrium Hyatt** and **Forum** hotels. In 1867, Emperor Franz Josef was crowned King of Hungary here, and soil from across the nation was piled into a Coronation Hill, whence he flourished the sword of Saint Stephen and pledged to defend Hungary against any foe. Eighty years later, the square was renamed in honour of the late US president.

Dominating the eastern side of the square is the **Gresham Palace**, a grimy but splendid example of Art Nouveau, commissioned by a British insurance company in 1904. Its entrance passage leads into a T-shaped, glass-roofed arcade off which three staircases lead to different parts of the building. On the ground floor, below a warren of offices, are a pleasant bar and a luxurious Chinese restaurant.

The **Hungarian Academy** at the northern end of the square is another bequest from Count Széchenyi, who donated a year's income from his estates towards its foundation in 1825 (as depicted on the wall facing Akadémia utca). Unlike the Széchenyi Library, however, the public are not admitted to the building. The Nobel Prize winning scientist György Hevesy (1885–1966) – discoverer of the element hafnium – was born at Akadémia utca 1, behind the academy.

From here you can continue northwards to the Parliament building on Kossuth tér, or head back towards the Vigadó and then cut inland to Vörösmarty tér.

From Erzsébet Bridge to Astoria

The inner city is more or less bisected by the thoroughfare that crosses the Erzsébet Bridge, which changes its name with bewildering frequency. Near the bridge it is called Szabadsajtó út and flanked by the two imposing **Klothild Palaces** – beneath the fancy title, essentially ornate nineteenth-century office blocks. The wider section further inland, known in the Communist era as Feldszabadulás tér (Liberation Square), is currently named **Ferenciek tere** (Franciscans Square) after the church on the corner: there is talk of another change, reverting to the pre-World War I name of Kigyó tér (Snake Square).

Flanking Ferenciek tere to the north is the **Párizsi udvar** (Parisian Arcade), a slab of gilt and gingerbread architecture. There's a big *IBUSZ* office on the corner and an ice cream parlour facing the square, but it's the stained-glass Art-Nouveau passageway that draws you into the arcade. On Kigyó utca, around the corner, it's also worth looking into the *Apostolok* restaurant, whose salons are decorated with paintings of the apostles and towns that were lost to Hungary after World War I. At the far end of this street is Váci utca (see below).

Meanwhile, the main road becomes **Kossuth utca** as it runs to meet the Small Boulevard at **Astoria** – site of a famous hotel and a Metro station beneath the intersection. Once a haunt of spies and journalists, the **Astoria Hotel** was badly damaged in the 1956 Uprising and served as a Soviet *Komandantura* in the aftermath, but has now been restored to its former elegance. Across the road, on the corner of Semmelweiss utca, you can peek into the foyer of what is still (but unlikely to remain) the **Soviet House of Culture**, occupying the premises of the pre-war National Casino club. Until a few years ago, jackbooted officers could be seen swaggering in and out, attended by their lackeys.

From Váci utca to Vórósmarty tér

Visitors seem inevitably to gravitate towards **Váci utca**, the fashionable *korzó* running north from the Párizsi udvar. Lined with boutiques and street cafés, this bustling promenade has been likened to Bond Street in London or the Ramblas in Barcelona. Though neither is a very accurate comparison, you can see what they're getting at, as Váci utca combines hauteur and flirtatiousness in equal measure. During the Eighties, its vivid **streetlife** became a symbol of the "consumer socialism" that distinguished Hungary from other Eastern bloc states, and invariably featured in documentaries about the country.

Heading north up Váci utca you'll pass the **Pest Theatre** (no. 9), where the twelve-year-old Liszt made his concert debut, and lines of women selling embroidered quilts and tablecloths – the ones in traditional dress are from the ethnic Hungarian regions of Transylvania. While the police tolerate some dire one-man-bands, other **hustlers** are fair game for harassment, especially the Africans on roller-skates who hawk *Budapest Week*. Within a few blocks you can hear every language from Arabic to German, Italian to Yoruba.

VÖRÖSMARTY TÉR

The crowd flows on from here to **Vörösmarty tér**, breaking on a reef of portraitists to eddy about conjurers, violinists and other street performers. While children play in the fountains, youths congregate around the statue of Mihály Vörösmarty (1800–50), a poet and translator whose hymn to Magyar identity, *Szózat* (Appeal), is publicly declaimed at moments of national crisis. Its opening line – "Be faithful to your land forever, O Hungarians" – is carved upon the pedestal.

On the far side of the square, the famous **Gerbeaud patisserie** has been a haunt of Budapest high society since 1884, when the coffeehouse was bought by the Swiss confectioner Emile Gerbeaud. Though its gilded ceilings and china recall the Belle Époque, the waitresses no longer have time to discuss the customers in their private code language, and the octogenarian "Gerbeaud ladies" with their furs and lace gloves have been driven away by the tourists.

Beside Gerbeaud's terrace is the entrance to the **Millennial Railway** (Metro line l), the first underground on the European continent when it was inaugurated in 1896, following the construction of London's Metropolitan line. Coincidentally the **British Embassy** is just a stone's throw away on Harmancid utca: the street's name – meaning "one thirtieth" – recalls an old tax.

PETŐFI UTCA AND MARTINELLI TÉR

Petőfi utca, running parallel to the *korzó*, has none of the glamour of Váci utca and all the traffic, but it still manages a couple of places worth noting. At no. 13 is the **Central Post Office** with its *poste restante* department, followed by the **Central Telephone and Telegraph Bureau** at nos. 17–19. Where the street opens on to **Martinelli tér**, just north of here, look out for the **Rózsavölgyi House** (no. 5), which blends the National Romantic and Modernist styles, and the erstwhile **Turkish Banking House** (no. 3), its gable aglow with a mosaic of Hungaria – the Magyar equivalent of Britannia – flanked by shepherds and angels. From here, you can head past a multi-storey car park to reach Deák tér.

Deák tér and Erzsébet tér

Three Metro lines, two segments of the Small Boulevard and several important avenues meet at **Deák tér** and Erzsébet tér (which makes local addresses very confusing), but for all its importance as a transport hub there's little reason to hang around. You'll recognise the area by two landmarks: the dome of Saint Stephen's Basilica to the north, and the huge mustard-coloured, mansard-roofed Anker Palace to the east. Beneath this, in the Károly körút section of the pedestrian underpass, railway buffs can grow maudlin over ornate fixtures and tiling and yellow trams dating from the 1890s, in the **Metro Museum** (*FAV muzeum*; Tues–Sun 10am–6pm; admission by Metro ticket).

The entrance to the Metro proper lies across the main road, flanked by the **National Evangelical Museum** (Tues–Sun 10am–6pm), with relics pertaining to the Lutheran or *Evangélikus* faith, including a facsimile of Luther's last will and testament. Across the way is a Mercedes Benz showroom, occupying what used to be a propaganda bureau for the old German Democratic Republic – one of those jokes played by history that Marx was keen on. On Sütő utca, running off between the two, you'll find **TOURINFORM**, the capital's best source of **tourist information** (daily 8am–8pm; ☎117-9800).

In the other direction lies **Erzsébet tér bus station**, the place to board international services or embark on tours of the city in an open-topped bus – see *Omnibusz Tours* in the main building for details.

The Lipótváros

This section and the ones that follow cover the areas immediately beyond the Belváros, moving in a clockwise direction starting with the Lipótváros north of Vörösmarty tér. The **Lipotváros** (Leopold Town) started to develop in the late eighteenth century, first as a financial centre and later as the seat of government and bureaucracy. Though much of its architecture is ponderously Neoclassical, the main squares are enlivened by touches of Eclectic and Art Nouveau style. The following account assumes Vörösmarty tér as the starting point: coming from Erzsébet tér, it's logical to visit the Basilica first, then Szabadság tér and Parliament. Note, too, that the Lipótváros straddles the V and VI districts, but the actual demarcation line is a bit of a mystery. Thus you can have places as far north as Szent István körút assigned to the V district, while addresses halfway up Bajcsy-Zsilinszky út fall under the VI.

Szabadság tér

Immediately north of the Small Boulevard (József Attila utca), narrow streets lined with administrative buildings lead towards the government district, only to have their gloomy progress interrupted by Szabadság tér (Liberty Square). Here, opposite the vast Hungarian **Television Building** (originally the Stock Exchange) is the **National Bank** with its bas-reliefs symbolising honest toil and . profit, and a small **Museum of Banknotes and Coins** (Thurs 9am–2pm only) inside. Just north of here is the **US Embassy** (no. 12), where Cardinal Mindszenty spent fifteen years of "internal exile" after the 1956 Uprising (see p.125). A nearby statue commemorates General Harry Bandholtz of the US Army, who intervened with a dogwhip to prevent Romanian forces from looting the National Museum in 1920. Further north stands a monument to the Red Army, its plinth bearing tableaux from the siege of Budapest. The fascist Arrow Cross had its headquarters at no. 15, behind and to the left.

In the interwar years, the square boasted several **statues** loaded with symbolism, which the Communists removed but the present government has considered restoring. The Monument to Hungarian Grief – featuring a flag at half mast and a quotation from Mussolini – commemorated the loss of Hungarian territory to the Successor States (Yugoslavia, Czechoslavakia and Romania), as did four statues called North, South, East and West. For a few years, the square even had a statue titled "Gratitude", which was erected in 1949 on the occasion of Stalin's seventieth birthday – but nobody has proposed restoring that.

Parliament and Kossuth tér

Continue northwards and the **Parliament building** *(Országház)* suddenly appears. Variously described as "Eclectic" or "neo-Gothic" in style, it sprawls for 268 metres between the embankment and Kossuth tér, dominating the vicinity with a spiky facade embellished by 88 statues of Hungarian rulers. The symmetrical wings housing the Assemblies meet beneath a gigantic cupola 96 metres high, which can accommodate both chambers when they meet in ceremonial conclave. A vital force during the Reform Era, Parliament had grown sluggish by the time its grandiose seat was built (in 1884–1902). Under Fascism, opposition MPs learned to fear for their lives; after the Communist takeover in 1948, parliamentary politics became a mere echo of decisions taken by the Politburo and Secretariat of the Communist Party, at MSzMP headquarters on Akadémia utca. In the late Eighties it began to recover authority, and now functions as a parliament should. When not in session, there are **guided tours** of the splendid interior, arranged by *Budapest Tourist* on Roosevelt tér. The price (around 1000Ft) includes a visit to the National Gallery or the Mátyás Church on Castle Hill.

Kossuth tér itself, named after the leader of the 1848 Revolution, contains statues of Lajos Kossuth and Prince Ferenc Rákóczi II, an earlier hero of the struggle for Hungarian independence. The quote inscribed on the latter's plinth – "The wounds of the noble Hungarian nation burst open!" – refers to the anti-Habsburg war of 1703–11, but also perfectly describes the evening of October 23, 1956, when crowds filled the square chanting anti-Stalinist slogans at Parliament, and calling for the appearance of the popular reformist Imre Nagy – the prelude to the Uprising that night

Thirty-three years later, the wheel turned full circle as the Republic of Hungary was proclaimed to an enthusiastic crowd from the same balcony that Nagy had spoken from, and the People's Republic of Hungary was officially consigned to the dustbin of history. This watershed was also symbolised by the removal of the red star from Parliament's dome, and the replacement of Communist emblems by the traditional coat-of-arms, featuring the double cross of King Stephen.

A neo-Renaissance pile at Kossuth tér 12 houses the **Ethnographic Museum** (Tues–Sun 10am–6pm), whose richly frescoed foyer is as much an attraction as the diverse collection of Inuit furs and kayaks, African instruments and barkcloth and wonderfully carved Melanesian masks. Though often overlooked, this is one of the finest museums in Budapest.

St Stephen's Basilica and Bajcsy-Zsilinszky út

The restoration of **Saint Stephen's Basilica** is proceeding almost as slowly as its construction did, lack of funds being a problem now as then. Building originally began in 1851 under the supervision of József Hild, continued after his death under Miklós Ybl, and was finally completed by Joseph Krauser in 1905. At the inaugural ceremony, Emperor Franz Josef was seen to glance anxiously at the dome, whose collapse during a storm in 1868 had naturally set progress back. At 96 metres it is exactly the same height as the dome of Parliament – both allude to the date of the Magyars' arrival in Hungary.

The cavernous interior is poorly lit and undergoing restoration, but it's worth going inside to view the **mummified hand of Saint Stephen**, in a chapel behind the altar. Drop 20Ft into the cabinet and it will light up to reveal the *Szent Jobb* (literally, "sacred right"), which is paraded around the church on August 20, the anniversary of his death. There is also a one-room **treasury** of chalices and monstrances (daily May–Sept 9am–5pm; Oct–April 10am–6pm).

While Stephen is revered as the founder and patron saint of Hungary, the pantheon of national heroes includes a niche for Endre Bajcsy-Zsilinszky (1866–1944). Originally a right-winger, he ended up an outspoken critic of fascism, was arrested in Parliament (a statue on Deák tér captures the moment) and shot as the Russians neared Sopron. **Bajcsy-Zsilinszky út** runs northwards to terminate at **Marx tér**, where the *Skála-Metró* department store (a proto-capitalist competitor to the state-run *Centrum* chain in the mid-Eighties) faces **Nyugati Station**, an elegant, iron-beamed terminal built (1874–77) by the Eiffel Company of Paris, which now contains probably the ritziest *McDonald's* in the world.

The Terézváros and Andrássy út

The VI district or **Terézváros** (Theresa Town) was laid out in the late nineteenth century, under the influence of Haussman's redevelopment of Paris. At that time it was one of the smartest districts in the city – especially around the Városliget – but much of it is now run down and getting poorer. Hopes for its revival are pinned on the "Hungarian Broadway", which cuts across the main thoroughfare, Andrássy út, just below the Oktogon intersection.

ANDRÁSSY ÚT

Running for two and a half kilometres up to Hősök tere on the edge of the Városliget, this is Budapest's longest – and most renamed – avenue. Inaugurated as the Sugár (Radial) út in 1884, it later became **Andrássy út** (after a statesman of the era) – a name that stayed in popular use throughout the years when this was officially Stalin Avenue (1949–56) or the Avenue of the People's Republic (1957–89). The last name was always a jawbreaker for foreigners, being rendered as Népköztársaság útja in Hungarian.

With its parade of grand buildings laden with stone dryads and colonnades, its Opera House and coffee houses, the avenue retains something of the style that made it fashionable in the 1890s, when "Bertie" the Prince of Wales drove its length in a landau offering flowers to women passing by. Early this century it was also famous for a luxurious brothel – the House of Nations – and sleazier versions in the backstreets to the east.

The initial stretch up to the Oktogon is within walking distance of Erzsébet tér, but if you're going any further it's best to travel from sight to sight by Metro line

1 (running beneath the avenue) or bus (#1 or #4). At Andrássy út 3, a former residential block harbours the **Post Office Museum** (Tues–Sun 10am–6pm) in what used to be a seven-room apartment. Exhibits include a compressed-air mail tube, push-button displays of *Magyar Posta* in the telecommunications age, and blunderbuses and thigh-high boots which attest to the hazards of a postman's life in Habsburg times.

THE OPERA HOUSE AND "BROADWAY"

Founded by Ferenc Erkel (1810–93), composer of Hungary's national anthem, the **State Opera House** is a magnificent neo-Renaissance pile built (1875–84) by Miklós Ybl. The opera can boast of being directed by Mahler, hosting performances conducted by Otto Klemper and Antal Doráti, and sheltering hundreds of local residents in its huge cellars during the siege of Budapest. Unfortunately, you can't get inside except to see performances (see "Entertainments"). By way of compensation, though, you can probably see the interior of the **Arany János Theatre** in the backstreets across the road, which is a stunning Art Nouveau building, recently restored.

One block north of the Opera House, Andrassy út is crossed by **Nagymező utca** – nicknamed **"Broadway"** after the clubs and theatres that cluster here, either side of the avenue. A little further up on the right-hand side, the **MÁV Bookings Office** at no. 35 is the place to buy international railway tickets. Shortly afterwards, Andrássy út meets the Great Boulevard at the **Oktogon**, so-called after the octagonal configuration of the junction. During the Horthy period it rejoiced in the name Mussolini tér, but changed to November 7 tér in the Communist era.

TO THE KODÁLY KÖRÖND AND BEYOND

Andrássy út 60 was once the most terrifying address in Budapest – the **headquarters of the secret police**. Jews and other victims of the Arrow Cross were tortured here during World War II, and the ÁVO (see box) subsequently used the building for the same purpose. Prisoners were brought in by the side entrance on Csengery utca. When the building was captured by insurgents in 1956, no trace was found of the giant meat-grinder rumoured to have been used to dispose of corpses. On the exterior of the building (now the offices of a chemical trading company) are recently affixed memorial plaques.

THE AVO

The **Communist secret police** began as the Party's private security section during the Horthy era, when its chief, **Gábor Péter**, betrayed Trotskyites to the police to take the heat off their Stalinist comrades. After World War II it became the *Allamvédelmi Osztály* or **ÁVO** (State Security Department), its growing power implicit in a change of name in 1948 – to the State Security *Authority* or **ÁVH** (though the old title stuck). Ex-Nazi torturers were easily persuaded to apply their skills on its behalf, and its network of spies permeated society. So hated was the ÁVO that any members caught during the Uprising were summarily killed, and their mouths stuffed with banknotes (secret policemen earned more than anyone else). Re-organised under Kádár, they remained a force to be feared until the Seventies, waning in menace thereafter.

On the opposite side of the road a little further on, the building on the corner of Vörösmarty utca contains the **Liszt Memorial Museum** (Mon–Fri noon–5pm, Sat 9am–1pm), where the composer lived from 1879. His glass piano and travelling keyboard are the highlights of its extensive collection of memorabilia and scores. Another great Hungarian composer lends his name to the **Kodály körönd** junction, where Kodály spent the last years of his life at no. 1. Across the way stands a magnificent neo-Renaissance mansion with gold *sgraffiti* on its facade. Before and during World War II, the körönd suffered the indignity of being called Hitler tér.

By detouring a few blocks off the körönd, you can find the **Ráth Museum** at Gorkij fasor 12 (Tues–Sun 10am–6pm). Housed in a beautifully preserved Art Nouveau villa, this features a private collection of Chinese and Japanese art, worth a look if you're in the mood. The collection is complemented by the **Museum of Eastern Asiatic Art** at Andrássy út 103 (Tues–Sun 10am–6pm), a choice selection of Japanese and Indian silks, puppets, ivory and the like, trawled by Ferenc Hopp on his many voyages east.

The final stretch of the avenue, **up to Hősök tere**, is lined with plane trees and embassies. It was at the Yugoslav Embassy that Imre Nagy took refuge after the Uprising, but was tricked into emerging, arrested by the Soviets, spirited away to Romania, and finally returned home to be executed in 1958.

Hősök tere and the Városliget

Laid out in in 1896 to mark the thousandth anniversary of the Magyar conquest, **Hősök tere** (Heroes' Square) is appropriately grand. The **Millenary Monument** in the centre of the square consists of a 36-metres-high column topped by the figure of Archangel Gabriel who, according to legend, appeared to Stephen in a dream and offered him the crown of Hungary. Around the base are Prince Arpád and his chieftains, who led the Magyar tribes into the Carpathian Basin. As a backdrop to this, a semicircular colonnade displays statues of Hungary's most illustrious leaders, from King Stephen to Kossuth. During the brief Republic of Councils, when the country was governed by revolutionary soviets, the square was decked out in red banners, and the column enclosed in a huge red obelisk. More recently, it was the setting for the ceremonial reburial of Nagy and other murdered leaders of the Uprising (including an empty coffin to represent the "unknown insurgent"), on June 16, 1989 – an event which symbolised the dawning of a new era in Hungary.

THE FINE ARTS MUSEUM AND MŰCSARNOK

To the left of Hősök tere stands the **Museum of Fine Arts** (Tues–Sun 10am–6pm), whose diverse collection embraces everything from Egyptian funerary relics to Impressionist paintings, though ongoing reorganisation makes it difficult to predict what will be on show. Amongst the drawings, look out for Leonardo's *Head of a Warrior* and Raphael's *Esterházy Madonna*. Most of the Italian, Dutch and German Old Masters are represented, there's one of the best collections of El Grecos outside Spain, and Rodin, Renoir, Toulouse-Lautrec, Chagall and Picasso are only some of the big names in modern art. Temporary exhibitions are held at the **Műcsarnok** on the other side of the square (same hours), which often hosts foreign exhibitions on tour, or thematic, avant garde shows.

THE STALIN AND LENIN STATUES

Before venturing into the Városliget behind Hősök tere, spare a thought for the statues that once stood on Aréna út, the main road running alongside the park. Here, 200m south of the square, the Communist leaders used to review parades from a grandstand like their bigger brothers on Red Square. The 70-tonne **Stalin statue** was torn down during the Uprising, dragged to the Great Boulevard, decapitated, doused with petrol and set alight; the headless torso lay there for a week, surrounded by a constantly changing crowd, who hammered away at it for souvenirs. (One family donated an ear to the Rákosi-Stalin exhibition in 1990).

After the Uprising had been crushed, a **Lenin statue** was erected in its place, remaining until 1989, when it was carted away "for structural repairs", and never returned. There are now plans afoot to assemble all such discarded statues in a "Communist Theme Park" somewhere in the city (ask *TOURINFORM* about developments).

The Városliget

The leafy **VÁROSLIGET** (City Park) starts just behind Hősök tere, where the fairytale towers of **Vajdahunyad Castle** rear above an island girdled by an artificial lake used for boating or skating. Like the park, the castle was created for the Millenary Anniversary celebrations, so dramatic effects were the order of the day. This "stone catalogue" of architectural styles incorporates a **replica of the Chapel at Ják** in western Hungary and two Transylvanian castles (one of the originals, the Hunyadi Castle in Romania, gives its name to the building).

The main wing houses an **Agricultural Museum** (Tues–Sat 10am–5pm, Sun 10am–6pm) which is guaranteed to make vegetarians blanch and everybody else yawn, but children are delighted by the hooded **statue of "Anonymous"** outside. This nameless chronicler to King Béla is the prime source of information about early medieval Hungary, but the existence of several monarchs of that name during the twelfth and thirteenth centuries makes it hard to date him with any exactitude.

Leaving the island by the causeway at the rear, you're on course for the **Petőfi csarnok**, a "Metropolitan Youth Centre" that regularly hosts concerts, films, discos and other events (☎142-4327 for information in English). On the first floor is an **Aviation Museum** (April–Nov Tues–Sun 10am–6pm) whose vintage planes and genuine space capsule appeal to kids. In a similar vein, there is the **Transport Museum** at the back of the park, which includes antique cars, models galore, and mothballed steam trains (Tues–Sun 10am–6pm).

On the other side of the park's central promenade lie the **Széchenyi Baths**, fronted by a statue of the geologist Zsigmondy Villmos, discoverer of the thermal spring that feeds its outdoor pool (Mon–Sat 6am–7pm, Sun till 7pm in summer, 4pm in winter) and Turkish baths (Mon–Sat 6am–8pm, Sun till 1pm). Here you can enjoy the surreal spectacle of people playing chess whilst immersed up to their chests in steaming water. The baths are undergoing major renovation at the moment, but were still open at the time of writing.

THE ZOO, CIRCUS AND VIDÁM PARK

The northwestern side of the park beyond Állatkerti körút harbours Budapest's **Zoo** (daily April–Sept 9am–6pm; Oct–March 9am–4pm). When opened in 1866, its Art Nouveau pavilions by Károly Kós seemed the last word in zoological architecture, but by modern standards few of them look fit for bird or beast. A refit is underway, however, and there's nothing to stop you enjoying the Palm House (*Pálmház*). The hippos, too, seem to thrive, apparently because they can wallow in hot water whenever they like. The children's corner is signposted *Allatóvoda*.

Just down the road is the municipal **Circus**, which traces its origins back to 1783, when the Hetz Theatre played to spectators around what is now Deák tér. From mid-April to the end of August there are performances Wed–Sat at 7.30pm; Thurs–Sun at 3.30pm; and at 10am at weekends (☎142-8300 for details). Next door lies **Vidám Park**, an old-fashioned, rather shabby amusement park (daily 10am–8pm), known as the "English Park" before the war. It has all the usual rides, only a few of which operate over winter.

The Erzsébetváros

The VII district or **Erzsébetvaros** (Elizabeth Town), between Andrássy út and Rákóczi út, is mainly residential, composed of nineteenth-century buildings whose bullet-scarred facades, adorned with fancy wrought ironwork, conceal a warren of dwellings and leafy courtyards. It is also traditionally the **Jewish quarter** of the city, which was transformed into a ghetto during the Nazi occupation and almost wiped out in 1944–45, but miraculously retained its cultural identity. Though specific things to see are few, there is no better part of Pest to wander around, soaking up the atmosphere and discovering things for yourself.

Before Andrássy út was built in the 1890s, the quarter's boundary was defined by **Király utca**, a congested thoroughfare noted for its brothels, where – as Patrick Leigh Fermor was told in 1934 – "any man could be a cavalier for five pengöes". The street retains many buildings from the mid-nineteenth century (mostly at the Erzsébet tér end), and at least one dating from 1810, but nowadays they contain nothing more notorious than secondhand (*bizományi*) shops and outlets for cheap, slightly flawed (*alkami*) shoes and clothing. Approaching the area from the south, as most people do, the first landmark is the Central Synagogue just off Károly körút.

The Central Synagogue
Budapest's **Central Synagogue** is the largest in Europe, capable of holding 3000 worshippers, and part of a complex of buildings which includes the birthplace of Theodor Herzl, founder of the Zionist movement. It is also a spectacular example of the Byzantine Moorish style of synagogue architecture favoured in the 1850s, sporting onion domes, crenellations and geometric friezes. After decades of neglect, restoration is underway, largely funded from abroad by the Hungarian-Jewish diaspora, with Tony Curtis (born of Twenties emigrants) spearheading the drive.

Depending on its progress, you'll be able to see at least part of the *zsinagóga* complex (Mon–Thurs 10am–3pm, Fri & Sun 10am–lpm), and the **National Jewish Museum** (May–Oct Mon & Thurs 2–6pm; Tues, Wed, Fri & Sun 10am–lpm) on the first floor. Here, torahs and other Judaica dating back to the Middle Ages, along with examples of the Jewish cultural florescence of the nineteenth century, are opposed by a harrowing Holocaust exhibit, the memory of which casts a chill over the third section, portraying Jewish cultural life today. This current resurgence owes much to the increased contacts with international Jewry, and a revival of interest in religion and roots amongst the 80,000-strong

Jewish community of Budapest, which had previously tended towards assimilation and been reticent to proclaim itself in a country where anti-semitic prejudices linger.

In the courtyard is a weeping-willow shaped **memorial** to the dead of the ghetto, each leaf bearing the names of families massacred by the Nazis.

Around the backstreets

Fanning out behind the synagogue are backstreets where practically every apartment block contains a run-down yet beautiful courtyard with stained-glass panels inscribed in Hebrew characters, and sad memorial plaques naming those who perished during the "autumn that bled" in 1944, when Nazi squads rampaged through **the ghetto** leaving Jewish corpses piled in the streets, while gentiles walked by, averting their eyes. As the Zionist underground prepared for escape or last-ditch insurrection, the Wallenberg group (p.72) manoeuvred and bribed to gain time; unable to thwart the murderous Arrow Cross, they nevertheless succeeded in forestalling a final SS assault on the ghetto, as Soviet troops were encircling the city.

At the lower end of Dob utca stands a recently erected **monument to Carl Lutz**, a Swiss emigré who saved Jews by issuing them with foreign identity passes – the tactic adopted by Wallenberg. Lutz, however, was a more ambiguous figure, (ironically regarded as pro-Nazi by the British), who ceased issuing passes and tried to stop others from faking them after being threatened by the Gestapo. After the war, he was criticised in his homeland for abusing Swiss law; felt unjustly slighted, and proposed himself for the Nobel Peace Prize. His monument – a golden angel stooping to help a prostrate victim – is locally known as "the figure jumping out of a window".

Further north and to the left, **Rumbach utca** harbours a twin-towered, Romantic-style synagogue built from 1872 for the so-called Status Quo or middling-conservative Jews. This can also be reached by walking through a succession of courtyards behind the red-brick Thirties apartment block on Károly körút. Another destination is **Klauzál tér**, towards the Great Boulevard, which is noted for its Jewish restaurants (see "Eating and Drinking").

The Eighth District

The **VIII district** – otherwise known as Józsefváros (Joseph Town) – is separated from the VII district by Rákóczi út, which runs out to Keleti Station; and from the Belváros by Múzeum körút, part of the Small Boulevard. This quarter has a mixed reputation – the site of prestigious institutions but also something of a red-light district and thieves' hangout, nicknamed "Chicago" during the Twenties and Thirties.

Múzeum körút resembles Andrássy út in miniature, with trees, shops and grandiose piles curving round to meet Kálvin tér. Immediately below the Astoria junction stands the natural sciences faculty of **Eötvös Loránd University**, whence many of the scientists who worked on the US atomic bombs graduated before World War II, including Edward Teller, the "Father of the Hydrogen Bomb". Further on and across the street, remnants of the **medieval walls of Pest** can be seen in the courtyards of nos. 17 and 21. The walls gradually disappeared as the city was built up on either side, but fragments remain here and there.

THE HUNGARIAN NATIONAL MUSEUM

The **Hungarian National Museum**, like so many other institutions in Budapest, was the brainchild of Count Széchenyi, who donated thousands of prints and manuscripts to form the basis of its collection in 1802. Shortly after it opened, the Neoclassical edifice (designed by Mihály Pollock) became the stage for a famous event in the 1848 Revolution, when Sándor Petőfi first declaimed the *National Song* with its rousing refrain – "Choose! Now is the time! Shall we be slaves or shall we be free?" – from its steps. Since then, March 15 has always been commemorated here with flags and patriotic speeches.

The museum (Tues–Sun 10am–6pm) is divided into two main sections – before and after the Magyar conquest – of which the latter, on the first floor, is the more interesting. As most captions are in Hungarian only, a catalogue may be a worthwhile investment. Highlights include the captured tent of a Turkish general, Renaissance pews from Nyírbátor, and the **Coronation Regalia** – reputedly the very crown, orb and sceptre used by King Stephen. The Hungarian coat-of-arms faithfully reproduces the distinctive bent cross that surmounts the crown. As the symbol of Hungarian statehood for over a millennium, the regalia has been buried in Transylvania to hide it from the Habsburgs, taken by Hungarian fascists to Germany in 1945, and thence to the US, where it reposed in Fort Knox until its return home in 1978.

BRÓDY UTCA AND KÁLVIN TÉR

Bródy Sándor utca, flanking the museum grounds, seems an unlikely place for a revolution to start – yet one did outside the nondescript **Radio Building** (no. 7), when ÁVO guards fired upon students demanding access to the airwaves, an act which turned the hitherto peaceful protests of October 23, 1956 into an uprising against the secret police and other manifestations of Stalinism.

Street fighting was especially fierce around **Kálvin tér**, at the junction of Üllői út and the Small Boulevard, where insurgents battled tanks rumbling in from the Soviet base on Csepel Island. It seems almost miraculous that the ornate reading room of the **Szabó Ervin Library** (Mon, Tues & Thurs 9am–9pm, Sat & Sun 9am–1pm), on the corner of Baross utca, survived unscathed. Until recently a famous illustrator had lived all her life in an apartment over the square, where she witnessed three revolutions and two world wars from her window.

Beyond the Great Boulevard

The József körút section of the Great Boulevard marks the beginning of the **red-light district**, where topless bars vie with streetwalkers for custom around **Rákóczi tér** (see box below). Women would do well to avoid the area after nightfall (or even by day), although there's less risk if you stick to **Köztársaság tér**, where the **Erkel Theatre** draws crowds of respectable folk most evenings. Some way northeast of here are **Keleti Station** and **Baross tér**, whence you can reach the following places, further out.

KEREPESI CEMETERY

Kerepesi Cemetery, between the Ügetopálya racing track and Mező Imre út, is the Père-Lachaise of Budapest, where the famous, great and not-so-good are buried. From the main entrance (one stop from Baross tér by tram #23 or #24), it's a ten-minute walk to the **Pantheon of the Working Class Movement**, where former Party leader János Kádár and other Communists are interred. This used to

---

PROSTITUTION IN BUDAPEST

During the Habsburg and Horthy eras, **prostitution** was licensed much as it still is in Vienna, with fixed prices for each quarter of the city. In 1950, the Communists shut down the licensed brothels and compelled many of the prostitutes to undergo "re-education through labour" at Dunaújváros, but they gradually drifted back into Budapest in the Sixties, just as a wave of *digozok* or "amateurs" was emerging to cater for tourists. Today, with the sex industry booming, there is still a great divide between the highly-paid hookers of the Belváros nightclubs and the streetwalkers of the VIII district, who service Hungarians.

---

include the tomb of László Rajk – Kádár's predecessor as Minister of the Interior in 1949, from whom Kádár obtained a "confession" for which Rajk was shot, then posthumously "rehabilitated" with full honours – but Rajk's son László (a famous dissident in the Eighties) recently removed his body from the Pantheon.

Further south lie the florid **nineteenth-century mausoleums** of Kossuth, leader of the 1848 Revolution against the Habsburgs; Count Batthyány, whom they executed for rebellion; and Ferenc Deák, who engineered the "Compromise" between Hungary and the Empire. The great *diva* Lujza Blaha, the "Nation's Nightingale", is also buried in Kerepesi.

NÉPSTADION
The **Népstadion** district, north across Kerepesi út, is chiefly notable for the 76,000-seat **People's Stadium**, where league championship and international **football** matches and **concerts** by foreign rock stars occur. Stalinist statues of healthy proletarian youth line the court that separates it from the smaller **Kistadion** and the indoor **Sportscsarnok**, which also hosts occasional concerts. The **Népstadion bus station**, for services to most parts of the country east of the Danube, completes this concrete ensemble. All are best reached by Metro line 2 (from Keleti Station or downtown) or by #30 bus along Aréna út (from the edge of the Városliget).

Ferencváros and beyond

The IX district, **Ferencváros** (Francis Town), was developed to house workers in the latter half of the nineteenth century, and remains the most working class of Budapest's inner suburbs. During the Thirties and Forties, its population confounded Marxist orthodoxy by voting for the extreme right; in recent times, supporters of the local football team *Ferencvárosi Torna Club* have become notorious for thuggery.

Ferencváros begins at **Vámház körút**, the section of the Great Boulevard running from Kálvin tér to the Szabadság Bridge, where the largest section of the **medieval walls** of Pest can be found in the courtyard of no. 16. Nearer the bridge stands the **Vásárcsarnok**, Budapest's main **market hall**, noted for its ambience as much as its produce, with tanks of live fish and stalls festooned with strings of paprika at the back, where Mrs Thatcher endeared herself to locals by haggling during a visit in 1984. Currently shut for renovation, the hall is likely to resume normal hours (Mon 9am–5pm, Tues–Thurs & Sat 6am–6pm, Fri 6am–7pm) when it reopens. The embankment area is dominated by the **Economics**

University, which shed the name of Karl Marx in 1989. The backstreets behind the building shelter several clubs (see "Entertainments").

Along Üllői út

Don't bother with **Üllői út** unless you have a particular destination in mind, since this grimy thoroughfare of ponderous Neoclassical blocks runs for miles out to the Airport and Debrecen highways. Fortunately, its principal attraction lies only one block back from the Ferenc körút Metro stop at the junction with the Great Boulevard.

The **Applied Arts Museum** at Üllői út 33–37 (Tues–Sun 10am–6pm) occupies a grandiose pile designed by Ödön Lechner in a mixture of Art Nouveau and Turkic folk styles. Although layers of soot obscure the rich Zsolnay porcelain and yolk-coloured tiles cover the portico and facade, the interior is marvellous, modelled on the Alhambra in Granada. Since many of the exhibits are displayed only on a temporary basis, you could find anything from Transylvanian enamel-ware to Finnish glass – or scrolls and prayer rugs collected by Sándor Kőrosi Csoma (1784–1842), who tramped on foot to Tibet and compiled the first Tibetan-English dictionary.

Just beyond the Great Boulevard, the massive block on the right is the former **Kilián Barracks**, whose garrison was the first to join the 1956 insurgents. As the Uprising spread, this became the headquarters of Colonel Pál Maleter and teams of teenage guerrillas who sallied forth from the passages surrounding the nearby Corvin Cinema to lob Molotov cocktails at Soviet tanks. Maleter himself was arrested by the KGB whilst negotiating for an armistice, and executed along with Nagy (see below). Further out near the Nagyvárad tér Metro stop, the highrise **Semmelweiss Medical University** *(SOTE)* hosts one of the largest discos in town (see "Entertainments").

Further out

To the north of Üllői út beyond smoggy Könyves Kálmán körút (the continuation of Hungaria körút, named after King Kálmán the Booklover) lies the leafy **Népliget** or People's Park, at the entrance of which stands Budapest's **Planetarium**. There are separate shows for children and adults (☎134-4153 for details), including a **Laser Show** (see p.104). The Planetarium is about 100m from the Népliget Metro stop.

Further still, out in the X district, is the **Új köztemető Cemetery**, where Nagy, Maleter and other leaders of the 1956 Uprising were secretly buried in unmarked graves in 1958. The police removed any floral tributes left at **Plot 301** until 1989, when they were accorded a ceremonial funeral in Hősök tere, before being returned to their graves, subsequently dignified by the erection of 301 crosses. The plot lies in the farthest corner of the cemetery, a thirty-minute walk from the main entrance on Kozma utca (accessible by bus #95 from Zalka Máté tér in the Kőbánya district) .

Finally, you might enjoy the sleazy **Ecseri Flea-market**, some way to the south along Nagykörösi út in the XX district (bus #54 from Boráros tér, and ask when to get off). There are stalls selling everything from bike parts and jackboots to nineteenth-century peasant clothing and hand-carved pipes. Bargain hard and avoid being taken for an Austrian or German – they're always overcharged. Opening hours are a bit irregular, but when last heard the *Ecseri piac* operated Mon–Fri 8am–5pm, Sat 8am–3pm.

Eating and Drinking

Hungarians relish **eating and drinking**, and Budapest is great for both. Though Magyar cuisine naturally predominates, you can find everything from Middle Eastern to Japanese food, bagels to Big Macs. The diversity of cuisine is matched by the range of outlets and prices – from deluxe restaurants where a meal costs an average citizen's monthly wage, to backstreet diners that anyone can afford. Many restaurants and bars have live music in the evenings; places where music and dancing are paramount are covered under "Entertainments".

Coffee Houses and Patisseries

Daily life in Budapest is punctuated by the consumption of black coffee drunk from little glasses, and for anyone who can afford it, a pastry or ice cream. Together they make a quintessentially Central European interlude, although nowadays less prolonged than before the war, when Budapest's **coffee houses** *(kávéház)* were social club, home and haven for their respective clientele. Free newspapers were available to the regulars – writers, journalists, and lawyers (for whom the cafés were effectively "offices") or posing revolutionaries – with sympathy drinks or credit to those down on their luck. Today's coffee houses and **patisseries** *(cukrászda)* are less romantic but still full of character; whether fabulously opulent, with silver service, or homely and idiosyncratic.

The first three apart, all of the following are in Pest.

Ruszwurm, 1, Szentháromság tér 7. Diminutive Baroque coffee house near the Mátyás Church; almost impossible to get a seat. Delicious cakes and ices. Daily 10am–8pm.

Korona, 1, Dísz tér 16. Another tourist mecca on Castle Hill, with Hungarian literary evenings during the week (tickets $2/around 150Ft.). Daily 10am–9pm.

Angelika, 1, Batthyány tér 7. Old fashioned and quiet, next to the Watertown Parish Church. Also does cocktails. Daily 10am–8pm.

Gerbeaud, V, Vörösmarty tér 7 (hence its other name, Vörösmarty's). A Budapest institution with a gilded salon (daily 9am–10pm), a plainer side room (Mon–Fri 7am–9pm, Sat 8am–2pm), terrace and shop. Costly, and full of tourists.

Bécsi Kávéház, V, Apáczai Csere János utca 12. Exquisite cakes and smooth service, on the first floor of the *Forum Hotel*.

Pálma, VII, Erzsébet körút 36. Known for its creams in glasses and *parfait* specialities. Daily 8am–10pm.

New York, VII, Teréz kőrut 9–11. Wonderful Art Nouveau decor, worth the price of a cappucino or a cocktail. There is also a restaurant downstairs (see overpage). Daily 9am–10pm.

Fröhlich Cukiszda, VII, Dob utca 22. A kosher patisserie whose speciality is *Flodni*, an apple, walnut and poppy-seed cake.

Astoria Kávéház, V, Kossuth utca 19. Another famous turn-of-the-century coffee-house-cum-cocktail-bar, in the *Astoria Hotel*. Likewise pricey but enjoyable.

Művész Cukrászda, VI, Andrássy út 29. Frequented by writers and fur-hatted old ladies, currently united in outrage at a foreign buyer's plan to turn the *Művész* into a car showroom. Meantime, open Mon–Sat 8am–8pm.

Lukács Cukrászda, VI, Andrássy út 70. Vintage patisserie with Baroque and Thirties decor, confiscated from the Lukács family by the Communist authorities to serve as the secret police cafeteria. Cheaper than *Gerbeaud's* for delicious cakes. Daily 8.30am–8.30pm (summer 9.30pm).

Rétes, V, Bajcsy-Zsilinszky út 15. Cheap cakes and ices, eaten standing up. Mon–Fri 8am–7pm, Sat 8am–1pm.

Párizsi, VI, Andrássy út 37. Another stand-up patisserie with a tempting range of French ice-creams, just beyond the *MÁV* bookings office.

Zeigler Peter, VI, Andrássy út 92. An old-fashioned confectioners near the Kodály körönd, selling sweet and savoury wafer specialities. Tues & Thurs 9am–2pm, Wed & Fri 1–6pm.

Fast food, self-service and snack bars

Budapest has taken to **fast food** in a big way, and new outlets and **snack bars** are opening all the time. Another innovation are the **Étkezde** – small, lunch-time diners with shared tables and a rapid turnover, serving hearty home cooking. Conversely, the old dirt cheap **self-service** canteens (*önkiszolgáló*) face an uncertain future as their subsidies are withdrawn.

Arany Paprika A new fast food chain, serving Hungarian food – an agreeable alternative to *McDonald's*. Branches in Pest at Szent István körút 3, near the Margit Bridge; and Harmincad utca 4, beside the British Embassy (upstairs; downstairs is a costly restaurant) .

McDonald's, V, Régiposta utca 2, just off Váci utca; and in Nyugati Station's magnificently decorated erstwhile restaurant (both daily 8am–9pm). A Big Mac costs 120Ft.

Anna Terássz, V, Váci utca 7. Nice for reading the papers over breakfast indoors, or observing life on Váci utca outside, but expensive as such places go.

Taverna Grill, V, Váci utca 20. A fast food eatery with longer hours and more varied fare than *McDonald's* (including bagels).

City Grill, V, Alkotmány utca 20 and VI, Andrássy út 33. Both outlets are in a similar vein but a bit cheaper than the above.

Falafel, V, Paulay E. utca 53. Budapest's best *falafel* joint, with rooms upstairs (Mon–Fri 10am–8pm). Other, stand-up outlets at V, Régiposta utca 19 and XII, Böszörmenyi utca 3 (above Déli Station).

Izes Sarok, V, Bajcsy-Zsilinszky út 1. Good for open sandwiches, coffee and juices, on the edge of Erzsébet tér. Mon–Thurs 8am–7pm, Fri 8am–5pm.

Saláta Bar, VII, Asboth utca (just off Mádach tér and Károly körút); and on the corner of the *Grand Hotel Hungária* (across from Déli Station) – both offer a range of salads.

Kádár Étkezde, VII, Klauzál utca 10. The best cheap diner in Pest, with delicious home cooking (Jewish food on Fri), open lunchtimes only (Mon–Sat 11.30am–3.30pm).

Mini Étkezde A similar establishment just around the corner on Dob utca. Mon–Fri 11.30am–3pm.

Lotto Étterem, VII, Rákóczi út 57. Cheap, basic *önkiszolgáló* 200m from Keleti Station. Daily 8am–8pm.

Önkiszolgáló Étterem, XII, Alkotás út 7–9. A similar place across the road and just uphill from Déli Station. Daily 8am–8pm.

Restaurants

The city's **culinary scene** has diversified enormously in recent years, with many new places offering Chinese and Japanese food to wealthy tourists and nouveau riche natives. While you can still eat well and cheaply if you know where to look, **rip-offs** abound. A favoured tactic is to issue menus without prices (sometimes just to women, on the grounds that only men need to know*), or pad the bill. Insist on a proper menu (including prices for drinks) and don't be shy about querying the total. Also note that **Sunday evenings** are dire for eating out, with

---

*A more amusing example of Hungarian chauvinism is the old convention that men precede women through the door of a bar or restaurant, in case there's a brawl inside!

warmed-up leftovers the norm in most places. On other evenings, only **reservations** will ensure a table in the restaurant of your choice, but you can usually find an alternative within a couple of blocks.

As forint **prices** rise continuously, we have classified restaurants in comparative terms. Expect to pay no more than £5/$8 per head for a full meal with drinks in a cheap place; around £7/$12 in an inexpensive one; £10–15/$17–25 in a moderately-priced restaurant; and upwards of £20/$35 in an expensive one. Some of the places below are rough and ready, others glittering citadels of *haute cuisine* – it's worth checking out both ends of the spectrum. For places not on the list, you can generally reckon that the further from the Belváros or Castle Hill the cheaper they are likely to be. If they don't have a menu *(étlap)* in German (which most waiters understand) or English, the food and drink vocabulary in *Basics* should suffice for **ordering meals**. Simply pointing to dishes on the menu or neighbouring tables might result in some surprises.

Buda

Despite the plethora of tourist-traps on Castle Hill, **Buda** offers some excellent possibilities if you don't mind a bit of a journey. Of the following places – grouped according to locality – the best value for money are the *Marcello*, *Náncsi Néni* and *Régi Sipos Halászkert;* while the *Kisbuda* and *Hársfa* are recommended to those who can spend more.

CASTLE HILL AND THE WATERTOWN

All the **"historic" restaurants on Castle Hill** charge exorbitant prices for mediocre food, though the *Alabárdos* deserves a mention for its medieval furnishings and roaring fireplace. Some better options are:

Vörös Kaviar, I, Ostrom utca 19. Caviar, blinis, beef stroganoff and other Russian favourites a little way downhill from the Vienna Gate. Mon–Sat 4–11pm. Moderately priced.

Mama Rosa, I, Ostrom utca 31; farther down towards Mozkva ter. Excellent pizzas and spaghetti, including vegetarian options. Daily noon–9pm. Inexpensive.

Horgásztanya, I, F, utca 27 (☎115-4664). Enjoyable fish restaurant on the Watertown's main street. Daily noon–midnight. Inexpensive.

Tabáni kakas, I, Attila út 27 (☎175-7165). The "Tabán Rooster", on the other side of Castle Hill, specialises in game dishes. Mon–Fri noon–midnight, Sat & Sun lpm–midnight. Moderately priced.

RÓZSADOMB, HŰVÖSVÖLGY AND SASAD

Trombitas, II, Retek utca 12 (☎135-1374). Touristy, rip-off garden restaurant with a "folklore" show, by Moszkva tér. Expensive.

Aranyfácán, XII, Szilágyi Erzsébet fasor 33. Unpretentious Slovakian cellar place, 400m from Moszkva tér. Inexpensive.

Kislugas, Xll, Szilágyi Erzsébet fasor 77. Serbian garden restaurant with a lugubrious cimbalom player. Bus #56 from Moszkva tér stops nearby. Cheap.

Náncsi Néni, II, Ördögárok út 80 (☎176-5809). Popular garden restaurant in the leafy Hűvösvölgy, ten minutes' walk from the end stop of the #56 bus. Live music and excellent food. Bookings essential. Mon–Sat noon–9pm, Sun noon–5pm. Cheap.

Ezüst Ponty, XII, Németvölgyi út 96 (☎181-0139). Agreeable fish restaurant with summer garden; catch bus #157 from the Hűvösvölgy terminal. Reservations essential. Daily noon–midnight. Moderately priced.

Marcello, Xl, Bartók Béla ut 40 (☎166-6231). Inconspicuous basement place serving great pizzas, near Móricz Zsigmond körtér. Inexpensive.

ÓBUDA

Régi Sipos Halászkert, III, Nagy Lajos utca (☎168-6480). Near the Roman ampitheatre, three stops by bus #6, #60 or #86 from the Margit Bridge. Shabby and smoky, but the fish and music are good. Inexpensive.

Sipos Halászkert, III, Fő ter 6 (☎188-8745). A rip-off version of the above, nearer the bridge. The **Postakocsi** across the square and the **Vasmacska** on Laktanya utca, nearby, are also tourist traps.

Kisbuda, II, Frankel Leó út 34 (☎115-2244). Near the lane up to Gül Baba's tomb; the garden and musicians are delightful. Excellent food and service; bookings advisable. Mon–Sat noon–midnight, Sun noon–3pm. Moderate to expensive.

Hársfa, III, Királyok útja 132 (☎116-4002). Garden restaurant offering "hunters' suppers", accompanied by *Schrammel* music in the evenings. Hearty portions of typically Hungarian food. Tues–Sun noon–midnight. Moderate to expensive.

Pest

The number and variety of places is greater in **Pest**, especially within the Great Boulevard, where rip-offs await the unwary but you can also find some excellent restaurants. The *Tüköry, Csarnok, Bohémtanya, Szofia* and *Szemiramis* are the best options if you're on a tight budget, while the *Thököly* and *Kiskakukk* are worth trading up a bit. If money isn't an issue, go for the *Százéves, Szindbád, New York* or *Robinson* – or the *Japan* or *Szecsuán* for oriental cooking. Two **vegetarian** places provide welcome relief for non-carnivores.

WITHIN THE GREAT BOULEVARD

Of the dozens of places around the centre (as far out as the Great Boulevard), the ones to **avoid** are the *Napoletana* on Apáczai Csere János utca; the *Mátyás Pince* on Március 15. tér; the *Kárpátia* in the backstreets nearby; and the *Berlin-Alex* on Szent István körút. All of the following are **recommended** to some extent.

Szecsuán, V, Roosevelt tér 5 (☎117-2407). Mouthwatering Chinese food in opulent surroundings. Mon–Thurs 11am–3pm & 7pm–midnight, Fri & Sat until 1am. Expensive.

Százéves, V, Pesti Barnabás utca 2 (☎118-3608). Over a century old and justly famed for its game in wine and flambé dishes. Bookings essential. Expensive.

Vegetárium, V, Cukor utca 3, near Ferenciek tere. Vegetarian and macrobiotic cooking, agreeable service and ambience. Noon–10pm daily. Moderately priced.

Marco Polo, V, Vigadó tér 3 (☎138-3925). Wonderful Italian food and stylish decor. Daily noon–2pm & 7.30–11pm. Expensive.

Luan, V, Zoltán utca 16 (☎131-4352). Budapest's first Polynesian restaurant, located between Szabadság tér and the Danube. Moderately priced.

Csarnok V, Hold utca 11 (☎112-2016). Excellent Hungarian food, one block east of Szabadság tér. Specialises in mutton, lamb and bone-marrow dishes. Mon–Fri 9am–11pm. Inexpensive.

Tüköry, V, Hold utca 15 (☎131-1931). Another very good, cheap place, a few doors along. Mon–Fri noon–11pm. Cheap.

Szemiramis, VI, Alkotmany utca 20 (☎111-7627). Small, friendly restaurant just off Kossuth tér, offering tasty Middle Eastern food. No alcohol. Mon–Sat noon–9pm. Inexpensive.

Szofia, V, Kossuth tér 13. Serves good Bulgarian food, just north of Parliament, with 25 percent reductions on Sundays. Inexpensive.

Szindbád, V, Markó utca 33 (☎132-2966). An epicurean's paradise further north, named after the character invented by writer and gourmet Gyula Krúdy. Superb food and service. Expensive (especially the wine).

Kis Itália, V, Szemere utca 22 (☎111-4646). Simple, pleasant Italian restaurant, just off Szent István körút. Mon–Sat 11am–9pm. Moderately priced .

Sirály, VI, Bajcsy-Zsilinszky út 7. Sited opposite Erzsébet tér bus station, this tourist-oriented place does large portions at fairly reasonable prices. Daily noon–midnight.

Frutte de Mer, VI, Bajcsy-Zsilinzsky út 21 (☎121-1039). Fancy seafood menu, beautifully cooked and presented. Very expensive, especially the wine.

Bohémtanya, VI, Paulay E. utca 6 (☎122-1453). Popular, cheap place just off Erzsébet tér, serving huge portions of Magyar cooking. Bookings essential. Daily 11am–10pm. Cheap.

Hanna, VII, Dob utca 35 (☎142-1072). An unpretentious kosher diner, secreted in a courtyard. Mon–Sun 11.30am–4pm; closed Fri. Inexpensive.

Carmel, VII, Kazinczy utca 31 (☎142-4585). Non-kosher Jewish cooking, with a family atmosphere on Sundays, when cheap lunches are served. Inexpensive.

Kispipa, VII, Akácfa utca 38 (☎142-2587). The "Little Pipe" excels in the cuisine of Budapest's assimilated Jewish middle class. Daily noon–midnight. Moderately priced.

Fészek Klub, on the corner of Dob and Akácfa utca. Stunning decor, with a lovely summer courtyard, though the food and service can be a letdown. As a club, it charges 50Ft at the door; beware of waiters trying to add this to your bill. Moderately priced.

New York, VII, Erzsébet körút 9–11 (☎122-3849). Fabulous Art Nouveau decor, excellent food and service – definitely worth a splurge. Daily 11.30am–3pm & 6.30pm–midnight. Moderate to expensive.

Japan, VIII, Luther utca 4–6 (☎114-3427). Expensive, authentic Japanese restaurant between Rákóczi út and Köztársaság tér. Daily noon–midnight. There's a cheaper Chinese place, the **Tian Ma**, on the same street.

Góbé, VIII, József körút 28. Frequented by whores and pimps of the red-light quarter, the "Rascal" is only recommended to those seeking genuine lowlife. Almost always open (though not necessarily for eating), its lamb dishes are surprisingly good. Cheap.

FURTHER OUT

Most of the following are easily accessible from downtown Pest, but you should reserve a table to avoid a wasted journey.

Syros, VII, Csengery utca 24 (☎141-0772). A Greek cellar-restaurant near the Oktogon Metro stop, with live music on Wed & Sat. Daily noon–11pm. Moderately priced.

Vörös Sárkány, VI, Andrássy út 80 (☎131-8757). Variable Chinese meals, near Kodály körönd Metro stop. Daily noon–3pm & 6pm–1am. Moderately priced.

Great Wall, VII, Ajtósi Durer Utca 1. Another Chinese restaurant, near the southeastern corner of the Városliget. Moderately priced.

Gundel, XIV, Állatkerti körút 2 (☎122-1002). Sited near the Zoo in the Városliget, Budapest's most famous restaurant now caters almost exclusively to foreigners, and locals reckon that standards have slipped. Bookings and smart dress required. Daily noon–4pm & 7pm–midnight. Expensive.

Robinson, in the park behind the Fine Arts Museum, beside the lake (☎142-0955). A new top-flight international restaurant, with superb food and service. Daily noon–midnight on the terrace, noon–3pm & 7pm–midnight indoors. Very expensive.

Visegrádi, XIII, Visegrádi Utca 50A (☎140-3316). Agreeable vegetarian restaurant, west of the Lehel tér Metro stop. Daily noon–midnight. Inexpensive.

Kiskakukk, XIII, Pozsonyi út 12 (☎132-1732). The "Little Cuckoo" near the Margit Bridge does wonderful game dishes like wild boar in juniper sauce. Mon–Sat noon–11pm, Sun noon–4pm (closed over summer). Moderately priced.

Thököly, XIV, Thököly út 80 (☎122-5444). Delicious Transylvanian food, served outdoors or indoors, where the band can be a nusiance. Catch a #7 bus or #67 tram from Baross tér, by Keleti Station. Daily noon–midnight. Moderately priced.

Sport Étterem, XVI, Csömöri út 198 (☎183-3364). Next to the Metro Campsite in Rákosszentmihály; four stops by bus #130 from Örs vezér tere Metro terminal. Offers a huge range of dishes, including cock's balls. Good cooking, worth the forty-minute journey. Inexpensive.

Drinking

It's hard to draw a firm line between places to eat and places to **drink** in Budapest, since some patisseries double as cocktail bars, and restaurants as beer halls (or vice versa), while the provision of live music or pool tables blurs the distinction between drinking-spots and clubs. The scene is constantly changing as places open or close, revamp their image, become trendy or the pits.

Insofar as you can generalise, most places that style themselves **bars** (or "drink") are chiefly into cocktails. The majority of *borozó* or **wine bars** are less pretentious than in the West, offering such humble snacks as *zsíros kenyér* (bread and pork dripping with onion and paprika). Conversely, **beer halls** *(söröző)* are often quite upmarket, striving to resemble an English pub or a German *bierkeller*, and serving full meals. The addition of *pince* to the name of an outlet for wine *(bor)* or beer *(sör)* signifies that it is in a cellar; many of the new places stink of mould until the crowds arrive.

The following list is hardly exhaustive, excluding as it does various **club-ish places** (covered under "Entertainments") and **strip bars** (at the Margit and Erzsébet bridge ends of the Pest embankment and around Rákóczi tér) .

Buda

Café Pierrot, I, Fortuna utca 14. Stylish cocktail bar on Castle Hill, where you can ask the pianist to *Play it again Sam*, after 8pm. Mon–Sat 5pm–1am, Sun 10am–11pm.

Hattyú, I, Hattyú Utca 1. Typical cheap and cheerful neighbourhood wine bar, in the backstreets north of Castle Hill.

Kecskeméti Borozó Another such place, just off Moskva tér on the corner of Retek utca and Széna tér.

Marxim's, II, Kis Rókus utca 23, off Mártírok útja near Moskva tér. A "socialist nostalgia" theme bar, with busts of Lenin, red flags, and other symbols of the People's Republic and its fraternal allies (RIP).

Vinceller Borozó, I, Fő utca 71. Agreeable wine cellar near the Király Baths. Daily 8am–10pm.

Ászok Söröző, I, Győző utca 5. A rowdy joint northwest of Déli Station, offering videos, Ászok and Alpesi beers.

Te meg Én, II, Bem rakpart 30. Café-bar north of Batthyány tér, with cocktails and a pool table

Miniatűr Espresszó, II, Rózsahegy utca 1. Small bohemian bar run by a mother and daughter since the Sixties. If they like you, you get to sit in the inner room (pianist after 9pm); if they don't, you won't get in the door. Mon–Sat 7pm–3am.

Pest

Gresham Borozó, V, Merlég utca 4. In the atmospheric old Gresham Palace on Roosevelt tér (entrance around the corner from the *Szecsuán* restaurant). Inexpensive for its location.

John Bull Pub, V, Apáczai Csere János utca 17. A lifeless imitation of an English pub serving John Bull bitter and Skol lager at nigh-on London prices, with receipts for its business-type clients. Open till midnight.

Fregatt, V, Molnár utca 26. An earlier attempt at a pub in the backstreets south of Ferenciek tere, packed out by resident foreigners most nights. Offers Holsten beer and tasty chicken liver snacks, live jazz or taped rock oldies. The bell is rung when someone gives a tip. Open till midnight.

Gösser Sörpatika, V, Régiposta utca 4. The "beer pharmacy" prescribes Gösser beer and sandwiches, just off Váci utca. Daily 10am–11pm.

Dóm Sörbár, V, Szent István tér. A smaller place facing the Basilica, offering draught Wernesgrüner and a big selection of bottled beers. Daily 9am–5am.

Borsodi Söröző, V, Honvéd utca 18, around the back of the Ethnographic Museum. Stocks ten kinds of beer. Mon–Fri 8am–10.30pm, Sat 8am–8pm, Sun noon–4pm.

Razzia, V, Bajcsy-Zsilinszky út 36–38. A café-bar where the young go, on the ground floor of the Toldi cinema

Dani Drink, V, Szent István körút 21. Above a small shop on a rather sleazy boulevard, serving almost any cocktail imaginable. Mon–Fri 10am–10pm, Sat 9am–2pm.

Trojka Söröző, VI, Andrássy út 28. An all-night hang-out for oddballs,with videos upstairs. Does Ratskeller, Egger and other beers. Daily 10am–6am.

Pink Pussycats, VII, Wesselényi utca 58. Off the Great Boulevard two blocks north of Blaha Lujza tér; look out for the breast-like protrusions. Cellar "cave", billiards room and pianist – a trendy all-night place. Daily 9am–5am.

Hági Söröző, VIII, Huszár utca 7. A neighbourhood den just off Rákóczi út, near Baross tér, dispensing various Austrian beers. Daily 9am–5am.

Pragai Svejk Vendéglő, VII, Király utca 59B. Located in a sidestreet off "Broadway", this imitates the favourite Prague beer hall of the fictional Good Soldier Svejk, with great Czech beer and food, and a portrait of Emperor Franz Joseph.

Broadway Drink, VI, Nagymező utca 49. Pleasant cocktail bar on the other side of "Broadway" – try the *Zöld özvegy* (Green Widow).

Kaltenberger, IX Kinizsi utca 30–32 (☎118-4792). A liveried doorman sets the tone for this smartly appointed beer cellar, near the Applied Arts Museum on Üllői út. Kaltenberger beer brewed on the premises, hearty roasts and attentive service; reservations essential in the evening. Open daily till 11pm.

Sörcsárda, X, Jászberenyi út 7. Attached to the Kőbányai Brewery, so heaving with workers enjoying the fruits of their labours. Rowdy but fun. Mon–Fri 9am–8pm; Sat & Sun 9am–3pm. Bus #168 from Örs vezér tere.

Entertainments

The range of **entertainments** available in Budapest includes everything from nightclubbing to opera-going, jazz to folk dancing and Formula One racing to football. To find out **what's on**, check out *Programme* magazine, a free bi-lingual monthly put out by the tourist board, the listings in *Budapest Week*, or the Hungarian-language weekly *Pesti Műsor*. The latter's review columns are headed: *szinház* (theatre), *zene* (music), *pop*, *film*, *képzőművészet* (fine arts), and *TIT* (lectures). Another source is the monthly *Koncert Kalendárium* (free from *TOURINFORM*), giving a full rundown of classical music and opera performances, plus the agencies for **bookings**.

Festivals and events: the Budapest year

The highlights of Budapest's cultural calendar are the **Spring Festival** in late March – whose motto is "10 days, 100 venues, 1000 events" – and the **Autumn Arts Weeks**, from late September to late October. Both offer a wealth of music, ballet and drama (including star acts from abroad). The ten-day **Film Festival** used to be another fixture (in February), but may not survive in the future.

On **March 15**, Budapest decks itself out in flags and cockades in honour of the 1848 Revolution, and there are patriotic gatherings at the Petőfi statue and the National Museum. **Easter** is marked by church services and outbreaks of *locsolkodás* (splashing) – when men and boys visit their female friends to spray them with cologne and receive a painted egg or pocket money in return. The fall of Communism has put paid to grandiose parades on April 4 and May 1, but **Mayday** remains a workers' holiday, with beer tents and music in the Városliget and the Népliget, sponsored by rival trade unions.

While many theatres close down for the season, there are plenty of concerts and two major sporting events (see below) over **summer**. **Saint Stephen's Day** (August 20), honouring the founder of the Hungarian state, occasions day-long celebrations at the Basilica (see p.84) and a spectacular display of **fireworks** at 9pm. Over a million people line the embankments to watch them fired off from Gellért Hill, so prime vantage points like the Erszébet and Szabadság bridges are taken by 8pm, and the traffic jam that follows the display is equally mindblowing.

As the Autumn Arts Weeks wind down and trees in the parks turn russet and gold, it is nowadays permitted to honour the anniversary of the 1956 Uprising. **October 23** was a taboo anniversary for decades, then suddenly accorded cathartic, televised, recognition: interest now seems to be waning among the majority of Hungarians who are too young to have experienced the Uprising. On December 6, children hang up Christmas boots for "little Jesus" to fill, and people prepare for the **Christmas Eve feast** of jellied carp or turkey. Festivities build up towards **New Year's Eve**, when revellers gather on the Great Boulevard, engaging in trumpet battles at the junction with Rákóczi út.

Concerts, clubs and discos

Budapest attracts every Hungarian band worth its amplifiers and a growing roll-call of international stars, making it the best place for **rock concerts** in Hungary. Major foreign acts appear at the vast *Népstadion* or the nearby *Budapest Sportscsarnok* (see p.91), and their appearances are well publicised in the media. Don't get too excited by flyposters advertising Michael Jackson or the Cure, however, as these refer to light shows or DJs at clubs and discos. Posters around Ferenciek tere and the Astoria underpass also publicise concerts by **Hungarian bands**.

Concert venues
Local bands most often perform at the *Petőfi csarnok* (see below) or one of the following places in Buda:

R-Klub, XI, Műegyetem rakpart 9 (☎166-4011). In block R of the Technical University south of Gellert Hill.

KEK, XI, Villányi út 44 (☎185-0666). The club of the Horticultural University, 200m west of Móricz Zsigmond körtér.

I Kerületi Művelődesi Ház, I, Bem rakpart 6. The I district community centre, between the Chain Bridge and the Hotel Victoria.

Clubs and discos
Many clubs and discos in the city are still run under the aegis of universities, though there are an increasing number of private ventures, some of which have a fairly strict entrance policy. Clubbers are fickle, so places open and close, lose their credibility or acquire cachet – something to bear in mind as you check out the following venues. All but the last two are in Pest. The gay and jazz scenes are covered separately (see opposite).

Vén Diák, V, Egyetem tér 5 (☎119-4603). A jampacked disco opposite the Law faculty of Eötvös University, playing current hits and classic oldies. Its name – meaning "former student" – is abbreviated to *VD* on posters. Daily 10pm–5am.

Piaf, VI, Nagymező utca 20. This fashionable bar on "Broadway" has a selective entry policy in the evening – it helps to know a regular. Basically a room and a cellar graced by the odd film star and lots of wannabes, with occasional jazz or rock sets.

Levi's 501, VI, Nagymező utca 41(☎132-3857). Smart A/C disco bar with Levi-upholstered seats and clean-cut clientele, further up the road. 150Ft cover. Daily 9pm–4am.

Rock Café, VII, Dohány utca 18. A humid cellar near the Synagogue, harking back to Carnaby Street in the Sixties, with a nightly set of R&B or hard rock. 100Ft admission. Daily 6pm–2am.

Tilos az Á, VIII, Mikszáth Kálmán ter 2 (☎118-0684). A meeting place for *FIDESZ* supporters, entrepreneurs and social climbers, but not at all flash. Though its name (from the "Tresspassers W" sign in Winnie the Pooh, which is cult reading in Budapest) means "no entry", anyone can get in (70–100Ft). Headbangers gravitate to the cellar. Located near Kálvin tér. Closes 3–5am.

Total Car, VIII, Krúdy utca 19. A pool hall and sweaty disco, nearer József körút. Women admitted free, black people not at all – a place to boycott.

Fekete Lyuk VIII, Golgota út 3. Punky "Black Hole" in the backstreets between Keleti and the Népliget; bus #99 from Baross tér, or fifteen minutes' walk from Népliget Metro stop. Live music most nights – usually Thrash. 8pm–4am.

Blue Box, IX, Kinizsi utca 28 (☎118-0938). Hangout near the Economics University, with everything under one roof: art movies and a café-bar, with a disco uptairs (80–200Ft cover) . Normally 8pm–2am.

SOTE Club, IX, Üllői út 121 (in the Semmelweiss Medical University near Nagyvárad tér Metro stop). Two heaving discos, plus sideshows of anything from Irish folk music to art films. Generally Thurs–Sat 8pm–2am. Bring ID.

Petőfi csarnok, XIV, Zichy M. út (☎142-4327). A huge, purpose-built youth centre near the back of the Városliget, hosting the Holdfény-Csillagfény Disco on Saturday nights, when the 3–4000-strong crowd votes the top ten for the following week. Half-price admission for women. Also a venue for concerts, films, exhibitions and other events. You can phone for details in English. Daily 10am–10pm.

E-Klub, XI, Egri József utca 1 (in block E of the Technical University south of Gellért Hill). A cattle market for engineering students, with go-go dancers on stage, roulette tables at the back, and lukewarm beer. Fri & Sat 8pm–2am. Bring ID.

Cadillac Club, III, Szépvölgyi út 15 (☎180-5262). Day and night hang-out in an erstwhile Óbuda brothel, with a games room, restaurant and live music every night. 8am–4am.

Gay life

Budapest's **Gay scene** has taken wings in recent years, with new, overtly gay clubs replacing the old, covert hang-outs, and the appearance of a trilingual monthly listings magazine, *Mások* ("Outsiders"). However, gays must still tread warily and lesbians are several steps behind. (The Magyar euphemisms for gay and lesbian are *meleg* and *hideg*, "warm" and "cold".) Aside from places listed below, gays frequent the Király Baths (see p.72) and the Palatinus pool on Margit Island; and go cruising on the Danube side of Gellért Hill, around the Városliget and Népliget, and along the Pest embankment.

Angyal Bár, VIII, Szentkirályi utca 8 (☎118-4204). Budapest's premier gay club, with a nightly disco and drag shows at midnight on Tues and Thurs. Cheaper admission Mon–Wed; packed on Sat. 10pm–3am (or later).

Lokál, VII, Kertész utca 31. Now eclipsed by the *Angyal*, so less crowded. Nightly show, with discos on Fri and Sat (100–200Ft admission). 9pm–4am.

Mystery Bar-klub, V, Nagysándor József utca 3 (☎112-1436). Small bar near the Arany József Metro stop, for talking rather than dancing (no disco). Mon–Sat 9pm–4am.

Jácint Eszpresszó, V, Október 6. utca 5 (☎117-2802). Only exclusively gay after 8pm, with a show on Thurs from 11pm (100Ft admission). Daily 9am–midnight (or later) .

Darling, V, Szép utca 1. A beer-house and gallery that gets "warmer" after 9pm and stays open late.

Jazz and Billiards

Although jazz is currently fashionable in Budapest, regular venues are few in number. Some bands appear at local cultural centres; others in **billiard clubs**, which are all the rage at the moment – hence this unlikely pairing. Some more occasional jazz venues can be found under "Drinking" and "Clubs and Discos".

Merlin Jazz Club, V, Gerlóczy utca 4 (☎117-9338). Cool restaurant and cocktail bar off Károly körút, aimed at foreigners. Two sets nightly (200–300Ft admission); also English theatre with British actors during summer (tickets 1800Ft).

Kosztolányi Művelődesi Ház, IX, Török Pál utca 3 (☎118-0193). The world famous Benkó Dixieland Band plays here every Wednesday evening when not abroad.

MAHART Jazz Corso Klub, V, Vigadó utca 3 (☎118-1880). In the headquarters of the state shipping company on the Pest embankment, run by jazz-loving employees.

Közgáz Jazz Klub, IX, Kinizsi utca 2–4 (☎117-3033). Belongs to the Economics University and favours progressive jazz. Foreign artists play here.

Eötvös-Klub, V, Károlyi M. utca 9 (☎117-4967). An occasional venue for jazz or folk music, just off Ferenciek tere.

Kassác Klub, XIV, Uzsoki utca 57 (☎183-3974). The same goes for this place, near Mexikói út (Metro line 1).

Belvárosi Művelődesi Ház, V, Molnár utca 9 (☎117-5928). A cultural centre which sometimes hosts jazz or folk music, near the *Fregatt* pub (another irregular jazz spot).

Almássy téri Szabadidő Központ, VII, Atmássy tér 6 (☎142-4144). The Wei Wu Wei Jazz-Dance club meets here Mon 8pm.

Ballantine's Club, VI, Andrássy út 19. Extremely elegant and pricey, with jazz or other piano music, billiards, and fine whiskies. Mon–Fri 10pm–3am, Sat & Sun 6pm–3am (members only after 9pm).

Fél Tiz Biliard, VIII, Mária utca 48. Agreeable pool and billiard hall with draught beer and nightly live jazz, between Ferenc körút and Kálvin tér. Reserve your pool table early. Daily 2pm–midnight.

Folk music and Táncház

Hungarian **folk music and dancing** underwent a revival in the Seventies, drawing inspiration from communities in Transylvania, regarded as pure wellsprings of Magyar culture. Enthusiasts formed "Dance Houses" or **Táncház** to revive traditional instruments and dances, and get people *involved* in the process. Visitors are welcome to attend the weekly gatherings at selected clubs or community centres, where the 60–100Ft admission charge contributes to new instruments and costumes. Muzsikás and the Téka and Kalamajka ensembles play sounds from Transylvania, while other groups are inspired by South Slav music from Serbia, Croatia and Bulgaria.

Besides the following venues, folk music might also feature at the *MAHART*, *Eötvös* and *Kassák* clubs and the *Belvárosi Művelődesi Ház* (see "Jazz and Billiards"). Details of events are available from the information service of the *Petőfi csarnok* (☎142-4327), or in *Pesti Műsor* and *Budapest Week*.

Fővárosi Művelődesi Ház, XI, Fehérvári út 47 (☎181-1360). Márta Sebestyén and Muzsikás play every Tues at 7pm; the Falkafolk Balkan band on Wed at 7pm. Tram #18 from Szent Gellért tér or bus #3 from Móricz Zsigmond körtér.

Almássy téri Szabadidő Központ, VII, Almássy tér 6 (☎142-4144). The Téka ensemble plays every Friday at this community centre, north of Blaha Lujza tér. Kids' session 5–6pm; adults 7pm–midnight.

MOM Művelődesi Központ, XII, Csörsz utca 18 (☎156-8451). From April to October, the Budapest Dance Ensemble appears most nights at 8.45pm. More of a show than a *Táncház*, but still fun. Bus #12 from Moszkva tér can drop you nearby.

Opera, ballet and classical music

Opera is highly esteemed in Hungary, whose composers and writers have created such works as *Bánk Bán*, *László Hunyadi*, *The Queen of Sheba* and *Blood Wedding*. Fans prefer their opera "old style", with lavish sets and costumes and histrionic performances which they interrupt with ovations after particularly bravura passages. Operas by Mozart, Verdi, Puccini, Wagner and national composers are staged throughout the year, while six to eight new productions are premiered during the Spring and Autumn festivals, when you can also catch performances by the State Opera **ballet** and visiting foreign companies.

Budapest is even better for **classical music**, with several concerts every night of the year, especially during summertime and both festivals. Look out for performances by the Liszt Ferenc Chamber Orchestra and the Budapest Festival Orchestra; pianists Zoltán Kócsis and Desző Ránki, and cellist Miklós Perényi. The State Symphony Orchestra is conducted by Kobayashi Ken-Ichiro of Japan. Over summer, smaller concerts occur outdoors on Margit Island, and in historic buildings such as the Mátyás Church. It's also worth knowing about the season of concerts **at Vácratót** (p.130) and **Martonvásár** (p.142) – both within commuting distance of Budapest.

Pesti Műsor and the *Koncert Kalendárium* detail every event, while *Budapest Week* and *Programme* cover a selection. **Information** can also be obtained from *TOURINFORM* and the main ticket offices. **Tickets** for the Opera, Operetta and Erkel theatres are available from the *Central Box Office*, VI, Andrássy út 18 (☎111-2000), and II, Moszkva tér 3 (☎135-9136) in Buda. The *Central Ticket Office*, V, Vörösmarty tér 1 (☎117-6222), can supply tickets for concerts elsewhere, except for outdoor performances which are sold by box offices at VI, Jókai utca 24 (☎132-4721), VI, Teréz körút 106 (☎112-0430) and the Central Box Office on Andrássy út.

State Opera House, VI, Andrássy út 22 (☎153-0170). Budapest's grandest venue, with gilded frescos and three-ton chandeliers – a place to dress up for. Box office (Tues–Sat 10am–7pm, Sun 10am–1pm & 4–7pm) on Dalszínház utca, round the corner; **returns** also sold at Andrássy út 18. Higher prices for performances on Fri and Sat.

Operetta Theatre, VI, Nagymező útca 17 (☎122-6470 or 153-2172). Stages classical Hungarian operettas and modern musicals; located on "Broadway", a few blocks from the Opera House.

Erkel Theatre, VIII, Köztársaság tér 30 (☎133-0540). A modernised venue for operas, ballet and musicals, on the edge of the red-light district near Keleti Station.

Academy of Music, VI, Liszt Ferenc tér 8 (☎142-0179). Nightly concerts and recitals in the magnificent *Nagyterem* (Great Hall) or the smaller *Kisterem*. The former is usually shut during summer, as it gets too hot.

Vigadó, V, Vigadó tér 1 (☎118-9903). Another fabulously decorated hall, but the acoustics are inferior and concerts tend to be formal affairs attended by diplomats. Box office opens 1pm.

Mátyás Church Choral or organ recitals, usually on Fri and sometimes on Sat, at 8pm (June–Sept).

Saint Stephen's Basilica Organ concerts every Mon (July–Sept). Tickets from VII, Erzsébet körút 29.

Musicals, rock-opera and laser shows

Musicals are probably not what you have come to Budapest for, but for addicts there is at least an opportunity to review a couple of old favourites, plus one fascinating home-grown production. *Cats* is currently on at the Madách Theatre, VII, Erzsébet körút 29–33 (☎122-2015) while *Les Misérables* is playing at the Vígszínház, XIII, Szent István körút 14 (☎111-0430). Tickets are available for hard currency only at the Central Box Office (see above) and top hotels.

For an authentically Magyar **rock-opera**, you can't beat *István a király* (*Stephen the King*), which dramatises the conflict between paganism and Christianity at the birth of the nation. Written by Szörenyi and Bródy – the Lennon and McCartney of Hungary – it was the smash hit of the Eighties, when over a million copies of the record were sold. At time of writing it is staged at the National Theatre, VII, Hevesi Sandor tér 4 (☎122-0014).

If **Laser Shows** are your thing, there's an hour-long extravaganza to music by Genesis, Pink Floyd, Jean Michael Jarre and Dire Straits at the Planetarium in the Népliget (☎134-4513). Schedules vary, but you can ring to enquire about the *Lézerszinház*, or ask *TOURINFORM*. Tickets cost 250Ft. In a different vein, there are **Magic Lantern shows** combining film and mime at the Nulladik Színház ("Theatre #0"), VI, Csengery utca 68 (☎133-0512), usually on Saturdays at 8pm.

Theatre

If you're undeterred by the language barrier, **theatre** can also be a rewarding experience. The **Kátona József Company** won plaudits at the Old Vic in London and the Odéon in Paris, and remains the most exciting company in town. Their permanent repertory includes *The Government Inspector*, *Ubu Roi* and *Twelfth Night*. The Kátona Theatre is at Petőfi Sándor utca 6, next to the Párizsi Udvar. Its box office opens at 2pm, while tickets "for any unoccupied seat" are sold just before the show starts at 7pm.

During summer there are easy-to-understand performances at the outdoor theatre on Margit Island and in the courtyard of the *Budapest Hilton*, advertised in *Programme* and *Pesti Műsor*. Puppet theatres are covered under "For Kids . . . and Adults" below.

Films and Cinemas

Hollywood blockbusters and Euro soft-porn films currently dominate Budapest's **cinemas**, as evinced by the billboards along Rákóczi út and the Great Boulevard. During the summer, *Daily News* runs a column on films in English, and *Budapest Week* covers offerings in other languages as well. If you can deal with Hungarian, the fullest **listings** appear in *Pesti Műsor*, under the heading *Budapesti mozik műsora*. Here, the times of shows are cryptically abbreviated to *n8* or *1/4 8* for 7.15pm; *f8* or *1/2 8* for 7.30pm; and *h8* or *3/4 8* for 7.45pm. In the absence of *Mb.* (meaning "dubbed") you can assume that the film is subtitled in Hungarian.

Serious film buffs should investigate **Art Cinemas**, which specialise in the latest releases and obscure films from Eastern and Western Europe. Their provenance is indicated thus: *Angol* (British), *Lengyel* (Polish), *Német* (German), *Olasz* (Italian), and *Orusz* (Russian). Cinemas belonging to the *Art Kino* network include the *Blue Box* and *Toldi* (see "Drinking" and "Clubs and Discos"); the *Művesz*, VI, Teréz körút 88 (☎132-6726); and the *Hunnia*, VII, Erzsébet körút 26 (☎122-3471).

Sports

This is mainly about **spectator sports**. Details of swimming pools and billiards have appeared at various points in the text. **Tennis** courts are for hire at II, Nagkovácsi út (Mon–Fri 8am–2pm). Contact *Pegazus Tours* (V, Ferenciek tere 5; ☎117-1644) about **horseback riding** at the Petneházy school (II, Feketefej utca; Tues–Sun 9am–7pm). In winter, it's possible to **ski** at Normafa and Jánoshegy in the Buda Hills. Various types of **sporting equipment** can be hired from II, Török utca 2; VI, Jókai tér 7; and VIII, Jószef Körút 67.

Soccer

While **international matches** are held at the 76,000-seater Népstadion, national football revolves around the turf of two **premier league teams**. *Ferencvárosi Torna Club* (aka *FTC* or *Fradi*) are based at IX, Üllői út 129 (☎113-6025), near the Népliget Metro stop. Their colours are green and white and their fans are keen to fight with supporters of *Honvéd-Kispest*, whose ground is at XIX, Új temető út 1–3 (tram #42 from Határ út Metro stop to the end of the line). Matches are played on Saturday or Sunday afternoons, or occasionally on Wednesday evenings; see *Programme* and *Daily News* for details.

A day at the Races

Horse-racing was introduced from England by Count Széchenyi in 1827 and flourished until 1949, when flat-racing (*galopp*) was banned by the Communists. In the mid-Eighties it resumed at the **Lóversenyter**, north of the International Fair grounds (Pillangó utca Metro stop), where punters gather every Sunday afternoon during the racing season, and the **Hungarian Derby** is held on the second or third Sunday in July. Devoted fans also attend **trotting races** at the **Ügetőpalya** alongside Kerepesi út (bus #95 or trolleybus #80 from either Népstadion or Keleti Station), starting at 2pm on Saturday and Sunday and at 4.30pm on Wednesday and Thursday. The atmosphere at both tracks is informal, but photographing the race-goers is frowned upon, since many attend unbeknownst to their spouses or employers. Races are advertised in *Népsport*, *Daily News* and *Programme*.

The Hungarian Grand Prix

The **Hungarian Grand Prix**, first held in 1986, occurs every summer at the purpose-built **Formula 1 Racing** track at Mogyoród, 20km northeast of Budapest. It is usually but not always scheduled for early August; details are available from *IBUSZ, TOURINFORM* or any listings magazine. You can reach the track by special buses from the Arpád Bridge; trains from Keleti Station to Fót, and then a bus from there; or by HÉV train from Örs vezér tere to the Szilasliget stop, which is 1800m northeast of Gate C. The price of tickets (from *IBUSZ* or *Budapest Tourist*) ranges from £12–40/$21–70 depending on the location, and whether you book in advance or risk disappointment on the day.

The Budapest Marathon

An increasingly popular event held in late April or early May, the 20km-long **Budapest Marathon** follows a flat and scenic route from Népstadion to Római-Fürdő. If you want to participate, a Hungarian friend should be able to register you at the *IBUSZ* office on Ferenciek tere for under £1/$2, whereas admitted Western nationals have to pay £30/$50. **Jogging** is also becoming popular, particulary on Margit Island, where a circuit equals about 5km.

For Kids . . . and Adults

From Klauzál tér's scaled-down assault course to the folksy wooden see-saws and swings erected on Széchenyi-hegy, there are **children's playgrounds** all over Budapest. Adults could combine a visit to Jubilemi Park on Gellért Hill with some sightseeing, or extract a series of childish diversions from the Városliget (see p.87) with its mock castle and old trains, its **amusement park**, **circus** and **zoo**. The "railway circuit" of the Buda Hills (p.75) should also appeal to all ages, while the **Waxworks** on Castle Hill (p.65) could be just the thing for kids going through a gory phase.

If the Petőfi Csarnok or the MOM (p.103) have nothing suitable for children, you could take them to a dance club or one of Budapest's **puppet theatres**. Morning and matinée performances are for kids, while the evening's masked grotesqueries or renditions of Bartók's *The Wooden Prince* and *The Miraculous Mandarin* are intended for adults. Tickets are available from the Central Ticket Office or the *Bábszinház* themselves, at VI, Andrássy út 69 (☎142-2702) and VI, Jókai tér 10 (☎112-0622). The Arány János Theatre at VI, Paulay Ede utca 35 (near the opera) often features **musicals** aimed at children (☎141-5626), and most local cultural centres have children's **dance clubs** on Saturday afternoons or Sunday mornings. Children's films are advertised in *Pesti Műsor* under the heading *Gyermeknek ajánlott.*

Last but not least, there is "Kidstown" (*Kölyökvár*), a play and activity centre open every Sunday (10am–1pm) at VII, Almássy tér 6. This organises everything from face-painting to model-building – plus films, music and drama from mid-October to April (☎142-0387 for details).

Listings

Airlines *Aeroflot*, V, Váci utca 4 (☎118-5955); *Air Canada*, I, Lovás út 1 (☎175-4618); *Air France*, V, Kristóf tér 6 (☎118-0411); *Alitalia*, V, Ferenciek tere 1 (☎118-6882); *Balkan*, V, Párizsi utca 7 (☎117-1818); *Bnitish Airways*, V, Apáczai Csere János utca 5 (☎118-3299); *CSA*, V, Vörösmarty tér 2 (☎118-3045); *JAT*, V, Párizsi utca 9 (☎117-1595); *KLM*, V, Vörösmarty tér 2 (☎117-4742); *Lufthansa*, V, Váci utca 19–21 (☎118-4333); *Malév*, V, Váci utca 1–3 (☎118-7922); *SABENA*, V, Váci utca 1–3 (☎118-4111); *SAS*, V, Váci utca 1–3 (☎118-5582); *Swissair*, V, Kristóf ter 7–8 (☎117-2500); *TAROM*, VII, Károly körút 11 (☎122-5682).

Airport The journey to Ferihegy airport takes about an hour if all goes well, however you do it; but for safety you should probably allow two. Taxis out to the airport are less extortionate than those into the city, but you can still get stung. The alternatives are to take the Metro to Kobánya-Kispest and then a bus (red #95 to Terminal 1, black #95 to Terminal 2), or to book a seat on the private minibus shuttle (☎157-8993; 400–500Ft), which will pick you up anywhere in the city. **Terminal 1** (☎157-2122) serves all airlines except *Malév*, *Lufthansa* and *Air France*, which use **Terminal 2** (☎157-7212).

Banks Most *OTP* branches are open Mon–Fri 9am–4pm, but changing money and traveller's cheques is easier at almost any tourist office (24-hour service at V, Petőfi tér 3). You can transfer money from abroad through the *Magyar Külkereskedelmí Bank*, V, Szent István tér 11: this takes about a week – the *Kereskedelmí és Hitel Bank*, V, Arany János utca 24, is even slower.

Books in English from: Váci utca 32 & 33; Petőfi utca 2; Vörösmarty tér 4 and inside the Párizsi udvar. **Secondhand** (*Antikvárium*) bookshops: Váci utca 28 & 75; Múzeum körút 5; and on the corner of Deák tér and Bajcsy-Zsilinszky út. All in the Belváros.

British Council, VII, Benczúr utca 26. Library, newspapers and a noticeboard. Mon–Thurs noon–7pm, Fri 10am–5pm, Sat 9am–noon.

Bus stations The most useful are: *Népstadion* (Metro line 2; ☎118-7315) serving areas east of the Danube; *Erzsébet tér*, in the Belváros, for Transdanubia and abroad (☎118-2122); and *Árpád híd* (Metro line 3; ☎120-9229), covering both banks of the Danube Bend. Destinations and schedules are given in "Travel Details".

Camping and Caravanning Club, IX, Kálvin tér 9 (Mon–Fri 8am–4pm; ☎117-7248). Can supply canoeing maps of the Danube, advise on equipment and arrange reductions for *FICC* members.

Car rental *Avis*, V, Aranykéz utca 4–8 (☎118-4158); *Budget*, IX, Ferenc körút 43 (☎113-1466); *Főtaxi*, VII, Kertész utca 4–8 (☎122-1471); *Hertz*, V, Aranykéz utca 4–8 (☎115-7533); *Vólantourist/Europcar*, Ferihegy 1 (☎134-2540) and 2 (☎157-8570). *Avis, Budget* and *Hertz* are also represented at major tourist offices and hotels.

Car repairs *Fiat* models at XII, Boldizsár út 1–3 (☎126-1608 or 145-2908); *Mercedes* at XIII, Kárpat utca 21 (☎149-8507); *Ford, Opel, Toyota, Mazda* and *Suzuki* on the corner of Mexikói út and Besnyői utca (☎283-5975); *Peugeot, Renault* and *Citroen*, XXI, Jókai utca 25 (☎147-8533). The *Magyar Autó Klub* runs a **24-hour breakdown service** (☎169-1831 or 169-3714).

Church services in English on Sunday mornings: *Anglican Holy Communion*, VI, Vörösmarty utca 51, on the first and third Sun of the month, alternating with the *Scottish Mission Church*; *International Church of Budapest* in the Buda Cultural Centre, I, Corvin tér 8 (Pastor Glen Howard; ☎176-4518); *International Baptist Fellowship*, II, Tapolcsányi utca 7 (Pastor Ray Reynolds; ☎165-1081). The *Jesus Church of the Sacred Heart*, VIII, Mária utca 25 (☎118-3479) holds Mass every Saturday at 5pm.

Department Stores *Corvin*, VIII, Blaha Lujza tér 1–2; *Csillag*, VIII, Rákóczi út 20–22; *Divatcsarnok*, VI, Andrássy út 39; *Ifjúsági*, V, Kossuth utca 9; *Lottó*, VIII, Rákóczi út 36.

Embassies/consulates *Australia*, VI, Déliáb utca 30 (☎153-4233); *Austria*, VI, Benczúr utca 16 (☎122-9467); *Bulgaria*, XII, Levendula utca 15–17 (☎156-6378); *Canada*, II, Budakeszi ut 32 (☎176-7711); *China*, VI, Benczúr utca 17 (☎122-4872); *CIS*, Andrássy út 104 (☎131-8985); *Czechoslovakia*, XIV, Népstadion út 22 (☎251-1700); *Denmark*, II, Vérhalom utca 12–6 (☎115-2066); *Germany*, XIV, Izsó utca 5 (☎122-4204); *Israel*, II, Fullánk utca 8 (☎176-7896); *Netherlands*, XIV, Abonyi utca 31 (☎122-8432); *Norway*, XII, Határőr utca 35 (☎155-1811); *Romania*, XIV, Thököly út 72 (☎142-6941); *Sweden*, XIV, Ajtósi sor 27A (☎122-9800); *UK*, V, Harmincad utca 6 (☎118-2888); *USA*, V, Szabadság tér 12 (☎111-9629); *Yugoslavia*, still operating for the moment at VI, Aréna út 92A (☎142-0566).

Emergencies Ambulance: ☎04; Police: ☎07; Fire service: ☎05.

Hospitals and Dentistry There are 24-hour casualty departments at V, Hold Utca 19, behind the US embassy (☎111-6816), and at XII, Diosárok 1, off Szilágyi E. fasor in Buda (☎156-1122). The *Országos Traumatológiai Korház*, VIII, Mező Imre út 17 (☎133-7599), specialises in broken limbs; the *Szájsebészeti Klinika, Stomatológiai Intézet*, VIII, Mária utca 52 (☎133-0189) in dentistry. Embassies can recommend private, foreign language-speaking doctors and dentists.

International calls are best made from the Telephone and Telegam Bureau, V, Petőfi utca 17–19 (Mon–Fri 7am–9pm, Sat 7am–8pm, Sun 8am–1pm) or from direct-dial phone booths in the downtown area. International operator ☎09.

International railway tickets should be purchased 24 to 36 hours in advance, preferably at the **MÁV booking office**, VI, Andrássy út 35 (Mon–Wed 9am–5pm, Thurs & Fri 9am–7pm; ☎122-8049) where lines are shorter than at *Nemzetközi-jegy* (international tickets) counters in stations.

Lost property For items left on public transport, VII, Akácfa utca 18 (Mon, Tues & Thurs 7am–4pm, Wed & Fri 7am–6.30pm); otherwise Erzsébet tér 5 (Mon 8am–6pm, Tues & Thurs 8am–5pm, Fri 8am–3pm). Lost **passports** should be reported to *KEOKH*, VI, Andrássy út 93 (Mon 8am–4.30pm, Tues–Fri 8.30am–noon), and any found will be forwarded for collection there.

Motoring information *Magyar Autó Klub*, II, Rómer Floris utca 4A (☎115-2040); *Fővinform* for traffic conditions in Budapest (☎117-1173); *Útinform* (☎122-2238) for national conditions.

Naturism is catching on with the support of the *Naturisták Egyesülete* (XIII, Karpát utca 8), a Naturist Union which runs a nudist camp at the Délegyháza Lakes, 40km southeast of Budapest (by route 51 or train from Józsefváros Station). Closer at hand, nude sunbathing is permitted on the single-sex terraces of the Gellért and Palatinus baths, and the *strand* at Csillaghegyi in the III district.

Pharmacies The following are all open 24 hours: II, Frankel Leó út 22 (☎115-8290); VI, Teréz körút 95 (☎111-4439); VII, Rákóczi út 86, at Baross tér (☎l22-9613); XI, Kosztolányi Dezső tér 11 (☎166-6494); XII, Alkotás utca lB, at Déli Station (☎155-469); XIV, Bosnyák utca lA (☎183-0391). For **herbal remedies** try *Herbária*, VIII, Rákóczi út 49 and V, Bajcsy-Zsilinszky út 58.

Photomats Passport-sized photos available from V, Dorottya utca 9; VIII, Somogyi utca 18 (Mon–Fri 9am–6pm); and the third floor of the *Corvin* department store on Blaha Lujza tér.

Post Offices Main office/*poste restante* at V, Petőfi utca 13 (Mon–Fri 8am–6pm, Sat 8am–2pm); **24-hour** *postas* at VI, Teréz körút 51 and VII, Baross tér 11C (near Nyugati and Keleti Stations, respectively).

Record Shop Rock, pop and jazz (including bootlegs) from *DOB Records*, VII, Dob utca 71; *Lemezkucko*, VI, Király utca 67; and *WAVE Records*, V, Bajcsy-Zsilinszky út 15. *HUNGARATON*, *V*, Vörösmarty tér 1, for own-label classical music; *Rózsavölgyi*, V, Martinelli tér 5, for folk.

Radio *Radio 102* (102 FM) broadcasts in English with Voice of America news every hour on the hour. *Radio Danubius* (100.5 & 103.3 FM) is another commercial channel, broadcasting in German. *Calypso 873* plays rock oldies (873 KHz); *Radio Bartók* classical music and jazz (69.38 MHz).

Taxis *Volántaxi* (☎166-6666), *Fötaxi* (☎122-2222), *Budataxi* (☎120-4000), *Citytaxi* (☎153-3633), *Gábriel Taxi* (☎155-5000), *Rádió Taxi* (☎127-1271).

Television Uncut, subtitled *BBC News* on Mon, Tues, Thurs & Fri after 11pm on Channel 1. The main *Hungarian news* programmes are at 7.30pm on Channel 1, 9pm on Channel 2.

travel details

For reasons of space, these travel details are limited to the most obvious destinations and routes.

Trains

From Déli Station to Balatonfüred (every 1–2hr; 2hr–2hr 30min); Balatonszentgyörgy (every 1–2hr; 3–4hr); Dombóvár (7.30am, 10.10am, 12.50am & 4pm daily; 2hr 15min); Pécs (7.30am, 10.10am, 12.50am & 4pm daily; 3hr); Siófok (9.30am, 12.40am, 12.55am, 3.40pm, 5.15pm, 6.50pm & 10pm daily; 2hr 30min); Székesfehérvár (every 60–90min; 1hr); Szekszárd (7.40am, 1.35pm & 6pm daily; 3hr); Szombathely (6am, 12.30am, 1pm, 3pm & 5.20pm daily; 3hr 30min); Veszprém (11.35am, 12.30am, 3pm, 5.20pm & 5.45pm daily; 2hr 15min–3hr); Zalaegerszeg (6.35am & 11.55am daily; 4hr).

From Keleti Station to Békéscsaba (9.10am, 2.10pm, 3.30pm & 5.20pm daily; 2hr 30min); Eger (7.45am, 12.30am & 5.30pm daily; 2hr); Győr (7am, 8.30am, 9.50am, 10am, 12.30am, 1pm, 1.30pm, 3pm, 4pm & 6pm daily; 2hr 30min); Miskolc (6.10am, 7am, 10am, 12am, 1pm, 2.30pm, 4pm, 5pm, 6pm, 7pm & 8pm daily; 1hr 45min–2hr 15min); Sopron (7am, 10am, 1pm, 4pm

& 6pm daily; 3hr 30min); Tata (7am, 10am, 1pm & 6pm daily; 1hr 15min).

From Nyugati Station to Debrecen (7.10am, 8am, 10am, noon, 1pm, 2pm, 3pm, 4pm, 4.30pm, 5pm & 6pm daily; 2hr 30min–3hr 30min); Kecskemét (6.25am, 8.15am, 10.25am, 12.25am, 2.25pm, 4.25pm, 6.15pm & 7.25pm daily; 1hr 30min); Nyíregyháza (6.10am, 7.25am, 8am, 10am, 12am, 1pm, 2pm, 3.30pm, 4pm, 4.30pm & 7pm daily; 3hr–3hr 30 min); Szeged (6.25am, 8.15am, 10.25am, 12.25am, 2.25pm, 4.25pm, 6.15pm & 7.25pm daily; 2hr 30min).

Intercity buses

From Árpád híd to the Danube Bend: Dobogókő (1–3 daily; 2hr 30min); Esztergom via the Bend (every 90min; 3hr) or Dorog (every 30min; 2hr); Pomáz (hourly; 45min); Szentendre (hourly; 1hr); Vác (every 30min; 30min); Visegrád (hourly; 2hr).

From Erzsébet tér to Lake Balaton and Transdanubia: Balatonfüred (6.30am & 3.40pm daily; 2hr 15min); Dunaújváros (7.20am, 9am, 2pm & 2.20pm daily; 1hr 30min); Győr (every 40–60min; 1hr 15min–2hr); Harkány (6.20am daily; 4hr 30min); Herend (2.40pm & 4.10pm daily; 2hr 40min); Hévíz (6.30am & 3.40pm daily; 4hr); Keszthely (6.30am & 3.40pm daily; 3hr 45min); Mohács (6.40am & 1.20pm daily & Sat 3.20pm; 4hr); Nagyvázsony (Mon–Sat 9.40am & 2.20pm; 3hr); Pécs (6.20am, 7.20am, 9am, 2pm & 4.20pm daily; 4hr); Siklós (6.40am daily; 5hr); Siófok (8am & 12.40am daily; 1hr 45min–2hr 15min); Sopron (8am & 3pm daily; 3hr 45min); Sümeg (2.40pm & 8pm daily; 4hr 30min); Szekszárd (6.20am, 7.20am, 9am, 11.40am, 2pm, 2.20pm 3.40pm & 4.20pm daily; 3hr 15min); Székesfehérvár (every 40–60min; 1hr 15min); Szombathely (6.45am & 8am daily; 4hr 15min); Veszprém (every 60–90min; 2hr 15min); Zalaegerszeg (3.40pm daily; 4hr 45min); Zirc (6.45am, 7.30am, 3pm & 4.20pm daily; 2hr 30min).

From Népstadion to Northern Hungary and the Great Plain: Aggtelek (6.15am daily; 5hr); Baja (every 1–2hr; 3hr 15min); Balassagyarmat (every 1–2hr; 2hr 30min); Békéscsaba (6.25am, 1.45pm & 4.15pm daily; 4hr); Eger (every 90min; 3hr); Gyöngyös (hourly; 2hr); Kalocsa (every 1–2hr; 2hr); Kecskemét (15–20 daily; 1hr 45min); Kiskunfélegyháza (8–10 daily; 2hr); Lillafüred (8am daily; 3hr 30min); Mátraháza (7.10am, 8.10am, 5.10pm & 6.45pm daily; 2hr); Szeged (9pm daily; 3hr 45min); Vác (hourly; 30min).

International trains

Although destinations should remain the same, the departure times of express services below will doubtless change – so double check. Bookings are required on all routes, but it may not be possible to obtain them on trains leaving from Kőbánya-Kispest. This also applies to services from Zugló Station, which sometimes handles international traffic (though not at time of writing). The Vienna-bound *Wiener Waltzer* often runs late, so reserve sleepers on from Austria in Budapest. Also bring drinks, as the buffet staff overcharge shamelessly.

From Déli Station to Vienna (7.10pm daily; 3hr 30min); Zagreb (June–Sept 1pm daily & June–Aug 0.10am daily; 7hr).

From Keleti Station to Athens (midnight daily; 29hr); Arad (9.10am, 7.45pm & 11.20pm daily; 5hr 30min); Basel (5.30pm daily; 14hr 30min); Belgrade (6.20am, 11.20am, 3.20pm & midnight daily; 6hr); Berlin (8am & 2pm daily; 5hr 30min); Braşov (9.10am, 2.10pm, 7.45pm & 11.20pm daily; 13hr); Bratislava (8am, 2pm, 2.10pm & 3pm daily & June–Sept 6.30pm daily; 5hr 15min); Bucharest (9.10am, 2.10pm, 7.45pm & 11.20pm daily; 17hr); Cologne (8.30am daily; 14hr); Częstochowa (9pm & 11.30pm daily; 18hr); Dresden (8am & 2pm daily & June–Sept 6.30pm daily; 13hr); Frankfurt (8.30am daily; 11hr); Gdansk (3pm daily; 18hr 30min); Istanbul (6.20am daily; 26hr); Katowice (3pm, 7pm & 11pm daily; 10hr); Kiev (8.15am & 11.50pm daily & Wed & Thurs 7.25am; 25hr); Košice (6.10am & 7.20pm daily; 4hr 15min); Kraków (7.20pm daily; 12hr); Leipzig (June–Sept 6.30pm daily; 15hr); Lódz (9pm daily; 20hr); Moscow (8.15pm & 11.50pm daily & June–Sept Mon & Sun 7.25am; 38hr); Munich (12.30am, 3.30pm & 9pm daily; 9hr); Novi Sad (3.20pm daily; 3hr 15min); Nürnberg (8.30am daily; 9hr); Paris (3.30pm daily; 18hr); Plovdiv (6.20am daily; 19hr); Poprad Tatry (6.10am daily; 6hr 15min); Poznan (7.30pm daily; 14hr 30min); Prague (8am daily & June–Sept 6.30pm daily; 10hr); Saint Petersburg (8.15pm daily; 68hr); Sibiu (2.10pm & 7.45pm daily; 10hr 45min); Sighişoara (9.10am & 11.20pm daily; 10hr 30min); Skopje (midnight daily; 16hr); Sofia (6.20am & 3.20pm daily; 16hr); Szczecin (7.30pm daily; 17hr 30min); Thessaloniki (midnight daily; 22hr); Venice (9.50am daily; 12hr); Vienna (6am, 8.30am, 9.50am, 12.30am, 1.30pm, 3.30pm, 5.30pm & 6.30pm daily; 3hr 30min); Warsaw (7pm &

11.30pm daily; 17hr 30min); Wroclaw (7.30pm daily; 12hr); Zagreb (6.45am daily; 6hr 30min).

From Kőbánya-Kispest Station to Arad (June–Sept Thurs–Sat 3.15am; 6hr 15min); Bratislava (June–Sept Mon, Sat & Sun 9.20pm; 3hr 45min); Burgas (June–Sept 6.30am daily; 28hr); Katowice (June–Sept 11pm daily; 10hr); Prague (June–Sept Mon, Sat & Sun 9.20pm; 10hr); Ruse (June–Sept 6.30am daily & Thurs–Sat 3.15am; 20hr); Timişoara (June–Sept Thurs–Sat 3.15am; 9hr); Varna (June–Sept Thurs–Sat 3.15am; 21hr); Warsaw (June–Sept 11pm daily; 17hr).

From Nyugati Station to Arad (6am daily & June–Sept 11.45am daily; 5hr 15min); Baia Mare (1pm daily; 9hr); Braşov (6am & 2.55pm daily; 17hr 30min); Bratislava (3pm, 5pm, 9.25pm & 11.50pm daily; 4hr 30min); Berlin (3pm, 5pm & 11.50pm daily; 16hr 30min); Bucharest (6am & 2.55pm daily; 18hr 30min); Burgas (June–Sept 11.45am daily; 27hr); Chop (6.10am daily; 7hr); Cluj (6am & 2.55pm daily; 8hr 30min); Dresden (3pm, 5pm & 11.50pm daily; 14hr); Oradea (6am & 2.55pm daily; 6hr); Prague (3pm, 5pm, 9.25pm & 11.50pm daily; 10hr); Satu Mare (1pm & 9pm daily; 8–9hr); Sighişoara (6am & 2.55pm daily; 13hr 30min); Sofia (6am daily; 26hr); Timişoara (June–Sept 11.45am daily; 7hr).

International buses

Verify departure schedules and book tickets 24 hours in advance. Tickets must be purchased at the bus station in hard currency.

From Erzsébet tér to Amsterdam (June–Sept 9am daily; 26hr); Arad (6am daily; 7hr); Athens (June–Sept 10am & 6pm daily; 28hr); Banská Bystrica (6.45am & 11am daily; 4hr); Berlin (11pm daily & June–Aug 2am daily; 16hr); Bologna (June–Sept 1.30pm; 20hr); Bratislava (6.25am & 6.50am daily; 4hr 30min); Brussels (June–Sept 9am daily; 22hr); Cluj (6am & 8pm daily; 9hr 30min); Dresden (11pm daily & June–Aug 2am daily; 13hr); Florence (June–Sept 1.30pm daily;

21hr); Friedberg (4.15pm daily; 5hr 30min); Galanta (6am daily & Tues, Thurs & Sun 6.50am; 4hr); Gdansk (June–Aug 11am daily; 21hr); Gheorgeni (6am daily; 16hr 30min); Graz (4.30am daily & Nov–April 6.30am daily; 7hr); Hamburg (11pm daily; 20hr); Helsinki (June–Aug 2am daily; 55hr); Istanbul (7am daily; 25hr); Komarnó (6am daily & Tues, Thurs & Sun 6.50am; 3hr 30min); Kraków (6.45am daily & June–Aug 11am; 15hr); Levice (Tues, Thurs & Fri 6.30am, Wed, Thurs & Sat 4pm; 3hr); Lučenec (June–Oct 5pm daily; 3hr); Miercurea Ciuc (6am & 8pm daily; 15hr); Munich (6.30am & 8pm daily; 9hr); Nitra (Tues, Thurs & Fri 6.30am; 4hr); Nürnberg (6.30am, 8am & 3.15pm daily; 13hr); Oradea (6am & 8am daily; 6hr); Paris (June–Sept 9am daily; 24hr); Prague (Mon, Wed & Sat 6am & June–Aug 2am daily; 11hr); Propad-Tatry (6.45am daily; 5hr); Rimavská Sobota (Tues & Fri 6.45am; 6hr); Rome (June–Sept 1.30pm daily; 22hr); Rožňava (6.10am daily; 4hr 45min); Sfîntu Gheorghe (8pm daily; 16hr 30min); Sighişoara (6am daily; 13hr 30min); Stockholm (June–Aug 2am daily; 40hr); Stuttgart (8pm daily; 11hr 30min); Subotica (6.40am daily; 5hr); Tatranská Lomnica (6.45am daily & June–Oct 6am daily; 7hr 30min); Timişoara (6am daily; 8hr 30min); Tîrgu Mureş (6am & 8pm daily; 11hr 45min); Velké Kapušany (Aug–Sept 3.30pm daily; 7hr); Venice (April–Oct 6.30am & 6pm daily & June–Oct 8pm; 14hr); Vienna (6am, 7am & 5pm daily & June–Aug 2pm daily; 4hr); Warsaw (6.45am daily; 14hr); Zakopane (6.45am daily; 8hr).

Hydrofoils and Ferries

From the Belgrád rakpart international landing stage to Vienna at 8am (April 1–Oct 6) and 1.30pm (April 13–Sept 15) daily. 5hr.

From the Vigadó tér pier to Esztergom (7am, 7.30am & 2pm daily; 5hr); Szentendre (7.30am, 10am & 2pm daily & June–Aug 8.30am & 3pm daily; 90min); Vác (7am daily; 2hr 45min); Visegrád (7am, 7.30am, 10am & 2pm daily; 3hr).

CHAPTER TWO

THE DANUBE BEND

To escape Budapest's humid summers, people flock north of the city to the **Danube Bend** (*Dunakanyar*), one of the grandest stretches of the river, outdone only by the Kazan Gorge in Romania. Entering the Carpathian Basin, the Danube widens hugely, only to be forced by hills and mountains through a narrow, twisting valley, almost a U-turn – the "Bend" – before parting for the length of Szentendrei Island and flowing into Budapest. The **historic towns and ruins** of Szentendre, Esztergom and Visegrád can be seen on a long day trip from Budapest to the west bank, but with the chance of **hiking** or **horse-riding** in the neighbouring Pilis and Börzsöny highlands, it would be a shame not to linger.

The **Danube** is the second longest river in Europe after the Volga, flowing 2857km (1775 miles) from the Black Forest to the Black Sea. Between the confluence of the Bereg and Briach streams at Donauschingen and its shifting Delta on the Black Sea, the Danube is fed by over 300 tributaries from a catchment area of 816,000 square kilometres, with ten nations along its banks. Known as the *Donau* in Germany and Austria, it becomes the *Duna* from Czechoslovakia down through Hungary, Slovenia, Croatia, Serbia, Bulgaria, Romania and Moldova, forming the frontier for much of the way.

This "dustless highway" for armies and tribes since antiquity impressed the German poet Hölderlein as an allegory for the mythical voyage of the ancient German forefathers to the Black Sea, and Hercules' journey from Greece to the land of the Hyperboreans. Attila Jószef described it as "cloudy, wise and great", its waters from many lands as intermingled as the peoples of the Carpathian Basin. While the Danube's strategic value ended after World War II, economic and environmental concerns became live issues in the 1980s, when the governments of Hungary, Czechoslovakia and Austria agreed to dam the river between Gabčikovo and Nagymaros. The public opposition that compelled Hungary to abandon the project was a milestone along the road to democracy, mobilising society in a way that more overtly political causes would never have been allowed to.

THE WEST BANK

By building a line of *castra* to keep the barbarians on the far side of the Danube, the Romans unwittingly staked out the sites of the future castles of Magyar kings, who had to repel the Mongols – these are the most tourist-ridden places along the **west bank** today. Baroque **Szentendre**, around forty minutes by HÉV train from Batthyány tér in Budapest, is the logical place to start.

Buses on from Szentendre are very frequent, making it easy to move on to the medieval ruins of **Visegrád**, and then continue westwards to **Esztergom**, the

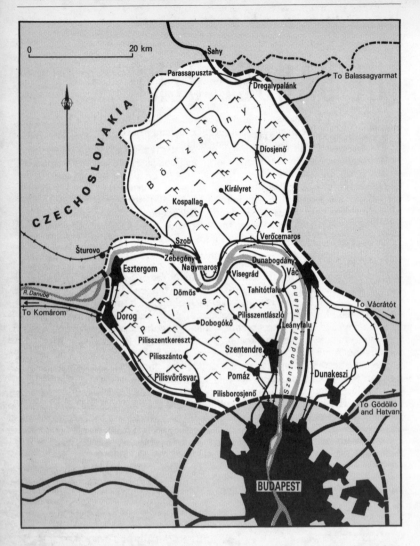

heart of Hungarian Catholicism. Both of these are also accessible direct from Budapest, with hourly buses from the Árpád híd terminus following an anticlockwise route around the Bend – although Esztergom can be reached more directly by the less scenic clockwise route that goes via Dorog (this is also the route taken by trains from the capital's Nyugati station). Various sites in **the Pilis range** can be reached by bus from Esztergom, Szentendre or Budapest's Árpád híd terminus, though services are pretty irregular. In view of its hairpin bends and heavy traffic, **cycling** is not permitted along the main west bank road (route 11).

Boat journeys

Between May and mid-September another option is to travel by **boat**. Discerning visitors opt for the scenic ride between Visegrád and Esztergom (2hr) rather than the dreary stretch of river between Budapest and Szentendre (1hr 30min), or the full five-hour journey from the capital to Esztergom. There are two services from Budapest's Vigadó tér pier to Esztergom via Szentendre and Visegrád (leaving at 7.30am & 2pm) plus another which terminates at Visegrád (10am). From June to late August there are also additional ferries to Szentendre (8.30am & 3pm). Should you board the wrong boat, or feel like a change of scenery, there are regular car ferries between towns on opposite banks.

Szentendre

> *Szentendre is the Montmartre of the Danube*
>
> Claudio Magris

Having cleared the bus and HÉV terminals and found their way into its Baroque heart, visitors are seldom disappointed by **SZENTENDRE**. Ignoring the outlying housing estates and the rash of boutiques in the centre, "Saint Andrew" is a friendly maze of houses painted in autumnal colours, secretive gardens and lanes winding up to hilltop churches – the perfect spot for an **artists' colony**.

Before the artists moved in at the turn of the century, Szentendre's character had been formed by waves of refugees from Serbia. The first influx followed the catastrophic Serbian defeat at Kosovo (1389), which foreshadowed the Turkish occupation of Hungary in the sixteenth century, when Szentendre itself fell into ruin. In 1690, after the Turks had been expelled by the Habsburgs, eight hundred families of Serbians, Albanians, Bosnians and Greeks arrived here under Patriarch Crnojevič, who made Szentendre the seat of the exiled Serbian Orthodox church. Prospering through trade, the immigrants replaced their wooden churches with stone ones, and built handsome town houses. Most returned to Serbia after the 1880s, however, and only about seventy families of Serbian descent still live here today.

The Town

Walking from the HÉV or bus station into the centre takes ten or fifteen minutes, unless you detour off Kossuth utca to examine a hoard of **Roman stonework** at Dunakanyar körút 1 (May–Oct Tues–Sun 10am–6pm). The eroded lintels and sarcophagi belonged to *Ulcisia Castra*, a military town named after the Eravisci, an Illyrian-Celtic tribe subdued by the Romans during the first century.

Further north along Kossuth utca you'll encounter the first evidence of a Serbian presence – the **Požarevačka Church**, just before the Bükkos stream. Typically, this was built in the late eighteenth century to replace an older wooden church, although its Byzantine-style iconostasis was inherited rather than specially commissioned. Beyond the stream, Dumtsa Jenő utca continues past the birthplace of Serbian novelist Jakov Ignjatovic (1822–49). Opposite is the **Barcsay Collection** (Tues–Sun April–Sept 10am–6pm; Oct–March 9am–7pm) of drawings and paintings by Jenő Barcsay, who was born in Transylvania but worked in Szentendre after 1928.

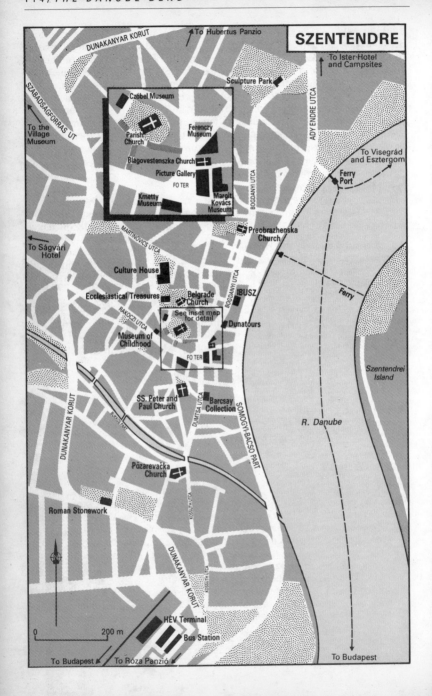

SZENTENDRE

To Hubertus Panzio

To Ister-Hotel
and Campsites

DUNAKANYAR KORUT

Sculpture Park

ADY ENDRE UTCA

SZABADSAGFORRAS UT

To the
Village
Museum

Czóbel Museum

Parish
Church

Ferenczy
Museum

Blagovestenszka Church

Picture Gallery

FO TER

Kmetty
Museum

Margit
Kovács
Museum

BOGDANYI UTCA

To Visegrád
and Esztergom

Ferry
Port

MARTINOVICS UTCA

Preobrazhenska
Church

To Ságvári
Hotel

Culture House

Ecclesiastical Treasures

Belgrade
Church

IBUSZ

BOGDANYI UTCA

Ferry

RAKOCZI UTCA

See inset map
for detail

Dunatours

Museum of
Childhood

FO TER

Szentendrei
Island

SS. Peter and
Paul Church

DUMTSA UTCA

Barcsay
Collection

R. Danube

DUNAKANYAR KORUT

RAKOCZI PAK

SOMOGYI-BACSO PART

Pozarevacka
Church

KOSSUTH UTCA

Roman Stonework

FINO

DUNAKANYAR KORUT

HEV Terminal

Bus Station

0   200 m

To Budapest

To Róza Panzió

To Budapest

A little further on the road is crossed by Péter-Pál utca, where a left turn brings you to the **Peter-Paul Church**, whose original furnishings were taken back to Serbia after World War I. From here, or from the last uphill stretch of Dumtsa utca, it's just a block to the main square, which by 1989 had reverted to its traditional name (spurning "Marx tér") – a year before other municipalities took the plunge.

Around Fő tér

Swarming with buskers and tourists over summer, **Fő tér** can be a place to savour – or escape fast. Horse-drawn carriages can be hired near the Plague Cross erected by the merchants' guild after Szentendre avoided infection in 1763; alleys run off in all directions; or you can duck into one of the many galleries and museums around the square.

If your appetite for such things is limited, don't waste time on the **Szentendre Picture Gallery** of contemporary work by local artists (Tues–Sun April–Oct 10am–6pm; Nov–March 9am–5pm), occupying three Baroque houses united under a single roof. As in the *Műhely* or **Workshop** opposite (same hours), the bulk of the exhibits are touristy dross. An alley beside the *Műhely* leads to the **Kmetty Museum** (Tues–Sun April–Oct 10am–6pm; Nov–March 9am–5pm), containing sombre daubs by János Kmetty (1889–1955) that would never be chosen to adorn anyone's fireplace.

Far more appealing is the **Margit Kovács Museum** (daily 9am–5pm) at Vastagh György utca 1, behind the Szentendre Picture Gallery. This wonderful museum never fails to delight visitors with its graceful sculptures and reliefs, for the artist's themes are legends, dreams, love and motherhood. Given its universal appeal, it's a shame that her work isn't better known abroad. In Hungary, however, Kovács (1907–77) is duly honoured as the nation's greatest ceramicist.

Almost as striking, but utterly different in spirit, are the icons within the Annunciation or **Blagoveštenska Church**. Painted by Mikhail Zivkovič of Buda early last century, they evoke all the richness and tragedy of Serbian history. The building itself is thought to have been designed by András Mayerhoffer in the 1750s. Look out for the tomb of a Greek merchant of Macedonian origin to the left of the entrance, and the Rococo windows and gate facing on to Görög utca (Greek Street). Next door, a portal carved with emblems of science and learning is the entrance to the former Serbian school, now the **Ferenczy Museum** (Tues–Sun 10am–5.30pm), devoted to an artistic family. Károly Ferenczy (1862–1917) pioneered Impressionism and *plein air* painting in Hungary, while his eldest son Valér (1885–1954) swung towards Expressionism. The younger twins Nóemi (1890–1957) and Béni (1890–67) branched out into textiles and bronzeware, with diminishing returns.

Alternatively, cross the square and walk up past the former Pálffy House (no. 17), whose Baroque gate bears the sign of the merchants' guild, combining the patriarchal cross of Orthodoxy with an anchor and a number four, representing Danube trade and the percentage of profit that was deemed appropriate. At Rákóczi utca 1, 50m further up, is the **Museum of Childhood** (Tues–Sun 10am–5.30pm), a fascinating collection of toys, cribs, imagery and tableaux.

Templom tér and beyond

From Fő tér or Rákóczi utca you can ascend an alley of steps to gain a lovely view of Szentendre's rooftops and gardens from **Templom tér**, where **crafts fairs** are frequently held to help finance the restoration of the Catholic **Parish Church**. Of medieval origin, with Romanesque and Gothic features, it was rebuilt in the Baroque style after falling derelict in Turkish times; the frescoes in its sanctuary were collectively painted by the artists' colony. Across the square, the **Czóbel Museum** (Tues–Sun April–Oct 10am–6pm; Nov–March 9am–5pm) exhibits paintings whose fierce brush strokes challenged the Neoclassicism of the Horthy era, by Béla Czóbel (1883–1976) and his wife Mária Modok (1896–1971).

Beyond Templom tér, the burgundy spire of the Orthodox episcopal cathedral or **Belgrade Church** pokes above a walled garden dark with trees. Its sexton (who lives in a nearby house marked *plebánia csengője*) is reluctant to open up for tourists, but the finest of the icons and *objets d'art* are displayed in a **Museum of Ecclesiastical Treasures** (Wed–Sun 10am–5.30pm) in the grounds. The entrance is around the corner at no. 5 Engels utca (a street name that's sure to change).

From the Belgrade Church you can follow a lane down to Bogdányi utca, where another painterly couple are commemorated by the **Imre Ámos–Margit Anna Collection** at no. 12 (Tues–Sun April–Oct 10am–6pm; Nov–March 9am–5pm). Further along, Bogdányi utca opens on to a square flanked by the **Lazar Cross** honouring King Lazar of Serbia, whom the Turks beheaded in revenge for the death of Sultan Murad at Kosovo.

The **Preobraženska Church**, 400m on, was erected by the tanners' guild in 1741–76, and its embonpoint enhanced by a Louis XVI gate the following century. Though its lavish iconostasis merits a look, the church is chiefly notable for its role in the Serbian festival on August 19. Another guild raised the **Vinegrowers' Cross** at the end of Bogdányi utca, which is fittingly wreathed in grapevines.

Across the road at no. 51 is the **Szentendre Artists' Colony** itself, which has temporary exhibitions by current and past members in its gallery (March 15–Oct 31 Tues–Sun 10am–6pm). Having come this far, you might as well check out the hulking creations of Jenő Kerényi (1908–75) in the **sculpture park** at Ady utca 5 (Tues–Sun April–Oct 10am–6pm; Nov–March 9am–5pm).

Szentendre Village Museum

The **Szentendre Village Museum** (April–Oct Tues–Sun 9am–5pm), 4km out of town, is by a long way the most enjoyable local attraction, so visit it before your energy flags. It is Hungary's largest open-air museum of rural architecture (termed a *Skanzen*, after the first such museum, founded in a Stockholm suburb in 1891), and will eventually include "samples" from ten different regions of the country. The museum lies along Szabadságforrás út, west of town, and is accessible by hourly buses from stand 8 of the bus terminal near the HÉV station. Get off when you see the spires in a field to the right.

Downhill from the entrance is a composite village from **Szabolcs-Szatmár** county, culled from isolated settlements in the Erdőhát region (see Chapter Six). The brochure on sale at the entrance points out the finer distinctions between humble peasant dwellings like the house from Kispalad, and the cottage from Uszka, formerly occupied by petty squires, that rise amongst the barns and woven pigsties (which could be erected on the spot). Rural carpenters could execute highly skilled work, as you can see from the circular "dry mill", the wooden bell tower from Nemesborzova, and the carving inside the church from Mand (on a hilltop).

> The Szentendre telephone code is ☎ 26

The second village "unit" seems far more regimented, originating from the ethnic **German** communities of the *Kisalföld* (Little Plain) in Transdanubia. Neatly aligned and whitewashed, the houses are filled with knick-knacks and embroidered samplers bearing homilies like "When the Hausfrau is capable, the clocks keep good time".

Demonstrations of weaving, pottery, baking and other skills take place on the first and third Sunday of each month, with **folkloric programmes** on traditional feast days (☎12-304 for details). A stand outside the entrance sells good pancakes; walk 100m up the main road and you'll find the stop for buses back into town.

Practicalities

Dunatours at Bogdányi utca 1 (Mon–Fri 8am–6pm, Sat 9am–1.30pm, Sun 9am–noon; ☎11-311) and *IBUSZ* (similar hours; ☎10-315) at no. 11 can supply **information**, and guide you around the diverse events of the *Szentendrei Nyár* **summer festival** (late June to late Aug), which culminates in a pop concert and fireworks on August 20. On the day before that, a **Serbian festival** with *kolo* dancing occurs outside the Preobraženska Church. Szentendre's main **post office** is at Rákóczi út 4, and the **police** can be found at Martinovics utca 11.

Accommodation

Both tourist offices can arrange **private rooms** (②), which can also be directly obtained from rentiers (look for *Zimmer Frei* signs around town). Some could well be located in outlying suburbs such as Tyukos-Dűlő or Leányfalu, off route 11. Aside from the options listed below, there are two **campsites** north of the centre. *Aquatours Camping* (May–Sept; ☎11-106;) at Ady utca 9–11 is 200m past the sculpture park. On Pap-Sziget or "Priest's Island", opposite the *Hotel Ister*, the larger, noisier *Pap-Sziget* site (April 15–Oct 15; ☎10-697;) has two- to four-person bungalows (②–③), a motel (②) and restaurant. The camping fee includes use of the swimming pool on the island.

The following **pensions** and **hotels** are listed according to location, the southernmost first:

Róza Panzió, Pannónia út 6B (☎11-737). A small pension to the south of the bus terminal. ②.

Bükkos Panzió, Bükkos-part 16 (☎12-021). A larger, comfier place, 200m west of the Požarevačka Church. ③.

Wiking Hajó Panzió, Ady utca 3 (☎11-707). Another comfy pension, near the sculpture park (May–Sept). ③.

Coca Cola Panzió, Dunakanyar körút 50 (☎10-410). Less attractively sited, and further out. ③.

Horvath Fogadó, Daru utca 2. Small and friendly, but not very convenient, in the backstreets off Dunakanyar körút. (③).

Ister Hotel, Ady utca 28 (☎12-511; telex 22-4300). Located near Pap-Sziget, 1km north of the centre, this hotel may appear on maps as the *Danubius*. ④.

Hubertus Panzió, Tyukos-dűlő 10 (☎10-616). Signposted off Ady utca, but too far out for anyone but motorists. ③.

Eating, drinking and nightlife

Restaurants in Szentendre are pricey by Hungarian standards, and crowded over summer. Perennial favourites include the *Görög Kancsó Vendéglő*, Görög utca 1; the *Béke Étterem*, Fő tér 19; and the *Rab-Rábi Vendéglő*, Péter-Pál utca 1A (daily noon–midnight; ☎10-819). However, there's better service at the *Régimondo Étterem*, Dumtsa utca 2, or the *Muskátili Étterem* at Rakoczai utca 1 (west of Rákóczi utca). Campers can use the *Szigetgyöngye Étterem* on Pap-Sziget. At the Brazilian *Pampa Churrascaria*, Somogy-Bacsó part 2 (Tues–Sat noon–11pm, Sun noon–4pm), around 600Ft will get you a meat platter and there's live South American music on Friday and Saturday nights. Though all these places serve alcohol, the *Kanizsa Sörbár*, opposite the Szentendrei Island ferry wharf, is a cheaper **drinking** spot. During the summer festival there's plenty going on in the way of **entertainment**, including plays and concerts. The rest of the year, the main form of nightlife is **discos**. Most venues are transitory (look for flyposters in the centre), but there's usually a disco at the *Szigetgyöngye Étterem* (8pm–2am).

Buses and ferries

There are two docks for **Danube ferries**: one for boats across to Szentendrei Island; the other – 500m further north – for services between Budapest and Esztergom. However, it's quicker to travel north using the hourly **buses** to Visegrád and Esztergom, or the more frequent local services (*Helyvonat*) to Leányfalu and Dunabogdány. Nothwithstanding the construction of a highland road via Pilisszentlászlo – intended to relieve congestion between Szentendre and Visegrád – most buses stick to the embankment route.

Szentrendrei Island, Leányfalu and Dunabogdány

Szentendre's northern suburbs merge into **LEÁNYFALU**, a leafy resort first popularised in the late nineteenth century by writers like Zsigmond Móricz. There is a *strand* for swimming, and numerous **rooms** and villas for rent. Also signposted along the main road are the *Duna Panzió* (☎26/23-161; ③) and *Dunakanyar* **camping** (April 15–Oct 15; ☎26/23-154), which has chalets (②) and tennis courts.

Between Budapest and Visegrád the Danube is split in two by **Szentendrei Island**, an attenuated slab of mud and vegetation, whose villages are linked to the east or west bank by small ferries. From the wharf between Szentendre and Leányfalu you can cross over to SZIGETMONOSTOR, where the *Horány Gyöngye Panzió* (☎26/23-544; ③) supervises a campsite (April 15–Oct 15) that caters to **nudists** from June to August. TAHITÓFALU, 4km further north, has one foot on the island (where architect Mihály Pollack once resided) and the other on the west bank (where there are two campsites and many rooms for rent), connected by a bridge. From Tahitófalu a road runs to the eastern side of the island, where you can catch a boat across to Vác (see p.131). There is a **golf course** at KISOROSZI, at the northern end of the island, accessible by ferry from Verőcemaros on the east bank (see p.133).

Sticking to the west bank, the land starts to rise and orchards and vineyards flourish around **DUNABOGDÁNY**, a picturesque village where many Budapesters have weekend cottages. Its Germanic traditions are commemorated by a **Local History Collection** at Kossuth utca 93 (Mon–Fri 9am–noon, Sat 2–4pm), and help attract many German tourists to the village **campsite** (May–Sept). A few kilometres further on, the Danube Bend and Visegrád heave into sight.

Visegrád and around

When the hillsides start to plunge and the river twists, keep your eyes fixed on the mountains to the west for a first glimpse of the citadel and ramparts of **VISEGRÁD** – "its upper walls stretching to the clouds floating in the sky, and the lower bastions reaching down as far as the river", still almost as it appeared to János Thuroczy in 1488. At that time, courtly life in Visegrád – the royal seat – was nearing its apogee, and the palace of King Mátyás and Queen Beatrice was famed throughout Europe. The papal legate Cardinal Castelli described it as a "*paradiso terrestri*", seemingly unperturbed by the presence of Vlad the Impaler, who resided here under duress between 1462 and 1475.

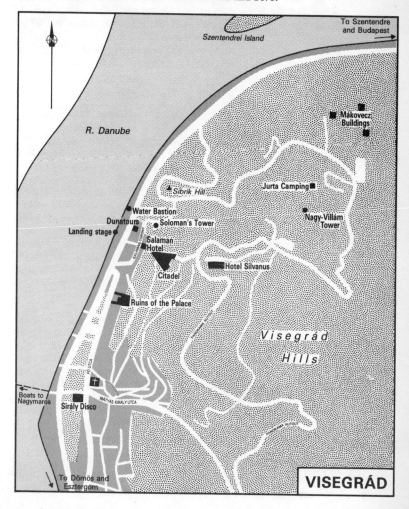

Today, visitors come to the village to admire the ruins of the palace and the gorgeous view from the surrounding Visegrád Hills, an unexpected but appropriate setting for several works by the visionary architect Imre Mákovecz (see below). While the ruins can be seen on a flying visit, the hills require a full day and a fair amount of walking, with the option of longer hikes or pony-trekking.

The Ruins of Visegrád

The layout of the **ruins of Visegrád** (whose Slavic name means "High Castle") dates back to the thirteenth century, when Béla IV began fortifying the north against a recurrence of the Mongol invasion. Its most prominent features are the Citadel on the hill, and the Water Bastion and Solomon's Tower near the riverside below. The palace itself is inconspicuously sited, further inland and 500m south of Solomon's Tower. As Visegrád fell into dereliction after the Turkish occupation, mud washed down from the hillsides gradually buried the palace entirely, and later generations doubted its existence until János Schulek unearthed one of the vaults in 1934.

The palace
Now largely excavated and partially reconstructed, the **Royal Palace** spreads over four levels or terraces at Fő utca 27–29 (Tues–Sun April–Oct 9am–5pm; Nov–March 8am–4pm). Originally founded by the Angevin king Charles Robert, it was the setting for the Visegrád Congress of 1335, attended by the monarchs of Central Europe and the Grandmaster of the Teutonic Knights, who failed to agree upon a response to the growing Habsburg threat but managed to consume 10,000 litres of wine and vast amounts of victuals in the process. In February 1991, Visegrád played host to another, less extravagant, summit, when the prime ministers of Hungary, Czechoslovakia and Poland met here to put together a joint strategy for trade and EC membership in the post-Communist era.

Although nothing remains of Charles Robert's palace, the **cour d'honneur** built for his successor Louis, which provided the basis for subsequent building by Sigismund and, later, Mátyás Corvinus, is still to be seen on the second terrace. Its chief features are the pillastered **Renaissance loggia** and two panels from the **Hercules Fountain**. The upper storey – which was made of wood, heavily carved and gilded – disappeared long ago.

A legend has it that Beatrice, desiring to rule alone, eventually poisoned Mátyás, so a chalice with toxic contents might have passed between the **royal suites** that once stood beneath an overhang on the third terrace, separated by a magnificent **chapel**. Reportedly, the finest sight was the garden above the bath corridor, embellished by the **Lion Fountain**. A perfect copy of the original (carved by Ernő Szakál) bears Mátyás's raven crest and dozens of sleepy-looking lions, although, unlike the original, it's not fed by the gutters and pipes that channelled water down from the citadel.

During summer, the ruins provide the setting for **historical pageants** and/or films intended to recreate the splendour of Visegrád's Renaissance heyday.

The Water Bastion and Solomon's Tower
North along Fő utca past the Mátyás Statue, you can follow the embankment highway to the decrepit **Water Bastion** near the ferry landing stage.

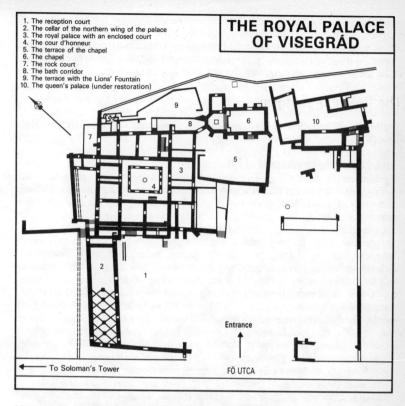

1. The reception court
2. The cellar of the northern wing of the palace
3. The royal palace with an enclosed court
4. The cour d'honneur
5. The terrace of the chapel
6. The chapel
7. The rock court
8. The bath corridor
9. The terrace with the Lions' Fountain
10. The queen's palace (under restoration)

THE ROYAL PALACE OF VISEGRÁD

← To Soloman's Tower

Entrance

FŐ UTCA

Alternatively, head up Salamán-torony utca to reach **Solomon's Tower**, a mighty hexagonal keep buttressed by concrete slabs. The **Mátyás Museum** (May 1– Nov 7 Tues–Sun 9am–5pm) inside the tower exhibits finds from the palace, including the white Anjou Fountain of the Angevins and the red marble "Visegrád Madonna" carved by Tomaso Fiamberti – the probable sculptor of the Lion and Hercules fountains.

Rather than walking on to the **ruined Roman fort** atop Sibrik Hill, save your energy for the climb to Visegrád's citadel.

The Citadel

Dramatically sited on a crag, Visegrád's triangular **Citadel** (daily 9am–5pm) served as a repository for the Hungarian crown jewels until they were stolen by a treacherous maid of honour in the sixteenth century. Though only partly restored, the Citadel is still mightily impressive, commanding a superb view of Nagymaros and the Börzsöny Mountains on the east bank.

You can reach the Citadel by the "Calvary" footpath (25min) that starts just above Nagy Lajos utca (signposted *Fellegvár*), or by catching a bus (June–Aug only) from the Mátyás Statue, which follows the scenic Panorama autóút into the hills.

The Visegrád Hills

Thickly wooded and crisscrossed with paths, the **Visegrád Hills** are a popular rambling spot. From the car park near the citadel, you can follow the autóút and then a signposted path to the **Nagy-Villám observation tower** (daily 9am–5pm), offering a view that stretches into Czechoslovakia. If you feel like **hiking**, there's a twelve-kilometre trail marked with blue stripes running from the tower, via Paprét (Priest's Meadow), to Pilisszentlászló, which takes two to three hours. **Horse-riding** can be arranged through the *Dunatours* office in Visegrád (see below).

Imre Mákovecz at Visegrád

A kilometre north of the observation tower lies Mogyoró-hegy (Hazelnut Hill) and its amazing wooden **buildings by Imre Mákovecz**. As a promising architect in the Kádár years, Mákovecz was branded a troublemaker for his outspoken nationalism, banned from teaching, and "exiled" to the Visegrád forestry department in 1977. Over the next decade he refined his ideas and acquired a host of student followers, holding annual summer schools where they would create temporary structures from twigs and branches, learning to build cheaply, and with low technology, in a specifically Magyar way suitable for poor communities.

Now duly esteemed as Hungary's foremost architect, Mákovecz holds classes on trains as he shuttles from one building site to another, in provincial towns and villages. What you see here is mainly the result of Mákovecz's forestry department commissions, along with a few of the smaller structures that are designed to decay. The shingled Community Centre is the focal point, a cluster of helmet-shaped domes around a central plumed dome with elaborate arched entrances, the whole appearing to rise organically out of the earth. Other notable examples of work by the architect's *Mákona* company include the community centres in Sárospatak, Zalaszentlászló and Szigetvár, and the oesophagus-like crypt of Farkasréti cemetery in Budapest. Mákovecz also designed the much admired Hungarian Pavilion at the 1992 Expo in Seville.

Practicalities

At the time of writing, it's hard to be categorical about most practicalities. While *Dunatours* at Fő utca 3 (Mon–Thurs 8am–4pm, Fri 8am–3.30pm; also Sat & Sun during summer) is closed for renovation, you have to seek **information** at Rév utca 12, the home address of the man who runs it.

Accommodation

Aside from booking **private rooms** (②) in Visegrád (or Nagymaros, across the river), the options are somewhat uncertain, with several places due to be revamped – or closed down – in the future. Bearing this in mind, start with the former tourist hostel – now the *Salamán Hotel* – at Salamán-torony utca 1 (☎26/28-278; ②). Just along from this is the *Üdüllő-Szálló*, one of two erstwhile trade union homes, now renting **bungalows** (②) to all comers. The other – renamed the *Hotel Matias Rex* – is at the northern end of Fő utca, on the way into town. Quieter is the *Elte Hostel* at Fő utca 117 (☎26/28-165; ②), on the other side of Visegrád.

Wealthier travellers can enjoy the *Hotel Silvanus* on Fekete-hegy **in the hills**, which has a sauna, tennis courts and bowling green (☎113-6063; ⑤). Near Mogyoró-hegy there is a well-equipped **campsite** (April 15–Oct 15; ☎26/28-217) – known as *Jurta* or *Natours Bellevue Camping* – which rents chalets (②–③) but is difficult to reach. When last heard of, the smaller "youth" campsite at Széchenyi utca 7, in Visegrád itself, was no longer operating.

Eating, entertainments and moving on

Fried-fish and sausage stalls along the promenade are augmented by several **restaurants**. On Rév utca you'll find the *Fekete Holló* and the *Sirály Étterem* (Mon–Sat 8am–2pm), not far from the *Diófa Kisvendéglő* at Fő utca 48. In summer there are **discos** at the *Sirály*, and sporadic disco **cruises** between Visegrád and Esztergom (which leave from the main landing stage as advertised). Although Visegrád itself has nowhere to swim, there is a salubrious *strand* and warm-water **pool** at Lepence, 3km towards Dömös (see below).

You can easily move on using **buses** or thrice-daily **ferries** for Esztergom (from the main landing stage), or the small car-ferry that sails to Nagymaros every forty minutes from the jetty near Rév utca.

Dömös and Pilismarót

Seven kilometres round the Bend, **DÖMÖS** is a verdant straggle of overgrown houses and holiday homes, with a nice **campsite** (May–Sept) by the river. Less conspicuous signposts indicate the start of **trails into the Pilis range**, abounding in raspberries during early summer. Follow the Malom tributary 2.5km upstream and you'll reach a path that forks right for the Rám precipice (3hr) and Dobogókő (4–5hr), and left for the Vadallo Rocks (3hr) beneath the towering "Pulpit Seat"– a 641-metre crag that only the experienced should attempt to climb.

PILISMARÓT, 4km on, has two **ferry crossings** for the east bank. Ferries run to Zebegény from the village itself, and to Szob from another landing stage at Basaharc, 2km beyond Pilismarót.

Esztergom

Beautifully situated in a crook of the Danube facing Czechoslovakia, **ESZTERGOM** is dominated by its Basilica, whose dome is visible for miles around. The sight is richly symbolic, for although the royal court abandoned Esztergom for Buda after the thirteenth-century Mongol invasion, this has remained the centre of **Hungarian Catholicism** ever since Stephen imposed Christianity on his subjects in 1000 AD. As a pillar of the *ancien regime*, the Church was ruthlessly attacked during the Rákosi era, when hundreds of priests were tortured and jailed; but after 1971 the regime settled for a *modus vivendi*, hoping to enlist the Church's help with social problems and to harness the patriotic spirit of the faithful. Since an avowedly Christian government was elected in 1990, the Church has striven to regain its former influence. Parochial schools and religious education have been restored, and the government is considering restrictions on abortion and divorce.

The Town

Arriving by bus from Visegrád, alight near the Basilica Hill or down in the centre rather than staying on to the bus terminal on Simor utca, in the south of town. Should you arrive at the railway station, 1km farther south, buses #1 and #5 run into the centre. Ferries from Budapest tie up alongside the island to the west of the lower town, fifteen minutes' walk from the centre.

Esztergom's craggy **Basilica Hill** is the natural focus of attention. It was here that Prince Géza established the royal seat, and that his son Stephen built Hungary's first cathedral, where his coronation by a papal envoy on Christmas Day 1000 signified the country's recognition by Christendom. In 1991, the hill was

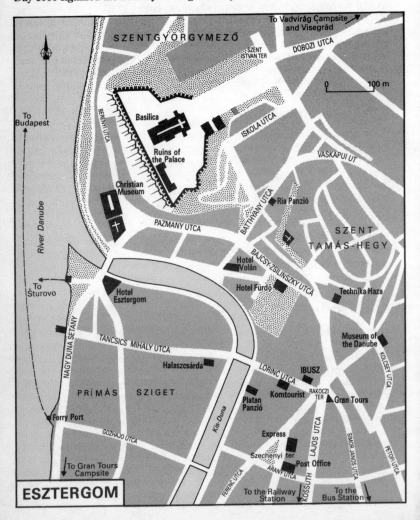

ESZTERGOM

the setting for two events symbolising the Church's triumph over Communism: the reburial of the exiled Cardinal Mindszenty and the first papal visit to Hungary.

The Basilica

Esztergom's **Basilica** (March–Dec daily 9am–5pm; Jan & Feb Tues–Sun 9am–3pm) is the largest in Hungary, measuring 118m in length and 40m in width, capped by a dome 100m high. Built on the site of the medieval basilica ruined by the Turks, it was begun by Pál Kühneland and János Packh in 1822, and finally completed by József Hild in 1869. However, it was actually consecrated in 1856, as soon as the dome was in place; Liszt's *Gran Mass* was composed for the occasion (*Gran* being the German name for Esztergom).

As befits what is claimed to be the fifth largest church in the world, its nave is on a massive scale, clad in marble, gilding and mosaics. To the left of the entrance is the lavish red marble **Bakócz Chapel**, with an altar by Florentine craftsmen, salvaged from the original basilica for which it was commissioned by Archbishop Tamás Bakócz, whose papal ambitions were dashed when "his" crusade turned into the great peasants' revolt of 1514. The Basilica's main altarpiece was painted by the Venetian Michelangelo Grigoletti, based on Titian's *Assumption* in the Frari Church in Venice.

Don't miss the **crypt**, resembling a set from a Dracula film, with giant stone women flanking the stairway down to gloomy vaults full of entombed prelates. Though several other mausolea look more arresting, it is the **tomb of Cardinal Mindszenty** that transfixes Hungarians (see box below). The walls of the crypt are 17m thick, to support the weight of the Basilica.

Buy tickets at the main entrance if you intend to visit the treasury (*kincstar*) or belltower (*harangtorony*). Having seen the overpowering collection of bejewelled crooks and chalices and kitsch papal souvenirs in the **treasury** (daily May–Oct 9am–5pm; otherwise 10am–4pm; closed Jan), it is almost a relief to climb the seemingly endless stairway to the **belltower** (May–Oct daily 9am–5pm). The stifling heat inside the cupola and the pigeon droppings within the bellroom are forgotten the moment you step outside and see the magnificent view of Esztergom, with Czechoslovak Štúrovo across the water.

THE RETURN OF CARDINAL MINDSZENTY

When the much-travelled body of **Cardinal József Mindszenty** was finally laid to rest with state honours in May 1991, it was a vindication of his uncompromising heroism – and the Vatican *realpolitik* that Mindszenty despised.

As a conservative and monarchist, he had stubbornly opposed the Communist takeover, warning that "cruel hands are reaching out to seize hold of our children, claws belonging to people who have nothing but evil to teach them". Arrested in 1948, tortured for 39 days and nights, and sentenced to life imprisonment for "treason", Mindszenty was freed during the Uprising and took refuge in the US Embassy in Budapest. He remained there for fifteen years, appalled by the miniskirts and pop music that he witnessed from a window overlooking Szabadság tér.

When the Vatican struck a deal with the Kádár regime in 1971, Mindszenty had to be pushed into resigning his position and going into exile, where he died in 1975. Although his will stated that his body should not return home until "the red star of Moscow had fallen from Hungarian skies", his reburial occurred some weeks before the last Soviet soldier left, in preparation for the pope's visit in August. Nowadays the Vatican proclaims his greatness, without any hint of apology for its past actions.

Palace ruins: The Castle Museum

South of the Basilica are the ruins of the palace founded by Géza, now known as the **Castle Museum** (Tues–Sun April–Oct 9am–5pm; Nov–March 10am–4pm). In its former life the royal palace entertained Louis VII and Frederick Barbarossa on their way to the Crusades, and after Buda became the capital in 1249, the widowed Queen Beatrice and sundry archbishops lived here. According to the chronicler Djelalzade, the Turks "knocked down idols in the churches and destroyed the symbols of infidelity and error" when they sacked Esztergom in 1543, but left intact the wheel and "narrow copper tube" which piped water up to the castle from the Danube.

Excavations in the 1930s uncovered a twelfth-century **chapel** with a beautiful rose window and Byzantine-style frescoes. You can also visit Beatrice's suite, and the study of Archbishop Vítez – known as the **Hall of Virtues** after its allegorical murals depicting Intelligence, Moderation, Strength and Justice. During June and July, **historical pageants** are staged at the open-air theatre nearby (look out for advertisements).

Coming back down the hill, look out for the monumental **Dark Gate** beneath it. Constructed to facilitate access between church buildings on either side of the hill, this tunnel was later exploited by the Red Army, who maintained a base below "Peace Square" until 1989.

The Watertown and Prímás-Sziget

Below the hill, the sound of choirs seems always to be floating through the Baroque streets of the **Watertown** district. Turning into Pázmány utca, you pass the Cathedral Library at no. 21, and a small **Museum of Local History** (Tues–Sun 9am–5pm) at no. 63 (which may move to no. 77). The latter is named after the poet Bálint Balassi (1554–94), who perished in the battle to recapture Esztergom from the Turks; a campaign in which the Italian composer Monteverdi also fought.

Further west stands the Italianate Baroque **Watertown Parish Church**, fronted by an equestrian statue of King Stephen. A few doors along, the old Primate's Palace at Berényi utca 2 makes a worthy setting for the **Christian Museum** (Tues–Sun 10am–5.30pm), Hungary's richest hoard of religious art. This includes the largest collection of Italian prints outside Italy; Renaissance paintings and wood carvings by German and Austrian masters; and the *Lord's Coffin of Garamszentbenedek*, a wheeled, gilded structure originally used in Easter Week processions.

From the Parish Church cross Archbishop Mindszenty Square and the Kossuth Bridge onto **Prímás-Sziget** (Primate's Island). A popular tourist spot, with two campsites and an outdoor *halaszcsárda* (Fisherman's Inn), it faces Štúrovo, across the river. The towns were linked by a wrought-iron **bridge** until it was blown up in World War I. Its elegant stump – decorated with a freshly painted Hungarian coat of arms – rises between the ferry landing stages. Having admired the scene, head east along Táncsics utca and over the Bottyán Bridge, into the lower town.

Szent Tamás-hegy and the lower town

Should you come directly from Watertown instead, it's worth a detour up to **Szent Tamás-hegy** (St Thomas' Hill), if only for the view. The hill is named after the English martyr Thomas à Becket, honoured here with a chapel by Margaret Capet, formerly the wife of Prince Henry of England, whose father Henry II had caused Thomas' death by raging, "Who will rid me of this turbulent priest?". In

The Esztergom telephone code is ☎ 33

the way of medieval royalty, Margaret later married Béla III of Hungary, but her conscience would not let her forget the saint. The existing chapel was built after the Turkish occupation.

Walking down Bajcsy-Zsilinszky utca, you might consider another detour to Esztergom's former Synagogue, a flamboyant, Moorish-style edifice on Imház utca, now a science club or **Technika Háza**. From here you can cut across Vörösmarty utca to the **Museum of the Danube** (March–Oct Tues–Sun 10am–5.30pm) at Kölcsey utca 2, containing exhibits on the history and ecology of this great river. Among them is a model of the *Vidra*, the first steam dredger in Hungary, introduced from England by Count Széchenyi.

Otherwise, carry on to Rákóczi tér and the older **lower town** beyond. By following the pavement cafés, you should emerge onto **Széchenyi tér** – a pleasant square culminating in a Town Hall with Rococo windows. A couple of blocks further south stands the eighteenth-century **City Parish Church**, built on the site of a medieval monastery where Béla IV and Queen Mária were buried. The marble plaque to the right of the gate shows the level of the flood of 1832. More exciting and only slightly further from the square is the outdoor **market** halfway along Simor János utca.

Practicalities

All the **tourist offices** are near Rákóczi or Széchenyi tér. While *Komtourist* at Lőrinc utca 6 (☎12-082) is useless, *IBUSZ* (Mon–Fri 8am–4pm; June–Aug also Sat 8–11.30am; ☎12-552), on the corner of Rákóczi tér, can be helpful, as can *Gran Tours* (April–Oct Mon–Fri 8am–4.30pm, Sat 8am–noon; Nov–March Mon–Fri 8am–3.30pm; ☎13-756) and *Express* (Mon–Wed 8am–3.30pm, Thurs 8am–4pm, Fri 8am–3pm, Sat 8am–noon; ☎13-113) on Széchenyi tér.

Accommodation
The cheapest accommodation in July and August is **beds** (①) in colleges like the *Martos Flóra Kollégium* (☎12-813) at Szent István tér 16, below the Basilica – contact *Express* or *Gran Tours* for bookings. The next best deal are **private rooms** (①–②), available year round from *IBUSZ* or *Gran Tours*; the latter also has apartments sleeping four to five (④).

HOTELS AND PENSIONS
Hotel Esztergom, Prímás-Sziget (☎12-883). Stylish and comfortable, with a restaurant and sports facilities. Rooms are cheaper off-season. Breakfast included. (⑥).
Hotel Fürdő, Bajcsy-Zsilinszky utca 14 (☎11-688). Attached to a thermal bath complex. Doubles with baths (④) or without (②).
Hotel Volán, József Attila tér 2 (☎12-714; telex 27-752) Rather shabby, but handily located. Rooms with (③) or without (②) baths.
Platan Panzió, Kis-Duna sétány. A new pension opposite Prímás-Sziget. (③).
Ria Panzió, Batthyány utca 11 (☎13-155). A small pension below the Basilica hill (March–Oct). ③.
Bánomi Fogadó, behind the Bánomi estate 1km east of the Basilica; bus #3 or #4 from Béke tér stops nearby. ②.

Csüki Kocsma, Dobogókői út 110 (☎11-584). A small pension out along the road to Dobogókő. Bus #7 or #9. ③.

Oktáv Motel, Wesselényi utca 35–39 (☎11-755). A quiet place in the Kertváros (garden district), south of town. ④.

CAMPSITES

Kis Duna, by the *Halászcsárda* on Prímás-Sziget. Handy location, but only functions from mid-June to late Aug.

Gran-Tours Camping, (☎11-327), 300m south of the ruined bridge on Prímás-Sziget. Noisy but well equipped, with bungalows (②–③). Open May–Oct 15 (bungalows until late Sept).

Vadvirág Camping, (☎12-234), 3km along the road to Visegrád, near the tail-end of the #6 bus route. Rents grassy tent-space and two-person bungalows (①). May–Sept 15.

Gyopár or **Vaskapu**, on Siplóhegy, 1km from the end of the #1 bus route, on Vaskapui út. A simpler, smaller site with huts (①), open April 15–Oct 15.

Eating, drinking and entertainments

Most of the **restaurants** around the centre are pretty touristy, but none the worse for that. The best one in Watertown is the *Annonym Étterem* at Berényi utca 4 (noon–9pm); another place near Basilica Hill is the *Csülök Csárda*, at Batthyány utca 9. In the lower town you'll find a pizzeria between the tourist offices on Lőrinc utca; the *Vadászkert Vendéglő* on Széchenyi tér; and the *Kispipa Étterem*, one block to the east at Kossuth utca 19 (daily 8am–10pm). On Prímás-Sziget, violinists serenade diners at the outdoor *halászcsárda* (8am–10pm), and there's an excellent but expensive restaurant in the *Hotel Esztergom*.

Should you happen to visit during the first half of August in an odd-numbered year, look out for posters advertising the **Guitar Festival**. Summer is also the time for **concerts** of choral or organ music in the Basilica and the Watertown Parish Church (details from *IBUSZ* or *Gran Tours*), and Saturday and Sunday night **disco cruises** to Visegrád (advertised around the centre). To boogie on terra firma, check out the *Galeria Disco* (Fri & Sat 9pm–4am), near the cinema on Rákóczi tér. By day, you might care to soak in the **thermal bath** (May–Sept daily 9am–5pm) behind the *Hotel Fürdő*.

Moving on

Buses from the depot on Simor utca serve most parts of the west bank and the Pilis range, with a couple of long-distance services to Veszprém (5am & 2.40pm), Győr and Sopron (5am & 1.40pm) in western Hungary. Most services to Budapest go via Dorog rather than the west bank.

As the hourly **car ferry** between Esztergom and ŠTÚROVO only carries Hungarians and Czechoslovaks, the nearest points for **crossing into Czechoslovakia** are KOMÁROM, 60km to the west, or PARASSAPUSZTA, in the Börzsöny range on the east bank.

The Pilis Range

Whether you describe it as mountains or hills, the **PILIS RANGE** (*Pilis hegység*) offers scope for **hiking** amidst lovely scenery. The beech and oak woods on these limestone slopes are most beautiful in the autumn, but always hold the possibility of encounters with red deer or wild boars. Ruined lodges and monasteries attest to the royal hunting parties and hermits of the Order of St Paul who frequented the hills in medieval times.

The Pilis is directly accessible by bus from Esztergom, Szentendre or the Árpád híd terminus in Budapest, or you can hike up by various routes – from the Nagy-Villám Tower (see p.122), or from Dömös to Dobogókő (p.123). If you're planning any walking, get hold of a **map** that marks the paths (*turistaút/foldút*), caves (*barlang*), and rain shelters (*esőház*) throughout the highlands.

Dobogókő

DOBOGÓKŐ, in the shadow of 756-metre-high Pilis-tető, has been a hiking centre since the late nineteenth century, when one of Hungary's first hostels was established here, and is still the best base for walking in the Pilis. Today, the hostel building is a **Museum of Rambling and Nature Tourism** (Thurs–Sun 10am–4pm), which leaves no cheaper alternative to the *Hotel Dobogókő* (☎26/27-681; ③) or the *Hotel Nimród* (☎26/27-644; ⑤). From June to August, however, **accommodation** in isolated hunting lodges (②–④) can be booked through *Natours Travel* in Budapest (XII, Győri út 2B).

Pilisborosjenő and Pomáz

The southern foothills of the Pilis are good for **pony-trekking**, which can be arranged through *Natours Travel*, or on the spot. In **PILISBOROSJENŐ**, off the Dorog–Budapest road, contact the *Zsíros Panzió* at Var utca 14 (☎26/34-059), which also does rooms (③). **POMÁZ**, on the HÉV line between Budapest and Szentendre, has a **riding school** (9am–6pm) at Mártírok útja 1, and a couple of **pensions**: the *Rákos Panzió* at Beniczky utca 63 (☎26/25-355; ③) and the *Tutti Panzió* at Lévai út 14 (②).

Many residents of Pomáz are of Serbian or Croatian extraction, giving a different flavour to the local *Táncház* (Dance House). This is the meeting place of the **Vujicsics Ensemble** (named after its founder, Tihamer Vujicsics, who died in 1975), which plays **South Slav music**. Concerts are usually advertised in Szentendre or Budapest.

THE EAST BANK

The **east bank** has fewer monuments than its western counterpart, so tourists are thinner on the ground. As the only sizeable town, with a monopoly on historic architecture, **Vác** styles itself the "city of churches". More or less en route to Vác are the **Dunakeszi** riding school and the beautiful botanical garden at **Vácrátót**. Farther north are **Zebegény** and **Nagymaros**, which have the finest scenery in the Danube Bend and, like other settlements beneath the **Börzsöny range**, mark the start of trails into the highlands.

Starting **from Budapest**, you can reach anywhere along the east bank within an hour or two by train from Nyugati station, or bus from the Árpád híd terminus. The slower alternative is to sail from Budapest's Vigadó tér pier to Vác (2hr 30min), or on to Nagymaros and Zebegény. Approaching **from the west bank**, there are regular ferries across from Visegrád to Nagymaros; Pilismarót to Zebegény; and from Basaharc, north of Pilismarót, to Szob. Vác is accessible by ferry from the far side of Szentendrei Island, 4km from Tahitófalu.

Dunakeszi, Göd and Vácrátót

DUNAKESZI, 18km north of the capital, is the home of the **Alag Riding School**, patronised by Budapest's diplomatic corps. Less illustrious mortals may join the cross-country rides (held weekly Sept–Nov) providing they have some equestrian experience and book in advance – for details, contact *Pegazus Tours* in Budapest (V, Károlyi utca 5; ☎171-552) or Dunakeszi's *Magyar Loverseny Vallalat* (☎27/41-656).

Holidaymakers here for the fishing, swimming and sunbathing are catered for with a variety of **accommodation**. The *Hotel Dunakeszi* at Tábor utca 2 (☎27/41-611; ⑤) has sports facilities and all mod cons. Cheaper options include the *Fészek Panzió* on Malomárok (☎27/41-653; ③), which has a **campsite** next door (May–Sept), and the *Kikelet Panzió* at Kikelet utca 1 (☎27/42-554; ③). The larger *Dunakeszi* campsite (May 15–Sept 15; ☎27/42-358) is on Liget utca beside the Danube, north of *Dunatours*, which can book private rooms (②).

Heading north, the next settlement is **GÖD**, a mass of holiday homes, where workers' sports camps provided a cover for underground activism during the Horthy era. Appropriately, the local Arts House or *Fészek* (literally "nest") contains an exhibition on the history of the workers' sports movement (May–Oct Tues–Sun 10am–6pm). There is good bathing at SZŐDLIGET, 5km up the road to Vác.

The Botanical Garden at Vácrátót

VÁCRÁTÓT is famous for its **Botanical Garden** (April–Oct Mon–Fri & Sun 8am–6pm, Sat 8am–4pm), founded in the 1870s by Count Vigyázó, who subsequently bequeathed it to the Academy of Sciences. Complete with waterfalls and mock ruins, the garden contains thousands of different trees and shrubs from around the world, providing a wonderful setting for **concerts** of classical music on summer evenings. Concert tickets (from Vörösmarty tér in Budapest or *Dunatours* in Vác) allow free admission to the park after midday, encouraging you to make a day of it. As bad weather can disrupt concert schedules, look out for *rossz idő esetén*, signifying an alternative date.

Motorists can reach Vácrátót by turning east off the main road a few kilometres north of Sződliget. The village is otherwise accessible in ninety minutes by train from Nyugati station; or by bus or rail from Vác. It also has **connections** with the Northern Uplands (see Chapter Six), namely a branch line to Aszód, where one can board trains for Balassagyarmat, and regular buses to Gödöllő. The nearest **accommodation** is the *Kastély Panzió* at Veres utca 3 (☎27/11-014) in VÁCHARTYÁN, midway between Vácrátót and Vác.

Vác

The small town of **VÁC** has a worldlier past than its present sleepy atmosphere suggests. Its bishops traditionally showed a flair for self-promotion, endowing monuments and colleges like the cardinals of Esztergom. Under Turkish occupation (1544–1686) Vác assumed an oriental character, with seven mosques and a public *hammam*, while during the Reform Era it was linked to Budapest by Hungary's first railway line (the second carried on to Bratislava). In modern times, Vác became notorious for its (now defunct) prison, used to incarcerate leftists under Admiral Horthy and "counter-revolutionaries" under Communism.

Though its legacy of sights justifies a visit, it's not worth staying unless you're planning to visit Vácrátót or Zebegény as well.

The Town

Arriving by bus, train or ferry, you can walk into the centre in around ten minutes. From the railway station, head 400m along Széchenyi utca to reach Március 15 tér, passing the tourist offices on the way. Coming from the bus station, cross over Dr. Csányi László körút to get on to Széchenyi utca. Disembarking at the landing stage for ferries from Budapest, you can see the prison and triumphal arch before following Köztársaság út or the riverside promenade into the centre. Ferries from Szentendrei Island dock only two blocks from Március 15 tér.

Around Március 15 tér

The triangular square at the heart of Vác rivals Szentendre for its handsome melange of Baroque and Rococo. The latter style was developed to a fine art locally, as evinced by the gorgeous decor of the **Dominican Church**. At no. 6 stands the original Bishop's Palace, converted into Hungary's first Institute for the Deaf and Dumb in 1802. It was Bishop Kristóf Migazzi who erected the Baroque **Town Hall** across the square, its gable adorned with two prostrate females bearing the coats of arms of Hungary and Migazzi himself. This ambitious prelate was the moving force behind Vác's eighteenth-century revival, which impressed Empress Maria Theresa sufficiently to make him Archbishop of Vienna.

Aside from Migazzi's triumphal arch and Vác prison, all the sights are south of here. There's a small but lively **market** in the side street behind the Dominican Church, and an **art gallery** (Tues–Sun 10am–6pm) of local artists' work on Kaptalan utca, nearby. Heading south along Köztársaság út you'll pass a Baroque Piarist Church and Trinity Statue on Szentháromság tér, before emerging on to Konstantin tér, dominated by Vác Cathedral.

Vác Cathedral and Museum

Chiefly impressive for its gigantic Corinthian columns, Migazzi's **Cathedral** is a temple to self-esteem more than anything else. Its Neoclassical design by Isidore Canevale was considered revolutionary in the 1770s, the style not becoming generally accepted in Hungary until the following century. Migazzi himself took umbrage at one of the frescoes by Franz Anton Maulbertsch, ordering the *Meeting of Mary and Elizabeth*, above the altar, to be bricked over. It's worth looking, too, at the exquisitely embroidered chasubles and intricate gold filigree in the **treasury**.

From here you can walk along Múzeum utca to the **Vak-Bottyán Museum** (Tues–Sun 10am–noon & 1–5pm), named after the blind general of the Rákóczi War of Independence. The pre-Turkish era is reduced to a sorry collection of broken masonry, silver coins from Vác's fourteenth-century royal mint, and some lovely, though fragmented, mosaics. There are also some fine paintings of nineteenth-century markets, and unintelligible exhibits on the development of craft guilds. Múzeum utca continues round to Géza király tér, the centre of Vác in medieval times, where there's a Baroque **Franciscan Church** with magnificent pulpits, altars and organ.

Along the waterfront

For a break from churches or a pleasant stroll towards the prison, follow one of the side streets off the main squares down to the **riverside promenade** (*sétány*) that runs the length of town. On Ady Endre sétány, level with Március 15 tér, is the wharf for **ferries to Szentendrei Island**, where townsfolk go to dine at the *Pokol Csárda* (Hell's Inn). From here you can walk across the island to Tahitófalu (4km), or perhaps thumb a lift.

The northern stretch of promenade – named after Liszt – runs past the **Round Tower**, the only remnant of Vác's medieval fortifications. There are rooms for rent in the side streets past here, while beyond the dock for ferries to Budapest and Esztergom rises the forbidding hulk of Vác prison.

The Prison and Triumphal Arch

Ironically, the building that became **Vác Prison** was originally an academy for noble youths, founded by Maria Theresa. Turned into a barracks in 1784, it began its penal career a century later, achieving infamy during the Horthy era, when two Communists died of beatings after going on hunger strike to protest against maltreatment. Today, their memorial plaque is set to be joined by one honouring the victims of the Stalinist period and their mass escape in October 1956. Thrown into panic by reports from Budapest, where their colleagues were being "hunted down like animals, hung on trees, or just beaten to death by passers-by", the ÁVO guards donned civilian clothing and mounted guns on the rooftop, fomenting rumours among prisoners whose hopes had been raised by snatches of patriotic songs overheard from the streets. A glimpse of national flags with the Soviet emblem cut from the centre provided the spark: a guard was overpowered, locks were shot off, and the prisoners burst free*.

The **Triumphal Arch** flanking the prison was another venture by Migazzi and his architect Canevale, occasioned by Maria Theresa's visit in 1764. Migazzi initially planned theatrical facades to hide the town's dismal housing (perhaps inspired by Potemkin's fake villages in Russia, created around the same time), but settled for the Neoclassical arch, from which Habsburg heads grimace a stony welcome.

Practicalities

If *Dunatours* (Mon–Thurs 8am–4pm, Fri 8am–3pm, Sat 8am–noon; ☎27/10-940) at Széchenyi utca 14 is closed for renovation, *IBUSZ* (Mon–Fri 7.30am–3.30pm; summer also Sat 7.30–11am; ☎27/12-011) at no. 4 can supply **information** and book private **rooms** (②). These can also be rented directly at Liszt sétány 13 (☎27/12-683; ①) and Molnár utca 1 (①), near the Round Tower. Otherwise, there is the small *Tabán Panzió* at Dombay utca 3 (☎27/11-607; ②), or the option of staying at Váchartyán or Verőcemaros (see above and below).

Whereas the medieval traveller Nicolaus Kleeman found Vác's innkeepers "the quintessence of innkeeperish incivility", modern visitors should enjoy two

---

*One who didn't was the Englishwoman Dr Edith Bone, who came to Budapest as correspondent for the *Daily Worker* at the age of 68, and was arrested in 1949 on Rákosi's personal orders. Happily, she was released by insurgents from a prison in the capital in 1956, emerging frail but self-educated in Greek after many years of solitary confinement at Vác.

outdoor **restaurants**: the *Halászkert* at Liszt sétány 9 and the dearer *Pokol Csárda* on Szentendrei Island (closed Tues). Other places include the *Kőkapu Étterem* at Dózsa utca 5, near the triumphal arch, and, for snacks, the *Széchenyi Ételbár* on the corner of Széchenyi utca and Galcsek utca, near the railway station.

Aside from **moving on** up the east bank by boat or rail, you can catch a bus or train (5–7 daily) northwards through the Börzsöny towards Balassagyarmat, which allows for a night in Diósjenő (see p.135). Buses to other Börzsöny villages follow such roundabout routes that hitching or walking might be a quicker way of getting there.

Verőcemaros

Not content with his work in Vác, Migazzi plumped for another Baroque church and a summer mansion at **VERŐCEMAROS**, 10km further round the Bend. However, the only "sight" that's accessible is a **memorial museum** (Tues–Sun April–Oct 10am–6pm; Nov–March 9am–5pm) in the home of the ceramicist **Géza Gorka** (1894–1971) at Szamos utca 22. The settlement sprawls along the Danube, merging into **KISMAROS** (or *Verőcemaros-Felső*, as its railway halt is designated), a resort with a more youthful profile. It is here that you'll find the terminal of the *Kis-vasút*, a **miniature railway** leading up to Királyrét in the Börzsöny (see the end of this chapter). From Verőcemaros itself there are ferries to Kisoroszi on Szentendrei Island (see p.118).

Should you care to stay for the swimming, riding or fishing, both places offer **accommodation**. Verőcemaros proper has the *Orgona Tourist Hostel* on Magyarkút (☎27/50-045; ①), and the *Treff* or *Salon Panzió* at Árpád utca 67 (②). In Kismaros, the youth travel agency *Express* maintains the *Hotel Touring* (April 15–Oct 15; ④), *Express Motel* (April 15–Oct 15; ③), a **campsite** (June–Sept) and bungalow complex (May–Sept; ②), all located near the *Kis-vasút* terminal, and sharing the same phone number (☎27/50-166).

Nagymaros and the Dam

A quietly prosperous village with an air of faded grandeur (nobles lived here in the age of royal Visegrád), **NAGYMAROS** seems an unlikely focus for years of environmental protest. The cause is not Nagymaros itself, where a drunk's ejection from an *italbolt* still counts as a major disturbance, but a short way upriver, where the aborted **Dam** languishes amid the detritus of its construction (see box overleaf).

The village lies across the river from Visegrád, with a superb view of the latter's citadel, ("Visegrád has the castle, but Nagymaros has the view", locals have always boasted). From the Gothic church by the railway station, white-washed houses straggle up the hillside; and social life centres around the patisseries and leafy squares. From the station, duck under the bridge to reach the main road and head up the principal backstreet towards the hills above. One kilometre uphill, the path divides at a car park – one fork heads south to Hegyes-tető, where you can enjoy a **panoramic view of the Bend**, the other heads up **into the Börzsöny**, towards Törökmező (see below).

THE GABČIKOVO–NAGYMAROS DAM

A question mark still hangs over the **Gabčikovo-Nagymaros Hydroelectric Barrage**, a megalomaniac project dreamed up by Hungarian and Czechoslovak planners in 1978, with the collusion and capital of the Austrians, who sought cheap electricity at someone else's environmental expense. The barrage was intended to harness 200km of river, diverting it for 25km and tapping it for energy with two dams. While work at Nagymaros was abandoned in 1989, after five years' opposition by *Duna Kör* (Danube Circle), the Gabčikovo dam was almost completed by the time of the Velvet Revolution. Having invested hugely in the project, and desperate to find an alternative source of energy to the brown coal that is killing its forests, Czechoslovakia is now considering a toned-down "C Varient" to produce a quarter of the electricity originally planned. Whether this happens or not, the work has already had adverse effects, with once-perfect cropland along the upper reaches of the Danube beginning to dry up.

Private **accommodation** in Nagymaros can be booked through *Dunatours* in Visegrád, or obtained direct from rentiers at Kassák utca 2 (☎27/54-394; ②), Bajcsy-Zsilinszky utca 97, Váci út 39 and Sólyomszigeti út 64. Alternatively, you can stay among the beech woods at the *Törökmező Hostel* (☎27/50-063; ①), which is 5km by footpath (marked with blue signs) from the car park, or slightly further if you follow the Panorama út road. Beds here can be reserved through *IBUSZ*.

Zebegény and Szob

At **ZEBEGÉNY** the Danube turns south before taking the Bend, and the magnificent scenery has lured painters ever since István Szőnyi (1894–1960) first put brush to canvas here, and his **memorial house** at Bartóky út 7 (Tues–Sun March–Nov 9am–5pm; Dec–Feb 10am–6pm) began hosting an international **art school** every summer. Another sign of Zebegény's bold horizons is the **Navigation Museum** (April–Oct Tues–Sun 9am–5pm) at Szőnyi utca 9, housing the private collection of Captain Vince Farkas, who has sailed the world and amassed some nifty carved figureheads in the process. The local **Catholic Church** deserves a mention as the only one in Hungary to be built in the National Romantic style (an amalgam of Art Nouveau and folk art). Its frescoes, by Aladár Körösfői Kreisch, depict the vision of Emperor Constantine and Saint Helena finding the Holy Cross in Jerusalem.

With no **accommodation** in Zebegény, Nagymaros and Szob are the nearest options. Alternatively, you could hike up to the *Törökmező Hostel* (see above) in three to four hours, or take the **ferry** across to Pilismarót on the west bank, to stay at Dömös, Esztergom or Visegrád. Zebegény does, however, have a couple of **restaurants**: the *Mátyás Vendéglő* at Magyar utca 24 and the *Maros Vendéglő* at Kossuth tér 2.

Szob

Depots, dust and *ennui* sum up most frontier posts, and **SZOB** is no exception. As trains merely pass through, and motorists can't drive across, few tourists come here. For chance visitors, however, the **Börzsöny Museum** at Hámán utca

14 (Tues–Sun 10am–5pm) is ready with peasant costumes, carved tombstones, and a piece of the petrified primeval tree found at Ipolytarnoc and now distributed among several provincial museums. **Accommodation** boils down to camping at the *Sportcentrum* beside the ferry landing stage or staying at the agreeable *Malomkert Fogadó*, Malomkert utca 5 (☎27/70-233; ③).

Although trains cross the border **into Czechoslovakia** at Szob, you cannot board them here (or at any other point along the east bank). The nearest road crossing is 30km northeast at **PARASSAPUSZTA**, on the Ipoly River which demarcates the frontier. The neighbouring village of DRÉGELYPALÁNK is on the Vác–Diósjenő–Balassagyarmat line (trains roughly every 2hr).

Walking in the Börzsöny

The **Börzsöny Range** sees few visitors despite its scattering of hostels and forest footpaths, and the abundance of rabbits, pheasants and deer watched by circling eagles. Though the frontier zone should be avoided, it's otherwise feasible to camp rough here, but most of the following sites offer some kind of accommodation. Would-be walkers should buy Cartographia's *Börzsöny-hegység* map, which shows paths and the location of hostels (*túristáház*).

The only peak requiring climbing experience is **Mount Csóványos** (939m), the highest in the Börzsöny. Hikers usually approach it from the direction of **DIÓSJENŐ**, a sleepy mountain village that's accessible by bus or train from Vác. Unfortunately, Diósjenő's **campsite** (May–Sept; ☎ Diósjenő 10-660;) lies 1km from the village and 2km from the railway halt, and its small stock of rooms (②) can only be reserved through *Nógrád Tourist* in Salgótarján (see p.231).

An alternative route into the mountains begins at Kismaros beside the Danube (see p.133), whence narrow-gauge trains trundle every couple of hours up to **Királyrét** between 7.40am and 5.30pm. Supposedly once the hunting ground of Beatrice and Mátyás, this "Royal Meadow" is now the site of a forking path; one trail (marked in red) leads 3km to the **Magas-Tax Hostel**, the other to the "Big Cold" peak, **Nagy Hideg**. The latter has excellent views and its own **hostel**, the starting point for walks to Mount Csóványos and two villages – Nagybörzsöny and Kospallag.

Nagybörzsöny

From Nagy Hideg, a trail marked by blue squares leads westwards to **NAGYBÖRZSÖNY**, 20km from Szob; motorists can get there by turning off the Parassapuszta road beyond Ipolytölgyes. A wealthy town during the Middle Ages, Nagybörzsöny declined with the depletion of its copper, gold and iron mines, and is now a mere logging village. Visitors can see the thirteenth-century Romanesque **Church of St Stephen** and the fifteenth-century Gothic **Miners' Church**; plus an exhibition of folk costumes and gems in the **Mining Museum** (Sat & Sun 10am–5pm) at Petőfi utca 19. More enticing is the prospect of **horse-riding**, which can be arranged through the *Kastély Hotel* (☎80/64-109; ③) at Kossuth utca 10 – the only **accommodation** going.

Kospallag

The other trail from Nagy Hideg (red markings) runs south down to **KOSPALLAG**, another prosaic village, redeemed only by a **hostel** (①) with a

restaurant, and **buses** to Vác until 9pm. However, things improve beyond the Vác–Szob road junction below the village, where the path wanders through beech woods to a lovely open meadow graced with a solitary tree and the first view of the Danube. Cutting southwest across the meadow puts you back on the path to the *Törökmező Hostel*, or you can head west towards Zebegény when the path divides by the exercise camp in the woods. This leads eventually to a car park at the junction of paths to Hegyes-tető and Nagymaros.

travel details

Trains

From Budapest to Esztergom (every 40–90min; 1hr 15min); Szentendre (every 15–30min; 45min); Vác (every 30min; 45min); Vácrátót (7.20am, 9.40am, 11.35am, 2.15pm, 3.20pm, 5.10pm & 6.15pm daily; 1hr 20min).

From Esztergom to Budapest (every 40–90min; 1hr 30min); Komárom (7.45am, 12.25pm, 2.50pm & 8.30pm daily; 45min).

From Kismaros to Királyrét (7.40am, 9.45am, 12.40pm, 3.30pm & 5.30pm daily; 45min).

From Vác to Balassagyarmat (7.30am, 11.40am, 1.55pm, 2.40pm, 5.35pm, 7.35pm & 10.35pm daily; Mon–Sat also 6.35am & 4.25pm; 2hr); Budapest (every 30min; 45min); Diósjenő (7.30am, 11.40am, 1.55pm, 2.40pm, 5.35pm, 7.35pm & 10.35pm daily; Mon–Sat also 6.35am & 4.25pm; 45min).

From Vácrátót to Aszód (12.35pm, 2.55pm & 5.25pm daily; 1hr 30min); Vác and Budapest (6.15am, 7.45am, 9.30am, 11.20am, 12.20pm, 2.40pm, 3.35pm, 4.40pm, 6.40pm & 8pm daily; 15min/1hr 20min).

Buses

From Budapest *Árpád híd* terminus to Esztergom via the Bend (every 1hr 30min; 3hr) or Dorog (every 30min; 2hr); Dobogókő (1–3 daily; 2hr 30min); Vác (every 30min; 30min); Visegrád (hourly; 2hr). From *Népstadion* terminus to Vác (hourly; 30min).

From Esztergom to Budapest (every 30min; 2hr); Győr (5am & 1.40pm daily; 2hr); Komárom (hourly; 90min); Sopron (5am & 1.40pm daily; 4hr); Szentendre (hourly; 1hr 45min); Visegrád (every 20–40min; 1hr).

From Szentendre to Dobogókő (3–4 daily; 1hr 30min); Esztergom (hourly; 1hr 45min); Visegrád (hourly; 30min).

From Vác to Budapest (hourly; 30min); Diósjenő (5–7 daily; 1hr); Kospallag (every 90min; 90min); Szob (every 20–40min; 30min); Vácrátót (hourly; 45min).

From Visegrád to Budapest (hourly; 2hr); Dömös (every 20–40min; 15min); Esztergom (every 20–40min; 1hr).

Ferries

Most ferries between Budapest, Esztergom, Szentrendre, Vác and Visegrád operate only from May to September 15, though services marked below with an asterisk also run at weekends and on public holidays at other times of the year. All other ferry services operate year round.

From Budapest (Vigadó tér) to Esztergom (7am*, 7.30am* & 2pm daily; 5hr); Szentendre (7.30am*, 10pm & 2pm daily; also June–Aug 8.30am & 3pm daily; 1hr 30min); Vác (7am* daily; 2hr 45min); Visegrád (7am*, 7.30am*, 10am & 2pm daily; 3hr); Zebegény (7am*, 7.30am* & 2pm; 3hr 45min).

From Esztergom to Budapest (May to mid-Sept 8.30am, 3.30pm & 4.30pm daily; mid-Sept to April Sat & Sun 2.30pm & 3pm; 4hr); Szentendre (May to mid-Sept 8.30am, 3pm & 4.30pm daily; mid-Sept to April Sat & Sun 3pm; 2hr 45min); Vác (May to mid-Sept 3.30pm daily; mid-Sept to April Sat & Sun 2.30pm; 2hr); Visegrád (May to mid-Sept 8.30am, 3.30pm & 4.30pm daily; mid-Sept to April Sat & Sun 2.30pm & 3pm).

From Kisoroszi to Kismaros (every 30–90min 6.55am–10.40pm).

From Kismaros to Kisoroszi (every 30–90min 6.15am–10.45pm).

From Leányfalu to Pócsmegyer (every 20–60min 6am–11pm).

From Nagymaros to Visegrád (every 45–60min till 10.45pm).

From Pilismarót to Szob (hourly 6.50am–6.50pm); Zebegény (hourly 6.10am–6.10pm).

From Szob to Pilismarót (hourly 7.40am–6.40pm).

From Tahitófalu to Vác (hourly 6am–11pm).

From Vác to Budapest (May to mid-Sept 5.45pm daily; mid-Sept to April Sat & Sun 4.45pm; 1hr 45min); Tahitófalu (hourly 5.50am–11.50pm).

From Visegrád to Budapest (May to mid-Sept 9.50am, 4.50pm & 5.50pm; mid-Sept to April Sat & Sun 3.50pm & 4.20pm; 4.30pm daily; 2hr 30min); Esztergom (10.20am*, 10.35*am & 5pm daily; 1hr 45min); Kisoroszi (every 45–90min 6.25am–11.25pm); Nagymaros (every 45–60min till 10.55pm); Vác (May to mid-Sept 4.50pm daily; mid-Sept to April Sat & Sun 3.50pm; 45min); Zebegény (10.20am*, 10.35am* & 5pm daily; 45min).

CHAPTER THREE

LAKE BALATON AND THE BAKONY

F ew Magyars now would subscribe to the old romantic view of **Lake Balaton** as the "Hungarian sea" but, despite rising prices pushing out natives in favour of Austrians and Germans, it is still very much the "nation's playground". Holiday resorts line the lake's **southern shore**, almost wholly given over to the pleasures of guzzling, swimming and sunbathing. With **Siófok** as the archetype, one place here is much like another. Nature only reasserts itself at the western end of the lake, where the Zala River flows through the reeds to **Kis-Balaton**, a bird reserve. The **northern shore** is equally crowded, but waterfront development has been limited by reedbanks and cooler, deeper water, giving tourism a different slant. Historic **Tihany** and the wine-producing **Badacsony Hills** offer fine sightseeing, while anyone whose social life doesn't take off in **Keszthely** can go soak themselves in the thermal lake at **Hévíz**.

Another centre for bathing and boozing is **Lake Velence**, midway between the Balaton and Budapest. Close by is **Martonvásár**, where Beethoven concerts are held in the grounds of the Brunswick Mansion during summer. And while you're visiting the Balaton area, it would be a shame not to see the romantic-looking Belváros and "Bory Castle" at **Székesfehérvár**, or something of the hills that roll picturesquely into **the Bakony**. A wine-producing region dotted with small villages and ruined castles, the Bakony is dominated by the historic towns of **Veszprém** and **Sümeg** and exploited for its mineral wealth at **Tapolca**.

Approaches

There are several possible approaches from Budapest, and your choice depends largely on which shore of Lake Balaton you're aiming for. Most **trains** from Déli station to Siófok call at Lake Velence, Székesfehérvár, and the main settlements along the southern shore, before veering off towards Nagykanizsa at Balatonszentgyörgy. From mid-July to late August *MÁV* even runs **steam trains** to Siófok – though you have to be a real enthusiast to last the ten-hour journey (over twice as long as the regular train). Regular services to Balatonfüred are likewise routed through Székesfehérvár, and continue along the northern shore to the Badacsony Hills, where they head off towards Tapolca. All of these towns – plus Keszthely, Veszprém and Sümeg – are also accessible by **buses** from the capital's Erzsébet tér depot.

Since the M7 motorway bypasses everywhere en route to Siófok, **drivers** wishing to keep their options open should use route 70 instead, which permits you to switch to route 71 (for the northern shore) at Polgárdi or the junction outside Balatonaliga, or stay on course for the southern shore. At weekends and throughout summer, heavy traffic and long tailbacks can be expected on all major approaches.

LAKE VELENCE AND SZÉKESFEHÉRVÁR

Lake Velence resembles a diminutive version of the Balaton, with hills to the north and two contrasting shorelines. The southern shore – followed by route 70 and the railway – is awash with holiday homes and tourists, while the opposite bank is too reedy for swimming, but ideal for birds. If none of this appeals, there is always **Martonvásár**, where the Brunswick Mansion hosts a season of Beethoven concerts. Otherwise, the focus of attention is **Székesfehérvár**, Hungary's capital in the days of King Stephen – with ruins to prove it.

The telephone code for Lake Velence, Martonvásár and Székesfehérvár is ☎22

Lake Velence and Martonvásár

It's hard not to smile when told that **LAKE VELENCE** (*Velencei-tó*) is named after Venice, since anywhere less romantic would be hard to imagine. The **southern shore** is one continuous strip of holiday homes, campsites, and enclosed *strand* where you have to pay for a swim and the dubious privilege of using the changing rooms. If it wasn't for their individually named railway stations, you'd never realise that there used to be three separate settlements along the shore: **Velence**, **Gárdony** and **Agárd**. Just about the only good thing to say for them is that this an ideal place to learn **windsurfing**, since the lake is only one to two metres deep and therefore warms up to 22°C or more over summer (but often freezes solid in winter). Facilities for windsurfing and other water sports are widely available along the southern shore.

The reedy **western end** is a nesting ground for some 30,000 **birds**, which migrate here in spring; according to legend, three sisters who turned themselves into herons to escape the Turks return home every year. Permission to visit this **nature reserve** (*Madárrezervátum*) must be obtained in Budapest (XII, Költő utca 21; ☎156-2133); the entrance is 2km north of the Dinnye train halt, beyond Agárd.

The less built-up **northern shore** is accessible by ferry from Velence or Agárd to a small peninsula near the village of **Pákozd**. From the landing stage, it's a short walk up to **Mészeg Hill**, where an obelisk commemorates the first Hungarian victory in the 1848–49 revolution, and you can gaze across the lake or the Velence Hills. Geologically speaking, these are the oldest in Hungary, formed from magma and granite. Atop the 351-metre-high **Meleg Hill** are several colossal **"rocking stones"** (*ingókövek*) that sway perceptibly in the wind.

Lakeside practicalities

Wherever you get off the train, simply head for the lake – it would be hard to lose your way round here. **Information** is available from *Albatours*, Szabadság utca 24 (Mon–Fri 8am–3.30pm) in Agárd, and on the *Panorama* campsite in Velence (☎68-043), both of which can book private rooms (③–④). Many householders also let rooms directly (look for *Zimmer frei* signs), but these are just as expensive as the rest of the **accommodation** here. Places to try include:

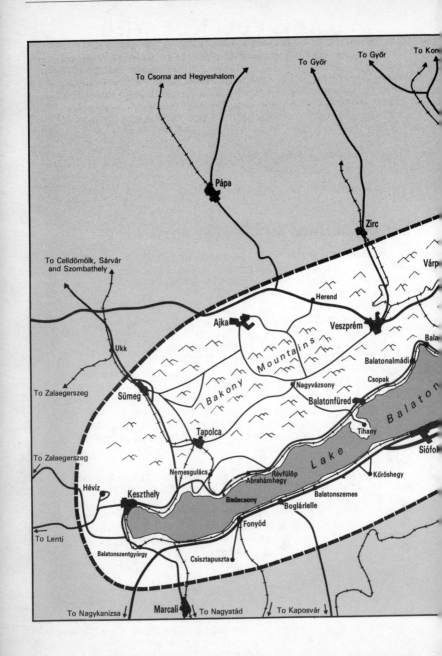

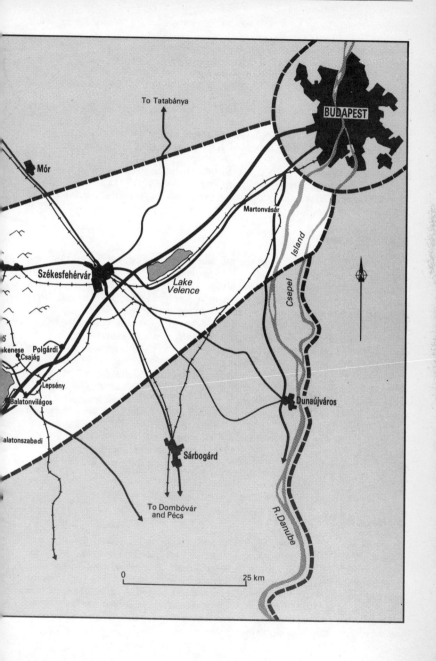

Juventus Hotel, Tópart utca 25A (☎68-159). Near the lake and Velence station, with a sauna, tennis and watersports. ⑤.

Helios Hotel, Tópart utca 34 (☎68-159). Smaller, with fewer facilities, not far away. ④–⑤.

Panorama Camping, Kemping utca. A huge site on the northeastern shore of the lake, 2km from Velence station, with watersports gear and bungalows (③) for rent. April–Oct.

Fortuna Panzió, Vörösmarty utca 53 (☎68-125). A tiny pension in Kápolnásnyek, 1km east of Velence. ④.

Touring Hotel, Tópart utca 1 (☎55-019). Another place with sports facilities, beside the lake in Agárd. May–Oct. ④–⑥.

Viking Hotel, Gallér utca 2 (☎55-287). In a similar vein, nearby, but open all year. ⑤.

Agárd Hotel, Akácfa utca (☎55-016). Next to the campsite 100m east and inland of Agárd station. ④–⑤.

Nemeskócsag Camping, Akácfa utca (☎55-016). Sandwiched between the railway tracks and the main road in Agárd; noisy and grossly overcrowded. April 15–Oct 15.

Termál Camping, Határ utca (☎55-294). By the thermal baths on the southern edge of Agárd. May–Sept.

Martonvásár

Visiting **MARTONVÁSÁR** – on the rail line roughly halfway between Budapest and Velence and just fifteen minutes from the lake – you are transported into another era. The road opposite the station leads to the neo-Gothic **Brunswick Mansion** (Tues–Sun 10am–5pm), set in a lovely 64-acre park, where **Teréz Brunswick** founded Hungary's first nursery school in 1828. Her sister **Josephine** may have been the "immortal beloved" of **Beethoven**'s love letters, and the inspiration for his *Moonlight* and *Appassionata* sonatas. Certainly the composer was a regular visitor, though others reckon that his muse was **Giulietta Guiccardi**, the "beautiful devil", whom he also met here between 1800 and 1806.

Whatever the truth, a small Beethoven **museum** exhibits manuscripts and personal belongings, and on summer evenings **performances of Beethoven's symphonies** are held on an island in the middle of the park, beneath a great bower of beech and sycamore. Armed with mosquito repellent and a couple of bottles (there's a bar-buffet), you can watch the sun set and hear the soaring music. **Tickets** are available from the Central Ticket Office in Budapest (V, Vörösmarty tér 1) or *Albatours* in Székesfehérvár. Should you miss the last train back to the capital (around 11.30pm on Sat), **accommodation** is available at the *Macska Panzió*, Szabadság út 21 (☎79-127; ④).

Székesfehérvár

Reputedly the site where Árpád pitched camp and founded his dynasty, **SZÉKESFEHÉRVÁR** was probably the earliest Hungarian town. Its name (pronounced "SAIKesh-fehair-var") comes from the white castle (*fehérvár*) founded by Prince Géza, whose son Stephen made it his royal seat (*szék*). As the centre of his efforts to civilise the Magyars, it was named in Latin *Alba Civitas* or *Alba Regia*. Since this medieval town was utterly destroyed by the Turks, Székesfehérvár as it exists today owes its Belváros to the Habsburgs, and its high-rise suburbs to the final German counter-attack in 1945, which levelled everywhere else.

Arriving at the railway station, 1km south of the centre, catch any bus heading up Prahószka út – which subsequently becomes Vár körút – and get off near the *Hotel Alba Regia*. The intercity bus station on Piac tér is only a few minutes' walk from the Belváros.

The Town

Székesfehérvár's **Belváros** occupies approximately the same area as the great castle once did, as evinced by a section of the medieval walls alongside the **Romkert** (April–Oct Tues–Sun 9am–6pm). Amongst the stonework in this "Garden of Ruins" is a richly carved Roman sarcophagus, found in 1803 and believed to hold the remains of King Stephen. Directly across the road are the excavated **foundations of the cathedral** where Stephen was buried – it was designed for him by Italian architects, in an attempt to rival Saint Mark's in Venice. Thirty-eight Hungarian kings were crowned here, hence its name of the Coronation Church. After the town fell to the Turks in 1543, the cathedral was plundered of its gold and jewels, and blown up.

Szabadság tér recalls Székesfehérvár's revival under Maria Theresa, with its Baroque town hall, Franciscan church and Zopf-style **Bishop's Palace**, built with stones from the ruined cathedral by Bishop Milassin, whose coat of arms appears on the gable. Március 15. utca, running off to the north, is so perfectly preserved that you expect to see crinolined ladies emerging from the **Fekete Sas Pharmacy Museum** at no. 9 (Tues–Sun 10am–6pm). This eighteenth-century apothecary, the *Black Eagle*, was open right up to 1971: today you can still see the original fittings and fixtures, along with displays on traditional remedies. Like the Baroque Church of Saint John across the street, it was founded by the Jesuits.

On Bartok tér, around the back of the church, the **Csók Museum** (Tues–Fri 10am–7pm, Sat & Sun 10am–6pm) displays paintings by István Csók (1865–1961). Initially associated with the Nagybánya School, he fell under the influence of Vuillard and Bonnard in Paris and returned to Hungary to practice *plein air* painting. More interesting, though, is the **István Király Museum** on Ország Zászló tér (Tues–Sun 10am–6pm). Its archaeological finds and domestic treasures are laid out to form a vivid exhibition on local history; especially notable are the eastern Celtic pottery and nineteenth-century court dress.

More historic architecture clusters south of Szabadság tér. Directly behind the town hall is the only remainder of medieval Székesfehérvár, a modest **Chapel of Saint Anna** that the Turks spared for use as a mosque – notice the Koranic inscriptions and arabesque murals. Across the way stands **Saint Stephen's Cathedral**, a much rebuilt edifice that is now essentially Baroque although it dates back originally to the thirteenth century. By continuing south along Arany utca, you'll come to the fanciful Zopf-style **Budenz House** (no. 12) and a **Carmelite Church** with Rococo carvings and frescoes by the Austrian painter Maulbertsch.

Bory's Folly

The town's best sight, however, is out in the eastern suburbs, beyond the microchip and TV factories. Accessible by #26 bus from Piac tér to Máriavölgy utca, **Bory's Castle** (*Bory Vár*; Mon–Fri 9am–5pm, Sat & Sun 10am–noon & 3–5pm) is a bizarre product of matrimonial obsession; an eclectic structure combining features of Scottish, Romanesque and Gothic architecture, built of reinforced concrete, ceramics and stone by a group of students directed by the artist Jenő Bory (1879–1959). The rooms and courtyards are filled with statues and paintings of Ilona Komocsin, his wife and model, whose memory the castle enshrines. Although the overall effect of Ilona's multiple images is slightly morbid, this is a marvellous place to wander around.

Practicalities

Information is available from *Albatours*, Városház tér 1 (Mon–Fri 8am–4.30pm, Sat 8am–1pm; ☎12-494) or *IBUSZ*, Ady utca 2 (☎11-510). Ask *Albatours* about plays at the **Vörösmarty Theatre** near the *Hotel Magyar Király*, or recitals at the **Bartók Concert Hall**. The main **post office** is on the corner of Kossuth utca and Petőfi utca; the **police** are at Dózsa tér 12.

Accommodation

Albatours, *IBUSZ* and *Cooptourist*, Rákóczi utca 3 (☎14-391), can book private **rooms** (②–③) – though not for one night only. *Express*, Rákóczi utca 4, may be able to arrange beds in college dorms (①) over summer. The other options are:

Hotel Alba Regia, Rákóczi utca 1 (☎13-484). A central, three-star Seventies block. Breakfast included. ⑤.

Magyar Király Hotel, Március 15. utca 10 (☎11-262). Built in the 1870s, its grand facade hides ordinary rooms with baths. Breakfast included. ⑤.

Arév Hotel, József utca 42 (☎14-441). This high-rise workers' hostel 400m east of the centre also takes tourists. Rooms with sinks and shared bathrooms. ②.

Törökudvar Tourist Hostel, Jókai utca 2 (☎24-975). Beds in rooms sleeping 8–12. Booking advisable. (①).

Két Góbé Panzió, Gugásvölgyi út 2 (☎27-857). A small pension just off the outer ring road, 2km from the centre. ③.

Renzó Panzió, Krasznai utca 46 (☎10-624). Another pension, in the Öreg-hegy district off the Budapest highway. ③.

Eating and drinking

The *Ósfehérvár Étterem*, opposite the Romkert, serves hearty meals at moderate prices, while the *Korzó Söröző*, at the junction of Március 15. utca, is good for breakfast and offers a couple of vegetarian dishes. Other **restaurants** include the *Fehérvár*, Sallai utca 25; the *Kis Kulacs* on the corner of Vár körút and Budapesti út; and the dining room of the *Hotel Magyar Király*. You can go **drinking** at the *Korzó Söröző*, which has Czech beer, or sample Badacsony wines at the *Ezerjó* on Ország Zászló tér.

On from Székesfehérvár

Moving on from Székesfehérvár you have a choice of destinations and routes. Aside from international trains to Vienna or Leipzig, and long-haul buses to Szekszárd in Transdanubia and Kecskemét or Szeged on the Great Plain, there are basically three options.

North through the Vértes

Komárom-bound trains and buses heading for Győr (both covered in Chapter Four) take a scenic route **through the Vértes Hills**. Most trains call at **BODAJK**, where the *Galyavölgye Hostel* at Petőfi utca 93 has rooms (②), bookable through *Albatours* in Székesfehérvár; and serves as a base for hikes to **CSÓKAKŐ**, overlooked by a **ruined castle** (6km further on). Buses and trains also usually stop at **MÓR**, another starting point for **walks**, and the centre of a wine-producing region. You can enjoy a tipple in the **wine museum** opposite the run-down *Vértes Tourist Hostel*, Ezerjó utca 2 (②).

West towards Veszprém

Travelling **towards Veszprém** in the Bakony by bus or train (a convenient bus leaves Székesfehérvár daily at 3pm, heading for Zalaegerszeg via Veszprém, Balatonfüred, Badacsony and Hévíz), **VÁRPALOTA** appears through a haze of lignite smoke. Even though emissions from its power plant and aluminium foundry are quietly falling as acid rain upon the Bakony's forests, ecological concerns are ignored in the **Museum of the Chemical Industry** (April–Oct Tues–Sun 11am–5pm), and you're unlikely to be tempted to stop by this or the **Roman weir** constructed of gigantic stones, whose remains stretch for almost 1km near the suburban swimming resort of **PÉTFÜRDŐ**. Motorists, however, might consider a stopover at **ÖSKÜ**, 9km further west, which boasts an extraordinary **circular chapel** with a mushroom-shaped cupola, dating from the eleventh century.

Towards the Balaton

Heading for the southern shore of Lake Balaton, people with transport (or willing to get off at Szabadbattyán train station and hope for a local bus) can make a detour to **TÁC**, 5km off route 70, where signs point towards the **Roman ruins of Gorsium**. This began life as a military camp at the junction of two roads, but by the beginning of the second century had become the religious centre of Lower Pannonia. The site (daily 8am–dusk) covers two square kilometres, and includes the walls of a palace, a temple, Forum and houses. Carved stonework and other finds are displayed in a **museum** (Tues–Sun May–Oct 9am–6pm; Nov–April 10am–5pm).

LAKE BALATON

With 197km of shoreline to exploit, **Lake Balaton** is a huge money-spinner, generating over a third of Hungary's income from tourism. Since 1987, massive sums have been invested to create five new harbours and belatedly clean up the lake's water and beaches. In truth, little of the shoreline has escaped being embanked in concrete and turned into *strand* (the generic term for any bathing place but rarely what you'd call a beach), and holiday homes have virtually filled the spaces between once separate settlements. The result isn't to everyone's taste, but it certainly tries hard to be. While the southern shore is unabashedly hedonistic, the northern shore can boast of historic monuments, cultural events and scenic landscapes. Tennis, horse-riding and water sports are easily arranged, and most resorts offer some kind of nightlife.

The lake itself is the largest in Europe (unless you count Lake Baikal in Siberia), stretching for almost 80km and varying in width from 14km to 1.5km (at the point where it's almost cut in two by the Tihany peninsula). With an average depth of only three metres, it warms up quickly and maintains a pleasant temperature from May to October, but often freezes over in winter, when the ice can grow as thick as 25cm, and horse-drawn carts can drive across.

Though its **history** is hardly writ large, the region was first settled in the Iron Age, and has been a wine-growing centre since Roman times. During the sixteenth century, it formed the front line between Turkish and Habsburg-ruled Hungary, with an Ottoman fleet based at Siófok and an Austrian one at Balatonfüred. Spas and villas appeared from 1765 onwards, but catered largely to the wealthy until the Communists began promoting holidays for the masses after World War II. During the Sixties, footloose youths started flocking to the *Bacsi* (Balaton's familiar nickname), while the Seventies and Eighties witnessed a boom in private holiday homes and room-letting, fuelled by an influx of tourists from Germany and Austria.

Accommodation around the Balaton

The Balaton has more tourist **accommodation** than anywhere else in Hungary, but there can still be a shortage during the summer. Especially at the main resorts and scenic spots (Siófok, Balatonfüred, Tihany, Badacsony and Keszthely), you'll be lucky to find a room in any of the cheaper **hotels** or **pensions**. Unless you have a **reservation**, your best option is a **private room** from one of the **tourist agencies** – foremost amongst which are *Siótour* (on the southern shore) and *Balatontourist* (on the north). However, it's often cheaper to

STORM WARNINGS

From May to September the Balaton is prone to occasional **storms**. Storm **warnings** are given by flashing lights: 30 flashes per minute indicates winds of 40–60km per hour; 60 flashes per minute winds over 60km per hour. Windsurfers or sailors should head for land at once.

rent directly from householders: the signs to look for are *Zimmer frei* or *Szoba kiádo*. Balaton's **campsites** are amongst the dearest in Hungary: most of the large ones operate from May to September, whilst auxiliary sites open to handle the overfill in many resorts from June to August.

Transport

Though all the main resorts are accessible by rail from Budapest or Székesfehérvár, it's worth knowing that the so-called *Balaton Express* is actually a slow train, stopping everywhere as it encircles the lake. Such **trains** are the easiest way of travelling along the southern shore, and between Balatonalmádi and Badacsony on the opposite bank, whereas **buses** are better for the journeys between Balatonfüred and Tihany, Badacsony and Keszthely, and Veszprém and Siófok.

From mid-April to late September or mid-October, fairly regular **passenger ferries** zigzag from Siófok to Balatonfüred on the other bank, then west to Tihany-rév and back across the lake to Balatonföldvár. During July and August, another service runs the length of the lake from Balatonkenese to Keszthely (5hr), making regular stops on both banks en route. Additionally, **car ferries** ply between Tihany-rév and Szántódrév (April–Nov), Révfülop and Balatonboglár, and Badacsony and Fonyód (both mid-April to mid-Oct). See "Travel Details" at the end of this chapter for more information.

The southern shore from Siófok to the Kis-Balaton

Approaching **the southern shore** from the direction of Budapest by train, you'll catch your first glimpse of the Balaton at **BALATONVILÁGOS**. As one of the lushest, least commercialised resorts, built on wooded cliffs and along the shore, it was formerly reserved for Party officials, while boats – even those seeking refuge from storms – were forbidden to dock in the harbour. Unlike other resorts, Balatonvilágos has something that could properly be called a beach. At time of writing it is being refurbished as an upmarket resort, but private **rooms** (②–③) can be arranged at Csok sétány 36 (☎84/30-027), and the *Volán Hotel*, Zrínyi utca 135 (☎84/30-022; ④) is ready for business. If you can find a room, it's a very pleasant place to stay.

Siófok

SIÓFOK is the largest port on the southern shore: a plebeian, open-armed place that was the first resort to introduce video-discos in the Eighties, and strip bars in more recent years. Its vitality and tackiness might appeal for a while, but you're unlikely to want to stay for long – and the accommodation situation is dire. A string of high-rise hotels – their communal beach always crammed with bodies – typifies the modern resort, belying its pre-war reputation as a centre of quiet elegance. A token reminder of this past can be found in the **Petőfi sétány**, a leafy promenade lined with sedate villas that terminates by a rose garden in **Jókai Park**.

You can trace some of the history of Siófok and the lake at the **Beszédes József Museum** (Tues–Sun 9am–1pm & 2–6pm) at Sió út 2 by the Sió canal, just south of the obvious landmark of the meteorological tower on Szabadság tér. Among the items covered are the first canal and locks – initiated by Emperor Galerius in 292 AD; the Turkish occupation, when an Ottoman fleet of 10,000 men was stationed in Siófok; and an assortment of old boats. As you can see from some of the vessels exhibited, crossing the lake must have been a hazardous business before steam boats were introduced by Count Széchenyi in the 1840s.

Practicalities

The bus and railway **stations** are a couple of blocks apart, on either side of **Fő utca**, the town's main axis. Ferries **dock** to the west of the park, at the mouth of the Sió canal. *Siótour*, Szabadság tér 6 (summer Mon–Sat 8am–8pm, Sun 9am–noon & 3–6pm; winter Mon–Fri 8am–4.30pm, Sat 8am–noon; ☎10-900), and *IBUSZ*, Fő utca 174, are the main sources of **information** – easily located by heading for the meteorological tower – but they can get overwhelmed in summer. If the queues are horrendous and you just want to book a room, try *MÁV Tours* in the railway station, *Cooptourist* at Fő utca 148 (☎10-279), or *Safeta Tours*, Fő utca 216.

ACCOMMODATION

During summer, you may find it impossible to get a **private room** (②–③) without trying several agencies, and even then you might have to settle for one in a distant suburb. Solo travellers or people wishing to stay less than three nights are likely to be disappointed. The alternatives are to reserve ahead (or hope for a vacancy) at a **pension**; pay through the nose at a lakeside **hotel**; or resign yourself to a **campsite** far from the centre. A selection of each follows – the first five can be reserved through *Pannonia Tourist* (VIII, Rákóczi út 9; ☎138-4225) in Budapest:

Hotel Napfény, Mártírok útja 8 (☎11-408). A nondescript Seventies low-rise between the park and the promenade. Summer rates include half-board; closed over winter. ⑤–⑥.

Hotel Balaton, Petőfi sétány 9 (☎10-655). A bit smarter and further along the promenade, also with half-board in summer; closed winter. ⑥.

Hotel Lídó, Petőfi sétány 11 (☎10-633). Another Seventies low-rise, next door to the *Balaton* and with similar arrangements. ⑥.

Hotel Hungária, Petőfi sétány 13 (☎10-677). Another modern place, even dearer. ⑥.

Hotel Európa, Petőfi sétány 15 (☎13-4111). As above. ⑥–⑦.

Magistral Hotel, Beszédes sétány 72 (☎12-544). On Aranypart *strand*, 200m east of the above. ④–⑤.

Diana Panzió, Szent László utca 41 (☎13-360). A couple of blocks inland from the *Magistral*, with only 15 beds. ②–③.

Oázis Panzió, Szigliget utca 5 (☎13-650). Single, double and triple rooms one block in from the lake, 500m west of the canal. ③–④.

Ezüsztpart Camping, November 7 tér. Fairly large, shadeless site, 4km west of the centre (bus #1 from the Baross Bridge).

Aranypart Camping, directly on the waterfront, 5km east of the centre, where Siófok merges into Balatonszabadi. No shade, but a great waterchute. Mid-May to mid-Aug.

Activities and nightlife

Although the stretch of waterfront in the centre consists of paying **beaches** (8am–7pm daily), there are free *strand* 1km out at and Aranypart and Ezüsztpart, to the east and west respectively. On most of the beaches and at many campsites you can rent **windsurfing** boards and small **sailing** boats. *Siótour* can arrange **horse-riding** and various **excursions** and **pleasure cruises**. The latter should not be confused with cruises on the *Love Boat*, a sex emporium moored on the canal, which together with the *Intim Kiss Kiss*, *Hawaii Bar* and *Tengerszem Disco*, leads the field in sleazy **nightlife**.

Between Siófok and Fonyód

Blink as you pass through **ZAMÁRDI**, the next settlement, and you'll miss it – which isn't a great shame. Red signs lead from the station to **Szamárkő** (Donkey Rock), thought by archaeologists to have been a sacrificial site of the ancient Magyars, and claimed by some Christians to bear the hoof-print of Christ's donkey. Nearer to the main street is a **Tájház** displaying peasant pottery, tiled ovens and old agricultural equipment. Otherwise Zamárdi offers the standard beach'n'bars set-up. *Auto-camping I* (mid-May to mid-Sept) and *II* (June–Aug) are both on the shore road, the *Touring Hotel* is at Petőfi utca 146 (☎84/31-008; ④–⑤) and *Siótour* is at Kossuth utca 12.

Neighbouring **SZÁNTÓD** has the expensive *Rév Camping* (April–Aug; ☎84/31-159) and *Touring Hotel* (☎84/31-096; ⑤–⑥), sited near the docks for **car ferries** to Tihany on the northern shore. Further inland by the main road, a collection of eighteenth- and nineteenth-century farm buildings, known as the **Szántódpuszta**, houses **exhibitions** of crafts and local history, a blacksmiths, aquarium, and two *csárdas* (summer daily 9am–5pm; winter Tues–Sat 8am–4.30pm, Sun 8am–noon).

BALATONFÖLDVÁR is in a similar vein but on a larger scale. Swimming began here at the turn of the century, and now thousands come to amble from snack bar to snack bar through carefully laid out parks and holiday complexes. The cheapest places **to stay** are the pleasant *Magyar Tenger* campsite (☎84/40-240) down by the *Hotel Neptun* (☎84/76-038; ⑥); and the *Hotel Juventus* (☎84/40-379; ④) and bungalows (May–Sept; ☎84/40-371; ②–③) on József utca – both owned by *Express*. **KŐRÖSHEGY**, 3km inland, boasts a fifteenth-century **church** where **chamber-music concerts** are held on summer evenings. If you're in the mood for **walking**, the villages further south are pretty, and the hills beyond resound with the choruses of mating deer.

Balatonszárszó and Balatonszemes

The boundary of **BALATONSZÁRSZÓ** is marked by a cemetery containing the **grave of Attila József**, the tragic proletarian poet (see p.281). Dismissed by his literary peers and rejected by his lover and the Communist Party, he threw himself beneath a local freight train on December 3, 1937. Every year, a few desperate souls emulate his suicide. Attila spent his last days in a pension that's now a **memorial museum** (Tues–Sun April–Oct 10am–6pm; Nov–March 10am–2pm). You'll find it at József utca 7, 100m from *Tura Camping*, by the railway tracks (mid-June to Aug). There is a *Tourist Hostel* at Fő utca 37 (☎84/40-492; ①).

BALATONSZEMES, 5km west, has an old coaching inn converted into a **Postal Museum** (June–Sept Tues–Sun 10am–6pm), with antique stage coaches in the courtyard. Besides rooms in the *Lídó Fogadó*, Ady utca 53 (May–Sept; ☎84/45-112; ②), there are several **campsites**: *Lídó Camping*, Ady utca 8 (April–Sept; ☎84/45-112); *Hullám Camping*, Kaza utca (☎84/45-116); and the *Bagódomb* site (July–Aug; ☎84/45-117), uphill towards the **ruined Bagolyvár Castle**.

Boglárlelle

BOGLÁRLELLE consists of two settlements that were merged during the Kádár era but intend to separate again. In BALATONLELLE, nearer Balatonszemes, a former mansion at Kossuth utca 2 hosts performances of **folk-dancing** in July and August. BALATONBOGLÁR is known for its **wine harvest festival** (*Boglári Szürét*) from August 18 to 20, and **exhibitions** by artists in the two chapels atop Cemetery Hill (*Temetődomb*), further inland. On neighbouring Castle Hill, a spherical **lookout tower** commands a sweeping view from Keszthely to Tihany.

There are *Siótour* **information** offices at Dózsa György utca 1 in Boglár (mid-May to mid-Sept daily 8am–noon & 3–7pm; otherwise Mon–Fri 8am–4.30pm, Sat 8am–noon), and Szent István utca 1 in Lelle (same hours; ☎84/51-086). Both can book private **rooms** (②–③), and the Boglár branch handles college beds (①) over summer. Boglár also features *Sellő Camping* (June–Sept; ☎85/50-800) near the landing stage, and more **bungalows** at the *Guiseppe Hotel*, Köztársaság út 36–38 (June–Sept; ☎85/50-074). Lelle has three bungalow complexes: *Hullám*, Köztársaság utca 14 (mid-May to mid-Sept; ☎84/50-440), *Liget*, Kikötősétány 3 (same dates; ☎84/50-687) and Hunyadi utca 32 (open all year; ☎84/51-118). They all charge about the same (②–③).

The *Albatross Étterem* on the main road between Lelle and Boglár is a good place to **eat**, while draught Holsten can be quaffed at the *Zöld Lugas* on Honvéd utca in Lelle.

Fonyód, Nagyberek and the Kis-Balaton

FONYÓD grew up between the Sipos and Sándor hills and subsequently spread itself along the lakeside; the symmetry of its setting is best appreciated from the far shore. A built-up *strand* and bleak modern architecture make this an unlikely setting for the grand passion that inspired Fonyód's **"Crypt Villa"**. Raised above a red marble crypt with room for two, this was built by a grieving widower who lived there in seclusion for many years, waiting to join his wife below, and is now undergoing restoration as a "sight" in a place otherwise bereft of curiosities. Most people, however, come here only for the **ferries to Badacsony** on the northern shore.

Should you need **information**, *Siótour* (summer daily 8am–noon & 2–7pm; otherwise Mon–Fri 8am–4.30pm; ☎85/61-816) are in the station, and *IBUSZ* (summer Mon–Sat 8am–6pm, Sun 9am–noon; winter Mon–Fri 8am–4pm; ☎85/61-816) at Szent István utca 4. During summer, they might be able to find beds (①) in a local *kollégium*. Otherwise, **accommodation** boils down to private rooms (through the same agencies; ②–③), camping or a bungalow (②–③) at the

Napsugár complex Komjáth utca 5 in Fonyód-Bélatelep,(☎84/61-211) 2km east of the centre; or the *Korona Panzió*, Szent István utca 3 (☎85/61-608; ⑤).

Nagyberek and Cisztapuszta

Behind the lakeside sprawl of Balatonfenyves and Balatonmáriafürdő (see below) lies an extensive swampland that was partially drained in the Sixties, under the auspices of the **NAGYBEREK** state farm. This produced fewer benefits than expected and spoiled a rich breeding ground for fish, so the emphasis has now switched to conservation. The **primal swamp of Fehérvíz** (*Fehérvízi őslap*) is a nesting ground for little and white egrets, spoonbills, purple and night herons and other **birdlife**. The area can be visited on a **narrow-gauge railway** running from Balatonfenyves to Csisztapuszta. Trains run every day except Monday – three times a day over winter and every couple of hours during summer, when there's a *nosztálgia* **steam train** in the morning. At **CSISZTAPUSZTA**, where drilling for oil unexpectedly yielded warm springs instead of "black gold", you can wallow in the **baths** or go **horse riding** in the surrounding countryside (*Siótour* has details).

From Balatonkeresztúr to the Kis-Balaton

The final stretch of the southern shore is partially banked by reeds and very shallow. Whole tribes of swimmers decamp to rafts anchored offshore, armed with crates of beer and piles of *lángos*. **BALATONMÁRIAFÜRDŐ** has private **rooms** (②)– look for the signs; a **hostel** (☎84/46-383; ①–②) and a basic **campsite**; plus **ferries to Balatongyörok** on the northern shore.

Consider a brief stopover at **BALATONKERESZTÚR** to see the **Baroque church** at the main crossroads, entirely decorated with gorgeous frescoes in the style of Maulbertsch. These include portraits of the Festetics family, who owned most of the land around Keszthely. Count Kristóf appears at the rear of the church and to the left of the altar, accompanied by his wife Judit Szegedi. A former Festetics mansion at Ady utca 26 now serves as a **hostel** (☎85/76-779; mid-May to late Aug; ①–②); beds can be booked through *Siótour*.

BALATONSZENTGYÖRGY, several kilometres inland, has nothing to recommend it but the *Csillagvár* restaurant, Berzsenyi utca 50–58 (daily 7am–10pm); and **buses** to Keszthely and **trains** to Nagykanizsa in southern Transdanubia. Lakeside **BALATONBERÉNY**, however, features the only **nudist beach** on the southern shore, the agreeable *Kócsag* **campsite** (☎85/77-154; June–Aug) and two agencies letting **rooms** (②–③): *Halló Ungarn*, Botond utca 2 (☎84/77-408; open year round), and *Fortuna Kft*, Kossuth utca 14 (☎84/77-163; June & July).

Kis-Balaton

At the far end of the lake, reeds obscure the mouth of the River Zala, and stretch for miles upstream to the **Kis-Balaton** (Little Balaton). This lake once covered forty square kilometres, but was half-drained in the Fifties to provide irrigation for new cropland, while the dumping of pollutants into the Zala nearly killed it during the Eighties. Its regeneration is currently top priority for the Office of Environmental Protection, which has declared it a **nature reserve** for over eighty breeds of **bird**, including spoonbills, egrets and cormorants. Visits require permission from the *National Office for Nature Conservation* in Budapest (V, Arany utca 25; ☎132-7371). KESZTHELY, at the western end of Lake Balaton, is covered on p.160.

The northern shore to Balatonfüred

To reach Lake Balaton's **northern shore** by road from Budapest, turn off route 70 just outside Balatonaliga and follow the shoreline round through **BALATONKARATTYA**, distinguished only by the dead trunk of the *Rákóczi fa* – a tree where the freedom fighter is said to have tied his horse – and *FKK Piroska Camping*, a **nudist campsite** (☎80/81-084; May–Sept). Neighbouring **BALATONKENESE** features a **Baroque church** and **peasant houses** along Bajcsy-Zsilinszky, Kossuth and Fő utca; while above the settlement are **caves** dug into the clay banks by refugees from the Turks, which continued to be inhabited until the end of the last century.

Balatonalmádi, Alsóors and Csopak

Beyond the smelly nitro-chemicals plant that disfigures Balatonfűző, the main road approaches the first town on the northern shore, **BALATONALMÁDI**, a resort since 1877. Now modern looking, only the medieval **Chapel of Saint Job** – originally part of Buda Castle but transplanted here towards the end of the nineteenth century – built into its Catholic church (decorated with mosaics by Károly Lotz) engenders any historical interest.

Should the paying *strand* induce you to stay, **accommodation** ranges from the *Hotel Auróra*, Bajcsy-Zsilinszky utca 14 (☎80/38-810; ⑥), and *Tulipán Hotel*, Városház tér 1 (☎80/38-317; ⑤–⑥), to rooms from *Balatontourist*, Petőfi utca 11 (☎80/38-707; ②–③), and two campsites. *Yacht Camping* (mid-May to mid-Sept; ☎80/38-906) by the lake rents out boats and bungalows (②); *Kristóf Camping* (mid-April to mid-Oct; ☎80/38-902) is situated inland from the railway station.

Ferries and trains continue around to **ALSÓORS**, formerly a mining village where the rock was used to make millstones. Although that's no reason to linger here, there's an odd remnant of the Ottoman occupation at Petőfi köz 7: a **Gothic manor house** once inhabited by the local Turkish tax collector, distinguished by a turban-topped chimney (a sign of wealth in the days when smoke left most houses through a hole in the roof). **FELSŐÖRS**, 1km inland, has a **Baroque church** built from purple-red sandstone, whose tower is carved with the "Knots of Hercules", ancient ornamental reliefs designed to ward off demons.

A campsite, the *Pelikán Hotel* (☎86/47-149; ⑥) and the *Szivárvány Panzió* (Szegfű utca 13; mid-April to mid-Sept; ☎86/47-124; ②) notwithstanding, you're unlikely to want to stay at Alsóors. Neighbouring **CSOPAK** – with a reputation for its *Olaszrizling* and *Furmint* **wines** – is marginally more attractive, with bungalows for rent on Sport utca (May–Sept; ☎86/46-035); the *Forrás Fogadó* at Füredi út 99 (☎86/46-317; ②); and the flashier *Hotel Forrás* at Forrás út 5 (mid-March to Dec; ☎86/46-3111; ⑤). Otherwise, there's nothing to stop you from pushing on to Balatonfüred.

Balatonfüred

Seventeenth-century chronicles tell of pilgrims descending on **BALATONFÜRED** to "camp in scattered tents" and benefit from the mineral springs. Nowadays some 30,000 people come every year for treatment, mingling with hordes of tourists to make this one of the busiest and liveliest of the Balaton resorts. **Arriving** at the bus or railway station, northwest of the centre, walk to Jókai utca and down to the waterfront (15min), or catch bus #1, which takes a roundabout route to the embankment before heading west along Széchenyi út. Ferries dock near the start of the Tagore sétány promenade, named after the Bengali poet who came here in 1926 and planted a tree in gratitude for his cure. Other celebrities followed his example – the origin of the memorial grove which opens on to the main square.

The sights

Gyógy tér (Health Square) is aptly named. Its columned, pagoda-like **Kossuth Well** gushes carbonated water, while other springs feed the trade union sanatorium and cardiac hospital – whose **mineral baths** are reserved for patients – which flank the northern and eastern sides of the square. Excavated villas suggest that the Romans were the first to exploit the springs, using the waters to treat stomach ailments and, when mixed with goats' milk whey, as a cure for lung diseases.

Across the square stands the eighteenth-century **Horváth House**, one of the first inns in a land where inn-keeping developed late. Magyars tended to consider such work beneath them: Petőfi complained that his landlord wouldn't utter a word of welcome until he had been paid, and served food "as if by the special grace of God"; another traveller reported that his host was "capable of giving his guests a good hammering or throwing them out" on impulse. The inn was patronised by writers and politicians during the Reform era, and is now a sanatorium for uranium miners – it has recently started taking tourists.

Beyond this lies Blaha Lujza utca, named after the "Nation's Nightingale", Lujza Blaha (1850–1926), who spent her summers in a villa at no. 2, and had her tea at the *Kedves Cukrászda* across the road. Opposite the **Round Church**, at the junction with Jókai utca, stands the **Jókai Memorial House** (April–Oct Tues–Sun 9am–6pm). The novelist Jókai came to Balatonfüred at the age of 37, half-expecting to die from a serious lung infection; built this villa so that he could return each year, and lived to the ripe old age of 84.

Heading northeast, Jókai utca becomes Ady utca once it crosses the railway tracks; an ironic juxtaposition of names, since the poet Ady died of syphilis at the age of 42. Bus #1, #2 or #3 can drop you at the far end, in the original centre of town, where old houses in the traditional local style line Siske and Vázsonyi utca, and there's a touch of village atmosphere about the **market** off Arácsi út. During summer there may be **concerts** in the Calvinist church.

Information and accommodation

Balatontourist, Blaha Lujza utca 5 (summer Mon–Sat 8.30am–6.30pm, Sun 8.30am–noon; winter Mon–Fri 8.30am–4.30pm, Sat 8.30am–noon; ☎86/42-823), is the best source of **information** and also the best place to book **private rooms** (①–②), the cheapest of which are in the old town. Rooms (②–③) are also available from *IBUSZ*, Petőfi utca 4A (☎86/42-251), a few blocks from the station; *Volántourist*, Petőfi utca 49 (☎86/42-259); and *Cooptourist*, Jókai utca 23 (☎86/42-677). Other options include:

Horváth House, Gyógy tér. Quadruple rooms in this historic building are sometimes rented out to tourists. ⑤.

Korona Panzió, Vörösmarty utca 4 (☎86/43-278). A decent pension next to *IBUSZ*, open all year. ②–③.

Ring Panzió, Vörösmarty utca 7. Smaller place across the road, likewise featuring clean rooms and shared baths, with breakfast included. ②–③.

Hotel Aranycsillag, Zsigmond utca (☎86/43-466). A grand old place that's seen better days, off Petőfi utca, a few blocks north of *IBUSZ*. Rooms with shared showers; breakfast included. ③.

Hotel Blaha Lujza, Blaha Lujza utca 4 (☎86/42-603). Opposite *Balatontourist*, off Gyógy tér. Closed Jan & Feb. ②–③.

Hotel Uni, Széchenyi utca 10 (☎86/42-239). On the main street 1km west of the centre, with tennis courts, boat hire and private *strand*. ④–⑤.

Hotel Marina, Széchenyi utca 26 (☎86/43-644). Classier and nearer the waterfront, with half-board over summer. April–Sept. ⑤–⑥.

FICC Rally Camping, Széchenyi utca 24 (☎86/43-823). A huge site with bungalows (②–③), tennis and watersports, beyond the *Hotel Marina* (bus #1 or #2). Mid-April to mid-Oct.

Activities

Balatontourist has details of **horse-riding** in the Koloska Valley outside town, where there is a riding school. You can hire **bicycles** outside the big hotels and campsite (300Ft per hour, 700Ft for three hours, plus 1000Ft deposit), and pedal-loes and **windsurfing** boards at every *strand*. The *Gagarin*, moored alongside a small pier, hires out **yachts** (9am–8pm; closed Thurs) for 300Ft an hour, plus a fee for the skipper if you haven't got a licence. The only **waterskiing** on Lake Balaton is practised at *FICC Rally Camping*, using an electric-powered towing cable.

There are paying **beaches** (daily 8am–6pm; July–Aug till 7pm) either side of the harbour; the one by the *Hotel Marina* is best for swimming (though not for kids, as it drops away very quickly). On the eastern edge of town is a free *strand* where you can bathe at night – though this too may be turned into a paying beach soon.

Eating, drinking and moving on

The *Halászkert* on Széchenyi tér and the *Blaha Lujza* on the street of the same name are the best value **restaurants** downtown, but you can get a better deal at the *Nimrod Vendéglő* on Ady utca, just across the tracks. Opposite the latter is a fabulous wine cellar – a better place for **drinking** than the *Borozó Bitburger* on Jókai utca. To enjoy some fresh air and **music** with your meal, take a trip out to the *Tölgyfa Csárda* (daily 10am–10pm) in the Koloska Valley (bus #3 or #4), which specialises in game dishes.

Moving on, the obvious destinations are Tihany (see below) or Nagyvázsony and Veszprém in the Bakony (covered later in this chapter) – all served by frequent buses. Ferries sail to Tihany and to Siófok on the far side of the Tihany peninsula: the railway line skips the peninsula as it forges eastwards.

Tihany

A rocky peninsula that was declared Hungary's first national park in 1952, **Tihany** is historically associated with the Benedictine order and a redoubtable castle (no longer in existence) that withstood 150 years of Turkish hostility. As one of the most beautiful regions of the Balaton, Tihany gets swamped with visitors over summer, but you can always escape the crowds by hiking into the interior. The coastal road from Balatonfüred passes through Dios (where Avar graves have been discovered) and Gödrös, entering Tihany village, where flights of steps climb up from the mole at which ferries from Balatonfüred dock. Arriving by ferry from Szántód or Balatonföldvár, on the southern shore, you'll land instead at TIHANY-RÉV at the tip of the peninsula, dominated by the *Club Tihany* complex.

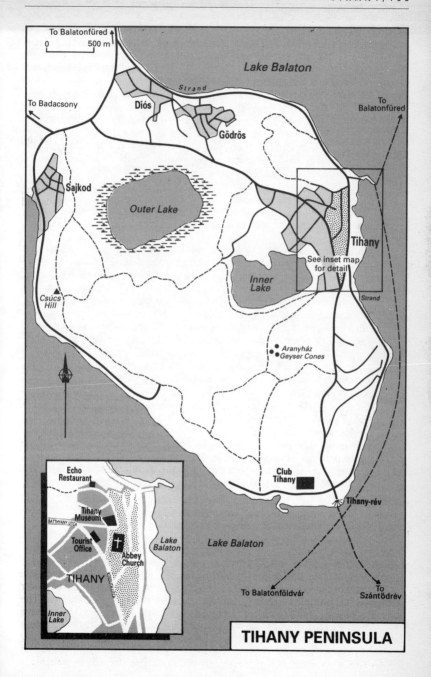

To Balatonfüred

0   500 m

To Badacsony

Lake Balaton

Strand

Diós

Gödrös

To
Balatonfüred

Sajkod

Outer Lake

Tihany

See inset map
for detail

Strand

Inner
Lake

Csúcs
Hill

Aranyház
Geyser Cones

Echo
Restaurant

Tihany
Museum

BATTHYÁNY UTCA

Tourist
Office

Abbey
Church

Lake
Balaton

TIHANY

Inner
Lake

Club
Tihany

Lake Balaton

Tihany-rév

To Balatonföldvár

To
Szántódrév

TIHANY PENINSULA

Around Tihany village

In contrast to Tihany-rév, **TIHANY** village remains a traditional-looking place, with many old houses built of grey basalt tufa with porticoed terraces, their windows and doors outlined in white. In days gone by, the village was dominated by a Benedictine abbey, established here in 1055 at the request of Andrew I, and founded – true to the biblical injunction – upon a rocky promontory overlooking the Balaton. Andrew's body lies in the crypt of the **Abbey Church** – the only one of the Árpád line to remain where he was buried – but the building itself is Baroque, the original having succumbed to wars and time. Inside are virtuoso **woodcarvings** by Sebestyén Stulhoff, who lived and worked in the abbey for 25 years after his fiancée died (her features are preserved in the face of an angel to the right of the altar) and grandiose **frescoes** by Lotz, Székely and Deák-Ebner. The church, (open 10am–6pm, except during masses), provides a magnificent setting for **organ concerts** over summer which should resume once restoration is complete. The abbey's foundation deed (held at Pannonhalma Monastery in Transdanubia, p.183) is the earliest document to include Hungarian words among the Latin.

The **Tihany Museum** (Tues–Sun 10am–6pm) in the former priory (which four monks are currently trying to reclaim) exhibits Balaton landscapes and an interesting collection of costumes, implements and musical instruments gathered from far-flung communities in the Ural Mountains and the *taiga* beneath the Arctic circle – whence the Magyars originated (see box). In the basement are Roman altars and bits from the Paulite Monastery at Nagyvázsony.

From the museum, the **Pisky promenade** leads past an old **Fishermen's Guild House** (Tues–Sun 10am–6pm) where **folk dancing** performances occur over summer, to the scenic vantage point of **Echo Hill**, whose echo seems to have disappeared. By following a well-marked path onwards, you can circumambulate the **Óvár** (Old Castle), a volcanic outcrop riddled with cells carved by Russian Orthodox monks, where hot springs gush forth.

Lakes and geysers

To escape the crowds and enjoy the beauty of the peninsula, go walking inland. The **Inner Lake** (*Belső-tó*) – whose sunlit surface is visible from the Abbey Church – fills a volcanic crater 25 metres above the level of the Balaton. From its southern bank, you can follow a path through vineyards, orchards and lavender fields to the **Aranyház geyser cones** – rock funnels forced open by hot springs.

THE ORIGIN OF THE MAGYARS

When the **Magyars** swept into the Carpathian Basin and raided deep into western Europe (896–995), they were identified with the invading **Huns** of the fifth century (hence the appellations "Hungarian", *Ungarn, Hongoris,* etc). This association persisted until linguistic and ethnographic investigations by János Sajnovics (1733–85), Antal Reguly and others traced their descent from the **Finno-Ugric peoples** of what is now Siberia. The language of the **Chuvash**, for example, has many similarities with old Hungarian, and their folk songs are based on the same pentatonic scale. More recently, however, the idea of a link between the early Magyars and the Huns has been revived following the decipherment of **inscriptions** on the "Treasure of Attila", which have much in common with ancient Magyar runes.

The northerly **Outer Lake** (*Külső-tó*) was drained for pasture in 1809, but refilled after 1975. Its reedbeds are harvested by hand over winter in the traditional manner, and provide a sanctuary for mallards, gadwalls and other **birds**. On the eastern side of the peninsula, a lookout tower atop **Csúcs Hill** (232m) offers a **panoramic view** of the Balaton. The trail, marked in red, takes about one and a half hours to hike.

Practicalities

The **tourist office** at Kossuth utca 20 in Tihany village (summer Mon–Sat 8am–6.30pm, Sun 8am–1pm; otherwise Mon–Fri 8am–4pm, Sat 8am–1pm; ☎86/48-519) can book **rooms** (②–③) over summer, or you'll see plenty of *Zimmer frei* signs if you simply wander the streets. Aside from this, there are just two (expensive) **hotels**, both in Tihany-rév. *Club Tihany* (☎86/48-088; ⑥) is a holiday village run by a Hungarian-Austrian-Danish consortium, offering luxury bungalows and rooms with half-board; the *Park Hotel* (☎86/48-611; ⑤–⑥) is similarly equipped with every sports facility, but only open from April to October.

While **bars** and snack stalls cluster round the dock at Tihany-rév, **restaurants** are concentrated in the village. Locals eat at the *Kecskeköröm Csárda*, Kossuth utca 19; the *Fogas Csárda* at no. 1 (11am–11pm); and the *halásztanya* at Visszhang utca 11 (11am–9pm). The *Echo Restaurant* on Echo Hill is dearer, but offers a lovely view (Mon–Sat 10am–10pm). Besides the paying **beaches** by *Club Tihany* and Tihany docks, there are free *strand* along the reedier shores between Gödrös and Dios, and south of Sajkod on the other side of the peninsula.

Tihany is connected to Balatonfüred by hourly **buses**, and **ferries** from the village dock, whence other services sail to Badacsony over summer. From April to November, there are boats from Tihany-rév to Balatonföldvar and Szántód (the latter a car ferry) on the southern shore every half hour or so. Buses to Balatonudvari, Balatonszepezd or Badacsony are the best means of **heading west**.

West towards Keszthely

For thirty kilometres west of Tihany **the shoreline** is infested with holiday homes and nondescript resorts; perhaps worth stopping for if you hit upon a beach or campsite to your taste, but generally nothing special. **ASZÓFŐ**, where the peninsula road meets the highway, has a good **campsite**, *Diana Camping* (☎86/45-013; June–Sept 6). At **ÖRVÉNYES**, 2km west, an eighteenth-century **watermill** is still operating (May–Sept 8am–5pm; Oct–April 8am–4pm) – one of the few that wasn't demolished in the Fifties to clear the way for state milling collectives. Nine kilometres further on, the cemetery in **BALATONUDVARI** features **heart-shaped tombstones** (also a popular motif in Austria and Germany during the eighteenth century).

BALATONAKALI, known for its *Akali muskotály* white **wine**, has four **campsites**. The huge *Holiday* (☎86/44-514; late May to mid-Sept) and *Strand* (☎86/44-513; June to mid-Sept) sites are on the eastern side of town, while *Privát Camping*, Kossuth utca 14 (May–Sept); and *Pacsirta Camping*, Pacsirta utca 1–4 (mid-June to Aug); are smaller and more central. There are **private accommodation** bureaux at Kossuth utca 17, Petőfi utca 4, and outside the railway station.

A fortress-like miners' rest home guards the road into **BALATONSZEPEZD**, where you can book **rooms** at Rózsa utca 122 (☎87/48-558; ②–③), and *Venusz Camping* (mid-May to mid-Sept; ☎87/48-048) awaits visitors by the waterside, 1km east of the railway station. Both are preferable to the overpriced *Napfény* site (mid-May to mid-Sept; ☎87/44-309) in neighbouring **RÉVFÜLÖP**, whence there are **ferries to Boglárlelle** on the southern shore. **ÁBRAHÁMHEGY**, 5km west, contains the **Folly Aboretum** of cedars and pines from all over the world, and a refreshingly unbuilt-up *strand*. Shortly afterwards comes **BADACSONYÖRS**, which has *Balaton Camping* (May–Sept; ☎87/31-253) and the *Szürkebárat Panzió* (③). The village is named after the massif that looms just around the coast.

The Badacsony

A coffin-shaped hulk with four villages prostrated at its feet, backed by dead volcanoes ranging across the Tapolca basin, **the Badacsony** is one of the Balaton's most striking features. When the land that was to become Hungary first surfaced, molten magma erupted from the seabed and cooled into a great semicircle of **basalt columns**, 210 metres high, which form the Badacsony's southeastern face. The rich volcanic soil of the lower slopes has supported vineyards since the Age of Migrations, when the Avars buried grape seeds with their dead to ensure that the afterlife wouldn't be lacking in **wine**. Nowadays, the harvest is blended into *Badacsonyi Kéknyelű, Zöldszilváni, Szürkebárat* ("Grey Monk") or *Olaszrizling*, and there's a **harvest festival** during the first week in September.

Although trains and buses also call at Badacsonytomaj, Badacsony Lábdihegy and Balatontördemic, it is Badacsony proper that gets all the tourists, and ferries from Boglárlelle, Fonyód and Szigliget. If you don't fancy embarking on the wine trail immediately, pay a visit to the **Egry Museum**, on the left just over the railway level crossing (May–Sept Tues–Sun 10am–6pm). József Egry (1883–1951) was born into a poor local family and worked as a locksmith and roofer before winning a scholarship to the Academy of Fine Arts. His paintings capture the ever-changing moods and light of the Balaton.

Otherwise, hop into one of the jeep-taxis that run 3km uphill through the vineyards (100Ft) to the **Róza Szegedi House**. This charming residence is also called the Kisfaludy House after Róza's husband, Sándor Kisfaludy, who lauded the Balaton's beauties in verse. When last heard it was closed for restoration, but the nearby restaurant (in a former winepress) was doing fine. From the last turn on the road up to the house, a side road runs 1km west to the **Borászati Wine Museum** (mid-May to mid-Oct Tues–Sun 10am–6pm).

Walking in the Badacsony

From Szegedi's house you can follow a path up to the **Rose Rock** (*Rózsakő*), of which it's said that if a man and woman sit upon it with their backs to the Balaton and think about each other, they'll be married by the end of the year. The trail continues through the beechwoods to the **Kisfaludy Lookout Tower** (at 437m) and on to the **Stone Gate** (*Kökapu*), where sightseers ooh-aah at two massive basalt towers flanking a precipitous drop.

Longer hikes into the hills further north offer an escape from the crowds. A four-kilometre walk from the Stone Gate will bring you to **Gulács-hegy**, a perfectly conical hill (393m) near the NEMESGULÁCS halt for trains en route to Tapolca. The **Szent György-hegy** (415m), on the far side of the tracks, boasts some impressive basalt **organ pipes** and the region's finest vineyards, where *Szürkebarát* is produced. A few kilometres to the east, 375-metre-high **Csobánc-hegy** is crowned by a **ruined castle** that was once defended against the Turks by women. Serious hikers might consider pushing on to SZENTBÉKKÁLLA and the beautiful **Seas of Stone**, created from layers of sand and pebbles deposited by the ancient Pannonian Sea.

The last three hikes will probably take the best part of a day and leave you closer to Tapolca than the Balaton. It's advisable to buy a 1:80,000-scale map of the region.

Practicalities

Maps and **information** are available from *Balatontourist*, Park utca 10 (Mon–Fri 8.30am–4.30pm, Sat 8.30am–noon; summer Mon–Sat till 6.30pm, also Sun 8.30am–noon; ☎87/31-249), near the railway station in Badacsony. They also rent private **rooms** (②), as do *Midi TOURIST*, Park utca 53 (June–Sept 8am–10pm; ☎87/31-028), *Cooptourist*, Kossuth utca 76, and households advertising *Zimmer frei*. Otherwise, there's a **campsite** south of the landing stage (mid-May to mid-Sept; ☎87/31-091); the *Harsfa Panzió* at Szegedi Róza út 1 (☎87/31-293; ③); or the *Egry József Panzió*, Kisfaludy utca 2, in Badacsonytomaj (mid-April to mid-Sept; ☎87/31-057; ①).

After Badacsony the railway veers northwards up to Tapolca in the Bakony, so although you can switch **trains** there and ride back down to Keszthely, it's easier to continue along the shore **by bus**, changing at Balatonederics if necessary.

Szigliget and beyond

The **Szigliget** peninsula beneath the Kamonkő cliffs looks most dramatic when viewed from a ferry, at which point you can imagine the Hungarian fleet moored under the protection of **Szigliget Castle**, as it was in Turkish times. Originally commissioned by Pannonhalma Monastery in the wake of the Mongol invasion, the now ruined stronghold can be reached by a path that starts behind the white church sited on the highest spot in the village. Below the ruins are a lush park containing over five hundred kinds of ornamental shrubs and trees, plus a former Esterházy mansion used as a holiday resort by the Writers' Union. Non-members may look around the grounds with permission.

BALATONEDERICS, 5km on, is notable only for the **hostel** at Kültelek 10 (mid-May to mid-Sept; ☎87/36-131; ②), and as a train station and the junction for route 84 to Sümeg. Sticking to buses, you can carry on round the lake to **BALATONGYÖRÖK**, still partly a village of white-porticoed, thatched houses, with a **campsite** on the beach. Its **Szépkilátó Lookout** affords a vista encompassing the Szent György and Csobánc hills to the north, and the twin peaks behind Fonyód, across the lake.

After this comes **VONYARCVASHEGY**, where coach parties pack the outdoor *Fészek Vendéglő*, and the lakeside *Horgász* **campsite** (May–Sept) comes under the auspices of *Zalatour* in Zalaegerszeg (p.206). There is another campsite (April–Oct) and a private accommodation bureau on Kossuth utca in **GYENESDIÁS**, which merges into the suburbs of Keszthely.

Keszthely and Hévíz

A tradition of free thinking that dates back to the eighteenth century gives **KESZTHELY** a sense of superiority over other resorts, and its university ensures that life isn't wholly taken over by tourism. The Belváros and *strand* somehow absorb thousands of visitors gracefully, without looking bleak and abandoned out of season. With the Festetics Palace to admire, and a thermal lake awaiting bathers at Hévíz, nearby, Keszthely is the best hangout on the Balaton.

Arriving by ferry near the main *strand*, you can walk up Erzsébet királyné útja into the centre (10–15min). The railway and intercity bus stations are further south, at the bottom end of Mártirok útja, but most buses entering town drop passengers on downtown Fő tér, sparing them a 600-metre trudge along Kossuth utca.

Walking up from the station, you'll pass the **Balaton Museum** (Tues–Sun 10am–6pm), which covers the region's zoology, ethnography and archaeology, with artefacts dating back to the first century AD, when road-building Romans disrupted the lifestyle of local Celtic tribes. Downtown Keszthely begins around Fő tér – an ambiguous square with a much-remodelled Gothic Parish church. From here on, **Kossuth utca** is given over to cafés, buskers and strollers, with a **flea market** on Wednesday mornings.

Heading up towards the palace, you'll pass the **birthplace of Karl Goldmark** (1830–1915) on the corner of Fejér utca. The son of a poor Jewish cantor who enrolled him in Sopron's school of music, Goldmark went on to study at the Vienna Conservatory. Almost shot as a rebel for giving concerts in Győr during the 1848 Revolution, he survived to write *Merlin*, *Zrínyi* and *The Queen of Sheba*.

The Festetics Palace and Georgikon

The aristocratic Festetics family are chiefly remembered for Count György (1755–1819), founder of Keszthely's agricultural university and the Baroque **Festetics Palace** (Tues–Sun April–Sept 10am–6pm, midsummer till 7pm; Oct–March 9am–4.30pm). During the early nineteenth century, the palace's salons attracted the leading lights of Magyar literature (now recalled by memorial trees) as Hungary's first public forum for criticism. The palace's highlights are its gilt, mirrored ballroom and the **Helikon Library**, a masterpiece of joinery by János Kerbl, containing 52,000 books in diverse languages. Chinese vases and tiled stoves jostle for space with portraits of the family racehorses and dachshunds (whose pedigrees are proudly noted), and the pelts and heads of tigers, bears and other animals shot by Count Windishgrätz. There are **concerts** here over summer.

Count György's most useful contribution was an agricultural college, or **Georgikon**, the first of its kind in Europe. Students attending the three-year course lived and worked together in a cluster of whitewashed buildings at Bercsényi utca 67, which now displays dairy and viticulture equipment, cartwright's tools, old Ford tractors and suchlike (April–Oct Tues–Sat 10am–5pm, Sun 10am–6pm). The Georgikon was the forerunner of today's **Agrártudományi University**, a green and daffodil-yellow pile halfway along Széchenyi utca.

Keszthely is in the process of changing its telephone code. Most places still use the old ☎82, but some may change to ☎92

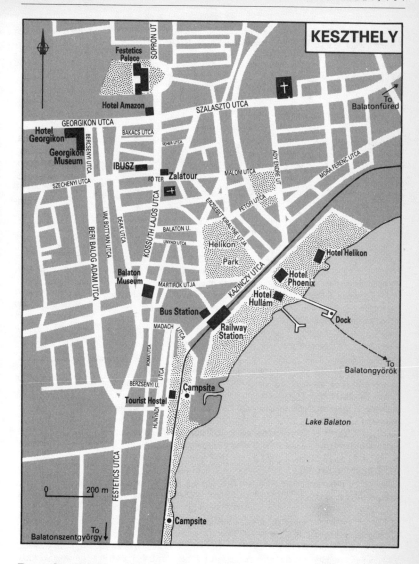

Practicalities

Three **tourist offices** cluster downtown: *IBUSZ* at Széchenyi utca 1–3 (Mon–Sat 8am–6pm; also Sun 9am–1pm over summer; ☎12-951); *Zalatour*, Fő tér 1 (summer Mon–Fri 8am–5pm, Sat 8am–4pm, Sun 8am–noon; rest of year Mon–Fri 8am–5pm, Sat 8am–noon; ☎12-560); and *Express*, Kossuth utca 22 (April–Oct Mon–Sat 8am–8pm; Nov–March Mon–Sat 8am–5pm; ☎12-032).

Private rooms (②–③) are bookable through any of the above or from *Volántourist*, Kossuth utca 43 (☎12-733); *Helikon*, Erzsébet királyne útja 1 (☎12-596); *Hongarije Tours*, Erzsébet királyne útja 26; and an *IBUSZ* branch at Római út 2. The last three are all relatively near the station. *Non-Stop Tourist*, Bakacs utca 12, functions **24-hours** during the high season, but charges more than other agencies. You can avoid their charges altogether by finding a room yourself: try the backstreets south of the station, or any house advertising *Zimmer frei*. The alternatives are:

Hotels and Pensions

Hotel Amazon, Georgikon utca 1 (☎74-213). Run-down, eighteenth-century premises near the palace. Singles (①–②) and doubles (②–③) with or without baths. Usually full.

Hotel Georgikon, Georgikon utca 20 (☎11-730). A renovated manor house of similar vintage, four blocks west. All rooms with baths; breakfast included. ②–④.

Attika Panzió, Jókai utca 16 (☎11-232). Small, family-run pension, just off Fő tér. ③.

Hotel Hullám, Balaton-part 1 (☎18-950). Palatial old mansion on the waterfront, with use of the facilities at the *Hotel Helikon*. Breakfast included. Closed Jan & Feb. ③–④.

Hotel Phoenix, Balaton-part 3 (☎92/12-630). A motel-style place just behind the Hullám, open April–Oct. ③–⑤.

Hotel Helikon, Balaton-part 5 (☎18-944). Luxury high-rise eyesore with sauna, pool and tennis courts, open year round. Breakfast included. ⑤–⑥.

Forras Panzió, Római út 1 (☎11-418). A few blocks southwest of the station. ②–③.

Teréza Panzió, Honvéd utca 28 (☎12-466). Further south, past the tourist hostel, in an area full of rooms signs. ②–③.

Hostels and Campsites

Tourist Hostel, Honvéd utca 22 (☎11-424). Dormitory beds 10-min walk from the station. Reserve through *Express* or *Zalatour*. April to mid-Oct only. ①.

Sport Camping, Csárda utca (☎12-842). An unappealing site beyond the railway tracks, behind the hostel. April–Oct.

Zalatour Camping, Balaton-part (☎12-782). Bigger, more attractively located site, 10-min walk south. May–Sept.

Castrum Camping, Móra F. utca 48 (☎92/74-423). Aimed at motorists, and far from the shore 1km north of the station. Very expensive. April–Oct.

Eating and drinking

Keszthely is the best place on the Balaton for **eating and drinking**, but it's difficult to make specific recommendations – the scene is constantly changing as good spots turn bad, while new ones open up. Places entirely frequented by tourists are likely to overcharge or give lousy service; these include the *Gösser* on Fő tér and the *Kert* on Széchenyi utca, around the corner.

Better alternatives are the *Pizzeria da Francesco*, on Szabad nép utca, one block north, for its tasty pizzas, and the friendly *Bár Picolo* just along the road. Don't miss the *American Hamburger* on the corner of Kossuth and Csók utca, 500m south of Fő tér, which offers 36 varieties of sandwich with whimsical names like "Mafia" (9am–1pm & 3–10pm). The once cheap *Béke Vendéglő* at Kossuth utca 50 has moved upmarket, so locals now frequent the 24-hour *Rózsa Étterem* on the corner of Bercsényi and Széchenyi utca – try their potato pancakes (*tocsi*).

A nameless outlet beside the *American Hamburger* does delicious ice cream, while the *Muskátali Cukrászda* at the upper end of Kossuth utca has fine cakes, coffee and a selection of newspapers to peruse.

Activities and entertainments

Keszthely has two **beaches**: the *Városi strand* – with its own mole – near the ferry dock, and the *Helikon strand* between the two campsites further south (both daily 8.30am–7pm). You can rent **windsurfing** gear at either, and play **tennis** or **mini golf** by the waterfront hotels. Enquire at *Zalatour*, the *Hotel Helikon*, *Forrás Panzió* or *Sport Camping* about **horse-riding** in Keszthely-Újmajor.

During the annual **Helikon Festival of chamber and orchestral music** (June–Aug), concerts are held in the palace every Monday and sometimes at weekends. The future of Keszthely's biennial **Interforum Festival of avant-garde music** is less assured, but it's worth asking *IBUSZ* or *Zalatour* if the event is still scheduled. Otherwise, summer is enlivened by **rock, folk and jazz concerts** on Fő tér (as advertised), plus buskers and jugglers along Kossuth utca. If there are no discos advertised in Keszthely, neighbouring Hévíz can always provide some lurid **nightlife**.

Moving on

Aside from Hévíz – which is best visited as an excursion (see below) – there are various possibilities for **moving on**. From June to mid-September, **ferries** sail twice daily (8am & 2pm) for the Badacsony and Tihany, continuing to Siófok in July and August. The **railway** around the lake's curve to Balatonszentgyörgy, (change there for Nagykanizsa), is a continuation of the main line down from Tapolca and Sümeg – which provides the easiest means of reaching the Bakony. Over summer (June 23–Sept 9 Tues–Sun 11.45am) a wonderful old **steam train** runs up to Tapolca and down to Badacsonytomaj. Tickets cost only 300Ft, and there's a bar on board.

Buses leave from the bus stand on Fő tér for a range of destinations in Transdanubia, including Nagykanizsa, Szombathely, Zalaegerszeg, Győr and Sopron. The depot outside the railway station is the point of departure for buses to Hévíz (every half-hour), Balatongyörök and overnight to Budapest.

Cyclists heading towards Zalaegerszeg, Szombathely or Sárvár might enjoy the tree-lined road that follows the River Zala through ZALASZENTGRÓT – which has a picturesque bridge and manor and a good restaurant, the ill-named *Grót Étterem*. On the road to VASAR, oxen and horse-drawn carts are more common than cars.

Hévíz

HÉVÍZ, 8km outside Keszthely, boasts the second largest **thermal lake** in the world (the biggest is in New Zealand). Indian waterlilies flourish on its surface, since the temperature rarely drops below 30°C even during winter, when steam billows from the lake and its thermal stream. The lake is constantly replenished by eighty million litres of water gushing up from springs one kilometre underground, so that it is completely flushed out every two days. Exploited for curative purposes as well as for tanning leather, since medieval times, it was subjected to scientific enquiry and salubriously channelled into a bath-house by Count György. By the end of the nineteenth century, Hévíz had become a grand **resort**, briefly favoured by crown princes and magnates like those other great spas of the Habsburg empire, Karlsbad and the Baths of Hercules. They'd be hard pressed to recognise it today, with high-rise hotels and tacky bars setting the tone.

Although the wooden terraces and catwalks surrounding the **baths** (*Tófürdő*) have a vaguely *fin-de-siècle* appearance, the general ambience is contemporary, with people sipping beer or reading newspapers while bobbing on the lake in rented inner tubes. Prolonged immersion isn't recommended on account of the slightly radioactive water, though mud from the lake is used to treat locomotive disorders. The baths are open all year (daily 7am–4pm).

Practicalities – and Alsópátok

With half-hourly buses from Keszthely, there's no need to stay here, but plenty of **accommodation** should you feel like it. Private rooms (②–③) are available from *Cooptourist* and *Zalatour* on Rákóczi utca and *Volántourist* in the bus station. Hotels run the gamut from the high-rise *Aqua* (☎84/18-947; ⑥) and *Thermál* (☎84/18-130; ⑥) on Kossuth utca to the elegant old *Park Hotel*, Petőfi utca 26 (☎84/18-130; ③–④) and a former workers' hostel at Attila út 10 (☎84/12-960; ③). There are also the *Piroska Panzió*, Kossuth utca 10 (☎84/12-698; ③); the *Tischler Panzió*, Attila út 113 (☎84/16-137); and the four-star *Kurcamping Castrum*, which lets plots to caravaners at exorbitant rates (☎84/13-198), open year round.

Nightlife revolves around the *Bar Romantica* on Tavirózsa utca (Mon–Sat 6pm–4am) – with a disco, sex show and go-go dancers – and the even seedier *Autos* strip-bar near the market place. Alternatively, you could catch a bus (every 15min) to the neighbouring village of **ALSÓPÁHOK**, where the *Disco Sello* plays very loud Eurorock, and tourists hang out at the low-priced *Tranzit Büfe Kaffeeteria* – a café-bar with friendly, English-speaking staff. Alsópáhok is a nicer, cheaper place to stay than Hévíz, with lots of private **rooms** for rent (②). The British company *New Millennium Holidays* stashes its tourists here.

THE BAKONY

The Bakony range cuts a swathe across central Transdanubia, as if scooped from the ground to provide space for the lake, and piled as a natural embankment behind the lowlier Balaton hills. Abundant vineyards testify to the richness of the volcanic soil and, more recently, mineheads to the mineral wealth beneath it. With dense woods and narrow ravines, this was the Hungarian equivalent of Sherwood Forest during the centuries of warfare and turmoil, and the setting for a dozen castles, the finest of which stand at **Sümeg** and **Nagyvázsony**. The regional capital **Veszprém** boasts a wealth of historic architecture and serves as a base for trips to the highwaymen's inn at **Nemesvámos** and the **Herend** porcelain factory. Or you can get away from everything by walking in the hills around **Zirc** or **Bakonybél**. During autumn, pink crocuses spangle the meadows between Sümeg and the Balaton, and huge sunflower fields and red-podded trees abound nearer Sárvár.

Tapolca and Sümeg

From Szigliget on the Balaton, the railway heads up to **TAPOLCA**, a blot on the landscape devoted to bauxite mining and aluminium processing. Until recently, Tapolca was slightly redeemed by the **Tavas Caves**, whose main grotto was used as a sanatorium for asthma and bronchitis sufferers, but mining operations caused its karstic spring to dry up and a cave-in has rendered the grotto unsafe. Now there is nothing to see except a **Museum of the Aluminium Industry** (Mon–Fri 9am–3pm) at Batsányi tér 2, which is every bit as dull as you'd imagine.

Although the *Gabriella Hotel*, Batsányi tér 7 (☎87/12-642; ③); and the *Aspa Panzió*, Kossuth utca 19 (☎87/11-695; ③) offer **accommodation**, it's best to stay on the train until Sümeg or head straight out on a local bus to Nagyvázsony and Nemesvámos (8 daily). There are also regular **buses** and trains down to Keszthely, including *nosztálgia* **steam trains** over summer (Tues–Sun at 4pm). *Balatontourist* at Deák utca 2 (☎87/11-179) has **information**.

Sümeg

SÜMEG, 14km north, is an altogether different proposition, with a dramatic-looking castle overshadowing a Belváros dating from the eighteenth century, when the town was the seat of the Bishops of Veszprém. Baroque mansions and parts of the medieval walls line Deák utca, leading to a **Parish Church** containing magnificent **frescoes** by Franz Anton Maulbertsch (1724–96). With a team of assistants, he was able to cover the whole interior within eighteen months, mostly in Biblical scenes. Exceptions are the rear wall, which depicts his patron, Bishop Biró (the man kneeling before him has Maulbertsch's features, as does the shepherd in the Adoration scene), and the wall facing the choir, showing the churches Biró sponsored in Sümeg and Zalaegerszeg. Apropos of Biró, it was another Hungarian, László Biró, who invented the biro, or ballpoint pen.

Even more impressive is **Sümeg Castle** (8am–sunset), which dominates the town from a conical limestone massif, a unique Cretaceous outcropping among the basalt of the Bakony. The citadel to the south, built during the thirteenth century, provided the basis for successive fortifications – including the outer wall and gate tower – which kept the Turks out, but succumbed to the Habsburgs in 1713. A few years back, the castle was rented out to a man who is gradually restoring it; **historical pageants and jousts** are held in the courtyard over summer. The steep ascent is worth it for the views alone, but there's also the **Museum of Saddlery** (daily 8–11.30am & 2–5pm) in the former bishop's stables at the bottom of Vak Bottyán utca.

Practicalities – and moving on

The *Vár Hotel*, Vak Bottyán utca 2 (closed Jan; ☎87/52-414; ②), and the *Király Fogadó*, Udavarbiró tér 5 (☎87/52-605; ②), can provide **accommodation**, while the *Vár Csárda* near the former is a good place to **eat**. Contact the *Király Fogadó* about **horse-riding** in the surrounding countryside.

Travellers heading **into Transdanubia** by rail may have to change at UKK (for Zalaegerszeg) or CELLDÖMÖLK (for Győr or Szombathely). Heading **towards Veszprém**, direct buses are quicker but less regular than trains (which entail changing at BOBA). More frequent services **from Tapolca** pass through Nagyvázsony and Nemesvámos en route to Veszprém.

Nagyvázsony and Nemesvámos

Buses **along the Tapolca–Veszprém road** can drop you at two places redolent of the Bakony's history – Nagyvázsony (also accessible by bus from Balatonfüred) and an old highwaymen's inn near Nemesvámos (only 6km outside Veszprém).

NAGYVÁZSONY, 20km from Tapolca, harbours **Kinizsi Castle** (April–Oct 9am–dusk), given by King Mátyás to Pál Kinizsi, a local miller who made good as a commander. Formidably strong, he is said to have wielded a dead Turk as a bludgeon, and danced a triumphal jig while holding three Turks, one of them between his teeth. During the sixteenth century, this was one of the border fortresses between Turkish and Habsburg-ruled Hungary. Its keep exhibits weapons and fetters, while the chapel across the way contains Kinizsi's red marble sarcophagus.

Towards the end of July, three or four days of **show-jumping and jousting** in the grounds enliven what is otherwise a sleepy market town. If you're planning to attend the festival, it's worth reserving a room (④) or bed (①) in the **Kastély Hotel** and **hostel**, which occupy a former Zichy mansion at Kossuth utca 12 (☎80/64-109). The *Vázsonykő*, Sörház utca 2, is a good place to eat.

Approaching Veszprém, you can't miss the roadside *Vámosi csárda* (or *Betyár csárda*), an **eighteenth-century Bakony inn**. If you ignore the odd modern fixture and today's clientele, it's possible to imagine the inn's appearance in olden days: servants hurrying from the tap-room with its huge casks into the cellar, where swineherds, wayfarers and outlaws caroused, seated upon sections of tree trunk. Poor though most were, Bakony folk were proud of their masterless lives among the oak forests, esteeming the *kondás*, with his herd of pigs, and the highwaymen who robbed rich merchants. These latter called themselves *szegénylegények* – "poor lads" – and the most audacious, Jóska Savanyú, claimed the tavern as his home.

The village of **NEMESVÁMOS** lies 600m south of the inn. Nearby are the **ruins of a Roman villa** at BALÁCAPUSZTA (May–Sept Tues–Sun 10am–6pm). Its reconstructed frescoes and mosaics convey an impression of the lifestyle of wealthy Roman colonists in the early centuries of the Christian era. The Hungarian government asserts that the famous **Seveso Treasure** came from another such villa in the Balaton region – although its claim is disputed by Lebanon, Turkey and what used to be Yugoslavia, whose own claims to ownership are currently being judged in the courts.

Veszprém

VESZPRÉM spreads over five hills, cobbled together by a maze of streets twisting up towards its old quarter, on a precipitous crag overlooking the Bakony forest. Like Székesfehérvár, it became an episcopal see in the reign of Prince Géza (who converted to Christianity in 975). In 997, it was here that King Stephen crushed a pagan rebellion with the help of knights sent by Henry of Bavaria, father of his queen Gizella. During medieval times, Veszprém was the seat of the queen's household and the site of her cornonation – hence its title the "Queen's Town". Utterly devastated during the sixteenth century and rebuilt after 1711, its Castle Hill and downtown parks are now juxtaposed with blocks of flats, a technical university and chemical factories.

Being only 20km from Lake Balaton, Veszprém could serve as a base for visiting the resorts without having to stay there, and for excursions to Nagyvázsony, Nemesvámos or Herend. Motorists coming in from the west will cross the 150-metre-long Valley Bridge over the River Séd, glimpsing Castle Hill en route to the centre. **Arriving** at the railway station 2km out, catch bus #1 to the big *Áruház* store near downtown Szabadság tér; the intercity bus depot (which has a left-luggage office) is fifteen minutes' walk east. From Szabadság tér, you can head north towards Castle Hill or strike out into the lower town.

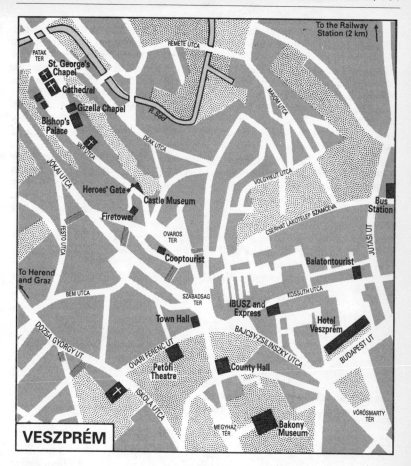

VESZPRÉM

Castle Hill

The Castle district is presaged by **Óváros tér**, a triangular plaza flanked by Baroque and Rococo buildings painted in pinks, blues and the shade known as "Maria Theresa yellow" (which she ordained as the colour scheme for public buildings throughout the Habsburg empire). Behind nos. 7–8 rises the Baroque **Firetower** (*Tűztorony*), whose medieval base once formed part of the castle; a carillon in the dome plays a traditional recruiting tune every hour on the hour.

For a closer look at the tower, bear left down an alley beyond the **Heroes' Gate**, a neo-Romanesque portal commemorating the dead of World War I. The right-hand gate-tower contains a **Castle Museum** (May–Sept Tues–Sun 10am–6pm) recalling sieges of the *vár*, which the Habsburgs demolished in 1702, replacing it with the mansions and churches that ennoble Castle Hill today. Following Vár utca uphill, you'll pass a **Piarist Church and Monastery** – now used for temporary exhibitions (May–Oct 9am–5pm) – whose facade bears three Greek letters, encapsulating the Piarist credo "Mary, Mother, God".

The **Bishop's Palace** on the main square is a typically massive Baroque pile by Jakab Fellner. During its construction in the 1760s, workmen unearthed part of the medieval queen's palace. This vaulted chamber, dubbed the **Gizella Chapel**, contains Byzantine-style frescoes of the apostles from the thirteenth century (May–Oct Tues–Sun 10am–5pm). Across the square, at no. 35, you can view an **Ecclesiastical Collection** of votive statues, chasubles and suchlike to the sound of taped Mass, and a **Museum of Brick Manufacturing** (both May–Oct 9am–5pm).

Beyond the Trinity Statue looms Veszprém **Cathedral**. Having been razed and resurrected half a dozen times since the eleventh century, its current, neo-Romanesque incarnation (1907–10) has only a Gothic crypt to show for its origins. However, a glass dome behind the cathedral shelters the excavated remains of **Saint George's Chapel**, where Stephen's son Imre is said to have taken an oath of celibacy. His canonisation – like that of Stephen and the latterday king László – cemented the Árpáds' adherence to Catholicism, and gave the Hungarians their own saints to identify with.

Statues of Stephen and Gizella duly watch over the parapet at the far end of Vár utca, while a flight of steps round the side of the cathedral leads down to **Benedek Hill**, which commands a panoramic view of the Séd Valley and the Bakony forest. During summer, the Castle district is the setting for open-air **concerts**.

The lower town

Returning to Szabadság tér, head past the Baroque **Town Hall** (originally the mansion of the Kaposvári family) and right along Óvári Ferenc út to find the Art Nouveau **Petőfi Theatre**. The first large building in Hungary to be constructed from reinforced concrete (in 1908), it boasts a circular stained-glass window entitled *The Magic of Folk Art*, whose symbolic figures represent the attachment of Hungarians to their land. Its designer, Sándor Nagy, was one of the Gödöllő Pre-Raphaelites; his *Hunting of the Magic Deer* (a Magyar myth) decorates the rear of the building.

A short walk past the Eclectic-style **County Hall** brings you to Megyház tér, flanked by Kálvária Hill and the **Bakony Museum** (March–Oct 10am–6pm; Nov–Feb 10am–4pm; closed Tues). The collection of exhibits includes Roman mosaics unearthed in the villa at Balácapuszta, regional folk costumes, and material on the Bakony's *betyár*, or highwaymen. Next door stands the **Bakony House** (same hours), a Thirties clone of a traditional homestead, filled with peasant artefacts.

Three more sights lurk 700m west of the centre, off Kittenberger utca, which can be reached by walking from Dózsa György út, itself accessible by bus #5 or #10. First comes an antique **watermill** – one of many that once lined the banks of the Séd – followed by a **Game Park** (daily 9am–5pm) named after the nineteenth-century zoologist Kálmán Kittenberger. In the Fejes Valley 330m further south is a **Village Museum** of cottages and implements from the Bakony region (May–Oct Tues–Sun 10am–6pm).

The Veszprém telephone code is ☎80

Practicalities

Information is available from *Balatontourist Nord* at Kossuth utca 3 (Mon–Fri 9am–5pm; summer also Sat 9am–5pm; ☎13-750) and Szabadság tér 21 (same hours; ☎26-630), or from *IBUSZ*, Kossuth utca 6 (☎12-425). Both agencies can book private **rooms** (②), as can *Cooptourist* at Óváros tér 2 (Mon–Fri 8am–5pm), whilst *Express* above *IBUSZ* may be able to find **beds** (①) in the student hostel at Egyetem utca 12, beyond the Chemical Technical University 1km south of the centre (bus #2Y, #4, #8 or #14Y). Other options are:

Hotel Veszprém, Budapest út 6 (☎24-876). Centrally located Seventies low-rise. Rooms at the back are quieter. Breakfast included. ②–③.

Ingaforg Hotel, Házgyari út 1 (☎23-304). A former workers' hostel 500m south of the railway station. ②.

Erdei Motel, Kittenberger utca 14 (☎26-751). Bungalows (April–Oct; ②) and a campsite (May–Sept) on a hilltop above the Game Park. Reserve through *Balatontourist Nord*.

Élőgyöngy Panzió, József A. utca 1. At the start of the Nagyvázsony road, 400m southwest of the Petőfi Theatre. ②–③.

Eating and drinking

Several upmarket **brasseries** cluster around Óváros tér and Szabadság tér; the former also has an Italian restaurant offering a couple of vegetarian dishes. Other **restaurants** include the *Puszta Étterem*, with a nice garden, on Buhim utca (just off Szabadság tér); the cheap *Vadasztanya kisvendéglő*, József A. utca 2; and the *Tiszafa* on Dózsa György út, which offers Jewish dishes from Transylvania, and claims to be open 24 hours. There is also the famous *Vámosi Csárdá*, out along the Tapolca road (see p.166).

On from Veszprém

Leaving aside the places already covered in this chapter, you have a choice of destinations when it's time to move on. Heading northwest towards **Szombathely** (see the following chapter, p.198), it's easy to visit the famous porcelain factory at Herend, with the possibility of scenic detours for those with their own transport. The route more directly north towards **Győr** plunges through the heart of the Bakony, emerging onto the Little Plain to pass by Pannonhalma, with its famous monastery.

West towards Szombathely

HEREND, 12km west of Veszprém, makes an enjoyable excursion from town or an interesting stopover en route to Szombathely. The origins of its famous **Porcelain Factory** go back to 1826, when Vince Stingl founded a pottery in the village. Herend porcelain gained international renown at the Great Exhibition of 1851, when Queen Victoria ordered a Chinoiserie dinner service. Other famous purchasers have included Tsar Alexander II, Kaiser Wilhelm I, the Shah of Iran and the British royals Charles and Diana. The factory's **museum** (April–Oct Tues–Sun 8.30am–4.30pm; Nov–March Mon–Sat 8am–4pm) displays handpainted dinner services, vases and statuettes – many of which go right over the top.

After Herend the scenery deteriorates around AJKA, but 6km beyond DEVECSER (where the rail line turns northwards towards Celldömölk) there's a great view of the Bakony from a lookout tower near **SOMLÓVÁSÁRHELY**. In clear weather Mount Kőris (see below) and even the Austrian Alps may be visible.

North towards Győr

Heading north towards Győr, both railway and route 82 follow the River Cuha through the Bakony Hills. The only town en route is **ZIRC**, whose former Cistercian **Abbey Church** has altar paintings by Maulbertsch. The adjacent abbey now contains a **Natural History Museum** (Tues–Sun April–Oct 9am–5pm; Nov–March 9am–1pm) and a **library** with Empire-style furnishings, named after Antal Reguly (1819–58), the pioneer of Finno-Urgic linguistic research who was born in Zirc. The *Erdőalja Panzió* has rooms and bungalows (mid-May to mid-Sept; ②–③).

If you fancy walking in the hills, **BAKONYBÉL**, 17km west and accessible by local buses from Zirc, is situated at the foot of **Mount Kőris**, the highest peak in the Bakony (713m). Several **hiking** trails emanate from the village, where you can stay at the *Bakony Panzió*, Fürdő út 57 (②). The main route continues northwards via **CSESZNEK**, where a **ruined castle** on a steep hill affords a fine view of the region. Although trains stop some distance away (at Porva-Csesznek), the railway journey is a scenic one, winding between cliffs, over bridges and through tunnels, along a line built in 1896. Most Győr-bound trains stop at Pannonhalma Monastery along the way; for details, see Chapter Four.

travel details

Trains

From Budapest (Déli Station) to Balatonfüred (every 1–2hr; 2hr–2hr 30min); Siófok (9.30am, 12.40pm, 12.55pm, 3.40pm, 4.50pm, 5.15pm, 6.50pm & 10pm daily; 1hr 30min); Székesfehérvár (every 60–90min; 1hr); Veszprém (11.35am, 12.30pm, 3pm, 5.20pm & 5.45pm daily; 2hr 15min–3hr).

From Balatonfenyves to Csisztapuszta (Tues–Sun every 60–90min; 45min–1hr 30min).

From Balatonfüred to Budapest (every 1–2hr; 2hr–2hr 30min).

From Balatonszentgyörgy to Nagykanizsa (every 1–2hr; 45min).

From Székesfehérvár to Balatonfüred (hourly; 30min–1hr); Budapest (every 60–90min; 1hr); Komárom (every 60–90min; 1hr 15min–1hr 45min); Siófok (hourly; 30min); Szombathely (6.45am, 7.10am, 12.25pm, 1.20pm, 3pm, 6.20pm & 6.50pm daily; 2hr 30min–3hr 45min); Veszprém (hourly; 45min–1hr).

From Tapolca to Celldömölk (every 60–90min; 1hr 15min); Sümeg (every 60–90min; 1hr 30min); Szombathely (9.30am, 2.50pm, 7.15pm & 7.45pm daily; 1hr 30min).

From Veszprém to Budapest (7.45am, noon, 1.40pm & 2.40pm; 1hr 45min–2hr 15min); Győr (8.40am, 2.30pm, 5pm & 6.30pm daily; 2hr 30min); Szombathely (7.45am, 2.15pm, 4.45pm & 7pm daily; 1hr 15min).

Buses

From Budapest (Erzsébet tér) to Balatonfüred (6.30am & 3.40pm daily; 2hr 15min); Herend (2.40pm & 4.10pm daily; 2hr 45min); Hévíz (6.30am & 3.40pm daily; 4hr); Keszthely (6.30am & 3.40pm daily; 3hr 45min); Nagyvázsony (Mon–Sat 9.40am & 2.20pm; 3hr); Siófok (6am, 8am & 12.40pm daily; 1hr 45min–2hr 15min); Sümeg (2.40pm & 8pm daily; 4hr 30min); Székesfehérvár (every 40–60min; 1hr 15min); Veszprém (every 60–90min; 2hr 15min); Zirc (6.45am, 7.30am, 3pm & 4pm daily; 2hr 30min).

From Badacsony to Keszthely (hourly; 1hr); Székesfehérvár (7.15am & 3.35pm daily; 2hr 15min).

From Bakonybél to Budapest (7am, 11am & 3.40pm daily; 3hr 15min).

From Balatonfüred to Győr (every 30–90min; 2hr); Nagyvázsony (every 1hr 30min; 45min); Sopron (3.15pm daily; 4hr); Tapolca (Mon–Sat 1.30pm; 1hr 30min); Tihany (hourly; 30min); Veszprém (every 30–90min; 30min).

From Hévíz to Keszthely (every 30min; 15min); Pécs (5.40am & 3.40pm daily; 4hr 15min); Zalaegerszeg (7.25pm daily; 2hr).

From Keszthely to Hévíz (every 30min; 15min); Pécs (8.25am & 4.55pm daily; 3hr 45min); Sümeg (3.55pm daily; 1hr); Szombathely (hourly; 2hr 30min); Zalaegerszeg (9.50am; 1hr).

From Siófok to Győr (7.45am daily; 3hr); Mohács (5.30pm daily; 3hr); Pécs (6.40am daily; 3hr); Szekszárd (5.30pm daily; 1hr 45min); Veszprém (4.30pm daily; 1hr).

From Sümeg to Győr (5.35am, 11.25am & 4.45pm daily; 2hr 15min); Keszthely (3.30pm daily; 45min); Sárvár (6.15am & 4.10pm daily; 1hr 15min); Sopron (6.15am & 4.10pm daily; 2hr 15min).

From Székesfehérvár to Badacsony (3pm daily; 2hr 30min); Budapest (every 40–60min; 1hr); Kalocsa (Sun 7.35am; 3hr); Pécs (5.35am daily; 4hr); Szekszárd (8am & 4.25pm daily; 2hr); Veszprém (every 40–90min; 1hr); Zalaegerszeg (5.20am & 3pm daily; 4hr 15min).

From Tapolca to Balatonfüred (Mon–Sat 5.30am; 1hr 30min); Nagyvázsony (8 daily; 45min); Sümeg (hourly; 30min); Veszprém (every 2hr; 1hr).

From Veszprém to Budapest (every 60–90min; 2hr 15min); Győr (4.30pm, 5.30pm, 6pm & 7.15pm daily; 2hr); Harkány (6.10am daily; 4hr); Herend (hourly; 30min); Nagyvázsony (7am, 10.20am, 1.10pm & 2.20pm daily & Mon–Sat noon, 3.30pm & 4.50pm; 25min); Nemesvámos (hourly; 25min) Siófok (7.30am daily; 1hr 30min); Székesfehérvár (every 60–90min; 1hr); Szekszárd (6.30am & 2.50pm daily; 3hr 45min); Tapolca (7am, 10.20am, 1.10pm & 2.20pm daily & Mon–Sat noon, 3.30pm & 4.50pm; 1hr).

From Zirc to Budapest (7.35am, 11.35am & 4.25pm daily; 2hr 30min).

International Trains

From Balatonszentgyörgy to Zagreb (9.05am daily; 4hr).

From Fonyód to Dresden (June–Sept 6.40pm daily; 15hr); Leipzig (June–Sept 6.40pm daily; 17hr); Zagreb (June–Sept 2.15am & 3.10pm daily; 2hr).

From Siófok to Dresden (June–Sept 7.40pm daily; 14hr); Leipzig (June–Sept 7.40pm daily; 16hr); Prague (June–Sept 7.40pm daily; 10hr); Vienna (12.15pm daily; 5hr); Zagreb (8.10am daily & June–Sept 1.40am & 2.25pm daily; 2hr 30min).

From Székesfehérvár to Dresden (June–Sept 8.20pm daily; 12hr); Leipzig (June–Sept 8.20pm daily; 14hr); Prague (June–Sept 8.20pm daily; 9hr); Vienna (11.40am daily; 5hr 45min); Zagreb (7.40am daily & June–Sept 1am & 1.45pm daily; 6hr).

International buses

From Balatonboglár to Vienna (July–Aug Sat 1.45pm; 5hr 15min).

From Balatonföldvár to Banská Bystrica (July–Oct Sat 5pm; 5hr 30min).

From Balatonszeped to Vienna (July–Aug Sat 1.45pm; 5hr 15min).

From Hévíz to Vienna (July–Aug 3.35pm daily; 6hr 30min).

From Keszthely to Graz (Wed & Sat 4pm & June–Sept 7.25pm daily; 4hr 30min).

From Siófok to Amsterdam (June–Sept Mon 10pm; 24hr); Bratislava (July–Aug 4pm daily; 5hr 15min); Brno (July–Aug 3.45pm daily; 7hr); Frankfurt (June–Sept Mon 7am & 10pm; 18hr); Galanta (July–Aug 5.45pm daily; 4hr 15min); Semmering (July–Aug 2.40pm daily; 6hr); Trnava (July–Aug Sun 4.30pm; 5hr 30min); Vienna (July–Aug Sat 2.10pm; 5hr).

From Veszprém to Nitra (6am daily; 4hr 30min); Vienna (Mon, Thurs & Fri 5.50am; 4hr 30min).

From Zalakros to Vienna (5.30am daily; 4hr 45min).

Ferries

Unless specified otherwise, most of the following services run from mid-April until late August or mid-September. Bear in mind that schedules can change, so all departure times should be verified on the spot.

From Badacsony to Balatonboglár (July–Aug 9.55am, 12.40pm, 4.15pm, 5.50pm & 6.10pm daily; 1hr); Balatonföldvár (July–Aug 4.15pm daily; 2hr 45min); Fonyód (mid-April to mid-Oct 8.45am, 10am, 11.25am, 12.45pm, 2.25pm, 3.45pm, 4.15pm, 5pm, 6.20pm, 7.25pm & 7.40pm daily; 45min); Siófok (June–Aug 4.25pm daily; 4hr 30min); Tihany (June–Aug 4.25pm daily; 3hr).

From Balatonboglár to Révfülöp (July–Aug 9.10am, 10.45am, 12.15pm, 2.25pm, 3.30pm, 5pm & 6.20pm daily; 30min); Badacsony (July–Aug 8.45am, 10am, 11.25am, 12.45pm, 2.25pm, 3.45pm, 4.15pm, 5pm, 6.20pm, 7.25pm & 7.40pm daily; 30min).

From Balatonföldvár to Balatonfüred (8am, 11.10am, 2.30pm & 5.15pm daily; 1hr); Keszthely (July–Aug 9.25am daily; 5hr); Siófok (8am, 11.10am, 2.30pm & 5.15pm daily; 2hr); Tihany (8am, 11.10am, 2.30pm & 5.15pm daily; 30min).

From Balatonfüred to Balatonföldvár (8.30am, 12.10pm, 2.30pm & 6.20pm daily; 1hr); Tihany (8.30am, 9.20am, 11.50am, 12.10pm, 2.30pm & 6.20pm daily; 30min); Siófok (8.40am, 9am, noon, 12.15pm, 2.30pm, 3.40pm, 4.30pm & 6.25pm daily; 1hr).

From Fonyód to Badacsony (mid-April to mid-Oct 8am, 9.25am, 10.45am, noon, 1.45pm, 3pm, 4.25pm, 4.50pm, 5.40pm & 6.50pm daily; 30min).

From Keszthely to Badacsony (July–Aug 8am, 10.40am, noon, 2pm & 5.50pm daily; 45min); Balatonföldvár (2pm daily; 5hr).

From Révfülöp to Balatonboglár (July–Aug 9.40am, 11.40am, 12.50pm, 3pm, 4.25pm, 5.40pm & 7pm daily; 30min).

From Siófok to Badacsony (July–Aug 8am daily; 4hr 30min); Balatonföldvár (7.40am, 11.20am, 1.40pm & 5.30pm daily; 2hr); Balatonfüred (7.40am, 8.30am, 11am, 11.20am, 1.40pm, 4pm & 5.30pm daily; 1hr); Tihany (7.40am, 8.30am, 11am, 11.20am, 1.40pm & 5.30pm daily; 1hr 15min).

From Szántódrév to Tihany-rév (April–Nov every 40–60min; 10min).

From Tihany to Badacsony (July–Aug 9.20am daily; 2hr 30min); Balatonföldvár (8.55am, 12.35pm, 3pm & 6.45pm daily; 30min); Balatonfüred (8.35am, 11.45am, 3pm & 5.50pm daily; 30min); Siófok (8.35am, 11.45am, 3pm & 5.50pm daily; 1hr 15min).

From Tihany-rév to Szántódrév (April–Nov every 40–60min; 10min).

CHAPTER FOUR

TRANSDANUBIA

Travelling between Budapest and Vienna it's easy to gain a poor impression of **Transdanubia** – the *Dunántúl* – from the monotonous *Kisalföld* (Little Plain) or the industrial dreck around Tatabánya. What you don't see in passing is lakeside Tata, Győr's antique waterfront, Sopron's cobbled streets, deer in the Forest of Gemenc, or the rolling Mecsek Hills. More than other regions in Hungary, Transdanubia is a patchwork land, an ethnic and social hybrid. Its valleys, hills, forests and mud flats have been a melting pot since Roman times, when the region was known as *Pannonia*. Settled since by Magyars, Serbs, Croats, Germans and Slovaks, it has been torn asunder and occupied by Turks and Habsburgs; and only within the last 150 years has it been raised from a state of near feudalism.

Though **Szombathely** with its Temple of Isis and other ruins has the most to show for its Roman origins, all the main **towns** display evidence of this evolution. **Castles** (*vár*) are at the heart of them: survivors of the centuries of warfare that decimated medieval culture, leaving only a few superb churches – for example at **Ják** and **Velemér** – and living evidence in the form of **Pannonhalma Monastery**. Around each weathered *vár* stands a *Belváros*, with rambling streets and squares overlooked by florid Baroque and the odd Gothic or Renaissance building. **Tata**, **Kőszeg** and **Győr** provide fine examples of the genre; so too does **Sopron**, the most archaic, and **Pécs**, which boasts a Turkish mosque and minaret.

While several towns host spring or summer **festivals** of classical music, drama, folk music and dancing, the most interesting event is the masked *Busó Carnival* at **Mohács** in March. During summer, concerts are also held in two unique settings – the **Esterházy Palace** at **Fertőd** and the rock chambers of **Fertőrákos** – both close to Sopron and **Nagycenk**, where you can ride antique **steam trains** on the Széchenyi Railway. At the monthly **market** in Pécs, you'll sense the peasant roots underlying many Transdanubian towns, whose sprawling *lakótelep* house recent immigrants from the countryside.

NORTHERN TRANSDANUBIA

Northern Transdanubia consists of the low-lying Kisalföld, bounded by the Vértes Hills and the Danube. Aside from the hills and the Szigetköz region bordering the river, its scenery is uninspiring, focusing one's attention on the towns. Lakeside Tata is delightful, and often overlooked by tourists travelling between Budapest and Győr – as is Komárom, the main crossing into Czechoslovakia. Besides the intrinsic appeal of its lovely Belváros, Győr is an ideal base for excursions to Pannonhalma Monastery. All these towns lie along the main rail line to Mosonmagyaróvár, served by frequent **trains** from Budapest's Déli or Keleti stations, and most can also be reached by **bus** from the Erzsébet tér depot. **Motorists** should avoid the unfinished M1 motorway between Budapest and Győr – where traffic is lethal – and use the more northerly route via Tata and Komárom.

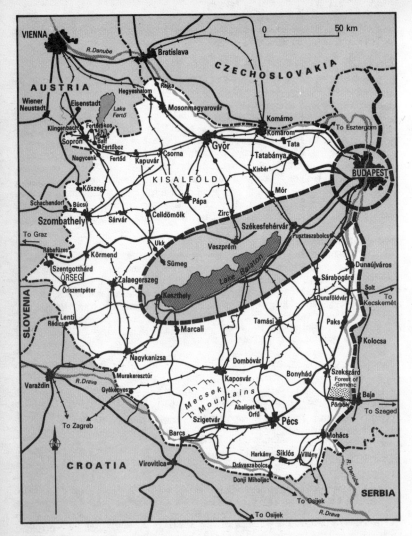

Zsámbék and Tatabánya

Heading out from Budapest, the Vértes Hills form a prelude to the Kisalföld, worth a brief detour if not an extended visit. **ZSÁMBÉK**, 33km west, deserves a mention for its **ruined thirteenth-century Romanesque church**, whose arches and walls look as romantic as a Piranesi drawing. Built for the Premonstratensians by the Ainard family (of French descent, they came over during the Angevin monarchy), the church later passed to the Pauline order, and was destroyed by an earthquake in 1763. Zsámbék can be reached by bus from

Széna tér (near Moszkva tér) in the capital – bring a picnic and make an afternoon of it. To get an idea of what the church once looked like, check out the replica constructed on Élmunkás tér in Budapest during the 1930s.

Tatabánya

Following the direct Budapest–Vienna route, you can't miss **TATABÁNYA**, an ugly industrial town surrounded by ravaged countryside. Its only "sight", the giant bronze **Turul statue**, can be glimpsed from a train carriage window, perched on a mountain top overlooking the grimy sprawl. Erected to commemorate the thousandth anniversary of the Magyar conquest, this great monument shows the legendary bird of prey clutching the sword of Árpád in its talons. The only reasons for a closer encounter with Tatabánya are the **Jazz Festival** (some time in summer) and the chance to go **walking in the Vértes Hills**, where the **ruined Vitány Castle** broods on a crag 5km south of town (catch a bus to Vértessomló and walk up). Legend has it that the cowslips that grow around here during April are able to guide you towards hidden treasure.

Accommodation in Tatabánya's Újváros district includes the *Árpád Hotel* on Fő tér (☎34/10-299; ④); private rooms (②) from *Komturist*, Győri út 1A (☎34/11-936); and *Nomád Camping*, Tolnai út 14 (April–Sept; ☎34/11-507).

Tata

A small, sleepy town interlaced with canals and streams, **TATA** derives its charm from its lakes. Misty mornings enhance the romance of the **Old Lake** (*Öreg-tó*), with its castle and pillared riding school, slender trees and spires.

Following Tópart utca round past a statue of the "Tata mermaid", you'll come to a thatched building that was once an abattoir and now contains a **Butchers Museum** (May–Sept Tues–Sun 10am–6pm), and then to an ornate **Mill** built in 1753. Beyond lies Tata's moated **Castle** (Tues–Sun 10am–6pm), originally the hunting lodge of King Sigismund. Badly damaged by the Turks and Habsburgs, its now contains a museum of Roman miniatures and faience by Domokos Kuny (1754–1822), a local craftsman.

From here you can wander up Rákóczi utca into the old town, reconstructed under Jakab Fellner after the Turkish and Rákóczi wars. Tata's former synagogue is now home to a **museum** of replica Greek and Roman statuary, including life-sized plaster casts of the Elgin Marbles, Hercules and Laocoön (May–Oct Tues–Sun 10am–6pm; Nov–April Tues–Fri 10am–2pm, Sat & Sun 10am–4pm). The mental **hospital** to the north of Hősök tere occupies an Esterházy mansion where the Habsburg king Francis took refuge from Napoleon in 1809. At the top of the hill, alleys lead off Kossuth tér towards **Calvary Hill** with its crucifixion monument, **nature reserve** and outdoor **Geological Museum** (Sat & Sun 10am–4pm).

Alternatively, head east from the castle along Alkotmány utca, where the old Nepomucenus Mill at no. 1 houses an **Ethnographic Museum** devoted to the German communities of the Little Plain (May–Oct Tues–Sun 10am–6pm; Nov–April Tues–Fri 10am–2pm, Sat & Sun 10am–4pm). As always the costumes are best: the men wearing jackboots with braided black and stovepipe hats, the women swathing their layers of petticoats and ruffles with embroidered shawls. Amongst the *Volk*, Tata was known as *Totis*.

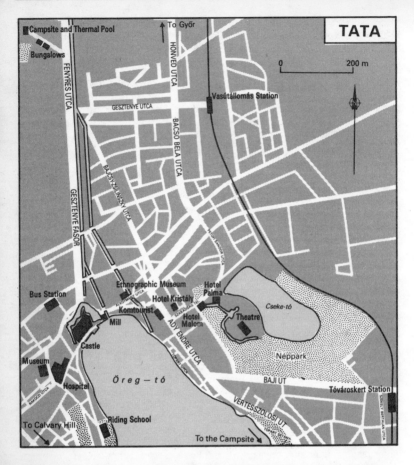

Beyond the stretch of main highway dubbed Ady Endre utca, peace returns as you follow Szabadság tér into the **Néppark** surrounding the **Small Lake** (*Cseke-tó*). Also known as Angol Park – the "English Park" – this contains an outdoor **theatre** and swimming **pool**, and a fake ruined church cobbled together from Roman and Benedictine stonework. Hungary's Olympic team has its main training facility along the southern edge of the park.

Riding, Remetségpuszta and Kocs

Tata's **Riding School** (*Lovasiskola*) is over a century old, with a grandiose ring modelled on the Spanish Riding School in Vienna. It offers lessons, point-to-point races through the woods, extended riding tours and (in the autumn) hunting. *Komturist* or the *Hotel Kristály* (see below) can supply details, and tell you about **fishing**. There is an outdoor **thermal pool** on the edge of town (bus #3 to the end of the line). Rowing **boats** (*csónakázás*) and pedal boats (*vízibicikli*) can be hired beside the Old Lake.

REMETSÉGPUSZTA, south of town, is a **Game Park** with a hotel catering to wealthy hunters, a nice place to visit outside the hunting season (bus #4 to the end of the line). Lastly, it would be churlish not to mention KOCS, 11km southwest of Tata, where the **coach** (far lighter and more comfortable than the wagons used up to then) was invented in the seventeenth century – not that the village has anything to show for it.

Practicalities

Arriving by train, you'll be deposited at the main Vasútallomás station 1km from the centre (bus #1), or at the Tóvároskert station, 600m east of Öreg-tó (bus #5). The intercity bus station is a couple of blocks behind the castle. *Komtourist,* Ady utca 9 (summer Mon–Fri 9am–5pm, Sat 8am–noon; winter Mon–Fri 8am–4pm; ☎34/81-805), can supply **information** and book private rooms (②–③), which can also be arranged by *Cooptourist,* Tópart-sétány 18 (☎34/81-602). Other **accommodation** includes:

Hotel Kristály, Ady Endre utca 22 (☎34/83-577). Noisy location, but its 200-year-old dining room is appealing. Doubles and singles with showers or baths; breakfast included. ③–④.

Hotel Malom, Erzsébet tér 8 (☎34/83-530). A nicer place nearer the park, closed over winter. Shared bathrooms. ②.

Pálma Hotel, in the Néppark (☎34/83-577). Even better setting and ambience, but likely to be full over summer. Shared bathrooms. ②.

Motel Magyar Aszfalt, Fényesfasor (☎34/82-771). The latest name for a clutch of **bungalows** with tennis courts and a sauna, near the thermal baths (bus #3). ③–④.

Fényes-Fürdő Camping, Fényesfasor (☎34/81-591). By the thermal baths beyond the motel, where bus #3 terminates. April 1–Oct 15.

Öreg tó Camping, Fáklya utca (☎34/83-128). Bungalows (②–③) and tennis courts, between the lake and the motorway. To get there from Tóvároskert station, follow Székely B. utca to the end, then Öveges J. utca. April 1–Oct 15.

Moving on

Trains are best for reaching Budapest, Győr or Sopron, but **buses** run more frequently to Tatabánya, Komárom and Esztergom. To reach Esztergom by rail entails changing at Almásfüzitő or Komárom.

Komárom

KOMÁROM is the main crossing between Hungary and Czechoslovakia, linked by a road and rail bridge to Komárno, across the Danube. The two towns formed a single municipality until 1920, and ethnic Magyars still predominate in Czechoslovak Komárno, where shops and streets are signposted in both languages. Though neither town has much to offer in the way of sights, the easy crossing and good **connections** between Komárno and Bratislava make this a useful stepping-stone en route to the Slovak capital.

From Komárom railway station it's a five minute walk to **the Hungarian side** of the 500m-long bridge, thronged by locals walking across the border. Since Roman times, the crossing has been secured by a fortress at the confluence of the Danube and the Váh. The existing **Csillag Fortress** was built by the Habsburgs, captured by the Hungarians in 1849, and occupied by Soviet troops until a few years ago. Just downriver and set back from the water, there is a **thermal bathing complex** (Tues–Sun 8am–6pm) open year round.

Should you cross over to **Czechoslovak Komárno**, its bus and railway stations are 2km northwest of the main street, Zahradnichka Slovanská. Just in from the bridge, on ulica Gábora Steiner, is a small **museum** (Tues–Sun 10am–noon & 2–4pm) that pays tribute to two local sons, **Franz Lehár** and **Mór Jókai**. The former, the composer of the *Merry Widow*, was born here in 1870 and initially followed in his father's footsteps as bandmaster with the local garrison; Jókai was an extremely nationalistic Hungarian novelist who would not approve of the town's modern-day split nationality. In the museum grounds stands a small **Orthodox church** built by Serbian refugees from the Turks early in the eighteenth century.

Practicalities

Accommodation in Komárom clusters around the thermal baths, where you'll find the *Thermal Hotel* at Táncsics utca 38 (☎37/446; ③–④), and the marginally cheaper *Hotel Juno* across the road. Next door to the former is a pleasant **campsite**, open year round. If you'd rather stay in Komárno, rooms in its three hotels can be booked through *ČEDOK* on Zahradnichka Slovanská.

Crossing the border is quite straightforward, with both country's passport controls at the Czechoslovak end of the bridge. The information desks in Komárom and Komárno railway stations can tell you the time of the next bus running from one to the other (every couple of hours) if you don't fancy walking. There are regular local trains from Komárno **to Bratislava** (110km), eliminating the need to use international services (which cross the border here at night). If you're **entering Hungary**, there are fairly frequent trains and buses from Komárom to Budapest, Esztergom (for the Danube Bend) and Győr.

Győr

The industrial city of **GYŐR** (pronounced "Dyur") harbours a waterfront Belváros stuffed with Baroque mansions and churches, where streets bustle and restaurants vie for custom. With so much to enjoy around the centre, you can easily forget the high-rise blocks and factories that form the rest of Győr, whose Rába Engineering Works – producing trucks and rolling stock – is the third largest industrial complex in Hungary. The city also makes an excellent base for excursions to Pannonhalma Monastery.

Győr's **history** owes much to its location at the confluence of three rivers – the Rába, the Rábca and the Mosoni-Duna – in the centre of the Little Plain. The Romans called the place *Arrabona*, after the local Celtic tribe whom they subjugated, while its current name derives from *gyürü*, the Avar word for a circular fortress. During the Turkish occupation of Hungary, its castle was a Habsburg stronghold and the town was known as *Raab* (after the Rába River). After its military role diminished, Győr gained industrial muscle and a different kind of clout. In the 1956 Uprising, its Town Hall was occupied by a radical Provisional National Council that pressed the government to get Soviet troops out, and quit the Warsaw Pact, immediately. As an indication of how Hungary has changed since then, a neo-Nazi cell with links to Austrian and American fascists was recently unearthed in Győr.

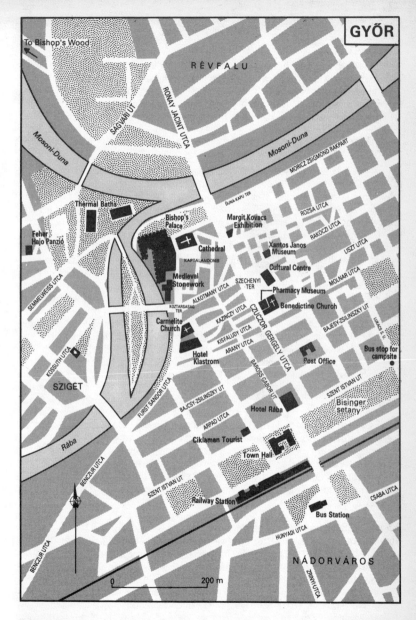

GYŐR

RÉVFALU

To Bishop's Wood

RÓNAY JÁCINT UTCA

SAGVARI UT

Mosoni-Duna

Mosoni-Duna

MÓRICZ ZSIGMOND RAKPART

DUNA KAPU TÉR

Thermal Baths

Bishop's Palace

Margit Kovacs Exhibition

ROZSA UTCA

RÁKÓCZI UTCA

LISZT UTCA

Feher Hajo Panzió

Cathedral

Xantos Janos Museum

KAPTALANDOMB

SEMMELWEISS UTCA

Medieval Stonework

Cultural Centre

MOLNAR UTCA

SZECHENYI TÉR

ALKOTMANY UTCA

Pharmacy Museum

KOZTARSASAG TÉR

Benedictine Church

KAZINCZY UTCA

CZUCZOR GERGELY UTCA

Carmelite Church

BAJCSY-ZSILINSZKY UT

KOSSUTH UTCA

KISFALUDY UTCA

LUKÁCS S. U.

Hotel Klastrom

ARANY UTCA

Bus stop for campsite

SZIGET

FURST SANDOR UTCA

BAROSS GABOR UTCA

Post Office

BAJCSY-ZSILINSZKY UT

Hotel Rába

SZENT ISTVAN UT

Bisinger setany

Rába

ARPAD UTCA

Ciklamen Tourist

Town Hall

BENCZUR UTCA

SZENT ISTVAN UT

Railway Station

CSABA UTCA

Bus Station

BENCZUR UTCA

HUNYADI UTCA

NÁDORVÁROS

ZRINYI UTCA

0   200 m

Orientation

Arriving at the bus or railway station you can seek lodgings in the vicinity first, or head straight for the Belváros, a ten- to fifteen-minute walk over the Baross

> The Győr telephone code is ☎96

Bridge which crosses the railway line, and across Szent István út, a wind tunnel of an avenue which, until a new bypass is built, serves as the main route to Vienna. Assuming you make it safely across, it's easy to find *Ciklámen Tourist* at Aradi vértanúk útja 22 (Mon, Tues & Fri 8am–4pm, Thurs 10am–6pm, Sat 8am–1pm; ☎11-557), where you can book rooms and obtain **information**.

Around the Belváros

A web of streets and alleys stretching from Széchenyi tér to Káptalandomb, the **old quarter** is covered by preservation orders and traffic restrictions, making it a pleasure to wander around. Heading up pedestrians-only Baross Gábor út, antique sidestreets beckon on your left, narrow and shadowy with overhanging timbered houses – the setting for a conspiracy. Indeed, Communists met secretly during the Horthy years at no. 15 on Sárlo köz, a cobbled alley forking off Kazinczy utca.

Chances are you'll emerge on to **Köztársaság tér**, overlooking the River Rába, which reputedly escaped flooding in the eighteenth century thanks to a miracle-working statue of Mary of the Foam, occupying a chapel beside the former **Carmelite Church**. Entering through a portal whose inscription proclaims "I worked zealously for the Lord of Hosts", you'll find a richly decorated high altar and other furnishings carved by Franz Richter, a lay brother in the order. Behind the church stands the erstwhile monastery, subsequently used as a refugee centre and military prison, and now converted into the *Hotel Klastrom*.

On the eastern side of the square are two **mansions** with finely wrought ironwork. The Zichy Palace (no. 13), built in 1778–82, has a balconied, Zopf-style facade bearing the coat of arms of the Ott family, who owned it at a later date. Next door stands the Altabek House (no. 12), with two corner oriel windows dating back to the sixteenth century, and a Baroque portico. Just around the corner at Alkotmány utca 4 is the so-called Napoleon House where the Emperor stayed during a visit in 1809, and which now contains a **Picture Gallery** of mostly nineteenth-century works (Tues–Sun April–Oct 10am–6pm; Nov–March 10am–5pm).

From Köztársaság tér you can head uphill past the surviving bastions of Győr's sixteenth-century **castle**, where visitors can see a courtyard full of medieval stonework and underground casements (April–Oct Tues–Sun 10am–6pm). The castle successfully resisted the Turks for decades – unlike the town, which was frequently devastated.

Káptalandomb and the waterfront

Káptalandomb (Chapter Hill) has been crowned by a **Cathedral** (daily 9.15am–noon & 2–6pm) ever since King Stephen made Győr an episcopal see in the eleventh century, so the existing building incorporates Romanesque, Gothic and Baroque features. Just inside the entrance, the Gothic Hederváry Chapel contains a **reliquary bust of Saint László**, preserving a fragment of the skull of this canonised monarch (1077–95). Sensitively moulded and richly enamelled, it is a superb example of the goldsmith's art from the workshop of the Kolozsvári brothers. The frescoes inside the cathedral were painted by Maulbertsch, who decorated numerous Hungarian churches in the eighteenth century; while the Bishop's throne was a gift from Empress Maria Theresa.

The building to the southeast of the cathedral houses the **Miklós Borsos Collection** of paintings and sculptures by the self-taught artist who designed the Kilometre Zero monument in Budapest (Tues–Sun April–Sept 10am–6pm; Oct–March 9.30am–4.30pm). In the other direction lies the **Bishop's Palace** (*Püspökvár*), a much remodelled edifice whose oldest section dates from the thirteenth century (Tues–Sun April–Sept 9am–6pm; Nov–March 10am–5pm).

From here you can walk down Káptalandomb utca past the Zopf-style Provost House (no. 15) to reach the **Ark of the Covenant**, a splendid Baroque monument erected by Emperor Karl III by way of an apology for the Habsburg soldiers who knocked the monstrance from a priest's hands during a Corpus Christi procession in 1727. Just beyond lies **Duna-kapu tér**, a waterfront square alongside which Danube grain ships once moored, and where food **markets** are still held on Wednesdays and Saturdays. Notice the iron weathercock on top of the well, an allusion to the one that the Turks fixed above the town's gate, boasting that they would never leave Győr until it crowed.

Across the river

Should you want a change of scenery, cross the Mosoni-Duna River to the **Révfalu** district, where a fifteen-minute walk will bring you to the **Bishop's Wood** (*Püspök-erdő*), an attractive park with deer and other fauna. Alternatively, you can cross the Rába via a small island linked by bridge to Köztársaság tér and the **Sziget** district. There is an outdoor **thermal bath** (currently closed for repairs) at the northern tip of Sziget, and a domed former **Synagogue** at Kossuth utca 15.

Around Széchenyi tér

There's more to see, however, behind Duna-kapu tér, starting with the **Margit Kovács Collection** at Rózsa Ferenc utca 1 (Tues–Sun April–Sept 10am–6pm; Oct–March 10am–5pm). This is just as delightful as the museum of her work in Szentendre (p.115), but closer to home, as Kovács (1902–77) was born in Győr. On the other side of the road, Bread Alley (*Kenyér köz*) and Soap Alley (*Szappanos köz*) lead to **Széchenyi tér**, traditionally the main square, overlooked by eye-like attic windows from the steep roofs of surrounding buildings.

Notice the **Iron Stump House** (no. 4) on the northern side of the square, so-called after a wooden beam into which travelling journeymen hammered nails to mark their sojourn. The building now contains the **Imre Patkó Collection** of paintings and African art (April–Oct Tues–Sun 10am–6pm), which deserves a visit. Next door is the **Xantos János Museum** (Tues–Sun April–Sept 10am–6pm; Oct–March 10am–5pm), named after a locally educated archaeologist (1825–94) who emigrated to America and subsequently travelled in China. You can buy a leaflet in English describing the varied and fascinating artefacts relating to local history, while the collection of tiled stoves needs no explanation.

Further east, take a look into the Tuscan Renaissance-style courtyard of the erstwhile **Hospice** at Rákóczi utca 6; a second courtyard at the back contains a fountain embellished with statues of birds. Back on Széchenyi tér, with its ornate **Marian Column** commemorating the recapture of Buda Castle from the Turks, the **Benedictine Church of Saint Ignatius** was designed by the Italian Baccio del Bianco in the 1630s. A painting in the sanctuary by the Viennese artist Troger (1794) depicts the saint's apotheosis. Beside the adjacent monastery is the **Pharmacy Museum**, a beautifully furnished seventeenth-century apocethary that still functions as a pharmacy (Mon, Tues, Thurs & Fri 9am–5pm; Wed & Sat 2–5pm; Sun 9am–1pm).

Practicalities

From mid-July to mid-August, the cheapest **accommodation** available is **dormitory beds** (①) in the Technical College at Ságvári Endre utca 3, on Révfalu. Bookings can be made through *Express* at Bajcsy-Zsilinszky út 41 (Mon–Fri 8am–5pm; ☎18-853). Regular **private rooms** (②–③) are bookable through *Ciklámen Tourist* (see above) or *IBUSZ*, at Szent István út 31 (Mon–Fri 8am–5pm, Sat 9am–noon; ☎14-224). You might also enquire about the sporadically open tourist **hostel** at Révai Miklós utca 5 (☎14-629), near the railway station. Other options are:

HOTELS

Hotel Klastrom, Fürst Sándor utca 1 (☎15-611). Behind the Carmelite church, with a beautiful restaurant and courtyard in the old priory – very classy. ⑤–⑥.

Hotel Raba, Árpád út 34 (☎15-533). A well-equipped Seventies block near the main street. ⑤.

Hotel Aranypart, Áldozat utca 12 (☎26-033). Modern, sports-oriented budget hotel in Révfalu, accessible by bus #16 from the Town Hall. ③–④.

Budaflax Hotel, Kandó Kálmán utca 1 (☎11-344). On the edge of the industrial *Gyárváros*, 1km east of the centre. ②–③.

Graboplast Hotel, Mészáros Lőrinc utca 20 (☎16-999). A few blocks east of the bus station, beyond the *Corvin Panzió* (see below). ③.

PENSIONS

Corvin Panzió, Csaba utca 22 (☎12-171). A small pension three blocks east of the bus station. ③.

Kuckó Panzió, Arany János utca 33. Attached to a restaurant, right in the centre. ③–④.

Pető Panzió, Kossuth Lajos utca 20 (☎13-412 or 12-195). On Sziget, accessible by bus #1 or #1Y from Aradi vértanúk útja. Breakfast included. ③.

Fehér Hajó Panzió, Kiss Ernő utca 4 (☎18-050). A larger pension sited near the thermal baths. ③.

Révesz Panzió, Ságvári Endre utca 22 (☎20-667). Between the Technical College and the *Hotel Aranypart* in Révfalu. ③.

CAMPING

Ciklámen Camping, Kiskút-liget (☎18-986). A big site with bungalows (②–③) near the stadium beyond the industrial district; catch bus #8 from Szent István út, opposite Lukács Sándor utca. April 15–Oct 15.

Napsugár Camping, Külső Veszprémi út (☎11-042). A motorists' stopover miles out along the Veszprém road. May 15–Sept 30.

Balázs Béla Camping, Vajcsuk L. utca 70 (☎29-033). Small private site near a housing estate in the Nádorváros district (bus #5 or #22 from the Baross Bridge). June 15–Aug 25.

Eating and drinking

Most **restaurants** in Győr close early, around 10pm. If money isn't a problem, indulge yourself at the *Várkapu Étterem*, Köztársaság tér 7, or the *Apostolok* on Széchenyi tér. Less pricey options include the *Matróz Csárda* at Duna-kapu tér 3 and the *halászcsárda* at Rózsa Ferenc utca 4 – for game and fish, respectively – and the Chinese restaurant above the *Jereván* bar on the island opposite Kóztársaság tér. The friendly *Szalai Vendéglő*, Kisfaludy utca 34, does tasty cheap pizzas, while the *Tejivó Salatbár* at no. 30 offers salads and real fruit milkshakes. For cheap snacks and grills, try the *Duna-kapu Ételbár* on the corner of that square, or the *Korzó Étterem* at Baross Gábor út 13 – both are self-service. Spicy fish soup can be eaten at the *Magyar Büfe* wine cellar, Árpád út 18.

Two cellars for **drinking** are the *Szürkebarát Borozó*, Arany János utca 20, and the *Vár-borozó*, midway along Alkotmány utca. The *Jereván* on the island is a cheaper late-night haunt than *Charly's Night Klub*, Nagy István utca 12, whose dance floor is almost deserted due to the 300Ft admission charge. Cocktails and spirits can also be drunk in **patisseries** like the *Rába Cukrászda* at Baross Gábor út 30. Alternatively, catch a #4 bus out to the Nádorváros to enjoy the old-fashioned ambience of the *Bergmann Cukrászda*, at József Attila utca 29 (Wed–Sun 10am–6pm).

Entertainments

Ciklámen Tourist can give you a rundown of **entertainments** on offer, including its own boat and fishing trips. Culture vultures should look out for performances by the **Győr Ballet Company**, which achieved international renown under its founder Iván Márko, formerly the lead dancer of Maurice Béjarat's Twentieth Century Ballet Company. Although Márko has moved on and foreign critics now disparage the company, locals still cherish it, and performances at the brashly-tiled **Kisfaludy Theatre** on the corner of Bajcsy-Zsilinszky út and Czuczor Gergely utca always sell out.

Another source of pride is the city's **football** team, Rába ETO, which has in the past humbled such foreign clubs as Manchester United at their stadium in the eastern suburbs (bus #8). Undubbed foreign **films** are often screened at the cinema at the back of the park to the north of the Baross Bridge.

Other things: moving on

The main **post office** is at Bajcsy-Zsilinszky út 46, while **police** headquarters are at Zrínyi utca 54, near the bus station. There are several **hospitals** along Felszabadulás útja, 1km further south. If you're planning to visit Lébénymiklós (see overpage), it might be worth **hiring a car** from *Hertz* at Bartók utca 10 (☎13-013).

Moving on, the obvious destination to the west is Sopron (see p.187), which is easily reached by train. Heading for Vienna or Bratislava instead, the only significant place en route is Mosonmagyaróvár (described below). Szombathely in western Transdanubia can be reached by trains routed through Papa, while another branch line runs south to Veszprém (p.166) via Pannonhalma. Express trains and buses to Budapest take about two hours.

Pannonhalma Monastery

Twenty kilometres southeast of Győr the low-lying Kisalföld meets a spur of the Bakony, a glorious setting for the fortress-like **Pannonhalma Monastery** atop Saint Martin's Hill (282m). According to Anonymous, it was here that Árpád was "uplifted by the beauty of Pannonia" after the Magyar conquest, and Prince Géza invited the **Benedictine Order** to found an abbey in 969. The Order helped Géza's son Stephen weld the pagan Magyar tribes into a Christian state, and remained influential until its suppression in 1787 by Emperor Josef II. Re-established by his successor, the Benedictines thereafter confined themselves to prayer and pedagogy.

Tourists are admitted to the monastery– whose imposing hillside buildings manifest a wide variety of styles and antiquity– only on **guided tours** (Tues–Sun 9am–4pm, every hour on the hour except midday; 200Ft or 400Ft depending on duration). The Gothic **cloisters** date from the first quarter of the thirteenth century, when Pannonhalma was remodelled under Abbot Oros, who later gave King Béla IV 220 kilos of silver to help him rebuild the country after the Mongol invasion. The wings are chiefly Romanesque, contrasting with the Baroque exterior of the **church** and a Neoclassical **tower**. Purists lament the church's neo-Romanesque interior, remodelled by Ferenc Storno in 1867. Notice the exquisitely carved portal and marble sepulchres containing the bones of two abbots and a princess.

Although Pannonhalma's most sacred **treasures** are displayed only on a couple of days around August 20, its medieval codices and ancient books are permanently on show in the Empire-style **library**. The 300,000-volume collection includes the foundation deed of Tihany Abbey, dating from 1055 – the earliest known document to include Hungarian words (55 of them) amongst the customary Latin. A one-room **art gallery** displays a portrait of King Stephen and paintings by Italian, Dutch and German artists of the sixteenth and seventeenth centuries.

Believers have a choice of two **masses** on Sunday: with (9am) or without (10am) a sermon and organ music. Fully fledged **organ recitals** usually occur on Easter Monday, Whit Sunday, August 20, October 23 and December 26, drawing crowds of music lovers. Book at least a week in advance through *Ciklámen Tourist* in Győr, or the local tourist office.

Practicalities

The monastery can be reached from Győr by any bus or train heading for Veszprém (or vice versa), although the railway station is 2km from the monastery. In the village below, *Pax Tourist* at Vár utca 1 (closed Mon; ☎96/70-191) can arrange private **accommodation** if you can't afford the *Pax Hotel* at Dózsa György utca 2 (☎96/70-006; ③–⑤), or point you towards a campsite with huts (May 1–Sept 30). There are several **restaurants** in the village.

Towards Mosonmagyaróvár

Driving to (or from) Vienna or Bratislava, one has the option of stopping over at Mosonmagyaróvár, or detouring off Route 1 to visit Lébénymiklós or the Szigetköz region. Since neither is accessible by bus or rail, however, travellers relying on public transport may reckon that it's not worth interrupting their journey for Mosonmagyaróvár alone.

Detouring off the highway to **LÉBÉNYMIKLÓS** is only recommended if you're a fan of ecclesiastical architecture, since the village's sole attraction is a thirteenth-century **Benedictine Church** that once came under the jurisdiction of Pannonhalma. Though touted as one of the oldest and finest examples of Romanesque architecture in Hungary, it was actually restored to its original style after receiving a Baroque facelift from the Jesuits in the mid-seventeenth century. If this sounds enticing, you can reach Lébénymiklós by turning west off the highway at Öttevény, 16km from Győr.

On the other side of the highway lies **the Szigetköz** or "Island region", bounded by the meandering Mosoni-Duna and the "Old" or main branch of the

Danube. This picturesque wetland abounds in rare flora, **birdlife** and fish, making it something of a paradise for hikers and naturalists alike. Unfortunately, the completion of the **Gabčikovo hydroelectric barrage** further upriver threatens to dry up the Szigetköz, ruining its ecology. Győr's *Reflex* environmental group (☎96/10-988) are hoping to prevent this and, with the help of the World Wildlife Fund, create a Trilateral National Park embracing the whole Danube region from Hainburg to Komárom, with responsibility going to Hungary for the Szigetköz.

Meantime, you can traverse the Szigetköz by a minor road running between Győr and Mosonmagyaróvár, which is ideal for **cyclists**. The village of LIPÓT, 2km off the road, offers **accommodation** in the form of the *Holt-Duna Panzió* (☎98/16-196; ②) and a basic campsite (May–Sept).

Mosonmagyaróvár

MOSONMAGYARÓVÁR is a fusion of two settlements near the confluence of the Mosoni-Duna and Lajtha rivers. While Moson – one side of the highway – is utterly prosaic, Magyaróvár on the other is a pleasant old town with a picturesque castle and bridges. Both are visibly prosperous, for hordes of Austrians come here to shop or for inexpensive medical attention, while townsfolk travel to work in Austria and return home to draw the dole, commuting by Mercedes. If you've got a choice, the best time to visit is late autumn, when the first pressing of grapes takes place at **vineyards** in the locality.

Entering town by the Győr road, you'll pass a couple of sights along Fő utca. The **Hanság Museum** at no. 135 is one of the oldest provincial collections in Hungary, covering local history since Roman times – but was closed for restoration when last heard. Once reopened, it is sure to include material on the event which made the town notorious in 1956 (see box). Further up the road at no. 103 stands the Baroque Cselley House (Tues–Sun April–Oct 10am–6pm; Nov–March 10am–5pm), hosting an **Exhibition of Fine and Applied Arts** from the seventeenth century onwards.

MASSACRE AT MOSONMAGYARÓVÁR

Three days after the Uprising begun in Budapest, a quarter of Mosonmagyaróvár's population staged a peaceful march on the Town Hall, demanding an end to Stalinism. ÁVO guards opened fire on the crowd without warning, killing 100 people and wounding 250. An Italian journalist was present, and news of the massacre was flashed around the world.

While most of the perpetrators were lynched shortly afterwards, the officer in charge escaped to enjoy a peaceful retirement in the Kádár era. Following the demise of Communism, the popular wish that such crimes should be punished led Parliament to pass the **Zétényi–Takács Law** (named after the two MPs that drafted it) in November 1991. However, others feared that it could be used against anyone associated with the Communist regime, and argued that Hungary had already suffered enough from political witch-hunts. Amongst its critics were President Árpád Göncz and MPs Imre Mécs and László Rajk Jr, who had been gaoled under Communism. In March 1992, Hungary's Constitutional Court overturned the law on the grounds that "the ethical glory of punishing a villain is not worth risking the legal guarantees of our constitutional state".

However the chief attraction is **Magyaróvár Castle**, just beyond Szent László tér (follow the signposts for Bratislava). Founded in the thirteenth century to guard the western gateway to Hungary, it gave the town its medieval name, *Porta Hungarica*. Much remodelled since then, it now houses a section of Keszthely's Agricultural University and a small exhibition on the fauna of the Hanság (Mon–Fri 10am–6pm), which enables you to gain access to the castle.

Practicalities

Both halves of town have their own **tourist office**. In Magyaróvár, *Ciklámen Tourist* is at Fő utca 8 (☎98/11-078), whilst in Moson you'll find their office at Szent István király út 108 (☎98/16-554). Either can book **private rooms** (③) if you don't fancy the **hostel** at Fő utca 119 (May–Oct; ☎98/11-780; ②) opposite the tourist office in Magyaróvár. You can try any of the following:

Szent Flórian Hotel, Fő utca 127 (☎98/13-177). A comfortable three-star establishment with wheelchair access. ④.

Fekete Sas Hotel, Fő utca 93 (☎98/15-842). Smaller place nearer the centre. ③.

Solaris Hotel, Lucsony utca 19 (☎98/15-300). Well equipped, and just east of the castle. ④.

Lajtha Hotel, Palánk utca 3 (☎98/11-824). A one-star place with tennis facilities and wheelchair access. ③.

Minerva Hotel, Engels út 2 (☎98/11-367). More basic and a bit cheaper. ②–③.

Magyar Autóklub, Gabona rakpart 6 (☎98/15-883). An unpleasantly overcrowded motorists' campsite by the river, with bungalows (②–③). May 1–Oct 15.

Jóker Camping, corner of Alkotmány and Baratság utca, next to the Polish Market (bus #4). A smaller, private site.

Restaurants and border crossings

Aside from various cheap **restaurants** along Fő utca, you might investigate the *Széchenyi Étterem* at Városház utca 2 and the *Várpince Étterem* at Vár utca 2. The *Ambrozia Kávéház* on the corner of Szent László tér in downtown Magyaróvár serves delicious cappucino and apple-poppyseed *retes*.

Mosonmagyaróvár is the last stop before two major **border crossings**. RAJKA, 19km north, handles traffic bound for the Slovak capital of Bratislava (15km), while HEGYESHALOM is the main road and rail crossing into Austria, whence it's 45km to Vienna. While the Czechoslovak border has relaxed considerably since the Velvet Revolution, controls along the Austrian border have been tightened up again since 1990 (see box).

THE AUSTRO-HUNGARIAN BORDER

The **Austro–Hungarian border** used to be wired and mined, with guards authorised to shoot would-be escapers. Then in the spring of 1989, the removal of life-threatening barriers encouraged thousands of East Germans to use Hungary as an escape route to the West, precipitating the dramatic events that led to the fall of the Berlin Wall. Hungarians gained the right to travel anywhere with the introduction of the so-called *Világ* (World) passport in 1988, but for citizens of Romania and the former USSR the border is still a barrier unless they have a Western visa, which the average person has no chance of getting. Hence the tragi-comic scenes as trains approach Hegyeshalom, with young Romanians torn between hiding under the seats (where guards always check) or hoping to reboard the train just before it pulls out (another ruse that the Austrian *Grenzpolizei* have sussed).

WESTERN TRANSDANUBIA

Western Transdanubia, bordering Austria and Slovenia, has a sub-Alpine topography and climate, ideal for wine-growing and outdoor pursuits. Its Baroque towns and historic castles evince centuries of Habsburg influence and doughty resistance against the Turks. From the beautiful town of Sopron, you can visit the Esterházy Palace before heading south to Kőszeg and Szombathely, and thence to Sárvár or the picturesque Őrség region. This itinerary suits regional **transport**, since Sopron is easily accessible by express trains and coaches from Budapest or Győr, whereas other places are easier to reach using local services. Starting from the Balaton, however, it's easier to work your way north via Szombathely or Zalaegerszeg (in which case, backtrack through the following sections).

Sopron

With its 115 monuments and 240 listed buildings, **SOPRON** can justly claim to be "the most historic town in Hungary". Never having been ravaged by Mongols or Turks, the inner town retains its medieval layout, with a fusion of Gothic and Baroque architecture that rivals Castle Hill in Budapest. Sopron is also a major wine-producing centre and the base for excursions to the Esterházy Palace, the vintage steam railway at Nagycenk, and other sites. The only drawback is its proximity to Vienna, which means that Austrians come here in droves to shop, eat out and get their teeth fixed, swamping the town over summer.

Arriving at the main railway station south of the centre, head 500m up Mátyás király utca to reach Széchenyi tér and the Belváros. Coming in by intercity bus, a five-minute walk along Lackner Kristóf utca will bring you to Ógabona tér, on the edge of the Várkerület körút surrounding the old quarter. Once inside the horseshoe-shaped Belváros, **orientation** is simple. The following account progresses northwards through the quarter.

Around the Belváros

Heading up Templom utca, turn right along Fegyvertár utca to reach **Orsolya tér**. This cobbled square gets its name from an Ursuline convent that once occupied the site of the **Church of the Virgin**, sandwiched between two neo-Gothic edifices dripping with loggias. The one on the left hosts an **Exhibition of Catholic Artefacts** (June–Sept Mon & Thurs 10am–6pm, Sat & Sun 11am–4pm), while the arcaded building at no. 5 contains a small **Guild Museum** focusing on local craft traditions (Tues–Sun summer 9am–5pm; winter 9am–1pm). In olden days, animals were butchered under the arcades and the square was the site of the Salt Market.

Új utca (New Street), running off to the northwest, is actually one of Sopron's oldest thoroughfares, a gentle curve of arched dwellings painted in red, yellow and pink, with chunky cobblestones and pavements. During the Middle Ages it was called *Zsidó* (Jewish) utca and housed a flourishing community of Jewish merchants. As elsewhere, however, they were accused of conspiring with the Turks and expelled from Hungary in 1526, only returning to Sopron in the nineteenth century. At no. 22 on the left is a tiny medieval **synagogue** with a ritual bath in the courtyard (April–Oct 9am–5pm; Nov–March 9am–4pm; closed Tues).

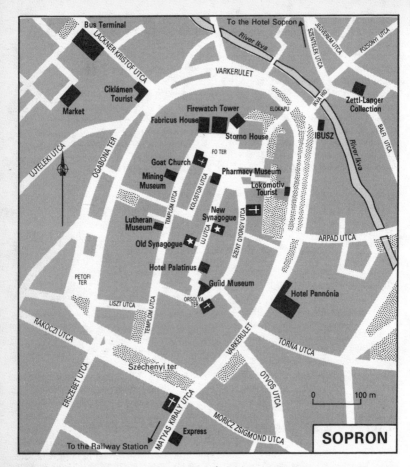

SOPRON

When last heard, the northern end of Új utca was closed due to work on the water mains, compelling visitors to return to **Templom utca**. Heading up past the ornamental Töpler House (no. 22), you'll reach the **Lutheran History Museum** at no. 12 (April–Sept Mon, Thurs, Sat & Sun 10am–1pm). The adjacent Lutheran **church** dates from 1782, but only acquired its tower eighty years later, due to restrictions on the faith decreed by Emperor Josef II – as related in the museum.

Another, more interesting exhibition can be found in the former Esterházy Mansion at no. 2, now a **Mining Museum** covering the industry's history (April–Oct 10am–6pm; Nov–March 10am–4pm; closed Wed). Directly across the street at no. 1 stands the **Chapter House**, whose beautiful vaulted interior dates from the fourteenth century, with allegorical images of the seven deadly sins decorating the capitals of its pillars and the bosses of its cross-vaulting (Tues–Sun 10am–noon & 2–4pm). Beyond them lies Sopron's historic main square.

Fő tér

The focal point of **Fő tér** is a magnificent **Trinity Statue** crawling with cherubim, which local protestants took as an affront when it was erected in 1700 by Cardinal Kollonich, who threatened: "First I will make the Hungarians slaves, then I will make them beggars, and then I will make them Catholics". Behind it stands the triple-aisled **Goat Church** built for the Franciscans in 1300, where three kings were later crowned and Parliament convened on seven occasions. Its curious name stems from the legend that the church's construction was financed by a goatherd whose flock unearthed a cache of loot – in gratitude for which, an angel embraces a goat on one of the pillars of its Baroque interior.

Before crossing the square to visit the mansions on its northern side, check out the **Pharmacy Museum** at no. 2, which preserves the Angel apothecary founded by Tóbiás Marb in 1601. Though remodelled since then, its Biedermeier-style walnut furnishings and artefacts from the Dark Ages of pharmacology certainly deserve a look (Tues–Sun April–Oct 10am–6pm; Nov–March 9am–5pm).

Directly opposite the church stands the **Fabricus House** at no. 6, (Tues–Sun 10am–6pm), which unites a Baroque mansion built upon Roman foundations with a patrician's house from the fifteenth century. A Renaissance stairway leads up to a small museum of archaeological finds, also noted for its "whispering gallery", while the Gothic cellar contains three large Roman statues unearthed during the construction of the Town Hall. Next door at no. 7 is the **Lackner House**, named after the seventeenth-century mayor who bequeathed it to Sopron; his motto *Fiat Voluntas tua* (Let your will be) appears on the facade.

The Renaissance **Storno House** at no. 8 has the finest pedigree, however. King Mátyás stayed here in 1482–83, as did Franz Liszt in 1840 and 1881. It is still owned by descendants of Ferenc Storno, painter, architect and master chimney-sweep, who restored Pannonhalma and other medieval churches during the nine-teenth century. The family's private collection of Liszt memorabilia and Roman, Celtic and Avar relics can be seen only on group tours (Tues–Sun summer 10am–6pm; winter 10am–4.30pm).

The Firewatch Tower

North of the square rises Sopron's symbol, the **Firewatch Tower** (*Tűztorony*), founded upon the stones of a fortress built by the Romans, who established the town of *Scarbantia* here during the first century AD. As its name suggests, the tower was intended to give warning of a fire anywhere in town; while standing watch, the sentries blew trumpets to signal the hours. Ascending from its square, tenth-century base up through a cylindrical, seventeenth-century mid-section, you emerge on to a Baroque balcony offering a stunning **view** of Fő tér and the inner town (Tues–Sun April–Oct 10am–6pm; Nov–March 10am–4pm).

At the base of the tower is the **Gate of Loyalty**, erected in honour of the town-folks' decision to reject the offer of Austrian citizenship in 1921. The motif shows Hungaria surrounded by kneeling citizens and Sopron's coat of arms, which henceforth included the title *Civitas Fidelissima* (The most faithful town). Walking through it, you'll emerge onto **Előkapu** (outer gate) street, where the houses are staggered for defensive purposes; and "errant burghers" and "gossiping, nagging" wives were once pinioned in stocks for the righteous to pelt with rotten food.

From its junction with **Várkerület körút** you can cross the road to examine the colourfully-tiled facade of the **Golden Lion Pharmacy** at no. 29, or head south along the boulevard to espy a section of the **medieval town walls** on the left.

Beyond the Belváros

Ikva híd (crossing a narrow stream which flooded noxiously in the nineteenth century) points towards a couple more sights. Off to the right at Balfi utca 11 is the private **Zettl-Langer Collection** of porcelain, earthenware and weaponry (daily 10am–noon), assembled by a nineteenth century businessman.

For a longer walk, follow Pozsonyi út uphill past the **House of the Two Moors** (so-called after the turbaned statues flanking its gate) to the partially Gothic **Church of Saint Michael**, whose gargoyles leer over a decaying thirteenth-century Chapel of Saint Jacob. Nearby stand the cross-less tombstones of Soviet soldiers killed liberating Sopron from the Arrow Cross puppet-government, which massacred hundreds of hostages before fleeing with the Coronation Regalia in April 1945.

The Fool's Castle

In the western garden suburbs lurks a bizarre "**Fool's Castle**" built by a local eccentric early this century, similar to "Bory's Folly" in Székesfehérvár. The *Taródi-vár* is still inhabited by his descendants, who allow visitors to enter several rooms crammed with paintings and curios, and have recently started taking paying guests. There are no set hours, but you can usually gain admission whenever someone's at home; the curator charges whatever she can get away with. The Fool's Castle is located at Csalogány köz 8 (square C5 on up-to-date town plans). Bus #1 from Széchenyi tér can drop you near the covered pool (*Fedett Uzsoda*) outside town; walk 50m back, turn left on to Tölgyfa sor, and then left again at the end.

The Lővérek and the Bürgenland

South of town, the sub-Alpine **Lővérek Hills** are a standing invitation to hikers. Bus #1 or #2 will drop you at the *Hotel Lővér* near the start of the path up to the **Károly Lookout Tower** (April–Oct 9am–6pm; Nov–March 9am–4pm), which offers marvellous views of the surrounding countryside. Although several **hiking** trails continue into Austria, only locals may pass through the low-key checkpoints. Both sides of the border are inhabited by bilingual folk engaged in viticulture, following the division of the **Bürgenland** region between Hungary and Austria (which got the lion's share) after the collapse of the Habsburg empire – an amicable partition, it seems, since nobody complains about it today.

Practicalities

The best sources of **information** are *Ciklámen Tourist* at Ógabona tér 8 (April–Oct Mon–Thurs 7.30am–4pm, Fri & Sat 7.30am–8pm, Sun 8am–noon; Nov–March Mon–Sat 7.30am–4pm; ☎12-040), and *IBUSZ* at Várkerület körút 41 (Mon–Fri 8am–4pm, Sat 8am–noon; ☎13-28). *Express*, Mátyás király út 7 (Mon–Fri 8am–noon, 1–3.30pm, Sat 8am–1pm; ☎12-024), is strictly for booking college beds, whilst *Lokomotiv Tourist*, Várkerület körút 90 (☎11-111), deals with trips on the Széchenyi Railway (see p.194).

The Sopron telephone code is ☎99

Accommodation

During July and August cheap **dormitory beds** (①) might be available at Damjanich utca 9 (just off Lackner Kristóf utca) or the Jereván high school – *Express* can make bookings and point you in the right direction. Though **private rooms** (②–③) are scarce over summer, it is worth enquiring at *IBUSZ* and *Ciklámen Tourist*, since most of the alternatives are dearer:

Jégverem Panzió, Jégverem utca 1 (☎12-004). A renovated inn named after the old ice pit in the middle of its restaurant, located just off Pozsony út. Breakfast included. ④.

Royal Panzió, Sas tér 13 (☎14-481). Slightly cheaper and just around the corner. ④.

Hotel Sopron, Fövényverem utca 7 (☎14-254). Plush establishment with nightclub, sauna, solarium and tennis courts, further north. ⑥.

Hotel Pannónia, Várkerület 74 (☎12-180). Decent, if a bit old fashioned – formerly the *Golden Stag Inn*, where Johann Strauss stayed. ④–⑤.

Palatinus Hotel, Új utca 23 (☎11-395). Sited in the heart of the Belváros, with an agreeable ambience. ⑤.

Átrium Vendégház, Kőszegi út 3 (☎13-799). A simple pension in the southeastern suburbs (bus #12M). ③.

Talizmán Panzió, Ady Endre út 85. Similar place, 1km east of the centre (bus #10). ③.

Solar Club Hotel, Panoráma út 16 (☎11-675). About 2km from the centre, and hard to reach by public transport. ⑤.

Panoráma Üdülő-Hotel, Panoráma út 38 (☎12-745). A cheaper bungalow complex, formerly a trade union resort, on the same street. ③.

Hotel Sziesta, Lővér körút 37 (☎14-260). Likewise once reserved for trade unionists, but easier to reach (bus #1). ③.

Lővér Hotel, Vársi utca 4 (☎11-061). Sited further south below Károly Hill (bus #1 or #2). Sauna, gym and restaurant. Breakfast included. ⑤.

Lővér Camping, (☎11-715). Located 4km south of the centre; bus #12 runs hourly from Deák tér and the intercity bus station. Camping from mid-April to mid-Oct, with chalets (②–③) over summer. Reserve through *Ciklámen Tourist*.

Ózon Camping, Erdei Malom köz 3 (☎11-322). Smaller, private site with a few rooms (②), in the garden district 5km outside town, off the #10 bus route.

Festivals, eating and drinking

Sopron is at its liveliest during the **Spring Days** (late March) and **Festival Weeks** (mid-June to mid-July), when all manner of concerts and plays are staged at the Petőfi Theatre on Petőfi tér and the Liszt Cultural Centre on Széchenyi tér – *Ciklámen Tourist* can supply details.

There are **restaurants** attached to all the main hotels, but except for the one in the *Hotel Palatinus* – which does excellent, inexpensive set meals in the evening – you'll eat better elsewhere. For traditional Hungarian nosh, try two places on Várkerület körút – the *Tramini Vendéglő* (Mon–Sat 9am–9pm) at no. 63 and the *Várkerület Söröző* at no. 83 – or the *Deák Étterem* on the corner of Deák tér and Erzsébet utca, which specialises in game dishes. The *Corvinus Pizzeria* by the Storno House offers a range of pizzas and other, dearer items, while the cheapest place in town is the self-service *Önkiszolgáló Étterem* on the western side of Széchenyi tér (daily 7am–3pm).

Hearty red *Kékfrankos* and white, apple-flavoured *Tramini* are best sampled in **wine cellars** such as the *Gyógygödör Borozó* at Fő tér 4 (Tues–Sun 9am–9pm) and the *Poncichter Borozó* at Szentlélek utca 13. The *Cezár Pince* on the corner of Oroslya tér and Hátsókapu utca (9am–9.30pm) boasts vintage oak butts and leather-aproned waiters, but they can get a bit sniffy if you don't order a platter of *wurst* to go with your wine. For beer and disco-beat, try the *Holsten Söröző* in the *Hotel Palatinus* (noon–10pm). Cocktails and spirits can be enjoyed in the elegant, old world café in the *Hotel Pannónia*, or the *Stefánia Cukrászda* at Szent György utca 12 – both are recommended for **cakes** and coffee.

Moving on

Excursions to nearby atttractions aside (see below), the most obvious destinations are Kőszeg or Szombathely. With no trains **to Kőszeg** and three of the five daily buses leaving before 7am, you have to be sure to catch the 12.50pm or 3pm service. Szombathely is served by four trains (mostly in the afternoon) and five buses daily. Other **buses** run to Bük, Sárvár, Veszprém, Komárom, Esztergom, Hévíz and Balatonfüred. Services **to Austria** cover a host of towns including Vienna (Mon–Sat 8am; also Mon, Thurs & Fri 9.20am), which is also served by train (arrive at the station one hour early to clear customs); and there is a daily bus **to Bratislava**.

Excursions from Sopron

To the east of Sopron lies **the Hanság** region, a once extensive swampland that has gradually been drained and brought under cultivation since the eighteenth century. Prone to thick fogs, the area is traditionally associated with tales of elves and water sprites, and with the dynastic seats of the Esterházy and Széchenyi families, at Fertőd and Nagycenk. The most obvious feature on the map is the shallow, reedy expanse known to Hungarians as **Lake Fertő** and to Austrians as the *Neuseidler See,* which was out of bounds to prevent escapes until recently, but can now be reached by bus from Sopron (every 90mins–2hrs) and attracts naturalists and birdwatchers.

There are hourly buses to all of the following places from the depot on Lackner Kristóf utca.

Fertőrákos Quarry

FERTŐRÁKOS, 8km north of town, presumably gets its name "Cancerous slough" from the local **quarry** (May–Sept Tues–Fri 8am–7pm, Sat & Sun 9am–5pm), where limestone has been hewn since Roman times. Vienna's Saint Stephen's Church and Ringstrasse were built with stone from Fertőrákos, where quarrying only ceased in 1945. The result is a Cyclopean labyrinth of gigantic chambers and oddly skewed pillars, resembling the mythical cities imagined by H.P. Lovecraft: animal and plant fossils attest that the land was once submerged beneath a prehistoric sea. **Concerts** are staged in the quarry during the Sopron Festival Weeks.

Fertőrákos itself boasts a former Bishop's Palace at Fő utca 153, containing a small **museum** of antique furniture (May–Sept Tues–Fri 9am–3pm, Sat & Sun 9am–5pm). Should you feel like **staying**, beds at the *Kastély Hotel* (☎99/55-040; ③) in the palace or the *Vízmalom Hostel* at Fő utca 41 (☎99/12-040; ①–②) should be reserved through *Ciklámen Tourist*, which also handles concert tickets.

The Esterházy Palace at Fertőd

The Esterházy Palace lies 27km east of Sopron along a minor road that connects with the route to Fertőrákos at **BALF**, a bathing resort since Roman times. Its fin-de-siècle **spa** and gazebo are appealing, but not so much that you're tempted to check into the *Kurhotel-Schloss Balf* (☎99/14-226; ⑤). Also worth noting in passing are the traditional cottages and barns in **FERTŐSZÉPLAK**, 5km before Fertőd.

FERTŐD itself began life as an appendage to the palace and was known as "Esterháza" until the family decamped in 1945. As you enter the village, post-war housing gives way to stately public buildings endowed by the Esterházys, presaging the palace at the eastern end. So long as you stay on the main street, it's impossible to miss.

The Esterházy Palace

Built on malarial swampland drained by hundreds of serfs, the **Esterházy Palace** was intended to rival Versailles and remove any *arriviste* stigma from the dynasty (see box). Gala balls and concerts, hunting parties and masquerades were held here even before it was completed in 1776, continuing without a let-up until 1790, when Prince Miklós "the Ostentatious" died. Neglected by his successor, who dissolved the orchestra and moved his court back to Eisenstadt, the palace rapidly decayed. Its picture gallery, puppet theatre and Chinese pavilions disappeared, while its salons became storerooms and stables. Though basic repairs were made after World War II, restoration only began in earnest during the Fifties, and is still unfinished due to the prodigious cost.

Ornate Rococo wrought-iron gates lead into a vast horseshoe courtyard where Hussars once pranced to the music of Haydn, Esterházy's resident maestro. The U-shaped wings and ceremonial stairway sweep up to a three-storey Baroque facade, painted a rich ochre. **Guided tours** (Tues–Sun May–Sept 8am–noon & 1–5pm; Oct–April 8am–noon & 1–4pm) cover only a fraction of the 126-room interior, which seems rather lifeless owing to a lack of furniture. The highlights of the ground floor are the panelled and gilded **Sala Terrena** and several blue and white **Chinoiserie salons**. On the ceiling of the **Banqueting Hall** upstairs is a splendid fresco by J.B. Grundemann, so contrived that Apollo's chariot seems to be careering towards you across the sky whatever angle you view it from.

THE ESTERHÁZY FAMILY

Originally of the minor nobility, the **Esterházy family** began its rise thanks to **Miklós I** (1583–1645), who married two rich widows and sided with the Habsburgs against Transylvania during the Counter-Reformation, to be rewarded with the title of Count. His son Paul was content to make his mark by publishing a songbook, *Harmonia Celestis*; but **Miklós II** "the Ostentatious" (1714–90) celebrated his inheritance of 600,000 acres and a dukedom by commissioning the palace in 1762. Boasting "anything the Kaiser can do, I can do better!", he spent 40,000 *gulden* a year on pomp and entertainments. Thereafter the family gradually declined, until under the Communists they were expropriated and "un-personed". Today, one descendant drives trams in Vienna, while two others (from a separate branch of the family) are respected figures back home: the writer **Péter Esterházy** and his cousin, **Marton Esterházy**, centre forward on the national football team.

An adjacent room displays **Haydn memorabilia** from the period following his appointment as the Esterházy *Kapellmeister* in 1761. Haydn subsequently took over the direction of palace orchestra, opera house and marionette theatre, and wrote six great masses for performance here between 1796 and 1802. The palace also witnessed the premiere of Beethoven's Mass in C, conducted by Ludwig in 1807. The tour over, you can wander around the **French Gardens** at the back, whose formal beds and hedges have grown wild through neglect.

Practicalities

The prospect of **staying at the palace** is almost irresistible. Proper rooms (②) in the east wing are available year-round, but must be booked in advance (☎99/70-971). From April to September there are also dormitory beds (①), bookable through *Ciklámen Tourist*. Less romantic, but handier for eating out, are three places **in the village**: the *Kastély Hotel*, Bartók utca 2 (☎99/45-971; ③); the *Udvaros Ház*, Fő utca 1 (☎99/45-921; ②); and the *Eszterházi Panzió*, Fő utca 20 (②). For food and drink, try the *Grenadier House* opposite the palace gates (closed Mon), or the restaurants and supermarket in the village.

The Széchenyi Mansion and Steam Railway at Nagycenk

Another feudal seat worth investigating lies 13km southeast of Sopron, near **NAGYCENK**. Buses from town can drop you at the **Széchenyi Mansion** (*kastély*), 1.5km from the village. As the family home of Count Széchenyi, "the greatest Hungarian" (see box), it has never been allowed to fall into ruin, and was declared a memorial museum in 1973. The museum (Tues–Sun April–Oct 10am–6pm; Nov–March 10am–2pm) includes a fascinating reconstruction of his household – the first in Hungary to be lit by gas-lamps and have flush toilets – and details his achievements, leading naturally into an exhibition on Hungarian industry since Széchenyi's day.

Across the road is a shining example of the heritage industry – the **Széchenyi Railway**. This outdoor museum of **vintage steam trains** comes alive every weekend from April to October, when 100-year-old engines run along a special line that terminates at FERTŐBOZ, 4km away (though some turn back earlier). Advance details and tickets can be obtained from *Lokomotiv Tourist* in Sopron, or you can just turn up and hope for the best.

In the **village** stands a neo-Romanesque **Church of Saint Stephen** (designed by Ybl in 1864) whose portal bears the Széchenyi motto "If God is with us, who can be against us?". Across the road is a cemetery containing the **Széchenyi Mausoleum**, with a chapel decorated by István Dorfmeister, and a crypt including the graves of István and his wife Crescentia Seilern.

Practicalities

Accommodation is polarised between comfy rooms in the *Kastély Hotel* (☎99/60-061; ⑤–⑥) occupying an outbuilding of the mansion, and unheated chalets without bathrooms at the *Hársfa Panzió* (☎99/60-015; ②) around the back. There's a similar dichotomy between the hotel restaurant and the cheaper *Pálya Vendéglő* near the railway. Should you travel to Fertőboz by steam train, bear in mind that this village is on the Sopron–Fertőd road, and has a tourist hostel at Fő utca 11 (☎99/12-040; ②).

COUNT SZÉCHENYI

Count István Széchenyi (1791–1860) was the outstanding figure of Hungary's Reform era. As a young aide-de-camp he cut a dash at the Congress of Vienna and did the rounds of stately homes across Europe. The "odious Zoltán Karpathy" of Bernard Shaw's *Pygmalion* (and the musical *My Fair Lady*) was based on his exploits in England, where he steeplechased hell-for-leather, but found time to examine factories and steam trains. Back in Hungary, he pondered solutions to his homeland's backwardness and offered a year's income from his estates towards the establishment of a Hungarian Academy. In 1830 he published *Hitel* (Credit), a hard-headed critique of the nation's feudal society.

Though politically conservative, Széchenyi was obsessed with **modernisation**. A passionate convert to steam power after riding on the Manchester–Liverpool express, he invited Britons to build railway lines and the Chain Bridge; imported steamships and dredgers; promoted horsebreeding and silk-making; and initiated the taming of the River Tisza and the blasting of a road through the Iron Gates of the Danube. Alas, his achievements were rewarded by a melancholy end. The 1848 Revolution and the triumph of Kossuth triggered a nervous breakdown, and although Széchenyi resumed writing after his health improved, he committed suicide during a relapse.

Kőszeg and Bükfürdő

Nestled amidst the sub-Alpine hills along the Austrian border, the small town of **KŐSZEG** cherishes its status as the "Hungarian Thermopylae", and a Belváros of chocolate box prettiness. While its castle recalls the medieval Magyar heroism that saved Vienna from the Turks, its Baroque houses and *bürgerlich* ambience reflect centuries of Austrian and German influence, when Kőszeg was known as Güns. Despite a summer blitzkrieg of tourists that briefly arouses avarice and excitement, this is basically a sleepy, old-fashioned town where folk are honest enough to leave fruit for sale (and the takings) lying unguarded in the streets.

Arriving at the bus station on the corner of Liszt and Kossuth utca, walk 150m up the latter to reach the Belváros, encircled by a road called the Várkör, which follows the line of the long-demolished medieval town walls. To get there from the railway station in the south of town, catch a #1, #1A or #1Y bus as far as the junction of Fő tér and the Várkör.

Around Fő tér and Jurisics tér

From **Fő tér**, where the **Church of the Sacred Heart** stands aloof from two hotels and three tourist offices, an alley flanked by twin saints leads off to the **Heroes' Tower**. Erected to mark the 400th anniversary of the siege of Kőszeg, this fake medieval portal was one of several commemorative gates raised in the Twenties and Thirties, when Hungary was gripped by nostalgia for bygone glories and resentment towards the Successor States.

Beyond the archway lies **Jurisics tér**, a cobbled square whose antique buildings are watched over by two churches and a statue of the Virgin. The most eye-catching facades are those of the **Town Hall** (embellished with oval portraits of worthies) and no. 7, on the eastern side of the square, where the pillory stood in medieval times. An eighteenth-century apothecary is preserved as a **Pharmacy**

Museum (Tues–Sun 10am–6pm) at no. 11, while the Baroque General's House by the tower is now the **Jurisics Museum** (Tues–Sun 10am–6pm), containing examples of bookbinding and other historic crafts.

Beyond the well and Virgin statue (where a brass band often plays on Sundays and holidays), the Baroque **Church of Saint Emerich** precedes the older **Church of Saint James**, a handsome Gothic edifice containing the tomb of Miklós Jurisics (see below) and frescoes dating back to 1403. From here you can follow Chernel or Rajnis utca off the square, to find Kőszeg Castle.

The castle

The Turks swore that Kőszeg's **Castle** was "built at the foot of a mountain difficult to climb; its walls wider than the whole world, its bastions higher than the fish of the Zodiac in heaven, and so strong that it defies description". Since the castle is actually quite small, with not a mountain in sight, the hyperbole is probably explained by its heroic defence during the month-long **siege of 1532**, when 400 soldiers under Captain Miklós Jurisics resisted 100,000 Turks, halting Sultan Süleyman's advance on Vienna. After nineteen assaults the Sultan abandoned campaigning until the following year, by which time Vienna was properly defended. Weapons and other relics are displayed in the castle **museum** (Tues–Sun 10am–6pm), while another hall off the courtyard serves as a bar-cum-disco.

Other sights

The former **synagogue** at Várkör 41 resembles an outlying bastion of the castle, having two crenellated towers with slit windows. Built in 1859, the redbrick complex originally included a *yeshiva* and a ritual bath. Its dereliction is a sad reminder of the provincial Jewish communities that never recovered from the Holocaust, for – unlike the Budapest ghetto – their extermination was scheduled for the summer of 1944, when Eichmann's death-machine still ran at full throttle.

Where earlier editions left an ominous blank, recent maps of the **hills** around Kőszeg show the entire border region, with trails crossing the frontier that locals may now leave the country by. If you fancy hiking 6km, there is a well-signposted trail to the highest summit in the region (833m), where **Írottkő Lookout Tower** straddles the border. Tourists with passports can ascend the tower (April 1–Oct 15), but not cross over into Austria. Lastly, should you feel the need to cool off, there is a public **swimming pool** just across the river from the centre of town: follow Kiss János utca eastwards from the Várkör.

Practicalities

Maps and **information** are available from *Savaria Tourist* at Várkör 57 (Mon–Fri 7.45am–4.30pm, Sat 8am–noon; ☎94/60-195), or *IBUSZ* at Varosház utca 3, just off Fő tér towards the Heroes' Gate (Mon–Fri 8am–noon & 1–4pm; May–Aug also Sat 8am–noon; ☎94/60-376). Both offices can book private **accommodation**, while *Express* (☎94/60-376) next door to *Savaria Tourist* handles reservations at its own places outside town (see below).

Írottkő Hotel, Fő tér 4 (☎94/60-373). Central, modern, but pricey. Breakfast included. ⑥.

Strucc Hotel, Várkör 124 (☎94/60-323). A fine old hotel opposite *Savaria Tourist*. Doubles with showers; breakfast included. ③.

Tourist Hostel, Rainis utca 9, opposite the castle. Dormitory beds (①) and a few double and triple rooms (②). April to mid-Oct.

Kóbor Macska Fogadó, Várkör 100. Friendly seven-room pension with a restaurant, on the corner of Hunyadi utca. ③.

Hotel Park, Park utca 2 (☎94/60-363). Quiet nineteenth century pile at the western end of Hunyadi utca. Breakfast included. Book through *Express*. ②–③.

Hotel Panoráma (aka *Napsugár Turistaszalló*). An *Express*-owned bungalow complex on Szabó-hegy (Tailor's Hill), southwest of town (bus #2 from the railway station). ①–②.

Campsite on Strand sétány, by the swimming pool (☎94/60-981). No huts, but good for sunbathing. May 1–Sept 30.

Eating, drinking and moving on

Aside from hotel **restaurants**, the centre can offer the *Kulacs Étterem* at Várkör 12 (daily 6am–10pm), the *Szarvas Étterem* at Kossuth utca 6, and the *Alpesi Vendéglő* opposite the bus station (Mon–Sat 9am–9pm). The *Gesztenye Étterem* further down Kossuth utca often hosts **discos**, as do the castle and the *Park Hotel*. For **drinking**, try the *Bécsikapu Söröző* on Rajnis utca, opposite Saint James' Church, or the beer garden on the corner of Schneller utca at the north-eastern edge of the Várkör (summer only).

Short of **moving on** to Bükfürdő (see below), you're likely to head for Sopron or Szombathely. There are five buses daily to each (mostly in the afternoon), plus ten trains **to Szombathely** (30mins). Motorists can cross **into Austria** at Mannersdorf, 3km northwest of town.

Bükfürdő and around

BÜKFÜRDŐ, 16km east of Kőszeg, is a major new development designed to attract western tourists. Its **thermal spa** is one of the best equipped in Hungary, but the real selling point is the **Birdland Golf Club**, an 18-hole course and golfing village run by a Swedish-Austro-Hungarian consortium. Though foreigners can easily afford the daily fee (£9/$15), the course is effectively out of bounds to the average Magyar, and lodgings, too, are aimed at wealthy tourists, making this an expensive place for budget travellers. To economise, stay 3km down the road in **BÜK**, which musters some cheaper pensions and campsites. **Private rooms in Bük** (②–③) can be rented directly at Petőfi utca 22 (☎94/58-412); Kossuth utca 58 (☎94/58-623); Szabadság utca 7 (☎94/58-304); and Szabadság utca 13 (☎94/58-165). Motorists intending to head for Austria might also consider staying at **CSEPREG**, 5km west of Bük. It is close to the border for an early start, with a nice family-run **campsite**, *Ottó Kemping*, at Bognár utca 1 (mid-March to mid-Oct; ☎94/65-393). Otherwise, accommodation in Bükfürdő includes:

Thermal Hotel Bük (☎94/58-500). Unmissable, brand new four-star hotel with sports and bathing facilities, in the centre of Bükfürdő. ⑥–⑦.

Hotel Bük (☎94/58-028). A smaller, less palatial rival just across the way. ⑤.

Romantik Camping, Termál körút 12 (☎94/58-362). Bükfürdő's well-equipped and costly camper-van haven.

Elizabeth Camping-Panzió, Kossuth utca 72 (☎94/58-414). A smaller site with a few rooms (②) to let, in Bük.

Sziszi Kemping, Kossuth utca 70 (☎94/58-280). A similar outfit next door, also open year round.

Szombathely

Commerce has been the lifeblood of **SZOMBATHELY** ("Saturday market") ever since the town was founded by Emperor Claudius in 43 AD to capitalise on the Amber Road from the Baltic to the Mediterranean. *Savaria* (as it was then called) soon became the capital of Pannonia, and a significant city in the Roman empire. It was here that Septimus Severus was proclaimed emperor (193 AD) and Saint Martin of Tours was born in 317. Under Frankish rule in the eighth century, the town – known as *Steinamanger* – prospered through trade with Germany. Nowadays, it is Austrians who boost the economy, flooding across to shop, get their hair done or seek medical treatment in the town which they have nicknamed "the discount store".

From a tourist's standpoint, the chief **attractions** are the outdoor Village Museum and Roman ruins, a Belváros stuffed with Baroque and Neoclassical architecture, and the finest collection of Socialist art in Hungary. Szombathely is also the base for trips to Sárvár Castle – where the "Blood Countess" Báthori acquired a taste for murder – and the beautiful Romanesque church at Ják.

The heart of town

Arriving at the railway station, you can walk along Szell Kálmán utca into the centre (800m), or catch a #2, #3, #5, #7, #7Y or #11 bus to Mártírok tere or Köztársaság tér. The intercity bus station is next to the Romkert near the cathedral, so arriving there makes things even easier. As is often the case, the Belváros is compact enough to cover on foot with no risk of getting lost, but a town plan is useful for **orientation** once you venture outside the centre.

Exploring the Belváros doesn't take long unless you spend time in its museums and galleries. If your appetite for exhibitions is limited, it's best to make a beeline for the cathedral or the Temple of Isis, and conserve some enthusiasm for the Village Museum (see below). Otherwise, it's not a bad idea to begin with the **Savaria Museum** at Kisfaludy utca 9 (Tues–Sun 10am–6pm), a local archaeology display which starts with mammoth tusks and works through to Roman times, represented by reliefs of mythical figures and other stonework.

Further west, the Belváros turns monumental around **Berzsenyi Dániel tér**, dominated by the **County Hall** and a huge eighteenth-century **Bishop's Palace** whose stuccoed facade is crowned by allegorical statues of Prudence, Justice, Fortitude and Temperance. The **Smidt Museum** (Tues–Fri 10am–6pm), which occupies one wing of the palace, represents the fruits of a life-long obsession. As a boy, Lajos Smidt scoured battlefields for souvenirs and collected advertisements and newspapers; after qualifying as a doctor he diversified into furniture and pictures. The destruction of many items during World War II only spurred him to redouble his efforts during retirement; and finally, he founded this museum to house his extraordinary collection.

On the other side of the square, the Revolutionary History Museum that once occupied the **Eölbey House** has been evicted, and temporary exhibitions may soon be replaced by a Museum of Religious Art. Much depends on the outcome of negotiations between the churches that once owned prime real estate in Szombathely and the authorities who expropriated it after World War II – a situation that affects many towns in Hungary.

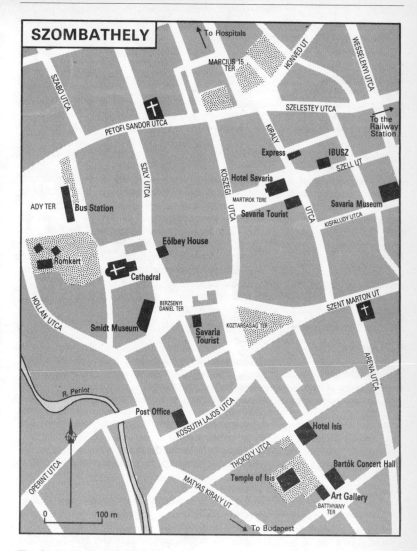

The Cathedral and Romkert

Szombathely's **Cathedral** postdates the great fire that ravaged the town in the late eighteenth century, which explains why it is Neoclassical rather than Baroque or Gothic. Unfortunately, its exuberant frescoes by Maulbertsch were destroyed when US bombers attacked the town in the last months of World War II, and painstaking structural restoration has stopped short of recreating his work. Around the corner lies the **Romkert** or Garden of Ruins (May–Oct Tues–Sun 10am–6pm), comprising a crossroads and a mosaic floor from Roman

Savaria, and the remains of the Basilica of Saint Quirinus – the largest church in Pannonia when it was built with stones from the Roman governor's palace during the Dark Ages.

The Temple of Isis

The most interesting relic of ancient Savaria only came to light in 1955, when construction work along Rákóczi utca uncovered a **Temple of Isis** (May–Oct Tues–Sun 8am–6pm), dating from the second century AD. One of three such *Iseum* extant in Europe, it is centered around a sacrificial altar which the rising sun illuminates, and decorated with a pantheon of deities. Reliefs depict Isis riding the dog Sothis, Victoria holding palm leaves, a glum-looking Fortuna-Abundantia, and Mars-Harpokrates.

This mixed bag of deities reflects the eclectic religious life of the Roman Empire in its waning era. The custom of daily Isis-worship at sunrise originated in Egypt, where the "Great Mother" was believed to have given birth to Horus, the divine avatar of the Pharaohs, and avenger of the murder of Osiris by his brother Seth, Lord of Chaos. Of all the cults that spread from the Middle East into Europe, it had the widest appeal; some argue that the Virgin Mary was Christianity's riposte to Isis in the battle for hearts and minds.

The *Iseum* in Szombathely was destroyed in an earthquake in 455. Since being partially restored in the 1960s, it has provided a setting for performances of the aria *Isis and Osiris,* from Mozart's opera *The Magic Flute*, during the annual Savaria Festival. Though the festival has temporarily bitten the dust, the temple still hosts events during the Spring Days.

Socialist art: the Group of Eight

The **Szombathely Gallery** (Tues–Sun 10am–6pm), just south of the temple, contains Hungary's finest collection of **Socialist art**. Unlike the hack painters and sculptors of the Rákósi era, radical artists of the Twenties and Thirties were inspired by genuine vision and commitment. **Gyula Derkovits** (1894–1934) was a member of the **Group of Eight** (*Nyolcak*) who "declared war on all those ideologies and styles of art that begin and end with the 'I'". Living amongst the working class – his subject matter – Derkovits strived to rid his art of "every element of illusion", moved towards Cubism and studied at the Nyergesújfalu Free School during the heady days of the Republic of Councils. Its supression left him desolate, as can be seen from *The Last Supper*, where Christ – with the artist's features – sits amidst a group of weary workmen.

The baton was taken up by another son of Szombathely, **István Dési Huber** (1895–1944), a goldsmith by trade. Abandoning Naturalism for Cubism to express his Marxist beliefs, he joined *Nyolcak* in the unequal struggle against the dominance of the "School of Rome" (modelled on Italian fascist art) during the Thirties and Forties. During the Communist era the group finally received due honour – but were simultaneously tarnished by association with the regime. Now, with political and cultural values turned upside down, they have become tragic – or kitsch – exemplars of the light that failed. Hopefully, the museum (Tues–Sun 10am–6pm) will continue to exhibit their work.

Across the road stands Szombathely's former Synagogue, a lovely piece of neo-Byzantine architecture similar to the one in Pest, which is now the **Bartók Concert Hall** and music college – another venue for performances during the Spring Days.

Further out – the Village Museum

Northwest of the centre lie **Lake Gondola** (*Csónakázótó*) and the **Anglers' Lake** (*Horgásztó*), two smallish ponds where locals fish and go boating near an outdoor **thermal bath**. A #7 bus from Operint utca takes you right to the **Village Museum** (April–Oct Tues–Sun 10am–6pm) by the Anglers' Lake. Reconstructed here are eighteenth- and nineteenth-century farmsteads culled from 27 villages in the Őrség region, furnished with all the necessities and knick-knacks – an architectural progression from log cabins to timber-framed wattle and daub dwellings. On six Sundays a year there are demonstrations of traditional folk crafts and dances of the region.

Other sights

The green-belt district south of the lakes includes a small **Game Park** (*Vadaszkert*) with deer, pheasants and other wildlife – nothing to get excited about, but okay for a picnic. The park is situated off Középhegyi út, southwest of the *Hotel Liget*; alight from bus #7 on Jókai utca and walk from there.

Szombathely's northern suburbs harbour two more attractions which can be reached by #2 bus from Petőfi utca. The **Kámoni Arboretum** (Tues–Sun 8am–5pm) contains 2500 different kinds of trees, shrubs and flowers, with an especially varied assortment of roses. Just up the road is the grandly named **Gotthárd Astrophysics Observatory** (Mon–Fri 9am–4pm), with an interesting exhibition on cosmology.

Practicalities

Information can be obtained from *Savaria Tourist*, Mártirok tere 1 (Mon–Fri 8am–4pm, Sat 8.30am–noon; ☎12-348) or *IBUSZ*, Széll utca 3 (☎14-141), both of which can arrange private **accommodation** (②). *Express*, Mátyás király út 12 (☎11-230), can find dormitory beds (①) over summer and at weekends the rest of the year – probably in the *kollégium* facing the cathedral, or one of the colleges 50m west of the bus station. Other options are:

Hotel Savaria, Mártirok tere 4 (☎11-440). Centrally located, turn-of-the-century establishment with a ritzy restaurant. Breakfast included. ⑤.

Hotel Claudius, Bartók körút 39 (☎13-760). A modernistic pile where the ring road passes near Lake Gondola. Sauna, gym and restaurant. Breakfast included. ⑤

Hotel Liget, Szent István Park 15 (☎14-168). Motel-style lodgings further south on the ring road (bus #7 from the railway station). ④

Tópart Camping, Kondics utca 4 (☎14-766). Huts sleeping two (②) or four (④), near a swimming pool 10 minutes' walk from the Village Museum. May–Sept.

Szőllős Camping, Szőllős utca 11 (☎25-674). A simpler site with no huts, out along route 87 (bus #17 from Hunyádi út). May to mid-Oct.

Eating, drinking and entertainment

The best value **restaurants** in Szombathely are the *Gyöngyös Étterem*, Szell Kálmán utca 8 (closed Mon); the *Pelikán Étterem*, Huszár út 6, which does vegetarian dishes; and the *Vendéglő* between the two lakes. The elegant restaurant in the *Hotel Savaria* doesn't deign to list prices on its menu, but they're high. The

The Szombathely telephone code is ☎94

beer garden in **Jókai Park**, just south of the *Hotel Liget*, is something of a youth hangout; or you can **drink** at the *Ferences Söröző*, near the Franciscan church on Savaria tér.

Lack of funds has recently put an end to the annual **Savaria Festival** of music, dance and drama, but a future revival is possible – it's worth checking if you're likely to be here in late September or early October. Meantime there are the **Spring Days** in late March, featuring all kinds of music – plus whatever occurs at the Bartók Concert Hall and the cultural centres on Március 15. tér and Ady tér any time during the year. There's also a tradition of lively **Easter processions** in Szombathely and other towns in the region.

Moving on

With transport to Ják, Szentgotthárd and the Őrség region covered under the following sections, other possibilities can be briefly summarised. Most **trains** head eastwards through Sárvár to Celldömölk (for Sümeg, Tapolca and the Balaton) or Pápa (for Győr), or south towards Zalaegerszeg and Nagykanizsa (for connections to southern Transdanubia, with an early morning express to Pécs). There are daily **buses** to Keszthely, Zalaegerszeg and Győr, and a weekly service to Vienna (Wed). However, most people travel **to Austria** by train to Graz, or drive across at Búcsú, 14km west of town. Railway **information and tickets** are available from *MÁV Tours*, Thököly utca 39.

Ják and Sárvár

With hourly buses from Szombathely to **JÁK**, 10km southwest, you can easily pay a visit to Hungary's most outstanding **Romanesque Abbey Church** (daily April–Oct 8am–6pm; Nov–March 10am–2pm), far more impressive than the scaled-down replica you may have seen in Budapest. The church is sited on a hilltop overlooking the feudal domain of its founder Márton Nagy (1220–56), who personally checked that his serfs attended Sunday services – and whipped any who failed to do so.

The church is similar in **plan** to its ruined contemporaries at Zsámbek and Lébény, and likewise influenced by the Scottish Benedictine Church in Regensburg, the point from which Norman architecture spread into Central Europe. Its most striking feature is the magnificent **portal** on the western facade, where Christ and his apostles surmount an arch ribbed with complex patterns, guarded by whimsical lions. The twin towers and rose windows were restored in the 1890s by Frigyes Schulek, who performed a similar job on the Mátyás Church in Budapest. For a small fee, you can turn on the light to view the **frescoes**, which the English-speaking priest may take the time to explain.

A tourist kiosk outside sells books on the surrounding area, but there's nothing else to see – and nowhere to stay – in the village, so you might as well return to Szombathely or push on to Körmend (see p.204).

Sárvár

SÁRVÁR, 27km east of Szombathely, has more to offer. Its **thermal spa** is the newest in Hungary, since the hot springs were discovered only 25 years ago. A **riding centre** offers lessons and pony trekking for the actively inclined, while beer drinkers will enjoy the small **Kaltenberg brewery**, where you can sample the product as you watch it being made. The brewery marks a renewal of ties between Sárvár and Bavaria, whose nineteenth-century monarchs owned the fortress that gives the town its name – "Mud Castle".

Sárvár Castle

Though that may have been a fair description of what stood here in the Dark Ages, it hardly applies to **Sárvár Castle** (Tues–Sun 10am–6pm) today. Successively modified by many owners over the centuries, its pentagonal layout is credited to the **Nádasdy family**, particulary Tomás Nádasdy, who hired Italian architects and made this a centre of Renaissance humanism in the sixteenth century. It was here that the first Hungarian translation of the New Testament was printed (1541). The **festival hall** is decorated with Dorfmeister frescoes of Biblical episodes, allegories of art and science, and murals depicting the "Black Knight" Ferenc Nádasdy routing the Turks. There is much about Tomás and Ferenc in the **museum**, but only a passing mention of the latter's wife – the infamous Countess Báthori.

Practicalities

Sárvár is accessible by hourly trains and irregular buses from Szombathely. To reach the castle, take bus #1 or #1Y from the railway station, or walk east along Batthyány utca from the bus terminus. The thermal baths beyond the castle are

---

COUNTESS ERZSÉBET BÁTHORI

Countess Erzsébet Báthori was possibly the first female serial killer in history. Born in 1560, the offspring of two branches of the noble Báthori family (whose intermarriage could explain several cases of lunacy in the dynasty), she was intelligent and well educated, but subject to fainting spells and fits of uncontrollable rage. A horrific experience in childhood (see Nagyescsed, p.308) and an illegitimate pregnacy that was hushed up so that she could marry Ferenc at the age of fifteen may have precipitated her psychosis.

While he was away at war, she began torturing serving women at Sárvár, cudgelling or sticking pins into them for any misdemeanour. A dozen maids were forced to lie naked in the snowy courtyard, doused with cold water, and froze to death as she watched. Though not averse to brutalising servants himself, Ferenc balked at such extremes on his return, and it wasn't until after his death (1604) that she could give full rein to her lusts. With the assistance of two maids (one of whom was her lover), her son's wet-nurse and a male retainer, she tortured to death over 600 women and girls – sometimes biting chunks of flesh from their necks and breasts – the origin of **legends** which say that she bathed in the blood of virgins to keep her own skin white and translucent.

While *Die Blutgräffin* preyed exclusively on commoners – who could always be enticed into service at Sárvár and her later residences at Beckov and Čachtice (now in Slovakia), there was little risk that any accusations by the victims' relatives would be taken seriously. It was only after the demise of her lover Darvulia that she started killing aristocratic girls, making her **downfall** inevitable. In December 1610 sheriffs raided Castle Čachtice, catching her literally red-handed. Tried *in camera* to spare her family shame, she was walled up in one room of the castle and died there four years later. All mention of the case was prohibited, but after protests from relatives of her victims, her body was moved to the family vault at Nagyescsed.

well signposted. En route you'll see *Savaria Tourist*, Várkör 33 (Mon–Fri 9am–5pm, Sat & Sun 9am–noon; closed Sun in winter; ☎94/578), which can supply **information** and book private **accommodation** (②–③). Note that some of the alternatives below have no direct telephone connection, so can only be contacted through the Sárvár operator.

Good, inexpensive **meals** and loud music are the order of the day at the *Kinizsi Étterem*, across the road from the baths. Alternatively, you can eat at the upmarket restaurant above the Kaltenburg brewery (aka the *Vár Söröző*) near the *Thermal Hotel* on Rákóczi út.

Plátán Fogadó, Hunyadi utca 23 (☎Sárvár 623). A small pension en route to the castle. ③.

Hotel Thermal, Rákóczi út 1 (☎96/16-088). The town's smartest hotel, with a sauna, gym, and other facilities. Another hotel of similar stature is being built across the road. ⑥.

Vadkert Fogadó, Vadkert utca vége (☎96/24-056). A pleasant pension on the "strip" between the castle and the thermal baths. ④.

Mini Motel, Vadkert utca 2 (☎Sárvár 228). Exactly what its name says, situated opposite the baths. ②.

Thermal Camping, Vadkert utca 1 (☎Sárvár 292). Likewise by the baths; take bus #1Y to the end of the line. April 15–Oct 15.

Körmend, Szentgotthárd and the Őrség

The hilly region to the **south of Szombathely** is defined by the River Rába, which flows from the Styrian Alps across the Little Plain to join the Danube at Győr. Its valley forms a natural route into Austria, straddled by two small towns with a sub-Alpine ambience and historic links with the newly independent state of **Slovenia**. Though neither merits a special trip, Körmend and Szentgotthárd make pleasant stopovers en route to the border, and good jumping-off points for the Őrség region, further south. Both towns are accessible by train from Szombathely.

KÖRMEND, 16km south of Ják, boasts a massive Baroque **Batthyány-Strattman Mansion**, incorporating four corner towers from a medieval castle. The surrounding park is a nature conservation area with many old trees and the finest magnolias in Hungary. Should you care **to stay** overnight, private rooms (③) from Rákóczi utca 11 are cheaper than the *Rába Hotel* at Bercsényi utca 24 (☎ Körmend 89; ④). Places **to eat** include the *Rába Étterem*, Rákóczi utca 2, and the *halászcsárda*, Bajcsy-Zsilinszky utca 18.

SZENTGOTTHÁRD, 29km west of Körmend, grew up around a Cistercian abbey founded in the twelfth century. Many Slovenes subsequently settled here, as evinced by a collection of their costumes in the **Pável Ágoston Museum** (Tues–Sun 10am–6pm) which, like the Dorffmeister fresco in Szentgotthárd's **Baroque church**, also commemorates the Battle of Mogersdorf (the town's German name) in 1664, when European mercenaries under General Montecuccoli repulsed a Turkish army. Tradition has it that one hundred Turks drowned in the River Lapincs, which joins the Rába at Szentgotthárd. A mere stream in summer, it becomes an icy torrent as the snow thaws in the Styrian Alps.

With its hotel closed for renovation, **accommodation** is limited to private rooms from Eötvös utca 6, but there is a choice of **restaurants**: the *Hármashatar Étterem* and *Zöldfa Halászcsárda* on Széchenyi utca, and the *Makk Hetes Vendéglő* on Árpád utca. Szentgotthárd lies 5km off the main road, where traffic queues presage the Rábafüzes/Heilingenkreutz **border crossing**.

The Őrség

The forested **Őrség region** has guarded Hungary's southwestern marches since the time of the Árpáds, with hilltop watchtowers and isolated hamlets where every man was sworn to arms in lieu of paying tax. Moist winds from the Jura Mountains make this the rainiest, greenest part of Hungary; its heavy clay soil allows no form of agriculture except raising cattle, but provides ample raw material for the local pottery industry. Until well into this century, when the region declined as villagers migrated to Zalaegerszeg, houses were constructed of wooden beams plastered with clay. Whether tourism and the encouragement of crafts will revive the Őrség remains to be seen; meanwhile, its soft landscapes and folksy architecture are a powerful attraction.

There are several **approaches**, depending on your starting point. Trains from Szombathely to Szentgotthárd are met by buses to Őriszentpéter via Szalafő – two of the nicest villages. Alternatively, you could head for Zalalövo by train from Körmend or Zalaegerszeg (4 daily) and travel on to Őriszentpéter (14km) via Pankász, hitching or hiking if a bus doesn't materialise. Given the limited services and quiet roads, cycling is the best way of **getting around**. Bikes can be hired at several villages, but it's wise to bring a rainproof garment for those inevitable drizzles.

Őriszentpéter and Szalafő

ŐRISZENTPÉTER is the obvious base, having bus connections to Szentgotthárd, Körmend and Zalalövo, and the best tourist facilities in the region. For local **information**, visit *Savaria Tourist* at Városszer 23, or, if closed, Kovácsszer 16; or ask at the *Őrség Fogadó*, Városszer 57 (☎Őriszentpéter 155), by the campsite opposite the church. While private **rooms** are pricey (④), the *Dominó Motel* (☎Őriszentpéter 248) 1km outside the village has excellently appointed self-contained units, sleeping 4–6 (②).

On the western outskirts stands a **Romanesque church** with traces of frescoes and fine carvings around the doorway, dating from the thirteenth century. The denomination of Őrség churches can be a contentious issue, since many of the Protestant ones built by German settlers (whose religious freedoms had been guaranteed as early as the eleventh century) were appropriated by the Catholics during the seventeenth-century Counter-Reformation.

Protestants whose ancestors had smuggled Lutheran Bibles in wine barrels claimed retrospective victory in the Eighties, when the church at **SZALAFŐ**, 6km up the road, was deemed to be of *Református* origin – the proof being newly discovered sixteenth-century murals depicting the duties of women! The village consists of eight hamlets, sited apart on high ground to reduce the risk of flooding. Its most distictive feature is the hilltop **Pityerszer** of heavy-timbered houses surrounding a courtyard, with connecting porches designed to allow neighbourly chats despite the rain. Nearby, you can rent similar houses **sleeping** five to ten people (① per head, minimum four persons) and **bicycles** for 160Ft per day.

Other villages

Approaching the Őrség from Zalalövo, you can stop to admire the rustic **wooden belltower** at **PANKASZ**, 7km east of Őriszentpéter. **Bikes** and **rooms** can be rented at **HEGYHÁTSZENTJAKAB**, 3km north off the road between Zalalövo and Pankasz.

More appealing, though, are two villages along a minor road **south of Őriszentpéter**, well off the public transport routes. In the hills along the Slovenian border, 12km away, the tiny village of **MAGYARSZOMBATFA** (pop. 300) preserves the old tradition of **Habán pottery**, sold through the local *Fazekasház* (*fazekas* is the Hungarian for "potter"). The road continues 6km southeast to **VELEMÉR**, whose single-aisled Romanesque church contains beautiful frescoes from 1380. To view them, ask for a key at the signposted school house 400m before the church. There's nothing to fear from the armed border guard nearby.

CROSSING INTO SLOVENIA

Midway between Őriszentpéter and Magyarszombafalva is a turn off for Hodos/ Salovci, Hungary's only border **crossing into Slovenia**. The new republic is keen to attract tourists, so **visas** are issued on the spot with minimal fuss. Slovenian independence now seems assured, and the country should remain peaceful however bad the conflict in the other former Yugoslav republics, since Serbia no longer seeks control of its territory.

Zalaegerszeg

The county capital **ZALAEGERSZEG** – familiarly known as Zala – began to metamorphose after the discovery of oil in 1937, and is now the most industrialised town in southwestern Hungary (pop. 70,000). Despite the futuristic television tower featured on tourist brochures, its main interest lies in the past, represented by vestiges of folk culture from the surrounding region, preserved in two museums and an annual festival.

The town itself consists chiefly of housing estates and landscaped plazas, as you'll discover on **arrival** at the railway station south of the centre (bus #1, #7, #10 or #11), or the intercity bus depot east of the main square. **Downtown** centres around three squares running into each other. Kazinczy tér is for local transport and information; Szabadság tér features a Baroque parish church, Trinity Statue and county hall; while Deák tér – named after the local politician (1803–76) who negotiated the historic Compromise with the Habsburg Empire – is the site of a lively **market** selling Göcsej cheese and other local produce.

Museums and other sights

In the old town hall at Batthyány utca 2, off Szabadság tér, the **Göcsej Museum** (Tues–Sun 10am–5pm) displays a rich haul of antique folk costumes from the region. Less colourful but more amusing are the **sculptures by Zsigmond Kisfaludi Strobl** (1884–1975). The son of a sculptor, he enjoyed early success with busts of British Royals and Hungarian aristocrats, then switched to producing glorified Workers (and the Liberation Monument in Budapest) under Communism, earning himself medals and the nickname "Step from Side to Side".

On the northwestern outskirts of town near a dead tributary of the River Zala are two more museums (bus #1, #1Y or #8Y). Giant pumps, drills and other hardware dominate the **Oil Museum** (Tues–Sun 10am–6pm), which examines the history of the petroleum industry in Hungary. Unfortunately for the economy, exploratory drilling in the Fifties and Sixties discovered far more hot springs than

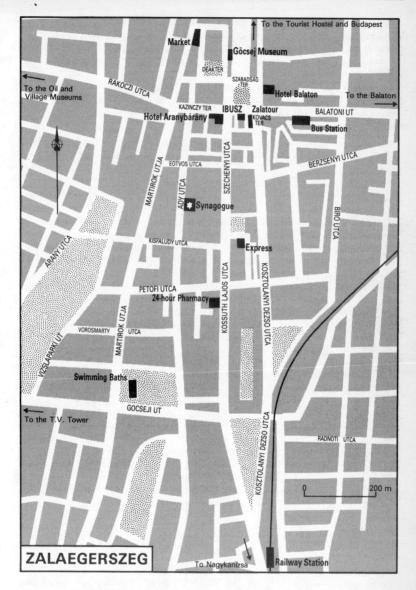

To the Tourist Hostel and Budapest

Market

Göcsej Museum

DEÁKTÉR

SZABADSÁG TÉR

To the Oil and
Village Museums

RÁKÓCZI UTCA

Hotel Balaton

To the Balaton

KAZINCZY TÉR

IBUSZ

Zalatour

Hotel Aranybárány

KOVÁCS TÉR

BALATONI ÚT

Bus Station

MÁRTÍROK ÚTJA

EÖTVÖS UTCA

ADY UTCA

SZÉCHENYI UTCA

BERZSENYI UTCA

Synagogue

ARANY UTCA

KISFALUDY UTCA

BÍRÓ UTCA

Express

KOSSUTH LAJOS UTCA

KOSZTOLÁNYI DEZSŐ UTCA

PETŐFI UTCA

24-hour Pharmacy

MÁRTÍROK ÚTJA

VÖRÖSMARTY UTCA

VÍZSLAPARKI ÚT

Swimming Baths

GÖCSEJI ÚT

To the T.V. Tower

RADNÓTI UTCA

KOSZTOLÁNYI DEZSŐ UTCA

0   200 m

ZALAEGERSZEG

To Nagykanizsa

Railway Station

oil, and the most promising field was found to straddle the Romanian border, so
domestic production amounts to a fraction of Hungary's requirements.

The **Village Museum** next door (April–Oct Tues–Sun 10am–5pm) assembles
traditional dwellings, barns and artefacts from the surrounding **Göcsej region**.
Traditionally, this was so poor and squalid that no one would admit to being a

part of it, and enquirers were always hastily assured that its boundaries began a few miles on, in the next village. Nowadays, Göcsej folk spend their weeks working and sleeping in hostels in Zala, returning home on weekends; some have bought apartments in town and are saving up to build a new holiday home in the hills.

Back in town, it's a short walk from Kazinczy tér to the town's former **Synagogue**, an unmistakable, lilac-painted edifice at Ady utca 14. Should there be a temporary exhibition on, you'll be able to see the interior, designed by József Stern in the Eclectic style in 1903. Lastly, there is the aforementioned **Television Tower**, on a hill to the southwest of town (bus #30 from Göcseji út), whose observation deck (Tues–Sun 10am–4pm) offers a panoramic vista of Zalaegerszeg.

Practicalities

Information is available from *Zalatour,* Kovács tér 1 (Mon–Fri 8am–4pm, Sat 8am–noon; ☎92/11-443), and *IBUSZ* next door (same hours; ☎92/11-458), which can both arrange private rooms (②). Aside from the chance of dormitory beds (①) from *Express*, Dísz tér 3 (8am–4.30pm daily; ☎92/14-144), other **accommodation** includes:

Hotel Aranybárány, Széchenyi tér 1–3 (☎92/14-100). The "Golden Lamb" is a fine old building in the centre. ③–④.

Hotel Balaton, Balatoni út 2A (☎92/14-400; telex 33-408). Not so attractive, but modern and likewise central. ③–④.

Göcseji Fogadó, Kaszaházi utca 2 (☎92/11-580). Beds in dorms (①) and quadruple rooms (②), 500m from centre (bus #3, #3Y or #5).

Hotel ZÁÉV, Vizslaparti út 32 (☎92/11-561). Apartments (④), doubles (②) and triples (③) with baths, near Youth Park, west of the synagogue.

ZÁÉV Vendégház, Alsóerdő (☎92/14-310). Doubles (②) and triples (③) with baths, near the television tower.

Though its future is uncertain, it's worth asking about the **Göcsej Days**, a folklore festival previously held in August. Otherwise, entertainments boil down to whatever's on at local cultural centres or the Sportscsarnok two blocks east along Balatoni út. Besides the **restaurants** in downtown hotels and the *Göcseji Fogadó* (which specialises in fish and game dishes), try the *Göcseji Étterem* at Dózsa liget 1, or the *Nefelejcs Étterem* on Dísz tér.

While **trains** run to Budapest and Pécs, Keszthely and neighbouring areas are better served by **buses** from Kovács tér.

SOUTHERN TRANSDANUBIA

Heading for **southern Transdanubia** from Zala, Budapest or the Balaton, it's best to aim directly for **Pécs**, the region's attractive capital. Although the **Völgység**, or valley region between Lake Balaton and the Mecsek Hills is pretty to drive through, none of the towns are really worth stopping for. Travelling from the Balaton by train, however, you might find it necessary to change at Nagykanizsa or Kaposvár. Express trains from Budapest to Pécs usually run via Dombóvár, while intercity coaches are routed through Szekszárd.

Nagykanizsa and Kaposvár

NAGYKANIZSA (pronounced "Nodge-konizha") is an old fortress town straddling the Principális River, 60km south of Zala. Together with Szigetvár and Siklós, it bore the brunt of Turkish assaults during the first decades of the occupation, and, like them, ultimately succumbed. The fort has long since disappeared, but its masonry was used to build the Parish church, containing the **tomb of Mustafa Pasha**, Nagykanizsa's last Turkish overlord, into which baptismal fonts have been cut. Other downtown sights include two Baroque houses on Szechényi tér (nos. 5 & 7); Celtic and Roman artefacts and regional folk costumes in the **Thury György Museum** (Tues–Sun 10am–6pm) on Szabadság tér; and modern **sculptures** in a pleasant municipal **park**. The local **brewery** produces *Gold Fassel* and *Dreher* beer.

When last heard, the town still had its Communist street-names; for up-to-date **information**, contact *Zalatour* at Lenin út 13 (Mon–Fri 8am–5pm, Sat 8am–noon; ☎93/11-185) – or whatever this main street is now called. Aside from private rooms (booked through *Zalatour*, ②), you can **stay** at the *Marika Panzió*, Cserfa utca 9 (☎93/19-186; ②); the *Hotel Central*, Szabadság tér 23 (☎93/14-000; ③); the *Pannonia Hotel*, Vörös Hadsereg út 4 (☎93/14-000; ③); or *Autóscamping* motel, Vár utca 1 (May–Sept; ☎93/19-119②), 2km out towards Letenye on the Croatian border. The *Ady Étterem*, Ady út 5, serves good food from 9am to 10pm. There are five **trains** daily to Pécs, via Szigetvár. The nearest road **crossing into Croatia** – which is *not* recommended at time of writing – is at Letenye, 26km west of town.

Kaposvár

The industrial town of **KAPOSVÁR** (pop. 75,000), capital of Somogy county, is also a stepping stone for Szigetvár or Pécs, but offers little inducement to stay. Arriving at the bus or railway station, sited one block apart on Nagy Budai Antal utca, south of the centre, it's best to check travel connections before heading up Teleki or Dózsa György utca to investigate the sights. Most things worth noting can be found along or just off the main, pedestrianised street, currently still known as Május 1. utca.

The **Somogy County Museum** (Tues–Sun 10am–6pm) at no. 12 contains the usual mix of ethnographic and historical material*, and stands next door to the seventeenth-century **Golden Lion Pharmacy**, where József Rippl-Rónai (1861–1927), the "father of Hungarian Art Nouveau", was born. Some of his paintings can be seen in the **Rippl-Rónai Museum** (Tues–Sun 10am–6pm) one block east at no. 10, while other local artists are showcased in the **Kaposvári Gallery** (Tues–Sun 10am–6pm) at Rákoczi tér 4, just up from the railway station. Directly opposite is the **Csiky Gergely Theatre**, whose company has attracted kudos abroad (tickets from the *Színház Jegypéntzár*, Május 1. utca 8).

Practicalities

Information and private rooms (②) are available from *Siótour*, Május 1. utca 1 (Mon–Fri 8am–5pm, Sat 8am–noon; ☎82/14-640), or *IBUSZ*, Teleki utca 3. Next

---

* Most likely, this will soon include a section on **Imre Nagy**, Hungary's Premier during the 1956 Uprising, who was born in Kaposvár.

door to *Siótour* is the renovated, eighteenth-century *Csokonai Fogadó* (☎82/12-497; ②) – the nicest **accommodation** in town, but often full. One block west on Kossuth tér stands the ugly modern *Kapos Hotel* (☎82/14-580; ③); 150m in the other direction is the small *Pálma Panzió* Széchenyi tér 6, (③). *Deseda* **campsite** lies 6km northeast of town (bus #8 from the station, or get off at the Toponár stop on the Siófok–Kaposvár branch line). Inexpensive **meals** are served at the *Ipar Vendéglő*, Teleki utca 8 (closed Sun).

Buses run to Pécs (every 1–2hrs), Szigetvár (5 daily), Keszthely, Siófok and Kecskemét (one of each daily). You're required to have seat reservations on the three to four daily express **trains** to Pécs; for these, and tickets, contact *MÁV Tours* on Csokonai utca (through the passageway from Május 1. utca 21).

Pécs and the Mecsek Hills

If there was ever a uranium mining town worth visiting, **PÉCS** – pronounced "Paych" – is it. Tiled rooftops climb the vine-laden slopes of the Mecsek Hills, and the nearby mines of Újmecsekalja (aka "Uranium City") haven't contaminated Pécs's reputation for art and culture. As Transdanbuia's leading centre of education, its population of 150,000 includes a high proportion of students, giving Pécs a youthful profile. The city boasts some fine examples of Islamic architecture, several wonderful museums and galleries, and the biggest market in western Hungary. It is also a base for exploring Siklós, Szigetvár and Mohács, further south, and the Mecsek Hills above the city.

Settlements existed here in prehistoric times, but the city's **history** really began with *Sopianae*, a Celtic town developed by the Romans and later raised to be the capital of the new province of *Pannonia Valeria*. Made an epicospal see by King Stephen, the town – known as *Quinqua Ecclesiae* or *Fünfkirchen* (Five Churches) – became a university centre in the Middle Ages. Under Turkish occupation (1543–1686) its character changed radically, and its Magyar/German population was replaced by Turks and their Balkan subjects. Devastated during its "liberation", the city slowly recovered thanks to local viticulture and the discovery of coal in the mid-eighteenth century. While the coalmines now face closure due to bankruptcy, Pécs's uranium mines – dating from the early 1950s – are still going strong.

Around the Belváros

Most of the sights, hotels and tourist offices lie within the Belváros, encircled by a road marking the extent of the medieval town walls. **Arriving** at the railway station, you can stash your luggage in a small building by platform one before catching a bus into the centre. Any bus up Szabadsag utca can drop you at the Zsolnay monument on Rákoczi út, while bus #30 follows Bajcsy-Zsilinszky utca as far as the main square – this passes close to the intercity bus station, but from there you can easily walk to the centre, in less than ten minutes.

If you do walk this way, take a bearing on the *Konzum* department store, near which you can turn on to Kossuth tér to find an elegant **Synagogue** built in 1865 (May–Oct 9am–1pm & 1.30–5pm; closed Sat). The carved and stuccoed interior is beautiful but haunting, with Romantic frescoes swirling around space emptied by the murder of over four thousand Jews now listed in a Book of Remembrance;

ten times the number that live in Pécs today. Thanks to local efforts, state support and contributions from abroad, this was one of the first synagogues in Hungary to be restored in the 1980s.

Further up Bajcsy-Zsilinszky utca, notice the **Zsolnay Fountain** outside the church on the right. Local Zsolnay ceramics are typified by polychromatic, metallic-looking glazes; the bulls' heads on the fountain are modelled on a gold drinking vessel from the "Treasure of Attila" (see p.281). One block north, the road meets **Király utca**, traditionally the *korzó* where townsfolk **promenade**. Amongst the buildings worth noting on this street are the newly restored Art Nouveau **Hotel Palatinu**s; the Nendtvich House (no. 8) with its ceramic ornamentation; the **National Theatre**, surmounted by a statue of Genius; and the Vasváry House (no. 19), with its allegorical figurines. However, there's more to see around Széchenyi tér, at the top of Bajcsy-Zsilinszky utca.

Széchenyi tér

With its art galleries and tourist offices, modern-day **Széchenyi tér** is centuries removed from its Turkish predecessor, a dusty square crowded with "caravans of camels laden with merchandise from India and the Yemen". At its top end stands a Catholic church whose ornate window grilles and scalloped niches denote its origins as the **Mosque of Gazi Kasim Pasha**, which the Turks built from the stones of a medieval, Gothic church. The vaulted interior and Islamic *mihrab* decorated with Arabic calligraphy can be viewed during sightseeing hours (summer Mon–Sat 10am–4pm, Sun 11.30am–4pm; winter Mon–Sat 11am–noon, Sun 11.30am–2pm).

Contemporary artwork is exhibited in a **Gallery** on the western side of the square. It's worth a quick look in case there's anything remarkable, but with so many art collections in Pécs, it pays to be selective. The **Archaeological Museum** (Tues–Sun 10am–6pm) on the northern side of the square – covering the history of the region from prehistoric times to the Magyar conquest – is lacklustre compared to the real Roman tombs further west, and the **Mining Museum**, not far away at Mária utca 9 (same hours), is also disappointing, for all the sparkle of its crystals. At this point, you have the option of three routes to the cathedral – along Káptalan, Janus Pannonius or Apáca utca – via a clutch of museums.

Káptalan utca

Káptalan utca (Chapter street) has no fewer than five museums virtually next to each other, all of them open Tuesday to Sunday from 10am to 6pm. The **Zsolnay Museum** at no. 2 is a must for its vases, plaques and figurines from the Zsolnay Ceramics Factory, founded in 1868 by Vilmos Zsolnay and the chemist Vince Wartrha, the inventor of eosin glaze. Some pieces are exquisite, others totally kitsch, but they deserve a look either way. In the basement are sculptures by Amerigo Tot (1909–84), whose *Erdély family* with its clamped grave-posts symbolises the plight of the Magyars in Romania.

Across the road at no. 3, the **Vásárely Museum** exhibits Op-Art canvases by Viktor Vásárely, who was born in this house in 1908, but made his name in Paris and New York. The **Modern Magyar Keptár** next door to the Zsolnay Museum presents a *tour d'horizon* of Hungarian art since the School of Szentendre, with a large section devoted to Constructivist evocations of the proletarian struggle by Béla Uitz (1887–1972), who lived for fifty years in the Soviet Union. The **Nemes**

To Hotel Hunyor

JURISICS UTCA

BALICSI UT

Idris Baba Mausoleum

NYAR UTCA

KODALY UTCA

Kollégium

ALKOTMANY UTCA

ALKOTMANY UTCA

IFJUSAG UTJA

Hospital

Jakovali Hassa
Mosque

Medical University

SZIGETI UT

PETOFI SANDOR UTCA

JOZSEF ATTILA UTCA

TUZER UTCA

MEGYERI UTCA

KOLOZSVAR UTCA

N

0   200 m

PÉCS

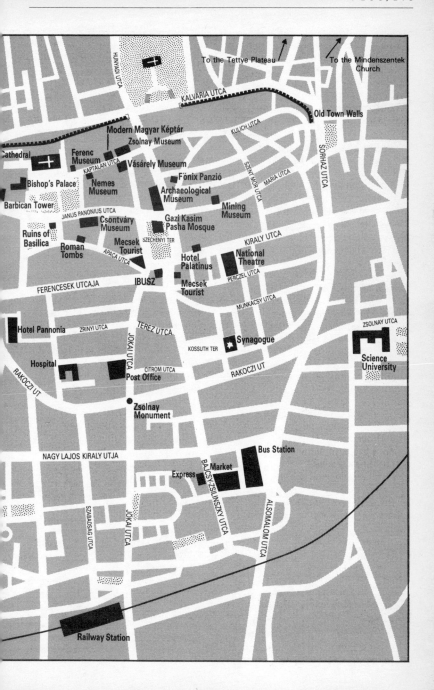

Museum at no. 5 honours the surrealist Endre Nemes (1909–85), who was born in nearby Pécsvárad but spent most of his life in Sweden. Diagonally across the street at no. 6, right by Dóm tér, the **Ferenc Museum** showcases work by Martyn Ferenc (1899–1986), an early exponent of non-figurative painting.

The Csontváry Museum

If you only visit one place in Pécs, make it the **Csontváry Museum** at Janus Pannonius utca 11–13 (Tues–Sun 10am–6pm). Kosztka Tivadar Csontváry (1853–1919) was born in the same year as van Gogh, and his artistic career was similarly affected by madness and the pursuit of "the path of the sun". His fascination with Hebrew lore and the Holy Land was expressed in huge canvasses – *Baalbek*, *Mary's Well at Nazareth*, and *Pilgrimage* – while his hallucinatory vision of nature produced *Tatra*, *Storm on the Great Hortobágy* and *Solitary Cedar*.

After his death, these works were almost sold as tarpaulin but purchased by an architect at the last moment. When Picasso later saw an exhibition of his work in Paris, he asked to be left alone in the room for an hour, then remarked, "I did not know there was another great painter in our century besides me", and later told Chagall, "There you are, old master, I bet even you could not paint something like this".

Roman remains on Apáca utca

The necropolis of Sopianae lay more or less beneath Apáca utca (Nun street), where several **Roman tombs** decorated with scenes of the Gates of Paradise have been excavated in the courtyard of no. 9. After the Romans went home and waves of migrating tribes swept across Hungary, the tombs were used as refuges and modified accordingly. Across the road are the less impressive **remains of a chapel**, likewise dating from the third or fourth century AD. Opening hours for both sites are irregular, but the tombs are worth seeing if they're open. If not, another excavated ruin can be found on Szent István tér, nearby.

Around Dóm tér and the Cathedral

Szent István tér, the lower, park-like extension of Cathedral Square, harbours a subterranean **ruined basilica** or **early Christian mausoleum** (there is doubt as to which it actually is; Tues–Sun 10am–6pm), containing a chapel dating from around 350 AD, decorated with frescoes of the Fall and Daniel in the Lion's Den, and containing a white marble sarcophagus and skeletal remains.

Up the steps past the Szepesy statue, Dóm tér is dominated by a huge, four-towered **Cathedral** that has been endlessly rebuilt since a Basilica was founded here in the eleventh century. Though a crypt and side chapels from eleventh- to fourteenth-century churches have been incorporated in the cathedral, its outward form is neo-Romanesque, the style chosen to replace Mihály Pollock's previous Baroque design. Its lavish blue and gold murals are by Lotz, Székely and other historicist painters of the 1890s.

The neo-Renaissance **Bishop's Palace** to the west is embellished with a modern statue of Liszt waving from the balcony, which might have amused Janus Pannonius (1434–72), the humanist poet and bishop of Pécs, or Bishop György Klimó, founder of its library, who said to borrowers: "You don't have to pay for anything. Depart enriched. Return more frequently". Around the corner to the south, a circular **Barbican tower** punctuates the old town walls, giving access to Klimó György utca.

The Pécs telephone code is ☎72

Around the periphery

From here, you can head uphill and on to Aradi vértanuk útja to see a section of the **old town walls** – once a massive crenellated rampart 5500 paces long, buttressed by 87 bastions– erected after the Mongol invasion of the thirteenth century. Above the tunnel 300m along is a small garden with a decaying **Calvary Chapel**, offering a fine view of the Belváros.

Alternatively, head downhill around the peripheral boulevard – henceforth Rákóczi út – to find the inconspicuous **Jakovali Hassan Mosque** (10am–1pm & 1.30–6pm; closed Wed). Unlike its counterparts at Szigetvár and Eger, this sixteenth-century mosque is still intact (though its minaret is closed), with friezes, a superbly-carved *minbar* (pulpit), and Turkish carpets adorning its cool white interior. Around the corner on Sallai utca, you can see the ruins of a Turkish bath outside the *Minaret* restaurant.

A small **Ethnographic Museum** (Tues–Sun 10am–6pm) containing folk costumes from the Baranya region can be found at Rákóczi út 19. The nearby **Zsolnay Monument** gazes benevolently over the junction with Szabadság utca. Heading back towards the centre, notice the Romantic-style **Post Office** on Jókai utca.

Further out

Unless you're fascinated by Turkish death rites, it's not worth tracking down the *türbe* or **mausoleum of Idris Baba** at Nyár utca 8, off Kodály utca, 1km west of the centre, which is touted as a local attraction. Further out lies the Medical (*Orvostudományi*) faculty of **Pécs University**, Europe's fifth when it was founded in 1367. The Science (*Tudományi*) faculty is on the other side of the Belváros; buses #M14 and #30 run between the two campuses, which are still a couple of the liveliest parts of town.

For a fresh perspective on Pécs, catch bus #33 from Kossuth tér up to the **Tettye plateau**, where a ruined palace – once used as a Dervish monastery – stands in a park. Higher up and further out, **Misina Hill** (534m) is crowned by a **Television Tower** with an observation platform, accessible by bus #35 from Kossuth tér or the railway station, which runs past a **Zoo** (daily 9am–6pm) on Ángyán János utca. Should you care to walk back from the plateau, Havihegyi út* offers a succession of views as it winds around the hillside, with several picturesque backstreets slinking down past the **Mindenszentek Church**, whose pastor supplements his income by selling poultry.

All kinds of livestock appears at the monthly **Pécs Market**, a huge country fair held on the first Sunday of every month at a site in the southeast of town – take bus #50 from outside the *Konzum* store on Rákóczi út and ask to be dropped off at the *Vásártér*. Be sure to buy a bus ticket from the newspaper kiosk, as inspectors are on the prowl. On other Sundays, there is a lively market for clothes and junk on the same site.

---

*Old town plans show this as Mező Imre út, and Áangyán J. utca as Beloiannisz utca. My favourite discarded streetname is I. Ötéves terv utca – "First Five Year Plan street".

Practicalities

Mecsek Tourist, Széchenyi tér 1 (Mon–Fri 8am–4pm, Sat 8am–noon; ☎13-300), is the best source of **information**, though *IBUSZ* at no. 8 (same hours; ☎12-169) can also help. Private **rooms** (③) are bookable through either, and they can also find **dormitory beds** (①) in vacant colleges – or ask at *Express*, Bajcsy-Zsilinszky utca 6. Out of hours, a direct approach to the *kollégium* at Kodály utca 30 (500m west of the cathedral) or the *Pollack Mihály Kollégium* at Boszorkány út 2 (☎24-277; bus #30 to the end of the line) might pay off. Other options include:

Hotel Palatinus, Király utca 5 (☎33-022). Recently restored fin-de-siècle pile with a magnificent lobby and modern rooms (no singles). Breakfast included. ⑥.

Hotel Főnix, Hunyadi út 2 (☎11-682). A small, modern place just off Széchenyi tér, with single (③), double (④) and triple (⑤) rooms.

Hotel Pannónia, Rákóczi út 3 (☎13-322). A Seventies block off the ring road. Breakfast included. ⑤.

Hotel Hunyor, Jurisics Miklós utca 16 (☎15-677). Northwest of town (bus #32), with a nice wine garden and restaurant. Double rooms (④) and apartments (⑤).

Fenyves Hotel, Szőlő utca 64 (☎15-996). West of the Tettye plateau, accessible by bus #33 or a five-minute walk from the *Toboz Panzió*. Breakfast and great views of the city included. ③.

Toboz Panzió, Fenyves sor 5 (☎25-232). A former trade union hostel now open to anyone. Take bus #34 or #35 to Károlyi utca, or walk uphill from the *Fenyes Hotel*. ③–④.

Mediterranean Hotel, Dömörkapu (☎15-987). An ex-tourist hostel gone upmarket, further into the hills (bus #35 to the end of the line). ④.

Mandulás Hotel and **Panzió**, Ángyán János utca 2 (☎15-981). Rooms with or without baths, and motel doubles with showers, on a **campsite** in the woods below the TV tower, near the penultimate stop on the #34 bus route. April 15–Oct 15. ②–③.

Free camping – with minimal facilities and no security – is possible at the site of the monthly market, where Romanian and Polish traders sleep in their cars.

Entertainments, eating and drinking

Pécs's **opera and ballet** companies are highly regarded, so it can be hard to obtain tickets for performances at the National Theatre on Király utca – ask about cancellations at the box office an hour before the show starts. There is a **puppet theatre** on the corner of Mária and Szent Mor utca. *Mecsek Tourist* can give details of **concerts** and other events at local cultural centres. Live music and rock 'n' roll dancing are occasionally on at the *Pepita Bar* in Balokány park, 400m beyond the Science University (bus #21). The *Pinnochio Bar* on the corner of Teréz and Jókai utca often hosts **discos**.

Klimó György utca has a couple of good places to **eat and drink**, namely the Serbian restaurant on the corner of Kodály utca, and the *Bástya Söröző* down from the Barbican tower. On Jókai ter, there is the *Elefánt Söröző* (named after the statue on the corner of the building), which has a bar and an upstairs restaurant. The historic *Iparos Ház* at the top of Szabadság utca by the Zsolnay Monument also does good food (11.30am–10pm; entrance around the block). Cakes and ices can be enjoyed at the *Capri Cukrászda* on Citrom utca (Lemon street).

Moving on

Aside from various possible **excursions** from Pécs (see the following sections), it's worth remembering that the city has bus **connections** to Baja, Kecskemét and Szeged on the Great Plain; and Siófok, Hévíz and Székesfehérvár around Lake Balaton. Before the civil war in Yugoslavia, it was also the point of departure for coaches to Osijek and Vukovar (now defunct, for obvious reasons) and trains to Osijek (still operating when last heard).

The Mecsek Hills

The karstic **Mecsek Hills** north of Pécs offer panoramic views and trails fanning out from the television tower through groves of sweet chestnuts and almond trees. If you fancy some **hiking**, invest in a 1:40,000 map of the hills, available from bookshops. Alternatively, you could catch an hourly bus from the intercity depot out to Örfü or Abaliget, two popular resorts.

ÖRFÜ features two artificial **lakes** surrounded by sports facilities, restaurants and accommodation, with a museum-piece **mill** to the east of the smaller lake. A few kilometres west along the road is the larger settlement of **ABALIGET**, with an outdoor pool and a 640-metre-long **stalactite cave** inhabited by blind crabs beside one of its lakes. Should you wish to stay, it's wise to book **accommodation** through *Mecsek Tourist*. Örfü has several campsites on terraced slopes, private rooms for rent (②–③; look for the *Zimmer Frei* signs), and bungalows with baths at Dollár utca 1 (☎78-070; April 15–Oct 15; ③). In Abaliget, there is a camping motel offering doubles with communal bathrooms (①), bungalows with private showers (②), and discos on Friday and Saturday nights (9pm–1am).

Szigetvár

SZIGETVÁR, 33km west of Pécs, rivals Kőszeg for its heroic resistance against the Turkish invasion. Every Hungarian child is taught the story, which is enshrined in poetry and music. Even today the town has a military presence – nothing heavy, but a reminder of the war just across the border in Croatia. Though Szigetvár has recently acquired a striking **community centre** by the architect Imre Mákovecz, and has an agreeable **thermal bath** 250m off the main square (head up Tinadi utca), it is the castle and relics of the Turkish occupation that are the main attractions.

Arriving at the railway station, follow Rákóczi út 500m north to reach the centre. Starting from the bus station, you have the option of a preliminary detour round the corner of the **market** to see a ruined **Koran school** on Szecsadi Máté utca, before heading up Rákóczi út to **Zrínyi tér**. The Baroque church on this central square has Turkish-style windows that betray its origins as the **Mosque of Ali Pasha** (1596). Directly across the square, with its defiantly snarling lion statue, Vár utca leads off towards the castle.

The Castle

As its name – **Island Castle** – suggests, this quadrilateral fortress was once surrounded by lakes and marshes. Under local strong man Bálint Török it resisted siege by the Turks in 1541 and 1554, but its finest hour came in 1566, when 2400 soldiers under **Miklós Zrínyi**, Governor of Croatia, resisted the onslaught of 100,000 Turks for 33 days. Enraged by the loss of 20,000 troops and the failure of his seventh attempt to march on Vienna, **Sultan Süleyman** died of apoplexy before the siege finally wore down the defenders: spurning offers of surrender, Zrínyi donned his court dress before leading a final, suicidal sally when they could no longer hold out.

The Sultan's followers buried his heart and innards outside town where his tent had stood, and erected a **mosque** in the grounds of the castle (Tues–Sun April–Oct 8am–6pm; Nov–March 10am–3pm). Its minaret has since disappeared, but the interior – with ornamental grilles and Koranic inscriptions – survives. In an adjacent **museum**, coloured miniatures of Turkish life are counterpointed by praise for Magyar heroism, including copies of the epic *Szózat* (Appeal) penned by Zrínyi's grandson, himself a general. A cry for liberty and a call for endurance, this seventeenth-century poem was adapted as a chorale by Kodály in 1956, and its single performance at the Budapest Academy was an emotional occasion. Crowds chanted its refrain, *Ne Bántsd a Magyarat!* – "Let the Magyars alone!" – as a symbolic protest against the Rákosi regime, causing the government members present to walk out.

Practicalities

Mecsek Tourist in the *Hotel Oroszlán* on Zrínyi tér (☎70/12-817; ④ including breakfast) can find you private **rooms** (②) or make advance bookings at the **hostel** in the castle (☎70/12-817; ①) – advisable, since soldiers or school parties are often billeted there. Alternatively, there is the *Kumilla Hotel* at Ságvári út 4 (☎70/10-150; ④), just off Zrínyi tér.

Szigetvár is accessible by regular **buses** from Pécs, and is a stopover for slow **trains** on the Nagykanizsa–Pécs line. **BARCS**, 31km southwest, has the nearest road **crossing into Croatia** (Terezino Polje) – not that this is safe at the time of writing. If you have to spend the night at Barcs, the *Határ* campsite and hotel, Nagyhíd utca 28, are cheaper than the *Hotel Boróka* (☎ Barcs 321), at Bajcsy-Zsilinszky utca 39.

Harkány and Siklós

Thirty-four kilometres south of Pécs, **HARKÁNY** draws visitors thanks to its open-air **thermal pool** (daily June–Aug 8am–4pm & 5–11pm; Sept–May 9am–5pm), with a section for wallowing in **hot mud** that is therapeutically rich in sulphur and fluoride. Aside from this, however, there is only a small **market** near the bus station and a dull **Bulgarian Army Museum** (Tues–Sun 10am–6pm), neither of which are any inducement to linger.

Should the mud baths tempt you into **staying**, the *Hotel Dráva* (☎72/80-434; ④) and the *Baranya Hotel* (☎72/80-160; April–Oct; ②) are on Bajcsy-Zsilinszky utca, opposite the baths, while at the end of the street is a campsite with a motel (③) and bungalows (②), open from mid-April to mid-October.

Thankfully, most buses plough on 6km across the dusty plain to **SILKÓS**, another small town huddled around a castle. The birthplace of **George Mikes** (known for his humorous writings in the West), Siklós is sleepier but more appealing than Szigetvár – in short, a nice one-horse town. The **castle** (Tues–Sun 10am–4pm), visible from the bus station, has been continuously inhabited since its construction in the fifteenth century. Bastions and rondellas form an impressive girdle around the Baroque mansion at its heart, once occcupied by the enlightened Casimir Batthyány, who freed his serfs in 1849. His tomb is in the Gothic chapel that is located (with no sense of incongruity according to medieval values) within whipping distance of a dungeon filled with instruments of torture and rank air.

CROSSING INTO CROATIA OR SERBIA

At the time of writing, despite a ceasefire and the deployment of UN peacekeeping forces, much of **Croatia** is still a **war zone**, where only journalists or aid workers have any reason to venture. If it's essential that you travel southwards through Yugoslavia, the only semi-**safe route** is across **Serbia**. From the Rözske crossing south of Szeged, the E75 and railway run via Subotica and Novi Sad to Belgrade. Truckers who've just driven through are the best source of information about conditions, which can change overnight.

Siklós practicalities

Lodged in separate wings of the castle are the **Hotel Tenkes** (☎73/11-433; ④) and a **tourist hostel** (☎73/11-433; ①) – best reserved through *Mecsek Tourist* – while a wine cellar-cum-**restaurant** lurks below the hotel. A cheaper, shabbier place to eat is the *Sport Vendéglő* opposite the bus station. **Buses** depart every hour for Harkány and Pécs, and less frequently for Villány. The Drávaszabolcs/ Donji Miholjac **border crossing** 14km south of Harkány is heavily militarised due to the situation in Croatia (see box).

Villány and Mohács

Fifteen kilometres east of Siklós, acres of vineyards lap the slopes of Mount Szársomlyo, producing red wine under the appellation **VILLÁNY**. Although the village's viticultural tradition goes back two thousand years, its chief attraction is a modern **sculpture park**, where bronze totems and concrete erections on the hill-side testify to the activities of an **artists' summer camp**. With no reason to stay, and no tourist accommodation, it makes sense to carry on 25km to Mohács.

Travelling there directly from Pécs one passes a range of hills to the north, where SZÉKELYSZABAR (*Samar*) and HIMESHÁZA (*Nimmersch*) were founded by Germans in the Middle Ages, but occupied after World War II by **Székely folk** from Romania, making them of interest to ethnographers. In Transylvania and Moldavia, where most of their kinsfolk live, the Székely are noted for erecting elaborately carved gateways outside their farms.

Mohács

The small town of **MOHÁCS**, hot and dusty beside the pounding Danube, is a synonym for defeat. As a consequence of a single **battle** here in 1526, Hungary was divided and war-torn for 150 years and lost its independence for centuries thereafter. The state was tottering before Mohács, however: its treasury depleted with an indecisive teenager on the throne. Only after Süleyman "the Magnificent" had taken Belgrade and was nearing the Drava did the Hungarians muster an army, which headed south without waiting for reinforcements from Transylvania, and engaged the Turks on August 29.

Legend has it that an olive-tree planted two hundred years earlier by Louis the Great suddenly became barren on the day, while the King's scribe records how Louis II gave orders for the care of his hounds before riding out to meet his fate. Attacking first, the Magyars broke ranks to loot the fallen and suffered a crushing counter-attack by Turkish Janissaries and cavalry, which caused a rout. Louis was crushed to death by his horse when trying to ford a stream, and the 25,000 dead included many of Hungary's nobles and prelates, leaving the country unable to organise resistance as the Turks advanced on Buda.

Memorials

The **battlefield**, 7km south of town, is known as Sátorhely – the "Place of Tents". Amidst fields of sunflowers and corn and clumps of blue flossflowers, statues of dying horses and men convey the chaos of battle, faces contorted in agony as the wind tinkles the pendants adorning the head of Süleyman's figure. There's no public transport to the site, so idle visitors will have to content themselves with the commemorative **museum** on Szerb utca (Tues–Sun 10am–6pm); an ugly **Votive Church** erected to mark the 400th anniversary; and a peep into the **town hall**, where the Sultan's calligraphic signature is engraved on one of the windows.

The Mohács Carnival

Aside from these, the River Danube rolling through town disconcertingly near street level is the only "sight" for 364 days of the year. The exception manifests itself on March 1, when the streets come alive with the annual **Busójárás Carnival**. With its procession of grotesquely masked figures waving flaming torches, the carnival assumes a macabre appearance at night. Originally, it was probably a spring ritual intended to propitiate the gods, but over a length of time participants also began to practise ritualistic abomination of the Turks to magically draw the sting of reality. Similar carnivals are also traditional in Serbia and Croatia, whence come many of the revellers at Mohács. At time of writing, the town is a reception centre for refugees from both republics.

Practicalities

Mecsek Tourist, Tolbuhin utca 2 (Mon–Fri 8am–4.30pm, Sat 8am–noon; ☎711/10-961), can supply information – including details of a recently opened **nudist campsite** on an island – and book private rooms (②). The only time when there's an **accommodation** shortage is during the carnival, so if you're planning to attend, make reservations. The *Hotel Korona*, Jókai utca 2 (☎711/10-541; ③), costs less than the smarter *Hotel Csele*, Kisfaludy tér 6–7 (☎711/11-825; ④–⑤), but the cheapest option is a bed (①) at the local *kollégium*, Hősők tér 6 – ask there.

There are daily **buses** to Szekszárd and Budapest (leaving around 7am & 2.40pm); and to Baja and Kecskemét or Szeged on the Great Plain (5–6 daily). Mohács is not on the railway line, but **trains** for Pécs, Szekszárd or Baja can be caught at Bátaszék, 28km to the north. Depending on the situation in Croatia, coaches might run to Osijek, Novi Sad or Slavonski Brod via the **border crossing** at Udvar, 11km south of town.

Szekszárd and the Forest of Gemenc

The chance to sample red wine from vineyards dating from Roman times and to buy inexpensive black pottery makes **SZEKSZÁRD** the prime stopover between Pécs and Budapest. With its somnabulent air and pleasant architecture, the town itself is more restful than interesting, but the chance to visit the beautiful Gemenc Forest might tempt you to stay longer. Everything of interest in town lies along, or just off, Hunyadi út, the main street, running up from the bus station. On the landscaped stretch designated Martírok tere, you will see a neo-Renaissance pile containing the **Béri Balogh Museum** (Tues–Sun 10am–6pm), with a rich collection of peasants' and nobles' artefacts.

After crossing Széchenyi utca, head uphill to Béla tér, where porticoed buildings tilt perceptibly around a statue marking the plague of 1730. The Neoclassical palace here stands on the site of an abbey church from the time of the Árpáds. Nearby, Babits utca runs off towards the **house of Mihály Babits** (Tues–Sun 9am–6pm), a homely residence exhibiting photos and manuscripts related to *Nyugat* (West). This avant-garde journal edited by Babits published the Village Explorers' exposés of rural life in interwar Hungary, and launched the literary careers of Endre Ady and Gyula Illyés. Alas for Attila József, the finest poet of that era, Babits hated him and refused to publish his work in *Nyugat*.

Practicalities

Information is available from *Tolna Tourist* (Mon–Fri 8am–4.30pm; also Sat 8am–4pm & Sun 8am–noon in summer; ☎74/12-144) at Széchenyi utca 38, or *IBUSZ* (☎74/11-947) at no. 19, both of which can book private **accommodation** (②). The *Hotel Gemenc*, Mészáros Lázár utca 4 (☎74/11-722; ⑤), lies one block behind the Balogh Museum, while the *Alisca Hotel* (☎74/12-228; ④) is at the top of Kálvária utca, off to the right of Béla tér, with lovely views of the Sió Hills. There is a fairly grotty campsite on the spur road between Szekszárd and route 6 (March 15–Nov 15; ☎74/12-458).

The *Hotel Gemenc* has a decent **restaurant**, or you have a choice between the *Kispipa Vendéglo*, Széchenyi utca 51 (9am–10pm), the *halászcsárda*, Zrínyi utca 60 (for fish), or the *Krokodil*, Oseri J. utca 114. There are several cellars near Széchenyi utca where you can try **Szekszárd wine** – a heavy, dark red "ox-blood" exported as far afield as Britain, Holland and Turkey in the 1700s. Franz Liszt, Pope Pius IX and Emperor Haile Selassie all reportedly imbibed *Szekszárd Vörös*.

Visiting the Forest of Gemenc

The **Forest of Gemenc** is a remnant of the wilderness of woods, reeds and mudland that once covered the Danube's shifting, flood-prone banks. Only at the beginning of this century was the river tamed and shortened by 60km, ending the annual flooding of its backwaters and the *Sárköz* (Mud region). However, marshes and ponds remained to provide habitats for boar, wildcats, otters, deer, ospreys, falcons, bald eagles, black storks and other **wildlife**. Nowadays, the forest is a nature reserve of sorts (although the deer are fair game for Western hunters), with **boat trips** on its backwaters and a **miniature railway** through the forest.

Unfortunately, its terminals at BÁRÁNYFOK (bus #7 from town) and PÖRBÖLY (on the main line between Bátaszék and Baja) are awkward to reach, and there are only three trains a day (leaving Báránfok at 10am & 2pm; Pörböly at 7.30am). All in all, it's easier to sign up for a *Tolna Tourist* **excursion** which includes a visit to DECS. Traditionally, this Sárköz village was isolated yet *au courant*, as its menfolk worked as bargees, bringing home the latest news and fabrics. Their wives wore be-ribboned silk skirts and cambric blouses with lace inserts, and later acquired a taste for metallic thread, lime green and yellow, making their **costumes** as lurid as Rave attire. Nowadays, these are only worn at Decs' biennial **Marriage Festival**, a Sárköz folk bash next scheduled for July 1993.

Between Szekszárd and Budapest

The road and railway **between Szekszárd and Budapest** passes through some dreary countryside which could be improved by removing the main towns along the way. If you're driving, consider a **scenic detour** along minor roads through the pretty villages of HŐGYÉSZ, GYONK and CECE, before rejoining the trunk route at Dunaföldvár, which – aside from Baja – has the only bridge across the Danube. Irregular **car ferries** from Fadd-Dombori, Gerjen, Paks and Dunaújváros also enable motorists to cross over to the Great Plain (see Chapter Six).

Paks and Dunaújváros

PAKS, 52km north of Szekszárd, is the site of Hungary's first **nuclear power station**, a Soviet-designed VVER 440 which supplies about sixteen percent of the country's electricity. After Chernobyl, the public opposed plans to build another reactor, but the current Minister asserts that Hungary must make a strategic choice between further nuclear- or coal-powered generating plants, and favours another reactor at Paks. However, the plant's director (who has been reappointed after resigning in disgust at how it was run in the old days) says that no new energy sources are needed until 2020, and consumption is actually falling. Another reactor would entail a huge increase in radioactive waste, which the industry wants to **dump** in the hills south of Bonyhád, as its present site at Puspökszilágy, outside Budapest, is almost full.

The reactor aside, Paks is notable for its **Railway Museum** (Tues–Sun 10am–6pm), where vintage steam trains are displayed in an old station, and a new **Catholic church** designed by Imre Mákovecz. Should you need them, private **rooms** are available through *IBUSZ,* Táncsics utca 2, or directly from Kossuth utca 71A (☎74/31-1131). The reputation of the 24-hour *halászcsárda* (**fish restaurant**) at Dunaföldvár utca 5A hasn't suffered from the reactor, a mile downstream.

Dunaújváros

DUNAÚJVÁROS (Danube New Town), 40km upriver, is a monument to Stalinist economics, created around a vast steelmill which the Party saw as the lynchpin of its industrialisation strategy for the 1950s. The construction of *Sztálinváros* (as the town was originally called*) was trumpeted as a feat by Stakhanovites, though much of the heavy work was performed by peasant women and "reformed" prostitutes, living under appalling conditions. Nowadays, of course, the **steelworks** is regarded as an economic liability, and was recently forced to shut down its blast furnaces for 25 days because the local electricity supplier cut off its power for non-payment of bills.

---

*Since another industrial town created in the Fifties changed its named from Leninváros to Tiszújváros (Tisza New Town) in 1990, such names have vanished completely from the map of Hungary.

travel details

Trains

From Budapest (Déli or Keleti Station) to Győr (7am, 8.30am, 9.50am, 10am, 12.30pm, 1pm, 1.30pm, 3pm, 4pm & 6pm daily; 2hr 30min); Komárom (7am, 8.30am, 9.50am, 10am, 12.30pm, 1pm, 1.30pm, 3pm, 4pm & 6pm daily; 1hr 30min–2hr); Pécs (7.30am, 10.10am, 12.50pm & 4pm daily; 3hr); Sopron (7am, 10am, 1pm, 4pm & 6pm daily; 3hr 30min); Székesfehérvár (every 60–90min; 1hr); Szekszárd (7.40am, 1.35pm & 6pm daily; 3hr); Tata (7am, 10am, 1pm & 6pm daily; 1hr 15min).

From Dombóvár to Pécs (every 60–90min; 1hr–1hr 30min).

From Fertőboz to Nagycenk (April–Oct Sat & Sun 11am, 1pm, 3pm & 5pm; 30min).

From Győr to Sopron (9am, 11am, noon, 3.20pm, 4pm & 6pm daily; 1hr); Veszprém (6.55am, 11am, 3.40pm & 6.25pm daily; 2hr 30min).

From Körmend to Szentgotthárd (every 1–2hr; 30min); Szombathely (every 1–2hr; 30min); Zalalövő (6.40am, 10.50am, 3.20pm, 5.20pm, 6.40pm & 11.20pm daily; 30min).

From Kőszeg to Szombathely (every 60–90min; 30min).

From Mohács to Pécs (5.20am & 5.15pm daily; 2hr 30min); Villány (every 1–2hr; 30min).

From Nagycenk to Fertőboz (April–Oct Sat & Sun 10.15am, 12.15pm, 2.15pm & 4.15pm; 30min).

From Nagykanizsa to Balatonszentgyörgy (every 1–2hr; 45min); Budapest (every 1–2hr; 3–4hr); Pécs (7am, 10.45am, 3.15pm, 7pm & 9.20pm daily; 1hr 30min–3hr).

From Pécs to Dombóvár (every 60–90min; 1hr–1hr 30min); Mohács (5am, 4.50pm & 8.50pm daily; 1hr 30min); Nagykanizsa (5.45am, 10.35am, 1.10pm, 3.45pm & 4.45pm daily; 1hr 30min–3hr); Szombathely (5.45am & 4.45pm daily; 4hr 30min); Villány (every 1–2hr; 1hr).

From Sopron to Budapest (6.30am, 9.30am, 12.30pm, 3.30pm & 6.30pm daily; 3hr); Győr (6.30am, 9.30am, 12.30pm, 3.30pm & 6.30pm daily; 1hr); Szombathely (6.40am, 11.15am, 2.30pm, 4.10pm, 5.25pm & 7.25pm & 10.30pm daily; 1hr 30min).

From Szekszárd to Budapest (6.35am, 1.30pm & 6.35pm daily; 3hr).

From Szentgotthárd to Körmend (every 1–2hr; 30min); Szombathely (every 1–2hr; 1hr).

From Szombathely to Körmend (every 1–2hr; 30min); Kőszeg (every 60–90min; 30min); Nagykanizsa (7.35am, 11.35am, 2.20pm & 3pm daily; 1hr 30min–2hr 30min); Pécs (5.30am & 5.35pm daily; 4hr 30min); Sopron (7.10am, 10.10am, 11.40am, 3.10pm, 4.35pm, 6.10pm, 8pm & 9.40pm daily; 1hr 30min); Székesfehérvár (6am, 8.30am, 10.10am, 12.50pm, 6.15pm & 7.10pm daily; 2hr 15min–2hr 45min); Szentgotthárd (every 1–2hr; 1hr); Tapolca (6.35am, 7am, 7.30am & 2.30pm daily; 1hr 45min).

From Zalaegerszeg to Budapest (5.35am, 11.50am & 5.15pm daily; 3hr 30min); Zalalövő (7.25am, 11am, 1.15pm, 3pm, 5.15pm, 6.45pm & 10.40pm daily; 30min).

From Zalalövő to Körmend (8.40am, 12.30pm, 4pm & 7.30pm daily; 30min); Zalaegerszeg (6.30am, 8.35am, noon, 2pm, 4.20pm, 7.45pm & 8.45 daily; 30min).

Buses

From Budapest (Erzsébet tér) to Dunaújváros (7.20am, 9am, 2pm & 2.20pm daily; 1hr 30min); Győr (every 40–60min; 1hr 15min–2hr); Harkány (6.20am daily; 4hr 30min); Mohács (6.40am & 1.20pm daily & Sat 3.20pm; 4hr); Pécs (6.20am, 7.20am, 9am, 2pm & 4.20pm daily; 4hr); Siklós (6.40am daily; 5hr); Sopron (8am & 3pm daily; 3hr 45min); Szekszárd (6.20am, 7.20am, 9am, 11.40am, 2pm, 2.20pm, 3.40pm & 4.20pm daily; 3hr 15min); Szombathely (6.45am & 8am daily; 4hr 15min); Zalaegerszeg (3.40pm daily; 4hr 45min).

From Bukfürdő to Budapest (11am daily; 5hr); Győr (11am daily; 2hr 15min); Szombathely (noon daily; 1hr).

From Győr to Balatonfüred (every 30–90min; 2hr); Budapest (every 40–60min; 1hr 15min–2hr) Kalocsa (Sun 5.35am; 5hr); Pannonhalma Monastery (every 30–90min; 30min); Siófok (4.20pm daily; 3hr); Sümeg (7.40am, 12.25pm, 1pm, 2.15pm & 4.40pm daily; 2hr 15min); Székesfehérvár (5.35am daily; 2hr); Szombathely (6.50am & 4.25pm daily & Mon–Sat 1pm; 2hr 30min); Tapolca (Mon–Sat 10.55am; 4hr); Veszprém (4.20pm daily; 2hr); Zalaegerszeg (6.35am & 1.35pm daily; 4hr 30min).

From Harkány to Budapest (3.20pm daily; 4hr 15min); Pécs (2.10pm, 3.20pm & 4.20pm daily; 35min); Siklós (hourly; 1hr); Szekszárd (2.10pm, 3.20pm & 4.20pm daily; 2hr 15min).

From Kaposvár to Hévíz (7.20am & 6pm daily; 2hr 30min); Pécs (every 60–90min; 2hr); Siófok (2.20pm daily; 2hr); Szekszárd (7am daily & Mon–Sat 1.30pm; 2hr 15min); Zalaegerszeg (6am daily; 3hr).

From Komárom to Esztergom (7.50am, 4.30pm & 7.40pm daily; 1hr 30min); Sopron (6am & 3pm daily; 1hr 45min).

From Kőszeg to Budapest (7am & 2.40pm daily; 4hr); Sopron (5 daily; 2hr); Szombathely (7.20am, 8.10am, 9am, 2.15pm & 6.15pm daily; 30min).

From Mohács to Siófok (6am daily; 3hr); Szekszárd (6am daily; 1hr).

From Pécs to Abaliget (hourly; 1hr); Békéscsaba (3.30pm daily; 5hr 30min); Harkány (8.45am, 9.45am & 10.20am daily; 45min); Hévíz (5.40am daily; 4hr 30min); Kaposvár (every 60–90min; 2hr); Keszthely (5.40am, 7am, 3.30pm & 4.20pm daily; 4hr); Orfű (hourly; 1hr); Siklós (hourly; 1hr); Siófok (2.45pm daily; 3hr); Székesfehérvár (2.45pm daily; 4hr 30min); Szekszárd (every 1–2hr; 1hr 15min); Szigetvár (every 60–90min; 1hr); Zalaegerszeg (6.30am & 2.25pm daily; 4hr 15min).

From Sárvár to Sopron (7.15am & 5.15pm daily; 1hr 15min); Sümeg (6.35am & 4.50pm daily; 1hr); Szombathely (9.45am daily & Mon–Sat 12.10pm; 1hr).

From Siklós to Budapest (1.40pm daily; 5hr); Harkány (hourly; 1hr); Pécs (hourly; 1hr).

From Sopron to Baja (6am daily; 9hr 30min); Balatonfüred (5.45am daily; 4hr); Budapest (6am, 10am & 2.20pm daily; 3hr 45min); Esztergom (5.10am daily, Sun–Fri 1.50pm, Sat 5pm; 4hr); Fertőd (hourly; 1hr); Fertőrákos (hourly; 1hr); Győr (6am, 10am & 2.20pm daily; 2hr); Hévíz (5am, 6am & 3pm daily; 3hr); Komárom (5.10am daily, Sun–Fri 1.50pm, Sat 5pm; 2hr 45min); Kőszeg (6.30am, 6.50am, 12.50pm & 3pm daily; 2hr); Sárvár (5.20am & 3.35pm daily; 1hr 15min); Sümeg (5.20am, 12.50pm & 1.35pm daily; 2hr 15min); Szekszárd (6am daily; 8hr); Szombathely (3pm daily; 1hr 45min); Zalaegerszeg (3pm daily; 3hr).

From Szekszárd to Baja (2.50pm & 6.50pm daily; 1hr); Budapest (8am, 3.40pm & 4pm daily; 2hr 30min); Mohács (7.15am daily; 1hr); Pécs (every 1–2hr; 1hr 15min); Siófok (7am daily; 2hr);

Székesfehérvár (2.10pm & 6.20pm daily; 2hr); Veszprém (6am & 2.30pm daily; 3hr 45min).

From Szigetvár to Nagykanizsa (Mon–Fri 3.55pm; 2hr 30min); Pécs (every 60–90min; 1hr).

From Szombathely to Budapest (10am & 2.40pm daily; 3hr 45min); Bukfürdő (10am & 2.40pm daily; 1hr); Ják (hourly; 30min); Keszthely (6.35am, 7.55am & 2.50pm daily; 2hr 30min); Nagykanizsa (6.50am, 1.20pm & 4.55pm daily; 2hr 45min); Körmend (hourly; 1hr); Kőszeg (8.20am, 9.45am & 2.25pm daily; 25min); Sárvár (6.15am & 2.40pm daily; 1hr); Sopron (6.55am, 8.20am, 9.45am & 2.25pm daily; 3hr 15min); Zalaegerszeg (6.50am, 9.40am, 1.20pm, 2.30pm, 4.15pm & 4.55pm daily; 1hr 30min).

From Tata to Esztergom (every 60–90min; 1hr 30min); Komárom (hourly; 1hr); Tatabánya (every 20min; 15min).

From Zalaegerszeg to Győr (5.40am & 1.55pm daily; 4hr 30min); Kaposvár (4.10pm daily; 3hr); Keszthely (hourly; 1hr); Körmend (8.50am daily; 1hr); Nagykanizsa (4pm daily; 1hr); Pécs (5.40am & 2pm daily; 4hr 30min); Sopron (6.55am; 3hr 15min); Szigetvár (5.40am & 2pm daily; 3hr 45min); Székesfehérvár (5.40am & 2pm daily; 4hr 15min); Szombathely (6.55am daily; 1hr 20min).

International trains

From Győr to Berlin (10.10am & 3.30pm daily; 13hr); Bratislava (3.30pm, 4.40pm & 4.45pm daily; 5hr); Cologne (10.10am daily; 11hr 30min); Dresden (3.30pm daily; 10hr); Frankfurt (10.10am daily; 9hr 45min); Gdansk (4.40pm daily; 18hr); Munich (2pm & 5pm daily; 7hr 15min); Paris (5pm daily; 16hr 30min) Prague (3.35pm daily; 8hr); Vienna (7.30am, 10.10am, 2pm, 3pm, 5pm, 7.40pm, 8.35pm & 10.35pm daily; 1hr 45min); Warsaw (4.40pm daily; 14hr).

From Pécs to Osijek (5.45am & 7.10pm daily; 4hr).

From Nagykanizsa to Zagreb (June–Sept 3.50am & 4.45pm daily; 3hr 30min).

From Sopron to Vienna (6am daily; 1hr); Wiener Neustadt (6am, 6.30am, 9.30am & 12.30pm daily; 1hr).

From Szombathely to Graz (6am, 10.10am & 2.30pm daily; 3hr).

From Tatabánya to Bratislava (3.50pm daily; 6hr); Gdansk (3.50pm daily; 19hr); Warsaw (3.50pm daily; 15hr).

International buses

From Bükfürdő to Forchtenstein (Tues & Fri 3.30pm; 3hr); Graz (3pm daily; 4hr); Schwarzenbach (4pm daily; 4hr); Stegersbach (July–Aug 4.30pm daily; 5hr) Vienna (July–Aug 4pm daily; 4hr).

From Dunaújváros to Komárno (6.25am daily; 4hr 30min); Vienna (Tues & Wed 4am; 7hr).

From Győr to Galanta (4pm daily; 2hr 30min).

From Kaposvár to Bratislava (June–Oct Wed & Sat 6am; 5hr).

From Lenti to Ljubljana (4pm daily; 5hr 30min).

From Letenye to Prague (July–Aug 8.25pm daily; 10hr).

From Mohács to Novi Sad (1.50pm daily; 5hr).

From Mosonmagyaróvár to Bratislava (Tues & Fri 7.45am; 1hr 30min); Vienna (Wed & Thurs 6.30am & 5pm; 2hr).

From Sárvár to Neunkirchen (July–Aug 4.20pm daily; 4hr); Vienna (June–Sept Tues 12.30pm; 3hr); Wiener Neustadt (4.20pm daily; 5hr).

From Sopron to Baden (6.35pm daily; 3hr 30min); Bratislava (6am daily; 3hr); Forchenstein (Tues & Fri 5.15pm; 1hr 30min); Oberpullendorf (2pm daily; 1hr 30min); Semmering (7.40am daily; 5hr); Vienna (Mon–Sat 8am & Tues 2pm; 1hr 45min).

From Szombathely to Bratislava (6.15am daily; 3hr 30min); Oberpullendorf (7.40am daily; 2hr 45min); Oberwart (Wed & Sat 7.30am & 2.30pm daily; 1hr 45min); Stergersbach (July–Aug 5pm daily; 2hr 30min); Vienna (6.40am & 3.40pm daily; 3hr).

CHAPTER FIVE

THE NORTHERN UPLANDS

The **Northern Uplands** of Hungary are generally hilly and forested, but otherwise defy easy characterisation. They take in the famous **wine-producing** towns of **Eger** and **Tokaj**, whose appeal goes beyond the local beverage, and a succession of **castles**, either well-preserved as at Sárospatak, or squatting in picturesque decrepitude on crags above the villages of Hollókő, Somoskő, Boldogkőváralja and Füzér. This part of Hungary was the first to be industrialised, and the idyllic woodlands of the **Bükk and Mátra mountains** lie cheek to cheek with drably utilitarian **Miskolc**, the coal mines of the Borsod Basin and the despoiled Sajó Valley, which are less than 50km from the amazing **Aggtelek stalactite caves**. Like the environment, lifestyles run the gamut between two extremes – at one end, skinheads prowling the housing estates of Ózd and Miskolc; at the other, horse-drawn carts clopping around tiny **Zempléni villages** where the siesta reigns supreme.

Approaching the Uplands

Although the westerly Cserhát mountains are adjacent to the Börzsöny Mountains (see Chapter Two), and thus accessible from Vác and Balassagyarmat, the commonest **approaches** to the uplands are **from Budapest** or the Great Plain. Several trains daily leave the capital's Keleti station, passing through Hatvan and Füzesabony en route to Miskolc and Szerencs – all places to change on to **branch lines** heading further north. **Hatvan** is the link with the Mátra; trains from **Füzesabony** run to Eger; **Miskolc** is the starting point for journeys in to the Bükk; while from **Szerencs** you can reach Tokaj, Sárospatak and many Zempléni villages. Balassagyarmat is accessible by train from Aszód, or by bus from Hatvan (where buses also depart for Hollókő).

Coming **from the Plain**, trains are again the easiest mode of transport. From Nyíregyháza, frequent services run through Tokaj to Szerencs, before branching off towards Miskolc or Sátoraljaújhely; while Karcag, Tiszafüred and Szolnok are linked by rail to Hatvan and Füzesabony.

Gödöllö, Aszód and Hatvan

Most fast trains pass straight through, but if you're driving to Gyöngyös or Miskolc, it's worth considering a brief stopover at **GÖDÖLLÖ**, 30km from Budapest, which is also easily reached by HÉV train from the capital's Örs vezér tere station (50min). This small Baroque town used to be a summer residence of the Habsburgs, boasting a palace that rivalled the "Hungarian Versailles" at Esterháza.

The former **Grassalkovich Palace** dominates the south side of Szabadság tér, where the Budapest–Aszód and Vác–Isaszeg roads meet near the centre of town.

Commissioned by Count Antal Grassalkovich, a confidante of Empress Maria Theresa, the palace was designed by András Mayerhoffer, who introduced the Baroque style of mansion to Hungary in the 1740s. "Sissy", the wife of Emperor Franz Josef, preferred living here to Vienna. Comandeered by Béla Kun's General Staff in 1919, and by Admiral Horthy a year later, the palace was pillaged by Nazis and the Red Army in 1944. One wing was subsequently turned into an old people's home, but the rest of the palace was allowed to rot until a few years ago, when restoration began. Though not officially open to tourists yet, one can usually stroll around without being challenged.

At no. 5 on the same square, a **Local History Museum** (Tues–Sun 10am–6pm) displays material on the **Gödöllö Artists Colony** (1901–20), which emulated the English Pre-Raphaelites and the Arts and Crafts movement of William Morris and John Ruskin. Members included Aladár Körösfoi Kreisch (who wrote a book about Ruskin and Morris), Sándor Nagy (whose home and workshop may become a separate museum) and Károly Kós (the architect of Budapest's zoo). The museum will move into the palace once restoration is complete.

If you feel like a walk, there's a lovely **aboretum** on the road to Isaszeg. Gödöllö's *Uno-Ring Hotel*, at Szabadság út 199 (☎28/20-602; ②), offers comfy **accommodation**.

Aszód

Five kilometres beyond Gödöllö by car or bus, heading east along route 30 towards Aszód, you'll pass a Transylvanian-style wooden gateway leading to a former Capuchin church and monastery where several Grassalkovichs are buried. In **ASZÓD** itself, 10km further on, look out for the former **Podmaniczky Mansion** on Szabadság tér, another decrepit Baroque pile, whose main hall has a ceiling fresco by the Austrian painter JL Kracker. In the vicinity stands an erstwhile Lutheran grammar school where Sándor Petőfi studied for three years, hence a small **Petőfi Museum** on the premises (Tues–Sun April–Oct 10am–6pm; Nov–March 9am–5pm).

Besides mainline services to Budapest and Miskolc, there are **trains** to Balassagyarmat (4 daily; 90min) and Vácrátót (2 direct trains; otherwise change at Galgamácsa). Regular **buses** shuttle between Aszód and Hatvan.

Hatvan

Straddling the crossroads between Budapest, the Northern Uplands and the Great Plain, **HATVAN** was traditionally a market town until its wholesale industrialisation this century. While modern Új-Hatvan is unremarkable, the old centre retains another **Grassalkovich Mansion**, which has been used as a hospital since the last war. Its previous occupants were the Hatvany family, who owned the local sugar-beet factory and much of the surrounding countryside. The **Local History Museum** on Kossuth tér (Tues–Sun 2–6pm) is named after Lajos Hatvany (1880–1961), local writer, critic and literary historian.

As befits a town whose name reflects its distance from Budapest (*hatvan* means "sixty" in Hungarian), **buses** fan out from here to the capital, Szolnok (see p.292), Gyöngyös, the Mátra settlements, and as far afield as Eger. Moderately priced rooms can be found at the **hotels** *Park*, Kossuth tér 14 (☎38/12-870; ②); *Mini*, Hórvath utca 15 (☎38/12-469; ②); and *Strand*, Teleki út (☎38/11-200; ②).

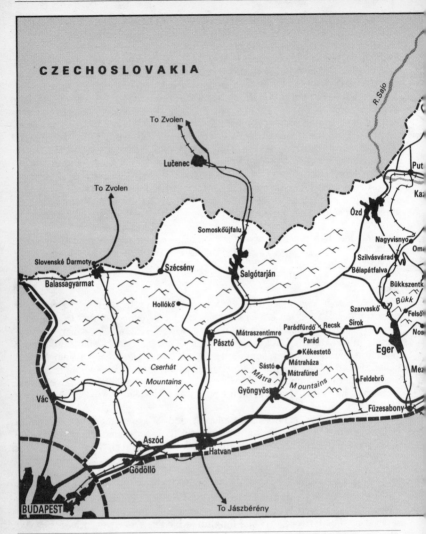

The Cserhát Region

The Cserhát range, like its more impressive neighbours, the Mátra and the Börzsöny, was once continuous forest. Farming and railways in the Nógrád and Zagyva valleys have made inroads, however, and today there's little magic about the northern slopes or the monotonous flatlands around the Ipoly River, which marks the border with Czechoslovakia. What colour there is is provided by the indigenous **Palóc ethnic group**, who sport fantastic costumes that have long since become museum pieces elsewhere: evidence of a backward agricultural economy or an eye for the tourist trade rather than any "separatist" feelings.

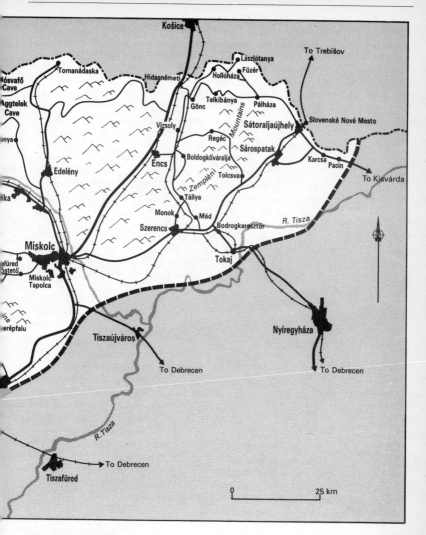

Balassagyarmat

After losing its medieval fortress and most of its inhabitants to the Turks, **BALASSAGYARMAT** (pronounced "Bolosho-dyurmot") was repopulated by a mixture of Germans, Slovaks and Czechs, and prospered during the eighteenth century, splashing out on several Baroque buildings – including a church decorated by the famous Maulbertsch – which were erected along its main street. Today, however, the town looks seedy and depressed, with little to show for its status as the "Palóc capital" except for a fine museum in the park off Bajcsy-Zsilinszky út.

Housed in an eclectic-style building, the **Palóc Ethnographical Museum** (Tues–Sun 9am–5pm) contains a fantastic collection of **costumes** from the Palóc community, which is thought to be of Slovak origin. For committed culture vultures, there are also two rooms devoted to local writers. **Imre Madách** (1823–64) began his career as a clerk in Balassagyarmat's County Hall, and went on to write *The Tragedy of Man* in 1860, commonly held to be Hungary's greatest classical drama – although performances were banned during the 1950s, when its pessimistic portrayal of human nature was regarded as contrary to the lofty ideals required of "Socialist Realist" art. Conversely, the satirical short stories of **Kálmán Mikszáth** (1847–1910), exposing the shortcomings of the landed gentry, encountered no ideological difficulties. Another section is devoted to **Gyula Benczúr**, whose narrative paintings won him a teaching post at the Academy of Fine Arts, but were denounced as "reactionary art" during the short-lived Republic of Councils, when Benczúr was exiled here as a punishment.

Practicalities

With the closure of the *Hotel Ipoly* on Bajcsy-Zsilinszky út, **accommodation** is limited to a small campsite on the edge of town (run by the Sports Society) and whatever the **tourist office** in the *Képtár* gallery (☎35/12-186) can muster in the way of private rooms. Rákóczi utca has two **restaurants**: the *Palóc* at no. 23 and the *Balassa* at no.34.

From the terminus on the main street, **buses** run to Szécsény, Hollókő, Pásztó and Salgótarján (see below), and once a day to Lučenec in Czechoslovakia.

Szécsény and Hollókő

Less than an hour's bus ride from Balassagyarmat, the small town of **SZÉCSÉNY** is ennobled by **Forgách Castle**, a graceful eighteenth-century mansion occupying the site of a medieval fortress that was blown up by the Habsburgs during the War of Independence (1703–11). It was here that the Hungarian Diet elected Ferenc Rákóczi II ruling prince and commander in chief of the Magyar forces, and declared the union of Hungary and Transylvania in 1705.

The castle now serves as a **museum** of hunting and local archaeology and the caretaker's lodge contains a collection of religious artefacts collected by Sándor Csoma Körösi, who travelled widely in Asia and compiled the first Tibetan-English dictionary. Down the road, a bastion from the old fortress exhibits instruments of torture and engravings demonstrating their use (all open Tues–Sun summer 10am–6pm; winter 9am–4pm).

Hollókő

From Szécsény you can catch another bus south to **HOLLÓKŐ** (Raven Rock), where a **ruined fortress** once owned by the Illés family overlooks a **museum village** on UNESCO's world cultural heritage list. How the locals feel about hordes of camera-clicking foreigners ambling down their two dirt streets, past whitewashed Palóc dwellings with broad eaves and carved gables and fences, is anybody's guess, but Hollókő has obviously grown dependent on the tourist trade. Its apotheosis comes on August 20, when local dance groups and international folk troupes in gorgeous costumes perform at the **Palóc Festival** (*Palóc szötés*).

At other times, traditional Palóc dress is chiefly only worn by old ladies attending vespers at Hollókő's restored **church** – outwardly austere, but decorated inside with vibrant colours and flowers. Traditionally, however, each village had its own style of homespun attire: in nearby Örhalom, for example, the Hollókő-style cap was transformed into a bonnet by the insertion of a stiff cardboard lining. Fine examples from various Páloc localities are displayed in the **Folk Museum** at Kossuth utca no. 82 (April–Sept Wed–Sun 10am–4pm; winter Thurs 10am–2pm, Fri noon–2pm, Sat & Sun 10am–4pm); the *Szövőház* or **Weaving House** at no. 94 (April–Oct Tues & Thurs–Sun 9am–5pm); and the **Tájvédelmi Kiállitás** at no. 99 (April–Oct Tues–Sun 10am–6pm), which also contains Palóc furniture.

Weaving, woodcarving and folk-dancing **courses** can all be booked through *Nógrád Tourist* in Salgótarján, which will also reserve **rooms** (②; sometimes furnished with Palóc wardrobes and embroidered bolsters) – a safer bet than relying on the local **tourist office** at Kossuth utca 68 (closed Mon & Tues; ☎Hollókő 4). The village has several places which serve food, and a couple of bars. **Buses** run regularly to Szécsény (except between 9am and noon), and twice daily to Pásztó and Hatvan, the jumping-off points for Salgótarján or the Mátra.

Salgótarján and Salgó Castle

After folksy Szécsény and Hollókő, **SALGÓTARJÁN** whacks you with grim modernity. This mining town – scarred since the nineteenth century by industrial squalor and poverty – was extensively rebuilt during the Sixties, a tardy response to workers' demonstrations in 1956, when the ÁVO shot dead 131 strikers in the aftermath of the Uprising. However modern housing and downtown supermarkets failed to efface bitter memories, reinforced during the late Eighties by local pit closures and unemployment, so that when the (renamed) Communists chose Salgótarján as the venue for their 1991 congress, massive protests compelled them to think again.

Aside from the huge statue of a partisan toting a machine gun which menaces one of its central squares, Salgótarján's only "sight" is the *Bányamúzeum* or **Mining Museum** (Tues–Sun 9am–5pm), buried in the inclined shafts of the now-defunct "József" pit and entered from Ady út, a block behind the outdoor market. Cramped and muddy, filled with props, tools and cables, the tunnels lack the dust, danger and noise of a working mine, but the explanatory leaflet still bids visitors "good luck", the traditional miners' greeting.

Practicalities

The **bus and train stations** (separated by the railway tracks) lie just south of the town centre, close to the market and Mining Museum. For **information**, look up *Nógrád Tourist* at Erzsébet tér 3 (☎32/10-660), around the corner from the *Karancs Hotel* (☎32/10-088; ③) on Tanácsköztársaság tér, Salgótarján's main square (which is sure to be renamed). Cheaper **accommodation** is available in private rooms (②) from the tourist office, a bungalow at the *Cserfa Fogadó* on Rózsafa út (②), or chalets at *Tó-Strand Camping* (April 1–Oct 10; ☎32/11-168; ①–②), at the end of the #6 bus route. There's also the option of staying at Salgó or Somoskő (see below).

Salgó Castle and Somoskő

In contrast with the grimness of the town, the surrounding countryside features volcanic rock formations and picturesque ruins. Regular buses from Salgótarján's terminal run 8km northwards to the village of **SALGÓ**, overlooked by a **ruined castle** which broods atop a 625-metre-high basalt cone. Constructed after the Mongol invasion of the thirteenth century, it later belonged to Count István Werbőczy, author of the Tripartium law which bound the peasants to "perpetual serfdom" following the peasants' revolt of 1514. Despite being blown up during the Turkish occupation, the castle (Tues–Sun 9am–5pm) still commands a superb view of the highlands further north. A little way past Salgó, on the same bus route, is a **hotel** (②).

Most buses carry on to **SOMOSKŐ**, a hamlet near the Czechoslovak border. Just across the border, another **ruined castle** squats upon vast blocks of eroded stone. Founded during the fifteenth century, its five towers survey impressive **basalt formations** (*bazaltömlés*) resembling giant organ pipes. It used to be possible to visit both sites on organised tours, but this arrangement has now lapsed and they can only be reached from Czechoslovakia. However, you can stay at the *Fogadó* (①) in the village (which is on Hungarian soil).

Moving on

If you're dependent on public transport, **moving on** from Salgótarján amounts to heading northeast towards Ózd or south towards the Mátra region, assuming that you don't take the early morning **bus to Lučenec in Czechoslovakia**, or the *Polonia Express* **train to Warsaw** (leaving around 1.25am).

Since the remote Aggtelek caves are the only reason for passing through Ózd, and bus connections are unreliable, **south** seems the obvious direction to take. Along the way to Hatvan (by bus or train), ore-buckets and slag hills disappear, giving way to vineyards and fields, and you can change buses at PÁSZTÓ and head **into the Mátra** by a scenic route. Services from Hatvan to Gyöngyös are likely to run more frequently, however.

Gyöngyös and the Mátra Mountains

Hungarians make the most of their highlands, and **the Mátra** – where Mount Kékestető just tops 1000 metres – is heavily geared to domestic tourism. Mount Kékestető is a popular place for winter sports, despite the relatively lacklustre resort facilities at Mátraháza and Mátraszentimre, while, in the summer, families ramble the paths between picnic sites and beer gardens, ignoring the wild boar and deer that live deeper in the thickets of oak and beech. Few of the Mátra settlements have much of interest beyond their amenities, but the mountains and forests are, in any case, the main attraction.

Gyöngyös

Most visitors approach the Mátra via **GYÖNGYÖS** (pronounced "Dyurn-dyursh"), the centre of the Gyöngyös-Visonta **wine** region, where white *Muskotály* comes from. It's a pleasant enough town, but nothing to write home about. The town's bus station lies roughly midway between the two centres of interest, the main square – called just that, Fő tér – and the Mátra Museum.

Turning left out of the bus station down Kossuth utca, you'll soon encounter a parade of nineteenth-century buildings painted in garish reds and blues, presaging the grander edifices around Fő tér. At the northern end of the square stands St Bartholomew's Church (open mornings only), originally Gothic but heavily remodelled in the eighteenth century. Beyond the wine stalls outside the *Hotel Mátra*, a street leads off to Nemecz József tér, where a Franciscan Church endowed by the Báthori family displays their coat of arms in its chancel. To the west of Fő tér, across the Nagy-patak stream, a Baroque County Hall and a derelict Synagogue (dating from 1816) flank Vármegye tér.

Heading in the opposite direction from the bus terminus, Kossuth utca runs past the landscaped grounds of the former Orczy mansion, fronted by benevolent-looking stone lions. The mansion itself, at no. 40, houses the Mátra Museum (Tues–Sun 9am–5pm), with a reconstructed mammoth's skeleton and a dazzling collection of butterflies, among other dead Mátra wildlife.

A bit further on is the terminus of the *Mátravasút*, a narrow gauge railway up to Mátrafüred in the mountains. Trains depart roughly every hour until nightfall.

Practicalities

Information on the Mátra region, including skiing during the winter, is available from *Mátratourist* on Fő tér (Mon–Fri 8am–5.30pm, Sat 8am–1pm; ☎37/11-565), which can also arrange private accommodation. A cheaper alternative to the three-star *Hotel Mátra* (☎37/12-057; telex 25-212; ④–⑤) on the main square is the *Vincellér Panzió*, Erzsébet királyné utca 22 (☎37/11-691; ②). The Mátra resorts offer other possibilities (see below).

The Mátra Settlements: Mátrafüred

The settlements detailed below are easily reached by bus, with routes allowing you to visit several villages in one day. From Gyöngyös, there are frequent (every 60–90min) services to Mátrafüred and Mátraháza, and four or five buses a day pass through Parad, Recsk and Sirok on their way to Eger, though check that these don't follow the E71 route; Recsk and Sirok are also accessible via the branch rail line down from Mátramindszent to Kál-Kápolna (the station before Füzesabony on the Budapest–Miskolc line). Anyone intending to visit Sirok or Feldebrő, or go walking in the mountains, should buy a large-scale tourist map (*A Mátra turistatérképe*) beforehand. But be warned that there's no tourist accommodation at either village.

The *Mátravasút* is the fun way to get from Gyöngyös to MÁTRAFÜRED, and takes no longer than the bus. Passengers arrive at the lower end of this sloping, touristy settlement, a short walk from the local *Mátra Tourist* at Vörösmarty utca 4. Here you can arrange private rooms (②) that cost slightly less than the *Hotel Diana*, Turista utca 1 (☎37/12-922; ②), and a fraction of what the three-star *Hotel Avar* (☎37/13-195; ④) charges. Tennis courts and horse-riding can be organised through the *Hotel Avar*.

Alternatively, you could stay at Sás-tó (Sedge Lake), 4km uphill from Mátrafüred, on the bus route between Gyöngyös and Mátraháza. It's a friendly place, full of Hungarians boating and fishing amid the usual *lángos* stands, with a campsite (☎37/74-025) and bungalows (②) open from April 1 to October 15. At 8pm the restaurant closes and action shifts down to the disco and bars in Mátrafüred. Heading on, you can easily walk from Sás-to to Mátraháza, on a footpath with wild boars reputedly lurking in the forests to the west.

Mátraháza and Mount Kékestető

Nine kilometres to the north, **MÁTRAHÁZA**, the next settlement, consists mainly of Trade Union hostels, set on an incline with a few bars and lots of walks in the vicinity. Though it's hard to think of any reason to linger, you can easily make a quick return bus journey from Mátraháza to **Mount Kékestető**, the highest point (1015m) in the Mátra range. Two **ski runs** (*sípálya*) descend from the summit, which is crowned by a nine-storey telecommunications **tower** offering an impressive view of the highlands (Tues–Sun 9.30am–3pm, until 4pm in summer).

Parád and Parádfürdő

Roughly 10km to the northeast, a group of similarly named villages gathers around **PARÁD**, where Count Károlyi tried to set an example to other nobles in 1919 by distributing land to his serfs. The commune has an old **Palóc House** full of costumes and artefacts (Tues–Sun 9am–5pm), and an exhibition of **woodcarving** signposted *Fafaragó Kiállitás* (daily 9am–7pm). Cheap **rooms** are available at the *Palócz Fogadó* (☎36/64-008; ②), along Kossuth utca, towards Parádfürd .

A popular **thermal spa** where the sulphurous, fizzy water is said to benefit digestive complaints, **PARÁDFÜRDŐ** really deserves a visit for its **Coach Museum** (April–Oct daily 9am–5pm; Nov–March Tues–Sun 9am–4pm). The *Kocsimúzeum*'s splendid collection includes vehicles for state occasions, hunting and for gallivanting around. For the record, the coach – which superseded the cumbersome wagon throughout Europe – was actually invented in a Hungarian village called – one might have guessed it – Kocs. Some beautiful horses can be seen in adjacent stables, which were designed for the Károlyi family by Miklós Ybl, the architect of Budapest's Opera House.

Follow the signposts from the main road to the far end of the commune to find cheap **rooms** (②) in the *Muflon Fogadó* at Peres utca 8 – which has a **restaurant** (4–10pm; closed Thurs) – or at no. 37 on the same street.

Recsk

Mention **RECSK**, a village 2km east of Parádfürdő, and many older Hungarians will share recollections of terror. During the late Forties and early Fifties, thousands of the tens of thousands of citizens arrested by the ÁVO were sentenced to labour in the quarries southwest of here. Half-starved and frequently beaten by their jailers, prisoners died of exhaustion or in rockfalls, but more usually while sleeping at night in muddy pits open to the sky.

Closed by Imre Nagy in 1953, **Recsk concentration camp** was effaced by a tree plantation during the Kádár years, and not until 1991 were its victims commemorated. A stone **monument** symbolising repression and a bronze model of the camp stand near the still-working quarry, 4.5km up from the village (look for the *Kőbánya* signs).

Sirok and Feldebrő

SIROK, 8km further east, is worth visiting if you're wild about romantic views. On a mountain top above the village, 1.5km northeast of the train station, there's a **ruined thirteenth-century castle** from which you can admire the mingled peaks of the Mátra, the Bükk and Slovakia.

A considerable detour – recommended only to antiquity buffs who have their own transport or are willing to hitch patiently – takes you to **FELDEBRŐ**, a village with one of the oldest church crypts still extant in Hungary. Therein you'll find beautiful twelfth-century **frescoes**, influenced by Byzantine art, and the **grave of King Aba** (1041–44), one of the ephemeral monarchs between the Árpád and Angevin dynasties. Keys for the crypt (Tues–Sat 10am–noon & 2–4pm, Sun & holidays 11am–noon & 3–4pm) are held at the *plébánia* (presbytery) behind the church. The local **linden leaf wine** (*Debrői hárslevelű*) is good for refreshing weary travellers.

Eger and around

Situated in its own sunny valley between the Mátra and the Bükk, **Eger** is famed for its wine, its minaret, and the heroic legend attached to its castle. From town, buses and local trains head to various villages bordering the Bükk national park, notably **Szilvásvárad** near the beautiful Szalajka Valley to the north, and Cserépváralja to the northeast, just below the "rocking" stones in the Felső-szoros ravine. Thus you can enter the Bükk mountains from the west, or cut straight through on a bus to Miskolc, and re-enter them by train from Lillafüred (see "The Bükk Mountains" p.242) after you've finished with Eger.

The Town

With its colourful architecture suffused by sunshine, **EGER** seems a fitting place of origin for *Egri Bikavér*, the potent, throat-rasping red wine marketed as *Bull's Blood* abroad, which brings hordes of visitors to the town. The *Szüret* or **Harvest Festival** in September is when Eger is at its liveliest, with two weeks of numerous wine-related events around town, including folk dancing and a parade of floats. Despite occasional problems with accommodation, it's a fine place in which to hang out and wander around, not to mention all the opportunities for drinking. Travellers **arriving** at the bus terminus can easily stroll into the centre; coming from the railway station, walk up the road to Deák Ferenc út, catch a #10 or #12 bus and get off just before the cathedral.

The Cathedral and Lyceum

Occupying a site hallowed since the eleventh century, Eger **Cathedral** looms above a flight of steps flanked by statues of saints Stephen and László, Peter and Paul, by the Italian sculptor Casagrande. Constructed between 1831 and 1836, this ponderous Neoclassical edifice was architect József Hild's rehearsal for the still larger basilica at Esztergom. Its interior was largely decorated by JL Kracker, who spent his last years working in Eger. Particularly impressive is the frescoed cupola, where the City of God arises in triumph as evildoers flee the sword. Close by, facing Széchenyi utca, stands the **Archbishop's Palace**, a U-shaped Baroque pile with fancy wrought-iron gates. One wing now serves as the headquarters of *Egervin*, the local wine company.

The florid, Zopf-style **Lyceum**, opposite the Cathedral, was founded by two enlightened bishops whose proposal for a university was rejected by Maria Theresa. Now a teacher training college (named after Ho Chi Minh during the Communist era), the building is worth visiting for its **library** (Tues–Sun 9.30am–noon), which has a huge ceiling fresco of the Council of Trent by Kracker and his son-in-law. The lightning bolt and book in one corner symbolise the Council's decision to establish an Index of forbidden books.

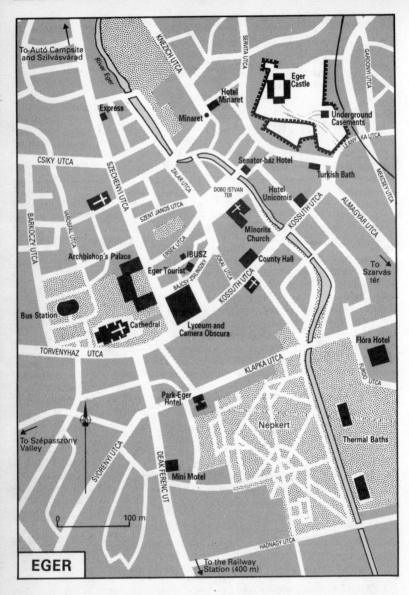

EGER

Even better, check out the **Observatory** (Tues–Fri 8.30am–1.30pm, Sat & Sun 9.30am–noon; closed winter) atop the tower in the east wing, where a nineteenth-century **camera obscura** projects a view of the entire town from a bird's-eye perspective. The camera's monocled curator gleefully points out lovers kissing in the backstreets, unaware of surveillance.

Kossuth utca and Dobó tér

From the Lyceum and Provost House across the way, **Kossuth utca** leads past a Franciscan Church (where a mosque stood in Turkish times), and the **County Hall**, whose magnificent gates were wrought by Henrik Fazola, (notice the stork with a snake in its beak and a vine in its claws, on the county coat of arms). On the other side of the road, across the bridge, stands the "Buttler House" that featured in Mikszáth's novel *A Strange Marriage*. Alternatively, follow Bajcsy-Zsilinszky or Érsek utca into **Dobó István tér**, the starting point for further sightseeing. Along one side of the square stands the former **Minorite Church**, a twin-towered Baroque edifice completed in 1771. The Latin inscription above its entrance asserts that "Nothing is Enough for God". Equally striking are the action-packed statues of warriors that commemorate the two sieges of Eger during the Turkish invasion – a tale of heroism known to every Hungarian.

The first **siege of 1552**, described in Géza Gárdonyi's panegyrical novel *Egri csillagok* (Stars of Eger), was an unexpected victory for the Magyars. Ensconced in the castle under the command of **István Dobó**, two thousand soldiers and Eger's **women** (who hurled rocks, hot soup and fat) repulsed a Turkish force six times their number – shattering the impetus of the Ottoman advance until 1596. In their second attempt, however, the Turks triumphed: Eger's garrison of foreign mercenaries surrendered after a week and the Ottoman troops sacked the town, leaving only "blackened walls and buildings razed to the ground" and "the naked bodies of Christians baking in the sun, in some places four yards high".

A short distance from Dobó tér are two relics of the Turkish occupation (which lasted until 1687). Eger's most photographed structure is a slender, fourteen-sided **minaret**, rising forty metres above Knezich utca. Despite looking rather forlorn since its mosque was demolished in 1841, the minaret offers fine views from its balcony (daily 9am–5pm). A passing glance suffices for the unimpressive remains of a **Turkish Bath**, en route to Eger Castle.

Eger Castle

With every approach covered by batteries of cannons, you can easily appreciate why **Eger Castle** was so formidable. Ascending from its lower gate past the Gergely Bastion, you enter the inner section of the castle through the Várkoch Bastion. On top of this lies the **tomb of Geza Gárdonyi**, on which is inscribed "Only his body lies here". Separate tickets for the Bishop's Palace, the underground *Kazamata* and a historical video are sold at the ticket office straight ahead (daily 9am–5pm; Mon *Kazamata* and Hall of Heroes only).

One of the few Gothic structures left in northeastern Hungary, the **Bishop's Palace** harbours a **museum** containing tapestries, Turkish handicrafts and weaponry. On the ground floor are temporary exhibits and a **"Hall of Heroes"** (*Hősök terme*) where István Dobó is buried amid a bodyguard of siege heroes, the latter carved in best Stakhanovite style. The adjacent **art gallery** boasts several fine Munkácsys and three romantic Transylvanian landscapes by Antal Ligeti.

To the east of this complex lies a jumble of medieval foundations signposted as a *Romkert* or **Garden of Ruins**. Here stood Eger's Gothic cathedral, which was damaged by fire in 1506 and used as a gunpowder magazine during the first siege; the Turks used it as an arsenal "to spite the Christians". To the south, tour groups gather outside the concrete tunnel entrance to the *Kazamata* or **underground galleries**: a labyrinth of sloping passages, gun emplacements, deep-cut observation shafts, and mysterious chambers which you can sneak off to explore. A fifteen-minute **video** on the castle's history is shown at regular intervals by the entrance.

> The Eger telephone code is ☎36

Wine and the Szépasszony Valley

Sights aside, drinking is obviously a major part of anyone's stay here. Local vineyards produce four types of **wine** – *Muskotály* (Muscatel), *Bikavér* (Bull's Blood), *Leányka* (medium dry white with a hint of herbs) and *Medoc Noir* (rich, dark red and sweet, it coats your tongue black).

Although the **Wine Museum** at Városfal utca 1 (Tues–Sat noon–10pm) offers a display of viticultural implements to whet your palate, it's more fun to go drinking in the **Szépasszony Valley**, just west of town (accessible by taxi). The "Valley of the Beautiful Woman" is surrounded by dozens of vineyards and **wine cellars**. Finding the right one is a matter of luck and taste: some are dank and gloomy and some have their own **musicians** (who otherwise go wherever there are most people). Cellar 38 is dry and spacious and takes its wine seriously. Most are open daily until 6–8pm or later, depending on custom.

Practicalities

The best source of **information** is *Eger Tourist*, at Bajcsy-Zsilinszky utca 9 (June 1–Aug 20 Mon–Sat 8am–6pm; otherwise Mon–Fri 8am–4.30pm, Sat 8am–noon; ☎11-724). Failing that, try *IBUSZ* (☎12-526), in the passage just behind.

Accommodation

As well as the booking services offered by *Eger Tourist* and *IBUSZ*, Eger has two agencies that deal solely with accommodation: *Express* at Széchenyi utca 28 (Mon–Fri 8am–4pm, Sat 8am–noon; ☎10-757) and the privately owned *Villa Tours* at Deák út 55 (April–Sept Mon–Fri 10am–8pm, Sat 10am–6pm, Sun 2–6pm; Oct–March Mon–Fri 10am–6pm; ☎17-803). The cheapest lodgings are **student hostels**, bookable through *Express* or *Villa Tours*. The most central one, at Dobó tér 6 (☎20-833; ①), has beds in dorms all year round. From late June to late August there are also two- to four-bed rooms in *kollégiums* at Leányka utca 2 (☎10-466; ①), 100m east of the castle; Széchenyi utca 17 (☎10-565; ①); and on Mátyás király út (①), south of the railway station. **Private rooms** (②) can be booked through *Eger Tourist*, *IBUSZ* or *Villa Tours* (which charges more than the others).

MOTELS AND PENSIONS

Tourist Motel, Mekcsey utca 2 (☎10-014). Just off Szarvas tér. Rooms sleeping 2–4 persons, with or without bathroom. ②.

Mini Motel, Deák út 11 (☎11-388). Between the railway station and the centre. Doubles without bathrooms; slightly cheaper. ②.

Köntös Vendégház, Servita utca 29 (☎15-722). Privately run pension below the castle. ②.

Fortuna Panzió, Kapás utca 35A (☎16-480). West of the first junction on Deák út as you come up from the railway station. ②.

Ködmön Fogadó (☎13-172). At the entrance to the Szépasszony Valley. ②.

HOTELS

Hotel Park-Eger, Klapka utca 8 (☎13-233; telex 63-355). Three-star establishment with the most expensive rooms in Eger. Breakfast included. ⑤.

Unicornis Hotel, Kossuth utca (☎12-886). The cheapest option. ②–③.

Flóra Hotel, Fürdo utca 5 (☎20-211; telex 63-440). Close to the entrance to the thermal baths. Only slightly cheaper than the *Park-Eger*. ⑤.

Senátor-ház Hotel, Dobó tér 11 (☎20-466; telex 63-355). Two-star hotel in a prime spot. ⑤.

Minaret Hotel, Knezich utca 2 (☎20-020; telex 63-238). Another well-situated two-star, facing the minaret. ④.

CAMPSITES

Autó Camping, 3km north of the centre by bus #10 or #11 (☎10-558). Two-person bunga-lows (②) and huts (①), tent space, a restaurant and snack bar. April 15–Oct 15. You can usually rent bicycles (200Ft per hour, 1000Ft per day) near the entrance.

Tulipán Camping (☎10-580), across the road from the riding centre at the entrance to the Szépasszony Valley. A newly opened, smaller site.

Eating and drinking

With a dozen restaurants and takeaways around the centre, eating out in Eger is never a problem. For **breakfast**, try the *Tejivó* milk bar opposite the Bishop's Palace on Széchenyi utca (Mon–Fri 6.30am–2.30pm, Sat 6.30am–noon), or get something savoury from one of the takeaways along Almagyar utca. The elegant *Dobos Cukrászda*, Széchenyi utca 6, and the outdoor *Pallas Presszó*, beneath the castle walls, are good for coffee and pastries. There's a good ice cream parlour on Kossuth utca.

The cheapest of Eger's **restaurants** is the *Várkapu Vendeglő* at Kossuth utca 26, which is self-service from 11am to 3pm, with waiters later on (from 4pm to 11pm). Somewhat dearer but still reasonable value are the *Mecset*, opposite the minaret, which has a nice garden and music (closed Mon), and the *Vadászkurt* at Érsek utca 4 (reservations advisable; ☎10-508). The *Fehér Szarvas* (White Stag), next to the *Park-Eger Hotel*, is also good, but very expensive (6.30pm–midnight). Recommended only for a look is the *Kazamata*, beneath the cathedral steps: a bizarre place resembling a set from *2001* crossed with the *Führerbunker*, all concrete and split levels and gloom.

For **drinking**, head out to the cellars of the **Szépasszony Valley** (see above) to sample the local wines. If you get hungry, you can eat there at the *Kulacs Csárda* or the *Ködmön Fogadó*. For those who prefer **beer**, there's the *HBH Söröző* on Dobó tér, in town.

Eger activities

Contact *Eger Tourist* (see above) if you're interested in **horse-riding** in the Szépasszony or Szalajka valleys, or **aeroplane tours** over town (May–Aug; 450Ft per person). Alternatively, head for the **thermal baths** and **swimming pool** (May–Sept daily 8.30am–7.30pm), where half the town comes to wallow and splash at weekends during summertime. Folk or rock **concerts** are sometimes held in the open-air theatre at the end of the Szépasszony Valley.

Moving on

There are five direct **trains** to Budapest daily; ten to Füzesabony on the Budapest–Miskolc line; five to Putnok (see "Stalactite Caves" below); and one direct train to Szeged every week. **Buses** from the terminus on Pyrker tér cover a range of destinations including Budapest (last express service 5.45pm), Mátraháza, Kecskemét, Szeged and the Aggtelek Caves (8.50am daily); hourly buses also run to Szilvásvárad, calling at Bélapátfalva along the way. At weekends there are two buses **through the Bükk mountains to Miskolc** (leaving at 7am and 11.25am) via Felsőtarkány, one of several villages accessible by bus where you can than head into the mountains **on foot** (see overpage).

Car rental is available from *Welcome Tours*, Jókai utca 5 (Mon–Fri 8am–4pm, Sat 8–11.30am; ☎11-711) for 600Ft a day.

Up to Szilvásvárad and the Szalajka Valley

The road and railway skirt the western foothills of the Bükk as they wiggle northwards towards Putnok, and 12km out from Eger the scenery is promisingly lush around **SZARVASKŐ** (Stag Rock), a pretty village with a nearby *fogadó* (April 15–Oct 15; ☎36/11-551) and very ruined thirteenth-century castle. However, quarries and an ugly cement factory spoil the view at **BÉLAPÁTFALVA**, where the sole reason to stop is a well-preserved Romanesque **abbey church** (Tues–Sun 9am–4pm) founded by French Cistercian monks in 1232. To get to the church, follow the signpost off the main road for 2km. On chilly days, the caretaker can be found at Rózsa utca 42 – look for the *"apátság gondnok"* sign on the right shortly after leaving the main road.

Szilvásvárad

Eight kilometres further north, **SZILVÁSVÁRAD** occupies a dell beside wooded mountains rising to the east. Once the private estate of the pro-fascist Pallavinici family, and then a workers' resort after 1945, nowadays it is chiefly known as a breeding centre for **Lippizaner horses** (see box) and the site of Hungary's annual coach-driving championship, the **Bükk Trophy** (usually held the last weekend in Aug).

You don't have to be mad on horses to enjoy the **Horsebreeding Exhibition** (Tues–Sun 9am–5pm) at Park utca 8, which is reached via the Transylvanian-style wooden gate just beyond the *Hotel Lipicai*. The exhibition includes a collection of coaches and a stable of beautiful white Lippizaners. The totemic columns in the park around the stud farm are dedicated to the memory of the farm director's beloved mount, Zánka, who died in harness of a heart attack – evoking the time of the Magyar conquest, when favourite horses were buried in graves.

Except during the coach-driving championships, there shouldn't be any problem with **accommodation**. Along the road in from Eger you'll find the *Hotel Lipicai* (☎36/55-100; ②) and the slightly cheaper *Szalajka Fogadó* (☎36/55-257; ②). At Park utca 6 are the reasonably priced *Szilvás Kastély Hotel* and *Panzió* (☎36/55-211; ②), with tennis courts and other facilities. There's a campsite (open year round) attached to the latter, and another one – *Hegyi Camping* (☎36/55-207) – at Egri út 36 (May 1–Oct 15). Private rooms (①) are available from the branch of *Eger Tourist* at Egri út 22 (☎36/55-268), whilst *Express* in Eger can make bookings at the cheap *Pluto Szálló* (☎36/20-155; ②).

The Szalajka Valley

If you don't fancy walking a couple of kilometres, it's possible to ride a narrow-gauge railway from Szilvásvárad into the **Szalajka Valley**, which really begins at *szikla-forrás*, a gushing rock cleft beyond the food stalls and captive **stags** that guard its approaches. Signposted just off the main path is an outdoor **Forestry Museum** (*Erdei Múzeum*) exhibiting weathered huts and tools (including an ingenious water-powered forge) once used by the charcoal-burners and foresters of the Bükk (April–Nov Tues–Sun 9am–4pm).

LIPPIZANER HORSES

Descended from Spanish, Arabian and Berber stock, **Lippizaner horses** are bred at six European stud farms. The original stud was founded near Trieste in 1580 by the Habsburg archduke Karl, but when Napoleon's troops invaded Italy its horses were brought to Mezőhegyes in southern Hungary for safekeeping. Lippizaner horses are comparatively small in stature (14.3–15.2 hands tall), with a long back, a short, thick neck and a powerful build. They are usually white or grey. Like their counterparts at the famous Spanish Riding School in Vienna, Szilvásvárad's horses are trained to perform bows, provettes and other manoeuvres that delight dressage cognoscenti.

Higher up, the valley is boxed in by mountains, with paths snaking through the woods to the triangular **Istállóskői cave** (*barlang*) and the barefaced **Mount Istállóskő** – which at 959m is the highest in the Bükk range, (the second highest, Bákvány, can be reached by footpath from Istállóskő (8km) or from NAGYVISNYÓ (9km), the next settlement after Szilvásvárad and on the same branch rail line).

The Bükk Mountains

Beech trees – *bükk* – cover the mountains between Eger and Miskolc, giving the region its name. Unlike most of the northern mountains, **the Bükk** were formed from sedimentary limestone, clay slate and dolomite and are riddled with sinkholes and caves that were home to the earliest tribes of *Homo sapiens*, hunters of mammoths and reindeer. As civilisation developed elsewhere, the Bükk declined in importance – except as a source of timber – until the start of the nineteenth century, when Henrik Fazola built a blast furnace in the Garadna Valley, exploiting the iron ore which today feeds the metallurgical works in Miskolc. While industry continues to shape the grim towns of Miskolc, Ózd and Kazincbarcika, almost four hundred square kilometres of the Bükk have been declared a **national park and wildlife refuge**. This can be explored superficially by train and bus, or thoroughly if you're prepared to do some hiking.

If you are planning to **hike**, a *Bükk hegység* **map** is essential. Since paths are well marked and settlements are rarely more than 15km apart, it's hard to go far astray walking, but a few **preparations** are advisable. Food and supplies should be purchased beforehand, together with insect repellent/bite cream and a canteen. Drinking water (*ivóvíz*) isn't always available, though many of the springs are pure and delicious. To be sure of **accommodation**, make reservations through *Eger Tourist* in Eger or *Borsod Tourist* in Miskolc. If need be, you can also sleep in shelters (*esőház*) dotted around the mountains.

The Bükk is particularly lovely in autumn, when its foliage turns bright orange and yellow, contrasting with the silvery tree trunks. Among the mountain flora are violet blue monk's hood which blooms at the end of summer, yellow lady's slipper, an endangered species in Europe, and the Turk's cap lily. The undergrowth is home to badgers, beech martens, ermines and other animals, and you might encounter rock thrushes and other birds in abandoned quarries, or see an Imperial eagle (*Aquila heliaca*) cruising overhead. The seldom-glimpsed "smooth" snake isn't poisonous.

Approaches from Eger

Starting **from Eger**, the most direct approach to the mountains is to take a bus, getting off somewhere along the route to Miskolc, or the railway branch line up to FELSŐTÁRKÁNY – and start walking from there. Paths also lead into the Bükk from Bélapátfalva, Szilvásvárad and Nagyvisnyó, north of the range (see above), and from villages to the **south**, accessible by bus from Eger. On the south side, arrowheads and other remains were found in the **Subalyuk Cave**, a Palaeolithic dwelling 2km from BÜKKZSÉRC and CSERÉPFALU at the start of one footpath, while further east, "rocking stones" and hollowed-out pillars – used by medieval beekeepers and known as "hive rocks" – line the rocky **Felső-szoros ravine** north of CSERÉPVÁRALJA.

Accommodation is offered by two villages on this side of the mountains. Felsőtárkány has the *Park-Hotel Táltos*, Ifjuság utca 1 (Mar 1–Nov 25; ☎36/20-760; ③) , and the cheaper *Szikla Fogadó*, Fő utca 313 (open year round; ☎36/20-904; ②). Noszvaj, 13km from Eger, features a Baroque mansion converted into the *De La Motte Kastély Hotel* at Dobó utca 10 (☎ Noszvaj 2; ②), and two pensions – the *Bükk Panzió*, Béke út 73 (②), and the *Pepsi Panzió*, József utca 10 (②) – all open year round.

Approaches from Miskolc

The Bükk can also be visited **from Miskolc** (described below), which offers a number of approaches. From Újgyőri főtér in the western part of the city (bus #101 from Tiszai Station) you can catch a #68 bus out to BÜKKSZENTLÁSZLÓ, and then walk or hitch via BÜKKSZENTKERESZT on to HOLLÓSTETŐ (6km further on) – which is on the Miskolc–Eger bus route, although services are infrequent. Bükkszentkereszt offers **private rooms** (☎46/50-694; ②), while Hollóstető features a **campsite** with **bungalows** (May 1–Sept 15; ☎46/92-983; ①).

The easiest approach, however, is to aim for **Lillafüred**, a small resort that's accessible by bus #5 or #105 from Majális Park in the west of the city (bus #1 from Tiszai Station), or by the narrow gauge railway from Miskolc's Killian Észak terminal (accessible by bus #101). Thronged by holidaymakers at weekends, Lillafüred is centred around the once elegant *Palace Hotel* (☎46/17-873; ②), offering pricier **accommodation** than the *Lilla Panzió* (☎46/51-299; ②) at Erszébet sétány 7. The train and buses #5 and #115 continue via Újmassa to Ómassa, further up the valley. The railway also runs northwards from Miskolc along the Csanyik Valley, but this route is less suitable for entering the Bükk. All these places are marked on the "Environs of Miskolc" map on p.247.

Lillafüred and its caves
LILLAFÜRED's principal attractions are three **stalactite caves** (*barlang*) that can be visited on guided tours, starting every hour or so from each cave entrance (daily April 16–Oct 15 9am–5pm; Oct 16–April 15 9am–4pm). Tucked away above the Miskolc road, the **Szeleta Cave** was found to contain Ice Age spearheads and tools. The **Anna Cave**, beside the road up to the hotel, has a long entrance passage and six chambers linked by stairs formed from limestone. If your appetite for stalactites is still unsatiated, walk 1km down the road towards Eger to find the **István Cave**, which is longer and less convoluted, with a "cupola hall" of stalactites, various pools and chambers.

Two hundred metres beyond this stands the wooden **house of Ottó Herman** (1835–1944), where this naturalist and ethnographer spent many years trapping and mounting local wildlife. Stuffed boars, birds and rodents, plus an extraordinary collection of giant beetles are the main attraction, but you can also see Ottó's top hat and butterfly nets, and a letter from Kossuth.

Lake Hámori, just north of Lillafüred, is used for **boating** in summer and **ice skating** during winter. The hill to the east is a military area with a "secret" underground base.

Újmassa and beyond

Open trains filled with shrieking children continue from Lillafüred up the Garadna Valley, which cleaves the Bükk plateau. At **ÚJMASSA**, the next stop, a **nineteenth-century foundry** (Tues–Sun 9am–5pm) attests to the work of **Henrik Fazola**, a Bavarian-born Eger locksmith, and his son Frigyes, who first exploited the iron ore deposits of the Bükk. Nearby are the sooty camps of **charcoal burners**, who still live for part of the year in the forest.

ÓMASSA, further up the valley, is the last stop on the train and bus routes. From here it's a few hours' walk up a well-marked path to **Mount Bálvány**, south of which lies the "Great Meadow" (*Nagymező*) where wild horses graze. A ski chalet and the summits of **Nagy-Csipkés** (822m) and **Zsérci-Nagy-Dél** (875m) can be reached to the east, but more impressive crags lie to the south – **Tárkő** (950m) and Istállóskő. South of Tárkő, the land drops rapidly, and water from the plateau descends through sinkholes, bursting forth in a spring at **Vörös-kő** (Red Rock). During winter, when the plateau is covered with snow, the entrances to these **sinkholes** are marked by rising steam.

MISKOLC AND THE AGGTELEKI RANGE

To the north and east of Bükk National Park are the three cities that comprise Hungary's "Rust Belt", a region afflicted by the collapse of its heavy industry. **Miskolc**, straddling the road and railway network, is hard to avoid, and maybe deserves a visit for its gritty character and the "thrashing" cave baths in its resort suburb. **Ózd** and **Kazincbarcika** have no such redeeming features, except that their transport links to more appealing destinations, including the wonderful **stalactite caves at Aggtelek**, near the Czechoslovak border.

Miskolc

MISKOLC (pronounced "*Mish*-koltz") is Hungary's second largest city, a drab conglomerate of high-rise apartment buildings ranged along windswept roads. Until a few years ago, a stint in the local administration seemed a shrewd move to ambitious functionaries, not least **Károly Grósz**, a native son who became Hungary's last Communist premier. Now, however, there are few takers for a job that entails closing down unprofitable steel and arms factories. The discontent bred by rising **unemployment** has found an outlet in Gypsy-bashing, to which the council responded by proposing that all the **Gypsies** be moved to an outlying

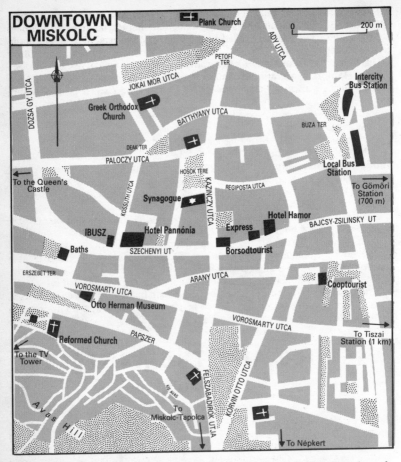

DOWNTOWN MISKOLC

0   200 m

Plank Church

ADY UTCA

PETOFI TER

JOKAI MOR UTCA

Intercity Bus Station

Greek Orthodox Church

BATTHYANY UTCA

BUZA TER

DOZSA GY. UTCA

DEAK TER

PALOCZY UTCA

HOSOK TERE

KOSSUTH UTCA

KAZINCZY UTCA

REGIPOSTA UTCA

Local Bus Station

To the Queen's Castle

Synagogue

IBUSZ

Hotel Pannónia

Express

Hotel Hamor

To Gömöri Station (700 m)

BAJCSY-ZSILINSKY UT

Baths

SZECHENYI UT

Borsodtourist

ERSZEBET TER

VOROSMARTY UTCA

ARANY UTCA

Cooptourist

Otto Herman Museum

PAPSZER

VOROSMARTY UTCA

To Tiszai Station (1 km)

Reformed Church

To the TV Tower

Avas Hill

FELSZABADIROK UTJA

KORVIN OTTO UTCA

To Miskolc-Tapolca

To Népkert

estate – a plan only dropped after a national outcry. At time of writing, the only cause for celebration is that the local **football** team, DVTK, has finally made it into the first division.

If all this sounds grim, there are some compensations. The city's summer festival features all kinds of performing arts, while the western suburbs harbour a medieval castle. And when the city palls, there are the cave baths in **Miskolc-Tapolca**, and enjoyable trips into the Bükk.

Arrival and orientation

Your likeliest point of **arrival** will be the main **Tiszai Station**, one kilometre east of the centre, or the **inter-city bus terminal** on Búza tér. From Tiszai Station you can catch a #1 or #101 bus to the castle or Majális Park (for Lillafüred: see below and "The Bükk Mountains", above), or a #1 or #2 tram into the centre, getting off at Széchenyi út. From Búza tér you can either walk into the centre, or head straight for Miskolc-Tapolca by bus (#2 or #102). Should you arrive at **Gömöri Station** instead, walk down to Zsolcai kapu, catch any bus heading west and alight near Ady utca.

For all kinds of **information**, contact *Borsod Tourist* at Széchenyi út 35 (Mon–Fri 7am–5pm; summer also Sat 8am–1pm; ☎46/88-036), or *IBUSZ* at Kossuth utca 2 (Mon–Fri 8am–4.30pm; ☎46/37-731), rather than *Express* or *Cooptourist*. Although a town plan is essential once you venture outside the downtown area, be warned that thirty **street names** are due to be changed soon.

The City

The main downtown street is **Széchenyi út**, whose eclectic mix of boutiques and restaurants, interspersed with Baroque facades painted pea green and sky blue or in the last stages of decrepitude, gives the impression of a boom and slump happening simultaneously. In the backstreets to the north and south, nineteenth-century artisans' dwellings crouch in gardens, overshadowed by concrete high-rises. Such contrasts make the downtown area the most appealing part of Miskolc.

One block north of the main stretch, **Hősök tere** is flanked by two imposing buildings. The still-functioning **Synagogue** was designed by Ludwig Förster, the architect of the great synagogue in Budapest. Its magnificent but crumbling interior seems painfully empty on major feast days: only 250 Jews now live in Miskolc, whose pre-war Jewish population numbered 118,000 (of whom 114,000 were taken to the death camps). Ask at the office behind the synagogue for the keys. On the northern side of the square stands a former **Minorite Church** and monastery, dating from 1729–40.

Off to the right and round the corner, trees screen a **Greek Orthodox Church** founded by descendants of the Greeks who fled here from the Turks in the seventeenth century. Beside the entrance, at Deák tér 7, is an **Orthodox Ecclesiastical Museum** (Tues–Sun April–Oct 10am–6pm; Nov–March 10am–4pm) containing religious art from all over Hungary. The church itself has a sixteen-metre-high iconostasis resembling a giant advent calendar, inset with the "Black Mary of Kazan" presented by Catherine the Great of Russia, and a jewelled cross from Mount Athos, both of which play a major part in Sunday services (liturgy at 10.30am). Until a few years ago, when their old homes were pulled down, the Greek quarter was situated around Búza tér.

Further north, beyond Petőfi tér, the spooky-looking **Plank Church** languishes like an unwanted import from Transylvania. Such Gothic-style wooden churches are rare in Hungary but common in northern Romania, where this kind of architecture reached its zenith in the eighteenth century. The interior is nothing special, however.

Avas Hill

To the south of Széchenyi út, a *fin-de-siècle* **bath house** (Tues–Sat 6–11am & 1–5pm, Sun 6am–noon) frames the view of **Avas Hill**. The Gothic **Reformed Church** at the bottom dates from 1560, although the pews – decorated with flower motifs – were added later. Its **wooden belfry** is separate from the church, as required by Counter-Reformation ordinances. From here, a maze of paths snakes upwards to the **Television Tower** and observation platform on the hill's summit. The right-hand paths climb through an extraordinary shantytown of miniature villas and rock-hewn wine cellars (some of them up to 50m deep), guarded by savage dogs. At the far end of Mendikás utca is an overgrown **Jewish Cemetery** with beautifully carved gravestones that date back to the eighteenth century.

The **Ottó Herman Museum**, at the bottom of the hill (Tues–Sun 10am–6pm), contains a dazzling collection of folk costumes, along with a section devoted to pottery. The pile of broken mugs owes to the tradition of drinking and then smashing your mug at wakes.

The Queen's Castle

The oldest building in Miskolc is the **Queen's Castle** or *Diósgyőr vár* (April–Oct Tues–Sun 9am–6pm), located in the western suburb of Diósgyőr, beyond the steelworks. Built for King Louis between 1350 and 1375, the castle marked the introduction of the southern Italian type of fortress to Hungary. Though eminently defendable, it served chiefly as a royal holiday home and a residence for dowager queens. Blown up in the Rákóczi wars, it has been crudely restored with breeze blocks and poured concrete, but the view from its towers, of Miskolc and the Bükk mountains, remains fine. To get there, catch a #1 or #101 bus to the Ady Endre Cultural Centre and walk towards the four stone towers poking above the rooftops.

Miskolc-Tapolca

Given the drabness of Miskolc itself, it's hardly surprising that so many people head out to **MISKOLC-TAPOLCA**, a resort suburb twenty minutes' ride from Búza tér (bus #2 or #102). Crammed with holiday homes and school parties, its main attractions are an outdoor **pool** (May 25–Sept 15 daily 8am–6pm) and the *barlang fürdő* or **cave baths** (daily 9am–1pm & 2–6pm), a series of dimly lit warm water grottoes, culminating in a "thrashing shower". Visitors who go **mushroom hunting** in the Bükk can have their fungi checked at the *Gomba Vizsgalat* hut (May 15–Nov 15 daily 1–6pm) near the #2 bus terminal. There are snack stands aplenty and a **disco** in the *Hotel Juno*.

Accommodation

As usual, student **hostels** arranged through *Express* or *IBUSZ* are the cheapest option for solo travellers. The best is the *Teréz Kollégium* (①) at Győri kapu út 156 (#1 bus or tram), open full time from late June to late August, and at weekends throughout the year. The University Town (*Egyetemváros*) in the hills south of town (bus #12 from Hősök tere) is another possibility.

Next in price come **private rooms** from *IBUSZ* or *Borsod Tourist* – almost certainly in a *lakótelep*, so check the location and accessibility before accepting. Chances are, the only places in the centre are **hotels** and pensions. The *Hotel Hámor*, Széchenyi út 107 (☎46/35-508; ②), is dowdy but fairly cheap, whilst the *Hotel Pannónia*, Kossuth utca 2 (☎46/16-434; ⑤), is plush and pricey.

As for **pensions**, the *Korona Panzió* (☎46/35-370; ②) at Kisavas 18 enjoys a nicer location, at the foot of Avas Hill, than the cheaper *Búzavirág Panzió* (☎46/26-987; ②) at Búza tér 6, near the bus station. The *Fauna Panzió* (☎46/40-243; ②), Bessenyői utca 22, is situated to the north of Gömöri Station.

ENVIRONS OF MISKOLC

To Kazincbarcika

Csanyik Valley

MISKOLC

Ómassa
Újmassa
Lake Hámori
THE
Lillafüred
Diósgyőr
Queen's Castle
Gömöri Railway Station
To Szerencs
Tiszari Railway Station

BÜKK
Hollóstető
Campsite
Bükkszentlászló
Bükkszentkereszt
Egyetem-Város
Campsite
Campsite
Miskolc-Tapolca

To Eger

0   1 km

To Budapest

MISKOLC-TAPOLCA

Private **rooms** in Miskolc-Tapolca can be arranged through *Borsod Tourist* at Martos utca 7 (☎46/68-917). There are numerous hotels along and just off the main road: try the *Mini Motel*, Branyiszkó utca 4 (☎46/68-104; ②–③); the *Hotel Lido*, Győri utca 4 (☎46/69-800; ②–③); or the *Park Motel*, Bak utca 4 (☎46/60-811; ②–③). There are dearer doubles along Martos utca, at the *Zenit Panzió* at no. 25 (③); and the *Flóra Panzió* at no. 35 (☎46/68-116; ③); and at the three-star *Hotel Junó*, Csabai utca 2–4 (☎46/64-133; ④). **Bungalows** and tent space can be rented at two **campsites**: *Éden Camping* (April 15–Oct 15; ☎46/68-421), a kind of manicured parking lot near the *Hotel Junó*; and *Autós Camping* (May 1–Sept 15; ☎46/67-171), a leafier site popular with motorists, 2km up along Iglói út.

Eating, drinking and entertainments

There are **restaurants** attached to the *Pannónia* and *Hámor* hotels on Széchenyi út, and a place specialising in Polish food, the *Katowice*, 300m north of Petőfi tér. For cheap snacks, check out the **market** beside the local bus terminal. The *Rori Cukrászda* by the *Hotel Pannónia* is a nicer place for coffee and cakes than the smoky *Rác Kávéház* further along, and excellent pancakes are served at the *Hagi Etterem*, Zsolcai kapu 5.

Nightlife boils down to **discos** at various cultural centres (as advertised on posters and at tourist agencies), and the "Bar Varíte" floorshow at the *Tokaj* penthouse overlooking Győri kapu út (which also has a disco, and a beer hall downstairs). Other places to go **drinking** include the flash *Spatzen Pince* beside the *Hotel Pannónia*; the *HBH Söröző* on Újgyőri főtér (off Győri kapu út); and the *Lokál Bar* on Budai József utca, south of the Népkert (park).

The city is at its liveliest during the **Miskolc Summer** (June–Aug), when rock and jazz concerts, plays and dancing take place at the castle and in Miskolc-Tapolca. One of the festival's highlights is the **Kaláka Folklore Festival** at the beginning of July, which attracts *Táncház* groups from all over Hungary and folkloric troupes from abroad. Events are advertised around town; ask *IBUSZ* or *Borsod Tourist* for details.

For those into **football**, the DVTK stadium lies out along Győri kapu út, towards the castle. Also worthy of a mention is the **Kossuth Cinema** (next to *IBUSZ*), which boasts a grand lobby and auditorium, dating from the turn of the century.

Moving on

If you're not heading into the Bükk (see p.242), there are regular **trains** from Tiszai Station to the Zempléni, Szerencs, the Great Plain and the capital. The fastest services to Budapest are the non-stop *Borsod, Hámor, Sajó* and *Lillafüred* expresses (1hr 45min). Tornanádaska-bound slow trains from Gömöri Station can drop you at the *Jósvafő-Aggtelek vá*, for the caves of Aggtelek (see below).

Aggtelek is also accessible by bus (Mon–Fri 7.30am, Sat 9.30am) from Búza tér. Other long-distance **buses** – to Debrecen, Eger, Kecskemét, Szeged, Nyíregyháza and Salgótarján – also tend to leave early in the morning.

International connections

There are also services from Miskolc **to Czechoslovakia and Poland**. *Volán* **buses** run to the Slovakian towns of Rožňava and Košice, while express **trains** depart from Tiszai station for Kraków (the *Cracovia*), Warsaw (*Karpaty*) and Poprad-Tatry (*Rákóczi*), all calling at Košice along the way.

Kazincbarcika and Ózd

A planner's dream and a resident's nightmare, **KAZINCBARCIKA** was created in the Fifties for the purpose of manufacturing chemicals and energy from the coal deposits of the north. Laid out in a grid, its endless rows of numbingly identical *lakótelep* are ineffectually separated from the smoggy industrial zone by 500 metres of withered grass. Of the three villages that originally stood here, only the **fifteenth-century churches** of Barcika and Sajókazinc and the **wooden belfry** of Berente remain. Though they're hardly worth staying the night for, the *Hotel Polimer Tours* (☎48/11-911; ③), on Ifjúsági körtér, lives in hope.

ÓZD, which likewise contributes to the pollution of the River Sajó, has been harder hit by industrial decline than anywhere else in Hungary and its prospects remain grim despite endless rumours of German investment. While its southeastern suburb of lace-curtained brick houses with gardens is reminiscent of small towns in the Rhondda or Ohio Valley, Ózd's modernised centre is utterly depressing, and notorious for gang violence. It's there that you'll find the bus terminal –

whose **services to Aggtelek** (daily around 8am, noon & 3pm) are the only reason to come here – and the *Hotel Kohász* (☎47/11-344; ③) at Ív út 9.

Stalactite Caves in the Aggteleki

Like the Bükk, the **Aggteleki range**, bordering Czechoslovakia, displays typical **karstic** features such as gullies, sinkholes and caves, caused by a mixture of water and carbon dioxide dissolving the limestone. The **Baradla caves** between the villages of **Aggtelek** and **Jósvafő**, and the **Béke caves** to the southeast, constitute an amazing subterranean world with stygian lakes and rivers, waterfalls, countless stalactites, and 262 species of wildlife. Set in remote countryside that's ideal for walking and cycling, the caves are deservedly popular with tourists.

Approaches and accommodation

Getting to the Aggteleki entails catching an early bus from Budapest, Miskolc or Eger; or travelling later in the day, starting from Ózd (see above) or from Putnok, where there are **buses** to Aggtelek and Jósvafő every hour and a half. **PUTNOK** (linked to Ózd, Eger, Miskolc and Kazincbarcika by rail) is the last outpost of *IBUSZ* and banks. Alternatively, slow **trains** from Miskolc to Tornanádaska can drop you at the Jósvafő-Aggtelek station, 10km east of Jósvafő, whence regular buses run to both villages (infrequently on Sundays).

Aside from the fortified church with its picturesque cemetery in **JÓSVAFŐ**, and the algae-green lake outside **AGGTELEK**, both villages are unremarkable. Shops are few and social life centres around the church and "drink shop" (active from 4pm). Aggtelek offers a choice of **accommodation**, having a campsite with two categories of four-person huts (May 15–Oct 15; ☎48/12-700; ②) and a tourist hostel (①), and the *Hotel Cseppkő* (☎48/64-331; ②), both open year round; whereas Jósvafő has only the *Hotel Tengerszem* (telex 64-294; ②). Both hotels contain **restaurants** and display local **bus schedules** in the lobby.

Visiting the caves

Both sets of caves are open daily from 8am to 5pm (Oct–April until 3pm), but hourly guided tours only begin when at least five people have assembled at one of the entrances (*bejárat*), so it makes sense to go for the most accessible.

The main **Baradla cave passage** twists underground for 22km, hence the option of one-hour, one-and-a-half-hour or three-hour **tours**. The **Aggtelek end** of the passage is more convoluted and thus more rewarding for shorter tours. Entering the caves from the **Jósvafő** end, the last medium (*kozep*) tour is at 3pm (1pm in winter) and the last short (*rovid*) tour at 5pm (winter 3pm). No description can do justice to the variety and profusion of **stalactites and stalagmites**, whose nicknames can only hint at the fantastic formations, glittering with calcite crystals or stained ochre by iron oxides. Among them is the world's tallest stalagmite, a full 25 metres high. In the "Concert Hall", boats sway on the "River Styx", and the guide activates a tape of Bach's *Toccata in D minor* to create a *Phantom of the Opera* type ambience.

Longer tours of the Baradla passage begin at the Vörös-tó entrance, situated in the Cool Valley (*Hideg völgy*) between the two villages, and require some stamina: three hours is a long time to clamber around dank, muddy caves, however beautiful they are.

Guided tours around the **Béke caves** are also fairly demanding. Although they contain a sanatorium, the underground air being judged beneficial to asthmatics, most of the caves are, in fact, untamed, even unexplored, and as recently as 1973 a new passage was found when cavers penetrated a thirty-metre waterfall. You'll need boots and warm, waterproof clothing, and visitors are issued with helmets. **Underground wildlife** – bats, rodents and bugs, mostly – keeps out of sight, and is easiest to view in the **Cave Museum** (Tues–Sun 10am–6pm) by the Aggtelek entrance, which also has photos and mementoes to gladden a speleologist's heart.

Excursions in the vicinity

The surrounding countryside is riddled with smaller caves and rock formations, clearly marked on the *Aggtelek és Jósvafő környékének* **map** sold at the Aggtelek cave entrance. This also shows the **border zone**, where armed guards still patrol with dogs, notwithstanding the demise of Communism. Always carry your passport when hiking. For those with a car or bike, lots of attractive **villages** are within reach in this part of the highlands, notably RAGÁLY, 11km back towards Putnok, and RUDABÁNYA, where the ten-million-year-old jawbone of *Rudapithecus hungaricus* – an ancient primate – can be seen at the mine where it was excavated.

THE ZEMPLÉNI RANGE

The **Zempléni range** is the region to see in the north – largely unspoiled by industry and tourism, and richly textured by nature and history. Its volcanic soil and microclimates favour diverse wildlife (particularly snakes and birds of prey), whilst the architecture reflects a tradition of trade and cultural exchanges between the Great Plain and the Slovakian highlands. **Tokaj**, in the Tokaj-Hegyalja wine-making district, absorbs most of the region's tourists, surprisingly few of whom make it up to **Sárospatak**, site of the superb Rákóczi castle, or to little **Zempléni villages** such as Füzér or Lászlótanya, where Hungary's Stalinist dictator enjoyed hunting.

Approaches via Szerencs

Approaching Tokaj and the northern Zempléni from Miskolc*, you're bound to pass through **SZERENCS**, a drab town with a reeking factory that's responsible for most of the chocolate produced in Hungary. If you've got time to kill between connections, pay a visit to the **fortified manor** at the far end of Rákóczi út, where István Bocskai (1557–1606) was elected Prince of Hungary. This event is recalled in the manor's **Zempléni Museum** (Mon–Fri 10am–noon), which also contains the world's third largest **collection of postcards** – 700,000 of them, donated by a local doctor. The other half of the manor is – for the moment – occupied by the *Hotel Huszárvár* (☎41/50-666; ②), but its future is uncertain.

Besides **trains** to Tokaj (7 daily; 35min), Szerencs is the starting point for the branch line up to Hidasnémeti, via villages on the western side of the Zempléni; and for **buses** to Monok, Mád and Tállya in the Tokaj-Hegyalja (see below).

---

*The Miskolc–Szerencs–Sátoraljaújhely road bypasses all the villages en route, having been built to allow the Soviet Army rapid access to the plains in the event of war. During its construction, house-building in the vicinity boomed, as contractors sold off materials on the quiet.

Tokaj and the Tokaj-Hegyalja

TOKAJ is to Hungary what Champagne is to France, and this small town has become a minor Mecca for wine snobs. Perched beside the confluence of the rivers Bodrog and Tisza, it's a place of sloping cobbled streets and faded ochre dwellings with wine cellars and nesting storks – all overlooked by lush vineyards climbing the hillside towards the "Bald Peak" and the inevitable television tower.

The Town

From the **railway station** it's ten minutes' walk under the arch and left along Bajcsy-Zsilinszky út to the **old town centre**, just past the bridge (which leads over to the campsite). Here are the first of the wine cellars (*bor pince*) which pop up along the main street to Kossuth tér, interspersed with fried fish (*sült hal*) shops, and the rainbow-striped *Hotel Tokaj*. Further along are the few architectural "sights" – the old Town Hall and Rákóczi-Dessewffy mansion – but inevitably it's **wine** that attracts most people's attention (see box).

Although lack of funds threatens to close it over winter, the **Tokaj Museum** at Bethlen Gábor utca 7 (Tues–Sun summer 9am–5pm; winter 9am–3pm) puts on a brave face with displays of wine labels from Crimea, France and the Rhineland – where attempts to reproduce Tokaj all failed – and a huge antique wine press.

The former Greek Orthodox church at Bethlen utca 17 hosts periodic **exhibitions** of contemporary paintings and sculptures (April–Oct Tues–Sun). In a back-street around the corner stands a derelict synagogue with a storks' nest upon its chimney. Other **architecture** worth a look includes the Zopf-style Town Hall at Rákóczi utca 44; the onetime Rákóczi-Dessewffy mansion at Bajcsy-Zsilinszky út 15–17 (now a college); and Zopf and Baroque houses on Bethlen Gábor utca.

If you fancy a walk, follow the road behind Kossuth tér uphill to the summit of Tokaj's 516-metre-high "Bald Peak". The route takes you past dozens of vineyards, each carefully labelled with its owner's name. From the summit you can scan the distant Great Plain and the lush green Tokaj-Hegyalja – the hilly wine-producing region. Other **activities** in Tokaj include rowing, water-skiing, and swimming in the Tisza, or fending off inebriated conscripts at the campsite discos.

TOKAJ WINES

The three main **Tokaj wines** – *Aszú* (sweet), *Hárslevelű* (linden leaf) and *Furmint* (which is usually dry) – derive their character from the special soil, the prolonged sunlight and the wine-making techniques developed here. Heat is trapped by the volcanic loess soil, allowing a delayed **harvest** in October, when many overripe grapes have a sugar content approaching sixty percent. Their juice and pulp is added by the *puttony* (butt) to 136-litre barrels of ordinary grapes, the number of butts determining the qualities of the wine: rich and sweet or slightly "hot", with an oily consistency and ranging in colour from golden yellow to reddish brown.

Though some may find *Aszú* too sweet, Tokaj wine has collected some notable accolades since the late Middle Ages. Beethoven and Schubert dedicated songs to it; Louis XVI declared it "the wine of kings, the king of wines"; Goethe, Voltaire, Heine and Browning all praised it; and Sherlock Holmes used it to toast the downfall of von Bork, after troubling Watson to "open the window, for chloroform vapour does not help the palate".

Accommodation

Private rooms are available at Bajcsy-Zsilinszky út 19 (②) and Ovar utca 6 (②). At Bethlen utca 49 (②), on the far (north) side of town, they come slightly cheaper because guests share a toilet – literally, as the loo has two doors, one from each room. Doubles with bathrooms (②) and quadruples without (②) can be found at the *Kollégium*, Bajcsy-Zsilinszky utca 15–17 (☎41/52-355), from June till late August, and possibly at weekends the rest of the year.

Another option is the *Makk-Marci Panzió* (☎41/52-336) at Liget köz 1, just off Rákóczi utca, with singles (②) and doubles (③). The two-star *Tokaj Hotel*, Rákóczi utca 5 (☎41/52-344), has comfortable but simple rooms (②).

Across the river are two **campsites**, one on either side of the road. At shady *Tisza Camping* (April 15–Sept 15; ☎41/52-012) you can rent two-bed chalets (①). *Camping Pelsöczi* charges slightly less for pitching a tent, and a faded notice in reception promises a free bottle of Tokaj to anyone booking two nights, which seems generous if true.

Drinking and eating

The venerable *Rákóczi* cellar at Kossuth tér 15 (daily 8am–noon & 12.30–7pm), where 20,000 hectolitres of wine repose in 24 cobwebbed, chandelier-lit passages, is the most famous in Tokaj and a favourite place of pilgrimage. However, you'll get a more personal service if you drink in the small private **wine cellars** that line the hillside in the backstreets above the main street. The *Vajtho* cellar opposite the bridge is recommended. As for **eating**, the options are limited. By the bridge you have the *halászcsárdá* at Bajcsy-Zsilinszky utca 23 and the restaurant in the *Hotel Tokaj*. Down by the river is the *Kikötő Pihenő*, a bar that also serves food during the summer; and the stand-up buffet at *Tisza Camping*. Or you might consider tracking down the *Horgony Vendéglő* at Bodrogkerestur út 4, an unpretentious place frequented by locals (8am–midnight). It's fifteen minutes' walk north from the centre, just past the old Jewish Cemetery on the left.

The Tokaj-Hegyalja

The southern slopes of the Zempléni form the distinctive region known as the **Tokaj-Hegyalja**, which is largely devoted to producing wine. Most of its beautifully sited villages are accessible by bus from Tokaj or Szerencs (many are also served by the branch line from the latter to Hidasnémeti). Since few have any accommodation for tourists, you'll have to visit on day trips – you can stop off at one or two villages a day, depending on schedules.

TOLCSVA, 2km off the road to Sárospatak and around 30km north of Tokaj, can be reached by the hourly bus from Tokaj to Komlóska. Its erstwhile Rákóczi manor is now a **Wine Museum** (Tues, Fri, Sat & Sun 10am–noon, Thurs 2–4pm) containing the usual implements. The hillside is honeycombed with 2.5km of cellars, full of the local **linden leaf wine** (*Tolcsvai Hárslevelű*).

MÁD, midway between Tokaj and Szerencs, boasts a folk Baroque-style **Synagogue**, built in 1765. Just downhill stands the former **Rabbi's house** and **Yeshiva** (religious school), a whitewashed building with graceful arcades (the keys are held by the council at Rákóczi utca 50–52, Mon–Fri 8am–4pm; at weekends seek out András Novak at Danesics utca 22). The old **Jewish Cemetery** is on the northern edge of the village.

Nine kilometres up the road, **TÁLLYA** is the second largest wine producer after Tokaj, with hundreds of barrels maturing in seventeenth-century cellars near a former Rákóczi mansion. In the village church you can view the font where Kossuth (see box below) was baptised.

MONOK, 10km northwest of Szerencs, was actually the **birthplace of Kossuth**, whose childhood home is now a **museum** (Tues–Sun 10am–1pm & 3–6pm). Monok's other famous son is **Miklós Németh**, Hungary's prime minister during the transition from Communism to democracy in 1989.

LAJOS KOSSUTH

Born into landless gentry in 1802, **Lajos Kossuth** began his political career as a lawyer, representing absentee magnates in Parliament. His parliamentary reports, advocating greater liberalism than the Habsburgs would tolerate, were widely influential during the Reform Era. Whilst in jail for sedition, Kossuth taught himself English by reading Shakespeare. Released in 1840, he became editor of the radical *Pesti Hírlap*, was elected to parliament, and took the helm during the 1848 Revolution.

After Serbs, Croats and Romanians rebelled against Magyar rule, and the Habsburgs invaded Hungary, the Debrecen Parliament proclaimed a republic with Kossuth as *de facto* dictator. Having escaped to Turkey after the Hungarians surrendered in August 1849, he toured Britain and America, espousing liberty. So eloquent were his denunciations of Habsburg tyranny that London brewery workers attacked General Haynau, the "Butcher of Vienna", when he visited the city. Karl Marx loathed Kossuth as a bourgeois radical, and tried to undermine his reputation with articles published in the New York *Herald Tribune* and the London *Times*. As a friend of the Italian patriot Mazzini, Kossuth spent his last years in Turin, where he died in 1894.

The western Zempléni

The western flank of the Zempléni is dotted with **villages** whose remote and sleepy existence today belies their historic significance. Unlike the other parts of Hungary with medieval churches and ruined castles, there's rarely another tourist in sight, while the **scenery** is great everywhere. In contrast to the rounded sedimentary hills on the western side of the valley, the volcanically formed Zempléni often resemble truncated cones (called *sátor* – "tent" – in Hungarian). If all of this appeals, and you don't mind the lack of bright lights and facilities, the region is well worth exploring.

Though private **transport** is definitely advantageous, most places are accessible by local buses or trains up the Szerencs–Hidasnémeti branch line. The scarcity of **accommodation** could be more of a problem unless you bring a tent, or encounter sympathetic locals. Try to buy a *Zempléni hegység* **map** showing all the villages mentioned below, even if you don't intend to go **hiking**.

The route described on the following page approximately follows the **Hernád Valley** up towards the river's source in the Slovakian highlands, and the **border crossing** into Czechoslovakia at Tornyosnémeti (by road) and Hidasnémeti (by rail).

Boldogkőváralja and Vizsoly

Best reached by road since the village lies 2.5km from its train stop, **BOLDOGKŐVÁRALJA** is dominated by a massive **castle** built upon a volcanic mound. Erected in the thirteenth century to discourage a return visit by the Mongols, its partial ruination mocks its name – "Happy stone castle on the hill". There are **guided tours** (Tues–Sun 8am–4pm) of this Gothic hulk, and a tourist **hostel** (April 15–Oct 15; ☎50-694; ①) in one wing. Advance bookings should be made through *Borsod Tourist* in Miskolc.

At **VIZSOLY**, 2km from its railway station (Korlát-Vizsoly), a thirteenth-century **church** harbours fantastic frescoes of Jesus' Ascension (leaving his footprints behind) and Saint George and the dragon. It also contains an original edition of the **Vizsoly Bible**, the Magyar equivalent of the King James Bible. As the first Hungarian-language translation, by Gáspár Károlyi in 1590, this played a formative role in the development of Hungarian as a written language. Keys to the church are at the *reformátos lelkesz* at Szent János út 123, across the road.

Gönc

Accessible by buses from Hidasnémeti (7 daily) as well as by train, **GÖNC** is set in splendid countryside. This was once an important place, a thriving trade centre in the Middle Ages. The Vizsoly Bible was written here and Sárospatak's Calvinist College took refuge in the village during the Counter-Reformation. More recently, Gönc's fame has rested on the 136-litre oak **barrels** (*Gönci hordok*) used to store Tokaj wine – but even these are no longer made here.

The most concrete reminder of all this is the white **Hussite House** (Tues–Sun 10am–6pm) on Kossuth utca, where there's a weird bed that pulls out from a table and a Gönc barrel downstairs. Down in the cellar, the door to the left enabled the house's Calvinist inhabitants to escape into the maze of cellars beneath the village. If it's shut, the old woman at Rákóczi utca 80 (across the stream, and off to the right) can let you in: she was born in the Hussite House.

At weekends, visitors can rent **rooms** at the edge of the village (ask at Dózsa utca 39 or Kossuth utca 47). Some might enjoy a hard day's **hiking between Gönc and Regéc**, along an ill-marked path skirting the 787-metre-high Gergely-Hegy (bring a compass, food and water). There are two buses a day to REGÉC from Encs (on the Miskolc–Hidasnémeti line), leaving around noon and 2pm.

Telkibánya, Abaújvár and Kéked

Buses from Hidasnémeti to Gönc carry on to **TELKIBÁNYA** (also served by two buses from Sátoraljaújhely, on the other side of the mountains), whose museum has a fine collection of colourful pottery, outsized carved heads and Zempléni crystals. During summer, the Children's Camp (*Gyermektábor*) offers self-catering **accommodation**. Beds can also be had out of season if you phone beforehand (☎Telkibánya 7). Jordán Istvánné is the woman to ask for.

A more northerly bus service (2 on weekdays only) from Hidasnémeti to Hollóháza (see p.260), via a new road unmarked on most maps, calls at **ABAÚJVÁR**, whose picturesque Reformed church incorporates some Gothic bits and battered frescoes dating back to 1332. Abaújvár can also be reached by a separate service to Gönc and Hidasnémeti (6 daily). **KÉKED**, on the Hollóháza bus route, has a **fortified manor** containing rustic knick-knacks and antiques (Tues–Sun 8am–4pm), and you could also stop off at an **outdoor bath** in the forest, fed by a coldwater spring (May–Aug).

Sárospatak

SÁROSPATAK (Muddy Stream) basks on the banks of the Bodrog, half an hour's train journey from Szerencs. It's a town that once enjoyed a significant role in Hungarian intellectual life, thanks to its **Calvinist College**: Magyars given to hyperbole used to describe Sárospatak as the "Athens on the Bodrog". In the last twenty years, some delightful examples of **Mákovecz architecture** have drawn attention to the town, but Sárospatak's main claim to fame is rooted firmly in the past: its historic association with the **Rákóczi family**, whose **castle** is one of the main sights in town.

The Rákóczi family played a major role in Transylvania and Hungary during a turbulent era. Shortly after **György I Rákóczi** acquired Sárospatak Castle in 1616, his Transylvanian estates – and political influence – were augmented by marriage to the immensely wealthy **Zsuzsana Lorántffy**. In 1630 the nobility elected him Prince of Transylvania, hoping that György would restore the stability enjoyed under Gábor Bethlen – which he did.

György II, however, was as rash as his father was cautious, managing to antagonise both Poland and Vizier Mehmet, whose invasion of Transylvania forced the clan to flee to Habsburg-controlled Hungary in 1658. Here the Counter-Reformation was in full swing, and Magyar landlords and peasants reacted against Habsburg confiscations by sporadically staging ferocious revolts of "dissenters" (*kuruc*). Though the original revolt led by Imre Thököly was bloodily crushed, conspirators gathered around György's son **Ferenc I**.

In 1703, the insurgency had become a full-scale **War of Independence**, led by **Ferenc II**, whose irregular cavalry and peasant footsoldiers initially triumphed. But by 1711 the Magyars were exhausted and divided, abandoned by their half-hearted ally Louis XIV of France, and Ferenc fled abroad as his armies collapsed under the weight of Habsburg power, to die in exile (in Tekirdag, Turkey) in 1735.

The Town

As you walk from the train or bus station through the School Garden (*Iskola Kert*), you'll pass statues of Sárospatak's famous alumni – testifying to the pedagogical prestige of the town's **Calvinist College** (Mon–Sat 9am–5pm, Sun & holidays 9am–1pm; closed Easter, Whitsun & Oct 31), just across the garden. Founded in 1531, the college achieved renown under the rectorship (1650–54) of the great Czech humanist **Jan Comenius**, who published several textbooks with the support of György Rákóczi. During the Counter-Reformation, it was forced to move to Gönc, and then to Slovakia, before returning home in 1703. Illustrious graduates include Kossuth, Gárdonyi (see "Eger"), the writer Zsigmond Móricz and the language reformer Ferenc Kazinczy. Like the Calvinist College in Debrecen, it has long-standing ties with England and runs an international **summer language school**. Since regaining control in 1990, the church has been striving to make the college an educational powerhouse once again. Hour-long tours take in the Neoclassical **Great Library** (*Nagykönyvtár*) to the right of the main entrance and a **museum** of college history.

Sárospatak Castle

Sárospatak Castle is a handsome melange of Gothic, Renaissance and Baroque architecture. In the Renaissance wings grouped around a courtyard, the **Rákóczi**

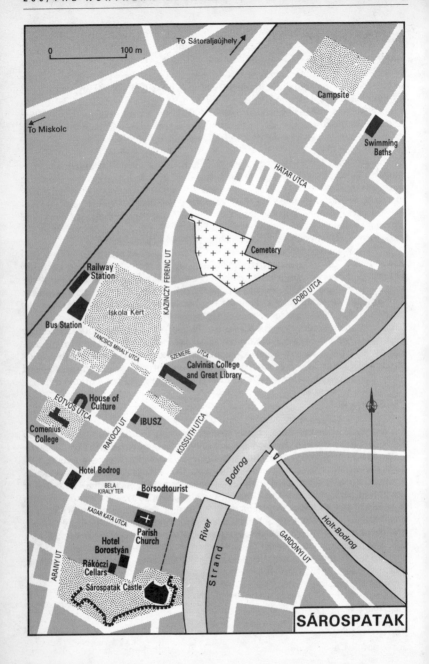

0   100 m

To Sátoraljaújhely

To Miskolc

Campsite

Swimming
Baths

HATAR UTCA

Cemetery

KAZINCZY FERENC UT

DOBO UTCA

Railway
Station

Iskola Kert

Bus Station

TANCSICS MIHALY UTCA

SZEMERE UTCA

Calvinist College
and Great Library

EOTVOS UTCA

House of
Culture

RAKOCZI UT

IBUSZ

KOSSUTH UTCA

Comenius
College

Bodrog

Hotel Bodrog

BELA
KIRALY TER

Borsodtourist

River

KADAR KATA UTCA

Holt-Bodrog

Parish
Church

GARDONYI UT

Hotel
Borostyán

ARANY UT

Rákóczi
Cellars

Sárospatak Castle

Strand

SÁROSPATAK

Museum (Tues–Sun March–Oct 10am–6pm; Nov–Feb 10am–5pm) dotes upon the dynasty, even down to a series of watercolours depicting the stages of Ferenc II's exile. Heavy inlaid furniture, jewellery, monstrous stoves, and a banqueting hall complete with piped court music recreate domestic life, while other rooms contain life-size paintings of fearsome cavalry and the mustachioed portrait of Ferenc II that's reproduced on 50Ft banknotes.

A romantic loggia, like a prop from *Romeo and Juliet*, links the residential wings to the fifteenth-century keep, known as the **"Red Tower"** (open similar hours). Guided tours take you around the dungeons and underground wells, the labyrinth of galleries used by gunners, and a series of impressive halls. The "Knights' Hall", remaining somehow austere despite its throne and stained-glass windows, hosted sessions of Parliament during the Independence War. Plots were hatched by Ferenc I in the adjoining circular balcony room, beneath a ceiling decorated with a stucco rose – hence the expression *sub rosa*, meaning conspiratorial.

The Parish Church and Rákóczi cellars

While in the vicinity of the castle, you can pay a visit to the **Parish Church** on Kádár Kata utca (Tues–Sun 10am–2pm). Though much remodelled since the fourteenth century, with painted-on rather than genuine vaulting, it remains one of the largest Gothic hall churches in eastern Hungary. Its huge Baroque altar was brought here from the Carmelite church in Buda Castle after their order was banned in 1784. Look out for posters advertising **organ recitals**.

On a more sybaritic note, the **Rákóczi cellars** behind the *Hotel Borostyan* offer tours and wine tasting for a price. The cellars are thickly coated in a black "noble mould", whose presence is considered so vital to the flavour of local **wine** that it's allowed to ferment in unsealed barrels. Although **tours** (Mon–Fri 7am–7.30pm) are only for groups of five or more, individuals can phone to find out if one is scheduled (☎41/11-902).

The Mákovecz buildings

Since 1972, Sárospatak council has commissioned a succession of buildings by the visionary architect Imre Mákovecz (see p.122). His first project was the *Bodrog Arúház* on Rákóczi út/Bartok utca, a humdrum modernist supermarket by Western standards, but far removed from the then prevailing brutalist style. Next came the **House of Culture** on Eotvos utca, whose silvery, insectile facade masks an amazing wooden auditorium. The **apartment block** on the corner of Eötvös utca and Rákóczi út displays his passion for asymmetry and organic forms, rooted in a fascination with ancient Celtic and Magyar culture. Mákovecz also designed the building in the courtyard of the Calvinist College, and the new **school** beyond the castle.

Practicalities

Orientation is easy in a small town like Sárospatak. You can get **information** from *Borsod Tourist* at Kossuth utca 50 (Mon–Fri 9am–3pm; ☎41/11-073), or from *IBUSZ* at Rákóczi út 3 (Mon–Fri 8am–4pm; May 15–Sept 15 also Sat). Out of hours – within reason – you can also contact the couple who run *Borsod Tourist* at home at Rákóczi út 37.

IBUSZ can organise summer beds in *kollégium* (①) or private **accommodation** (②). Rooms are also available direct at Szemere utca 5, near the Calvinist College, and at Katona utca 18, southeast of the castle. The low-rise *Hotel Bodrog*, on Rákóczi út (☎41/11-744; ④), has less ambience than the *Hotel Borostyan*, near the castle (☎41/11-611; ②). North of town, near the swimming baths, *Tengerszem Camping* (April 1–Oct 10; ☎41/11-753) has bungalows and good facilities, but rates are high and the staff are surly. Young Hungarians opt instead for the free **campsite** (*szabad kemping*) – with no facilities – on the *strand* across the river.

The *Borostyan*'s restaurant – occupying an old monastic chapel – is the nicest place to **eat** in town, but if cheapness is paramount you could join the locals at the unpretentious *Aszú Fogadó*, Kazinczy út 27. The *Kávéhaz* in the House of Culture (2–10pm) is a hangout for students and arty types, who also **drink** in the basement of the *Megyer Kisvendéglő*, opposite the *Hotel Bodrog*.

Ask at the House of Culture about concerts, plays and other events, especially during the **Music Days** or *Zenei Napok* (July–Aug). *Borsod Tourist* can arrange **horse riding** in the surrounding countryside, and have information on **fishing** in the Holt-Bodrog.

Moving on

There are five **trains** a day to Szerencs and Miskolc – three of which run on to Budapest (3hr 30min) – and a similar number 8km up the line run to Sátoraljaújhely, which is better served by buses. There are other **buses** up to Pálháza (2 daily) and across the river to Karcsa and Pácin (3 daily), plus **international services** to Trebišov (Wed, Fri, Sat & Sun) and Velké Kapušany (Wed–Sun) in Czechoslovakia, leaving late afternoon or evening from outside the Calvinist College or further along Kazinczy út (bookings from the main terminal).

Sátoraljaújhely and beyond

Easier to reach than it is to pronounce ("*Shar*-tor-all-yah-oowee-hay"), SÁTORALJAÚJHELY is the last Zempléni town before the border crossing to Slovenské Nové Mesto in Czechoslovakia. Formerly a thriving county town, it was relegated to a backwater by the Treaty of Trianon and the provincial mergers which made Sárospatak the Zempléni "capital". Today, people come here for buses to picturesque villages (see below) rather than for the town itself.

Walking up from the bus and railway station, you'll pass several monuments that have known better days. On the left stands a **Wooden Church**, similar to the one in Miskolc, while further up you'll find a **Gothic Piarist Church** and a cluster of Baroque edifices around Ady tér, the main square. It was from the balcony of the **Town Hall** at no. 5 that Kossuth first demonstrated his talent for oratory, during the Zempléni cholera epidemic and riots of 1830. Dózsa utca, running off the main street, harbours a deserted **Synagogue** at no. 13, and the dull local history displays of the **Kazinczy Museum** (Tues–Sun April–Oct 9am–5pm; Nov–March 9am–3pm).

If you fancy some walking, the wild ravines and forested slopes of **Mount Magas** (509m) loom just outside town. These heights saw bitter fighting between Magyars and Slovaks in 1919, and partisans and Nazis in 1944.

Practicalities

A cheaper option to the modern *Hotel Zemplén*, at Széchenyi tér 5–7 (☎41/22-522; ④), is the *Kossuth Panzió*, Várhegy utca 10 (April–Oct; ☎41/21-744;triples ②). Private **accommodation** can be obtained directly at Bányácska utca 20 (☎41/12-763), or through the **tourist offices** on Kossuth tér. *Express* (Mon–Fri 8am–4.30pm all year) can make bookings throughout the Zempléni; *IBUSZ* (Mon–Fri; May–Sept also Sat; ☎41/21-957) only locally.

Besides services to Miskolc (5 daily) and Budapest (3 daily), there are four **trains** a day to Slovenské Nové Mesto in Czechoslovakia, augmented between June and September by **international buses** to Trebišov (Wed, Fri & Sun 8pm) and Velke Kapušany (Wed–Sun afternoon or evening). However, it's the local buses that enable one to reach Zempléni villages such as Füzér (3 daily), Pálháza (8 daily), Hollóháza (6 daily), Karcsa and Pácin (hourly), or Telkibánya (twice daily on weekdays).

Into the Zempléni

The highlands beyond Sátoraljaújhely contain villages that are just as lovely as those on the western side of the Zempléni. With a car, you can visit half a dozen of them in a day and not feel cheated if a couple are less appealing than expected. Relying on local buses, you'll have to go for a simpler itinerary and be more selective. The following itineraries are basically structured around bus routes.

East to Karcsa and Pácin

Though easily reached from Sátoraljaújhely or Sárospatak, neither of these is officially a Zempléni village as they're located on the plain beyond the River Bodrog. They're not worth a journey in themselves, but merit a look if you're heading towards Kisvárda anyway (see Chapter Six).

On the edge of **KARCSA**, 20km from Sárospatak, stands a tenth-century **Romanesque church** with a Gothic nave and a freestanding belfry. The keys are next door, at the house with the *Belyegzes* sign. In **PÁCIN**, 4km further on, there's a **fortified manor** (Tues–Sun 10am–6pm; winter 9am–4pm) exhibiting peasant furniture. The kitchen cupboard carries a picture of a woman slaving over the stove, shouting "Hurry up, it's eleven o'clock!", to her husband who sits by the fire.

Towards Pálháza and Rostálló

This route can be a long excursion, or even a prelude to hiking over the Zempléni, depending on your inclinations. There are three buses daily from both Sátoraljaújhely and Sárospatak via Szépmalom and Füzérradvány to Pálháza, from where you can reach Rostálló in the mountains.

The first place worth a mention, 5km from Sátoraljaújhely, is **SZÉPMALOM**, where a park beside the road contains the **mausoleum of Ferenc Kazinczy** (Tues–Sun 10am–6pm). It was largely thanks to Kazinczy (1759–1831) that Hungarian was restored as a literary language in the nineteenth century rather than succumbing entirely to German, as the Habsburgs would have preferred.

At **FÜZÉRRADVÁNY**, 4km on, the **Castle Garden** (*Kastély Kert*) surrounding a derelict manor house has an arboretum of variegated oaks and pines which provides a haven for vipers and other wildlife. Buses stop by an avenue of pines that leads into the park (daily 9am–5pm). If the main gates are closed, follow the road round to the left and ask at the lodge. Füzérradvány village has a youth camp (*Ifusági Tábor*) which sometimes lets **rooms** from April to October (ask *Express* in Sátoraljaújhely), or you can stay at the *Nagy-Tanya Fogadó* (☎ Pálháza 59; ②) across the road. During summer it's wise to book through *Express* in Budapest or Sátoraljaújhely.

Another kilometre or so up the road lies **PÁLHÁZA**, the place to board the **narrow-gauge railway** that runs 8km up to Rostálló, in the mountains. This *erdei vasut* (forest railway) runs three times daily between April 15 and October 15, to coincide with the buses for Sátoralaújhely and Sárospatak. The railway terminal is near the *Pálháza Ipartelep* stop; to reach this by car from the main road, follow the signs to Kőkapu and then Hidasnémeti.

ROSTÁLLÓ is the starting point for **hikes** in various directions – mostly ambitious ones for which you need proper equipment and a map. A good objective is **István kut** (Stephen's Well), a silver birch wood between Rostálló, Háromhuta and Regéc, noted for its special flora and diverse butterflies.

Füzér, Hollóháza and Lászlótanya

If one excursion is your limit, the village to aim for is Füzér, a stopover for buses between Sátoraljaújhely and Hollóháza. Not only are the village and its castle beautiful, but you can also walk from here to the hunting lodge at Lászlótanya where Party bigwigs once cavorted – and maybe even stay there yourself.

FÜZÉR itself is an idyllic village of vine-swathed cottages, dignified elders and wandering animals. Depending on the time of day, its social centre shifts from the tiny church to the *Italbolt* and then the bus stop, for the last buses to Hollóháza (Mon–Fri 2.20pm; Sat, Sun & holidays 8.50pm) or Sátoraljaújhely (Mon–Fri 2.30pm; Sat, Sun & holidays 6.50pm).

The ruined **Perényi Castle** is almost directly overhead, although screened by trees and the precipitous angle of the hill. Erected in case the Mongols should return, it served as a repository for the Hungarian crown from 1301 to 1310, while foreign rivals squabbled over the throne. From the huge Gothic arches of its roofless chapel there's a magnificent view of blue-green mountains along the border, and the distant Plain, enlivened by flocks of swifts swooping and soaring on the powerful thermals. Due to the microclimate, the hillsides abound in **wildlife**, with special flora, vipers, birds of prey, and – sometimes – wolves and wildcats.

Accommodation can be found at the school on Kossuth utca (②; downhill from the bus stop; cross the bridge and turn right), where you should contact Bodnár Józsefné. With a bit of luck, however, you may be able to stay at Lászlótanya instead (see below).

The **porcelain factory** in the village of **HOLLÓHÁZA** was founded in 1831, and there's a **museum** relating its history (Tues–Sun May–Sept 9am–5pm; March, April, Oct & Nov 10am–4pm) with a shop (Tues–Sat 10am–4pm) selling unbelievably lurid, flowery examples. At the top end of the village is a small modern **church**, one wall bearing the stations of the cross (designed by the ceramicist Margit Kovács). However, the chief reason to come is to catch **buses** across the mountains to Kéked and Abaújvár (see p.254), leaving twice a day on weekdays; or to drive a few miles further north, up to Lászlótanya.

Accessible by road from Hollóháza, or a four-kilometre hike from Füzér, the tiny hamlet of **LÁSZLÓTANYA** gets its name from the former **hunting lodge** of László Károlyi, which stands only 400m from the Czechoslovak border. During the

Fifties, the lodge served as a holiday resort for top Communist officials – notably the then Party leader Mátyás Rákosi, the route being lined by ÁVO guards during his visits. It subsequently became a trade union resort, and from spring 1992 should be open to tourists, with rooms for around 1000Ft (☎Hollóháza 8). Hopefully, the mock-Tudor decor and cedarwood-panelled bar will stay but the tacky furniture won't. Should you feel like sleeping where the dictator once slept, the entrance to **Rákosi's suite** is via the doors at the top of the stairs.

travel details

Trains

From Budapest (Keleti station) to Eger (7.45am, 12.30pm & 5.30pm daily; 2hr); Miskolc (6.10am, 7am, 10am, noon, 1pm, 2.30pm, 4pm, 5pm, 6pm, 7pm & 8pm daily; 1hr 45min–2hr 15min).

From Balassagyarmat to Diósjenő and Vác (6.15am, 7.35am, 11am, 2.30pm & 7.10pm daily & Mon–Sat 1.30pm; 1hr/2hr).

From Eger to Budapest (7.10am, 1.30pm & 4.10pm daily; 2hr); Putnok (7.30am, 9.45am, 2.40pm, 4.45pm & 7.50pm daily; 3hr).

From Füzesabony to Debrecen (7.15am, 10.45am, 2.20pm, 5pm & 7.15pm daily; 2hr); Eger (every 60–90min; 30min); Hortobágy (7.15am, 10.45am, 2.20pm, 5pm & 7.15pm daily; 1hr); Tiszafüred (7.15am, 10.45am, 2.20pm, 5pm & 7.15pm daily; 30min).

From Gyöngyös to Mátrafüred (hourly; 1hr).

From Hatvan to Salgótarján (every 60–90min; 1hr–1hr 30min).

From Miskolc to Kazincbarcika (every 2hr; 30min); Putnok (every 2hr; 1hr); Nyíregyháza (every 60–90min; 2hr); Ózd (every 2hr; 2hr); Tornanádaska (8 daily; 2hr); Sártoraljaújhely (8.30am, 9.20am, 4pm, 6.30pm & 7.20pm daily; 1hr–1hr 30min); Szerencs (hourly; 30min).

From Szerencs Boldogkőváralja (6.35am, 9.15am, 2.30pm & 5.10pm daily; 1hr); Gönc (6.35am, 9.15am, 2.30pm & 5.10pm daily; 1hr 15min); Mád (6.35am, 7.50am, 9.15am, 10am, 12.40pm, 2.30pm, 4.10pm & 5.10pm daily; 15min); Tállya (6.35am, 7.50am, 9.15am, 10am, 12.40pm, 2.30pm, 4.10pm & 5.10pm daily; 30min); Tokaj and Nyíregyháza (frequently; 1hr/2hr).

Buses

From Budapest (Népstadion) to Aggtelek (6.15am daily; 5hr); Balassagyarmat (every 1–2hr;

2hr 30min); Eger (every 90min; 3hr); Lillafüred (8am daily; 3hr 30min); Mátraháza (7.10am, 8.10am, 5.10pm & 6.45pm daily; 2hr).

From Aggtelek to Budapest (3.15pm daily; 5hr); Eger (3.15pm daily; 4hr).

From Balassagyarmat to Budapest (every 1–2hr; 2hr 30min); Salgótarján (hourly; 1hr); Szécsény (hourly; 1hr).

From Eger to Abádszálok (5.45am & 3pm daily; 1hr 15min); Aggtelek (8.40am daily; 4hr); Békéscsaba (5.45am & 3pm daily; 5hr); Budapest (every 90min; 3hr); Debrecen (6.10am daily; 2hr 45min); Gyöngyös (7.45am daily; 1hr 30min); Gyula (5.45am daily; 5hr 30min); Hajdúszoboszló (6.10am daily; 3hr 15min); Hortobágy (6.10am daily; 2hr 30min); Jászberény (Mon–Sat 1.20pm & Sun 4.50pm; 2hr); Kecskemét (7.35am & 12.25pm daily; 4hr); Mátraháza (7.45am daily; 2hr); Miskolc via the Bükk (Sun 7am & 11.25am; 2hr 30min); Recsk (Mon–Sat 8.50am; 1hr 45min); Salgótarján (Mon–Sat 6.10am, 8.50am, 4.10pm & 5.30pm; 2hr); Sirok (Mon–Sat 8.50am; 1hr 30min); Szeged (5.25am daily; 5hr); Szilvásvárad (hourly; 1hr); Szolnok (2pm daily, Mon–Fri 8.15am & Mon–Sat 1.20pm; 2hr 30min); Tiszafüred (6.10am & 2pm daily; 1hr 15min).

From Füzesabony to Tiszafüred (hourly; 45min).

From Gyöngyös to Abádszálok (7.20am daily; 2hr); Debrecen (7.20am daily; 4hr 30min); Eger (1.45pm daily; 1hr 30min); Miskolc (1.45pm daily; 3hr 15min); Mátrafüred (every 20min; 30min); Mátraháza (hourly; 45min).

From Hatvan to Gyöngyös (hourly; 30min); Hollókő (3 daily; 1hr 30min).

From Hollókő to Szécsény (3 daily; 45min); Hatvan (3 daily; 1hr 30min).

From Mátraháza to Eger (1pm daily; 2hr); Gyöngyös (1pm daily; 45min); Miskolc (1pm daily; 4hr).

From Miskolc to Aggtelek (1pm daily; 3hr); Békéscsaba (2.30pm daily; 5hr); Bükkszentkereszt (Sun 6.25am; 1hr); Bükkszentlászló (every 20min; 45min); Debrecen (2.30pm daily; 2hr); Eger via the Bükk (Sun 6.25am & 3.15pm; 2hr 15min); Eger via Noszvaj (1.30pm daily; 2hr 15min); Hajdúböszörmény (2.30pm daily; 1hr 30min); Jászberény (1pm daily; 5hr); Lillafüred (every 20min; 30min); Mátraháza (6am daily; 4hr); Miskolc–Tapolca (every 10min; 15min); Nyíregyháza (Mon–Sat 5am; 2hr); Ómassa (every 20min; 45min); Recsk (Mon–Sat noon; 1hr); Sirok (Mon–Sat noon; 1hr 15min).

From Ózd to Aggtelek (3pm daily; 1hr 30min); Debrecen (10.30am & 11.55am daily; 3hr 45min); Miskolc (10.30am & 11.55am daily; 3hr 30min).

From Paradfürdő to Debrecen (5am daily; 4hr); Eger (5am daily; 1hr); Hajdúszoboszló (5am daily; 4hr 30min); Tiszafüred (5am daily; 2hr 45min).

From Putnok to Aggtelek (5–6 daily; 30min).

From Salgótarján to Eger (Mon–Sat noon, 1.30pm, 3.30pm & 4.10pm; 1hr 45min); Debrecen (5.30am daily; 2hr 15min); Gyula (5.30am daily; 5hr 15min); Hajdúböszörmény (every 30–90min; 1hr 45min); Hajdúszoboszló (7am daily & Mon–Sat 10.10am & 3.30pm; 2hr 30min); Hódmezővásárhely (5.30am daily; 6hr); Szeged (5.30am daily; 6hr 30min); Szentes (5.30am daily; 5hr 15min).

From Sárospatak to Sátoraljaújhely (hourly; 20min).

From Sártoraljaújhely to Füzér (hourly; 45min).

From Szécsény to Hollókő (3pm daily; 45min).

International trains

From Miskolc (Tiszai Station) to Bucharest (July–Sept 9.10am daily; 26hr 30min); Cluj (July–Sept 9.10am daily; 10hr 15min); Košice (8.25am, 8.45am, 3.40pm, 7.20pm & 9.20pm daily; 2hr); Kraków (3.45pm & 9.20pm daily & July–Sept 7pm daily; 11hr 15min); Poprad Tatry (8.45am daily; 3hr 45min); Varna (July–Sept 9.10am daily; 26hr 30min); Warsaw (1.20pm daily & July–Sept 7pm daily; 14hr).

From Salgótarján to Częstochowa (1.25am daily; 10hr 15min); Katowice (1.25am daily; 9hr); Warsaw (1.25am daily; 13hr).

International buses

From Balassagyarmat to Banská Bystrica (June–Sept 5.20pm daily; 3hr); Lučenec (June–Sept 7pm daily; 3hr 15min); Žilina (June–Sept 5.20pm daily; 4hr 45min).

From Eger to Banská Bystrica (June–Aug 5.10pm daily; 4hr); Lučenec (Mon–Sat 6.10am; 3hr 30min).

From Kazincbarcika to Moldava nad Bodvou (Mon–Fri 6.25am; 2hr 30min).

From Miskolc to Košice (2–4 weekly; 2hr 30min); Rožňava (Mon–Sat 7.15am & Wed, Fri & Sat 5.30pm; 3hr); Uzhgorod (5.20am daily; 7hr); Velké Kapušany (July–Sept Wed & Fri 3.30pm; 3hr); Zemplinska Širava (June–Sept Mon, Wed & Fri 4pm; 3hr 30min).

From Ózd to Rimavská Sobota (Mon–Fri 7am; 1hr 30min); Uzhgorod (4am daily; 8hr 30min).

From Salgótarján to Banská Bystrica (June–Aug 6.45pm daily; 3hr); Lučenec (Mon–Sat 8.15am; 1hr 30min).

From Sárospatak to Trebišov (6am daily; 1hr 45min); Velké Kapušany (July–Sept Sat & Sun 5pm; 2hr).

From Sátoraljaújhely to Trebišov (6.30am daily; 1hr 15min); Velké Kapušany (July–Sept Sat & Sun 5.30pm; 1hr 30min).

CHAPTER SIX

THE GREAT PLAIN

Covering half of Hungary and awesome in its flatness, the **Great Plain** or **puszta** can shimmer like the mirages of Hortobágy, or be as drab as a farmworker's boots. Chance encounters and fleeting details are often more interesting than "sights" on the Plain, and if vast herds no longer roam freely as in the nineteenth century, many villages look virtually unchanged, their whitewashed farmsteads (*tanya*) hung with strings of paprika, with their rustic artesian wells and clouds of geese. One-street affairs with names prefixed *Nagy-* or *Kis-* (Big or Little), they're at their most archaic in Szabolcs-Szatmár county, where the majority of Hungarian Gypsies live.

Residents of **Debrecen** and **Szeged** disagree over which is the more sophisticated city; Szeged deserves the accolade if restaurants, architecture and festivals are the main criteria, but both have lots of students and a high cultural profile. The **towns** of Kecskémet, Baja, Hajdúszoboszló and Nyírbátor all offer some excuse for a visit, and a few more have at least one redeeming feature, yet the main attractions are possibly the **national parks**, preserving the wildlife and landscape of the old puszta. The **Kiskunság**, due south of Kecskemét, is rather overshadowed by the **Hortobágy**, a mirage-prone steppe where an equestrian Bridge Fair is held on August 19–20. This more or less coincides with **festivals** in Debrecen and Szeged: a Flower Carnival on St Stephen's Day, plus the climax to the Szeged Weeks of music and drama. The *Téka Tabor* festival at Nagykálló in late July will delight anyone interested in Magyar folk arts, whilst the pilgrimages to Máriapócs cast a fascinating light on religious life in Hungary.

The Puszta: a brief history

The word *puszta* is nowadays practically synonymous with the Great Plain (*az Nagyalfold*), but it's actually a name that describes the transformation of this huge lowland. During medieval times **the Plain** was thickly forested, with hundreds of villages living off agriculture and livestock rearing, and the mighty **River Tisza**, fed by its tributaries in Transylvania and Maramures, determined all. Each year it flooded, its hundreds of loops merging into a "sea of water in which the trees were sunk to their crowns", enriching the soil with volcanic silt from the uplands and isolating the villages for months on end. But the Turkish invasion of 1526 unleashed a scourge upon the land: 150 years of nearly unceasing warfare. The peasants that survived fled to the safer *khasse* (tribute-paying) towns like Szeged and Debrecen, leaving their villages to fall into ruin, while vast tracts of forest were felled to build military stockades, or burned simply to deny cover to the partisans (*Hajdúk*). Denuded of vegetation, the land became swampy and pestilent with mosquitoes, and later the abode of solitary swineherds, runaway serfs, outlaws (*betyár*) and wolves. People began calling it **the puszta**, meaning "aban-

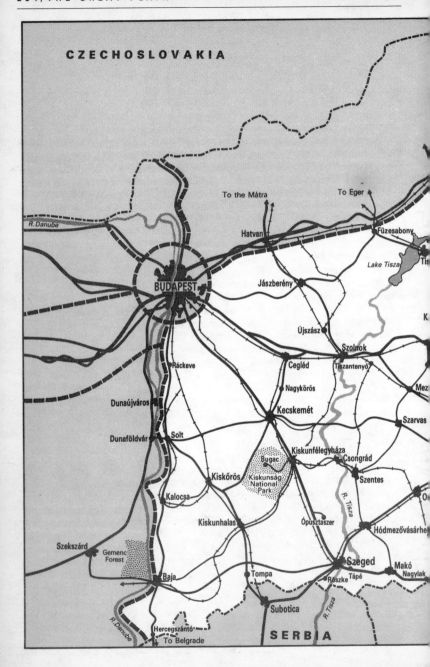

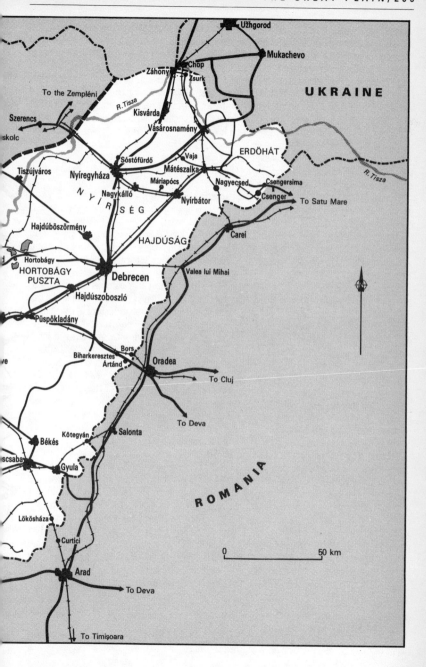

doned, deserted, bleak"; and something of its character is conveyed by other words and phrases with the same root, for example *pusztít* (to devastate), *pusztul* (perish, be ruined), and *pusztulj innen* (Clear out of here!). Not surprisingly, most folks shunned it, or ventured in solely out of dire necessity.

Yet another transformation began in the nineteenth century, as an unexpected consequence of Count Szechényi's flood-control work along the Tisza, when soil alkalinity increased the spread of **grassland**. Suitable only for pasturage, in time this became the "Hungarian Wild West", complete with rough-riding *csikós* (cowboys), and wayside *csárda* where lawmen, Gypsies and outlaws shared the same tables, bound not to fight by the custom of the puszta. It was a man's world – women and children remained in the farmsteads close to town – and nine-teenth-century romantics like Sándor Petőfi rhapsodised over it as the incarnation of Magyardom. "My world and home . . . the Alföld, the open sea."

By the 1920s reality had crushed romance. Irrigation enabled landowners to grow crops on, and enclose, common pasture. Mechanisation denied the evicted sharecroppers and herders even the chance of work on the big estates. Most of Hungary's landless peasants, or **"three million beggars"**, lived on the Plain, and their efforts to form Agrarian leagues were violently opposed by the gentry and gendarmerie, particularly around *Viharsarok* – the "Stormy centre", today's Békés county.

True to their promises, the Communists distributed big estates amongst the peasantry and **nationalised land** "for those who till it" in 1947, but, following the dictates of Stalinism, forced them to join state-run co-operative farms two years later. Treated as socalist serfs, they reverted to subsidence production; unami-mously dissolving "their" co-operatives in 1956, while vowing to prevent the land-lords from returning. Bearing this in mind, the Party pursued a subtler **agricultural policy** from the Sixties onwards, investing in ever larger co-operative and state farms, whilst allowing peasants to sell the produce of their "household plots" (limited to 1.5 acres), which accounted for half the meat and 70 percent of the fruit and vegetables produced in Hungary. By Eastern European standards the co-operatives were successful, producing a grain surplus that earned one third of Hungary's hard currency income; but the urge to be master of their own land remained strong amongst the peasantry.

During the 1990 election, the **Smallholder's Party** pledged to dissolve the co-operatives and return the land to its pre-1947 owners, winning a majority of votes cast on the Plain. Following intensive negotiations with the Democratic Forum, a compromise was agreed whereby co-operative farm workers could claim 3.7 acres, while previous owners would be entitled to compensation. The conse-quences of this are still uncertain, since no-one is sure how many co-operatives will remain viable, or whether the new **private farmers** will have enough land or be able to afford the machinery to work it. While many envisage a profitable future, others fear that the ex-Party "mafia" will appropriate the best land, or argue that large-scale farming is more rational, anyway. Opponents riposte that forty years of intensive agriculture has degraded the soil and rivers, and that only small-scale organic farming can restore the **environment** to health.

Getting There

With its often monotonous vistas and widely spaced towns, the Plain is something most people cross as much as visit, and if you're pressed for time, large areas can

THE "BLACK TRAIN"

Every Friday hundreds of migrant workers return to their homes in northeastern Hungary for the weekend, aboard the so-called "**black train**" (*fekete vonat*). The sobriquet actually applies to half a dozen trains leaving Budapest's Nyugati Station between 4pm and 7pm, bound for Debrecen and Nyíregyháza. Notorious for drunken passengers (home-brewed *pálinka* is sold in the toilets), gambling, theft and brawls, they are best avoided by women and the faint-hearted, but might appeal to adventurous types. As a foreigner, you are likely to be accosted by Gypsies, whom the trains' barmen describe as "good company, but then they drink all their wages and want to fight". I was once rescued from such a bunch by an elderly nurse; as she led me away, they shouted "she wants to fuck you in the toilet". However, at least you needn't worry about outlaws holding the train up, which happened in the 1860s when the famous *betyár* Sándor Rózsa preyed on the first railway across the Plain.

be skipped with a clear conscience. The region between the Danube and the Tisza is chiefly notable for Szeged, Kecskemét and Kiskunság National Park, while Debrecen, Hortobágy and the Nyírség are the highlights beyond the River Tisza. Few other places merit more than an excursion or a stopover, though visitors into rural life or cycling might want to consider more off-the-beaten-track destinations.

Intercity buses from Budapest's Népstadion terminal are the quickest way of reaching virtually everywhere as far east as Szeged or Szolnok, including towns such as Kecskemét and Baja, which are awkward or impossible to reach by train. **Trains** come into their own for the long hauls to Debrecen and Nyíregyháza (see box above), or for visiting the remote northeast (the only occasion when local *személyvonat* trains are useful). All these services from Budapest are covered under "Travel Details" at the end of Chapter One.

Although **hitchhiking** is feasible along the trunk routes to Baja, Szeged and Debrecen, it's not worth attempting it elsewhere unless there's no alternative. Conversely, **cyclists** are banned from major (single-digit) roads, but should find minor ones delightful. Carts and animals are more common than cars, and wild-flowers bloom along the verges.

BETWEEN THE DANUBE AND THE TISZA

Approaching from the direction of Budapest or Transdanubia, your first experience of the Plain will be the region **between the Danube and the Tisza**. Its chief attractions lie along two main routes from Budapest: Kalocsa and Baja, on the road following the Danube southwards; and Kecskemét and Szeged, on the trunk road towards Romania. If you're short of time and want to see something of the puszta grasslands, the second itinerary has a lot more to offer. Other towns, such as Cegléd or Jászberény, can easily be visited en route or as day trips.

South to Kalocsa and Baja

The route south from Budapest should only be undertaken if you like the sound of laid-back **Baja**, on the lower reaches of the Danube. Although **Kalocsa** certainly deserves a look along the way, it's not worth a special trip. Whether you visit **Ráckeve**, closer to Budapest, depends on your means of transport: a convenient stopover by car, but not by bus, it is most easily reached by train from Budapest as a separate excursion.

Ráckeve

Situated on the east bank of Csepel Island, 50km outside Budapest, the little town of **RÁCKEVE** harbours two monuments of unexpected splendour. To **get there** by car, turn off the main road just beyond Kiskunlacháza; alternatively, HÉV trains depart every twenty minutes from Budapest's Soroksári út terminal (bus #23 or #54 from Boráros tér), a journey of around an hour and a quarter.

A short distance from the HÉV terminal stands the **Savoy Mansion**, a grandiose fusion of Italian and French Baroque with a Neoclassical dome and other nineteenth-century additions. The original building overlooking the Danube was commissioned by Prince Eugene of Savoy, shortly after his armies drove the Turks from Hungary, and was built between was 1702 and 1722 according to the designs of JL Hildebrandt. Belatedly restored in the 1970s after decades of neglect, it now faces an uncertain future as an architects' resort and/or hotel-cum-conference centre – should either prove to be financially viable. Meanwhile, visitors can blag their way in to admire the opulent decor and octagonal stateroom.

Ironically, Ráckeve was founded by Serbs (*Rác* in Hungarian) fleeing from the advancing Turks some two hundred years earlier. Its **Serbian Orthodox Church**, at the west end of the town centre, is the oldest in Hungary – dating from 1487 – and is quite magnificent. A Baroque iconostasis and frescoes by Tódor Gruntovich glow within its vaulted Gothic nave like gems against velvet.

Ráckeve is easily visited on a day trip from Budapest, but if you do want **to stay** here, the *Keve Hotel* on Elnök tér (☎26/85-047; ③) is a less indulgent alternative to the expensive *Savoyai-Kastély* (☎26/85-25; ⑤).

Kalocsa

KALOCSA, around 120km from Budapest by bus, is promoted for its **"Painting Women"** and flowery **embroidery**, and as Hungary's **"paprika capital"** – all of which hold some appeal providing you avoid the tour groups and kitsch "folk displays". Together with other sights in town, they fully justify a stopover – but no more: an approach encouraged by regular buses on to Baja, further south. The bus station is within walking distance of all the sights.

The **Paprika Museum** on nearby Szent István út (May–Oct Tues–Sun 10am–noon & 1–5pm) lacks intelligible captions or the allure of paprika *al fresco*, but it's worth a quick look and you'll get the gist of the exhibits easily enough (see box below). A more rewarding stop is the **Viski Károly Museum** at Szent István út 25 (Tues–Sun 9am–5pm), ten minutes' walk past the tourist office and *Piros Arany* hotel. Upstairs you'll find a dazzling collection of nineteenth-century Magyar, Swabian (*Sváb*) and Slovak (*Tót*) folk costumes. The overstuffed bolsters and quilts on display were mandatory for a bride's dowry, recalling the woman in a Panaït Istrati novel who rages "Why should I spend months sewing them, for some fat pig to muddy with his boots?"

Carrying on into Szabadság tér, the old main square, you'll find Kalocsa's Baroque **Cathedral**, whose scruffy facade belies its delicate pink and gold interior. The nearby **Archbishop's Palace** dates likewise from the eighteenth century, but its grandeur recalls the medieval heyday of Kalocsa's bishopric, when local prelates led armies and advised monarchs. Its 120,000-volume **library** contains a Bible signed by Luther, and impressive paintings by Maulbertsch.

Following Kossuth utca off to the right as far as the hospital, you'll see a signpost for the thatched **Folk Art House** or *Népmüveszeti Szövetkezet* on Tompa utca (Tues–Sun 9am–5pm). Several of its rooms are decorated with exuberant floral murals, traditionally found in the *tiszta szoba* or "clean room" of peasant households, where guests were entertained. In Kalocsa, almost uniquely, these were painted by groups of women, who were respected artisans. Also displayed is a host of Kalocsa embroidery, which has changed a lot since the 1920s. Whereas nineteenth-century embroiderers used only red, blue, white and black yarns to produce assured designs, the modern stuff is multicoloured and rather twee.

Finally, for something completely different, check out the 22-metre-high **Chronos 8 light tower** that beams over Kalocsa; or the smaller, kinetic works of Nicolas Schöffer, the local-born Parisian conceptual sculptor, in the **Nicolas Schöffer Museum** at Szent István út 76 (Tues–Sun 10am–noon & 2–5pm).

Practicalities

Pusztatourist (Mon–Fri 7.30am–4.30pm; July & Aug also Sat 7.30am–noon; ☎78/779) at Szent István út 35 is next door to the run-down *Hotel Piros Arany* (☎78/62-220; ②). On Szabadság tér stands the more salubrious *Kalocsa Hotel* (☎78/11-931; ③). There are restaurants in both hotels, and other places to eat and drink on Petőfi utca. Buses leave for Baja every thirty to ninety minutes.

PAPRIKA

The countryside around Kalocsa and Szeged produces more **paprika** than anywhere else in Hungary, a country where this plant of the Capsicum genus is esteemed as "red gold" (*piros arany*). No one knows when paprika was introduced (during the Age of Migrations, via the Balkans, is one theory; from America, by Columbus, is another), but demand for it was assured by the continental blockades of the Napoleonic Wars, which compelled Europeans to find a substitute for pepper.

The nineteenth-century preference for milder paprika spurred cross-fertilisation and research, which led to the discovery of Capsaicin, produced by the plant in response to drought and sunlight, and responsible for its piquancy. Inventions like the Pálffy roller frame eased the laborious task of chopping and grinding, while the plant's nutritional qualities (shepherds were said to remain healthy on a diet of paprika and bacon) were investigated by **Dr Albert Szent-Györgyi** of Szeged University, who was awarded a Nobel Prize for synthesising vitamin C in 1933 (paprika is also rich in vitamin A).

The 23 villages around Kalocsa are devoted to paprika-growing. During **harvest season** (which traditionally begins on Sept 8), the countryside is an Impressionist dream of verdant shrubs and tapering scarlet pods, with carpets and garlands of paprika in every hue of red on the roadsides and houses for weeks afterwards.

Baja

BAJA, 76km further south, has an almost Mediterranean feel, with respectable citizens promenading up and down Eötvös utca, and young bloods revving their motorcycles around Béke tér. The languid atmosphere and the shady banks of the Sugovica-Danube are the main attractions, for this is basically a town in which to rest. If that sounds too sleepy, come during the **Danube Folklore Festival** (July 15–17) or the Baja **Summer Days** in late August.

From the bus station on Csermák Mihály tér, it's a ten-minute signposted walk to **Béke tér** (Peace Square), overlooking the Sugovica. Off to one side, on Roosevelt tér, the **Turr István Museum** (Tues–Sun 10am–6pm) contains an interesting exhibition on the Danube's history, and a picture gallery. The museum is named after a Hungarian general who fought alongside Garibaldi in Italy, just as many Poles and Italians aided Hungary against the Habsburgs.

Icon buffs should visit the **Serbian Orthodox Church** on Táncsics utca, one of two ministering to locals of Serbian descent. There is also a German high school catering to a smaller community of Swabians, whom the Habsburgs encouraged to settle here after the Turks were evicted. A left turn slightly further along will bring you to a Neoclassical **Synagogue** on Munkácsy utca, which now serves as a library.

Across the river from the main square lies **Petőfi Island**, where Baja's festivals are held: a nice place to go boating, swimming or fishing. It was from here that the last Habsburg emperor was ignominiously deported (see box below).

Practicalities

For **information** or private rooms, contact *Pusztatourist* (Mon–Fri 8am–4pm, Sat 8am–noon; ☎79/11-153) on Béké tér. Across the square is the old-fashioned *Hotel Duna* (☎79/11-765; ②), which, like the *Kolbri Panzió* at Batthyány utca 18 (☎76/21-628; ②), offers cheaper **rooms** than the *Hotel Sugovica* (☎79/12-988; ④) on Petőfi Island. Just beyond the latter is a shady campsite (May–Sept) with huts and chalets, where pheasants strut around at dawn.

Several cafés spill out on to Béké tér, where the *Belvárosi Cukrászda* sometimes features live music. Besides hotel **restaurants**, you can eat at the *Védió*

THE LAST OF THE HABSBURGS ?

Although the Habsburg Empire ended with the abdication of **Karl IV** and the establishment of republics in Austria and Hungary in 1918, the dynasty refused to die. In October 1921, Karl attempted to regain the Hungarian throne by flying into Baja, where a royalist force awaited him with lorries supplied by Major Lehár (cousin of Franz, composer of *The Merry Widow*). However, their advance on Budapest was swiftly halted by regular troops, and a British gunboat transported Karl into exile in Madeira. His widow **Zita** was barred from Austria until 1982 for refusing to renounce her claim, and only returned thereafter to be buried in Vienna.

Meanwhile, their son **Otto** had become a Euro MP and roving ambassador to the former Habsburg territories. An apocryphal story has it that when asked if he would be watching the Austria–Hungary football match, Otto replied, "Who are we playing?". Having retained Hungarian citizenship, he is also entitled to stand for parliament in Budapest, where nostalgia for the Dual Monarchy may yet restore a Habsburg to authority.

Étterem on Petőfi Island, or the *Csitanyica Vendéglő* at Szabadsag út 84. The *Belvárosi Cukrászda* and the *Hotel Sugovica* regularly host **discos**.

From the inter-city terminal on Csermák Mihály tér, there are regular **buses** to Kecskemét (8 daily; 3hr) and Szeged (1 daily; 5hr) on the Plain; and Mohács (4 daily; 40min) and Pécs (4 daily; 2hr) in Transdanubia. However, **trains** are really only useful for reaching Kiskunhalas (7 daily; 1–2hr).

Jászberény

JÁSZBERÉNY, 50km east of Budapest, with regular buses from the capital, Cegléd and Szolnok, and from Hatvan in the northern uplands, merits a passing mention for its historic links to the **Jász** (Jazygians), an Iranian-speaking people who migrated here from around the Caspian Sea at the beginning of the thirteenth century. Granted feudal privileges by Béla III, they prospered as cattle-breeders, tanners and furriers, each extended family owning several farms and a town house. A dozen settlements with names prefixed by "Jász-" denotes the extent of the Jászság region, which remained semi-autonomous until the 1890s, by which time they had become totally assimilated. As Patrick Leigh Fermor wrote, "this entire nation seems to have vanished like a will o' the wisp, and only these place-names mark the points of their evaporation".

Jász culture and history are explored in the **Jász Museum** (Tues–Sun 9am–5pm), which occupies the splendid old town hall on Lehel tér. The museum's star exhibit is the ivory **Lehel Horn**, intricately carved with hunting scenes. According to Jász tradition, this belonged to a Magyar general, Lehel, whom the German emperor Otto I defeated near Augsburg in 955. Legend has it that Lehel begged to be allowed to blow his horn before being executed, and, when the last notes had faded, suddenly stabbed Otto to death with it. Alas for legend, the horn is reckoned to be of eleventh- or twelfth-century Byzantine origin, and it was Lehel, not Otto, who perished at Augsburg.

You can **stay** at the *Hotel Touring*, Serház út 3 (☎57/12-051; ③), the *Kakukkfészek Panzió*, Táncsics út 8 (☎57/12-345; ②), or in rooms through *IBUSZ* (☎57/12-143) on Lehel tér. For **food**, try the *Lehel Gyöngye Étterem*, Fémnyomó utca 2, the *Lehel Étterem*, Lehel tér 34, or the *Mátyás Ételbár*, Déryné utca 2.

Cegléd and Nagykőrös

CEGLÉD straddles two major railway lines across the Great Plain, linking Budapest with Debrecen to the east, and Kecskemét and Szeged to the south. With an hour or so to kill between connections, you can check out the **Kossuth Museum** (Tues–Sun 10am–6pm) on Rákóczi út, between the railway station and the centre. A large oil painting in the foyer depicts the execution of György Dózsa, leader of the 1514 Peasants' Revolt, who was "crowned" upon a red-hot throne in Timişoara by the nobility. Some of his charred flesh was force-fed to his lieutenants, and the remainder impaled on the gates of five Hungarian cities as a warning. Three centuries later, the local peasantry responded enthusiastically to Kossuth's call for volunteers to defend the gains of the 1848 Revolution – principally the abolition of serfdom. The museum preserves the oak table on which he stood to speak, while a statue marks the site on Szabadság tér, near the bus terminal.

Another clue to the region's history is provided by **NAGYKŐRÖS**, further down the line towards Kecskemét. Like other settlements with names ending in "-kőrös", it recalls the so-called **Kőrös people**, who raised sheep and tumuli on the Plain during the Neolithic era (5500–3400 BC). Near the bus terminal in the town centre is an **ornamental garden** (*Cifrakert*) containing the **Arany János Museum** (May–Sept Tues–Sun 10am–6pm), which commemorates the life and works of the poet, librettist and balladeer, János Arany (1817–82). Motorists might consider lunching at the *csárda*, 500m outside town on the road in from Cegléd.

Kecskemét

Hungarians associate **KECSKEMÉT** with *barackpálinka* (the local apricot brandy) and the composer Kodály (who was born in what is now the railway station), but its cultural significance doesn't end there. The town centre boasts some of the finest architecture on the Plain, while its film studio and festivals impart a metropolitan pizzazz. Given this sophistication, you would never imagine that its name derives from the Hungarian word for "goat" (*kecske*).

Kecskemét is accessible from Budapest by train from Nyugati Station (6 daily; 2hr 30min) or bus from the Népstadion terminal (13 daily; 2hr 30min).There are equally regular services from Szeged, and less frequent buses from Baja and Cegléd. **Arriving** at the railway or bus station in the northern part of town, you are ten minutes' walk from the centre, a leafy conjunction of squares.

The Town

Although nothing remains of medieval Kecskemét, its size can be judged from the ring boulevard, which follows the old moat. Unlike most towns in the region, it was spared devastation by the Turks, as the Sultan took a liking to it. Waves of refugees settled here, and Kecskemét became the third largest town in Hungary. This fortunate history, underpinned by agricultural wealth, explains its air of confidence and the flamboyant, eclectic **architecture**, skilfully integrated with modern buildings by József Kerény.

Around Szabadság tér

Heading south into the town centre, on the northern side of Szabadság tér is the **Cifra Palace**, resembling a set from *Hansel and Gretl* on acid, ceramic mushrooms sprouting from psychedelic tiles above a gingerbread facade. Designed by Géza Markus in 1912, this wonderful example of Art Nouveau (termed the "Secessionist style" in Hungary) now serves as a trade union headquarters and an **art gallery** (Tues–Sun 11am–6pm).

The Transylvanian-Gothic hulk diagonally opposite the Cifra Palace is one of two buildings in Kecskemét in the style known as **National Romanticism**. Built between 1911and 1913 as a Calvinist college,this one is a "mature" example of the genre that coincided with Hungary's millennial anniversary and campaigns to "Magyarise" ethnic minorities, reflecting the triumphalist yet paranoid *zeitgeist* of the 1890s and 1900s. Its steeply pitched roofs and intimidating tower hark back to the vernacular architecture of rural Hungary and Transylvania, regarded as pure wellsprings of Magyar culture. It now houses a **library** and **Collection of Ecclesiastical Art** (Tues–Sun 10am–6pm); the entrance is on Villám utca.

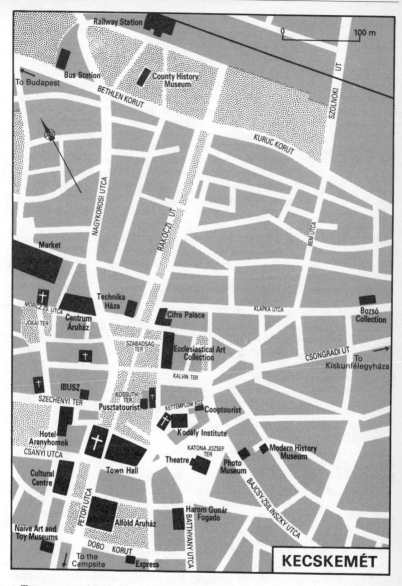

Temporary exhibitions of a scientific nature allow you to see inside the white, onion-domed **Technika-háza**, a former synagogue on Moricz Zs. utca, at the north end of the square. Built between 1862 and 1871 in the Moorish style, it was sacked by the Nazis when they deported local Jews in 1944. Another synagogue that died with its community can be found on Bajcsy-Zsilinszky utca, soon to become a museum of photography (see below).

Kossuth tér and around

To the south, across Kossuth tér, is the building that started the whole National Romanticism movement: the **Town Hall** designed by Ödön Lechner and Gyula Pártos in 1893. Like Lechner's later works in Budapest, it is richly ornamented with Zsolnay tiles inspired by the decorative traditions of Magyar folk art and nomadic Turkic cultures. However, the building itself is a Renaissance-Baroque pastiche whose lack of "authentic form" was criticised by later National Romanticists such as Károly Kós. Its Grand Hall (Mon–Fri 10–11am) contains gilded murals by Bertalan Székely, who decorated the interior of the Mátyás Church in Budapest. The bells outside play snatches of Kódaly, Handel, Beethoven, Mozart and Erkel at regular intervals.

With five churches in the vicinity you can afford to be selective; the three most interesting are on Kossuth tér. To the right of the town hall stands the so-called **Old Church**, which is Catholic and Baroque. Designed by Oswald Gáspár, an eighteenth-century Piarist father, its facade is decorated with reliefs commemorating the Seventh Wilhem Hussars and local heroes of the War of Independence. The **Calvinist Church**, behind *Pusztatourist*, was founded in 1683 and enlarged in the 1790s, when its "Red Tower" was added. Its meeting hall contains frescoes similar to those in the town hall. The **Franciscan Church**, to the east, is *really* the oldest one, but Baroque restoration has obscured its medieval features. Around the corner on Kéttemplom köz (Two Churches Lane) stands the former Franciscan monastery, which now houses the Kódaly Institute (see box opposite).

Kecskemét museums

Of the surprisingly large number of museums in Kecskemét, the best is undoubtedly the **Toy Museum** (Tues–Sun 10am–6pm) on the corner of Gáspár András and Hosszú utca. Exhibits cover toy design and manufacture through the ages, with sections on festive and foreign toys; at weekends you can play with some of them. The museum occupies an airy wooden building, specially designed by Kerényi. The **Naive Art Museum** (Tues–Sun 10am–6pm) next door is a close runner up, containing a delightful collection of naïve paintings from pre-World War I to the present day. Should you need an antidote to all this cuteness, wander round the corner to the **Medical Collection** (Tues–Sun 10am–6pm) at Kölcsey utca 3, which includes several gory exhibits.

Fans of Magyar folk art should head 500m south towards the junction of Petőfi utca and the ring boulevard (or take bus #1, #11 or #22). One block back, at Külső Szabadság út 19A, the **Museum of Hungarian Folk Craft** (Wed–Sun 9am–5pm) exhibits a wealth of textiles, pottery and embroidery from the 1950s onwards. Older artefacts, particularly furniture, are gathered in the **Bozsó Collection** (Fri–Sun 10am–6pm) at Klapka utca 34, 400m east of the Cifra Palace.

The **County History Museum** (Tues–Sun 10am–6pm), in the park near the station, has nothing much to offer, but two places around Katona tér might hold some interest. The soon-to-open **Photo Museum** occupies an old synagogue with a Star of David window and Hebrew writing on the ceiling, and will most likely display antique cameras. To see how Kecskemét has changed since the nineteenth century, track down the **Modern History Museum** (Tues–Sun 10am–6pm) on Bánk utca.

The Panonnia Filmstudió

Kecskemét is also the home of the **Pannónia Filmstudió**, whose entire output consists of **animated cartoons** – short films, television series, advertisements and

ZOLTÁN KODÁLY AND JÓZSEF KATONA

For a small town, Kecskemét has made a not inconsiderable contribution to national culture. The Spring Days festival, in particular (see "Festivals") offers a good opportunity to catch the work of its two famous sons.

Through his researches into the folk roots of Hungarian music, **Zoltán Kodály** (1882–1967) was inspired to compositions that eschewed the Baroque and Western strains his colleague Bartók termed "New Style". He also revolutionised the teaching of music, inventing the "Kodály method" that is now applied throughout Hungary and around the world. Kodály's belief that music can only be understood by actively participating in it remains the guiding principle of Kecskemét's **Institute of Music Teaching** (*Zenepedagógiai Intézet*). Students on the **one-year course** are exhorted to approach music through the human voice, "the most easily accessible instrument for all", and build upon their national folk traditions when teaching children – a task Kodály considered supremely important. "No one is too great to write for the little ones," he said, "in fact one has to strive to be great enough." For those who want to know more, there's an exhibition in the institute itself, at Kéttemplom köz 1–3.

The town can also boast of **József Katona** (1791–1830), the "father" of Hungarian romantic drama, who was born and died in Kecskemét. His masterpiece, *Bánk Bán* (later made into an opera by Erkel), revolves around the murder of Gertrude, the German-born queen of King Andrew II, by his vassal Bánk. Katona himself expired of a heart attack outside the town hall, the spot now marked by a cloven block. The fallible organ was preserved in a jewelled casket, and his name was bestowed upon Kecskemét's playhouse. During the 1980s, the **Katona Theatre** was directed by filmmaker Miklós Jancsó, whose avant-garde productions scandalised many townsfolk.

training films. Its parent company in Budapest made *Pumuckl* ("Goblins"), a big hit in Germany. The studio runs **guided tours** for groups of twenty or more by prior arrangement, so it's worth asking *Pusztatourist* if one is scheduled, or writing well beforehand to Dr Ferenc Miklós at the studio (Liszt Fő utca 21), which is located off Ceglédi út, beyond the railway station. Bus #18 from Rákóczi út runs past the door.

Practicalities

Kossuth tér is where you'll find *Pusztatourist* (Mon–Thurs 7.30am–4.30pm, Fri 8am–4pm; May–Sept also Sat 9am–1pm; ☎76/29-499), the regional **tourist organisation**; its competitor *IBUSZ* (Mon–Fri 7.30am–4pm, Sat 7.30–11am; ☎76/22-955) is nearby on Széchenyi tér, and *Cooptourist* (Mon–Fri 8.30–noon & 1–5pm) is on Kéttemplom köz. *Express* (Mon 10am–4.30pm, Tues–Fri 8am–4.30pm) is slightly further out, on the first floor of block 11, Dobó körút.

Accommodation

During the summer holidays, you may be able to get cheap **beds** in the colleges at Jókai tér 4 (☎76/21-977) or Izsáki utca 10 (☎76/21-611), bookable through *Express* or *IBUSZ*. **Private rooms** (①) from *Pusztatourist* and other agencies are also good value, and it's worth knowing that *Express* can arrange lodgings in converted **farmhouses** in the countryside. There's a **campsite** with chalets (April 15–Oct 15; ☎76/28-700) midway between the *Szauna* and *Tó* hotels, accessible by bus #22.

Otherwise, there are several **hotels** and **pensions** on offer:

Hotel Aranyhomok, Széchenyi tér 2 (☎76/20-211). Named after the "golden sands" of the puszta, but not at all romantic, its chief asset is the prime location. ④.

Három Gunár Fogadó, Batthyány utca 1 (☎76/27-077). A smart and comfortable hotel off Katona tér, with a restaurant. ⑤.

Szauna Hotel, Sport utca 3 (☎76/28-700; telex 26-227). Well equipped, with a sauna and gym, 1km south of the centre; bus #22 stops nearby. ④.

Tó Hotel, Sport utca 7 (☎76/28-166). Near a boating lake, 400m beyond the above. Also comfortable, but fewer facilities. ④.

Andi Panzió, Bácskai utca 13–15 (☎76/47-002). A very small place near the Budapest highway. ②.

Cassia Panzió An affordable, fairly central pension, situated on erstwhile Marx tér, northwest of Széchenyi tér. Cassia is the patron saint of chess – the owner is a fan. ②.

Colour Panzió, Jókai utca 26 (☎76/24-901). Another pension further west, along Móricz utca in the market district. ②.

Szőlőfürt Fogadó, István király krt 23 (☎76/21-239). A motel-cum-inn 4km out along the Békéscsaba road. ③.

Eating and drinking

Apart from the **restaurants** of the ritziest hotels, there are several decent places to eat in the town centre. Near *Pusztatourist* you'll find the *Liberté Kávéház*, a plush establishment serving wonderful stuffed mushrooms. The *HBH* is a Bavarian-style place on Csányi utca, around the corner from the Old Church. For a Magyar nosh-up, try the *Hírös Étterem* at Rákóczi út 3, 100m north of Szabadság tér. Further afield, there's the *Kisbugaci Csárda* at Munkácsy utca 10, beyond Széchenyi tér (daily noon–midnight); the *Akadémia Étterem* at Akadémia körút 19 (bus #20, #21 or #22); and the *Szélmalom Csárda*, 2.5km out along the Szeged road (closes 11pm).

All of the above are feasible **drinking** spots, while the bar opposite the *Három Gunár Fogadó* also serves food until late. Two **patisseries** worth a visit are the *Fodor Cukrászda* near the *Liberté Kávéház*, and the *Delicatesse Cukrászda* (7am–10pm) in an arcade on the corner of Kossuth and Széchenyi tér. The outdoor **market** is good for cheap snacks and fresh produce, while other purchases can be made in the *Centrum* department store on Móricz utca.

Festivals and other entertainments

Kecskemét is at its liveliest during the **Spring Days** (in late March, coinciding with the festival in Budapest), with numerous concerts and theatre performances; and over the summer, when folk groups from several countries perform at the **Danube Folklore Festival** (July 15–17). In late August, **historical pageants** and **wine-tasting** sessions enliven Szabadság tér and Petőfi utca. *Pusztatourist* has details of all these events.

Look out for posters advertising **discos** in the *Hotel Aranyhomok*, or in the Cultural Centre and *Júlia Presszó* (above the *Univer* supermarket) on Petőfi utca – generally at weekends.

Excursions and international connections

Kecskemét makes a good base for **excursions** to the Tisza resorts and the Kiskunság region (see p.277). A #2 bus from Széchenyi tér can drop you at the *Átrakó* terminal for narrow-gauge trains to Kiskunság National Park (see below).

The inter-city bus terminal near the railway station serves most other destinations, including Eger in the northern uplands.

It's from here that **buses to Romania** depart, bound for Miercurea Ciuc (Fri & Sun 6am), Oradea, Cluj and Tîrgu Mureş (Fri 6am). Note that these towns may be designated by their Hungarian names as Csíkszereda, Kolozsvár, Nagyvárad and Marosvásárhely. Depending on the political situation, there may also be services to Subotica in the Voivodina.

Lakitelek and Tiszakécske

Thirty kilometres east of Kecskemét are several low-key **resorts** where you can swim or wander beside the Tisza as it meanders through woodlands and meadows. Lakitelek and Tőserdő make for a relaxed excursion from Kecskemét or Kiskunfélegyháza, while Tiszakécske is more of a family holiday centre. **From Kecskemét**, five trains daily stop at Lakitelek en route to Kunszentmárton; to reach Tőserdő, you can take the same trains from Kecskemét, alighting at the Szikra station, or catch the bus. **From Kiskunfélegyháza**, the four daily Szolnok trains call at Lakitelek, Tiszakécske and Tőserdő.

The village of **LAKITELEK** is famous for hosting the **conference** that gave birth to the Hungarian Democratic Forum (MDF), which went on to win the 1990 elections. As the party struggles with the dilemmas of government and its own identity, the "spirit of Lakitelek" is invoked by politicians who return to press the flesh at the local **festival** (*Lakitelek Falunapok*) on the first weekend in July. Another attraction is the lovely **Tőserdő**, a sylvan nature reserve located 4km away.

Accommodation is available at the *Tölgyfa Panzió* (☎76/42-037; ③), in rented cottages arranged by *Pusztatourist* in Kecskemét (④), and at two campsites. *Autóscamping* (May–Sept; ☎76/42-012) is on the main road near the **thermal baths**, or *Tősfürdő* (open summer only). From there, a path runs 1km to the Holtág, a dead branch of the river that's nicer for swimming, with cheap **restaurants** and the other campsite (May 15–Sept 15; ☎76/42-011).

TISZAKÉCSKE, further north, has more of a tourist industry by the river. There are several restaurants, a free camping place, horse-drawn carts, a **children's railway** (May–Sept) and even **helicopter rides**. The **thermal baths** are open all year round. Buses run here hourly from Tiszakécske station, passing *Pusztatourist* at Béke utca 142 (☎76/41-012), and rooms for rent in the town centre.

The Kiskunság

The **Kiskunság** region, to the south of Kecskemét, is called "Little Cumania", after the Cumanian (*Kun*) tribes that settled here in the Middle Ages. This sandy tableland was unfit for anything but raising sheep until, in the nineteenth century, it was laboriously transformed by afforestation and soil husbandry to yield grapes and other fruit. While Magyars esteem this as "Petőfi country", where their national poet was born, its prime attractions for visitors are Kiskunság National Park and the exhibition complex at Ópusztaszer.

Kiskunfélegyháza

To Hungarian ears, **KISKUNFÉLEGYHÁZA** suggests people and paths converging on the "House of Cumania" – an apt name for a regional capital, even though the current town was created by Jazygian settlers in the 1740s, the Cumanian original having been wiped out by the Turks. This is a rural foil to urbane Kecskemét, a town that lives by geese-breeding and market gardening, with storks' nests on the chimneys and draw-wells in the courtyards.

Entering town by bus from Kecskemét, you'll pass the **Kiskun Museum** (Tues–Sun 10am–6pm), in an eighteenth-century manor house on the main street. Exhibits on the Cumanians and Jazygians and paintings of rural life by László Holló (1887–1976) pale before a section devoted to the **history of prisons**, in the very cell where the famous *betyár* Sándor Rózsa languished in 1860. The old **windmill** in the courtyard comes from the riverside village of Mindszent, where Cardinal Mindszenty was born.

Kiskunfélegyháza's main square strives to achieve the elegance of Kecskemét's, with a majolica-encrusted National Romantic **Town Hall** built by József Vass and Nándor Morbitzer in 1912. Diagonally opposite is the **Swan House** (*Hattyuház*), where Petőfi's father had a butcher's shop and the poet spent his childhood. His statue outside is decked with flowers and flags on March 15, the anniversary of the 1848 Revolution. You can also visit the **birthplace of Ferenc Móra** (1879–1934), writer, journalist and antiquarian, at Móra utca 19 (Thurs, Fri & Sat 10am–2pm); or soak in the town's **thermal baths**.

Practicalities

Coach parties **eat** at the *halászcsárda* on Petőfi tér and the *Aranyhegyi Csárda* out towards Kecskemét, making the *Arany Piva Étterem* on Blaha Lujza tér a preferable option. With most visitors just passing through, there's **accommodation** to spare at the *Hotel Kiskunság* on Petőfi tér (☎76/61-751; ②), the *Borostyán Panzió* at Szőlő utca 1 (☎76/62-573; ②), and the *Oázis Panzió* at Felszabadulás utca 13 (☎76/61-427; ②).

More likely, though, you'll simply catch the first **bus** out to Bugac (every 60–90min) or Ópusztaszer (2–3 daily), the highlights of this region.

Kiskunság National Park

The 30,000 hectares of **Kiskunság National Park** consist of several tracts of land, the largest of which starts 3km beyond the village of BUGAC. Buses from Kiskunfélegyháza can drop you near the entrance to the park (May–Oct daily 10am–5pm), whence a sandy track runs 3.5km past flower-speckled meadows and lounging shepherds, to a **farm** where *Csikós* in white pantaloons stage **equestrian displays**, riding bareback and standing up, with much cracking of whips.

Among the **animals** bred here are grey long-horned cattle, Merino sheep and Mangalica pigs (said to make the finest bacon). The surrounding reedy marshes support diverse birdlife and flora (including rare blue globe-thistles in August), and serve as baths for water buffalo, which plod back to their barns at sunset. In the wooden **Shepherds' Museum** (daily 10am–5pm) you can see felted cloaks and hand-carved pipes, and a grotesque tobacco pouch made from a ram's scrotum.

Practicalities

Apart from *Pusztatourist* excursions from Kecskemét, there are two ways of **getting to the park**. Buses from Kiskunfélegyháza drop you nearer to the entrance than narrow-gauge trains from Kecskemét to the *Bugacpuszta* station (a 90min walk from the farm), but the train ride is quicker and more fun. To catch the horse show you must get the first train (leaving 7.50am) or an early bus, since events are scheduled for groups, who then travel by buggy to a "typical" *csárda*.

You can stay near Bugac at the *Bugaci Lovas Hotel* (☎76/72-522; ③), which also offers bungalows (March 15–Nov 15); or in **rooms** in the village, reserved through *Pusztatourist*.

Kiskőrös and Kiskunhalas

Though hardly worth a visit, **KISKŐRÖS** should be mentioned as the **birthplace of Sándor Petőfi**, who made Byron look tame (see box overpage). The thatched **Petőfi House** sits incongruously in the centre, preserved as a museum (Tues–Sun 10am–6pm) that won't do much to enlighten non-Hungarian speakers. Nearby stands the first Petőfi statue in a country where every town has at least one feature named after him. Such is the cult of Petőfi (which the Communists tried to appropriate, but which Hungarian youth reclaimed as a symbol of rebellion) that Kiskőrös was elevated to the rank of a city on the 150th anniversary of his birth, in 1972. On the edge of town is a small nature reserve, the **Szücs Moorland Wood**.

If you want **to stay**, rooms are available from *Pusztatourist* (☎78/11-349) or the *Hotel Szarvas* (☎78/11-125; ②) on Petőfi tér; and **meals** are served in the hotel, the *Kurtakocsma* on József Attila utca, and the *fürdővendéglő* by the **thermal baths** (whose temperature is a constant 58°C).

Kiskunhalas

Somewhat more appealing, especially if you're interested in lace, **KISKUNHALAS** can be reached by train from Baja or Kiskunfélegyháza. The town's medieval **lace-making** industry owed its revival in the 1890s to local school teacher Maria Markovits, who studied patterns and samples from before the Turkish occupation. Her statue stands outside the **Lace House** at Kossuth utca 37A (Tues–Sun 9am–5pm), a treasury of tablecloths, ruffs and petticoats, some composed of 56 different types of stitches.

Other sights in the centre of town include a handsome **Town Hall**, and next to it, the **Thorma János Museum** (Tues–Sun 9am–5pm), which contains paintings by its namesake and colourful folk costumes. The newly opened **House of Collections** (Tues–Sun 9am–5pm) covers local history and the *oeuvre* of painter Tibor Csorba (1906–1985), who taught here before moving to Poland. Antiques and junk share stalls at the **flea market** on Wednesdays and Sundays, while saddlemaker Balázs Tóth Abonyi welcomes visitors to his workshop on Szász K. utca. At weekends, people make for the **thermal baths** (50°C) on the island in the river that flows through town, or go **fishing** north of town at Sóstó pond.

For **accommodation**, ask at *Pusztatourist* (☎77/21-455) or head straight for the *Hotel Csipke* (☎77/21-455; ②) on Semmelweiss tér, the *Malom Panzió* at Malom sor 4 (☎77/21-650; ②), or the *Sóstó Motel* (☎77/22-222; ③) and campsite (April–Oct). **Restaurants** include the *Városi Étterem* on the main square, the *Ezerjó Étterem* at Szilády utca 6, and the *Tölgyfa Étterem* at Brinkus utca 1.

Ópusztaszer Historical Park

Ópusztaszer Historical Park (April–Sept Tues–Sun 9am–5pm), just outside the village of the same name, commemorates the act of "**land taking**", when the seven Magyar tribes crossed the Carpathians and spread out across the Hungarian plains, each claiming a territory. The park supposedly marks the site of their first tribal "parliament" after the land taking – in around 896 – although the only evidence for this comes from Anonymous, writing 300 years later (see p.87). A huge memorial was erected here for the millennial anniversary celebrations of 1896, and in 1945 the Communists symbolically chose Ópusztaszer for the first distribution of land amongst the peasants.

Both themes are implicit in the diverse exhibits of the historical park. A **Village Museum** of households from southern Hungary is juxtaposed against combine harvesters, steam trains and aeroplanes. A ruined thirteenth-century monastery attests to Christian traditions, while the early freebooting, pagan Magyars are celebrated in the amazing **Cyclorama** by Árpád Feszty. This monumental canvas depicting Prince Árpád leading the tribes into the valley of Munkács was originally exhibited in Budapest's City Park. Damaged in the siege, it has only recently been restored and put back on show.

ÓPUSZTASZER itself lies 10km east of Kistelek on the Kecskemét–Szeged road. Direct **buses** to the village are scarce except on national holidays, but it's worth checking out the timetables in Kiskunfélegyháza or Szeged. Alternatively, you could try hitching from Kistelek, a stop for buses along the highway. Near the park are a basic **campsite** with huts (April 15–Oct 15; ☎62/75-123), and the *Nagy Tanya*, which serves tasty **meals**.

SÁNDOR PETŐFI

Born on New Year's Eve 1822–23, of a Slovak mother and a Southern Slav butcher-innkeeper father, **Sándor Petőfi** was to become obsessed with acting and poetry, which he started to write at the age of fifteen. As a strolling player, soldier and labourer, he absorbed the language of working people, writing lyrical poetry in the vernacular, to the outrage of critics. Moving to Budapest in 1844, Petőfi fell in with the young radical intellectuals who met at the Pilvax Café.

From this time on, poetry and deeds were inseparable. His *Nemzeti Dal* (National Song) was declaimed from the steps of the National Museum on the first day of the 1848 Revolution ("Some noisy mob had their hurly-burly outside so I left for home," complained the director). Mindful of the thousands of landless peasants encamped outside the city, Parliament bowed to the demands of the radicals and voted for the abolition of serfdom.

During the War of Independence, Petőfi fought alongside General Bem in Transylvania, and disappeared at the battle of Segesvár in July 1849. Though he was most likely trampled beyond recognition by the Cossacks' horses (as foreseen in one of his poems), Petőfi was rumoured to have survived. In 1990, entrepreneur Ferenc Morvai announced that Petőfi had been carted off to Siberia by the Russians, married a peasant woman and later died there. The Hungarian Academy refused to support Morvai's expedition to uncover the putative grave, and it was subsequently reported that forensic analysis had proved the corpse to be that of a Jewish woman.

THE LEGEND OF ATTILA

The lower reaches of the Tisza are associated with the **legend of Attila the Hun**, who died of a nasal haemorrhage following a night of passion with a new bride, Kriemhild, in 453. The body of the Scourge of God was reputedly buried in a triple-layered coffin of gold, silver and lead, and then submerged in the Tisza at an unknown spot – unknown because the pallbearers were slain before the Huns departed. Archaeologists have yet to find it, but the legend gains credence from the "treasure of Attila" (actually thought to have belonged to a Hun general) discovered at Nagyszentmiklós (in what is now Romania), and currently held by Vienna's Kunsthistoriches Museum.

Szeged

SZEGED, as cosmopolitan a place as you'll find on the Plain, straddles the Tisza like a provincial Budapest. Much of its friendly atmosphere is thanks to students from the university, while the old city's eclectic good looks have been saved by placing the ugly modern housing and industry over the river, in Újszeged. Though Kőrös folk settled here four to five thousand years ago, and the town flourished after 1225 because of its royal monopoly over the salt mines of Transylvania, Szeged's present layout dates from after the **great flood** of March 1879, which washed away all but 300 homes and compelled the population to start again from scratch. With aid from foreign capitals (after whom sections of the outer boulevard are named) the city bounced back, trumpeting its revival with huge buildings and squares where every type of architectural style made an appearance.

Arrival and orientation

Arriving at the railway station or inter-city bus terminal beyond the Belváros – the inner town, encircled by "Great" and "Small" boulevards – catch a #1 tram or a #70 bus to downtown Széchenyi tér. A few minutes' walk south from here is Klauzál tér, where you'll find *Szeged Tourist* (July & Aug daily 9am–7pm; otherwise Mon–Fri 9am–6pm, Sat 9am–2pm; ☎21-800), which is better for **information** and maps than *IBUSZ* (Mon–Fri 8am–4pm, Sat 8am–noon; ☎26-533), across the way.

Though the city's buses and trams are perfectly adequate for **getting around**, you can rent **bicycles** from the *Ezermester kölcsönző* at Stefánia utca 9 (near the *Hotel Hungária*). Western **cars** can be rented from *Avis/Cooptourist* in Kiss utca, cheaper Ladas from *Volántourist*, Fekete Sas utca 28. However, the downtown area is a pleasure to explore on foot, with the twin-spired Votive Church on Dóm tér an obvious landmark to aim for.

Around the Belváros

Heading southwest from Klauzál tér, you'll emerge on to Dugonics tér with its **Water Music Fountain**, where students congregate during breaks from the nearby **University**. The university is named, by way of restitution, after the poet **Attila József** (1905–37), whom it expelled in 1924 for a poem which began "I have no father, I have no mother, I have no god and I have no country" and

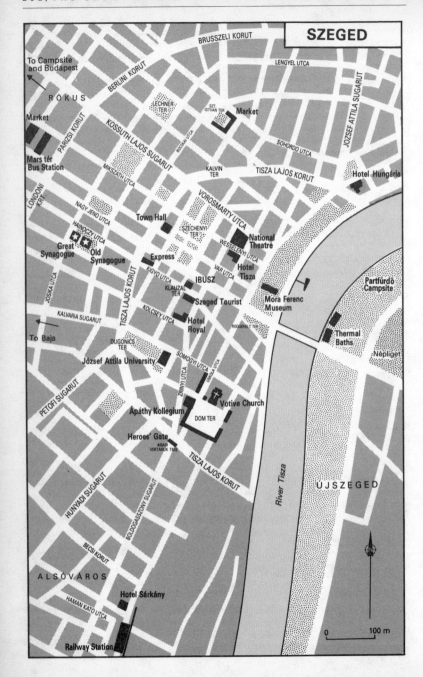

SZEGED

BRUSSZELI KORUT

LENGYEL UTCA

To Campsite
and Budapest

BERLINI KORUT

JÓZSEF ATTILA SUGARUT

RÓKUS

LECHNER
TER

SZT.
ISTVAN TER

Market

Market

PARIZSI KORUT

KOSSUTH LAJOS SUGARUT

SOHORDO UTCA

RÁKOSAI UTCA

Mars tér
Bus Station

MIKSZATH UTCA

KALVIN
TER

TISZA LAJOS KORUT

Hotel Hungária

LONDONI KRT.

NAGY JENO UTCA

VOROSMARTY UTCA

HAJNOCZY UTCA

Town Hall

SZECHENYI
TER

WESSELENYI UTCA

National
Theatre

JOSIKA UTCA

Great
Synagogue

Old
Synagogue

Express

KIGYO UTCA

VAR UTCA

Hotel
Tisza

TISZA LAJOS KORUT

IBUSZ

KLAUZAL
TER

Szeged Tourist

Mora Ferenc
Museum

Partfürdo
Campsite

KOLCSEY UTCA

Hotel
Royal

ROOSEVELT TER

Thermal
Baths

KALVARIA SUGARUT

To Baja

DUGONICS
TER

SOMOGYI UTCA

GOGOLA UTCA

Népliget

József Attila University

ZRINYI UTCA

PETOFI SUGARUT

Ápáthy Kollegium

DOM TER

Votive Church

Heroes' Gate

ARADI
VERTANUK TERE

TISZA LAJOS KORUT

HUNYADI SUGARUT

BOLDOGASSZONY SUGARUT

River Tisza

ÚJSZEGED

BECSI KORUT

ALSÓVÁROS

HAMAN KATO UTCA

Hotel Sárkány

0   100 m

Railway Station

continued "with a pure heart, I'll burn and loot, and if I have to, even shoot". Attila's bitterness was rooted in childhood, when his mother – a poor washerwoman – died of starvation. He was later also expelled from the Communist Party for trying to reconcile Marx and Freudian pyschology; lived in dire poverty; and finally jumped under a train at Lake Balaton. Though unappreciated in his lifetime, Attila's poetry now finds widespread favour. Elderly Hungarians weep upon hearing his sentimental "Mama", while anarcho-punks relish lines such as "Culture drops off me, like the clothes off a happy lover".

Head on past the university, take a left turn, and you'll come to the so-called **Black House** on the corner of Somogyi and Kelemen utca. This Romantic-style edifice is actually painted brown and white, but the ironmonger who lived here in the nineteenth century always told peasants "You can find me in the Black House". After this brief detour, walk along Zrínyi utca and turn right to reach Dóm tér.

Dom tér

Aside from the university, the main object of civic pride in Szeged is **Dóm tér**, flanked by arcades with twisted columns and busts of illustrious Hungarians. This 12,000-square-metre expanse was created in 1920 by demolishing a network of backstreets, to accommodate a gigantic **Votive Church** (Mon–Sat 9am–6pm, Sun 9.30–10am, 11–11.30am & 1–6pm) which the townsfolk had pledged to erect after the flood. Built of brown brick in the neo-Romanesque style, its portal is surmounted by a statue of the Virgin, whose image recurs inside the church in peasant costume, wearing embroidered "butterfly slippers". Visitors are dwarfed by the white, blue and gold interior, where the organ, with its 10,180 pipes and five manuals, benefits from superb acoustics.

The eight-sided **Demetrius Tower** out in front dates from the eleventh century, but was largely rebuilt by Béla Rerrich, who designed the square. A chiming clock plays the folk song "Szeged, a famous town" at midday. On the northeastern corner of Dóm tér stands an eighteenth-century **Serbian Orthodox Church** with a magnificent iconostasis framed in pear-wood.

Banked opposite the Votive Church are rows of seats for Szeged's festival, where I once caught an opera based on the life of Countess Báthori, featuring half-naked couples writhing in a vat of "blood". When performances (which start with everyone standing for the national anthem) finish, the crowds flood out towards the **Heroes' Gate** (*Hősök Kapuja*), which links Aradi Vértanúk tere with Boldogasszony sugárút. Though its origins are no longer publicised, the gate was raised to honour Horthy's henchmen, the "Whites", who gathered here in 1919, waiting for the Romanian army to defeat the Republic of Councils before they fanned out across Hungary to murder more than 5000 Jews and "Reds" in the "White Terror". Fascistic stone guardsmen still flank the archway, but Horthy's murals have been erased by dirt and time.

Around the waterfront and Széchenyi tér

By heading north past the Serbian church, you'll arrive at Roosevelt tér and the **Móra Ferenc Museum** (Tues–Sun 10am–6pm). Its Neoclassical facade of columns and decrepit statuary cloaks a typical mix of *objets d'art* and artefacts of local significance, notably a huge painting of the flood. Behind the museum you'll find the **remains of a castle** which in later times served as a prison for the outlaw Sándor Rózsa and for convicts who laboured on the river towpaths during the eighteenth century. As in Debrecen, this was a time of mass witch trials, when victims confessed to witchcraft under torture organised by the church elders.

From here you can walk up west past the **National Theatre** to spacious, verdant **Széchenyi tér**, Szeged's inner-city park. On the far (western) side stands a neo-Baroque **Town Hall**, likened by the poet Mihály Babits to "a lace-covered young woman dancing in the moonlight". The two allegorical **fountains** outside – known as "The Blessed and the Angry" – symbolise the benevolent and destructive aspects of the River Tisza. The town hall is linked to a neighbouring building by a charming "Bridge of Sighs", modelled on the one in Venice.

The Jewish Quarter and beyond

Outside its inner boulevard, Tisza Lajos körút, Szeged is shabbier and more utilitarian, but not devoid of sights. One area worth checking out is the old **Jewish quarter**, south of Nagy Jenő utca. The **Old Synagogue** on Hajinóczy utca, dating from 1843, bears a plaque showing the height of the water during the flood. Around the block on Gutenberg utca is the Secession-style **New Synagogue**, one of the largest in Europe (Mon–Fri & Sun 9am–noon & 2–5pm). Its magnificent dome represents the world, with 24 columns for the hours of day and night, white flowers for faith, and blue stars for the infinity of the cosmos. The stained-glass windows illustrate texts from *The Flora and Minerals of the Jews*, by Rabbi Immanuel Löw, and scenes from Jewish life.

Around the outer boulevard (bus #11, #21), to the south, parts of the **Alsóváros** or "lower town" resemble a village, with ochre-painted cottages and rutted streets. This quarter was traditionally inhabited by paprika growers, and centres around the **Alsóvárosi Church** on Mátyás király tér, begun in the late fifteenth century. Its reworked Baroque interior contains the *Black Madonna*, a copy of the famous Madonna of Częstochowa, and the focus of attention during the reconsecration ceremonies at the annual melon harvest festival.

The busy outdoor **markets**, on Mars tér in the Rókus quarter, and Szent István tér between the inner and outer boulevards, are well worth a visit.

Across the river and outside the city

On hot weekends people flock to the **swimming pool** or the grassy *Partfürdő strand* in Újszeged, across the river; they come in winter, too, for a wallow in the outdoor **thermal baths**. A less crowded place to get some fresh air is the **botanical garden** (*Füvészkert*) at the end of the #70 bus line.

There are opportunities for **excursions** from the city, using buses leaving from Mars tér. The fishing village of **TÁPÉ** (bus #73 or #73Y) has a couple of good restaurants, and a private Ethnographical Collection (Tues–Sun 3–6pm) at Vártó utca 4; **ALGYŐ** and **KISDOROZSMA**, 10km outside the city, have **nudist camps**. *Szeged Tourist* can arrange **birdwatching** trips to the **Fehér-tó Nature Reserve**, a haven for 250 kinds of migratory **birds**.

Practicalities

Szeged Tourist or *IBUSZ* can arrange **private rooms** (①) for considerably less than the cost of a hotel, but you should check that the location is central. These are also better value than the rooms that are available in vacant colleges (such as the *Apáthy kollegium* on Dom tér) during July and August (③). The latter are bookable through *Express* at Kigyó utca 3 (Mon–Fri 8am–4pm; ☎11-303). Local hotels, pensions and campsites are listed below; it is also feasible to stay in Makó or Hódmezővásárhely, a thirty-minute bus ride from the city. Carnivores can enjoy themselves in Szeged, which is famous for its sausages, and dishes such as *halászlé* (fish soup) and *halpaprikás* (fish in paprika sauce). As a student town, Szeged also has some good drinking places and a few discos, too.

Hotels

Hotel Hungária, Maros utca 2 (☎21-211). A three-star pile to the north of the Belváros. ⑤.

Hotel Napfény, Dorozsmai út 4 (☎25-800). Near the campsite at the start of the Budapest highway (bus #78). ③.

Hotel Royal, Kölcsey utca 1 (☎12-911). As comfortable as the *Hungária*, and dead central. Romanian gymnast Nadia Comanesti briefly took refuge here after defecting in 1989. ⑤.

Hotel Sárkány, Indóház tér 1 (☎10-514). A real dive in the vicinity of the railway station. ①.

Hotel Tisza, Wesselényi utca 1 (☎12-466). Another vintage place, between Szechényi tér and the waterfront. ④.

Pensions and campsites

Marika Panzió, Nyíl utca 45 (☎13-861). A small place in the Alsóváros, south of the railway station. ②.

Napfény Panzió, Dorozsmai út 4 (☎25-800). A bungalow-motel complex adjacent to the hotel of the same name. ② and ③.

Napfény Camping, Dorozsmai út 2 (☎25-800). Tent-space and huts, next to the above (May–Sept).

Partfürdő Camping, Középkikötő sor (☎53-811). A dearer site near the *strand* in Újszeged (May–Sept).

Restaurants

Debrecen Étterem, Széchenyi tér 9. Good for grills and salads; reasonably priced. Daily 11am–11pm.

Szeged Étterem, Széchenyi tér 13. Similar place with a terrace and violin music after 9pm. Open 9am–midnight, Sat until 2am.

Hági Étterem, Keleman utca 3. Good Brno beer and Slovak food, but patchy service. Open 11am–midnight. Cheap *Bisztró* and beerhall next door.

Alabárdos Étterem, Oskola utca 13. The smartest restaurant in town, specialising in fish and game dishes. Expensive. Mon–Sat 2–10pm; reservations advisable.

Tisza Halászcsárda, Roosevelt tér 12. Also aimed at tourists, but fish-oriented and less pricey.

Szőke Tisza Étterem. A boat restaurant serving grills, just beyond the museum. Open May–Sept.

Kiskörösi-Halászcsárda Smaller of two thatched restaurants out towards Tápé (bus #73 or #73Y), where the Prince of Wales (later Edward VIII) often came in the 1890s. Highly recommended.

Seherezáde Étterem, Szent Mihály utca 3. Arab-style place off Szent István tér, open noon–10pm.

Pagoda Étterem, Zrínyi utca 5. Unpretentious Chinese restaurant in the centre. Open noon–midnight.

Boszorkány Konyha, corner of Nagy Jenő utca and Széchenyi tér. Cheap, self-service "Witches' Kitchen".

Virág Cukrászda, Klauzál tér. Delicious cakes and ice cream. There's more of the same at the cheaper, stand-up *Kisvirág* shop across the square.

Drinking, nightlife and entertainments

Drinking spots include the *Brnoi Söröző* on Keleman utca; the *Borkostoló* wine and beer cellar at Somogyi utca 19 (8am–10pm, Fri & Sat until midnight); and the *Ring*, a dark "alternative" late-night bar at Deák utca 24-26. To shoot **pool**, look for places advertising *biliárd*, such as the *Boss Klub* on Fekete Sas utca.

Three venues host **discos**. The *JATE Klub* behind the university is a typical student hangout, usually bopping on Friday and Saturday (8pm–4am). The *Juhász Gyula Művelődési Központ*, Vörosmarty utca 5–7, has discos on Thursday and Friday, and live music on Saturdays. There may also be dancing at the *Tisza Gyöngye*, by the baths across the river. Other **entertainments** are likeliest during the concert season (Sept–May) and the **Szeged Weeks** (roughly July 20–Aug 20), a huge festival of drama and music. Events are advertised around town, and **tickets** (100–500Ft) are available from the *Szabadtéri jegyiroda* ticket agency at Klauzál tér 7 (Mon–Fri 10am–5pm, Sat 10am–1pm).

Moving on

There are express **trains** daily to Kecskemét (1hr) and Budapest (2hr 30min); to Pécs (leaving around 9.20am); and to Békéscsaba (2hr). Other places are easier to reach by bus from Mars tér, with frequent services to Makó and Hódmezővásárhely, and more sporadic **buses** to Veszprém, Eger, Ópusztaszer, Siófok and Miskolc. **International services** run to Arad and Timişoara in Romania; and Subotica, Zenta, Zrenjanin and Novi Sad in the Voivodina region of Serbia.

THE SOUTHERN PLAIN BEYOND THE TISZA

The **Southern Plain** beyond the Tisza is sunbaked and dusty, with small towns that bore the brunt of the Turkish occupation and often suffered from droughts, giving rise to such paranoia that "witches" were burned for "blowing the clouds away" or "selling the rain to the Turks". Resettled by diverse ethnic groups under Habsburg auspices, they later attracted dispossessed Magyars from Transylvania, who displaced the existing communities of Swabians, Serbs, Slovaks and Romanians. In the Fifties, geologists scoured the region for oil, but every bore hole struck thermal springs instead, hence the numerous spas in this region.

Many travellers miss this region altogether, and admittedly its attractions are rather low-key. **Approaches** are largely determined by where you cross the river. Crossing over at Szeged, the main trunk route heads towards Békéscsaba. Csongrád, further upriver, marks the start of a less clear-cut itinerary which might include Szarvas and Mezőtúr. The more northerly route from Szolnok to Debrecen is covered under the Northern Plain (see p.292).

Around Hódmezővásárhely and Makó

Heading on from Szeged there are two basic routes: northeast towards Békéscsaba via **Hódmezővásárhely**, or southeast through **Makó** to the Romanian border. While Makó could be a handy stop for motorists en route to Romania, neither is an essential stopover or an absolute "must". Counting the lovely park at nearby **Mártely**, Hódmezővásárhely is better endowed with sights than Makó, but the latter offers horse-riding and trips to the famous stud farm at **Mezőhegyes**.

Hódmezővásárhely and Mártely

HÓDMEZŐVÁSÁRHELY's tongue-twisting name can be translated as "marketplace of the badger's field", though it's disputed whether the *hód-* prefix really derives from the Magyar word for "badger". Either way, this long-established market town has diversified into leatherwork and pottery, consigning its rural past to the **Tanya Museum** (Tues–Sat 1–5pm), a converted former farmhouse and windmill you can find about 6km out along the Szeged road.

Downtown Kossuth tér is dignified by an eighteenth-century Calvinist church and an imposing town hall, across from which is the **Alföldi Gallery** (Tues–Sun 10am–6pm), displaying scenes of puszta life by local artist János Tornyai (1869–1936), whose *oeuvre* was recently enhanced by the discovery of 700 canvases in a Budapest attic. The paintings of other artists who worked here around the turn of the century hang in the **Tornyai János Museum** (Tues–Sun 11am–5pm) at Szánto Kovács utca 16, whose basement contains the *Venus of Kökénydomb*, a 5000-year-old statue of a fertility goddess. On the same street stands a fine Baroque **Greek Orthodox Church**, whose "Nahum iconostasis" from Mount Athos is named after an obscure seventh-century prophet. Another building worth a visit is the Secession-style **Synagogue** on what used to be Tanácsköztársaság tér.

Hódmezővásárhely is renowned for its black **pottery**, based on Turkish designs, which is fired in a manner dating back to Neolithic times. Examples are displayed in the **Csucsi Potter's House** (Tues–Sun 1–7pm) at Rákóczi utca 101, and alongside peasant costumes and furniture in the **Folk Culture House** on Árpád utca (Tues–Fri 10am–5pm, Sat 11am–5pm).

Practicalities

For **information**, contact *Szeged Tourist* at Szőnyi utca 1 (Mon–Thurs 7.30am–4.30pm, Fri 7.30am–4pm; summer also Sat 7.30am–noon; ☎62/41-325), which also arranges private **accommodation**. Alternatively, try the *Fáma Hotel* at Szeremlei utca 7 (☎62/44-444; ③), or the *Vándorsólyom Fogadó* at Tanya út 1447, out of town (☎62/41-900; ②). Adjoining the **campsite** – *Thermál Kemping* (June–Aug; ☎62/44-238), at Ady utca 1 – are the town's outdoor **thermal baths**, open year round.

The best **place to eat** is the *Bagólyvár* at Malinowsky utca 31, off the Szeged road (11am–11pm), although the *Akvárium*, by the campsite, and *Alföldi*, at Vidra utca 2, are more central.

Mártely

Regular buses run 10km north to **MÁRTELY**, a gorgeous **park** beside a tributary of the Tisza, with boats for rent and hand-woven **baskets** for sale. Ideal for picnics and **horse-riding**, it could also be a nice place in which to rest. The well-equipped **campsite** (May 15–Sept 30; ☎62/42-753) has chalets.

Makó and Mezőhegyes

The sleepy town of **MAKÓ** is the "onion capital" of Hungary, and notable for its therapeutic **baths in radioactive Maros mud**, but is otherwise unremarkable. Signposted off the main road is the **Attila József Museum** (Tues–Sun 10am–6pm), a typical collection of local paintings and artefacts, with a wagon-builder's workshop in the courtyard. The only other "sights" are an **Orthodox Synagogue** at Eötvös utca 15, and the **Attila Memorial House** at Kazinczy utca 8 (Tues–Sun 10am–6pm), where the poet lived all his life. More enticing is the prospect of **horse-riding** in the countryside, which can be arranged through *Szeged Tourist* (☎65/12-384), on the main square.

Aside from the *Hotel Korona* (☎65/11-384; ②), next door to the tourist office, Makó provides a choice of **campsites**, open from May to September. There are two beside the River Maros, 500m out towards Szeged, and another site 2km southeast of town, along the road to the Romanian border. There are also a few chalets and a grassy area for tents at MAGYARCSANÁD, a petrol stop 8km before the border crossing at NAGYLAK.

Enquire at *Szeged Tourist* about excursions to **MEZŐHEGYES**, 30km east of town, where a stud for breeding Lippizaner horses was founded in 1785. Today the **stud farm** breeds **Nonius and Gidrán horses**, the former having been introduced from Normandy in 1810 to produce resilient cavalry chargers. There is a covered **riding school** offering horse or carriage rides, and an expensive **hotel** at Korma utca 30 (☎65/11-045; ④).

Békéscsaba

Travelling between Szeged and Debrecen, **BÉKÉSCSABA** is practically unavoidable. Arriving at the railway station at the western end of Andrássy utca, catch bus #1, #1G, #2 or #7 to the start of the pedestrian precinct, and continue on foot towards the Körös canal. This route will take you past three **tourist offices**: *Express* at Andrássy utca 29–33; *Békéstourist* (Mon–Fri 8am–5pm, Sat 8am–noon; ☎66/23-448) at no. 10; and *Cooptourist*, a few doors along. Arriving by bus instead, it's a brief walk from the depot on Hunyadi tér to the main square, Szent István tér.

From here, follow Széchenyi utca past the Catholic church to the Derkovits embankment to find the **Munkácsy Museum** (Tues–Sun 10am–6pm). Exhibited alongside romantic canvases by Mihály Munkácsy (1844–1900) are oddments concerning the eighteenth-century Slovak settlers who revived Békéscsaba after a ruinous succession of earthquakes, invasions, plagues and fires. Slovak costumes and other artefacts are displayed in the ornate **Slovák Tájház** (Tues–Sun 10am–noon & 2–6pm) at Garay utca 21, a few blocks to the north.

From the Munkácsy Museum you can walk south along the **Promenade of Sculptures** beside the canal, or cross over the bridge to find another, albeit unofficial sight, the **István Malom**. This nineteenth-century flour mill, automated at the turn of the century, is crammed with wardrobe-sized shakers, rotating sieves and wooden chutes – objects of pride to the workers, who may show you around. Alternatively, you could catch bus #4 or #9 out along Gulyai út and walk on a bit from the end of the line to find the **Corn Museum** (*Gabonamúzeum*), a brick windmill in use as recently as 1953, which stands beside an old *tanya* (10am–6pm; closed Mon & Sat).

Practicalities

As usual, private rooms or dormitory beds (from *Békéstourist* or *Express*) are the cheapest **accommodation** going. If the *Csaba Hotel* on the corner of Szent István tér is still undergoing renovation, the only downtown alternative is the *Körös Hotel* on Széchenyi utca (☎66/21-777; ②). The *Fenyves Hotel* at Lencsési út 142 (☎66/39-017; ②) is on the József Attila housing estate, southeast of the centre (bus #17); and the new *Trófea Hotel* (☎66/21-622; ③) is at Gyulai út 61, on the eastern side of town (bus #4 or #9). There is also a **campsite**, *Pósteleki Camping* (June–Sept 15), in the suburb of Békéscsaba-Póstelek.

Cheap, filling **meals** can be eaten at the *Lencsési Étterem*, Lencsési út 17, or the *halászcsárda*, near the start of the pedestrian zone. Local youths go **drinking** in the bar of the *Körös Hotel*, and at the late-night *Rózsafa Disco Bar* (10pm–4am) on the corner of Degre utca and Dr Becsei utca, which has **discos** at weekends. The latter is near the **thermal baths** on the east bank of the canal; bus #8 runs fairly close.

From the inter-city depot on Hunyadi tér there are **buses** to Debrecen (8 daily; 3–4hr); Eger (2 daily); Kecskemét (1 daily); Hajdúszoboszló (leaving around 8.45am); and Gyula (hourly); plus **international services** to Subotica (5am), Arad and Timişoara (5.45am).

Gyula

GYULA, 20km from Békéscsaba en route to the Romanian border, is probably the prettiest town in the Körös region, with the most to show for its history. Named after a tribal chieftain from the time of the Magyar conquest, it became a twin town after the Turkish withdrawal, with Hungarians living in *Magyargyula* and Romanians and Germans living in *Németgyula*.

Gyula's chief monument is a chunky **brick fortress** (Tues–Sun 10am–5pm) dating from the fourteenth century, the only one of its kind left in Hungary. Its Powder Tower is now a wine bar, and the chapel a museum, while during July and August, the castle (*vár*) provides a setting for the **Castle Plays**, which are mostly on historical themes. The fortress is situated in a park to the east of the centre, near a **Greek Orthodox Church** on Groza tér, and a complex of twelve **thermal pools** known as the *Várfürdő*. The temperature of these pools ranges from 46°C to 92°C – the latter can only be borne after you've acclimatised yourself, and then only for a very short time.

"Erkel's Tree", in the park that runs alongside Béke sugárút, is named after Ferenc Erkel, the "father" of Hungarian opera and the composer of the national anthem, who often worked in the tree's shade. The great man is commemorated in the **Erkel Museum** (Tues–Sun 9am–5pm) on Dürer utca, which also contains works by the rather more famous German painter Albrecht Dürer, whose ancestors lived in Gyula. Marginally more interesting is the **György Kohán Museum**

(Tues–Sun 9am–5pm) in the park, containing some of the 3000 works that its namesake bequeathed to his home town – mostly bold depictions of horses, women and houses.

Practicalities

Information and private **rooms** are available from *Békéstourist* at Kossuth utca 16 (Mon–Fri 8.30am–5pm, Sat 8.30am–noon; ☎66/62-261) or *Gyulatourist* at Eszperantó tér 1 (Mon–Fri 8am–5pm; summer also Sat 8am–noon; ☎66/61-192). Across from the latter is the *Hotel Aranykereszt* (☎66/62-144; ③), which is under-cut by the *Hotel Hőforras* at Rábai Miklós út 2 (☎66/61-544; ②) and the cheaper *Hotel Komló* at Béke sugárút 6 (☎66/61-041; ②). There are two **campsites** with huts in the vicinity of the castle: *Thermál Camping* at Szélső utca 16, and the smaller *Mark Camping* at Vár utca 5.

The best place for cheap **meals** is the *gulyáscsárda* near the junction of Városház and Kossuth utca. Other options include the *Park Vendéglő* at Part utca 15; the *Komló Étterem* in the hotel of the same name; and the *Budrió Vendéglő* at Béke sugarút 69. Don't miss the small *cukrászda* at Jókai utca 1, which is the oldest patisserie in Hungary after *Ruszwurm's* in Budapest. For the benefit of trav-ellers arriving late from Romania, there's a **24-hour currency exchange** at Hétvezér utca 5.

Csongrád, Szarvas and Mezőtúr

An alternative route across the Tisza is via Csongrád, east of Kiskunfélegyháza, whence you can visit Szarvas and Mezőtúr before joining the main route to Debrecen at Kiszújszallas. In many ways this region has even less to offer than places further south, but frequent **buses** mean that you needn't stay long in a town if it doesn't appeal. Unless you strike lucky or juggle timetables, **trains** are not much use here. However, the country roads are good for **cycling** – especially in the late summer, when the verges are awash with purple sea lavender.

Csongrád

The county town of **CSONGRÁD** retains a core of thatched **peasant houses** and a Secession-style high school that lends charm to Kossuth tér, but there's no trace of the "Black Castle" from which its name derives (called *Czernigrad* by the Bulgar princes who ruled it in the ninth century). Originally, the castle occupied a strategic position near the confluence of three tributaries of the Körös, which regularly flooded the low-lying region. During the nineteenth century these rivers were gradually tamed by embankments, thrown up by day-labourers who wandered from site to site with their barrows; their lives are commemorated by the **Kubikus Museum** on Iskola utca (Tues–Fri 1–5pm, Sat & Sun 9am–noon). Like most towns on the Plain, Csongrád also features a **thermal bath**.

Should you fancy staying, cottages in the centre can be rented from *Szeged Tourist* at Felszabadulás útja 14 (☎63/31-232) from June to mid-October. More conventional **accommodation** is offered by the *Hotel Tiszavirág*, Fő utca 23 (☎63/31-536; ②), the *Erzsébet Hotel*, Felszabadulás útja 3 (☎63/31-690; ②), and a pleasant **campsite** beside the river. **Restaurants** include the *Bökény* at Muskátali utca 1, *Csuka Csárda*, Szentesi út 1, and *halászcsárda*, Kossuth tér 17.

SUICIDES

Csongrád county has the unenviable distinction of the highest **suicide** rate in Hungary, which has long been the world's most suicide-prone nation, with an average of 50 suicides per 100,000 people. Nobody is really sure why, although theories are legion. Some blame the stresses of a society in rapid transition, but other countries experiencing the same are nowhere near as badly hit (and the rate in Hungary actually declined during the worst years of Stalinist terror). Others cite racial melancholy – there's an old saying that "the Magyar takes his pleasures sadly" – or blame the vast puszta. Another explanation is that the local custom of displaying corpses before burial encourages attention-seeking suicides. Whatever the cause, instances are all too common, the most famous examples being that of Attila József (whose death under the wheels of a train at Lake Balaton is emulated by several people every year), and seventeen-year-old Csilla Molnár, who killed herself shortly after becoming Miss Hungary in 1986.

Travelling on by bus towards Szarvas, you will probably have to change services at SZENTES, across the river.

Szarvas

SZARVAS (Stag) looks eerily empty, with a broad main street intersected by wide roads. The town was laid out like a chess board in the eighteenth century by the enlightened thinker Samuel Tessedik, and originally populated by Slovak settlers. Aside from a bronze statue of a stag in the centre, there is nothing much to see beyond the **Tessedik Samuel Museum** on Vajda Peter utca (Tues–Sun 10am–6pm), and an old **Slovak House** (Sat & Sun 9am–5pm).

The town's principal attraction, however, is the **Arboretum** (Tues–Sun 8am–6pm), a few kilometres out along the road to Mezőtúr, beside a dead branch of the River Körös. This 84-hectare park contains 1700 different plants, laid out in emulation of the grounds of Schönbrunn Castle in Vienna by Count József Bolza, whose nickname – "Pepi" – gives the arboretum its sobriquet *Pepikert* (Pepi's Garden). You can also get there by rented boat – a nice excursion (☎67/13-400 for details).

Should you feel like **staying**, the outwardly grand *Hotel Árpád* (☎67/12-120; ③) is located at Kossuth utca 64 in the centre, while the *Aranyszarvas* campsite and motel can be found in the Erzsébet woods, out on the road to Kecskemét.

Mezőtúr and Túrkeve

Heading north from Szarvas to Mezőtúr – a quaint old ferry takes you over the river – you cross a region known as the *Sárrét* (Swampland), nowadays largely drained but still rich in flora, frogs and insects. **MEZŐTÚR** itself has an exhibition of local **pottery** in the former synagogue at Damjanach utca 1 (a sight in its own right), and serves as a base for trips to **TÚRKEVE**, 16km further north. Here one can see a big **exhibition of sculptures** by the Finta brothers, on the corner of Széchenyi and József utca (Tues–Sun 10am–6pm). The brothers left Hungary in the 1920s in search of fame and fortune, Sándor Finta moving to Paris and Gergely making it as far as New York. The most striking work displayed is Gergely's *Human Destiny*, a giant hand poised to absorb a helpless figure.

Accommodation is available in both towns. In Mezőtúr there is the *Berettyó Fogadó* (②) at Kossuth tér 8, while Túrkeve offers a choice between the *Kevi Fogadó* (②) at Kenyérmezei út 27, or private rooms (①–②) at Petőfi tér 3–5, Árpád utca 3A or Kenyérmezei út 8B.

Buses link both towns to KISÚJSZALLAS, along the main road and railway between Szolnok and Debrecen.

THE NORTHERN PLAIN BEYOND THE TISZA

The **Northern Plain** has more to offer than the south, with Hortobágy National Park, the friendly city of Debrecen, and picturesque villages around the headwaters of the River Tisza. In July and August, you can catch colourful festivals at Nagykálló, Hortobágy and Debrecen, while in September there's a carnival at Nyíregyháza and a major religious festival at Máriapócs.

Most travellers head directly for Debrecen along the trunk route from Budapest, which crosses the Tisza at Szolnok. Since the intervening towns have little to offer, and most places are best reached from Debrecen, the following sections have been structured accordingly.

From Szolnok to Debrecen

Sited at the confluence of the Zagyva and Tisza rivers, **SZOLNOK** has never been allowed to forget its importance as a bridgehead. When the Mongols stormed its castle in the thirteenth century, there was nothing to stop them from riding on to Buda, just as the town's seizure by the Red Army foretold their inexorable advance in 1944 and in 1956, the defeat of the Uprising. Given this history, it's not surprising that most of Szolnok consists of post-war blocks, or that the population turned out to jeer the Soviets goodbye in 1990.

Such sights as there are can be found in the Tabán district beside the Zagyva, which contains some old **gabled houses**. The local history **museum** (Tues–Sun 10am–6pm), at Kossuth tér 4, bears the name of János Damjanich, who trounced the Habsburg army in 1849, and is duly honoured inside along with members of the **Szolnok Artists' Colony**, whose work can also be seen past the bridge across the Zagyva. Another **art gallery** occupies an old synagogue on the corner of Ságvári körút and Kolói utca. The latter street also boasts a handsome Franciscan Church, where **organ concerts** are held in summer. Szolnok's **thermal baths** are to be found on the far side of the Tisza, in an ancient-looking (but actually modern) building with a colonnade.

Practicalities
Information and private rooms are available from *Tiszatour*, Szapáry utca 32 (Mon–Thurs 8am–5pm, Fri 8am–2.30pm; July 1–Aug 20 also Sat & Sun 9am–noon; ☎56/42-506). Other **accommodation** comes dearer, ranging from the *Tisza Hotel* at Verseghy park 2 (☎56/31-155; ⑤) and the *Pelikán Hotel* at Jászkúrt út 1 (☎56/43-855; ⑤), to the *Touring Hotel* on Tiszaligeti sétány (☎56/44-403; ④)

and the *Motel* (☎56/44-403; ③) at *Tiszaligeti Camping* (May–Sept), near the baths.

Aside from hotel **restaurants**, you can eat at the *Szolnok Étterem*, Jubileum tér 2, the *Aranylakat* on Tiszaligeti sétány, and the *Söröző* at Kossuth út 9. The last two have live music most evenings.

Szolnok is along the road and main rail line from Budapest to Debrecen; a terminus for **trains** to Kiskunfélegyháza via Lakitelek; and a nexus for **buses** to Jászberény, Cegléd, Tiszafüred and other towns on the Plain.

Karcag and Püspökladány

KARCAG, 85km east of Szolnok, was once a major settlement of the Cumanians, whose costumes and pottery are displayed in the **Győrffy István Museum** at Kálvin utca 4 (Tues–Sun 10am–noon & 2–6pm). Although much of the town's Cumanian identity has been lost, a couple of aspects still survive. **Food** based on traditional recipes such as *kunsági pandurleves* – a soup of chicken or pigeon, seasoned with ginger, garlic, nutmeg and paprika – can still be enjoyed at the *Kunsági Étterem*, Dózsa út 1; while there's also a thriving local tradition of **pottery**, as a visit to the **Kántor Sándor Fazekas Tájház** (April–Oct Tues–Sun 10am–noon & 2–6pm) at Erkel utca 1 will confirm. Karcag is also the location of the largest rice-hulling mill in Europe, which processes the rice grown around Hortobágy.

The industrial town of **PÜSPÖKLADÁNY**, 17km further east, is nowadays notable only for its branch line down to Békéscsaba, also used by international services to Romania. Before the demise of Communism, however, it was a stronghold of the **Workers' Militia**, founded by the Party to break strikes in the aftermath of the Uprising. This, the *Munkásrendőrség*, remained the Party's private army until it was dissolved in 1989 as a prelude to free elections, by which time the Militia had grown middle-aged and pot-bellied, with conspicuously few recruits from the younger generation.

The spa town of Hajdúszoboszló, around 30km further along the route to Debrecen, is covered after that city as part of the Hajdúság region (p.302).

Debrecen

Once upon a time, **DEBRECEN** was the site of Hungary's greatest livestock fair, and foreigners tended to be snooty about "this vast town of unsightly buildings" with its thatched cottages and a main street that became "one liquid mass of mud" when it rained, "so that officers quartered on one side were obliged to mount their horses and ride across to have dinner on the other". Even so, no-one can deny the significance of Debrecen (pronounced "DEB-retzen"), both economically and as the chief centre of Hungarian Calvinism. From the sixteenth century onwards, there wasn't a generation of lawyers, doctors or theologians that didn't include graduates from Debrecen's Calvinist College (the city is still renowned for its university and teacher-training colleges); while in the crucial years of 1848–49 and 1944–1945, it was here that Hungary's future was debated. During the late 1980s, local churches and employers helped to resettle thousands of refugees from Ceauşescu's Romania.

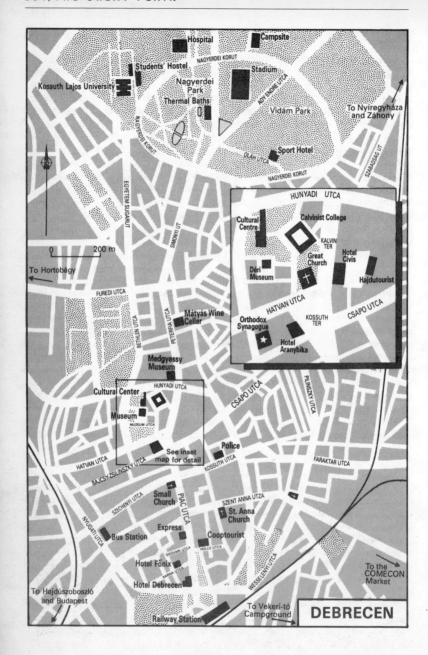

DEBRECEN

The City

Hungary's third largest city still follows the old, much maligned main street, which has reverted to its former name of **Piac utca** (Market Street) after forty years of being called Vörös Hadsereg útja in honour of the Red Army. The **bus station**, from where there are frequent services to the Hajdúság towns, is on Külső Vásártér, off Széchenyi utca; bus #1 runs from here to the railway station. Outside the railway station, in the southern part of town, you can board tram #1, which runs up Piac utca through the centre, continuing on to the University before looping back again – making sightseeing a doddle.

Along the way you'll pass the former **County Hall** at no. 54, whose facade crawls with statues of Hajdúks made from Zsolnay pyrogranite. Further up, on the other side of the road, are the nineteenth-century **Csanak House** (no. 51), and the Romantic-style **Small Church**, whose bastion-like top replaced an onion dome that blew off during a storm in 1909. Facing the church is a Secessionist pile with a gilded doorway, originally a Savings Bank whose premises rivalled Budapest's Gresham Building for lavish ornamentation. A little further on the road widens into **Kossuth tér** and **Kálvin tér**, dominated by two monumental edifices.

The Great Church and Calvinist College

The **Great Church** (*Nagytemplom*) is an appropriately huge monument to the *Református* faith that swept through Hungary during the sixteenth century and still commands the allegiance of roughly one third of the population. Calvinism took root more strongly in Debrecen than elsewhere, as local Calvinists struck a deal with the Turks to ensure their security and forbade Catholics to settle here after 1552. In 1673, the Catholic Habsburgs deported 41 Calvinist priests (who ended up as galley slaves), but failed to shake the faith's hold on Debrecen. A reconciliation of sorts was achieved during the pope's visit in 1991, when he laid a wreath at their memorial.

The church itself (Mon–Fri 9am–noon & 2–4pm, Sat 9am–noon, Sun 11am–4pm) is a dignified Neoclassical building designed by Mihály Pollock, with a typi-

---

WITCHCRAFT

The early Calvinists' hatred of popery was only exceeded by their animus towards pagan beliefs amongst the peasantry of the Plain, who regarded *táltos* (village wise men) with benevolence, while fearing *boszorkány*, their female counterparts. Until the eighteenth century, women accused of witchcraft were able to plead that they were beneficent *táltos* (for example Frau Bártha, who claimed to have learned *táltos* skills from her brother), but as the Calvinists' grip tightened this defence became untenable. Midwives were particularly vulnerable as it was popularly believed that the murder of a relative or newborn child was a prerequisite for acquiring their "magical" skills, but women in general suffered from the Calvinists' witch-hunting zeal, which also found scapegoats in herbalists, beggars and vagabonds.

Witch trials were finally banned by Maria Theresa in 1768 after the scandalous events in Szeged, when "witches" had confessions tortured out of them; and by the nineteenth century the bloody deeds of Debrecen's forefathers were buried beneath platitudes eulogising the "Calvinist Rome".

cally austere interior which accommodated the Diet of 1849 that declared
Hungary's secession from the Habsburg empire. The *Rákóczi-harang* – forged
from cannons used in the Rákóczi War of Independence – is the largest bell in
Hungary.

Around the back on Kálvin tér stands the **Calvinist College** (*Református
Kollegium*), where students were compelled to rise at 3am and be in bed by 9pm
until the end of the eighteenth century. The college motto, inscribed over the
entrance, is *orando et laborando* ("praying and working"). Though venerable in
appearance, this is not the original college founded in 1538, but an enlarged
version dating from the nineteenth century, where the Provisional National
Assembly of left-wing and centre parties met under Soviet auspices late in 1944,
unwittingly conferring legitimacy on the Soviet occupation. Visitors can inspect a
Museum of College History (Tues–Sat 9am–5pm, Sun 9am–1pm), whose exhibits include a meteorite which landed near town in 1857; as well as the **Oratory** and
Library (upstairs).

Museums

West of the college, on Déri tér, is the excellent **Déri Museum** (Tues–Sun April–
Oct 10am–6pm; Nov–March 10am–4pm), fronted by allegorical statues by Ferenc
Medgyessy. The museum is divided into various sections, including one devoted
to household interiors and the life of women in the nineteenth century. The
ethnographic collection features a dazzling display of **shepherds' cloaks** (*szűr*),
worth a little digression. Traditionally, a herdsman would "forget" to remove his
finest *szűr* from the porch when he left the house of the woman he was courting,
and if it was taken inside within an hour then a formal proposal could be made.
Otherwise, the cloak was hung prominently on the verandah – giving rise to the
expression *kitették a szűrét* ("his cloak was put out"), meaning to get rid of
somebody.

Another room contains **paintings** on romantic and patriotic themes by Viktor
Madarász, Bertalan Székely and **Mihály Munkacsy** (1844–1900). Pride of place is
given to the latter's vast canvas *Ecce Homo*, an allegorical representation of good
and evil, truth and falsehood, which toured the world in the 1890s. Having viewed
it in Dublin, James Joyce commented: "It is a mistake to limit drama to the stage; a
drama can be painted as well as sung or acted, and *Ecce Homo* is a drama".

Although the small **Postal Museum** at Bethlen Gabor utca 1 is strictly of interest to philatelists (Wed, Sat & Sun 2–4pm), you might consider visiting the
Medgyessy Museum at Péterfia utca 28 (Tues–Sun 10am–6pm), which honours
the locally born sculptor Ferenc Medgyessy (1881–1958).

Synagogues and other churches

Given the focus on Calvinism, it's easy to overlook the existence of other faiths in
Debrecen. A case in point is the pair of neglected synagogues in the backstreets
west of Kálvin tér. On Pásti utca stands an eclectic-style **Orthodox Synagogue**
dating from 1913, a block south from which you'll find the **Status Quo
Synagogue**, built to serve the so-called Status Quo or middling-conservative
Jews.

The Debrecen telephone code is ☎52

If ecclesiastical architecture is your thing, consider tracking down **St Anna's Church**, a couple of blocks east of Piac utca, which is Catholic and Baroque and originally belonged to the Piarist order. Above the portal you can discern the coat of arms of its founder, Cardinal Csáky, while next door is the former Piarist grammar school, with an exhibition on their educational methods (Sept 15–June 1 Mon–Fri 8am–2pm). The street on which it stands was previously called Béke útja (Peace Avenue), which raised a mordant chuckle amongst the townsfolk, since it leads to a slaughterhouse beyond the **Greek Orthodox Church** on Attila tér.

Nagyerdei Park and Kossuth Lajos University

North of Kálvin tér the city turns greener and quieter, with stylish residences lining the roads to **Nagyerdei Park** (formerly named after Lenin). In the western section you'll find the **thermal baths**, fed by springs of sulphurous "brown water" (*bárna-víz*) rising up from beneath the park. If it hasn't been removed by now, the plaque by the entrance reads: "Created with the support of the Workers' and Peasants' Revolutionary Party for the health of the workers".

Beyond the reedy lake and wooden footbridge rises the columned bulk of **Kossuth Lajos University**, fronted by fountains where newlyweds pose for photos. The university hosts a **Hungarian language summer course** (*Nyári-Egyetem*) usually in late July, which draws students from nations as diverse as Sweden and Vietnam – a good place to meet foreigners. Beyond the campus lies a **Botanical Garden**.

Markets

Though the great bi-monthly fairs "held here since time immemorial" no longer take place, Debrecen's **fruit and vegetable market** is a pungent, compulsive affair. The indoor *vásárcsarnok* (Mon–Sat 4am–3pm, Sun 4–11am), next to the supermarket on Csapó utca, is awash with kerchiefed grannies hawking pickles, meat, soft cheese and strange herbs; the air filled with smells and Magyar interrogatives ("*Hogy a . . . ?*" is slang for "how much is the . . . ?").

Until a few years ago, the wasteland at the back served as a "Polish Market", where traders from other Communist countries sold goods and exchanged currencies. Nowadays, this so-called **Comecon Market** (*KGST Piac*) is held on Wednesday and Saturday mornings in an industrial quarter of the city. Take a #30 bus from the railway station and get off with the crowd just past the cigarette factory (*Dohánygyár*). The market is across the road and through a portal, its 800-odd stalls selling clothes, tools, much junk and some antiques. It is also a place to exchange forints or hard currency for Romanian lei, Czech crowns and other currencies – and get ripped off, if you're not careful.

Practicalities

The most helpful place for **information** is *Hajdútourist*, in the mall on the eastern side of Kálvin tér (May–Sept Mon–Fri 3–5pm; Oct–April Mon–Fri 8am–4.30pm; ☎15-588). If this is closed, visit *IBUSZ* at Piac utca 11–13 (Mon–Fri 7.30am–4pm, Sat 8.30am–noon; ☎15-555). *Cooptourist* at Holló utca 4 (☎10-770) and *Express* at Piac utca 77 (Mon–Fri 8.30am–4.30pm; ☎18-332) are really only useful for booking accommodation.

Accommodation

The cheapest accommodation is **in colleges**, which charge by the bed (①). According to *Express*, there are vacancies on Friday and Saturday throughout the year, and daily throughout July and August. Likely venues include the *kollégium* at Jerikó utca 17–21, Kollos utca 17 (near the terminal of the #31 bus in the north of town), and the annexe behind the university. The next cheapest deal are **private rooms** (②), bookable through *Hajdútourist*, *Cooptourist* or *IBUSZ*. Other options are listed below.

HOTELS

Aranybika Hotel, Piac utca 11–15 (☎16-7777). A revamped nineteenth-century pile with sauna, gym and other facilities, including a wonderfully ornate restaurant. Rooms range from ④ to ⑦.

Cívis Hotel, Kálvin tér 4 (☎18-522). A newly opened three-star place across the square. ⑥.

Hotel Főnix, Barna utca 17 (☎13-355). Similarly rated but not so nice, near the station. ④.

Hotel Debrecen, Petőfi tér 9 (☎16-550). Another Sixties block, directly opposite the station. ③.

Hotel Sport, Oláh utca 5 (☎17-655). A well-equipped place in Nagyerdei Park. ③.

Üdülőbazis, Budai Ézsiás utca 4 (☎12-988). Another smaller one-star hotel, off Attila tér, east of the railway station. ②.

CAMPSITES

Thermál Camping, Nagyerdei körút 102 (☎12-456). Chalets and tent-space, north of Nagyerdei Park. May–Sept.

FICC Rally Camping (☎13-500), by Vekeri-tó lake 6km south of town: accessible by bus #26 from the bus terminal. Has huts and facilities for horse-riding and angling. Mid-April to Sept.

Eating

Most of the places to eat are on or just off Piac utca. Although the *Aranybika*'s restaurant is fabulously ornate, the food is nothing special, and if you're going to spend that sort of money it's better to go for **restaurants** such as the *Gambrinus* (11am–11pm;☎26-692); the entrance is via an alley just south of Kossuth utca. The *Régiposta* ("Old Post Office") at Széchenyi utca 6 occupies an arcaded building where Charles XII of Sweden stayed the night in 1714. Best of all, there's the *Csokonai* (Mon–Fri noon–11pm, Sat & Sun 4–11pm), opposite the theatre on Kossuth utca, with good food and attentive service. At the end of the meal customers roll three dice, and if the right symbols come up you don't have to pay anything. Booking is advisable.

For **cheaper meals**, try the all-night *Lordok Háza* ("House of Lords") at Piac utca 72, 300m from the Great Church, or the *Szabadság* at no. 28 (which can be rough late at night). Last but not least, there's *Gilbert Pizzas* (noon–10pm) in the shopping mall off Kálvin tér, or the new *McDonald's* opposite the *Lordok Háza*. The *Mandula Cukrászda* at Ember Pál utca 6, just off Simonyi út before Nagyerdei park, does good ice cream.

Drinking and nightlife

Aside from the restaurants or the bar of the *Hotel Aranybika*, the best area for **drinking** is the northern part of the city. The *Mátyás* cellar (daily 11.30am–midnight) on Péterfia utca has a nice ambience and an enjoyable rigmarole of serving wine from glass spigots. In the backstreets nearby, at Marothy György utca 38, is the *Fácán Kakas*, with a great patio and dreadful music.

During the Spring Days (see below), there is often something worth watching at the **Csokonai Theatre** on Kossuth utca, an exotic-looking Moorish structure named after the poet Mihály Csokonai Vitez, who was born and died in Debrecen. The liveliest (but hardly trendy) nightspot is the *Kiri-Giri* **disco** in the eastern section of Nagyerdei Park, active most nights until after midnight.

Festivals

Debrecen endeavours to dispel its austere image with three major festivals. The **Spring Days** (*Tavasi Napok*) of music and drama are timed to coincide with events in Budapest, though Debrecen claims to have originated the custom. Some time over summer, the city hosts a big **Jazz Festival** (*Dzsessz Napok* or *Jazzfeszt*), attracting the best Hungarian performers and a sprinkling of foreign acts. Details are posted around town and available from *Hajdútourist*.

A more predictable event occurs on August 20, when the **Flower Carnival** trundles north along Egyetem sugarút: thirty floats laden with flowers, bands and operatically dressed soldiers. People hang from windows en route, cheer wildly when the band plays tunes from *István a király* ("Stephen the King", a patriotic rock opera), and surge behind the last float towards the stadium, where the show continues into the late afternoon. In the evening there's a **fireworks** display outside the Great Church.

Listings

Bookshops at Piac utca 47 and opposite the Small Church stock maps, books in foreign languages, records and cassettes.

Hospital Károlyi Gáspar ter, west of Hunyadi utca.

International calls can be made from direct-dialling kiosks on Piac utca.

Pharmacy 24-hour service on Csapó utca.

Police Kossuth utca 20.

Post office Hatvan utca 5–9.

Hortobágy National Park

Petőfi compared **the Hortobágy puszta** of the central Plain to "the sea, boundless and green", and in his day this "glorious steppe" was astir with countless horses and cattle – tramping their way from well to water hole, urged on by mounted *csikós* – and Racka sheep grazing under the eyes of Puli dogs. Medieval tales of cities in the clouds and nineteenth-century accounts of phantom woods, or the "extensive lake half enveloped in grey mist" which fooled John Paget, testify to the occurrence of **mirages** during the hot, dry Hortobágy summers. Caused by the diffusion of light when layers of humid air at differing temperatures meet, these *délibáb* sporadically appear at certain locations – north of Máta, south of Kónya, and along the road between Cserepes and the *Kis-Hortobágyi Csárda*.

Cumanian tribes raised burial mounds (*kunhalom*) here in the Middle Ages that were later taken for hills; one of them served as the site of a duel between Frau Bártha of Debrecen and two rival *táltos*. Nowadays, the grasslands have receded and mirages are the closest that Hortobágy gets to witchcraft, but the puszta can still pass for Big Sky country, its low horizons casting every copse and hillock into high relief. You should however be prepared for a relatively costly touristic experience – the puszta comes packaged at Hortobágy.

Around the Hortobágy

The 630-square-kilometre **National Park** is a living heritage museum, with state-employed cowboys demonstrating their skills, and beasts strategically placed along the way to the **nine-arched stone bridge** (depicted in a famous painting by Tivadar Csontváry) that lies just west of **HORTOBÁGY** village.

In the village, immediately to the south of Hortobágy railway station, stands the much-restored **Great Inn** (*Nagycsárda*), a rambling thatched edifice dating from 1871 that's now a touristy restaurant. Across the road you'll find the *Pastormúzeum* or **Shepherds' Museum** (Tues–Sun 9am–5pm), whose embroidered *szűr*, carved powder horns and other objects were fashioned by plainsmen to while away solitary hours. Status counted within their world – horseherds outranked shepherds and cowherds, who in turn felt superior to the *kondás* or swineherd – although all slept equally beneath the stars, only building crude huts (*kunyhó*) or sharing a reed *szárnyék* with their animals in bad weather. Attached to the museum is a **natural history section**, with a slide show on Hortobágy wildlife (May 1–Oct 15 daily 9am–6pm). There is also an **Art Gallery** of mostly puszta-inspired, modern paintings (Tues–Sun April–Sept 9am–5pm; Oct–March 9.30am–4pm).

Across the bridge and 2km to the north lies the **Máta Stud Farm**, the place to witness equestrian displays and go riding in horse-drawn carriages; tickets are sold from the stall by the Shepherds' Museum. The village of Máta is also the venue for an international **Horse Show** (*Nemzetközi Lovas Napok*) on the first Sunday of July and the preceding Friday and Saturday; and the annual **Bridge Fair** (Aug 19–20), a Magyar rodeo occasioning the sale of leatherwork, knives and roast beef.

Wildlife

Silvery grey cattle and corkscrew-horned Racka sheep can be seen just behind Máta, but most of Hortobágy's **wildlife** is dispersed over 100,000 hectares. The Hortobágyi-halastó lakes (6km west of Hortobágy village) are the haunt of storks, buzzards, mallards, cranes, terns and curlews; dry sheep-runs are preferred by the little ringed plover, the stone curlew and the pratincole; while millions of migratory **birds** pass through during spring and autumn. Red-footed falcons here behave unusually for their species, forming loose groups in the low foliage. Although there's not much to see at the bird reservation southwest of Nagyiván, a large colony of storks nests in the village of Tiszacsege till the end of August.

Mammals can be found in marshy thickets – boars near Kecskéses, otters at Árkus and ground squirrels near Kónya – while roe deer can be found in the reeds, meadows and copses between Óhat and Tiszaszőlős. Rather than making the long walk south from the *Kis-Hortobágyi Csárda* to the water buffalo reserve (which is pretty unrewarding unless you bring binoculars), hang around the two white barns only 300m from the *csárda*, as this is where the beasts return in the evening.

Practicalities

A succession of small tourist inns gives advance notice of the park to drivers approaching via the Debrecen–Füzesabony road, but **getting there** by train offers a subtler transition from farmland to puszta. Services from Debrecen (towards Tiszafüred and Füzesabony) are better than trains from Nyíregyháza, which leave you stranded at Óhat-Pusztakócsi, several miles west of Hortobágy village; and during summer there might even be a "nostalgia" steam train from Debrecen.

Buses – calling at Hortobágy en route between Eger and Hajdúszoboszló (or direct from the latter during high season) – are another option.

Some of the sites listed above are within walking distance of train stations along the Debrecen–Tiszafüred, Tiszafüred–Karcag and Nyíregyháza–Óhat–Pusztakócsi lines. However, if you can rent a bike from the campsite (see "Practicalities") or from a local, cycling is the best way of **getting around**.

Near the Great Inn is a **tourist office** (May–Sept daily 8am–6.30pm; Oct Mon–Fri 8am–6.30pm; Nov–April Tues–Thurs 8am–4pm; ☎52/69-039), which can provide a **map** marking all the sites mentioned above, explain the various programmes on offer, and direct you to the campsite, *Puszta Camping* (May–Sept). Other **accommodation** includes the *Hotel Hortobágy* (☎52/69-010; ③), roughly 2km east of Hortobágy village along the road to Debrecen, and a cheaper, more basic *fogadó* (☎52/69-137; ②), which should be open from April to October, if not over winter as well. Wooden houses sleeping four people (②) can be rented in the village of Máta, though these are usually fully booked up in July and August; ask at no. 12, near the entrance to the village. Another option is to stay at one of the resorts around Lake Tisza, some 60km further west by rail.

Lake Tisza

Created by damming of upper reaches of the river, **Lake Tisza** has become a new centre for tourist developments, thankfully not yet so advanced as at Lake Balaton. Its most developed resort is **TISZAFÜRED**, a junction linking the Plain and the Northern Uplands by road and rail. The railway station is at the western end of the main street, Somogyi út; the bus terminus, *IBUSZ* (May 15–Sept Mon–Fri 8am–4pm; May 15–Sept also Sat 8am–noon; ☎59/52-047) and the town centre lie to the east. With so many private **rooms**, there's little call to use the *Vadász Hotel* at Szöllősy utca 4 (☎59/52-228; ②) or the *Füzes Panzió* at Huszőles utca 31B (☎59/11-855; ③). The *Thermal* **campsite** (May–Sept) is situated near a dead and pestilent tributary of the Tisza.

Other places around the lake remain less developed, with simple campsites at ABÁDSZALÓK to the south (which also has a pension: ☎56/38-103), and SARUD and POROSZLÓ on the western shore. The floodplain and ox-bow lakes are a paradise for **birdwatchers**, with black and white storks, bitterns, red-backed shrikes and magnificent golden orioles.

During summer there are **buses** to Abádszalók from Szolnok and Eger.

The Hajdúság

The Hajdúság region around Debrecen takes its name from the Hajdúk communities who occupied eight derelict villages here during the early seventeenth century. Originally cattle drovers and part-time bandits, their ranks were swollen by runaway serfs and homeless peasants, and they provided a fearsome army for István Bocskai's struggle against the Habsburgs. After Bocskai achieved his ambition to be Voivode of Transylvania, the Hajdúk were pensioned off with land to avert further disturbance. The result was a string of settlements with names prefixed *Hajdú-*, where the Hajdúk farmed, enjoyed the status of "nobles" (*natio*) and, if necessary, mustered to fight.

Hajdúszoboszló

The most attractive of the Hajdúság settlements is **HAJDÚSZOBOSZLÓ**, 24km from Debrecen, where many Hungarians, driven away from the Balaton by rising prices, now take their holidays. A **spa** has been operating here since 1927, the waters said to be good for arthritis and other muscular ills. These days Hajdúszoboszló gets about one and a half million visitors each year, and its **thermal baths** can be packed. Surveying the wallowing, guzzling crowds in the steaming brown waters (the consumption of beer and *lángos* is staggering), you might try the old Hajdúk war cry, *Huj, huj, hajrá!*, to clear some space before jumping in yourself. Away from the baths things are more relaxed, with **tennis courts** for rent in the park, and cafés and quaint old buildings around Bocskai and Hősök squares. Modern housing and supermarkets along the main street (called Szilvák alja or Debreceni út) nourish the illusion of a hedonistic urban environment.

Sixty feet of **fortress wall** – part of the fifteenth-century defences – lurk behind the inevitable Calvinist church, while a comically fierce statue of the Prince guards Bocskai tér. Around the corner at Bocskai utca 12, the **Bocskai Museum** (summer Tues–Sun 9am–1pm & 3–7pm; winter Tues–Sun 9am–1pm & 2–6pm) exhibits photos of nineteenth-century Hajdúk villagers, and assorted military relics – among them Bocskai's embroidered silk banner, given pride of place alongside the town's charter. Although Bocskai comes across as a benevolent leader, he didn't balk at betraying another group who fought for him: the Székely of Transylvania, who were butchered when they had outlived their usefulness during the so-called "Bloody Carnival". The room across the hall commemorates Hajdúszoboszló's spa, cultural achievements, and the natural gas extraction plant.

On the edge of town, around the railway station, the atmosphere is more rural: chunky whitewashed cottages – their vegetable gardens fringed with sunflowers – shimmer in the heat; while errant cows, old women, and wagon-loads of pigs move slowly in the dazzling sunlight.

Practicalities

Arriving at the **railway station**, 2km out, you'll find frequent buses into the centre, terminating at the **bus station** near the baths.

Hajdútourist (☎52/62-214) at József Attila utca 2 can supply **information** on various activities and arrange private **rooms** (②). Otherwise you'll find the modern *Béké Gyógyhotel* (☎52/61-049; ⑤) attached to the baths, and just down the road, the *Mikro Hotel* (☎52/62-744; ④) and the *Délibáb Hotel* (☎52/62-366; ⑤). The run-down *Hotel Gambrinus* (☎52/62-054; ②) on Bocskai tér may close in a year or so. Various categories of rooms and bungalows are available at the *Camping Hotel* (☎52/62-427), beside the **campsite** (May–Sept; ☎52/62-427) beyond the gasometers.

Nádudvar and Hajdúböszörmény

There are two other towns in the Hajdúság region that you might consider visiting. **NÁDUDVAR**, 18km west from Hajdúszoboszló by hourly bus, is particularly worthwhile if you're interested in **pottery**, as Lajos Fazekas continues a family tradition by producing black, unfired ceramics at his house and studio on the main street. Otherwise, this sleepy place offers two petite churches, a spanking new cultural centre, and, sprawled around its outskirts, the **Nádudvar Co-operative**

farm, where foreigners attending Debrecen's summer language course are sometimes taken for a glimpse of rural prosperity. In the past, some visits have culmi-
nated in a riotous *pálinka* binge, with students and workers riding pigs across
moonlit fields.

The Hajdúság's military heritage is apparent in the layout of
HAJDÚBÖSZÖRMÉNY, 20km north of Debrecen. Old houses stand in concen-
tric rings around a walled core that was once a Hajdúk fortress and is otherwise
notable for its Baroque town hall. Should you feel like staying, **private rooms** are
available from *Hajdútourist* at Karap utca 2 (☎55/11-416), and there's a simple
campsite at Polgári út 92–100, out along the Miskolc road (May–Sept; ☎55/11-
388).

Szabolcs-Szatmár County

North of Debrecen, the Plain ripples with low ridges of wind-blown sand,
anchored by birches, apple groves and tobacco fields. The soft landscape of the
Nyírség (Birch Region) makes a pleasant introduction to **Szabolcs-Szatmár**, an
area scorned by many Magyars as the "black country". More densely settled than
other parts of the Plain, Szabolcs would be wholly agricultural if not for industrialised Nyíregyháza, straddling the main routes to the Northern Uplands, the
Erdőhát villages and the Ukraine. Historically isolated by swamps, and then
severed from Transylvania and Ruthenia in 1920, the region has remained poor
and backward in comparison with the rest of Hungary.

If your interest in **rural life** is limited, stick to **Nyíregyháza** or **Nyírbátor**,
whose Village Museum and striking churches convey something of the region's
character. But for anyone seeking the challenge of remote areas, encounters with
Gypsies on their own turf, or the folk customs and architecture of old Hungary,
Szabolcs has much to offer, and there's the odd riding school and ruined castle to
add focus to your wanderings.

Nyíregyháza

NYÍREGYHÁZA has grown into the Big Apple of Szabolcs county, thanks to the
food processing industry developed to feed the Soviet market during the Sixties
and Seventies. The collapse of this market has hit the region badly, though other
businesses have sprung up in response to the flood of shoppers and traders from
the former USSR. The town itself (pop. 121,000) has a core of old buildings girdled
by factories and housing estates, with a garden suburb – **Sóstófürdő** – to the
north. The best time to come is the first Saturday in September, when a **carnival**
inaugurates the month-long **Nyírseg Autumn** arts festival.

Arrival and orientation

Arriving at the bus or railway station on Petőfi tér, 1km south of the centre, you
can obtain a street map from *Express* at Arany utca 2 before catching bus #8 or
#8A downtown, riding on to Sóstófürdő at the end of the line if you prefer. Most
other buses leave from Jókai tér, in the centre. For **information**, contact
Nyírtourist at Dózsa György utca 3 (Mon–Fri 7.30am–4.30pm; June & Aug also
Sat 7.30am–1pm; ☎42/11-544), or *IBUSZ* at Ország Zászló tér 10 (Mon–Fri
7.30am–4pm, Sat 7.30am–noon; ☎42/12-125).

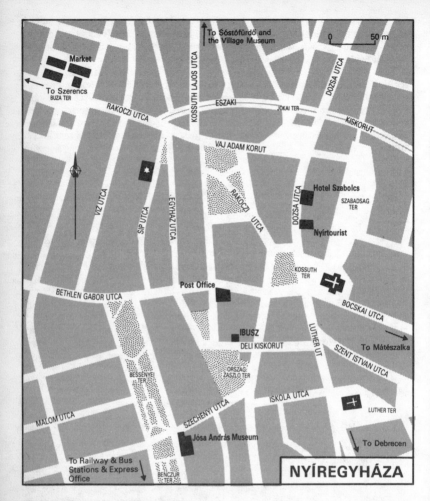

NYÍREGYHÁZA

Sóstófürdő and the Village Museum

Nyíregyháza's chief attraction is the leafy resort of **Sóstófürdő**, or "Salty Lake Bath". Should you fancy a wallow, the **thermal baths** are on Blaha Lujza sétány, near the lake and the Igrice tourist complex; but the real attraction lies beyond the sports ground on the other side of the main road.

The town's outdoor **Village Museum** (April–Oct Tues–Fri 9am–4pm, Sat & Sun 9am–3pm) feels eerier than its counterparts in Szombathely and Szentendre. With clothes on the washing-line, tables laid and boots by the hearth, the farmsteads seem to have been abandoned by their occupants only yesterday, leaving mute testimony to their lives in a nineteenth-century Szabolcs village. In this world, the size of the barns (*csűr*) and stables (*istálló*) denoted a family's wealth, as did the presence of a Beam Gate opening on to the street: "A gate on a hinge, the dog is big, the farmer is great", runs an old proverb. Other clues to social standing are the knick-knacks beloved of the "sandled noblity" or petty gentry, and the placing of a bench between two windows in Orthodox households. A single communal bowl speaks volumes about life in the poorest dwellings.

Downtown Nyíregyháza

A trawl of the downtown area yields several monuments that cast a bit more light on Nyíregyháza's history. Its confessional diversity is symbolised by three **churches** – Catholic on Kossuth tér, Lutheran on Luther tér, and Uniate on Bethlen utca – plus a former **synagogue** at the top of Síp utca. Ethnographic and archaeological material appears in the **Jósa András Museum** (Tues–Sun 9.30am–5.30pm), a couple of blocks beyond pastel-hued Orszag Zászló tér, along with rooms devoted to the painter Gyula Benczúr (1844–1922) and the epicurean writer Gyula Krúdy (1878–1933), both of whom were born in Nyíregyháza.

However, the most cosmopolitan place is the weekly **Comecon Market**, where Ukrainians, Magyars, Poles and Romanians barter and sell everything from fur hats to cars. Though invariably held beside the Szerencs road just beyond the railway tracks (where you should alight from bus #1), its timing varies, so you'll have to ask at the tourist office. This is not to be confused with the regular daily market on Búza tér, nearer the centre.

Practicalities

Accommodation is broadly divided between Sóstófürdő and the centre. In **Sóstófürdő** you'll find *Fenyves Camping* and its *hostel* (May 1–Oct 12; ☎42/15-171; ①) by the Village Museum turn-off; and *Igrice Camping* and *Summer Village* (same dates; ☎42/13-235), with a *fogadó*, flash bungalows (⑤) plus humbler chalets (②), near the baths. Another option is the comfortable *Ózon Panzió*, at Csalo köz 2 (☎42/11-084; ④), just off Sóstói út, halfway into town (bus #5, #7, #7A or #12). During summer, you may also be able to get beds in the *Tanárképző Fő iskola*, on the other side of the highway (ask at *Express* or *IBUSZ*). **Downtown** offers a straight choice between the *Palmero Panzió*, Széchenyi utca 16 (☎42/15-777; ②), and the *Hotel Szabolcs* (☎42/12-333; ③) on Dozsa utca.

The best **places to eat** are the *Ungvár Étterem* (11am–10pm) on the corner of Szent István utca and Luther út, and the *Bisztró* opposite *Fenyves* campsite. The *Korona Étterem* (11am–3pm), on the corner next to *Nyírtourist*, is a self-service joint. For **drinking** try the *Gosser Söröző* on Ország Zászló tér or the *HBH Bayer Söröző* on Hösők tere. The liveliest **nightspots** are the *Beatles Bar* in Sóstóhegy (across the railway tracks from Sóstófürdő), which plays classic rock until 2–3am, and the Friday and Saturday evening **disco** at the House of Culture on Ország Zászló tér.

Moving On

If you're hoping to explore the Szabolcs hinterland, it's worth enquiring about buses from the inter-city terminal on Petőfi tér before visiting the railway station. **Buses** will usually be quicker than trains, and the timetable is certainly easier to understand than the cryptic indicator board in Nyíregyháza station (to give you an idea, *"Debrecen – 7 balra"* means that the Debrecen train leaves from the left-hand side of the seventh track from the main building).

That said, Nyíregyháza is a major railway junction, straddling the line between Miskolc and Debrecen, and branch lines into Szabolcs county. There are half a dozen daily expresses to Budapest (4hr) via Debrecen and Szolnok, and twice that number of slower, Szerencs-bound **trains**, which call at Tokaj (20–30min). Szabolcs is served by three branch lines, with four or five slow trains along each (fewer on Sun). Trains bound for Zajtha can drop you off at Nagkálló, Nyírbátor or Mátészalka, while those for Vásárosnamény call at Vaja. Kisvárda is a stopover for slow trains to Záhony, but not for expresses originating in Budapest.

Nagykálló and Máriapócs

For those with private transport, it may be worth making a couple of stopovers on the way to Nyírbátor (see below). "Go to **NAGYKÁLLÓ!**" used to be a popular insult east of the Tisza, referring to the large mental asylum in this small town of converging houses painted a flaky ochre. Its sole attraction from a visitor's standpoint is the annual *Téka Tábor*, a workshop-cum-**festival of Hungarian folk arts**, held inside a weird "barn" shaped like a Viking's helmet, on the outskirts of town. The event lasts about a week, usually in late July. For details, contact the *Téka Együttyes*, PO Box 287, 1370 Budapest; tourist offices in Debrecen and Nyíregyháza should also have the dates. Apart from the festival, the only things to see are a few derelict Jewish monuments on Mártírok tere and Szarvas utca, mute reminders of a community that was annihilated in World War II.

With the fall of Communism, a tiny village off the road between Nagykálló and Nyírbátor has resumed its role as a place of pilgrimage for the Orthodox and Catholic faithful. Now that old identities are reasserting themselves across the Carpathians, **MÁRIAPÓCS** has become a spiritual focus for ethnic Magyars and Uniate Christians in Romania, Slovakia, the Ukraine and the Voivodina. In August 1991, 200,000 worshippers attended an open-air papal mass at Máriapócs, whose **Orthodox Church** contains an icon of the Virgin that has been seen to shed tears since 1696, as well as crutches and other tokens of infirmity attesting to miraculous cures. **Pilgrimages** occur on August 15 (the Feast of the Assumption) and the Saturday closest to September 8 – the latter festival is especially holy to Gypsies.

Nyírbátor

The tangled history of Trans-Carpathia has also left its mark on **NYÍRBÁTOR**, an attractive small town hosting **concerts** of choral and chamber music from mid-July to early September (details from *Hajdútourist* or *Nyírtourist*). Its name recalls the **Báthori family**, a Transylvanian dynasty which veered between psychopathic sadism and enlightened tolerance. Both attributes are subtly manifest in Nyírbátor's exquisite churches, which were equally funded by the Báthoris in an age when religious strife was the norm.

The Calvinist Church
The **Calvinist Church**, on a hill behind the main street, was originally founded as a Catholic place of worship in the 1480s, complete with a fourteen-seat pew now in the National Museum in Budapest. At the back of its web-vaulted Gothic nave lies the **tomb of István Báthori**, whose sleeping figure indicates that he died in bed, but reveals nothing of the character of this Transylvanian Voivode. Hungarian history judges him a shrewd ruler, forgiving his machinations against

the Transylvanian Saxons, and the periodic bouts of orgiastic cruelty for which István atoned by endowing churches. Most likely these had a hereditary origin, for similar hysterical rages and sadism were also characteristic of "Crazy" Gábor Báthori, a short-lived successor, and István's cousin Erzsébet (see "Nagyecsed" below).

When the church turned *Református* in the late sixteenth century, it was obliged to erect a freestanding **wooden bell tower**, since only Catholic churches were permitted stone belfries during the Counter-Reformation. From its wide-skirted base, the tower rises to a defiant height of thirty metres, with a spire like a wizard's hat sprouting four mini-towers known as *fiatorony* ("sons of the tower"), which symbolised a civic authority's right to execute criminals. Its hand-cut shingling and oak-pegged joists and beams can be inspected from the crooked stairway up to the balcony and bell chamber.

The Minorite Church and Báthori Museum

István Báthori's other legacy to Nyírbátor is situated on Károlyi utca, on the other side of the main street. Paid for by the spoils of war against the Turks (who, perhaps appropriately, gutted it in 1587), the **Minorite Church** contains fantastic Baroque wood carvings from Eperjes in Slovakia. The altars swarm with figures wearing disquieting expressions, suggestive of István's soul but actually commissioned by János Krucsay around 1730. To gain admission, ring at the side door marked *plebánia csengője*, which leads to an exhibition of photos of ancient Szabolcs churches.

Next door you'll find the **Báthori Museum** (Tues–Sun 10am–6pm), where various relics with unintelligible captions trace the history of the dynasty, whose estates included most of **Szatmár**. Though predominantly inhabited by Hungarians, this region was bisected as a result of the Treaty of Trianon, which allotted the provincial capital (nowadays called Satu Mare) and its surroundings to Romania. Relations have been awkward, if not hostile, ever since, which partly explains the small number of border crossings in these parts.

Practicalities

You can get **rooms** at the *Mátyás Panzió*, Hunyadi utca 2 (☎43/11-657; ②), or through **Nyírtourist** (☎43/11-525) on Szabadság tér, and there's a small **campsite** (June 15–Aug 30; ☎43/11-494). The *Kakukk* restaurant on Szabadság tér offers good cheap **meals** and the occasional video-disco. For fruit and vegetables, try the **market** at the junction of Váci and Fürst utcas. Men might enjoy the "old time" barber at Báthori utca 10. There are two **buses** (weekdays only) between Nyírbátor and Mátészalka, 21km away.

Mátészalka, Nagyecsed and Vaja

A shabby fusion of flaking estates and low yellow houses, **MÁTÉSZALKA**'s sole claim to fame is that it's the birthplace of Tony Curtis's parents, whose original family name was Kertes (Gardener). In the town centre – where each Sunday the population gravitates in homage to the Catholic and Orthodox churches and to enjoy a thermal bath – you'll find *Szátmar Tourist* at Bajcsy-Zsilinszky utca 3 (☎44/10-410), which can arrange private **rooms** or direct you to *Liget* **campsite** (May–Sept 15).

If you come here at all it's for **transport** to more interesting places, leaving from the western end of Bajcsy-Zsilinszky utca. There are regular buses down to Nagyecsed and across to Vaja (see below), whilst access to the Erdőhát region is facilitated by buses (10 daily; 2 at weekends) and trains (3–4 daily) to Csenger and Fehérgyarmat. Other slow trains (5 daily) run up to Vásárosnamény and Záhony, and across the border to Carei in Romania.

Nagyecsed and Vaja

The small town of **NAGYECSED**, 15km south of Mátészalka, deserves a passing mention as the **birthplace of the "Blood Countess" Erzsébet Báthori**, the most notorious of the Báthori clan, though her worst excesses took place at Sarvar (see p.203) and later in Transylvania. It was at the family château here that the young countess witnessed a Gypsy sewn into a horse's stomach and left to die – a formative experience which taught her that commoners could be killed with impunity, a practice she enjoyed in adult life. After Erszébet died a prisoner in her Slovakian castle and was buried nearby, the outraged parents of her victims protested until her body was transferred to the Báthori vault at Nagyecsed.

A less morbid attraction is the **fortified manor** (Tues–Sun April–Oct 9.30am–5.30pm; Nov–March 8am–4pm) 14km northwest of Mátészalka in **VAJA**, the feudal seat of Ádám Vaj, an early supporter of Rákóczi's campaign against the Habsburgs. Within its thick stone walls, visitors in felt slippers shuffle across the parquet from room to room, gaping at painted furniture and the grand meeting hall, the *Rákóczi-terem*. The school next door can sometimes provide accommodation.

The Erdőhát

The **Erdőhát** is Hungary's most isolated region, a state imposed by nature and confirmed by history. Meandering and flooding over centuries, the headwaters of the Tisza and its tributaries carved out scores of enclaves beneath the flanks of the Subcarpathians, where dense oak forests provided acorns for pig-rearing and ample timber for building. Though invaders were generally deterred by Escedi Swamp and similar obstacles, scattered communities maintained contact with one another through their intricate knowledge of local tracks and waterways. When the borders came down like shutters in the twentieth century, people were suddenly restricted to three tightly controlled frontier crossings, which have been only partially relaxed since the demise of Communism.

Roads are poor and motor vehicles are rare in these parts, but if you're interested in rural customs and architecture that's almost extinct elsewhere in Hungary, the Erdőhát **villages** are worth the effort. Two small towns – Fehérgyarmat and Vásárosnamény – serve as jumping-off points for the region.

Fehérgyarmat and Vásárosnamény

Much of the southern Erdőhát is accessible from **FEHÉRGYARMAT**, which has a **hotel** (②) at Móricz Zsigmond út 8 and a nice park entered via a Transylvanian-style portal. **Buses** fan out from here to Tivadar (hourly), Gyügye (less frequently), Csaroda (Mon–Sat 2 daily), Vásárosnamény and Csengersima (both Mon–Sat 5 daily; 1 on Sun), while **trains** to Zajta (2–3 daily) can drop you at Nagyszekres or Gacsály.

THE ERDŐHÁT

UKRAINE

Vámosatya

Csaroda

Tákos

Tarpa

Tiszacsécse

Gulács

Szatmárcseke

Sonkád

Uszka

River Tisza

Tivadar

Turistvándi

Botpalád

Mánd

Vámosoroszi

To
Vásárosnamény

Fehérgyarmat

Nemesborzova

Nagyszekeres

River Szamos

Gacsály

Mátészalka

Gyügye

Zajta

Csengersima

Nagyecsed

To Satu Mare

Petea

Csenger

ROMANIA

0   10 km

To Carei

Villages in the northern Erdőhát are generally easier to reach by bus from **VÁSÁROSNAMÉNY**, an erstwhile trading post on the "salt road" from Transylvania, whose **museum** displays local embroidery and cast-iron stoves from Munkachevo, with a room devoted to Erdőhát funerary customs. You'll have to see *Beregtourist* (Mon–Thurs 7.30am–4.30pm, Fri 7.30am–4pm) on the main square about private **rooms**, since the *Bereg Hotel* is closing for restoration. There's also a **campsite** (May–Sept 15; ☎71-076) just across the Tisza in

GERGELYIUGORNYA (hourly buses June–Aug 25), a small resort whose holiday homes are raised on stilts to avoid flooding. **Buses** run from Vásárosnamény to Tákos, Csaroda and Vámosatya every couple of hours.

Around Szatmárcseke and Turistvándi

If you don't fancy staying in Fehérgyarmat, there's a small **campsite** in TIVADAR, 10km north of town and within walking distance of Tarpa (see below). As far as sights go, however, there's more to recommend for villages on the other side of the river, further east.

The cemetery at **SZATMÁRCSEKE**, 20km northeast of Fehérgyarmat, contains "boat-shaped" oaken **grave markers** (*kopjafa*) that vaguely resemble the heads on Easter Island, while a pretty mausoleum commemorates **Ferenc Kölcsey**, the local-born poet (1790–1838) who penned the words to Hungary's national anthem. Between April and October, visitors can **stay** at the *Kölcsey Fogadó*, Honvéd utca 9 (☎ Szatmárcseke 9; ①), which has a **restaurant** attached.

A few kilometres to the south, **TURISTVÁNDI** has a picturesque **wooden watermill** whose workings are demonstrated should a group of tourists materialise. The key to the mill is kept at the house on the corner, across the main road.

Other fine examples of wooden architecture used to grace NEMESBORZOVA, VÁMOSOROSZI and BOTPÁLAD, until they were removed to Szentendre's Village Museum in the Seventies. However, **TISZACSÉCSE** retains the thatched cottage where the novelist and critic **Zsigmond Móricz** (1879–1942) was born, and also gives fine views across the plain towards the Carpathian mountains.

Further south

The southern Erdőhát is notable for its beautiful churches, which are folksy adaptions of Gothic or Baroque architecture. Slow trains bound for Zajta can drop you off at **NAGYSZEKERES** or **GACSÁLY**, whose churches feature striking wooden **bell towers**. Even more appealing is the tiny **church** in **GYÜGYE**, its coffered ceiling decorated with astrological symbols (illuminated in turn by a sunbeam during the course of the year, so the priest says). Gyügye is easily reached by bus from Fehérgyarmat, or you can walk there in an hour from Nagyszekeres.

Committed church buffs might also visit **CSENGER**, where the **Catholic church** dates from the Middle Ages. Built of red and black brick, it similarly features a superb coffered ceiling with folk Baroque paintings. Csenger is the terminal of the branch line down from Mátészalka; the last train back leaves at 8pm.

Although **CSENGERSIMA**, a few miles north, has been designated a 24-hour **crossing into Romania**, the Romanian officials at PETEA may refuse to admit travellers after dark. There are five **buses** daily (one on Sun) between Csengersima and Fehérgyarmat, but none across the border.

North of the Tisza

Another clutch of villages lies north of the Tisza, in the region known as *Bereg*. While some are only accessible from Vásárosnamény, others, such as Csaroda and Tákos, can also be reached from Fehérgyarmat.

TÁKOS harbours a wattle-and-daub Protestant **church** with bold floral designs on its gallery and coffered ceiling, painted by Ferenc Asztalos in 1766. As in most village churches, the men sit up front and the women at the back. If the church is shut, track down the old woman who has the key, at Bajcsy-Zsilinszky utca 40;

she might also be able to help with **accommodation**. The house opposite the church may become a *panzió* in the future.

In **CSARODA**, 2km east, a thirteenth-century **Gothic church** with a shingled spire contains **medieval frescoes** which the restorers brought back to life by covering them overnight with raw minced meat. The woman who lives opposite, at Kossuth utca 15, can open the church and explain their significance, blithely mixing up Biblical stories and folk myths, interspersed with tales of family misfortunes. Across the road, an old peasants' house has been turned into an exhibition of rural artefacts. **Rooms** at Csaroda's *Panzió* (②) are best reserved through *Beregtourist* in Vásárosnamény, but you can try your luck by asking at József utca 20, en route to the church.

The restorers have also been at work in **TARPA**, to the southeast, where a large horizontal "dry" **mill** (*szaraz-malom*) with an intricate conical roof stands amongst the cottages. Another formidable-looking **wooden belltower** can be found in **VÁMOSATYA**, 18km northwest of Csaroda.

Around Kisvárda and Záhony

The fruit-growing area northeast of Nyíregyháza is called the *Rétköz* (Meadow Land) or *Tiszakanyár* (Tisza Bend). Though pretty to drive through, there is little to attract visitors beyond Kisvárda, midway along the road and rail line to Záhony, the only border crossing into the Ukraine.

Kisvárda

KISVÁRDA is a backwater **spa** with a **ruined castle** used for staging plays in the summer. Despite being undamaged in the war, a random selection of buildings along the main street have been replaced by ugly modern structures, spoiling the look of Fő utca, which leads to the main square. Just off Fő tér stands an old **synagogue** with an ornamental ceiling and stained-glass windows, housing the **Rétköz Museum** of local history. The **tourist office** in the nearby House of Culture can tell you about **horse-riding** and book private **accommodation**. There's also a campsite and *fogadó* (May 1–Oct 15; ☎ Kisvárda 649; ②) with huts (①), down by the castle and swimming baths, where the *Amor* is a popular place to eat. Locals go **drinking** in the *Stilbar* at Fő utca 2, the *Várda* restaurant behind the town hall, or the seedy *Sport Falatózo* on Vár utca.

Záhony and Zsurk

ZÁHONY is currently the "front line" between relatively prosperous, Westernised Hungary and the impoverished masses of the former Soviet Union. When travel restrictions were eased in 1990, people flooded in from the Ukraine and Russia to trade goods for foodstuffs at the "**free**" **market** on the edge of town, until controls were reimposed the following year. Since then, spivs and dealers from Hungary and Poland drive across the border to do business in Uzhgorod, using Záhony as a base. Unless you relish hobnobbing with such characters however, the only reason to come here is another picturesque **church** with a wooden belfry, in the nearby village of **ZSURK**.

Should either prospect appeal, it's possible to rent private **rooms** at Szamuely utca 22, or stay at the *Kemény Fogadó*, Zalka M. utca 1 (②), in Záhony. There are **trains** from here down to Nyíregyháza and Debrecen, but you are not allowed to board international expresses running in either direction.

INTO THE UKRAINE

Since the spring of 1992 it has been possible to obtain **Ukrainian visas** on the spot at border crossings for around £30/$50 in any hard currency. The **road crossing** is a narrow bridge, easily found by following the traffic. Be warned, however, that **customs** at CHOP on the Ukrainian side may be out to extort cash or confiscate desirable items from travellers.

The reason for this becomes apparent once you enter Trans-Carpathia, the mountainous region traditionally known as **Ruthenia**, control of which has passed from Hungary to Czechoslovakia to the USSR to the Ukraine within the last eighty years. This forgotten corner of central Europe is as poor and backward as Albania, with a tradition of emigration that took Andy Warhol and Robert Maxwell to their adoptive countries. Its ethnic mix includes Hungarians, Slovaks, Gypsies and Romanians, not to mention a large number of Ruthenians (*Rusyns*), who cling to their Uniate faith.

The main road and rail line run through **UZHGOROD** (also a border crossing into Czechoslovakia), known as *Ungvár* to its Hungarian-speaking inhabitants. Another road heads east to **MUKACHEVO** (*Munkács*), the site of a last ditch battle against the Habsburgs during the Kuruc War. From here, the road continues across the mountains towards the Ukrainian city of Lvov, via the **Verecke Pass** through which Árpád led the Magyar tribes into the Carpathian Basin.

travel details

Trains

From Budapest (Keleti or Nyugati Station) to Békéscsaba (7.20am, 9.10am, 2.10pm, 3.30pm & 5.20pm daily; 2hr 30min); Debrecen (7.10am, 8am, 10am, noon; 1pm, 2pm, 3pm, 4pm, 4.30pm, 5pm & 6pm daily; 2hr 30min–3hr 30min); Kecskemét (6.25am, 8.15am, 10.25am, 12.25pm, 2.25pm, 4.25pm, 6.15pm & 7.25pm daily; 1hr 30min); Nyíregyháza (6.10am, 7.25am, 8am, 10am, noon, 1pm, 2pm, 3.30pm, 4pm, 4.30pm & 7pm daily; 3hr–3hr 30 min); Szeged (6.25am, 8.15am, 10.25am, 12.25pm, 2.25pm, 4.25pm, 6.15pm & 7.25pm daily; 2hr 30min).

From Baja to Kiskunhalas (8.45am, 11.50am, 3.45pm, 5pm & 7pm daily; 1hr 45min).

From Békéscsaba to Budapest (10.10am, 1.10pm, 3.20pm & 5.10pm daily; 2hr 30min); Szeged (6.55am, 7.40am, 9.15am, 11.10am, 2pm, 3.15pm & 6.20pm daily; 2hr).

From Debrecen to Budapest (7am, 9.15am, 11.20am, 1.10pm, 1.40pm, 3.10pm, 3.55pm, 5pm, 6.50pm & 7.35pm daily; 2hr 30min–3hr 30min); Hortobágy (10.45am, 11.30am, 2pm, 4.45pm & 7.45pm daily; 1hr); Mátészalka (10.20am, 11.20am, 3.10pm, 4.40pm, 6pm & 7.40pm daily; 1hr 30min); Nyírbátor (10.20am, 11.20am,

3.10pm, 4.40pm, 6pm & 7.40pm daily; 1hr); Nyíregyháza (every 30min; 30–45 min).

From Kalocsa to Kiskőrös (6.50am, 11.30am, 1.40pm, 4.40pm & 7.30pm daily; 1hr).

From Kecskemét to Bugac (7.55am, 10am & 2.30pm daily; 1hr); Szeged (6.20am, 9.20asm, 11.20am, 1.20pm, 3.20pm, 4.15pm & 6.15pm daily; 1hr 15min–2hr).

From Kiskőrös to Kalocsa (9.50am, 12.50pm, 3.35pm & 5.40pm daily; 1hr).

From Kiskunhalas to Baja (7.10am, 11am, 1.30pm, 3.30pm & 6pm daily; 1hr 45min).

From Mátészalka to Csenger (7.45am, 2pm & 5.20pm daily; 1hr); Vásárosnamény (7am, 12.15pm, 1.35pm & 5pm daily; 30min); Záhony (7am, 12.15pm, 1.35pm & 5pm daily; 1hr).

From Nyíregyháza to Mátészalka (8am, 10.40am, 2.40pm & 4.55pm daily; 1hr 15min); Nagykálló (8am, 10.40am, 2.40pm & 4.55pm; 15min); Nyírbátor (8am, 10.40am, 2.40pm & 4.55pm; 45min).

From Szeged to Békéscsaba (6.30am, 8.20am, 11.10am, 2.50pm, 4.25pm & 6.50pm daily; 2hr); Budapest (9.20am, 11.20am, 1.20pm, 3.20pm, 6.15pm & 7.35pm daily; 2hr 30min); Keceskemét (9.20am, 11.20am, 1.20pm, 3.20pm, 6.15pm & 7.35pm daily; 1hr 15min).

Buses

From Budapest (Népstadion) to Baja (every 1–2hr; 3hr 15min); Békéscsaba (6.25am, 1.45pm & 4.15pm daily; 4hr); Kalocsa (every 1–2hr; 2hr); Szeged (9pm daily; 3hr 45min).

From Baja to Budapest (every 1–2hr; 3hr 15min); Kalocsa (hourly; 1hr); Sopron (6.25am daily; 10hr); Szeged (6.30am, 7.20am, 9.20am, 11.20am, 1.20pm, 3.45pm, 4.20pm & 7.30pm daily; 2hr 15min); Szekszárd (6.25am daily; 1hr).

From Békéscsaba to Abádszálok (6am & 3.40pm daily; 3hr 15min); Békés (hourly; 30min); Budapest (5.30am, 7am & 1.40pm daily; 4hr); Debrecen (5.15am daily; 3hr); Eger (6am & 3.40pm daily; 5hr); Gyula (hourly; 1hr); Hajdúböszörmény (5.15am daily; 3hr 30min); Miskolc (5.15am daily; 5hr); Pécs (7.45am daily; 6hr 30min).

From Csongrád to Szeged (9.50am daily; 1hr 15min).

From Debrecen to Abádszálok (1.55pm daily; 3hr 15min); Békéscsaba (5.40am, 7.45am, 9.15am, 2.20pm, 4.15pm & 4.40pm daily; 3hr 30min); Eger (6.35am & 3pm daily; 3hr); Gyöngyös (1.55pm daily; 4hr; 45min); Gyula (7.40am daily; 3hr); Hajdúböszörmény (every 30–90min; 30min); Hajdúszoboszló (hourly; 45min); Hortobágy (3pm daily; 1hr); Jászberény (3pm daily; 2hr 30min); Miskolc (every 30–90min; 2hr); Nyíregyháza (6.40am daily; 2hr); Szeged (5.40am & 4.15pm daily; 5hr); Tiszafüred (6.35am & 3pm daily; 1hr 45min).

From Hajdúböszörmény to Debrecen (every 30–90min; 30min); Miskolc (every 30–90min; 1hr 45min);

From Hajdúszoboszló to Debrecen (hourly; 45min); Eger (2.40pm daily; 3hr 15min); Hajdúböszörmény (10.30am & 1pm daily; 1hr); Hortobágy (2.40pm daily; 1hr 15min); Miskolc (10.30am & 1pm daily; 2hr 45min); Nádudvar (hourly; 30min).

From Gyula to Abádszálok (3pm daily; 3hr 45min); Debrecen (2.15pm daily; 2hr); Eger (3pm daily; 5hr 30min); Miskolc (2.15pm daily; 5hr 15min).

From Hortobágy to Debrecen (8.10am daily; 45min); Eger (3.50pm daily; 2hr 15min); Hajdúszoboszló (8.10am daily; 1hr 15min); Tiszafüred (3.50pm daily; 1hr).

From Jászberény to Cegléd (9.30am, 2.25pm & 5pm daily; 1hr 15min); Debrecen (5.55am daily; 4hr 30min); Kecskemét (9.30am, 2.25pm & 5pm

daily; 2hr); Miskolc (6.30am daily; 4hr 45min); Paradfürdő (6.30am daily; 2hr 15min).

From Kalocsa to Baja (hourly; 1hr); Győr (Sun 2.55pm; 5hr); Székesfehérvár (Sun 2.55pm; 3hr).

From Kecskemét to Cegléd (hourly; 30min); Eger (7.45am & 12.35pm daily; 4hr); Gyöngyös (7.45am & 12.35pm daily; 3hr); Jászberény (7.45am & 12.35pm daily; 2hr); Kiskunfélegyháza (hourly; 45min).

From Kiskunfélegyháza to Bugac (every 90min; 1hr); Kecskemét (hourly; 45min).

From Nyíregyháza to Debrecen (4.20pm daily; 2hr); Miskolc (Mon–Sat 2.15pm; 2hr).

From Szeged to Békéscsaba (10.10am, 1pm, 2.45pm & 4pm daily; 2hr); Csongrád (1.40pm daily; 1hr 15min); Debrecen (5.50am & 4pm daily; 5hr); Hodmezővásárhely (1.50pm daily; 1hr 30min); Miskolc (1.50pm daily; 6hr 30min); Tiszafüred (1.50pm daily; 5hr).

From Szolnok to Eger (5.40am & 4.40pm daily & Mon–Fri 1.40pm; 2hr 30min); Jászberény (5.40am daily; 1hr 15min).

From Tiszafüred to Hodmezővásárhely (7am daily; 4hr 30min); Miskolc (Mon–Fri 6.40am & 6.45pm daily; 1hr 30min); Szeged (7am daily; 5hr); Szentes (7am daily; 3hr 45min).

International trains

From Békéscsaba to Arad (1.50am daily; 3hr); Bucharest (1.50am daily; 13hr)

From Debrecen to Baia Mare (4.30pm daily; 5hr 30min); Belgrade (9.25pm daily; 7hr 45min); Braşov (July–Sept 11.50am daily; 12hr); Bucharest (July–Sept 11.50am daily; 15hr); Cluj (July–Sept 11.50am daily; 7hr 30min); Csop (9am daily; 4hr); Kiev (2.30am & 11pm daily; 24hr); Moscow (2.30am & 11pm daily; 38hr); Satu Mare (12.45am daily; 6hr); Valea lui Mihai (12.45am & 4.30pm daily; 3hr); Varna (July–Sept 11.50am daily; 24hr); Warsaw (July–Sept 4.20pm daily; 16hr).

From Kecskemét to Belgrade (midnight daily; 5hr 30min); Chop (9pm daily; 6hr 45min); Kiev (4.50am daily; 23hr); Moscow (4.50am daily; 37hr).

From Szeged to Chop (7.50pm daily; 8hr).

From Szolnok to Arad (12.35am, 7.10am, 10.25am & 3.15pm daily & June–Sept 1pm daily; 4hr); Baia Mare (2.20pm daily; 4hr 30min); Belgrade (11.20pm daily; 6hr); Braşov (7.10am, 10.25am 3.15pm & 6.15pm daily; 11hr); Bucharest (12.35am, 7.10am, 10.25am, 3.15pm & 6.15pm daily; 13hr 45min); Burgas (June–Sept 1pm daily;

23hr); Cluj (6.15pm daily; 8hr); Kiev (5.40am daily; 36hr); Košice (1.20pm daily; 4hr 45min); Kraków (1.20pm daily; 14hr 30min); Moscow (1am & 5.40am daily; 50hr); Satu Mare (2.20pm & 10.35pm daily; 7hr 45min); Sibiu (3.15pm daily; 11hr 30min); Sighişoara (12.35am, 7.10am & 6.15pm daily; 16hr); Sofia (7.10am daily; 25hr); Warsaw (1.20pm daily; 17hr).

International buses
Services to Novi Sad, Subotica and Zrenjanin depend on the situation in Croatia and Serbia.

From Baja to Subotica (7.20am daily; 2hr).

From Békéscsaba to Arad (Mon, Tues, Wed & Fri 5.45am; 4hr); Timişoara (Thurs & Sat 5.45am; 5hr).

From Debrecen to Košice (Mon–Thurs 7am; 4hr); Mukachevo (Wed, Fri & Sun 1.30pm; 7hr); Oradea (March–Sept 6.30am daily; 3hr 30min); Satu Mare (March–Sept 5.30am daily; 5hr); Uzhgorod (5am daily; 6hr).

From Gyula to Subotica (4.45am daily; 5hr).

From Hajdúszoboszló to Oradea (March–Sept Tues, Thurs & Sat 6am; 4hr); Satu Mare (March–Sept Wed & Fri 5am; 5hr); Trebišov (June–Sept Wed & Fri 4.45pm; 5hr).

From Kecskemét to Subotica (Mon–Sat 5.40am; 3hr); Tatranská Lomnica (July–Aug 5.50am daily; 9hr).

From Nyíregyháza to Košice (6am daily; 3hr); Satu Mare (5.30am daily; 4hr); Uzhgorod (5.30am daily; 5hr).

From Szarvas to Arad (Fri & Sat 6.15am; 5hr); Timişoara (Fri & Sat 6.15am; 6hr).

From Szeged to Arad (6.30am daily; 4hr); Novi Sad (Mon–Sat 4pm; 4hr); Subotica (Mon–Sat 4–5 daily; 2hr); Timişoara (6.30am daily; 5hr); Zrenjanin (1pm daily; 4hr).

From Szolnok to Baia Mare (8am daily; 9hr); Oradea (8am daily; 4hr 30min); Satu Mare (8am daily; 7hr 30min).

HISTORICAL FRAMEWORK

The region of the Carpathian basin known as Hungary (*Magyarország*) changed hands many times before the Magyars arrived here at the end of the ninth century, and its history is marked by migrations, invasions, and drastic changes, as Asia and Europe have clashed and blended. Over the centuries borders have shifted considerably, so geographical limits as well as historical epochs are somewhat arbitrary. Transylvania, an integral part of Hungary for hundreds of years, was lost to Romania in 1920; the plight of its Magyar minority remains a contentious issue, while the situation of ethnic Hungarians in Serbia and Slovakia is also a cause for concern.

PREHISTORY

Although recorded history of the area now covered by Hungary begins with the arrival of the Romans, archaeological evidence of **Stone Age** (3,000,000–8000 BC) humans has been found in the Istállóskő and Pilisszántó caves in northern Hungary, suggesting that the earliest inhabitants lived by gathering fruit and hunting reindeer and mammoths. The end of the Ice Age created favourable conditions for the development of agriculture and the domestication of animals, which spread up through the Balkans in the Neolithic era, and was characteristic of the **Kőrös culture** (5500–3400 BC): clans herding sheep and goats and worshipping fertility goddesses, living alongside the River Tisza. As humans became more settled and spread into Transdanubia, evidence survives of mounds (*tell*) full of artefacts, apparently leading towards the rise of the **Lengyel culture** around Lake Balaton.

During the **Bronze Age** (2000–800 BC), warlike tribes arrived from the Balkans and steppes, introducing cattle and horses. Subsequent migrants brought new technology – iron came with the Cimmerians, and the Asiatic Scythians (500–250 BC) brought the potter's wheel and manufactured goods from Greek traders on the Black Sea coast – while the **Celts**, who superseded them in the early third century BC, introduced glassblowing and left mournful sculptures and superb jewellery (most notably the gold treasures of Szárazd-Regöly), before being subdued by the Romans.

THE ROMANS

The **Roman conquest** was initiated by Augustus at the beginning of the Christian era, primarily to create a buffer zone in **Pannonia** between the empire and the barbarians to the east. By the middle of the first century AD Roman rule extended throughout Transdanubia, from the Sava to the Danube, which was fortified with *castrum* and formed the *limes* or military frontier. Trade, administration and culture grew up around the garrison towns and spread along the roads constructed to link the imperial heartland with the far-flung colonies in Dacia (Romania) and Dalmatia (Yugoslavia). Archaeological finds at Pécs, Sopron, Szombathely and Buda show that these were originally Roman towns. The latter's amphitheatre and baths, the ruins of Gorsium and Szombathely's Temple of Isis are the best-preserved Roman remains.

During the fourth century the Romans began to withdraw from Pannonia, handing over its defence to the Vandals and Jazygians who lived beyond the Danube. In 430 they fell under the invading **Huns**, whose empire reached its zenith and then fragmented with the death of Attila (453). Other warring tribes – Ostrogoths, Gepidae and Langobards – occupied the region for the next 150 years, before being swept aside by the **Avars**, whose empire survived until the beginning of the eighth century, when the region once again came up for grabs for any determined invader.

THE MAGYARS

The **Magyars'** origins lie in the *Finno-Ugric* peoples who dwelt in the snowy forests between the Baltic and the middle Urals. Around the first century AD, some of these tribes migrated south across the Bashkiran steppes and fell under the influence of Turkic and Persian culture, gradually becoming tent-dwelling nomadic herders who lived on a diet of mare's milk, horse flesh, fish and berries. Some archaeologists believe that they mingled with the ancient Bulgars north of the Caspian Sea (in a land known as "Magna Bulgaria"), before the majority fled from marauding Petchenegs (in about 750) and moved westwards to settle on the far bank of the River Don in the so-called *Etelköz* region, around the year 830. Ties with the Huns and Avars have been postulated – including a common language – but there's more evidence to link the seven original Magyar tribes with three Kavar tribes; they were known collectively as the *Onogur*, or "Ten Arrows".

Overpopulation and Petcheneg attacks forced the Onogur to move westwards in 889, and tradition has it that the seven Magyar chieftains elected **Árpád** as their leader, pledging fealty to his heirs with a blood oath. Accompanied by smaller Kun (or Cuman) tribes, the Onogur entered the Carpathian basin in 896, and began the "**landtaking**" (*honfoglalás*) or conquest of the region. Six Magyar tribes settled west of the Danube and in the upper Tisza region; the seventh took the approaches to Transylvania, while the lower Tisza and the northern fringes of the Plain went to the Kuns and Kavars. For the next seventy years the Magyars remained raiders, striking terror as far afield as Constantinople and Orleans (where people thought them to be Huns), until a series of defeats persuaded them to settle for assimilating their gains.

Civilisation developed gradually, after Árpád's great-grandson Prince **Géza** established links with Bavaria and invited Catholic missionaries to Hungary. His son **Stephen** (*István*) took the decisive step of applying to Pope Sylvester for recognition, and on Christmas Day in the year 1000 was crowned as a Christian king and began converting his pagan subjects with the help of Bishop Gellért. Royal authority was extended over the non-tribal lands by means of the *megye* (county) system, and defended by fortified *vár*; artisans and priests were imported to spread skills and the new religion; and tribal rebellions were crushed. Stephen was subsequently credited with the **foundation of Hungary** and canonised after his death in 1038. His mummified hand and the Crown of Saint Stephen have since been revered as both holy and national relics.

THE MIDDLE AGES

Succession struggles raged for decades following Stephen's death, and of the sixteen kings who preceded Andrew II (1205–35), only the humane László I (also canonised), Kálmán "the Booklover", and Béla III (1172–96) contributed anything significant to Hungary's development. Fortunately, invasions were few during the eleventh and twelfth centuries, and **German and Slovak immigrants** helped double the population to about two million by 1200. Parts of **Transylvania** were settled by the Magyars and Székely, perhaps before the second half of the eleventh century, when the "lands of Saint Stephen" were extended to include **Slavonia** (between the Sava and Drava rivers) and the unwillingly "associated" state of **Croatia**. The growth in royal power caused tribal leaders to rebel in 1222, when Andrew II was forced to recognise the "noble" status and rights of **the Natio** – landed freemen exempt from taxation – in the *Golden Bull*, a kind of Hungarian Magna Carta.

Andrew's son **Béla IV** was trying to restore royal authority when disaster struck from the east – the **Mongol invasion** of 1241, which devastated Hungary. Hundreds of towns and villages were sacked; refugees fled to the swamps and forests; crops were burned or left unharvested; and famine and plague followed. Population losses ranged from sixty and even one hundred percent on the Plain to twenty percent in Transdanubia, and after the Mongol withdrawal a year later (prompted by the timely death of the Khan), Hungary faced a mammoth task of **reconstruction** – the chief achievement of Béla's reign, to which foreign settlers made a large contribution. Renewed domestic feuding (complicated by foreign intervention and the arrival of more Cuman tribes) dogged the reign of Andrew III; and worsened when he died heirless in 1301, marking the **end of the Árpád dynasty**.

FOREIGN RULE

Foreign powers advanced their own claimants, and for a while there were three competing kings, all duly crowned. **Charles Robert** of the French Angevin (or Anjou) dynasty eventually triumphed in 1310, when his rivals went home in disgust; and despite colonial skirmishes with Venice, Serbia and Wallachia, Hungary itself enjoyed a period of peace, for the Mongols and other great powers were occupied elsewhere. Gold mines in Transylvania and northern Hungary – the richest in Europe – stabilised state finances and the currency. Charles's son **Louis the Great** reigned (1342–82) during a period of expansion, when the population rose to three million; and by war and dynastic aggrandizement crown territory grew to include Dalmatia, the Banat, Gallicia and (in theory) Poland. Louis, however, sired only daughters, so that after his demise, another foreigner ascended the throne in 1395 – **Sigismund of Luxembourg**, Prince of Bohemia, whom the nobles despised as the "Czech swine". His extravagant follies and campaigns abroad were notorious, and while Sigismund recognised the growing threat of the Turks, he failed to prevent their advance up through the Balkans.

During the fourteenth century, the realm contained 49 boroughs, about 500 market towns, and 26,000 villages. Everyone benefitted from peace and expanded trade, but the rewards weren't shared evenly, for the Angevins favoured towns and guilds, and most of all the top stratum of the Natio, on whom they depended for troops (*banderia*) when war posed a threat. The burden fell upon the **peasantry**, who lacked "free" status and were compelled to pay *porta* (gate tax) to the state, tithes to the church, and one ninth of their produce to the landlords – plus extra taxes and obligations during times of war, or to finance new royal palaces.

Sigismund died in 1447 leaving one daughter, Elizabeth, just as **the Turks** were poised to invade and succession struggles seemed inevitable. The Turks might have taken Hungary then, but for a series of stunning defeats inflicted upon them by **János Hunyadi**, a Transylvanian warlord of Vlach (Romanian) origin. The lifting of the siege of Nándorfehérervár (Belgrade) in 1456 checked the Turkish advance and caused rejoicing throughout Christendom – the ringing of church bells at noon was decreed by the pope to mark this victory – while Hunyadi rose to be *Voivode* or Prince of Transylvania, and later regent for the boy king László. Following Hunyadi's death, László's early demise, and much skullduggery, Mihály Szilágyi staged a coup and put his nephew Mátyás (Matthias), Hunyadi's son, on the throne in 1458.

RENAISSANCE AND DECLINE

Mátyás Corvinus is remembered as the "**Renaissance King**" for his statecraft and multiple talents (including astrology), while his second wife **Beatrice** of Naples lured humanists and artists from Italy to add lustre to their palaces at Buda and Visegrád (of which some remains survive). Mátyás was an enlightened despot renowned for his fairness: "King Mátyás is dead, justice is departed", people mourned. By taxing the nobles (against every pre-cedent) he raised a standing force of 30,000 mercenaries, called the Black Army, which secured the realm and made Hungary one of Central Europe's leading powers; but when he died in 1490, leaving no legitimate heir, the nobles looked for a king "whose plaits they could hold in their fists".

Such a man was Ulászló II (whose habit of assenting to any proposal earned him the nickname "King Okay"), under whom the Black Army and its tax base were whittled away by the Diet (which met to approve royal decrees and taxes), while the nobility filched common land and otherwise increased their exploitation of the peasantry. Impelled by poverty, many joined the crusade of 1514, which under the leadership of **György Dózsa** turned into an **uprising against the landlords**. Its savage repression (over 70,000 peasants were killed and Dózsa was roasted alive) was followed by the **Werbőczy Code** of 1517, binding the peasants to "perpetual **serfdom**" on their masters' land and 52 days of *robot* (unpaid labor) in the year.

Hungary's decline accelerated as corruption and incompetence bankrupted the treasury, forts along the border crumbled, and the revived *banderia* system of mobilisation turned makeshift. Ulászló's son Louis II was only nine when crowned, and by 1520 the Turks, under Sultan Süleyman "the Magnificent", had resumed their advance northwards, capturing the run-down forts in Serbia. In August 1526 the Turks crossed the Drava and Louis hastened south to confront them at the **battle of Mohács** – a catastrophic defeat for the Magyars, whose army was wiped out together with its monarch and commanders.

TURKISH CONQUEST: HUNGARY DIVIDED

After sacking Buda and the south, the Turks withdrew in 1526 to muster forces for their real objective, Vienna, the "Red Apple". To forestall this, Ferdinand of Habsburg proclaimed himself king and occupied western Hungary, while in Buda the nobility put **János Zápolyai** on the throne. Following Zápolyai's death in 1541 Ferdinand claimed full sovereignty, but the Sultan occupied Buda and central Hungary, and made Zápolyai's young son ruler of Transylvania. Thereafter Transylvania became a semi-autonomous principality, nominally loyal to the Sultan and jealously coveted by the Habsburgs. The tripartite **division of Hungary** was formally recognised in 1568. Despite various official or localised truces, warfare became a feature of everyday life for the next 150 years, and the national independence lost then was not to be recovered for centuries afterwards.

Royal Hungary – basically western Transdanubia and the north – served as a "human moat" against the Turkish forces that threatened to storm Austria and Western Europe, kept at bay by Hungarian sacrifices at Szigetvár, Kőszeg and other fortresses. Notwithstanding constitutional arrangements to safeguard the Natio's privileges, real power passed to the Habsburg chancellery and war council, where the liberation of Hungary took second place to Austria's defence and aggrandizement, and the subjugation of Transylvania.

Turkish-occupied Hungary – *Eyalet-i Budin* – was ruled by a Pasha in Buda, with much of the land either deeded to the Sultan's soldiers and officials, or run directly as a state fief (*khasse*). The peasants were brutally exploited, for many had to pay rent both to their absentee Magyar landlords and to the occupying Turks. Their plight is evident from a letter to a Hungarian lord by the villagers of Batthyán: "Verily, it is better to be Your Lordship's slaves, bag and baggage, than those of an alien people". Peasants fled their villages on the Alföld to the safer fields around the expanding "agro-towns" of Debrecen and

Szeged, the nexus of the cattle trade which gradually supplanted agriculture, while neglect and wanton tree-felling transformed the Plain into a swampy wasteland – the *puszta*.

The Voivodes of **Transylvania** endeavoured to provoke war between the Habsburgs and Turks, in order to increase their independence from both and satisfy the feudal **Nationes**. The latter, representing the élite of the region's Magyars, Saxons and Székely, combined to deny the indigenous Vlachs political power, while competing amongst themselves and extending the borders of Transylvania (then much bigger than today). István Bocskai's *Hajdúk* forces secured the Szatmár region; Gábor Bethlen promoted economic and social development; but Prince György Rákóczi II aimed too high and brought the wrath of the Sultan down on Transylvania.

Religion was an additional complicating factor. The Protestant Reformation gained many adherents in Hungary during the sixteenth century, and while religious toleration was decreed in Transylvania in 1572, in Royal Hungary the counter-reformation gathered force under Habsburg rule. The Turks, ironically, were indifferent to the issue and treated all their Christian subjects (*Rayah*) with equal disdain. After the expulsion of the Turks, Protestant landowners were dispossessed in favour of foreign servants of the crown – a major cause of subsequent anti-Habsburg revolts.

HABSBURG RULE

After heavy fighting between 1683 and 1699, a multinational army evicted the Ottomans, and the Turks relinquished all claims by signing the **Peace of Karlowitz**. Yet for many years peace remained a mirage, for the Hungarians now bitterly resented Habsburg policy and their plundering armies. The **Kuruc revolt** (1677–85) led by **Imre Thököly** was but a prelude to the full-scale **War of Independence** of 1703–11, when peasants and nobles banded together under **Ferenc Rákóczi II**, György's grandson, and initially routed the enemy. Ultimately, however, they were defeated by superior Habsburg power and the desertion of their ally, Louis XIV of France, and peace born of utter exhaustion came at last to Hungary.

Habsburg rule combined force with paternalism, especially during the reign of Empress **Maria Theresa** (1740–80), who believed the Hungarians to be "fundamentally a good people, with whom one can do anything if one takes them the right way". The policy of *impopulatio* settled thousands of Swabians, Slovaks, Serbs and Romanians in the deserted regions of Hungary, so that in areas such as the "Military Border" along the Sava, **Magyars became a minority**. By the end of the eighteenth century they formed only 35 percent of the population of the huge kingdom. For the aristocrats it was an age of glory: the Esterházy, Grassalkovich and Batthyány families and their lesser imitators commissioned over 200 palaces, and Baroque town centres and orchestras flourished. Yet the masses were virtually serfs, using medieval methods that impoverished the soil, mired in isolated villages. Cattle, grain and wine – Hungary's main exports – went cheap to Austria, which tried to monopolise industry.

The **Germanisation** of culture, education, and administration was another feature of Habsburg policy. Whilst the richest nobles and most of the urban bourgeoisie chose the Habsburg style, however, the petty gentry and peasantry clung stubbornly to their Magyar identity. The ideals of the **Enlightenment** found growing support among intellectuals, and the revival of the **Magyar language** became inseparable from nationalist politics. **Ferenc Kazinczy**, who refashioned Hungarian as a literary language and translated foreign classics, was associated with the seven **Jacobin conspirators,** executed for plotting treason against the Habsburgs in 1795.

THE NINETEENTH CENTURY: NATIONALISM AND REFORM

Magyar nationalism, espoused by sections of the Natio, became increasingly vocal during the early nineteenth century. Hungary's backwardness was a matter for patriotic shame and self-interested concern, especially after the occurence of peasant riots in the impoverished, cholera-ridden Zempléni, and the publication of *Hitel* ("Credit"), which scathingly indicted the country's semi-feudal economy. However, most nobles were determined to preserve their privileges. One wrote that "God himself has differentiated between us, assigning to the peasant labour and need, to the lord, abundance and a merry life". Moreover, national liberation was seen in exclusively Magyar terms – the idea

that non-Magyars within the multinational state might wish to assert their own identity was regarded as subversive.

The **Reform Era** (roughly 1825–48) saw many changes. Business, the arts and technology were in ferment, with Jews playing a major role in creating wealth and ideas (although they remained second-class citizens). The **Diet** became increasingly defiant in its dealings with Vienna over finances and laws, and parliamentarians like Ferenc Deák, Count Batthyány and Baron Eötvös acted in the shadow of the "giants" of the time, Széchenyi and Kossuth, who expounded rival programmes for change. Count **István Széchenyi**, the landowning, Anglophile author of *Hitel*, was a tireless practical innovator, introducing silkworms, steamboats and the Academy, as well as an unprecedented tax on the Natio to pay for the construction of his life's monument, the Chain Bridge linking Buda and Pest. His arch rival was **Lajos Kossuth**, smalltown lawyer turned Member of Parliament and editor of the radical *Pesti Hirlap*, which scandalised and delighted citizens. Kossuth detested the Habsburgs, revered "universal liberty", and demanded an end to serfdom and censorship; but Magyar chauvinism was his blindspot. The law of 1840, his greatest pre-revolutionary achievement, inflamed dormant nationalist feelings among Croats, Slovaks, and Romanians by making Magyar the sole official language – an act for which his ambitions would later suffer.

REVOLUTION

The fall of the French monarchy precipitated a crisis within the Habsburg empire, which Kossuth exploited to bring about the **1848 Revolution** in Hungary. The emperor yielded to demands for a constitutional monarchy, universal taxation, widened voting rights and the union of Transylvania with Hungary; while in Budapest the nobles took fright and abolished serfdom when the poet **Sándor Petőfi** threatened them with thousands of peasants camped out in the suburbs. However, the slighted nationalities rallied against the Magyars in Croatia and Transylvania, and the reassertion of Habsburg control over Italy and Czechoslovakia closed the noose. The new emperor Franz Josef declared that Hungary would be partitioned after its defeat, in reaction to which the Debrecen Diet declared

Hungarian independence – a state crushed by August 1849, when Tsar Nicholas of Russia sent armies to support the Habsburgs, who instituted a reign of terror.

Gradually, brute force was replaced by a **policy of compromise**, by which Hungary was economically integrated with Austria and given a major shareholding in the Habsburg empire, henceforth known as the "Dual Monarchy". The compromise (*Ausgleich*) of 1867, engineered by **Ferenc Deák**, brought Hungary prosperity and status, but tied the country inextricably to the empire's fortunes. Simmering nationalist passions would henceforth be focused against Hungary as much as Austria, and diplomatic treaties between Austria and Germany would bind Hungary to them in the event of war. In 1896, however, such dangers seemed remote, and people celebrated **Hungary's millenary anniversary** with enthusiasm.

WORLD WAR AND ITS AFTERMATH

Dragged into **World War I** by its allegiance to the Central Powers, Hungary was facing defeat by the autumn of 1918. The Western or Entente powers decided to dismantle the Habsburg empire in favour of the **"Successor States"** – Romania, Czechoslovakia, and Yugoslavia – which would acquire much of their territory at Hungary's expense. In Budapest, the October 30 "Michaelmas Daisy Revolution" put the Social Democratic government of **Mihály Károly** in power. But the government avoided the issue of land reform, attempted unsuccessfully to negotiate peace with the Entente, and finally resigned when France backed further demands by the Successor States.

On March 21, 1919, the Social Democrats agreed on co-operation with the **Communists**, who proclaimed a **Republic of Councils** (*Tanácsköztársaság*) led by **Béla Kun**, which ruled through local Soviets. Hoping for radical change and believing that "Russia will save us", many people initially supported the new regime, but enforced nationalisation of land and capital, and attacks on religion, soon alienated the majority. Beset by the Czech Legion in Slovakia and by internal unrest, the regime collapsed in August before the advancing Romanian army, which occupied Budapest.

THE RISE OF FASCISM

Then came the **White Terror**, as right-wing gangs spread out from Szeged, killing "Reds" and Jews, who were made scapegoats for the earlier Communist "Red Terror". **Admiral Miklós Horthy** appointed himself regent and ordered a return to "traditional values" with a vengeance. Meanwhile, at the Paris Conference, Hungary was obliged to sign the **Treaty of Trianon** (July 4, 1920), surrendering two thirds of its historic territory and three fifths of its total population (three million in all) to the Successor States. The bitterest loss was **Transylvania**, whose 103,093 square kilometres and 1.7 million Magyars went to Romania – a devastating blow to national pride, reflected in the popular slogan of the times, *Nem, Nem, soha!* (No, No, never!).

During **the Twenties and Thirties**, campaigning for the overturn of the Trianon *diktat* was the "acceptable" outlet for politics; while workers' unions were tightly controlled and peasants struggled to form associations against the landlords and the gendarmerie, who rigged ballots and gerrymandered as in the old days. Politics were dominated by the *Kormánypárt* (Government Party) led by Count Bethlen, representing the Catholic Church and the landed gentry, which resisted any changes that would threaten their power. Social hardships increased, particularly in the countryside where the **landless peasantry** constituted "three million beggars" whose misery concerned the **Village Explorers** (*Falukutató*): a movement of the literary intelligentsia ranging across the political spectrum. With the Social Democrats co-opted by conservatism and the Communist Party illegal, many workers and disgruntled petit bourgeois turned to the **radical right** to voice their grievances, and were easily turned against Jews and the "Trianon Powers".

Resentment against France, Britain and Romania predisposed many Hungarians to admire **Nazi Germany**'s defiance of the Versailles Treaty; a sentiment nurtured by the Reich's grant of credits for **industrialisation**, and Nazi sympathizers within *Volksdeutsche* communities, commerce, the civil service and the officer corps. The rise of rampant nationalism and **anti-semitism** gave power to politicians like **Gyula Gömbös**, and Hungary's belated industrial growth was partly due to the acquisition of territory from Czechoslovakia, following Germany's dismemberment of the latter. The annexation of Austria made the Reich militarily supreme in Central Europe, and Hungary's submission to German hegemony almost inevitable.

WORLD WAR II

With the outbreak of **World War II**, the government's pro-Nazi policy initially paid dividends. Romania was compelled to return **northern Transylvania** in July 1940, and Hungary gained additional territory from the invasion of Yugoslavia a year later. Hoping for more, Premier Bárdossy committed Hungary to the Nazi invasion of the USSR in June 1941 – an act condemned by the former Prime Minister, Teleki (who had engineered the recovery of Transylvania), as the "policy of vultures". The Hungarian Second Army perished covering the retreat from Stalingrad, while at home, Germany demanded ever more foodstuffs and forced labour. As Axis fortunes waned Horthy prepared to declare neutrality, but Hitler forestalled him with *Operation Margarethe* – the outright **Nazi occupation of Hungary** in March 1944.

Under Sztójay's puppet-government, Hungarian **Jews** were forced into ghettos to await their deportation to Auschwitz and Belsen, a fate hindered only by the heroism of the underground, a handful of people organised by the Swedish diplomat Raoul Wallenberg, and by the manoeuvring of some Horthyite politicians. Mindful of Romania's successful escape from the Axis in August, Horthy declared a surprise armistice on October 15, just as the Red Army crossed Hungary's eastern border. In response, Germany installed a government of the native **Arrow Cross fascists**, or *Nyilas*, led by the deranged Ferenc Szálasi, whose gangs roamed Budapest extorting valuables and murdering people on the frozen Danube, while the Nazis systematically plundered Hungary. They blew up the Danube bridges and compelled the Russians to take Budapest by storm – a siege that reduced much of Buda to ruins. Meanwhile in Debrecen, an assembly of anti-fascist parties met under Soviet auspices to nominate a **provisional government**, which took power after the Germans fled Hungary in April 1945.

THE RÁKOSI ERA

In the November 1945 **elections** the Smallholders' Party won an outright majority, but the Soviet military insisted that the Communists and Social Democrats (with seventeen percent of the vote) remain in government. **Land reform** and limited **nationalisation** were enacted, while the Communists tightened their grip over the Ministry of the Interior (which controlled the police) and elections became increasingly fraudulent. **Mátyás Rákosi**, Stalin's man in Hungary, gradually undermined and fragmented the "bourgeois" parties with what he called "salami tactics", and by 1948 – officially called the **"Year of Change"** – the Communists were strong enough to coerce the Social Democrats to join them in a single **Workers' Party**, and neutralise the Smallholders. Church schools were seized, Cardinal Mindszenty was jailed for "espionage" and the peasants were forced into collective farms. More than 500,000 Hungarians were imprisoned, tortured, or shot in native concentration camps like Recsk, or as deportees in the Soviet Union: victims of the *ÁVO* secret police (renamed the *ÁVH* in 1949), who spread terror throughout society.

Soviet culture and the personality cults of Rákosi (known as "Baldhead" or "Asshole" to his subjects) and Stalin were stiflingly imposed. Hungarian classics like the *Tragedy of Man* were banned for failing to meet the standards of Socialist Realism. Under the 1949 **Five Year Plan**, heavy industry took absolute priority over agriculture and consumer production. To fill the new factories, peasants streamed into towns and women were dragooned into the labour force. Living standards plummeted, and the whole of society was subject to the laws and dictates of the Party. "Class conscious" workers and peasants were raised to high positions and "class enemies" were discriminated against, while Party *funkcionáriusok* enjoyed luxuries unavailable to the public, who suffered hunger and squalor.

Although the Smallholders retained nominal positions in government, real power lay with Rákosi's clique, known as the "Jewish Quartet". As elsewhere in Eastern Europe at this time, Hungary saw bitter **feuds within the Communist Party**. In October 1949, the

"Muscovites" purged the more independently-minded "national" Communists on the pretext of "Titoism". The former Interior Minister **László Rajk** was executed; and his friend and successor (and, later, betrayer), **János Kádár**, was jailed and tortured with others during a second wave of purges. Two years later, following Stalin's death in March 1953, Kremlin power struggles resulted in a more moderate Soviet leadership and the abrupt replacement of Rákosi by **Imre Nagy**. His **"New Course"**, announced in July, promised a more balanced industrial strategy and eased pressure on the peasants to collectivise, besides curbing the *ÁVO* terror. Nagy however had few allies within the Kremlin, and in 1955 Rákosi was able to strike back, expelling Nagy from the Party for "deviationism", and declaring a **return to Stalinist policies**. However, this brief interlude had encouraged murmurings of resistance.

1956: THE UPRISING

The first act of opposition came from the official Writers' Union: the *November Memorandum*, who objected to the rule of force. The Party clamped down, but also began to "rehabilitate" the Rajk purge victims. During June **1956** the intellectuals' **Petőfi circle** held increasingly outspoken public debates, and **Júlia Rajk** denounced "the men who have ruined this country, corrupted the Party, liquidated thousands and driven millions to despair". Moscow responded to the unrest by replacing Rákosi with **Ernő Gerő** – another hardliner – a move which merely stoked public resentment. The mood came to a head in October, when 200,000 people attended Rajk's reburial; Nagy was readmitted to the Party; and **students** in Szeged and Budapest organised to demand greater national independence and freedom.

In Poland, Gomulka's reform communists had just won concessions from the Kremlin, and Budapest students decided to march on October 23 to the General Bem statue, a symbol of Polish-Hungarian solidarity. About 50,000 assembled, patriotic feelings rose, and the procession swelled as it approached Parliament. A hesitant speech there by Nagy failed to satisfy them, and students besieged the Radio Building on Bródy utca, demanding to voice their grievances on the airwaves. The *ÁVH* guards opened fire, killing many. Almost immediately, this triggered a city-wide **uprising** against the *ÁVH*, which the regular police did little to control; and when Soviet tanks intervened, units of the Hungarian army began to side with the insurgents.

Over the next five days fighting spread throughout Hungary, despite Nagy's reinstatement as premier and pleas for order. **Revolutionary councils** sprang up in towns and factories and free newspapers appeared, demanding "*Ruszkik haza*" (Russians go home), free elections, civil liberties, industrial democracy and neutrality. Intellectuals who had led the first protests now found themselves left behind by uncontrollable dynamism on the streets. The Party leadership temporized, reshuffled the cabinet, and struggled to stay in control, as all the "old" parties reappeared and the newly liberated Cardinal Mindszenty provided a focus for the resurgent Right.

The negotiated **Soviet withdrawal**, beginning on October 29, was a delaying tactic. The Russians regrouped in the countryside and brought in fresh troops from Romania and the USSR. On November 1, Nagy announced Hungary's withdrawal from the Warsaw Pact and asked the UN to support **Hungarian neutrality**; that night, Kádár and Ferenc Münnich slipped away from Parliament to join the Russians, who were preparing to crush the "counter-revolution". America downplayed Hungary in the United Nations while the Suez crisis preoccupied world attention, but the CIA-sponsored **Radio Free Europe** encouraged the Magyars to expect Western aid. Having surrounded Budapest and other centres with tanks under cover of a snowstorm, the **Soviet attack** began before dawn on November 4.

Armed resistance was crushed within days, but the workers occupied their factories and proclaimed a **general strike**, maintained for months despite **mass arrests**. Deprived of physical power, the people continued to make symbolic protests like the "Mothers' March" in December. Inexorably, however, the Party and *ÁVH* apparatus reasserted its control. Over 200,000 **refugees** fled to the West, while at home, thousands were jailed or executed, including Nagy and other leading "revisionists", shot in 1958 after a secret trial.

KADAR'S HUNGARY

In the aftermath of the Uprising, the new Party leader **János Kádár** ruthlessly suppressed the last vestiges of opposition. After the mid-1960s, however, his name came to be associated with the **gradual reform** of Hungary's social and economic system from a totalitarian regime to one based, at least in part, on **compromise**. Kádár's famous phrase, "Whoever is not against us is with us" (a reversal of the Stalinist slogan) invited a tacit compact between Party and people. Both had been shaken by the events of 1956, and realised that bold changes – as happened in Czechoslovakia in 1967 and 1968 – only invited Soviet intervention, justified by the Brezhnev doctrine of "limited sovereignty".

Having stimulated the economy by cautious reforms in the structure of pricing and management, and overcome opposition within the Politburo, Kádár and Reszö Nyers announced the **New Economic Mechanism** (NEM) in 1968. Though its impact on centralised planning was slight, the NEM was accompanied by measures to promote "socialist legality" and make merit, rather than class background and Party standing, the criteria for promotion and higher education.

While generally welcomed by the populace, these reforms angered "New Left" supporters of either Dubček's "Socialism with a human face" in Czechoslovakia or of the Chinese Cultural Revolution, and also, more seriously, conservatives within the Party. With backing from Moscow, they watered down the NEM and ousted Nyers, its leading advocate, from the Politburo in 1973; expelling Hegedüs and other "revisionist sociologists" from the Party later.

Following a power struggle, Kádár was able to reverse the reactionary tide, and reduce constraints on the so-called "second economy". While structural reforms were extremely limited, consumerism, a private sector, and even "forint millionaires" emerged during **the Seventies**, when Hungary became a by word for **affluence** within the Socialist bloc – the "happiest barracks in the camp", as the joke had it. Mechanics and other artisans with marketable skills were able to moonlight profitably, as demonstrated by the boom in private home-building; and workers and unions acquired some say in the management of their enterprises. This **"market socialism"** attracted the favours of Western politicians and bankers, and before *perestroika* the "Hungarian model" seemed to offer the best hope for reform within Eastern Europe.

In **the Eighties**, however, economic and social problems became increasingly obvious – ranging from thirty percent **inflation**, whose effect was felt hardest by the **"new poor"** living on low, fixed incomes, to Hungary's $14.7 billion **foreign debt** (per capita, the largest in Eastern Europe). Despite reformist rhetoric, vested interests successfully resisted the logic of the market, whose rigourous application would entail drastic lay offs and mass **unemployment** in towns dominated by the unprofitable mining and steel industries. Although frank analyses of Hungary's economic plight started appearing in the media during the mid-Eighties, other issues ran up against the limits of state tolerance. These included fears for **the environment** in the wake of Chernobyl and the decision to build a dam at Nagymaros (see Chapter Two); an unofficial **peace movement** that quickly driven back underground; and any discussion of the Party's "leading role" or Hungary's alliance with the Soviet Union. Discussion of such topics could only be found in **samizdat** (underground) magazines like *Beszélő*, whose publishers were harassed as dissidents. Although in 1983 the Party announced that "independents" could contest elections, it proved unwilling to let them enter Parliament, as demonstrated by the gerrymandering used against László Rajk in 1986.

Yet the need for change was becoming evident even within the Party, where the caution of the "old guard" – Kádár, Horváth, and Gáspár – caused increasing frustration among **reformists**, who believed that Hungarians would only accept income tax and economic austerity if greater liberalisation seemed a realistic prospect. Happily, this coincided with the advent of **Gorbachev**, whose interest in the Hungarian model of socialism and desire to bring a new generation into power was an open secret.

THE END OF COMMUNISM

The **end of Communism in Hungary** was so orderly that it can hardly be termed a revolution, but it did set in motion the collapse of hardline regimes in East Germany and Czechoslovakia. Prefiguring the fate of Gorbachev, the politicians who created an opening for change hoped to preserve Communism by reforming it, but were swept away by the forces which they had unleashed.

At the **May 1988 Party Congress**, Kádár and seven colleagues were ousted from power by a coalition of radical reformers and conservative technocrats. The latter backed **Károly Grósz** as Kádár's successor, but his lacklustre performance as Party leader enabled the reformists to shunt him aside in July 1989, forcing conservatives and hardliners onto the defensive. As the ascendancy of **Imre Pozsgay**, **Rezsö Nyers**, **Miklós Németh** and **Gyula Horn** became apparent there was a "traffic jam on the road to Damascus" as lesser figures hastened to pledge support for reforms.

In mid-October 1989, the Communist Party formally reconstituted itself as the **Hungarian Socialist Party** (*MSzP*), dissolved its private militia and announced the **legalisation of opposition parties** as a prelude to free elections. To symbolise this watershed, the People's Republic was renamed the **Republic of Hungary** in a ceremony broadcast live on national television, on the thirty-third anniversary of the Uprising.

Meanwhile, the iron curtain was unravelling with astonishing speed. Ever since May, when Hungary began dismantling the barbed wire and minefields along its **border** with Austria, thousands of **East Germans** had seized their chance to escape to the West, crossing over via Hungary at a rate of 200 every day. Despite protests from the Honecker regime, Hungary refused to close the border or deport would-be escapers back to the DDR, and allowed 20,000 refugees encamped in the West German embassy in Budapest to leave the country. After the DDR sealed its own borders, frustration spilled over on to the streets of Leipzig and Dresden, where mass demonstrations led to the **fall of the Berlin Wall** (November 9, 1989) and ousting of Erich Honecker. A week later, the brutal repression of a pro-democracy demonstration in Prague's Wenceslas Square set in motion the **"Velvet Revolution"** in Czechoslovakia, which overturned forty years of Communist rule in ten days. The *annus mirabilis*

of 1989 climaxed with the **overthrow of Ceauşescu** in Romania (December 22).

THE 1990 ELECTION AND BEYOND

After such events Hungary's first **free elections** since 1945 – in 1990 – seemed an anticlimax. During the first round of voting (March 6) Pozsgay and the Socialist Party were obliterated, while two parties emerged as front runners. The **Hungarian Democratic Forum** (*MDF*), founded at the Lakitelek Conference of 1987, articulated populist, conservative nationalism, encapsulsated in the idea of "Hungarianness", whereas the rival **Alliance of Free Democrats** (*SzDSz*) espoused a neoliberal, internationalist outlook, similar to that of the **Federation of Young Democrats** (*FIDESz*). Two pre-war parties revived under octegenarian leaders also participated, namely the **Smallholders' Party** (under the slogan "God, Home, Family, Wine, Wheat and Independence") and the **Christian Democrats**.

Despite being diminished by voter apathy, the second ballot (March 25) gave a decisive majority to the Democratic Forum, which formed a coalition government under **József Antall**. The disappointed Free Democrats complained of an anti-Semitic dirty-tricks campaign by the *MDF*, but contributed to their own defeat by espousing a radical **transition to capitalism**, giving the impression that they welcomed unemployment as a cure for economic ills. Antall's government has played a shrewder hand, gradually withdrawing subsidies from loss-making firms until they go bust. Northeastern Hungary has been worst hit by **unemployment**, with two or three times the national average rate. While seventy percent of Hungary's population has suffered a drop in income or living standards, five percent has prospered enormously under the free market. Although the government need not face the voters for several years yet, its survival will be determined by the success or failure of capitalism to enrich the majority. Meanwhile, Hungary is receiving the largest share of **Western investments** in the former Eastern Bloc, and is tipped for **membership of the European Community** by the end of the decade.

MONUMENTAL CHRONOLOGY

8000 BC	Palaeolithic cave-dwellers in the Bükk Mountains.	Remains found at Subalyuk, Szeleta and other caves.
400 BC	Celts enter Transdanubia.	Pottery, glassware; gold treasure of Szárazd-Regöly.
1st–4th c.	**Romans** occupy Pannonia, founding numerous towns.	Ruins at **Aquincum, Gorsium, Szombathely, Pécs** etc.
896	Magyar conquest. The state and Christianity are established in Hungary by Stephen I during the eleventh century.	Ruins of the Székesfehérvár Basilica; eleventh-century crypts at Pécs and **Tihany** Abbey are virtually all that remain.
13th c.	Mongol invasion. Castles and new towns are founded during the reign of Béla IV.	**Romanesque churches** at **Ják, Zsámbék, Oskü,** and **Velemér** stand comparison with **Pannonhalma Monastery**. Ruined *vár* at **Esztergom, Füzér** and **Boldogkőváralja**, sited on precipitous crags.
14th–15th c.	Zenith of Hungarian power in Europe under the Angevin monarchs and then Mátyás Corvinus.	Remains of **Buda** and **Visegrád** where **Gothic and Renaissance architecture** attained great heights; **Diósgyőr** castle in Miskolc.
1526–1680s	After defeat at **Mohács**, Hungary is occupied for next 150 years by **Turks** and Habsburgs, and ravaged by warfare.	**Kőszeg, Sárospatak, Siklós**, and other **castles** have remained largely intact; as have a few **Turkish** *türbe*, ex-*djami* and **minarets** at **Pécs** and **Eger**; but most medieval towns were destroyed, although on the Plain, Szeged and Debrecen expanded vastly.
1703–11	Rákóczi War of Independence.	
17th–18th c.	Under **Habsburg rule**, many towns are wholly rebuilt around new centres; while Buda Palace and other monumental buildings are begun.	The **wooden belfrys**, pew-carvings and colourful coffered ceilings found at **Nyírbator, Zsurk, Csaroda**, and other remote churches in eastern Hungary are part-Gothic, and partly the "folk" equivalent of the **Baroque style**. This characterised much of seventeenth- and eighteenth-century architecture, eg in the Belváros of **Győr, Veszprém, Székesfehérvár** etc, and at the **Esterházy Palace** in Fertőd.
1830–1880s	After the Reform Era and the struggle for independence (1848–49), Hungary accepts the "Compromise" of 1868. Development of new centres of industry—Miskolc, Salgótarján, Csepel etc.	The **Chain Bridge** presages a spate of construction in Budapest, where large houses are built alongside the new **boulevards**. **Szeged** rebuilt after 1879 flood. The rise of **Neoclassicism**—with Ybl and Hild's huge Basilicas in Eger, Pest and Esztergom—but also **neo-Gothic**—the **Fishermen's Bastion** and **Vajdahunyad Castle** (in 1896, like the Metro)—plus Lechner's attempts to develop a uniquely "**Hungarian Style**" for the **Applied Arts Museum** and the public buildings in **Kecskemét**.
1896	1000th anniversary of the Magyar conquest.	

1918– 1919	Habsburg empire collapses; Hungary briefly becomes a "**Republic of Councils**."	Paintings by the **Group of Eight** (Szombathely Gallery)
1920s & 1930s	Hungary loses two thirds of its territory to neighbouring states. Regency of **Admiral Horthy**.	Deliberate evocation of past national glories—the erection of "Heroes' Gates" in **Szeged**, **Kőszeg** etc.
1944–45	**Nazis** occupy Hungary; massacre of Hungarian **Jews** and **Gypsies**. Heavy fighting with Soviet army.	Desecration of **synagogues**. Budapest and many towns incur massive damage. This is swiftly repaired.
1948–56	"**Rákosi era**" characterized by Five Year Plans, police terror, and a propaganda blitz.	**Dunaújváros** and other new towns; crash urbanisation and industrialisation; the **Liberation Monument** and other Soviet-style projects exemplify this phase.
1956	**Hungarian Uprising**.	Widespread urban damage—Budapest is worst affected.
1960s & 1970s	Emergence of "**Kádárism**"—economic reforms to encourage greater public affluence. During this period, Hungary becomes a by-word for "**consumer socialism**" in Eastern Europe.	The **Metro** is completed. **Modernistic** cultural centers at Győr and Sárospatak are notable examples of Sixties and Seventies **architecture**; while supermarkets, hotels and resorts around Balaton are more typical of the period.
1980s	Economic problems, made worse by energy shortfall after the Chernobyl disaster.	Go-ahead for construction of **Nagymaros dam** and more nuclear reactors at **Paks**. Closure of mines and other loss-making industries is proposed by the state.
1988	**Grósz** replaces Kadar as Party leader.	
1989	Grósz replaced by **Nemeth** and **Pozsgay**. Revolutions in neighbouring Czechoslovakia and Romania.	Nagymaros dam project abandoned. Removal of border fortifications.
1990	**Free elections** result in **MDF** government.	

BOOKS

Publishers are detailed below in the form of British Publisher/American Publisher, where both exist. Where books are published in one country only, UK or US follows the publisher's name. Hungarian Corvina publications are available at selected bookshops abroad and inside Hungary. Out of print books are designated o/p.

Gyula Antalffy, *A Thousand Years of Travel in Old Hungary* (Corvina, UK). Slightly stodgy in places, but with enough anecdotes and odd details to keep your attention as it surveys a millennium of Hungary through the eyes of foreign and native travellers.

Stephen Brook, *The Double Eagle: Vienna, Budapest and Prague* (Hamilton, UK). Taking their Habsburg traditions as a starting point, Brook's readable, personal exploration of three cities concludes that war and Stalinism have dissolved the bonds of common experience – a judgement which now rings less confidently than when this book was written in the late Eighties. Though more chapters are devoted to Vienna, it's the sections on Budapest, and above all Prague, that really shine.

Bob Dent, *Blue Guide Hungary* (A & C Black/WW Norton). A left-wing slant distinguishes this from other *Blue Guides*, enlivening the typically thorough coverage of monuments. The skimpy treatment of Kőszeg and Szombathely and a general lack of practical information are major flaws, however.

Gyula Illyés, *People of the Puszta* (Corvina, UK). An unsentimental, sometimes horrifying immersion in the life of the landless peasantry of pre-war Hungary, mainly set in Transdanubia. Illyés – one of Hungary's greatest twentieth-century writers – was born into such a background, and the book breathes authenticity. Highly recommended.

Patrick Leigh Fermor, *A Time of Gifts* (Penguin, UK/US); *Between the Woods and the Water* (Penguin UK/US). In 1934 the young Leigh Fermor started walking from Holland to Turkey, and reached Hungary in the closing chapter of *A Time of Gifts*. The Gypsies and rusticated aristocrats of the Great Plain and Transylvania are superbly evoked in *Between the Woods and the Water* (a third volume, covering Moldavia and Bulgaria, is underway). Lyrical and erudite.

Claudio Magris, *Danube* (Collins, UK). This highly praised account of the Danubian countries interweaves history and reportage in an ambitious attempt to illuminate their cultural and spiritual backgrounds. Though brilliantly successful in parts, it inevitably seems rather detached from post-Communist realities, and lacks the grittiness of a real travel book.

George Mikes, *Any Souvenirs?* (Deutsch, UK; o/p). Born in Siklós in southern Hungary, Mikes fled the country in 1956 and made a new life in Britain as a humorist. This wry account relates his first visit home in fifteen years.

John Paget, *Hungary and Transylvania* (o/p). Paget's massive book attempted to explain nineteenth-century Hungary to the English middle class, and within its aristocratic limitations, succeeded. Occasionally found in second-hand bookshops.

Walter Starkie, *Raggle-Taggle* (Murray, UK; o/p). The wanderings of a Dublin professor with a fiddle, who bummed around Budapest and the Plain in search of Gypsy music in the 1920s. First published in 1933 and last issued in 1964 – a secondhand bookshop perennial.

András Török, *Budapest; A Critical Guide* (Park). Just what its title proclaims, this witty, informative guide is written by a native of the city and fully revised every year. Available abroad and in Budapest itself; highly recommended.

HISTORY AND POLITICS

John Bierman, *Righteous Gentile* (Allen Lane/ Viking). The best biography of Raoul Wallenberg, the Swedish diplomat whose daring efforts partly frustrated Eichmann's attempt to exterminate the Jews of Hungary during 1944–45.

Miklós Haraszti, *A Worker in a Workers' State* (Penguin/Universe). Factual, gritty investigation of "Piecework" (the book's Hungarian title) in Budapest's Red Star factory, which earned Haraszti a prison term for "defaming socialism" in the Seventies. *The Velvet Prison: Artists Under State Socialism* (Penguin/Basic) is a later, tediously ideological critique, less specific to Hungary than *Worker*.

György (George) Konrád, *Antipolitics* (Quartet/H Holt & Co). Written in the mid-Eighties, when Konrád's strategy for the transformation of Hungarian society and East–West relations "from below" seemed highly optimistic, it now reads like a blueprint for the dissolution of Communism in Eastern Europe.

Paul Lendvai, *Hungary: The Art of Survival* (I B Tauris, UK). This readable account of how and why Kádár was ousted by Károly Grósz was overtaken by events, as Grósz fell by the wayside before the book came out.

Bill Lomax, *Hungary 1956* (Allison & Busby, UK). Probably the best – and shortest – book on the Uprising, by an acknowledged expert on modern Hungary. Lomax also edited *Eyewitness in Hungary* (Spokesman, UK), an anthology of accounts by foreign communists (most of whom were sympathetic to the Uprising) that vividly depicts the elation, confusion and tragedy of the events of October 1956.

George Mikes, *A Study in Infamy* (Deutsch, UK; o/p). Better known in the West for his humourous writings, Mikes here exposes the activities of the secret police during the Rákosi era, using captured documents which explain their methods for surveillance of the population and use of terror as a political weapon.

N M Nagy-Talavera, *Greenshirts and Others* (Stanford University Press, US; o/p). A well-written and researched study of the social dislocations, racism and paranoid nationalism which afflicted Hungary and Romania between the wars, giving rise to native fascist movements and bitter anti-semitism.

Peter F. Sugar et al, *A History of Hungary* (I B Tauris, UK/US). A scholarly but readable history from ancient times up until the late 1980s, with a postcript written just before the end of Communism. A revised edition deserves to be published in the future.

Nigel Swain, *Hungary: The Rise and Fall of Feasible Socialism* (Verso, UK/US). Analyses the "Hungarian model" of socialism in decline, and the prospects for a market economy in the Nineties. As throughout Eastern Europe, capitalism shows little sign of delivering prosperity *and* social justice.

ART, FOLK TRADITIONS, CINEMA AND COOKERY

Corvina publishes a number of books covering Hungary's folk traditions and artistic treasures, mostly translated into English or German. Some editions are available on import, and some of its British titles are available through US publishers of fiction and poetry. You can also browse through the range of them in Váci utca bookshops in Budapest.

Val Biro, *Hungarian Folk Tales* (Oxford University Press, UK/US). Merry tales of dragons and the like in a crisp, colloquial rendering close to original recountings; intended for children.

Susan Derecskey, *The Hungarian Cookbook* (Harper and Row, US). A good, easy-to-follow selection of traditional and modern recipes.

Tekla Dömötör, *Hungarian Folk Beliefs* (Corvina/Indiana University Press). A superb collection of social history, folk beliefs and customs.

Tamás Hofer et al, *Hungarian Peasant Art* (Oxford University Press, UK/US; o/p). An excellently produced examination of Hungarian folk art, with lots of good photos.

George Lang, *The Cuisine of Hungary* (Penguin/Atheneum). A well-written and beautifully illustrated work, telling you everything you need to know about Hungarian cooking, its history, and how to do it yourself.

Lesley Chamberlain, *The Food and Cooking of Eastern Europe* (Penguin, UK). A great compendium of recipes, nostrums and gastronomical history, guaranteed to have you experimenting in the kitchen.

Graham Petrie, *Hungarian Cinema Today: History Must Answer to Man* (Corvina/ Zoetrope). Though you wouldn't guess so from the title, this is an unpretentious and very readable account of Hungarian cinema, surveying its history from the beginnings to the work of directors like Bacsó, Szábó, Jancsó, Makk and Kézdi-Kovács. Could do with an update, though.

FICTION AND POETRY

Most **Hungarian classics in translation** are published by Corvina. Inside Hungary, you might find the swashbuckling romances of **Géza Gárdonyi**, novels by **Mór Jókai** and short stories by **Frigyes Karinthy**. Despite his stature, the romantic poems of **Sándor Petőfi** only appear in English thanks to the Hungarian Cultural Foundation in Buffalo, New York (1969; editor A Nyerges). The same publisher and editor are responsible for the collected poems of **Attila József** and **Endre Ady** (1973).

The number of **modern authors** in translation has increased since the mid-Eighties, when only **Gyula Illyés** (see "Travel Books" above), **József Lengyel** and **György Konrád** were published abroad. You can now read émigré writers such as **Tamás Aczel**, contemporary standbearers of Hungarian literature like **Peter Esterházy**, and a host of other writers in anthologies.

ANTHOLOGIES

István Bart ed, *Present Continuous: Contemporary Hungarian Writing* (Corvina). Short stories by twenty-five authors, many of them reportage in literary form, a genre that Hungarians term "sociography".

Lóránt Czigány ed, *The Oxford History of Hungarian Literature from the Earliest Times to the Present* (Oxford University Press, UK/US). Probably the most comprehensive collection in print to date. Chronological structure; good coverage of political and social background.

Lajos Illés ed, *Nothing's Lost: Twenty-five Hungarian Short Stories* (Corvina). Another rich anthology of post-war writing, including real stunners by Endre Vészi, Ferenc Karinthy and Erzsébet Galgóczi.

Albert Tezlsa ed, *Ocean at the Window: Hungarian Prose and Poetry since 1945* (University of Minnesota Press, US). A good selection.

Éva Tóth ed, *MA Today* (Corvina). An anthology of stories, poems and essays from the literary and art review *MA*, which constitutes a *tour d'horizon* of cultural trends since 1916.

Miklós Vajda ed *Modern Hungarian Poetry* (Columbia University Press, US). A reasonable selection of post-war poetry.

Paul Varnai ed, *Hungarian Short Stories* (Toronto: Exile Editions, o/p). A fine collection of modern work ranging from the "magical realist" to astringent social commentary.

POETRY

Endre Ady, *Poems of Endre Ady* (Hungarian Cultural Foundation, US). Regarded by many as the finest Hungarian poet of the twentieth century, Ady's allusive verses are notoriously difficult to translate. *Explosive Country* (Corvina) is a collection of essays about his homeland.

George Faludy, *Selected Poems, 1933–80* (University of Georgia Press, US). Fiery, lyrical poetry by a victim of both Nazi and Russian repression. Themes of political defiance and the nobility of the human spirit, the struggle to preserve human values in the face of oppression.

Ágnes Nemes Nagy, *Selected Poems* (University of Iowa Press, US; o/p). A major postwar poet, often speculating intellectually on knowledge and the role of poetry in trying to impose order on the world, despite the jarring and bitter realisation that it can't.

Jónas Pilzinsky, *Selected Poems* (Dufour, US; o/p). A major poet, with themes of humanity's suffering and sacrifice.

Miklós Radnóti, *Under Gemini: The Selected Poems of Miklós Radnóti with a Prose Memoir* (Ohio University Press, US). The best collection of Radnóti's sparse, anguished poetry. *The Complete Poetry* (Ann Arbor, US; o/p) is a fuller but poorly translated collection, ranging from exotic and erotic celebrations of nature to the agonies of repression and injustice. *Subway Stops: Fifty Poems* (Ann Arbor, US; o/p) has an over-scholarly introduction, but movingly contrasts love with the brutal surroundings of Radnóti's last years in a Nazi labour camp. His final poems before his murder appear in *Clouded Sky* (Harper & Row, US; o/p).

Sándor Weöres and Ferenc Juhász, *Selected Poems* (Peter Smith, US). Two successful modern poets. Weöres is more preoccupied with primitive myth and mystical themes; Juhasz, often quirkily, with folklore and rural culture and the folk oral poetic tradition.

FICTION

Tamás Aczel, *The Hunt* (Little Brown, US). A beautifully crafted allegorical novel of truth and falsehood, loyalty and betrayal, set on a remote rural estate in an unnamed country not unlike Hungary during the early Fifties.

Géza Csáth, *The Magician's Garden and Other Stories* (Columbia University Press; US); *Opium and Other Stories* (Penguin, UK/US). Both of these volumes of stories are in a "magical realist" genre, questioning "reality". Csáth himself was tormented by insanity and opium addiction, and committed suicide in 1918.

Tibor Dery, *The Portuguese Princess* (Northwestern University Press, US). Short stories by a once-committed Communist, who was jailed for three years after the Uprising, and died in 1977.

Peter Esterházy, *Helping Verbs of the Heart* (Weidenfeld & Nicolson, UK). A moving account of a mother's death and her son's grief, interwoven with ironic *pensées* by Hungary's foremost novelist and essayist, a descendant of the famous aristocratic family. Another sprig of the dynasty has achieved fame as a Hollywood screenwriter – Joe Eszterhaze, who wrote the controversial *Basic Instinct*.

Agnes Hankiss, *A Hungarian Romance* (Readers International, UK). A lyrical first novel by "Hungary's New Feminist Voice", dealing with a woman's quest for self-identity during the sixteenth century, and the timeless conflict between personal and public interests.

Mór Jókai, *Tales from Jókai* (Ayer Co Publishers, US); *The Dark Diamonds* (Corvina); *Dr. Dumany's Wife: A Romance* (Doubleday, US; o/p). Colourful stories by the Magyar equivalent of Dickens. Jókai wrote over 100 novels during his lifetime (1825–1904).

György (George) Konrád, *The Case Worker* (Penguin, UK/US); *The City Builder* (Penguin, UK/US); *The Loser* (Harcourt Brace Jovanovich,

US). In contrast with his optimistic *Antipolitics* (see above), Konrád's novels are overwhelmingly bleak, dealing with misery, alienation, escapism, hypocrisy and madness. Despite the subject matter, his powers of insight and rich use of language are seductive and compelling.

József Lengyel, *Acta Sanctorum* (Peter Owen, UK); *Prenn Drifting* (Peter Owen/Beekman Publishers); *From Beginning to End/The Spell* (Peter Owen/Englewood Cliffs; o/p); *The Judge's Chair* (Peter Owen/Beekman Publishers); *Confrontation* (Peter Owen/Lyle Stuart). A dedicated Communist since his youth, Lengyel apparently kept his faith through several years in the Gulag, but later began to display doubts. His colourful semi-autobiographical novels concern morality under stress, ambition, and the question of ends versus means. *The Bridgebuilders* (Corvina, UK) is the least gripping, although Lengyel reportedly considered it one of his best.

Peter Lengyel, *Cobblestones* (Readers International, UK). An absorbing, multi-layered detective story spanning two centuries, where an ingenious theft and an unexplained murder are tied into the Millenary celebrations of 1896, the Stalinist Fifties and the uncertainties of the Eighties.

László Nemeth, *Guilt* (Dufour, US). A Thirties novel of tragedy and its effect on a young couple.

Giorgio & Nicola Pressburger, *Homage to the Eighth District* (Readers International, UK). Evocative tales of Jewish life in Budapest, before, during and after World War II, by twin brothers who fled Hungary in 1956.

A Tezla, *Hungarian Authors: A Bibliographical Handbook* (Harvard University Press, US).

Stephen Vizinczey, *In Praise of Older Women* (Pan, UK;o/p). The memoirs of a randy egocentric lad growing up in refugee camps and in Budapest during the Rákosi years. Soft porn mixed with social comment and supposedly profound insights into the nature of women, which made a splash when first published in the West in 1967.

FOREIGN WRITERS ON HUNGARY

Heinrich Böll, *And Where Were You, Adam* in *Adam and the Train* (McGraw Hill, US). A superb short novel by one of the major post-war German novelists, consisting of loosely connected and semi-autobiographical short stories describing the panic-stricken retreat of Hitler's forces from the *puszta* before the Red Army in 1944. Told through both Hungarian and German eyes, these stories are a haunting evocation of the chaos, cruelty and horror of the retreat, but also of a rural culture that seems to resist everything thrown at it.

Franz Fühmann, *Twenty-two Days or Half a Lifetime* (Jonathan Cape, UK). Disjointed metaphysical and literary ramblings interspersed with musings on Budapest and Hungary, by an East German writer (1922–84).

Hans Habe, *Black Earth* (NEL, UK; o/p). The story of a peasant's commitment to the Communist underground, and his disillusionment with the Party in power; a good read, and by no means as crude as the artwork and blurb suggest.

Cecilia Holland, *Rakossy, The Death of Attila* (Hodder/Knopf; o/p). *Rakossy* is a bodiceripping tale of a shy Austrian princess wed to an uncouth Magyar baron, braving the Turkish hordes on the Hungarian marches; while the *Death of Attila* evokes the Huns, Romans and Goths of the Dark Ages, pillaging around the Danube. Two well-crafted historical romances.

MUSIC AND RECORDS

Hungarian music enshrines the trinity of Liszt, Bartók, and Kodály: Liszt was the founding father, Bartók one of the greatest composers of the twentieth century, and Kodály (himself no slouch at composition) created a widely imitated system of musical education. When you also take into account talented Hungarian soloists like Perényi, it's clear that this small nation has made an outstanding contribution to the world of music.

HUNGARIAN COMPOSERS

Franz Liszt (1811–1886), who described himself as a "mixture of Gypsy and Franciscan", cut a flamboyant figure in the salons of Europe as a virtuoso pianist and womaniser. The Hungarian Rhapsodies and similar pieces reflected the "Gypsy" side to his character and the rising nationalism of his era; while later work like the Transcendental Etudes (whose originality has only recently been recognised) invoked a visionary, "Franciscan" mood. Despite his patriotic stance, however, Liszt's first language was German (he never fully mastered Hungarian), and his expressed wish to roam the villages of Hungary with a knapsack on his back was a Romantic fantasy.

That was left to **Béla Bartók** (1881–1945) and **Zoltán Kodály** (1882–1967), who began exploring the remoter districts of Hungary and Transylvania in 1906, collecting peasant music. Despite many hardships and local suspicion of their "monster" (a cutting stylus and phonograph cylinders), they managed to record and catalogue thousands of melodies, laying down high standards of musical ethnography still maintained in Hungary today, while discovering a rich source of inspiration for their own compositions. Bartók believed that a genuine peasant melody was "quite as much a masterpiece in miniature as a Bach fugue or a Mozart sonata . . . a classic example of the expression of a musical thought in its most conceivably concise form, with the avoidance of all that is superfluous".

Bartók created a personal but universal musical language by reworking the raw essence of Magyar and Finno-Ugric folk music in a modern context; in particular his six String Quartets, although Hungarian public opinion was originally hostile. Feeling misunderstood and out of step with his country's increasingly pro-Nazi policies, Bartók left Hungary in 1940, dying poor and embittered in the United States. Since then, however, Bartók's reputation has soared, and the return of his body in 1988 occasioned national celebrations, shrewdly sponsored by the state.

Kodály's music is more consciously national: Bartók called it "a real profession of faith in the Hungarian soul". His *Peacock Variations* are based on a typical Old Style pentatonic tune and the *Dances of Galanta* on the popular music played by Gypsy bands. Old Style tunes also form the core of Kodály's work in musical education: the "Kodály method" employs group singing to develop musical skill at an early age. His ideas have made Hungarian music teaching among the best in the world, and Kodály himself a paternal figure to generations of children.

For others Kodály was a voice of conscience during the Rákosi era, writing the *Hymn of Zrínyi* to a seventeenth-century text whose call to arms against the Turkish invasion – "I perceive a ghastly dragon, full of venom and fury, snatching the crown of Hungary . . ". – was tumultuously acclaimed as an anti-Stalinist allegory. Its first performance was closely followed by the Uprising, and the Hymn was not performed again for many years; nor were any recordings made available until 1982.

HUNGARIAN FOLK MUSIC

Until Bartók and Kodály's research, **Hungarian folk music** (*Magyar népzene*) was identified with Gypsy bands in cafés, whose popular songs were influenced by the stirring *verbunk* (recruiting tunes) of the Rákóczi wars; and Austrian music – the sort of thing that Brahms and Liszt made into Hungarian Dances, and is still heard in Budapest restaurants. Bartók and Kodály were more excited by what the former called "Old Style" music: simple pentatonic (5-note) tunes stretching back to the days when Magyar tribes roamed the banks of the Don and Volga, where similar music has been handed down and recorded by ethno-musicologists.

In Hungary today, folk music has little connection with rural communities, whose taste in music (as in other things) has been transformed by urban influences, television and radio. Folk music and village life are still closely linked **in Transylvania**, however, which was seen as a repository of Magyar traditions even in Bartók's day, particularly the Kalotoság and Mezőseg regions near the city of Cluj, and the Csángó districts of the eastern Carpathians. In Hungary, by contrast, Magyar folk music has enjoyed a revival in towns and cities thanks to the **Táncház**. These dance houses are very popular with young people interested in traditional music and dances – mostly from Hungary and Transylvania, but also from the "South Slavs", Slovenia and Bulgaria.

RECORDINGS

Good quality **records and tapes** produced by *Hungaroton* retail for half or a third of what you'd pay abroad, which makes it well worth rooting through *zeneművesbolt* shops. After Western and Hungarian **pop**, the bulk of their stock consists of **classical music**. A full discography of the works of Liszt, Bartók and Kodály, directors like Dohnányi and Doráti, and contemporary Hungarian soloists and singers would fill a catalogue; and the following recordings (on tape or vinyl, sometimes in boxed sets with an English commentary) are merely an introduction to the equally wide field of Hungarian **folk music**.

VII. Magyarországi Táncház Találkozó. A great mixture of dances, ballads, and instru-

mental pieces from all over, recorded at the Seventh Dance House Festival in 1988. One of a series (MK 18152) – the Tenth Dance House Festival collection (MK 18190) is also especially good.

Magyar népzene 3. (Hungarian folk music). A 4-disc set of field recordings covering the whole range of folk music – Old and New style songs, instrumental and occasional music – that's probably the best overall introduction. In the West, the discs are marketed as "Folk Music of Hungary Vol.1".

Magyar hangszeres népzene. (Hungarian Instrumental Folk Music). A very good 3-disc set of field recordings of village and Gypsy bands, including lots of solos (Hungaroton LPX 18045-47).

Muzsikás. Beautiful arrangements of traditional ballads by the Muzsikás group and Márta Sebestyén, Hungary's leading Táncház singer. Highly recommended (Hannibal HNBL 1330).

The Prisoner's Song. More haunting songs by Márta and Muzsikás, released abroad on the Hannibal label (HNBL 1341).

Bonchidától Bonchidáig. The Kalamajka Ensemble, another Táncház group, plays Transylvanian and Csángó ballads and dances (Hungaroton MK 18135).

Este a Gyimesbe Jártam. Music from the Csángó region performed by János Zerkula and Regina Fikó; sparser, sadder and more discordant than other Transylvanian music (Hungaroton MK 18130).

Táncházi muzsika (Music from the Táncház). A double album of the Sebö Ensemble playing Táncház music from various regions of Hungary. Wild and exciting rhythms (Hungaroton SPLX 18031-32).

Jánosi Együttes (Jánosi Ensemble). Another young group, performing "authentic" versions of some of the folk tunes that Bartók borrowed in his compositions. A record that makes a bridge between classical and folk music (Hungaroton SPLX 18103).

Serbian Music from South Hungary played by the Vujicsics Ensemble. More complex tunes than most Magyar folk music, with a distinct Balkan influence (Hannibal HNBL 1310).

ONWARDS FROM HUNGARY

Hungary is linked to dozens of European cities by rail, and there are direct buses from Budapest's Erzsébet tér depot to many towns in Austria, Czechoslovakia and Romania, as summarised in the "Travel Details" at the end of Chapter One. Note that all the *Rough Guides* mentioned below are published in the US as *Real Guides*.

AUSTRIA

Austria, a few hours' journey from Budapest or western Transdanubia, is an expensive place to stay, but it's worth considering a stopover in imperially elegant **Vienna** (see "Getting There" in *Basics* for some accommodation hints). If you're Eurailing westwards, brief visits to **Graz** or lovely (but ultra-costly) **Salzburg** are also feasible. All three are covered in the *Rough Guide: Europe*. EC, US, Canadian, Australian and New Zealand citizens do not require a visa for Austria.

GERMANY

There are more options for budget travellers in **Germany**, which you can reach by bus or train, or even by hitching, from Budapest. Though details of everything from **Munich** nightlife to the **Bavarian Alps** appear in the *Rough Guide: Germany*, it's worth mentioning that the cheapest way to reach **Berlin** or **Dresden** from Budapest is by rail via Czechoslovakia. EC, US, Canadian, Australian and New Zealand citizens do not require a visa for Germany.

CZECHOSLOVAKIA

Since the "Velvet Revolution", **Czechoslovakia** has become a major tourist destination, particularly **Prague**, the loveliest city in Europe. Like the Slovak capital **Bratislava**, it is accessible by direct trains and buses from Budapest and western Hungary. Buses also run to Rožnáva, near Krásna Hôrka Castle and the dramatic Slovak Karst region;

Tatranská Lomnica in the **High Tatras** and the handsome town of Banská Bystrica; while the Rákóczi express runs from Budapest to Propad-Tatry, the gateway to the medieval **Spiš towns**, whose romance is only exceeded by the **castles of Bohemia**. All are detailed in the *Rough Guide: Czechoslovakia*; the *Rough Guide: Prague* covers the capital even more thoroughly. EC and US citizens do not require **visas**, but Canadians, Australians and New Zealanders must get one in advance from a Czechoslovak consulate. However, should the Czechoslovak federation split into two republics (as now seems likely), these rules might change.

POLAND

Poland has yet to become as popular as Czechoslovakia, so its attractions, particularly the lake district bordering the Ukraine, are far less overrun by tourists. The main cities are directly accessible from Budapest, with trains to **Warsaw**, several of which carry on to **Gdansk**, the birthplace of Solidarity; the *Polonia express* calls at **Częstochowa**, Poland's holiest shrine, along the way. There is also a weekly bus from Budapest to **Kraków**, the former capital, famed for its architecture and cabaret. Together with the lovely **Zakopane Mountains** and other, remoter areas, all are covered in the *Rough Guide: Poland*. EC and US citizens don't require a visa; other nationalities must apply to a Polish consulate (which can take up to fourteen days unless you pay extra for 24-hour service).

ROMANIA

Travel in **Romania** has become easier since the overthrow of the Ceauşescu dictatorship, but it remains a challenging experience. The best policy is to combine visits to the picturesque towns of **Transylvania** with remoter regions in the far north, such as **Maramureş**, with its amazing wooden churches and medieval-looking villages. Afterwards, you can follow the Iza Valley into **Moldavia** to see the **Painted Monasteries** or catch one of Romania's great folklore **festivals**. The capital, **Bucharest**, is chiefly notable for its raffish atmosphere and Ceauşescu's gigantic palace. Trains from Budapest to Bucharest are routed via **Cluj**, **Sighişoara** and **Braşov**, or **Sibiu** – all in

Transylvania, and worth a visit. Visas are available at border crossings, and the new, market exchange rate makes Romania reasonably cheap for tourists. The forthcoming *Rough Guide: Romania* contains everything you need to know.

BULGARIA

Crossing the Danube from Romania into **Bulgaria**, you can head down from **Vidin** to **Sofia**, and thence south to **Rila Monastery** and the beautiful small town of **Melnik**; or travel from **Ruse** to the historic cities of **Veliko Târnovo** and **Plovdiv**. Bulgaria's **Black Sea coast** improves the further south one goes, but **Varna**, accessible by the *Nord–Süd* or *Transdanubium* express, is a nice place to begin, with lots happening over summer. The forthcoming *Rough Guide: Bulgaria* is an obvious companion, and includes details of travelling on to Istanbul.

SLOVENIA

Having gained its independence from the rest of Yugoslavia, Slovenia is keen to attract tourists and totally safe to visit. The lively cultural scene in the capital, **Ljubljana**, is an obvious attraction; while the beautiful **Slovenian Alps** are great for hiking and skiing. Though a guide devoted to Slovenia has yet to be published, the 1990 edition of the *Rough Guide: Yugoslavia* is still pretty reliable in its coverage of this region (though not, for obvious reasons, the other republics). Visas are issued at the border if required.

THE UKRAINE AND RUSSIA

Like the Baltic states, the **Ukraine** has recently begun issuing visas (for the equivalent of £30) at the border with minimal fuss, making it possible to cross over from Záhony in eastern Hungary. However, tourism is still geared to the old, bureaucratic system, so that finding somewhere to stay (or eat) can present real problems. The off-on transition from the Soviet rouble to the Ukranian grivitsa makes everything more uncertain. US dollars are the best currency to bring (in small denomination bills).

As far as **Russia** goes, independent travel is still constrained by the hassle of getting a visa. If you're not booked on a package tour, it's necessary to obtain an official invitation, and pre-arrange some kind of accommodation. Although in 1992 it briefly became possible to slip into Russia from the Baltic states or the Ukraine without getting a visa, controls are being tightened up again. That said, it's possible to rent a private flat and stay for months, if you make the right contacts and know which strings to pull. Until a more up-to-date guidebook appears, Lonely Planet's *USSR: A Travel Survival Kit* is your best bet. A *Rough Guide* to Saint Petersburg is scheduled for 1993.

CHINA

Though no longer absurdly cheap, **trains from Budapest** via the former USSR are still the least expensive way of getting **to China**, with a one-way ticket costing around £120. Bookings are handled by *Pannonia-Intourist Kft.* in Budapest (V, József körut 45; ☎113-7062 or ☎113-4728), where Mrs Julia Ottmár can explain all the ins and outs. Basically, you travel to Moscow on one train, and then switch on to the *Trans-Mongolian Express* – nine days' journey in all. If you intend to return from Beijing by the same means (using the *Trans-Manchurian Express*), it's cheaper to buy a return ticket in Budapest than a single at either end.

Since **bookings** take at least a fortnight to arrange by telex, the whole process is extremely slow, and may be impossible between May and October, when demand is heaviest. Mrs Ottmár can give the latest rundown on **visas**, but when last heard travellers had to apply to the Chinese Embassy in Budapest (VI, Benczúr utca 17) first; then the Russian Embassy VI, Andrássy út 104) and finally at the Mongolian embassy (XII, Istenhegyi út 59–65).

Before leaving Budapest, buy plenty of food and drink for **the journey**, since catering on the *Trans-Mongolian Express* is dire, with the honourable exception of the *provodnitsa* who serve Russian tea from a samovar at any hour. Winning the favour of these formidable ladies may require some effort and a smattering of Russian, but a sympathetic *provodnitsa* will make your journey much smoother. Although the scenery goes on forever in a boring, steppe-ish way, other passengers – hailing from every continent and all over the former USSR – can be endlessly diverting.

LANGUAGE

Hungarian is a unique, complex and subtle tongue, classified as belonging to the Finno-Ugric linguistic group, which means that it's totally unlike any other language that you're likely to know. Its closest (though still distant) relatives are Finnish and the Siberian Chuvash language, although odd grammatical structures and words from Turkish have crept in, together with some German, English and (a few) Russian neologisms.

Consequently, foreigners aren't really expected to speak Hungarian, and natives are used to (but don't honestly appreciate) being addressed in **German**, the *lingua franca* of tourism. It's understood by older people – particularly in Transdanubia – and by many students and professional types, besides virtually everyone around the Balaton or in tourist offices. For a brief visit it's probably easier to brush up on some German for your means of communication, but a few basic Magyar phrases can make all the difference. However, **English** is gaining ground rapidly, particularly in schools and colleges, while French or **Italian** might also be understood in tourist areas or educated circles.

In addition to the following list of basic phrases, you'll find a detailed food glossary and a selection of basic words pertaining to transport in *Basics*. Berlitz's *Hungarian for Travellers* has an even wider range of phrases. If you're prepared to seriously study the language, *Colloquial Hungarian* (Routledge UK/US) is the best available book. As a supplement, invest in the handy little *Angol–Magyar/Magyar–Angol Kisszótár* dictionaries; available from bookshops in Hungary.

BASIC GRAMMAR AND PRONUNCIATION

Although its rules are fiendishly complicated, it's worth describing a few features of **Hungarian grammar**, albeit imperfectly. Hungarian is an agglutinating language – in other words, its vocabulary is built upon **root-words**, which are modified in various ways to express different ideas and nuances. Instead of prepositions – "to", "from", "in", etc – Hungarian uses **suffixes**, or tags added to the ends of genderless **nouns**. The change in suffix is largely determined by the noun's context, for example: (the) book = *könyv*; (give me the) book = *könyveket*; (in the) book = *könyvben*; (to the) book = *könyvnek*. It is also affected by complicated rules of vowel harmony (which you're bound to get wrong, so don't worry about them!). Most of the nouns in the vocabulary section below are in the subject form – that is, without suffixes. In Hungarian, "**the**" is *a* (before a word beginning with a consonant) or *az* (preceding a vowel); the word for "**a/an**" is *egy* (which also means "one").

Plurals are indicated by endings such as -*ek*, -*ok* or –*ak*, but *not* when qualified by a number: eg. *emberek* means "men", but "two men" is *ket ember* (using the singular form of the noun).

Adjectives precede the noun (*a piros ház* = the red house), adopting suffixes to form the comparative (*jó* = good; *jobb* = better), plus the prefix *leg* to signify the superlative (*legjobb* = the best).

Negatives are usually formed by placing the word *nem* before the verb. *Ez* (this), *ezek* (these), *az* (that), and *azok* (those) are the **demonstratives**.

PRONUNCIATION

Achieving passably good **pronunciation**, rather than grammar, is the first priority (see the box on p.340 for general guidelines). **Stress** almost invariably falls on the first syllable of a word and all letters are spoken, although in sentences, the tendency is to slur words together. Vowel sounds are greatly affected by the bristling **accents** (that actually distinguish separate letters) which, together with the "double letters" cs, gy, ly, ny, sz, ty, and zs, give the Hungarian **alphabet** its formidable appearance.

HUNGARIAN WORDS AND PHRASES

BASICS

Do you speak . . .	*beszél . . .*	good day	*jó napot*
English	*angolul*	good evening	*jó estét*
German	*németül*	good night	*jó éjszakát*
French	*franciaul*	how are you?	*hogy vagy?*
yes – OK	*igen – jó*	how are you? (more formal)	*hogy van?*
no/not	*nem*	could you speak more	*elmondaná*
I (don't) understand	*(nem) értem*	slowly?	*lassabban?*
please–excuse me	*kérem—bocsánat*	what do you call this?	*mi a neve ennek?*
two beers, please	*két sört kérek*	please write it down	*kérem, írja ezt le*
thank you (very much)	*köszönöm (szépen)*	today – tomorrow	*ma – holnap*
you're welcome	*szívesen*	the day after tomorrow	*holnapután*
hello/goodbye (informal)	*szia*	yesterday	*tegnap*
goodbye	*viszontlátásra*	the day before yesterday	*tegnapelőtt*
see you later	*viszlát*	in the morning – in the	*reggel – este*
I wish you . . . (formally)	*. . . kívánok*	evening	
good morning	*jó reggelt*	at noon – at midnight	*délben – éjfélkor*

QUESTIONS AND REQUESTS

Legyen szíves (Would you be so kind") is the polite formula for attracting someone's attention. Hungarian has numerous interrogative modes whose subtleties elude foreigners, so it's best to use the simple *van?* ("is there?"/"is it?"), to which the reply might be *nincs* or *azok nincsenek* ("it isn't"/"there aren't any"). Waiters and shop assistants often rely upon the laconic *tessék?*, meaning "What do you want?," "go ahead" or "next." *Kaphatok . . . ?* ("Can I have . . . ?") is politer, but less widely used than *Szeretnék . . .* ("I'd like . . ."); in restaurants you can also order with *Kérem, hozzon . . .* ("Please bring me . . ."); *Kérem, adjon azt* ("Please give me that"); *Egy ilyet kérek* ("I'll have one of those"); or simply *. . . kérek* (". . . please").

I'd like/we'd like	*Szeretnék/szeretnénk*	It's too expensive	*Ez nagyon drága*
Where is/are . . . ?	*Hol van / vannak . . ?*	anything cheaper?	*van valami olcsóbb?*
Take me to . . .	*Vigyen kérem a . . .*	a student discount?	*van diák kedvezmény?*
Hurry up!	*Siessen!*	Is everything	*Ebben minden*
How much is it?	*Mennyibe kerül?*	included?	*szerepel?*
per night	*egy éjszakára*	I asked for . . .	*Én . . . .-t rendeltem*
per week	*egy hétre*	The bill please	*Kérem a számlát*
a single room	*egyágyas szobát*	we're paying	*Külön-külön*
a double room	*kétágyas szobát*	separately	*kívánunk fizetni*
hot (cold) water	*meleg (hideg) víz*	what? – why?	*mi? – miert?*
a shower	*egy zuhany*	when? – who?	*mikor? – ki?*

SOME SIGNS

entrance – exit	*bejárat – kijárat*	room for rent	*szoba kiadó*
arrival	*érkezés*		(or *Zimmer frei*)
departure	*indulás*	hospital	*kórház*
open – closed	*nyitva – zárva*	pharmacy	*gyógyszertár*
free admission	*szabad belépés*	(local) police	*(kerületi) Rendőrség*
women's – men's	*női – férfi mosdó* (or *WC* -	caution/beware	*vigyázat!*
toilet	"Vait-say")	no smoking	*tilos a dohányzás*
shop – market	*bolt – piac*	no bathing	*tilos a fürdés*

DIRECTIONS

Where's the . . . ?	*hol van a . . . ?*	Do I have to change	*át kell szállnom*
campsite	*kemping*	for . . . ?	*. . .-be?*
hotel	*szálloda*	towards	*felé*
railway station	*vasútállomás*	on the right (left)	*jobbra (balra)*
bus station	*buszállomás*	straight ahead	*egyenesen előre*
(bus or train) stop	*megálló*	(over) there – here	*ott – itt*
Is it near (far)?	*közel (távol) van?*	Where are you going?	*Hova megy?*
Which bus goes to . . . ?	*Melyik busz megy . . .-ra/re*	Is that on the way to . . .?	*Az a . . . úton?*
a one-way ticket to . . .	*egy jegyet kérek . . .*	I want to get out at . . .	*le akarok szállni . . .*
please	*-ra/re egy útra*	please stop here	*itt álljon meg*
a return ticket to . . .	*egy retur jegyet . . .-ra/re*	I'm lost	*eltévedtem*

DESCRIPTIONS AND REACTIONS

and	*és*	good	*jó*	quick	*gyors*	ugly	*csúnya*
or	*vagy*	bad	*rossz*	slow	*lassú*	Take your	*ne fogdoss!*
nothing	*semmi*	better	*jobb*	now	*most*	hands off me!	
perhaps	*talán*	big	*nagy*	later	*később*	Help!	*Segitség!*
very	*nagyon*	small	*kicsi*	beautiful	*szép*	I'm ill	*beteg vagyok*

TIME

Luckily, the 24-hour clock is used for timetables, but on cinema programmes you may see notations like ¼4, ¾4 etc. These derive from the spoken expression of time which, as in German, makes reference to the hour approaching completion. For example 3:30 is expressed as *fél negy* – "half (on the way to) four"; 3:45 – *háromnegyed negy* ("three quarters on the way to four"); 6:15 – "*negyed hét*" ("one quarter towards seven") etc. However, ". . . o'clock" is . . . *óra*, rather than referring to the hour ahead. Duration is expressed by the suffixes *-től* ("from") and *ig* ("to"); minutes are *perc*; to ask the time, say "*Hány óra?*."

NUMBERS AND DAYS

1	*egy*	20	*húsz*	900	*kilencszáz*
2	*kettő*	21	*huszonegy*	1000	*egyezer*
3	*három*	30	*harminc*	half	*fél*
4	*négy*	40	*negyven*	a quarter	*negyed*
5	*öt*	50	*ötven*	a dozen	*egy tucat*
6	*hat*	60	*hatvan*	each	*darab*
7	*hét*	70	*hetven*	Sunday	*vasárnap*
8	*nyolc*	80	*nyolcvan*	Monday	*hétfő*
9	*kilenc*	90	*kilencven*	Tuesday	*kedd*
10	*tíz*	100	*száz*	Wednesday	*szerda*
11	*tizenegy*	101	*százegy*	Thursday	*csütörtök*
12	*tizenkettő*	150	*százötven*	Friday	*péntek*
13	*tizenhárom*	200	*kettőszáz*	Saturday	*szombat*
14	*tizennégy*	300	*háromszáz*	on Monday	*hetfőn*
15	*tizenöt*	400	*négyszáz*	on Tuesday	*kedden* etc.
16	*tizenhat*	500	*ötszáz*	day	*nap*
17	*tizenhét*	600	*hatszáz*	week	*hét*
18	*tizennyolc*	700	*hétszáz*	month	*hónap*
19	*tizenkilenc*	800	*nyolcszáz*	year	*év*

PRONUNCIATION

A o as in hot

Á a as in father

B b as in best

C ts as in bats

CS ch as in church

D d as in dust

E e as in yet

É ay as in say

F f as in fed

G g as in go

GY di as in medium, or d as in due

H h as in hat

I ee as in feet

Í ee as in see, but longer

J y as in yes

K k as in sick

L l as in leap

LY y as in yes

M m as in mud

N n as in not

NY ni as in onion

O aw as in saw, but shorter

Ó aw as in awe, with the tongue kept high

Ö ur as in fur, but without any "r" sound

Ő ur as in fur, as above, but with the lips tightly rounded

P p as in sip

R r pronounced with the tip of the tongue

S sh as in shop

SZ s as in so

T t as in sit

TY tty as in prettier, said quickly

U u as in pull

Ú oo as in food

Ü u as in the German "unter"

Ű u as above, but longer and with the lips tightly rounded.

V v as in vat

W v as in "Valkman," "vhiskey" or "WC' (vait-say)

Z z as in zero

ZS s as in measure

HUNGARIAN TERMS: A GLOSSARY

ABC national chain of supermarkets.

ALFÖLD plain; it usually means the Great Plain (*Nagyalföld*) rather than the Little Plain (*Kisalföld*) in northwestern Hungary.

ÁLLATKERT zoo.

ÁRUHÁZ department store.

ÁVO the dreaded secret police of the Rákosi era, renamed the *ÁVH* in 1949.

BARLANG cave; the most impressive stalactite caves are in the Aggteleki karst region.

BELVÁROS inner town or city, typically characterised by Baroque or Neoclassical architecture.

CALVINISM the Reformed (*Református*) faith, which established itself in Hungary during the sixteenth century.

CASTRUM (Latin) a Roman fortification.

CIGÁNY Gypsy (in Hungarian); hence *Cigánytelep*, a Gypsy settlement; and *Cigányzene*, Gypsy music.

CSÁRDA inn; nowadays, a restaurant with rustic decor.

CSÁRDÁS traditional wild dance to violin music.

CSIKÓS *puszta* horse herdsman; a much romanticised figure of the nineteenth century.

DOMB hill; *Rózsadomb*, "Rose Hill" in Budapest.

DJAMI or **DZAMI** mosque.

DUNA the River Danube.

ERDÉLY Transylvania; for centuries a part of Hungary, its loss to Romania in 1920 still rankles.

ERDŐ forest, wood.

FALU village; **FALUKUTATÓ** "Village Explorers" who investigated rural life and pressed for reforms in the countryside during the 1930s.

FŐ UTCA main street.

FORRÁS natural spring.

FÜRDŐ public baths, often fed by thermal springs.

GYÓGYFÜRDŐ mineral baths with therapeutic properties.

HAJDÚK cattle-drovers turned outlaws, who later settled near Debrecen in the **HAJDÚSÁG** region.

HAJÓÁLLOMÁS boat landing stage.

HÁZ house.

HEGY hill or low mountain (pl. **HEGYSÉG**).

HÍD bridge; *Lánchíd*, the "Chain Bridge" in Budapest.

HONVÉD Hungarian army.

ISKOLA school.

ITALBOLT "drink shop", or a village bar.

KÁPOLNA chapel.

KAPU gate.

KASTÉLY fortified manor or small castle.

KERT garden, park.

KÖRÚT boulevard. Some cities have semicircular "Great" and "Small" boulevards (**NAGYKÖRÚT** and **KISKÖRÚT**) surrounding their Belváros.

KÖZ alley, lane; also used to define geographical regions, eg. the "Mud land" (*Sárköz*) bordering the Danube.

KÚT well or fountain.

LAKÓTELEP high-rise apartment buildings.

LÉPCSŐ alley with steps ascending a hillside.

LIGET park, grove, or wood.

LIMES (Latin) fortifications along the Danube, marking the limit of Roman territory.

LOVARDA riding school.

MAGYAR Hungarian (pronounced "*Mod*-yor"). Also **MAGYARORSZÁG**, Hungary.

MDF (*Magyar Demokrátia Forum*) Hungarian Democratic Forum; the right-of-centre party that currently governs Hungary.

MEGÁLLÓ a railway station or bus stop.

MEGYE county; originally established by King Stephen to extend his authority over the Magyar tribes.

MIHRAB prayer niche in a mosque, indicating the direction of Mecca.

MSzMP (*Magyar Szocialista Munkáspárt*) the Hungarian Communist Party.

MŰEMLÉK historic monument, protected building.

MŰVELŐDÉSI HÁZ community arts and social centre; literally, a "Cultural House".

NYILAS "Arrow Cross"; Hungarian fascist movement.

OTTOMANS founders of the Turkish empire, which included central Hungary during the sixteenth and seventeenth centuries.

PALOTA palace; *Püspök-palota*, a Bishop's residence.

PÁLYAUDVAR (*pu.*) railway terminus.

PIAC outdoor market.

PINCE cellar; a **BOR-PINCE** contains and serves wine.

PUSZTA another name for the Great Plain, coined when the region was a wilderness.

RAKPART embankment or quay.

ROM ruined building; sometimes set in a garden with stonework finds, a **ROMKERT**.

STRAND beach, or any area for sunbathing or swimming.

SZIGET island.

TANÁCS council; also **TANÁCSKÖZTÁRSASÁG**, the "Republic of Councils" or Soviets, which ruled Hungary in 1919.

TEMETŐ cemetery.

TEMPLOM church.

TÉR square; **TERE** in the possessive case, as in *Hősök tere*, "Heroes' Square".

TEREM hall.

TÓ lake.

TORONY tower.

TÜRBE tomb or mausoleum of a Muslim dignitary.

UTCA (*u.*) road or street.

ÚT avenue; in the possessive case, **ÚTJA** – eg *Mártírok útja*, "Martyrs' Avenue".

VÁR castle.

VÁROS town; may be divided into an inner Belváros, a lower-lying *Alsóváros* and a modern *Újváros* section. Also **VÁROSKÓZPONT**, the town centre.

VÁSÁRCSARNOK market hall.

VASÚTÁLLOMÁS railway station.

VÖLGY valley; *Hűvösvölgy*, "Cool Valley".

ZSIDÓ Jew or Jewish.

ZSINAGÓGA synagogue.

INDEX

DIRECT ORDERS IN THE USA

Title	ISBN	Price
Able to Travel	1858281105	$19.95
Amsterdam	1858280869	$13.95
Australia	1858280354	$18.95
Berlin	1858280338	$13.99
Brittany & Normandy	1858280192	$14.95
Bulgaria	1858280478	$14.99
Canada	185828001X	$14.95
Crete	1858280494	$14.95
Cyprus	185828032X	$13.99
Czech & Slovak Republics	185828029X	$14.95
Egypt	1858280753	$17.95
England	1858280788	$16.95
Europe	185828077X	$18.95
Florida	1858280109	$14.95
France	1858280508	$16.95
Germany	1858280257	$17.95
Greece	1858280206	$16.95
Guatemala & Belize	1858280451	$14.95
Holland, Belgium & Luxembourg	1858280877	$15.95
Hong Kong & Macau	1858280664	$13.95
Hungary	1858280214	$13.95
Italy	1858280311	$17.95
Kenya	1858280435	$15.95
Mediterranean Wildlife	1858280699	$15.95
Morocco	1858280400	$16.95
Nepal	185828046X	$13.95
New York	1858280583	$13.95
Paris	1858280389	$13.95
Poland	1858280346	$16.95
Portugal	1858280842	$15.95
Prague	185828015X	$14.95
Provence & the Côte d'Azur	1858280230	$14.95
St Petersburg	1858280303	$14.95
San Francisco	1858280826	$13.95
Scandinavia	1858280397	$16.99
Scotland	1858280834	$14.95
Sicily	1858280370	$14.99
Thailand	1858280168	$15.95
Tunisia	1858280656	$15.95
USA	185828080X	$18.95
Venice	1858280362	$13.99
Women Travel	1858280710	$12.95
Zimbabwe & Botswana	1858280419	$16.95

Rough Guides are available from all good bookstores, but can be obtained directly in the USA and Worldwide (except the UK*) from Penguin:

Charge your order by Master Card or Visa (US$15.00 minimum order): call 1-800-255-6476; or send orders, with complete name, address and zip code, and list price, plus $2.00 shipping and handling per order to: Consumer Sales, Penguin USA, PO Box 999 – Dept #17109, Bergenfield, NJ 07621. No COD. Prepay foreign orders by international money order, a cheque drawn on a US bank, or US currency. No postage stamps are accepted. All orders are subject to stock availability at the time they are processed. Refunds will be made for books not available at that time. Please allow a minimum of four weeks for delivery.

The availability and published prices quoted are correct at the time of going to press but are subject to alteration without prior notice. Titles currently not available outside the UK will be available by January 1995. Call to check.

* For UK orders, see separate price list

DIRECT ORDERS IN THE UK

Title	ISBN	Price
Amsterdam	1858280869	£7.99
Australia	1858280354	£12.99
Barcelona & Catalunya	1858280486	£7.99
Berlin	1858280338	£8.99
Brazil	0747101272	£7.95
Brittany & Normandy	1858280192	£7.99
Bulgaria	1858280478	£8.99
California	1858280575	£9.99
Canada	185828001X	£10.99
Crete	1858280494	£6.99
Cyprus	185828032X	£8.99
Czech & Slovak Republics	185828029X	£8.99
Egypt	1858280753	£10.99
England	1858280788	£9.99
Europe	185828077X	£14.99
Florida	1858280109	£8.99
France	1858280508	£9.99
Germany	1858280257	£11.99
Greece	1858280206	£9.99
Guatemala & Belize	1858280451	£9.99
Holland, Belgium & Luxembourg	1858280036	£8.99
Hong Kong & Macau	1858280664	£8.99
Hungary	1858280214	£7.99
Ireland	1858280516	£8.99
Italy	1858280311	£12.99
Kenya	1858280435	£9.99
Mediterranean Wildlife	0747100993	£7.95
Morocco	1858280400	£9.99
Nepal	185828046X	£8.99
New York	1858280583	£8.99
Nothing Ventured	0747102082	£7.99
Paris	1858280389	£7.99
Peru	0747102546	£7.95
Poland	1858280346	£9.99
Portugal	1858280842	£9.99
Prague	185828015X	£7.99
Provence & the Côte d'Azur	1858280230	£8.99
Pyrenees	1858280524	£7.99
St Petersburg	1858280303	£8.99
San Francisco	1858280826	£8.99
Scandinavia	1858280397	£10.99
Scotland	1858280834	£8.99
Sicily	1858280370	£8.99
Spain	1858280079	£8.99
Thailand	1858280168	£8.99
Tunisia	1858280656	£8.99
Turkey	1858280133	£8.99
Tuscany & Umbria	1858280559	£8.99
USA	185828080X	£12.99
Venice	1858280362	£8.99
West Africa	1858280141	£12.99
Women Travel	1858280710	£7.99
Zimbabwe & Botswana	1858280419	£10.99

Rough Guides are available from all good bookstores, but can be obtained directly in the UK* from Penguin by contacting:

Penguin Direct, Penguin Books Ltd, Bath Road, Harmondsworth, West Drayton, Middlesex UB7 0DA; or telephone our credit line on 081-899 4036 (9am–5pm) and ask for Penguin Direct. Visa, Access and Amex accepted. Delivery will normally be within 14 working days. Penguin Direct ordering facilities are only available in the UK.

The availability and published prices quoted are correct at the time of going to press but are subject to alteration without prior notice.

* For USA and international orders, see separate price list

SLEEP EASY
BOOK AHEAD

AUSTRALIA
02 261 1111

CANADA
FREEPHONE 0800 663 5777

DUBLIN
01 301766

LONDON
071 836 1036

BELFAST
0232 324733

GLASGOW
041 332 3004

WASHINGTON
0202 783 6161

NEW ZEALAND
09 379 4224

IBN INTERNATIONAL BOOKING NETWORK

Call any of these numbers and your credit card secures a good nights sleep ...

in more than 26 countries

up to six months ahead

with immediate confirmation

HOSTELLING INTERNATIONAL

*Budget accommodation you can **Trust***

You are
A STUDENT

You travel
THE WORLD

You want
TO SAVE MONEY

Here's how

The International Student Identity Card

Available at Student Travel Offices Worldwide.

Entitles you to discounts and special services worldwide.

WHATEVER CORNER YOU'RE OFF TO, YOU CAN AFFORD IT WITH STA TRAVEL.

At STA Travel we're all seasoned travellers, so wherever you're bound, we're bound to have been. We offer the best deals on fares with the flexibility to change your mind as you go.
There are even better deals for students.

Call 071-937 1221 for your free copy of The STA Travel Guide.
117 Euston Road, NW1. 86 Old Brompton Road, SW7.
North America 071-937 9971, Europe 071-937 9921, Long Haul 071-937 9962,
Round the World 071-937 1733, or 061-834 0668 (Manchester).
USA freephone 1-800-777-0112.
Manchester, Leeds, Cambridge, Bristol, Oxford, London.

ABTA (99209) IATA

WHEREVER YOU'RE BOUND, WE'RE BOUND TO HAVE BEEN.   **STA TRAVEL**